CONCEPTS FOR ADVANCED NURSING PRACTICE
the nurse as a change agent

CONCEPTS FOR ADVANCED NURSING PRACTICE

the nurse as a change agent

Edited by

JEANETTE LANCASTER, R.N., Ph.D.

Professor, University of Alabama School of Nursing,
University of Alabama in Birmingham, Birmingham, Alabama

WADE LANCASTER, M.B.A., Ph.D.

Assistant Professor of Marketing, School of Business,
University of Alabama in Birmingham, Birmingham, Alabama

with **27** contributors and **59** illustrations

The C. V. Mosby Company

ST. LOUIS · TORONTO · LONDON   1982

MOSBY

A TRADITION OF PUBLISHING EXCELLENCE

Editor: Alison Miller
Manuscript editor: Judy Jamison
Design: Jeanne Bush
Production: Margaret B. Bridenbaugh

Copyright © 1982 by The C.V. Mosby Company

Printed in the United States of America

The C.V. Mosby Company
11830 Westline Industrial Drive, St. Louis, Missouri 63141

Library of Congress Cataloging in Publication Data

Lancaster, Jeanette, 1944-
    Concepts for advanced nursing practice.

    Bibliography: p.
    Includes index.
    1. Nursing—Social aspects. 2. Organizational
change. 3. Nursing—United States. 4. Medical
care—United States. I. Title. [DNLM: 1. Nursing
—Trends. 2. Delivery of health care—Trends.
3. Philosophy, Nursing. WY 86 C744]
RT86.5.L36   362.1′7   81-14061
ISBN 0-8016-2832-6   AACR2

VT/VH/VH 9 8 7 6 5   05/B/618

CONTRIBUTORS

KATHLEEN G. ANDREOLI, R.N., D.S.N., F.A.A.N.

Special Assistant to the President for Health Affairs,
University of Texas Health Science Center
at Houston, Houston, Texas

PAT BEARE, R.N., Ph.D.

Professor, School of Nursing,
The University of Texas Medical Branch at Galveston,
Galveston, Texas

ANNE ELIZABETH BELCHER, R.N., Ph.D.

Associate Professor, University of Alabama School
of Nursing, University of Alabama in Birmingham,
Birmingham, Alabama

LYNN W. BRALLIER, R.N., M.S.N.

Director, Stress Management Center of
Metropolitan Washington, Independent Practice of
Psychotherapy and Biofeedback, Washington, D.C.

JOHN G. BRUHN, Ph.D.

Dean, School of Allied Health Sciences,
Professor of Preventive Medicine and Community
Health, The University of Texas Medical Branch
at Galveston, Galveston, Texas

CECILIA H. CANTRELL, R.N., Ph.D.

Chairperson, School of Nursing,
Georgia State University, Atlanta, Georgia

F. DAVID CORDOVA, R.N., Ed.D.

Professor of Health Related Studies,
School of Allied Health Sciences,
The University of Texas Medical Branch at Galveston,
Galveston, Texas

CAROL DASHIFF, Ph.D.

Associate Professor, Psychiatric-Mental Health
Nursing, University of Alabama School of Nursing,
University of Alabama in Birmingham, Birmingham,
Alabama

ANNE J. DAVIS, R.N., Ph.D., F.A.A.N.

Professor, Department of Mental Health and
Community Nursing, University of California,
San Francisco, California

MARION R. DICKENS, R.N., Ph.D.

Associate Professor, School of Nursing,
Georgia State University, Atlanta, Georgia

W. JACK DUNCAN, Ph.D.

Professor of Management and Associate Dean,
Graduate School of Management,
University of Alabama in Birmingham,
Birmingham, Alabama

JEAN GOEPPINGER, R.N., Ph.D.

Associate Professor and Director, Primary Nursing
Care in Society Graduate Major, School of Nursing,
University of Virginia, Charlottesville, Virginia

CAROL J. GRAY, R.N., Ed.D.

Associate Dean, School of Nursing,
University of Texas Health Science Center,
Houston, Texas

MELVA JO HENDRIX, D.N.Sc.

Director, Division of Community Services for
Mental Health, Department of Human Resources,
Bureau of Health Services, Frankfort, Kentucky

DANIEL B. HILL, Ph.D.

Associate Professor, Graduate Program in Hospital
and Health Administration, School of Community and
Allied Health, University of Alabama in Birmingham,
Birmingham, Alabama

DANIEL H. KRUGER, Ph.D.

Professor of Industrial Relations, School of Labor and
Industrial Relations, Michigan State University,
East Lansing, Michigan

GRETCHEN E. LaGODNA, Ph.D.

Mental Health Nursing Associates,
Lexington, Kentucky

JEANETTE LANCASTER, R.N., Ph.D.

Professor, University of Alabama School of Nursing,
University of Alabama in Birmingham,
Birmingham, Alabama

WADE LANCASTER, M.B.A., Ph.D.

Assistant Professor of Marketing, School of Business,
University of Alabama in Birmingham,
Birmingham, Alabama

DALTON E. McFARLAND, Ph.D.

University Professor and Professor of
Business Administration, University of Alabama
in Birmingham, Birmingham, Alabama

ELIZABETH G. MORRISON, R.N., M.S.

Associate Professor, University of Alabama
School of Nursing, Instructor, Department of
Psychiatry, University of Alabama Medical School;
Doctoral Student, School of Nursing, University
of Alabama in Birmingham, Birmingham, Alabama

PAULA PURSE POINTER, M.A., C.A.S.E.

Consultant and Counselor, Human Dynamics,
Instructor, Division of Special Studies,
University of Alabama in Birmingham,
Birmingham, Alabama

CHARLOTTE RAPPSILBER, R.N., Ph.D.

Professor and Dean of Nursing,
West Texas State University, Canyon, Texas

CYNTHIA A. RECTOR, R.N., M.S.

Director of Nursing, Brattleboro Retreat,
Brattleboro, Vermont

ONA Z. RIGGIN, R.N., Ed.D.

Professor, University of South Florida,
Tampa, Florida

MARCIA STANHOPE, R.N., D.S.N.

Associate Professor, University of Kentucky
College of Nursing, Lexington, Kentucky

This book is dedicated to the memory of Drucilla Delate Mantle who was indeed a change agent in nursing. Her ideas and contributions to the advancement of nursing service administration will be long remembered through the accomplishments of the students whom she so steadfastly directed in their graduate studies at the University of Alabama in Birmingham. Her colleagues will miss her prodding and urging on to try new ideas.

PREFACE

As the eighth decade of the twentieth century advances, it is becoming increasingly apparent that human progress may have been purchased at a far greater cost than is recorded in accounting ledgers. Unexpected costs are being illuminated in the form of a severely damaged environment and a disintegration of traditional social institutions, including the family, and a national personality that radiates stress and anxiety. All of the hallowed institutions are feeling varying degrees of pressure for reorienting their priorities. Concurrently, there is a clamoring for heightened awareness, responsiveness, and humaneness in society. On the surface, this assessment and self-evaluation may be frightening; however, it may well herald the prelude to healthy and constructive change. In a dynamic environment, social forces are both ruthless and benevolent; ruthless in eliminating inappropriate social institutions and professions, benevolent in rewarding those who change to meet new and ever-changing pressures.

More change has occurred in the health care delivery system in the last five years than in the previous fifty. Instead of creating more uniformity in health care we are rapidly moving toward increased diversity and differentiation, which adds further stress to an already burdened health care system. Both professionals and consumers alike are becoming increasingly aware of and concerned with the nature and distribution of health resources as well as with the patterns for delivering and reimbursing for health care.

The health care system is interwoven into virtually all aspects of the American way of life. Health and illness are impacted upon by a wide array of variables in the physical environment, including climate, housing, sociocultural factors, political structure, the economy, and religion. During the past 10 years the financial expenditures for health care services have escalated at a frightening rate. In 1978, health expenditures in the United States totaled $192.4 billion or an average of $863 per person. During the 1970's, national health expenditures more than doubled, with an average increase annually of 12.6 percent. The nation's total health care expenses continue to consume an ever-growing proportion of the gross national product (GNP), which is a rough estimate of total national expenditures. In 1978, health care comprised 9.1 percent of the GNP, whereas health care accounted for an expenditure of $4.2 billion or 5.8 percent of the GNP in 1966 and 4.5 percent in 1950.

A simplistic conceptualization of the current health care system identifies its composition as being: (1) individuals who need health services, (2) an array of individuals and organizations that produce either health care goods or services, (3) organizational and administrative connections between providers and consumers, and (4) the societal system in which health endeavors occur. Currently the linkage among these subsystems is fragmentary and incomplete. Pressure is being exerted by government, as well as by consumers and selected groups of providers, to develop and implement new, efficient, well-organized, and cost-effective planning mechanisms. In this era of increased awareness of health care needs and costs, it is no longer justifiable to provide services merely because they seem desirable. Health care must become increasingly responsive to society's needs in an effective, businesslike manner that views assessment and planning as key features.

At present a diverse assortment of individuals, agencies, and institutions are involved in the production and distribution of those goods and services that constitute health care in the United States. Critics contend that priorities have been assigned to profits, research, and education, with health care happening only as a by-product rather than delivery systems being developed that are based on a thorough and rational assessment of the health care needs of the public. To date, a comprehensive, organized approach to health care delivery has not been developed. Thus, the label of "nonsystem" has been used in describing the current health care arena.

It is becoming increasingly imperative that we take a fresh look at our goals and carefully list our priorities. Uncomfortable and difficult questions must be raised and answered. For example, is health a right of all in the United States? If so, shall the "haves" pay for the health care of the "have nots"? If the answer to the second question is yes, then a third must be raised: "How?" What type of payment pattern will be adopted? Will cost-effectiveness be a consideration in the payment schema? Will nursing be an integral and reimbursable profession within the health payment system? Moreover, the ultimate question "What is health?" must be raised. Is health freedom from disease or an ultimate state of wellness for each individual?

Nursing must respect the rapid changes that are occurring within the health care system and become prepared to respond in a fashion that will move the profession forward. Currently, nursing is at a crossroad in its development as an integral profession within the health care system. Critics contend that nursing has no unique body of knowledge, that graduates of various types of programs fail to meet the needs of the employing institutions, and that the profession as a whole vacillates between apathy and open warfare.

As Pogo once said, "We have met the enemy and he is us." It is essential that nursing education recognize the sad fact that nursing can no longer stand back and wait to be invited to participate in the development of health care delivery plans for the near future. The present models for the delivery of health care will change—with or without nursing. Moreover, for the most part nursing's attempts to solve new problems with old solutions have fallen far short of the hoped-for goals. If and how the ever-present and increasingly complex problems facing nursing are to be solved will depend on how the profession as a whole perceives itself—how leaders within the profession elect to deal with the pressures both from within the body of nurses and from influential external groups.

At the present time nursing is experiencing phenomenal pressure from federal cutbacks, physician demands to define nursing practice, encroachment by labor unions, and an imminent threat related to exclusion from national reimbursement patterns. Never before have nursing students so greatly needed to pursue in-depth study relevant to leadership, change agent skills, and the notion of client responsibility for health care. The nurse who aspires to effect change in the future health care system must have a keen appreciation and knowledge of nursing, human dynamics, and business management concepts. It can no longer be ignored that nursing is "big business." Further, in order to secure a place for the profession within the health care arena, each nurse must employ highly refined human relations and group process skills in order to secure a niche yet avoid threatening the roles of other providers who hold complementary niches. As leaders emerge within nursing it will be because they have dared to risk forsaking old and obsolete dogmas and have launched forward in developing new solutions based on an informed, confident posture for communicating with both consumers and providers as well as reimbursement sources.

Concepts for Advanced Nursing Practice: The Nurse as a Change Agent was written to provide nursing students with a concise, easily accessible sourcebook that identifies, describes, and provides practical ways for dealing with key issues facing nursing in the 1980's. A paucity of resources is available for students in nursing who seek to understand and become involved in the future health care delivery system. Such a nurse not only must be well informed about specific clinical content in nursing but also must be knowledgeable regarding the social pressures, forces, and processes that influence if not determine the role of nursing.

The text is divided into three parts, each of which is supportive of the conceptualization of the role of change agent within nursing. Within each part, specific chapters are written by individuals with acknowledged expertise on the subject. The first part addresses the theoretical foundations that are integral to the discussion of change in Chapter 1. Theories selected include systems, organization, group process, role, leadership, communication, and de-

cision making. Also included are chapters on the use of both power and persuasion as facilitators of change.

The second part looks at the environment in which change occurs in terms of forces that facilitate as well as those that impede change. Forces selected for discussion include the current status of the health care delivery system, and the social, economic, political, professional, and ethical issues that influence nursing practice. Finally, an overview of labor relations is presented, with implications drawn for the future of nurses as change agents.

Part Three presents a conceptualization of the future health care delivery system as a preventive health model that focuses on client self-responsibility, new practice arenas, new models for both change and nursing practice, and an orientation of taking care of oneself. A special plea is made to direct attention to the necessity for a comprehensive assessment that should precede health planning activities, as well as the important nature of evaluation of any new program or plan of action.

Jeanette Lancaster
Wade Lancaster

CONTENTS

PART ONE

THEORETICAL FOUNDATIONS FOR CHANGE

Nurses rarely practice their profession in isolation. That is, the vast majority of nurses practice within the confines of an organization. Any consideration of the nurse as a change agent must address the organizational structure that supports or interferes with the implementation of nursing practice. Therefore, Part One provides an overview of the major theoretical foundations that are essential to understanding how to implement successfully strategies for change. Change occurs in any organization based on a multitude of factors including how communication takes place, the way decisions are made, the role each participant plays, and the power held by each one. The success of any change depends largely on the change agent's understanding of the system in which the change is being introduced as well as the organizational characteristics and individual qualities of the participants.

CONTRIBUTIONS OF WARREN G. BENNIS TO THE PROCESS OF CHANGE

Although many theorists have described the change process, the ideas of Warren Bennis have particular application to a discussion of change in nursing. Bennis (1966) speculates that the current form of social organization, bureaucracy, will not endure in the coming decades. He believes that society will eventually witness the end of bureaucracy as it exists and the rise of a new social system better suited to the demands of a changing industrialized nation. He anticipates that more democratic practices will take place in organizations, in which participants are held accountable for their actions with influence being based more on competence than position and a spirit of free communication and consensus is encouraged.

Bennis (1970) holds that the primary challenge facing all business enterprises is the need to evaluate clearly the constantly changing public and national goals in order to modify organizational objectives to become more relevant to social needs whenever possible. Businesses must move beyond responding and become leaders in anticipating, directing, and helping to create the forces of change. Thus organizations need to consider the impact of rapid change on the quality of life, develop new ways to help employees cope with change, and motivate people to make full use of their innate resources in order to find organizational life more meaningful (Bennis, 1966).

Bennis also contends that new styles of leadership will be needed for the changing organizations of the future. His concept of leadership is "an active method for producing conditions where people, ideas and resources can be seeded, cultivated, and integrated to optimum effectiveness and growth" (Bennis, 1968, p. 119). According to Bennis (1970, p. 185), leadership should embrace four sets of competencies: knowledge of large, complex human systems; practical theories of intervening and guiding these systems; interpersonal competence, especially the ability to understand the effect of your own behavior on others; and a set of values and competencies that enable you to know when to confront and attack, if necessary, and when to support and provide the psychological safety so necessary for growth (Bennis, 1970).

With this background about the nature of organizations and the type of leadership that is needed, Bennis (1969) identified eight types of change: indoctrinating, coercive, technocratic, interactional, socializing, emulative, natural, and planned. The key variables that differentiate these eight types include mutual goal setting and deliberateness of the change.

Although the aim of this book is to stimulate nurses to consider themselves as change agents in the area of planned change, it would be naive to discount participation in the other types of change as well. Often nurses participate in change without desiring to do so and without advance notice of this possibility. For this reason, all eight types of change are defined:

1. Indoctrinating—involves mutual goal setting, is deliberate, involves an imbalanced power ratio
2. Coercive—nonmutual goal setting, an im-

balanced power ratio, and one-sided deliberateness
3. Technocratic—bringing about change by
collecting and interpreting data
4. Interactional—involves mutual goal setting,
equal power distribution, no deliberateness
on either side
5. Socializing—has a direct kinship with the
interactional hierarchial control
6. Emulative—the process associated with a
formal organization in which there is no clear
superior-subordinate relationship
7. Natural—involves no apparent deliberateness and no goal setting
8. Planned—refers to a process of mutual goal
setting, equal power relationships, and deliberateness on the part of both sides

The theoretical formulations of Bennis are helpful in understanding the variety of change types and
also the responses of people to change. It is not
uncommon for people to resist change, which necessitates that change agents have considerable
interpersonal skill as they develop their change
strategies.

RESISTANCE TO CHANGE

Many people resist change because of a fear of
the unknown. The old way of doing things was
familiar and often comfortable. The old adage,
"We have always done it this way and it works" is a
logical rationale for not changing only if the context
of human functioning remains the same. In health
care delivery and specifically within nursing, innovations occur daily. The old responses and approaches are frequently unsuccessful attempts to
cope with innovation. Hence there is really no
question but that nurses will be involved in change;
the issue is whether they will be merely reactors to
or both effectors and reactors in the change process.
Bearing in mind that each participant typically has
a vested interest in the present way of doing things,
a few characteristics of successful change agents
will be described.

DEVELOPING A CHANGE-AGENT ROLE

The key issue in developing innovations is the
ability to introduce them so that they will be accepted by the people who will be asked to implement them (Levenstein, 1979). The change agent
often functions as a catalyst with others being instrumental in the actual implementation of the
change process; therefore a variety of considerations must be involved in ensuring that the project
will be accepted. For example, participants are not
likely to cooperate if the inconvenience outweighs
any perceived potential results. Cooperation may
also be impaired if the innovation is considerably
different from the present procedure or if the
change is introduced too rapidly.

The style evidenced by the change agent is just as
important as the timing of the innovation and its
compatibility with previous procedures. A knowledge of human behavior is a prerequisite to the
onset of change. The nurse who seeks to implement
a change-agent role must understand human motivations, needs, and roles and must also be able to
make decisions carefully and quickly. Further, the
change agent must recognize that not all innovations will be successful; some will be dismal failures, and the nurse responsible for them must
carefully assess the cause. Some failures result
from ineffectual planning, faulty implementation,
or low regard for the change agent, whereas others
result from situational variables outside the control
of the innovator.

In order to keep failures at a minimum, the
change agent must utilize carefully thought out
planning procedures. Planning in the change process involves problem-solving techniques that anticipate problems and devise alternative solutions in
advance of implementing the innovation. Good
planning also includes being aware not only of how
others view the change agent but also the potential
degree of resistance and the possible causes for lack
of responsiveness to change. If the person introducing the change is disliked or merely held in indifference by those who will be expected to participate, then potential cooperation will be limited.

Thus the change agent works to cultivate acceptance within the work group before introducing new ideas and procedures.

Change agents may not be in control of a great deal of organizational power, but they do have access to a wide selection of the tools of power, including credibility, the wise usage of interpersonal relationships, persuasion, and both formal and informal communication networks. Credibility is the key element in obtaining power in the change process. Peterson (1979) contends that credibility is built on honesty and is enhanced by directness and openness. In order to demonstrate credibility, the nurse as a change agent must evidence self-confidence and always appear well prepared.

Good interpersonal relationships depend to a large extent on productive communication upward, downward, and across the organizational hierarchy. In this context communication includes listening as well as speaking. The nurse as change agent must not only listen to what is said but also take note of critical aspects relative to the innovation that participants seem to avoid discussing. It is also important to observe for nonverbal reactions, because people may say that they are in favor of and will support an innovation while their nonverbal reactions convey either disinterest and apathy toward the project, or even visible negativism. When the gap between verbal and nonverbal communication is wide, the change agent needs to deal with it before continuing with the change process.

In order to effectively persuade participants of the positive features of the change proposal, the innovator must use language that everyone can understand. The effectiveness of persuasion depends on all participants clearly understanding the proposed project. The language used must be well matched to the level of understanding of the participants.

REFERENCES

Bennis, W.G.: Changing organizations, New York, 1966, McGraw-Hill Book Co.

Bennis, W.G.: New patterns of leadership for adaptive organizations. In Bennis, W.G., and Slater, P.E., editors: The temporary society, New York, 1968, Harper & Row, Publishers.

Bennis, W.G.: A typology of change processes. In Bennis, W.G., and Chin, R., editors: The planning of change: readings in applied behavioral sciences, ed. 2. New York, 1969, Holt, Rinehart & Winston.

Bennis, W.G.: American bureaucracy, Chicago, 1970, Aldine Publishing Co.

Levenstein, A.: Effective change requires change agent, J. Nurs. Adm. **11**:12-14, June 1979.

Peterson, G.G.: Power: a perspective for the nurse administrator, J. Nurs. Adm. **11**:7-10, July 1979.

Change has always been a part of the human condition. What is different now is the pace of change, and the prospect that it will come faster and faster, affecting every part of life, including personal values, morality, and religion, which seem almost remote from technology. . . . So swift is the acceleration, that trying to "make sense" of change will become our basic industry.

Ways, M.: Fortune, May 1964, p. 113.

1

CHANGE THEORY: AN ESSENTIAL ASPECT OF NURSING PRACTICE

Jeanette Lancaster

The inevitability of change is no longer a debatable topic. Change is with us whether we like it or not; the way in which we conceptualize change will determine our responses. Although no one can accurately predict the future, there is little question that change within the health care system will continue at an alarming rate. According to Toffler (1979), more change occurred in the health delivery arena between 1975 and 1980 than in the previous fifty years. In every aspect of American life, citizens are demanding increasing accountability, responsiveness, and relevance of health care to emerging societal trends and needs.

If nursing is to keep abreast of rapid societal change and remain a viable and valuable component of the health care delivery system, new approaches for looking at and ordering information about people, health, nursing, and change are required. It is becoming increasingly dangerous to address the complex health problems of the twentieth century as though a single causation could accurately explain the phenomenon under discussion. This chapter proposes that nursing adopt a role as change agent regardless of the practice arena. The context of the health care system is in constant flux, and nurses need to be at the forefront in initiating change. Concepts from nursing, business, sociology, psychology, and human ecology, to name a few contributing disciplines, are synthesized into a discussion of the nurse as a change agent. Specifically, this chapter addresses the role of the change agent by describing three types of change, examining the process of change, and considering ways to introduce and encourage the acceptance of change. In order to examine the acceptance of change, strategies for effecting change are discussed as well as sources of resistance and ways to overcome barriers to the acceptance of new ideas or plans.

Toffler (1979) enumerated five general categories of societal change that are influencing the role of nursing and will continue to do so:

1. The movement toward client self-care and responsibility for one's own health

2. The effect on health of environmental factors
3. A shift in emphasis in health care that is focusing attention on prevention of health disruption
4. The changing roles evidenced by health providers
5. New modes of decision making in health areas giving consumers an increasing amount of responsibility for health planning

People generally tend to be comfortable with change as long as it occurs at a reasonable rate and does not significantly affect strongly held values, beliefs, and ideals. Since the human organism consistently strives to maintain balance and equilibrium, change is frequently viewed as disruptive and as a force to be ignored or resisted. Toffler (1970) described future shock as the physical and psychological distress that results from an overload of the human system. The human response to continued overstimulation is often labeled the "disease of change." Nursing must maintain an astute perspective in relation to the changes currently affecting the profession, practice arena, and demarcation of roles. Modifications in the practice of nursing must be consistent with current societal trends if the value of the profession is to be recognized by society.

TYPES OF CHANGE

Change can be categorized into different types according to varying schemes. Duncan (1978) cited change as being either haphazard or planned. Haphazard change is generally random with no effort being made by the participants to prepare for the onset of the change cycle. In contrast, planned change results from deliberate and conscious actions taken to adjust the operations of a given system to meet the demands of the situation.

Similarly, Sampson (1971) categorized change according to developmental, spontaneous, or planned characteristics. Developmental change refers to that type that occurs as an individual, group, or organization progresses from infancy toward maturity. In each type of system—from individuals to large organizations—as growth occurs, frequent and rapid changes in physical size, complexity, and the nature of the interrelationships take place. In general, developmental change tends to be sequential, with one stage or phase of development leading into another in a more or less orderly fashion.

Spontaneous change occurs as a response to natural, uncontrollable events outside the system under consideration. This type of change is unpredictable and generally unanticipated; hence preplanning is not often possible. At present an astounding array of technological and knowledge advances are kindling spontaneous societal changes.

Planned change, common to the schemes of both Duncan and Sampson, is described as "an intentional effort to intervene in the on-going state in order to produce a new state" (Sampson, 1971, p. 226). Similarly, Bennis and others (1976, p. 4) define planned change as "conscious, deliberate, a collaborative effort to improve the operations of a human system, whether it be a self-system, social system, or cultural system, through the utilization of valid knowledge." This discussion will highlight planned change as a goal-directed action for nurses who envision themselves as facilitators for improved nursing practice.

PROCESS OF PLANNED CHANGE

The process of planned change is complex as a result of the interaction among the myriad of influencing forces. In general, planned change is a process by which new ideas are created or developed (invention), communicated to all participants (diffusion), and either adopted or rejected (consequences). For the purpose of this discussion, nurses need to pay particular attention to diffusion, since the method of communicating about any anticipated change will largely determine its adoption or rejection. Planned change requires a carefully thought out effort on the part of an individual or a group. Problem-solving and decision-making skills are necessary for the implementation of a change procedure, as is interpersonal competence (Welch,

1979). Since the ability to identify and implement planned change is an integral component of the professional nursing role, it is necessary to summarize some key aspects of change theory. The theoretical positions of Kurt Lewin, Everett Rogers, and Gordon Lippitt are set forth as a foundation for the development of a change-agent role in nursing. There is a considerable strand of commonality among these theoretical positions on change, although each does offer some unique and useful information.

Lewin's theory of change

The origin of classical change theory is credited to Kurt Lewin (1951), who described three steps in the change process: unfreezing, moving to a new level, and refreezing. *Unfreezing* includes motivating participants in the direction of readiness for change by "thawing them out." During this phase participants recognize the need for a change, work to diagnose the problem, and generate a solution by selecting from a number of alternative approaches.

At this stage the aim is to motivate the participants in the direction of the hoped-for change. Rapport must be established between the change agent and the group, so that they will listen to new ideas and eventually acknowledge the need and desirability of the proposed change. In order for a change agent to unfreeze a group effectively, a certain degree of trust and respect must be accorded to the one introducing the change. This stage is complete when the participants understand and accept the necessity or benefit of the change by viewing it as being in their best interest.

In the second phase of Lewin's change cycle the actual *moving to a new level* of behavior takes place. The move is brought about because participants have collected sufficient information about the situation to recognize the need to alter the status quo, and they have also agreed on an action plan. According to Lewin (1951), cognitive redefinition or looking at the problem from a different perspective takes place through a process of either identification or scanning. In identification, participants are influenced by the decision of someone they respect or who has some sort of power within the group. The leader sets forth one or more possible change strategies and the participants identify or agree with this approach. Identification tends to limit the number of alternatives presented in the moving phase but may increase acceptance and success of the project if the one introducing the change has sufficient power or respect within the group.

In the process of scanning, information about potential options is sought from a variety of sources. This approach yields a number of choices about a change approach and allows the participants more responsibility for narrowing down the possibilities and making a final decision. Scanning may take longer than identification, but it may also give participants a greater feeling of involvement in the change process (Welch, 1979). During this stage the problem is clarified and plans are made to move in a new direction. It is at this point that the change process can be pretested and the transition period commenced.

Refreezing is the stage in the change cycle when the newly acquired behavior is integrated into the participants' personalities. At this stage it is critical that the newly acquired behavior patterns not be extinguished; thus either continuous or intermittent reinforcement is important. In continuous reinforcement the behavior is acknowledged and rewarded every time it occurs, whereas intermittent reinforcement is only periodical. Intermittent reinforcement is generally more realistic and also longer lasting. During this stage positive feedback, encouragement, and constructive criticism reinforce newly learned behavior (Olson, 1979).

Lewin (1951) also introduced the concepts of driving and restraining forces that either help or hinder the change process. Driving forces are those that facilitate the change process by moving the participants in the direction desired by the change agent. In contrast, restraining forces impede the change cycle. When the driving and restraining forces are equal, the status quo is maintained.

Change occurs when one set of forces outweighs the other. It is important to identify both the driving and restraining forces in order both to line up a support system (driving forces) and to identify and learn to deal with the restraining forces.

In the history of nursing practice, a wide variety of situations have revealed Lewin's change cycle. Consider the introduction of unit or ward managers, which in many instances directly affected the role of the head nurse, who had previously performed management functions. With the addition of a non-nurse unit manager, head nurses were freed for increased involvement in patient care. Many head nurses had a great deal of difficulty returning to previously proscribed roles because of unfamiliarity with procedures and equipment and a subsequent fear of failing in this new role. While the following list is not intended to include all possible forces, those set forth are commonly identified as driving and restraining forces that surface with the introduction of a nonnurse unit manager. Driving forces include:

1. Freeing the head nurse of many routine, non-nursing functions
2. Improving patient care by allowing the head nurse to become a more involved provider and/or supervisor of direct care
3. Decreasing expenses
4. Centralizing unit management with one person

In contrast, restraining forces might include:

1. Threatening the head nurse by removing familiar functions
2. Increasing the head nurse's anxiety by expecting performance of unfamiliar or possibly forgotten tasks
3. Possible recruitment difficulties
4. Initial lack of ability of staff members and physicians to work with a unit manager
5. Preference on the part of some nurses for management rather than patient care activities

Change is more likely to be successful if the driving forces outweigh the restraining ones. It is better to focus on both sets of forces simultane-

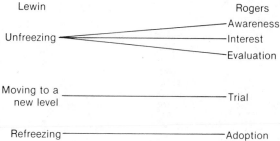

FIG. 1-1
Comparison between Rogers' and Lewin's phases of change.

ously, in that sudden emphasis on only driving forces will generally elicit a strong defensive assault from the restraining forces. Olson (1979) lists in order of effectiveness three factors that will increase the strength of the driving forces and three that can be used to decrease the restraining forces. Driving forces can be increased by:

1. Using a model or demonstration on one unit
2. Providing continuous support and encouragement throughout the change process
3. Using the change as an example when it works well

Likewise, the strength of the restraining forces can be decreased by:

1. Maintaining a forum for open-discussion meetings and conferences
2. Providing essential information at the appropriate time and level of cognition of the participants
3. Using a problem-solving approach (Olson, 1979, p. 329)

Rogers' theory

Planned-change theory has been discussed by many writers using Lewin's theory as a foundation. Everett Rogers (1962) expanded on Lewin's three phases of change by emphasizing both the background of those people participating in the change process and the environment in which the change takes place. Rogers described five phases in the change cycle: awareness, interest, evaluation, trial, and adoption.

In essence Rogers believed that the process of adopting any change was more complex than the three steps discussed by Lewin. Specifically, each participant in the change process could initially accept the change or reject it. In addition, although the change might initially be accepted, it could later be discontinued; or it could initially be rejected and later adopted. Hence Rogers calls attention to the fluid and sometimes reversible characteristics involved in change.

The relationship between Rogers' five phases and Lewin's three are depicted in Fig. 1-1.

Rogers maintains that the effectiveness of change depends on whether the participants are keenly interested in the innovation (the change) and have a commitment to work toward implementing it. Five factors are cited by Rogers and Shoemaker (1971) as determinants of successful planned change. These factors—relative advantage, compatibility, complexity, divisibility (trialability), and communicability (observability) are discussed later when the essential elements in the diffusion of a new idea are presented.

Lippitt's theory

Lippitt (1973) defines change as "any planned or unplanned alteration of the status quo in an organism, situation, or process," and planned change as "an intended, designed, or purposive attempt by an individual, group, organization, or larger social system to influence directly the status quo of itself, another organism, or a situation" (1973, p. 37).

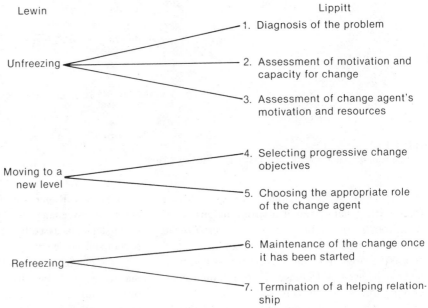

FIG. 1-2
Comparison between Lewin's and Lippitt's change cycle.

Lippitt contends that no one can escape change: the question is, "How do we handle change?" The complexity of the change cycle cannot be overestimated when we consider that human beings have nearly 10,000 thoughts pass through their heads daily. The key to dealing with change is to develop a thorough and carefully thought out strategy for intervention. To do this, Lippitt (1973, p. 52) identified seven steps in the change process: diagnosis of the problem, assessment of the motivation and capacity for change, assessment of the change agent's motivation and resources, the selection of progressive change objectives, choosing an appropriate role for the change agent, maintenance of the change once it has been started, and termination of a helping relationship. Fig. 1-2 presents a comparison between Lippitt's phases of change and those of Lewin.

Stage 1: Diagnosing the problem

Diagnosis of the problem requires that participants keep an open mind and avoid jumping to conclusions before all possible causes have been considered. Frequently participants think they know what is wrong and thus omit the critical first step of data collection and problem identification. Ideally all who will be involved in the change process or affected by the change should be included in this phase. They also need to be kept informed and feel free to raise questions and make suggestions. The more information the change agent has, the more likely an accurate assessment and problem identification will be made. Key people, especially those with considerable power and authority in the organization, need to be involved in the change process as early as possible (Welch, 1979).

Stage 2: Assessment of the motivation and capacity for change

Change seldom comes easily; on the contrary, successful planned change generally involves considerable hard work and commitment to the project. During this stage it is necessary to assess both the people involved and the environment in which the proposed change is to take place. Such factors as resources, constraints, and helpers must be identified. Since the majority of nursing practice takes place within the confines of an agency or institution, the organizational structure must be examined to determine whether the rules, policies, norms, and people involved will either help or hinder the change process. It is also necessary to think about the availability or limitations of financial resources. Can the institution afford to become involved in the project? Are those who control policies, budget, and personnel well informed and supportive of the change? During Stage 2, possible solutions are identified and prioritized by listing the pros and cons of each one.

Stage 3: Assessment of the change agent's motivation and resources

This stage requires a great deal of honest and critical self-assessment on the part of the change agent. The degree to which the change agent is trusted and respected within the organization will influence the acceptance of the idea. For example, if many of the change agent's ideas are viewed as radical, then proposals for change are likely to be viewed with skepticism, especially by more conservative members of the establishment. If more than one person is to be responsible for introducing the change, it is important that they have similar goals, objectives, and styles of leadership so that all involved receive similar messages about the project.

Stage 4: Selecting progressive change objectives

Once a diagnosis of the problem is made and the resources and constraints have been listed, it is time to develop a step-by-step strategy for implementing the change. This planning stage must be specific as to the steps to be taken, by whom, and when. Deadlines are especially helpful, and a trial period could be instituted at this time. If a trial period is used, careful and critical evaluation is necessary to determine the effectiveness of the change strategy. Goals can be reevaluated based on the trial ex-

perience, and alterations in the plan can be devised.

Stage 5: Choosing the appropriate change-agent role

The change agent may choose to be an expert role model, catalyst, teacher, or group leader. The change agent may actively gather information and demonstrate new procedures or may serve more as a motivator for others who will actually implement the project. It is facilitative of the change process if both the participants and the change agent have similar conceptions of the change agent's role. Lack of congruence between role perceptions breeds discontent and uncertainty, in that few people's expectations of one another are met.

Stage 6: Maintenance of the change

Once a change has been instituted the interest and enthusiasm seen during the developmental phase may wane, and old methods may spring up. When the change is implemented it is necessary to keep the lines of communication open so that questions, concerns, and ideas can receive attention. It is also helpful to provide frequent reports about the change to supervisory personnel as well as to participants. When the change has been successfully instituted, plans must be made for diffusion of information, since other people in the organization may want to become involved in a similar project. Members of the original change group may serve as resource people to other units, keeping in mind that the actual design of a change project may require modification to meet the unique needs of a different setting. Also, each setting has unique personality and structural qualities that may necessitate modification of the original plan.

Stage 7: Termination of the helping relationship

During this stage the change agent, following a prescribed plan, withdraws from the situation. This should be accomplished gradually so that participants can increasingly take more responsibility for the maintenance functions. The change agent may continue to serve as a consultant or resource person but should actively encourage autonomy on the part of the change implementers.

DIFFUSION OF NEW IDEAS

The success of any planned change often depends on how clearly the ideas are explained to the involved parties. The main elements in the diffusion of new ideas include the *innovation* itself, which is communicated through a variety of *channels,* over *time,* and among designated *participants* (adopters or rejecters). Simply stated, an innovation is brought to a receptive social (client) system by a change agent. Participants tend to evaluate an innovation according to five characteristics: relative advantage, compatibility, complexity, trialability, and observability (Rogers and Shoemaker, 1971, p. 22).

Characteristics of innovation

1. Relative advantage is the degree to which the new idea is considered superior to the old one. Although the degree of relative advantage may be measured in economic terms, it is often judged by social factors, convenience, time involvement, and general satisfaction with the idea. The participants' perception of the advantage is far more critical to its adoption than actual, objective advantage. The greater the perceived relative advantage the more rapid the adoption.

2. Compatibility refers to the degree of congruence between the innovation and existing values, habits, past experiences, and needs of the participants. The adoption of an incompatible innovation is slow because it often requires the prior adoption of a new set of values and attitudes. Because compatible ideas are more familiar, they tend to be less threatening and thus more readily accepted.

3. Complexity describes the amount of difficulty that participants have in understanding and subsequently using the innovation. Complexity of the innovation and adoption vary inversely. Often participants are embarrassed to acknowledge that they do not understand the process so they refuse to

participate lest their inability become widely known. Astute observation by the change agent is important in order to assess receptivity to ideas on a continuing basis.

4. Trialability is the degree to which the new idea can be pretested or tried on a limited basis. New ideas that can be tried on a small-scale basis are less frightening than massive changes and are more likely to be accepted. An innovation that can be pretested generally represents less risk, in that failure or difficulties are less obvious.

5. Observability refers to how visible the innovation is to participants and onlookers. The easier it is for an individual to see the results of an innovation, the more likely its adoption will be.

Communication channels

Communication is "the process by which messages are transmitted from a source to a receiver" (Rogers and Shoemaker, 1971, p. 23). Speaking from the perspective of change, source refers to the change agent who introduces the new idea, approach, or procedure and communicates it in the form of a message through a predetermined channel to the intended participants in the process (see Fig. 1-3).

The communication channel utilized is critical in determining whether the innovation will be accepted. In general the channel should be decided in light of the following conditions:

1. The purpose of the message may determine the channel used.
2. The characteristics of the audience to whom the message is being sent are a decisive factor.
   a. The flexibility and general receptiveness of the group are influential.
   b. If the audience is large and the change agent only wants to inform them, then the mass media are often effective and rapid.
   c. If the audience is not exceedingly large and the objective is to persuade them, then an interpersonal or small-group approach is most useful.

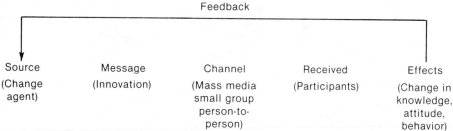

FIG. 1-3
Communication process for change.

3. The degree of ambiguity and controversy surrounding the innovation require sensitivity in communications.
4. The degree of institutional support for the innovation is decisive. If the change will be mandated regardless of participant response, then an announcement might be used, assuming acceptance by participants. However, if mandated and negative feelings abound, then small-group discussion would likely be useful.
5. The degree of urgency for the change is important.
6. The "personality" of the organization must be taken into account, including what usually works best and what the established lines and channels of communication are.

Timing

Timing is critical in the successful introduction of change. Any proposed innovation should be examined according to its timeliness for the expected participants. A good idea at the wrong time, for instance when participants are tired, upset, angry, or thinking about other more pressing ideas, is generally greeted with little enthusiasm. An effective change agent will critically assess whether A is the best solution to B at a given time and in the particular environment (Stevens, 1975). It is helpful to remember that "the wheels of change move slowly"; innovations take time for introduction,

acceptance, and implementation. Generally the larger the group involved, the more complex the innovation, and the greater the incompatibility with past procedures, the greater will be the amount of time involved. The process of change, then, includes general characteristics of change, the method of communication used, and the timing of the change occurrence. The person introducing change needs also to recognize general patterns often evidenced by those people responding to the change (adopters or rejecters). Responses to innovations typically can run the gamut from enthusiastic acceptance to active rejection.

Categories of adopters

Individual responses to change can be described according to six categories of adopters, actually forming a continuum from eager participation (innovators) to rejection (Rogers and Shoemaker, 1971, p. 357).

1. *Innovators.* These individuals are the "pacesetters." They are venturesome, curious, eager for new experiences, and enthusiastic. They are often considered radical and disruptive by colleagues but frequently bring great change, albeit often amidst controversy, to an organization.

2. *Early adopters.* This group seek to moderate their enthusiasm and vigor in introducing an idea according to the readiness of the organization. These individuals tend to be well-established members of the group who are often sought out as advis-

ers. Since the early adopters prefer to maintain esteem within the group, they do not usually introduce highly radical or controversial ideas.

3. *Early-majority adopters.* Accepting innovation just before the mass of participants do so, the early-majority adopters are followers with deliberate willingness and dedication to the innovation, but they rarely lead. This group generally constitute an effective support system for innovation.

4. *Late-majority adopters.* For this group adoption is an economic necessity. They view the innovation with skepticism, and though they may not be active dissidents, neither can they be counted on for support.

5. *Laggards.* Members of the category termed laggards tend to be socially isolated within the organization. They tend to be suspicious of change and may discourage others from participating by their attitude of general negativism.

6. *Rejectors.* Members of this group openly reject the innovation and actively encourage others to do so.

Individuals reacting to change can also be categorized as active accepters or rejecters, passive accepters or rejecters, and noncommitted individuals. Change can be advanced and resistance minimized by identifying and soliciting the support of the active accepters, locating and neutralizing the active rejecters, and persuading the uncommitted to accept the innovation. The passive adopters and rejecters have formulated their opinions about the innovation and have agreed neither to support it nor to attempt to influence others. These individuals, as well as the active rejecters, can often be converted to active accepters if they perceive they will benefit from the innovation by being offered new challenges, new experiences, or more responsibility.

Change rarely occurs in isolation; it has multiple effects on the individuals and organizations involved. Any alteration in one aspect of a living system has far-reaching effects on every other component. Hence attention is now directed toward an ecological perspective of change that nudges us to remember the impact and "ripplelike" or "snowball" effect of change.

ECOLOGICAL EXPLANATIONS FOR CHANGE

Nursing has always "reacted to" change rather than introducing it. This tendency is being altered dramatically as nurses increasingly assume leadership positions in health care. The "let's wait and see" attitude is being replaced by a deep appreciation of systems theory and the need to consider the entire scope of ramifications of an action before change commences. Selected principles from ecology can help structure one's thinking in order to remain cognizant of the necessity for considering the multiple effects of any innovation. Change is subject to the law of acceleration: change takes place at an ever-increasing rate, and the outcome of one action constitutes the potential for several additional reactions. Ecology's relevance to a discussion of change lies in its focus on the interaction between the human organism and the multiple environments that support existence. By definition, ecology refers to the continuous, complex interplay that occurs between living organisms and their environment. The main emphasis in contemporary human ecological thinking is on the essential holism of human interaction. Each person's behavior occurs within a context influenced by internal and external motivators. The ecological perspective on change aspires to obtain as complete and thorough a picture as possible of the current situation before action commences. Four ecological principles provide foundational discussion for change.

1. *Do not try to solve a complex problem with a simple solution.* Change typically results from multiple causation; that is, a variety of factors affect the actual event that produces the change. Change can be depicted simplistically as follows:

Stimulus → Organism → Processing → Reaction

While such a scheme looks quite simple, its complexity can be appreciated by considering the multitude of variables influencing each step in the process. For example, consider that human beings have approximately 10,000 thoughts pass through their heads each day. People are thus daily confronted with an unbelievable number of stimuli.

The ability to sort out stimuli and to direct a response to those having highest priority varies among people and is considerably influenced by perception and motivation. How and when an individual responds, as well as the complexity of the processing stage and ultimately the quality and magnitude of the reaction, depend to a large extent on how the stimulus was perceived. A basic premise of human dynamics holds that all behavior is motivated by conscious or unconscious forces. People move toward implementing or resisting change depending on their motivational state. The stance an individual takes in regard to change depends on whether movement in a specific direction is perceived as being of value. If people recognize no value to themselves in a change process, they are not likely to become actively involved. Thus perception is a key element in the process of change. Perception includes the processes of conscious cognition or awareness mediated through the sense organs. Not just the quality of an individual's sensory capacities (e.g., hearing, seeing, and smelling) affect the response to a stimulus; a person's needs, values, feelings, and self-esteem at any given time also influence perceptual acuity. Further, the meaning attached to any situation is influenced by the participants' repertoire of past experiences. Each individual responds to stimuli in the environment based on unmet needs, values, expectations, and the intensity of the stimuli. For example, nurses with low self-assessments might misinterpret an invitation to participate in a trial nursing project as an attempt to embarrass them, rather than as a genuine expression of recognition for capabilities not acknowledged by the nurse but obvious to colleagues.

2. *Interdependence is inherent in any human system*. Interdependence emphasizes the multiple causation inherent to change. Whenever one component in a natural ecosystem is altered, every other part is affected. In other words, we can never do just *one* thing. A respect for the interdependence of our actions motivates us to consider the ramifications of change before any alteration is attempted. Before the onset of any change process, it is useful to evaluate with care the content of the proposed action. Prior decisions and effects of our actions not considered in advance can seldom be disguised because of the impact on the total system involved. For example, consider the fate of patients who consume food or liquids after midnight Thursday when they are to have surgery at 7 AM on Friday. Not only do they miss their scheduled surgery, but they must anxiously wait until Monday for rescheduling.

3. *Too much or too little of anything is a bad thing*. As previously pointed out, too much or particularly too rapid a change can adversely affect the health and well-being of the participants. The rate of change thus has important consequences regarding the human organism's ability to maintain a sense of stability. People can adapt to gradual change and modify their coping abilities accordingly, but an excessive rate of change that calls forth new coping abilities often tends to perpetuate tension and anxiety. In contrast, too little change and the resultant deficit in stimulation fosters boredom, dissatisfaction, apathy, and frustration. Frequently the first week of nursing school constitutes an example of "too much of a good thing is a bad thing." New faculty, fellow students, assignments, places to go, and frequently novel living arrangements may cause considerable sensory overload. In contrast, persons hospitalized for many years in institutions for the chronically ill are likely to experience "too little of a good thing (solitude) is a bad thing."

4. *Any attempt to motivate others toward change can be facilitated by recognizing that everything and everyone has its niche*. The term niche refers to the functional role occupied by an organism within an ecosystem. In nonhuman systems, a niche is typically a place or structure, whereas in human systems niche refers to an individual's role. In human systems, roles or niches are continuously changing, thereby demanding alterations by occupants in other positions. Each individual "stakes out" a personal territory that includes role as well as actual physical space and constantly struggles to prevent others from stepping over the invisible role

boundaries. The concept of niche or personal territory will later be used to describe modes by which people resist change. The stresses and struggles that have emerged in recent years with the increasing popularity of nurse practitioners are an example of perceived "niche encroachment." In many cases other health providers have feared the increasing prevalence of nurse practitioners, believing such nurses might "take over" roles traditionally assigned to other disciplines.

STRATEGIES FOR EFFECTING CHANGE

Any discussion of strategies for effecting change must be preceded by a description of the four basic levels of change. Hersey and Blanchard (1977) identify four levels of change on an upward continuum of difficulty for accomplishment. These include (1) knowledge changes, (2) attitudinal changes, (3) behavioral changes, and (4) group or organizational performance changes.

As depicted in Fig. 1-4, knowledge change is the easiest to effect. It is far easier to alter levels of information than to change attitudes, which are generally invested with positive or negative emotional energy. Actual changes in behavior are considerably more difficult to bring about than either

knowledge or attitudes. Consider the issue of smoking among nurses. Few well-informed nurses would deny that research supports the hypothesis that smoking has deleterious effects on health; thus many nurses have knowledge that smoking is harmful. A segment of this group of nurses also holds a negative attitude toward smoking, yet they are unable to cease the habit considered harmful.

Group or organizational change is by far the most difficult to effect. The realization of change in more than one person is confounded by the often differing ideas, attitudes, and beliefs of each member of the group. Each participant may subscribe to a unique way of effecting the change. Moreover, individual members of a group involved in the change process must first go through the three preceding levels of change. It is especially crucial when attempting to bring about group change that the change agent decide in advance on the strategy that offers the greatest possibility for success.

Two schemes for change strategies prevail in the literature. The first scheme is divided by Chin and Benne (1976) into three types of strategies: empirical-rational, normative reeducative, and the application of power. The assumptions basic to empirical-rational modes of effecting change pur-

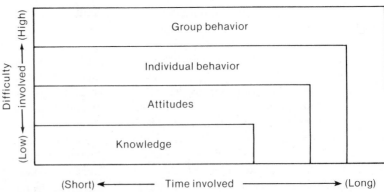

FIG. 1-4
Time and difficulty involved in making change.

(From Hersey, P., and Blanchard, K.H.: Management of organizational behavior: utilizing human resources, ed. 3, © 1977, p. 3. Reprinted by permission of Prentice-Hall, Inc., Englewood Cliffs, N.J.)

port that people are rational and will follow their own self-interests. Thus the task of the change agent using this approach is to convince the participants that the change is clearly in their best interest. When successful, this approach is fast, efficient, and long lasting.

The normative reeducative model for change, like the empirical-rational model, assumes that people are both rational and intelligent. This mode of change assumes that patterns of behavior are supported by sociocultural norms and that people change only after they have been involved in attitudinal as well as knowledge alteration. This approach, by involving self-improvement and enhancement of problem-solving ability, generally induces commitment from the participants although it takes longer to accomplish.

The third approach to change, the application of power or force, tends to be rapid and to involve the least amount of commitment from participants. This model requires that people adhere to the rules established for the implementation of change. Whereas each of the three models depends to some extent on the use of power, the third approach most clearly evidences its usage.

Hersey and Blanchard (1977) describe a change cycle that in effect is composed of two strategies for change: participative and coercive. Participative change is effected when new knowledge is made available to the participants in the hope that they will develop a positive attitude toward the innovation and demonstrate a commitment to support the new style of behavior. This approach works best when informal leaders can be utilized to assist in the dissemination of support for change. Clearly the participative approach to change incorporates several of the concepts involved in the preceding discussion of empirical-rational and normative reeducative approaches. When effective it tends to be long lasting, especially if introduced by leaders who have considerable personal power. It is also most effective when participants are highly motivated, achievement-oriented people.

In contrast, coerced change, which is similar to the previously discussed use of power or force, begins by imposing change on the total organization. Clearly a certain power base is essential for this mode of change to become operational. This model for change is most effectively used when participants are immature and willing to be dependent, especially in a new or novel situation. This type of change necessitates considerable personal power and the ability to dole out both rewards and punishment. In general, coerced change can be quickly effected but also has the potential to be volatile. If coerced change is the style chosen, it is important to watch for signs of subtle undermining of the project. Often participants will overtly support the goals of the proposed change but will covertly or subtly sabotage the activities, for example, by quietly rallying support for noncompliance with identified goals.

INDIVIDUAL REACTIONS TO CHANGE

Within any human system forces are operational that serve either to promote or to resist change. Each system attempts to maintain equilibrium and stability by resisting innovations, which are viewed as threatening to the maintenance of homeostasis. Forces that operate to resist change can either produce growth as they maintain order and stability or act as barriers to the change process. Resistance is often a protective measure undertaken when the impending change threatens the integrity of someone or a group. Two statements add color to a discussion of resistance to change.

1. Everything must go somewhere; nothing simply goes away.
2. There is no such thing as a free lunch; every gain is won at some cost.

Both of these statements redirect our attention to the ecological principles supportive to change, which emphasize the interdependence of parts in any living system. All living systems need a dynamic interplay between change and stability, so resistance is not always a negative term. Attention needs to be focused on the motivation for stability as well as on methods for interrupting resistance that seems nonproductive.

Change is more likely to be accepted if those who will be affected are well informed about the project's goals, the method of operationalization, and the effects on them of the innovation. It is equally important to prepare the participants for any emotional shifts that may arise during the implementation of the innovation.

Emotional cycle of change

Kelly and Conner (1979) describe an "emotional cycle of change" as moving from uninformed optimism to rewarding completion. This cycle begins before the participants have any knowledge that they are going to be approached about participating in a change project and continues until the innovation is completed. Such a cycle takes into account only those people who choose to participate in the innovation; it omits consideration of any individuals who may decline participation. Fig. 1-5 graphically depicts the change cycle.

Three key assumptions are set forth as explanatory of the emotional cycle of change. First, people who actively engage in an innovation tend to be optimistic concerning the adventure. This optimism is often directly related to the person's expectations of what will be involved in the project. Second, the more the person learns about the project, the greater the tendency to doubt whether participation is a good idea. Third, the level of pessimism or optimism about the project is related to the information available concerning what will be required both of each person and of the organization as a whole.

The first stage, *uninformed optimism,* is the "honeymoon" phase when the idea looks great, the obstacles look trivial, and those who are opposed are obviously just uninformed. Feelings are running high at this point, and morale is at a peak. As the project moves along, the participants recognize that problems are going to interfere with the established goals and time frame: resources suddenly seem scarce, co-workers increasingly become viewed as obstacles, and energy begins to wane. Hence *informed pessimism* is now in full bloom. At this point critical problems have been identified but few resources and solutions seem evident. Morale begins to drop, and participants ask themselves why they ever got involved in this project anyway. Further, the positive energy and motivation of the honeymoon phase is neutralized by a negative re-

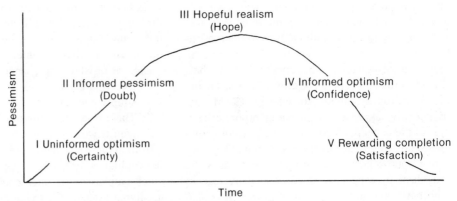

FIG. 1-5
The emotional cycle of change.

(From Kelley, D., and Connor, D.R.: The emotional cycle of change. In Jones, J.E., and Pfeiffer, J.W.: The 1979 annual handbook for group facilitators, LaJolla, Calif., 1979, University Associates, Inc., p. 118.)

sponse to the unforeseen problems of implementation. Such a balance between jealous optimism and caution is a healthy prelude to continued project development if the pessimism can be gradually turned into a more cautious and methodical optimism. In order to move on to *hopeful realism,* it is necessary to deal openly with the desire to withdraw from the project and possibly to modify goals.

During the *informed optimism* phase the project participants gain confidence in their abilities to succeed and begin to see evidence of the fruits of their labor. Encouragement, recognition, and support from the person guiding the project are imperative for continued progress. Finally, *rewarding completion* demonstrates a successful change experience. It is helpful to note here that the outcome may be somewhat or considerably different from what was expected. Each phase of the change process influences and is influenced by the perceptions, thoughts, beliefs, feelings, and needs of the participants. Therefore the end product is usually different, since the project accommodated the numerous individual and personal shifts that occurred as it progressed.

Resistance to change

Virtually all change meets with some degree of resistance. In general, two types of resistance are equated with the change process: resistance incurred because of the nature of the change and resistance resulting from misconceptions and inaccurate information about what the change might mean. Resistance seems to result from threats to the integrity of those faced with the change. Among the sources of resistance are a variety of social factors including the specific nature of the change, how and by whom it was suggested, the context and timing of the innovation, the perceived role threat, and the fear of how the change will affect the individuals involved as well as the total organizational system.

All resistance seems to spring from fear. Each time a change is suggested, those involved weigh the innovation against past experiences to determine whether it is consistent with attitudes and

value orientations, if its intent is clear and within the realm of possibility for the participants, and if there is something to be gained by participation. Those who oppose change may fear the unknown and untried; they may be afraid they will fail, not know enough to participate, or otherwise embarrass themselves. Resisters may also either be satisfied with the status quo or just be unwilling to take the time and energy required to make the effort to change. Other individuals may refuse to participate because they sincerely believe the change would hinder the goals of the system. Frequently resistance stems from insecurity, economic fears, or sociopsychological factors, such as beliefs that friends will not support the change.

It is important that nurses who function as change agents recognize that the degree of resistance will typically depend on the answers to the following questions:

1. How great is the change; how much does it deviate from the current norm of expectations?
2. How much emotional investment by the participants is there in the "old way?"
3. To what degree and in what manner are the people involved threatened? Most people when confronted with change ask themselves either consciously or unconsciously the following set of questions (Stevens, 1975, p. 24):

   Will the change alter my role by either increasing or decreasing my power or status?

   Will this change affect the activities or content of my job?

   Will my freedom to perform my job be altered? How will my range of choices be affected?

   Can I expect to be inconvenienced by this innovation?

   How will my financial status be affected?

   Exactly what advantages or disadvantages can I expect from this change?
4. How reasonable or profitable is this change?

5. Will new skills and procedures be expected? If so, how complex are they?
6. How much involvement at each level of the implementation can be encouraged?
7. How do participants feel toward the change agent?
8. How clear and well informed are the expected participants about the total change project and about what is expected of them?
9. How effective is the communication network surrounding the change process? Is two-way communication adequate?
10. What financial resources will be required?

On the other hand, resistance can often be minimized when:

1. All involved parties, including administration, are kept well informed.
2. The change is possible from a budgetary viewpoint.
3. The proposal is reasonably in line with established norms, procedures, and beliefs within the organization.
4. Communication is open and readily used for suggestions, questions, and feedback.
5. The project has been carefully thought out, potential problems identified and handled, and alternatives considered.

Certainly not all resistance is bad; it may in fact be a warning to assess the idea carefully before implementing it further. "Resistance has value in that it can force the leadership to clarify the purpose and results of the change" (Olson, 1979, p. 331). Resistance can call attention to the lack of effective communication about the proposed change: People may resist because they simply do not know what is going on; they feel left out, angry, or poorly prepared for future expectations of them. In truth, it is usually wise to listen carefully to dissenters; their hesitancy to participate may save the change agent and organization the embarrassment of embarking on an impossible or poorly thought out strategy. What is often seen as irrational resistance to change may in the long run help to maintain organizational integrity. Hence the resisters of change or those who quietly attempt to defend the status quo should be taken seriously.

No matter how irrational, hostile, or disruptive the resister or defender may be, this type of behavior communicates a great deal about the nature of the system. The change agent needs to determine what the resister is trying to protect and why such resistance is being evidenced. It may be helpful to modify the change strategy so as to gain the support of nonparticipants.

CHANGE AGENT

The change agent is defined as a "catalytic protagonist of the change process" (Broskowski et al., 1975, p. 173). Simply stated, the change agent generates ideas, introduces the innovation, develops a climate for planned change by overcoming resistance and marshaling forces for acceptance, and implements and evaluates the change. Any effective change agent respects the need for communication and group-process skills. Change agents must listen carefully to what is said as well as note what participants omit discussing. Often anger and ambiguity about the proposed change are disguised in silence. Change agents need self-awareness as well as skill in interpersonal relationships in order to recognize their own attitudes about the change, approach to people, and ability to handle disagreement and disappointments.

Change agents need also to assess whether they are functioning as insiders or outsiders. The diagnosed problem, the environment, and the characteristics of the participants determine whether it is better for a change agent to be an insider or an outsider. External change agents are often better able to view the situation clearly, in that they are less affected by vested interests and biases. Also the outsider is independent of the organizational power structure and cliques. The external change agent comes to the situation as a stranger, which may be a disadvantage until participants gain trust and confidence in this person's ability. It helps if the change agent has impressive credentials, is well informed about both the organization and the proposed change, and can communicate effectively with involved individuals and groups.

The internal change agent has the advantages of knowing the system, being able "both literally and figuratively to speak the language" of the participants, and being familiar to the organization (Olson, 1979, p. 325). The insider, though, may be influenced by vested interests and biases that impede clear examination of the situation. Internal change agents may also be handicapped by group impressions of their ability, by their past failures, and by jealousies within the group. There is no simple solution regarding which is consistently best: an internal or an external change agent. The needs and resources of each situation are unique. Although choice may not be possible because of administrative decisions, availability of competent people, or finances, the change agent needs to recognize the advantages and disadvantages of each option.

The change agent also needs to work toward agreement on priority tasks and procedures for implementing the project. For example, assume that all the head nurses in a hospital are involved in a project to improve the transportation system between the nursing units and various support departments. The clinical specialist has worked tirelessly with the head nurses to devise a plan whereby transport workers will arrive in the unit five minutes before the patient's appointment in another service area. One head nurse finds it tedious to call the transport department at the beginning of the day so that a daily schedule can be developed before 8 AM. This head nurse calls the transport service immediately before a scheduled appointment, which consistently upsets the mechanism. Had all head nurses agreed in advance that daily scheduling is essential, this disruptive behavior by one person might have been avoided. Perhaps this particular head nurse had a suggestion that was overlooked in the planning stage. Attention should be devoted toward finding out why the head nurse is not participating and what alterations could be considered.

The change agent assists the group to (1) define the problem; (2) list all possible alternatives and the positive or negative consequences of each; (3) determine the most suitable alternative at this time and for this setting; (4) organize an implementation plan; (5) provide ongoing supervision, direction, and support; and (6) work toward developing an evaluation format. The following guidelines for implementing change are offered to nurses in change-agent roles.

IMPLEMENTING CHANGE

1. *Involvement.* No one person knows everything, therefore respect the knowledge and wisdom of others and involve all who will be affected by the change in its development from the beginning. Listen carefully. People will usually cooperate and accept innovations that they perceive as nonthreatening and beneficial.

2. *Motivation.* People participate in activities toward which they are motivated. Generally, people are motivated if they feel that their contributions would be valuable for the outcome of the project, if their contributions are listened to, and if they feel respected.

3. *Planning.* This includes considering where the system is inflexible as well as what, how, and when change can be brought about.

4. *Legitimization.* Any change, to be accepted, must be sanctioned by the people in control of the organization, by the participants in the project, and ultimately by those who will be affected.

5. *Education.* Change typically implies reeducation or the switch from one way of thinking to another.

6. *Management.* The change agent finds a balance between leading and developing the leadership capacities of participants. It is helpful to manage by delegation of responsibility so that others may develop their talents.

7. *Expectations.* A variety of expectations should be held by change agents: Expect the outcome to be somewhat different than what was originally planned; expect resistance and unfore-

seen problems; also expect unbelievable reactions from participants.

8. *Nurturance.* Recognition and support for participants is imperative. People need to be acknowledged for what they do right, and they also need to discuss in private how their actions interfered with the project.

9. *Trust.* The key element in implementing change is developing trust. Participants must trust the change agent to think carefully before involving them in projects, and the change agent should trust the participants to do a good job.

The change agent serves as a vital communication link between each of the interacting parts of subsystems in the change project. To be effective the change agent must:

1. Be accessible to all who are involved in the change process.
2. Develop trust among participants.
3. Be honest and straightforward about goals, plans, priorities, and problems.
4. Keep the goals clearly in mind and assist others to do so and not get diverted by side issues or activities.
5. Define the responsibilities of others; allow participants the freedom to do their part.
6. Listen.

SUMMARY

Change is a complex, continuous process that can rarely be rushed or imposed on unwilling participants. Before the onset of any change process, a careful assessment must be performed as to the readiness to participate and support for the project of those who will invariably be involved. Each situation and organization has unique features that influence the response to innovation. Change is essentially goal-seeking behavior, and one key to success lies in careful delineation of the project goals. What is the need as defined by the change agent? Do others who will be involved perceive the need in a similar way? Once the goals of the change project are established, clarified, agreed upon, and prioritized, it is essential to determine what forces,

internal or external, will direct the project toward its goal. Not only helping forces but hindering factors must be identified so that the detrimental influences can be neutralized before the initiation of the change activity. Once the goals are established and resources and hindrances are identified, the change agent can begin to delegate and assign responsibility to participants.

The change agent will spend considerable time conveying information. All relevant information must first be sought, then clarified and synthesized into a logical format as a guide to action. The ideas and suggestions of a wide range of people must be listened to, elaborated on, and synthesized into a plan that allows all involved to feel that their ideas were heard. The wise change agent tests information against reality to determine whether proposed plans seem realistic, workable, and economically feasible. Often the overexpenditure of human, economic, and technical resources in the implementation of change can be directly attributed to poor or incomplete planning.

If at all possible it is helpful to try to implement a change strategy on a limited basis so that weak points can be assessed early and remedied before the complete process commences. Evaluation at each stage is crucial. Few projects could not be improved.

In summary, the following model for change is offered:

1. Stimulation of idea: diagnosis of need or problem
2. Assessment of motivation and resources for change
3. Assessment of resources and capability of change agent
4. Diagnosis of the type of change strategy needed
5. Development of the implementation strategy
6. Pretesting (trial) of the implementation strategy
7. Revision of strategy as needed
8. Implementation of the change project

9. Observation, handling, avoidance, or overcoming of resistance to the project
10. Evaluation of the effectiveness of the change
11. Formulation of recommendations for future actions or modifications

REFERENCES

Bennis, W.G., Benne, K.D., Chin, R., and Corey, K.E.: The planning of change, ed. 3, New York, 1976, Holt, Rinehart & Winston.

Broskowski, A., Mermis, W.J., and Khajavi, F.: Managing the dynamics of change and stability. In Jones, J.E., and Pfeiffer, J.W.: The 1975 annual handbook for group facilitators, LaJolla, Calif., University Associates, Inc.

Chin, R., and Benne, K.D.: General strategies for effecting changes in human systems. In Bennis, W.G., et al., editors: The planning of change, ed. 3, New York, 1976, Holt, Rinehart & Winston.

Duncan, W.J.: Essentials of management, ed. 2, Hinsdale, Ill., 1978, The Dryden Press.

Fessler, D.R.: Facilitating community change: a basic guide, LaJolla, Calif., 1976, University Associates, Inc.

Hersey, P., and Blanchard, K.H.: Management of organizational behavior, Englewood Cliffs, N.J., 1977, Prentice-Hall, Inc.

Kelley, D., and Conner, D.R.: The emotional cycle of change. In Jones, J.E., and Pfeiffer, J.W.: The 1979 annual handbook for group facilitators, LaJolla, Calif., 1979, University Associates, Inc.

Kinney, M., Millington, P., and Jackson, B.S.: Planned change in the critical care unit, Heart Lung **7**:85-90, Jan. 1978.

Klein, D.: Some notes on the dynamics of resistance to change. In Bennis, W.G., et al., editors: The planning of change, ed. 3, New York, 1976, Holt, Rinehart & Winston.

Lee, I.M.: Coping with resistance to change, Nursing '73 **3**:6-7, March 1973.

Levenstein, A.: Effective change requires change agent, J. Nurs. Adm. **9**:12-14, June 1979.

Lewin, K.: Frontiers in group dynamics: concept, method and reality in social science; social equilibria and social change, Hum. Relations **1**:5-41, June 1947.

Lewin, K.: Field theory in social science, New York, 1951, Harper & Row, Publishers.

Lewin, K.: Group decision and social change. In Maccoby, E., editor: Readings in social psychology, ed. 3, New York, 1958, Holt, Rinehart & Winston.

Lippitt, G.L.: Visualizing change: model building and the change process, LaJolla, Calif., 1973, University Associates, Inc.

Olson, E.M.: Strategies and techniques for the nurse change agent, Nurs. Clin. North Am. **14**:323-336, June 1979.

Rodgers, J.A.: Theoretical considerations involved in the process of change, Nurs. Forum **12**(2):161-173, 1973.

Rogers, E.: Diffusion of innovations, New York, 1962, The Free Press of Glencoe.

Rogers, E., and Shoemaker, F.: Communication of innovations: a crosscultural approach, New York, 1971, The Free Press of Glencoe.

Sampson, E.: Social psychology and contemporary society, New York, 1971, John Wiley & Sons, Inc.

Stevens, B.J.: Effecting change, J. Nurs. Adm. **5**:23-26, Feb. 1975.

Toffler, A.: Future shock, New York, 1970, Bantam Books.

Toffler, A.: Focus on the future, keynote address, National League for Nursing Convention, May 1979, Atlanta, Ga.

Watzlawick, P., Weakland, C.E., and Fisch, R.: Change: principles of problem resolution, New York, 1974, W.W. Norton Co.

Ways, M.: The era of radical change, Fortune **74**:113, May 1964.

Welch, L.B.: Planned change in nursing: the theory, Nurs. Clin. North Am. **14**:307-321, June 1979.

General systems theory, when applied to human personality and behavior, considers the human system to be an active, open one in which personality develops through interaction with other systems; problems within one system can produce ripple effects in others.

Marmor, J.: Hosp. Community Psychiatry **26**:807, Dec. 1975.

2

SYSTEMS THEORY AND THE PROCESS OF CHANGE

Jeanette Lancaster

From earliest history people have attempted to understand, interact with, and alter their environments. Numerous approaches have been developed that describe the human-environmental relationships. A particularly useful framework conceptualizes each person as a hierarchy of natural, living systems that are connected to one another by a variety of patterns of information and energy. This hierarchy of natural systems can cover the range from atoms, molecules, organelles, organs, individuals, families, communities, nations, to the entire planet Earth. The systems approach is useful in explaining change, in that it provides a format for looking at each level of interaction within a system. Since much of nursing practice takes place within a large system or an organization, an overview of systems concepts seems especially pertinent to understanding the change process.

In the past nursing has relied heavily on intuitive thinking and "hunches" in devising solutions to patient care problems. Starting in the middle 1960s a significant movement occurred in nursing: the mode of problem solving shifted from an intuitive approach to the development of a sophisticated scientific basis for practice. At present a major goal in nursing is to develop a "formal, explicit theoretical framework that can be used for the development of formal decisions and predictions" (Auger, 1976, p. 22). Since Chapter 18 describes in detail the usefulness of nursing theory and conceptual models for practice, the goal of this chapter is to consider systems theory as a way of planning, organizing, evaluating, and controlling nursing practice.

The basic mission of a systems approach is to organize knowledge about a specific phenomenon (person, group, organization) so as to focus on the interactional processes that occur among the parts. Hence the systems approach emphasizes process more than structure. As a dynamic, ever-changing process, systems theory provides a way of predicting the consequences of change within any part of the system by looking at interaction, boundaries, and energy exchange. The approach in this chapter is to set forth systems theory concepts first, and then

to apply it to nursing practice within an organizational context. The application is made within an organizational context because the majority of nursing activities occur in agencies rather than in independent practice.

SYSTEMS THEORY: OVERVIEW OF CONCEPTS

Varying definitions of systems have been developed in the past twenty years. Classic among them is Ludwig von Bertalanffy's definition of systems (1968b, p. 33) as "complexes of elements standing in interaction." Auger (1976, p. 21) defined a system as a "whole with interrelated parts, in which the parts have a function and the system as a totality has a function." Similarly, Hall and Fagen (1968, p. 81) define a system as "a set of objects together with relationships between the objects and between their attributes." In this definition, objects are the parts or components of a system that are unlimited both in number and in character; attributes refer to the properties of objects, and relationships are what tie the system together.

A final systems definition that can be easily applied to understanding health care organizations states that a system is a "group of interrelated but separate elements working toward a common objective" (Duncan, 1978, p. 76). This definition includes at least three implications. First, the arrangement of elements is orderly and has some recognizable structure. Second, since the parts of the system interact, there is some form of communication present; and third, since the system is goal oriented, the system's interactions are designed to achieve the goals or objectives that will maintain the viability of the whole.

The systems approach provides a comprehensive framework for assessing the human-environmental relationship due to its flexibility and mechanism for organizing information to look at the whole and also at how the parts interact and influence one another.

Systems theory is especially useful as a framework for viewing change within an organization since it provides a scheme for organizing information to examine how each part or element of the system can be studied and manipulated. A systems theory model emphasizes unity and holism and seeks to avoid fragmented, reductionistic approaches toward looking at selected aspects of the universe. The goal of a systems model is to provide a "framework by which otherwise unconnected parts are integrated and many different pieces fall into place" (Hazzard, 1971, p. 385). Systems theory provides a framework for setting forth each part of a whole in order to assess or predict what a change in one part will do to each of the other parts.

From a systems theory perspective the "organization is viewed as one element of a number of elements which interact interdependently" (Gibson, et al., 1976, p. 61). Every organization takes information, energy, or resources (its inputs) from the supra system (environment), processes these resources, and then returns them in a different form back to the environment (output). Society expects organizations to be both effective and efficient. That is, organizations are expected to function at maximal effectiveness, which refers to the ability to meet the goals and objectives of the organization within the confines of limited resources. Furthermore, the outputs of an organization must meet societal expectations with the greatest possible efficiency in order to produce the maximal amount of output at the least possible expenditure of resources (e.g., fiscal, energy, time, work force).

The health care system has long been accused of being one of the most inefficient and wasteful industries of contemporary society. From a management perspective, an inefficient organization cannot exist for long; this principle has in the past not held true for health care organizations because of the external funds available and the limited requirements for accountability. Waste and inefficiency in health care organizations may not come to a "screeching halt" in the near future, but it is unlikely that inefficiency will be tolerated at the same rate as it has been in the years since World War II. Systems concepts serve as a scheme for evaluating organizational effectiveness and ultimately help in planning for change.

Degree of openness of systems

It is possible to classify systems according to their degree of openness or interaction with the environment. Systems are generally described as open or closed. A closed system is defined as one that admits no matter or energy from the environment, nor does it expel matter or energy into the environment. Closed systems "are subject to the action of the Second Law of Thermodynamics, which states that the entropy (roughly a measure of disorder) of a closed system will always increase toward a maximum, attained in equilibrium" (Buckley, 1968, p. xviii). The status of a closed system is always directly related to the initial system parts, in that no alterations occur when a system lacks the capability to exchange resources with the environment.

For example, a closed system such as a rock has minimal interaction with the environment. Such a system is assumed to have a "leak-tight boundary" with little if any interaction across the boundary. The only practical use of the closed-systems concept is that variables can be artificially isolated for observation in a closed-system framework for the purpose of a controlled analysis. In this approach new elements can be introduced into the system on a limited basis to evaluate their impact on the system. For the purpose of looking at change from a systems perspective, emphasis is placed on open systems.*

Open systems freely exchange information, energy, and nutrients with the environment as they attempt to maintain balance or a steady state. Hall

---

*Although this presentation focuses on open systems as most applicable to social organizations, Kast and Rosenzweig (1972) postulate that systems should not always be dichotomized into two categories (closed or physical systems and open or biological systems). They hypothesize that social organizations may indeed seek a closed-systems status in order to increase efficiency.

and Fagen (1968, p. 83) define the environment of a system as a "set of all objects a change in whose attributes affect the system and also those objects whose attributes are changed by the behavior of the system." It is not always easy to distinguish exactly what is part of the system from what is in the environment. For the purpose of system analysis, arbitrary decisions may be made to form system boundaries at a certain point, including specifying some elements as subsystems and all other elements as part of the environment.

In discussing system openness, it may be helpful to visualize a system by drawing a large circle. Inside the circle are the system elements, parts, or variables, each of which affects the others as depicted by lines of contact (see Fig. 2-1). The lines can be thought of as rubber bands that shrink and expand as the system's parts interact. The rim or boundary of the circle specifies what is internal and external to the system.

As noted, systems tend to be made up of subsystems that are generally arranged in a hierarchy. For example, in considering a person as a system one might start with examining the cellular level, then move to organs, complete regulatory systems, and then to the total person. Systems can be approached for the purposes of analysis from either a micro- or macroscopic view. For example, highly complex systems can be studied by starting with the most minute hierarchy, assessing it thoroughly, and then moving to the next level of organizational complexity. Another method for studying systems is to go directly to an analysis of the whole and move to a study of the parts.

Hall and Fagen (1968) illustrate the differences between microscopic and macroscopic views by contrasting the techniques of physiologists and psychologists. The physiologist isolates and minutely studies the functioning of various internal organs. For example, when the physiologist is studying kidney structure, other organs such as the heart or lungs might be designated as part of the environment. In contrast, the psychologist employs a macroscopic approach to look at behavior patterns under varying environmental conditions. In a psychological study, stimuli need to be considered and ultimately isolated in order to determine precisely what internal and/or external environmental forces have an effect on behavior.

Open systems, while tending toward a steady state or balance, seldom maintain themselves at a point of equilibrium; instead, they continuously exchange input and output with the environment.

Boundaries

An important characteristic of a system is the boundary or the area that separates the system from the environment. The boundary may be real or artificial depending on the type of system being examined. By definition, a boundary refers to the "more or less open line forming a circle around the system" which regulates the exchange of energy and information that can take place between the system and its environment (Auger, 1976, p. 23). As mentioned, all living systems are continuously exchanging resources across their boundaries with elements in the environment. The degree of resource exchange depends on the porosity of the boundary. Since the boundary serves as a filter for the system, the more porous the filter the greater the interaction with the environment. Also the degree of porosity of the boundary corresponds with the

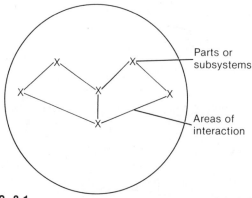

Parts or subsystems

Areas of interaction

FIG. 2-1
Visualization of an open system.

predictability credited to the system. A system with continuous, multiple, and widely divergent sources of input is less predictable than one whose boundary filters out a large portion of the potential input.

Consider patients in any type of critical care unit experiencing multiple sources of noise from machinery, multiple energy inputs from continuous monitoring, examinations, and intermittent episodes of pain. The boundary for these patients (systems) may be quite porous, frequently resulting in sensory overload and leading to psychological disequilibrium. In this example, the patient's ability to filter or screen stimuli is minimal because of physiological stress; the onslaught of further stimuli leads to greater degrees of stress.

Boundaries not only refer to physical and psychological attributes; they also include relationships such as roles, acts, expectations, influence, and power. As mentioned, a boundary is "the line forming a closed circle around selected variables, where there is less interchange of energy (or communication, etc.) across the line of the circle than within the limiting circle" (Chin, 1976b, p. 93). In assessing and diagnosing a potential situation for change, we need to tentatively examine the elements and assign each to a designated system with its unique boundary. As the system grows and develops the boundary may need to be renegotiated, in that some people are actually part of the system rather than external to it. For example, a student's graduate committee may serve as a system. The student may select five members, all of whom are interested in the student's research idea with each one bringing a different capability to the system. As work commences on the student's research it may become abundantly clear that a necessary type of expertise is missing. Often the student needs additional support from a statistician. To meet this system's need, the committee can be enlarged from five to six members, or one member can be asked to withdraw in order to add the person needed to meet the newly diagnosed system deficit.

Any discussion of system boundaries would be incomplete without considering both interfaces and linkages. An *interface* is the area of contact between two systems. Fig. 2-2 illustrates the relationship between boundaries and interfaces in two interacting systems.

As mentioned, the boundary serves as the filter for each system and also separates the system from the environment. In contrast, the interface is the area of overlap or connection between the two systems. In a human system a *link* is the person or persons assigned the responsibility for making contacts between systems. The tasks assigned to the link include obtaining input from other designated systems, interpreting this input for the system of origin, and providing information (feedback) to the other system.

Structure and function of systems

Theoretically, all natural phenomena can be discussed from a systems perspective. Systems are organized in hierarchial levels of complexity with the simpler systems constituting subsystems within the framework of the total complex system. For example, the largest possible living system that can be visualized clearly is the universe with its billions of human and nonhuman inhabitants (subsystems). Similarly, the family can be viewed as a system with each member representing a given subsystem. Likewise, a hospital or public health agency is a system comprised of multiple interacting subsystems.

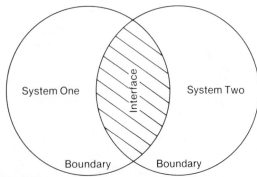

FIG. 2-2
System boundaries and interfaces.

The structure of any system refers to the unique arrangement of its parts or elements. On the other hand, function in systems terminology refers to the ongoing interaction among the parts. In a smoothly running system it should not be possible to discriminate the functioning of each part, in that each part should fit so well into the whole that we are generally aware of the entirety and not each part. A simplistic example of systems functioning is the human body. In a state of effective functioning the component body systems such as the gastrointestinal, urinary, or respiratory subsystems, should present a unified whole rather than a group of isolated systems. Only when an imbalance occurs do the discrete systems become obvious.

In a later section of this chapter the point of view is set forth that in an organization (e.g., a health care agency or institution) the actual functioning of system parts (subsystems) can bear little resemblance to the functions that seem to be proscribed by the formal structure. In many human systems the actual functional patterns more actively control the system than patterns outlined in formal organizational descriptions of structure.

Input–transformation–output

All systems exist to serve some function or reach some goal. No goal can be attained without energy expenditure, thus all open systems continuously take in energy, information, matter, or other resources as input; then they transform these resources and subsequently return them to the environment as output.

The output from any given system must be useful to the environment or suprasystem; if the products are undesirable to the environment, then they must either be changed or the system supplying them will no longer be needed and will be terminated. Thus inputs must be carefully processed and transformed into relevant and useful outputs, otherwise the viability of the system becomes limited.

An organization has two major categories of inputs: human and natural resources. Human inputs consist of the people who work in the organization and contribute their time, energy, and cognitive abilities in return for wages and other tangible or intangible rewards. Natural resources refer to the nonhuman inputs that can be processed so as to maintain the functioning of the organization. For example, universities take in resources (input) such as tuition, grants, tax monies, and endowment funds and gifts in order to teach students, conduct research, and provide services to society. The input must be sufficient to meet the demands of essential output (e.g., salaries, buildings and supplies, upkeep). In order to remain viable, the output and input must be fairly well balanced.

Likewise, in a hospital the inputs include personnel, equipment, supplies, and patients. The patients are processed by using the knowledge and technological resources available. To the extent that the patients are afforded the highest possible quality of care, the hospital is considered efficient and in a state of relative balance. Any organization's survival depends upon its (1) ability to adapt to environmental demands and (2) focus on the importance of a balanced input–processing–output cycle (Gibson et al., 1976).

Feedback

Feedback is the process whereby "output at one stage of a system's operation is returned to the system in the form of input for a successive stage" (Duncan, 1978, p. 79). A system makes alterations in its activities and operations on the basis of the feedback it receives. Feedback, then, is the "process by which an organism learns from its experiences with its environment" (Gibson et al., 1976, p. 62).

Any organization depends on its environment both for its input and for the acceptance of its output. For this reason feedback serves an invaluable purpose by providing information to the system as to how it is perceived by forces outside the boundary. Accurate feedback depends on a high degree of perceptiveness to both verbal and nonverbal cues in the environment.

Stevens (1979, p. 202) maintains that the feedback loop has three functions:
1. It produces information concerning the system's output.
2. It compares this information to preestablished goals and objectives.
3. It adjusts the system for better goal achievement. Typically system adjustment takes place during the processing or transformation phase but on occasion may be regulated through the filtering out of certain inputs so that they cannot serve as system disrupters.

Energy

All open systems require energy exchanges with the environment in order to maintain the functioning and integrity of the system. The continuous energy input from the environment can be dealt with in a variety of ways: (1) The energy can be used immediately by the system to perform necessary tasks; (2) it can be stored in the form in which it was taken in for later usage; or (3) it can be changed into an entirely different form either for immediate or later usage. Once energy is utilized or processed within the system it then serves as output or motivates other energy sources to be expelled as output from the system into the environment. In general, a system and its environment exist in a symbiotic relationship in which each serves as a source of energy for the other.

Every system requires a minimal reserve of energy in order to maintain viability and be able to interact with the environment. It is important to remember that the First Law of Thermodynamics holds that energy can neither be created nor destroyed but rather can only be changed from one form to another or moved from one place to another.

A key factor "governing the rate of energy transformation in a system is the level of ongoing activity within the system" (Auger, 1976, p. 27). If the activity level is high, then greater amounts of energy are necessary to sustain the work of the system. Certain types of mental and physical activities such as physical exertion, exercise, or strong emotions like fear and anger require considerable energy expenditures and may temporarily deplete the system's supply of available and usable energy. Each system has a certain gradient for tolerating energy deficits. When the deficit is great either in magnitude or the time involved, the system's integrity may be threatened. For example, the central nervous system can tolerate a deficit of oxygen for only four to six minutes before irreversible damage is likely to occur.

Moreover, every system must have a mechanism for storing energy in order to maintain some independence and autonomy from the environment. According to Auger (1976, p. 27), at any given time five different forms of energy are available for system utilization:
1. Energy that is entering the system in a nonfunctional form
2. Energy that is in the process of being transformed into a functional form
3. Energy that is being utilized
4. Energy by-products that are being dissipated to the environment
5. Entropic energy

The interaction among the first four sources of energy takes place at a relatively constant rate to maintain a state of balance. The system enters a state of disequilibrium when there is a lack of balance among the first four energy sources and activities.

Entropic energy has been defined as "that quantity of energy that is not capable of conversion into work" (Hazzard, 1971, p. 398). Whenever energy is transferred from one form into another, only a portion of this energy is actually available for work. The remaining energy is held in reserve as entropy or unavailable or "bound" energy. Entropy refers to a tendency toward disorder; maximum entropy is the "tendency toward maximum disorder within a system" (Hazzard, 1971, p. 398). The level of entropy (bound or nonusable energy) varies in an open system as a result of the continuous interaction with the environment.

In contrast, negentropy or negative entropy is the

energy in an open system that can be utilized by the system. Unlike entropy, negentropy represents order in the system and is available for carrying out necessary functions.

Information can be considered a form of energy that has considerable relevance for the application of systems theory concepts to nursing practice. Information processing, or communication, "is the change of information from one state to another or its movement from one point to another over space" (Hazzard, 1971, p. 397). As will be discussed in Chapter 8, the message sent is not always consistent with the message received. The transmission of information from one system to another or between subparts in a single system allows for distortion at several points. The perceptivity, biases, and frames of reference of system elements, as well as interference during the transformation process (e.g., from excess emotional discomfort or pain) affect the clarity of the message transmission.

In the late 1940s, Norbert Wiener (1968) introduced the concept of "cybernetics," which describes information and communication from a systems view. Cybernetics is essentially the "science of communication and control" (Buckley, 1968, p. xix). As such, it examines patterns of signals that transmit information from one system to another and also within a given system. The perspective taken in cybernetics is that transmission of energy is essential to control. Wiener (1968) maintains that the process of taking in and using information is central to determining an individual's relationship with the environment. He also purports that the information conveyed in a set of messages is directly related to the measure of organization present in the system. That is, disorganized systems transmit inaccurate, poorly timed, or incomplete messages. This process becomes circular in that inferior information militates against effective functioning and may breed further levels of inaccurate messages. Although cybernetics is not pursued here in any depth, recognition is given to its role as a systems-oriented study of information transmission.

Disorganization and equilibrium

Since systems are constantly engaged in the processes of taking in resources, processing or transforming them, and subsequently discharging output, they tend to be in a constant state of disequilibrium. Systems strive toward balance or a steady state, but rarely can such a state be sustained. Neither excessive input nor excessive output is useful to a system, since both situations tend to diminish the overall effectiveness of the system. For example, the excessive circulatory output in a hemorrhage is disruptive to effective physiological functioning. Likewise, a psychotic reaction precipitated by overstimulation (as in the critical care area) or from lack of stimulation (in an isolation or seclusion room) is illustrative of ineffective system functioning.

Chin (1976b, p. 94) distinguishes equilibrium, a "fixed point or level," from steady state, the "balanced relationship of parts that is not dependent upon any fixed equilibrium point or level." He uses body temperature to illustrate equilibrium or a fixed point toward which the body returns after any disturbance. Whereas the relationship between two work units represents a steady state, there are few pure examples of equilibrium because most human interactions are dynamic, and the relationships never really return to the preexisting point. A system in relative balance or steady state responds to excessive amounts of input in a variety of ways in order to resist the threatened disruption posed by the input. One way to resist a potential disturbance is simply to ignore its existence. For example, in a small work group one member may feel continually unrecognized as a valuable resource person. The group perceives their status as relatively balanced and comfortable, so they choose to ignore the member's overtures for a greater degree of inclusion.

The second mechanism for reacting to outside impingements is to recreate a state of balance immediately. For example, in the illustration cited above, the group may listen to the member's complaints about feeling useless and try to persuade the individual that the problem is merely a matter of perception; that is, the alienated member is just imagining that a problem exists.

The third way to resist outside forces is to create a new level of equilibrium. This can be done by directly addressing the perceived problem and working out a new distribution in the group's power and status relationships.

Tension, stress, strain, and conflict

Open systems do not maintain a static position. Because systems constantly interact with one another, and also because the elements of each system are different and not perfectly consistent in outlook and activities, tension and stress arise. For example, no two people think exactly the same way, nor would they consistently approach problem solving in the same manner. Marital partners are often required to deal with differences in the family system ranging from spending patterns to the discipline of children. The same types of differences occur in work groups when members see problems differently and have divergent goals and values, unique energy, and intellectual resources.

According to Chin (1976b, p. 93), tensions that are "internal and arise out of the structural arrangements of the system" are considered stresses and strains. Conflict arises when tensions accumulate and become polarized among two or more opponents. Human nature tends to be directed toward tension reduction and maintenance of comfort. Frequently this tendency to avoid stress and seek ways to reduce tension quickly and comfortably militates against creativity and originality. Tension may also be a warning sign that massive system problems are imminent. The task of any change agent is to remain attuned to even the slightest signs of stress and conflict in order to assess the origin of the tension early in the change process.

SYSTEMS THEORY AS A MODEL FOR NURSING PRACTICE

Models are often used to simulate reality by depicting representations of the real world. Finch maintains that "general systems theory makes pos-

sible the development of models that are abstractions of the real world" (1969, p. 182). The model identifies the parts or variables that can be manipulated to create new wholes. Such manipulation can be done through simulation so as to predict real-life events before they occur. Models also allow a comparison of the real with the ideal or "what is" with "what ought to be."

Chapter 18 discusses the process of model building and elaborates on the usefulness of models in nursing. The goal here is to describe models briefly and then to look at the components of a systems model. In solving any problem or critically examining any situation, it is necessary to describe the components, explain the relationships, and account for or predict the effect of usual functioning as well as the altered functioning that occurs with the introduction of any change.

It must be pointed out that in every instance of model building, our thoughts about such entities as components, relationships, or problems are merely abstractions based on our own perception of reality. Each of us makes abstractions and generalizations about reality based on our past experiences, values, beliefs, biases, and goals. By using abstractions we develop mental models or pictures of how we view reality.

Models can be classified in a variety of ways and Chapter 18 presents several examples. While systems can be modeled in many ways, this chapter will focus on the descriptive level.

According to Stevens (1979, p. 200), a framework for a systems model would contain at least eight categories. That is, a systems model for practice would be expected to:

1. Differentiate the system from its environment.
2. Describe the input–transformation–output process.
3. Identify the influence of energy in the system. (Where does it come from, what does it do?)
4. Discuss how the system maintains or strives toward balance or a steady state.

5. Identify the goals or objectives of the system.
6. Describe the throughput or transformation process in specific steps.
7. Identify the role of feedback.
8. Discuss the system in regard to the suprasystem of which it is a part as well as the system's constituent subsystems.

For the purposes of this discussion, a systems model is used as a tool for examining change. As such, a systems model for change focuses not just on ways to maintain stability but also on how change emerges out of the inevitable stresses and conflicts in the system. From this perspective the process of change takes place in order to reduce tension. A key area in examining the role of the change agent or innovator from a systems perspective is to pay careful attention to the connections between systems, which have previously been described as areas of interface or linkages. Since the change agent is often external to the actual client system, two distinct sets of boundaries, tensions, stresses, inputs, and outputs must be considered. Fig. 2-3 depicts the relationship between the change agent and the client system being changed. As can be seen in this illustration, the system as well as the change agent's own personal system go

through the processes of input, transformation, and output. Each of the two systems' output serves as input to the other system and influences subsequent system processes. Although Fig. 2-3 depicts the change agent as external to the system, this is not always the case. In many instances the change agent may comprise a subsystem of the overall system for which change is planned. That is, the change agent may already be an employee of the system who is assigned the responsibility of developing new policies, plans, or procedures.

A change agent must be especially sensitive to feedback in order to determine how activities, ideas, and new programs are being accepted. Feedback is found in what people say as well as in their obvious omissions in a discussion. For example, assume that a change agent presented a new model for patient education to the nurses on three units. After a week, evaluation forms were received from one unit that rated the program as quite useful. If no forms were returned from the other two units, the change agent would need to determine whether the lack of response represented forgetfulness or a passive-negative evaluation of the program. An active inquiry on the part of the change agent would be required to learn just how to interpret the feedback received from the two nonresponding units.

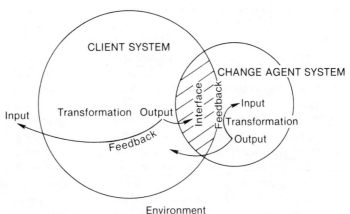

FIG. 2-3
System processing: change agent system and system to be changed.

The environmental components of the system

Now that the components of a systems model have been described, emphasis can be placed on the environment in which the system operates. All too frequently, change strategies are planned without sufficient respect for and knowledge of the environmental constraints and/or resources. In considering nursing practice within a health care organization the environment is of paramount importance. By definition, the environment refers to everything that is external to the system.

Chin (1976a) identifies five content aspects of the system's environment that have direct relevance for planned change. First, he addresses the *means available* in the environment for transforming the environment. For example, the rapid advances in technology, greater depths of knowledge, and changes in human impulses are all potential sources of environmental alteration. Perhaps never before in history have so many technological and social changes as well as possibilities for innovation existed that could dramatically and often rapidly alter the environment in which each of us lives.

Second, Chin focuses on the *patterns that structure power and authority* in the environment. The balances or ratios of power and influence determine whether the locus of control is within or external to the system. In any proposed change situation, it is extremely important to accurately assess where the power lies. It is not unusual for the greatest pool of potential power to lie in the most unexpected places. Persons who legitimately are expected to have considerable power by virtue of their position may in reality be virtually ineffectual either by choice or by loss of power to an overly controlling co-worker. It is not uncommon for people in a system to gain power by intimidation or threats of overaggressiveness. People also control others in varying covert and subtle ways, one of which is sabotage of new plans or projects. For these reasons the success of any change project relies heavily on determining "who holds power in the system—how and over whom?" The assessment provides information as to the relative strength of system inputs—that is, whose input has more influence. It is also helpful to remember that the balance of power can shift rapidly in any social system. Later chapters will discuss power and its influence on nursing practice more thoroughly, as well as ways of utilizing power to effect change.

The third aspect of the environment that affects the change process includes the *resources* available for innovations. Chin (1976a, p. 109) regards these resources as nutrients "with objects, functions and dynamics involved in them." For example, resources may include money, materials, time, and psychological need fulfillment. Items become resources when the system's survival is dependent on their intake. Too often people view resources as being finite and have an aversion to sharing among systems. We often think that if we share resources, praise, or encouragement we will somehow allow others to gain some sort of advantage. Hence, resources such as time, money, information, and psychosocial support often tend to be withheld rather than freely shared. Such thinking leads to a form of win-lose competition that carries the potential of motivating or impeding each system.

Fourth, the environment offers a virtually unlimited supply of *information* in the form of signals, symbols, communications, and actions (Chin, 1976a). The task of the change agent is to clarify the information in the environment so as to improve the system's functioning. Chapter 8 provides an overview of communication theory, which is vital to the change agent's knowledge of the system as well as its interacting environment. It is helpful to remember that information may present conflicts, distortions or misperceptions, and personal biases. The change agent must be astute to biased or erroneous sources of information, so that undue system disruption need not take place. Just as with nutrients, the information sources available in the system influence the output by determining the quality of the transformation or processing of system inputs. Scarcity of nutrients as well as inaccurate, scanty, or useless information makes system functioning difficult.

The fifth content aspect of a system's environment identified by Chin, potential *feedback loops* in the environment, must also be assessed. This stage is useful for analyzing, diagnosing, and planning improvements in the system. As mentioned earlier, feedback keeps systems functioning effectively because it regulates the information, energy, and resources in the system.

Luciano (1979) discusses the environmental view of systems in terms of five components that share several similarities with the environmental factors discussed by Chin. Luciano (1979, p. 140) says that "the systems view of organizations provides a framework for looking at the organization as a whole in terms of process-related subsystems." Each of the five subsystems is separate and definable yet intimately related so as to support the functioning of the total systems. These subsystems include: psychosocial, structural, objective, technological, and managerial.

The *psychosocial* subsystem "considers and is made up of individuals (psycho) and groups of individuals (social) within the organization" (Luciano, 1979, p. 141). This subsystem considers the unique and highly personal values, beliefs, attitudes, and motivations of each participant. This subsystem also contains the quality and openness of interactions; the degree of trust, acceptance, feelings of worth and belonging; and also the conflicts, envies, and fears of individuals. The psychosocial subsystem is especially difficult to diagnose because people often tend to portray to others views that may conflict with what they really think or feel. No matter how difficult, it is extremely important to assess this subsystem, and negative reactions to any plan need to be assessed early. This subsystem includes obvious elements as well as more subtle feelings and biases. Each of us responds to change based on our past experiences with similar situations; thus we are influenced by unobservable memories, ideas, beliefs, and feelings.

Luciano's second subsystem, the *structural*, refers to the lines of authority and responsibility within the organization. Just as with communica-

tion, there are both formal and informal structures within any organizational hierarchy. Often the informal structure has far more power and control than can be found in the designated positions ordinarily equated with power and authority. The organizational chart should depict what "ought to be" the structure of any agency or health care institution.

Detecting the informal structure is often a complex task requiring astute observational skills. For example, on some hospital patient care units the individual who wields the most control may be the aide or orderly who has worked on that unit for twenty years and remembers the chief of staff "from when he was a medical student" and the nursing supervisors from their days of basic nursing education. As head nurses come and go, they may fail to gain sufficient respect and recognition from the staff to be considered an appreciable force in the organization's structure. Often the most powerless person in this type of unit is the clinical specialist who has no authorized power when in a staff rather than a line position.

The third subsystem, which Luciano calls *objectives,* refers to the specific goals that comprise the overall mission of the organization with regard to the segment of a larger system or society that it serves. It is crucial that all components (people) in the system be cognizant of the goals and agree to work toward them in a manner that facilitates rather than hinders goal attainment. Just as there are formal and informal structural components or subsystems, there are both overt, readily identifiable objectives and covert, privately held goals. It is not unheard of for members of a work group to agree outwardly that certain goals should be set forth and that they will unequivocally support the delineated strategy for goal attainment. This overt display of allegiance is then countered by devious, subtle attempts to avert goal attainment. The chapter on communication discusses the role of rumors and the grapevine in an organization; both of these communication modes can be used to offset goal attainment.

The change agent, then, needs to establish checkpoints in any project in order to determine at frequent intervals what objectives are being met, how participants are responding to the project, and what suggestions others would offer. It is easier to evaluate whether objectives are being attained or not if they were clearly established and prioritized at the outset of the plan. Carefully monitoring the meeting of objectives also facilitates the processing stage.

The *technological* or fourth subsystem as identified by Luciano (1979) is that part of a system most taken for granted. This subsystem represents the tools, techniques, equipment, and whatever else would be required to implement a change strategy. In a narrow sense, technology refers to the actual physical resources. As has been mentioned, these are generally not infinite but need to be carefully allocated in order to obtain the greatest possible benefit. In a broader sense, technology includes the "know-how" or means to use the physical, intellectual, or emotional resources to the greatest advantage. No doubt some people are more gifted at the use of resources than are others. Likewise, most people would benefit from feedback on how (specifically) they could be more efficient and productive. This type of assistance can be obtained through continuing education, consultation, peer or supervisory evaluation, and suggestions. The technological subsystem is similar to what Chin considers the nutrients of the environment.

Luciano describes the fifth subsystem, *managerial,* as that part of any organization that organizes and controls the other subsystems. Few systems remain highly efficient when they are poorly managed. Moreover, the art of effective management within any living system includes far more than knowing how to organize and do things well yourself. Perhaps the most subtle yet powerful aspect of good management is knowing how to manage people so that they feel valued, appreciated, and respected. Encouragement, support, and praise (when justified) are potent ingredients for successful management. Each of these five subsystems starts with the system input and directly influences the quality of the processing or transformation phase and the subsequent output.

Defense as a part of system change

A change, whether major or minor, in any subsystem will have an impact on all other parts. Open systems frequently tend to resist change, often seeing it as a threat to the integrity and ultimate stability of the system and thus actively guarding against it. Individuals, groups, and communities may represent systems that feel quite adequate to meet ordinary challenges from the environment. The anticipation or introduction of change seems detrimental and threatening and is thereby actively resisted. Whether the threat is real or only represents lack of information or misperception, it instigates a form of resistance.

Frequently resistance to change can be minimized if the change agent keeps all parts of the system informed, and if information and opinions are solicited from individuals in the system as well as from influential elements in the environment. Too few planners of change are well grounded in the ability to collaborate with *all* who can be expected to be involved or affected. Often overlooked sources of input in the change process are the patients who are the recipients of nursing care. This omission increases the points at which resistance can occur, in that both project participants and recipients can resist an innovation that poses a threat to their conception of system functioning. Feelings of threat are particularly felt when the motives and plans of innovators are kept secret until just before the plan is to be implemented.

The defender role can be enacted by individuals as well as groups when threat to their integrity is perceived. This role is played out in a variety of both actively overt or subtly passive ways, depending on such factors as the setting, the type of change, the characteristics of the group or individuals involved, and the time frame for change. The defender role may be assumed by a senior, highly respected member of the group as well as by activists and rebels in the system.

How the change agent views the defender has

implications for the system's willingness to accept the innovation. No matter how irrational and unfounded the defender's reasons are for resisting the innovation, they must be heeded, since a valuable message is usually being communicated. In some instances the resistance provides an opportunity to refine plans for change, which may ultimately increase the likelihood of acceptance.

In order to appreciate fully the defender role from a systems-theory perspective, it is helpful to discuss briefly some basic concepts related to role theory. Each system is composed not only of a clearly designated organizational structure, but it also contains a network of positions occupied by individuals. A specific role is usually assigned to a position rather than a person, and expectations of how the person filling the role will behave are largely determined by the values, goals, and norms of the system. Thus the system provides guidance and parameters regarding what is considered acceptable behavior for the occupant of a given role. Not only does each system have input as to role-specific behavior, but other interacting systems have an opinion and influence on the appropriateness of the behavior of a role occupant. For example, consider from an organizational perspective the role of the staff nurse in a hospital unit. If a certain staff nurse wishes to make a change in the patient care unit, the nursing system on the unit will have a marked impact on determining whether such an innovation is part of the staff nurse role. Further, physicians, dieticians, technicians, and others may provide input as to the role appropriateness of the proposed change if it affects them in any way.

When any proposed change disrupts current role alignments, resistance is likely to occur. People tend to avoid any innovation that threatens old, often familiar and comfortable ways of doing things. For example, the creation of a new position in a nursing unit calls for a new set of roles. Not only is the occupant of the new position filling a new role, but all other system parts can be expected to feel the impact of this new role as role overlap; thus confusion and perhaps conflict result.

The role of change agent in any system is usually a challenging opportunity. The actual change-agent role may be ambiguous, with system members holding different expectations about what the change agent ought to do. Role expectations may not be clearly defined, or if defined clearly, may not be subscribed to by all involved parties. For example, a clinical specialist may be hired as a change agent with the task of improving patient care in a designated part of an institution. The staff may agree that clinical specialists "should" improve patient care, but they may firmly believe that the highest possible level of care is already being delivered, thereby negating the newly established role.

Not only may the change agent's role be ambiguous within the system, but the actual placement of the role often affects the success of the role occupant. That is, some change agents come from or function from within the system, whereas others function outside the system, possibly in a consultant role. The placement (i.e., inside or outside) of the change agent will often affect the degree to which defender roles emerge. Placement of a change agent should be determined by the resources available, the "personality" of the system, and the type of change desired.

The change agent in any system is generally in an insecure and risky position. The role ascribed to the change agent may be expendable. Thus if the innovation fails, the change agent may be out of a job. Change agents usually derive power from either expertise or ascribed position in the system. The amount of authority held by the change agent will significantly influence the nature and strategies for change. When the change agent advocates an innovation that is not satisfactory to the system, the defender role comes actively into play, and such resistance will frequently stifle the innovation.

SUMMARY

Systems theory provides a way of looking at both organizational structure and functioning. As a conceptual approach, systems theory allows for both analysis and synthesis. In order to analyze a given system, each part (subsystem) can be examined in isolation as well as in terms of interactions between and among the parts. A change in one subsystem has far-reaching ramifications, since all other subsystems are affected. System analysis provides a format for looking at how change in one subsystem does or can be expected to affect the total system as well as each subsystem.

As a synthetic approach, systems theory postulates that the "whole is greater than the sum of its parts." As the subsystems interact and are combined to form a total, unified system, new characteristics emerge. Thus systems development is not additive; the sum of three subsystems is not equal to the new synthetic system. The newly developed total system will include not only subsystems but will have unique characteristics of its own.

In an era of growing complexity, in society generally and the health care industry specifically, our conceptual approaches will largely determine the effectiveness of our practice. A systems view provides for a comprehensive approach to health care that acknowledges the complexity involved in looking at multiple, continuously interacting open systems where change is a way of life.

The human (organizational) system is open and continuously altered by inputs and the consequences of the system's own outputs. All living systems have a tendency to strive for a steady state by seeking a balance between inputs and outputs. An organizational steady state is rare in that many human subsystems influence the information-processing capacity.

This chapter has discussed basic elements and characteristics of systems theory and has applied the theoretical content to organizational functioning. System change and reactions to innovations were addressed from the viewpoint that systems often resist change in a variety of ways in order to maintain what participants view as a balanced position.

REFERENCES

Auger, J.: Behavioral systems and nursing, Englewood Cliffs, N.J., 1976, Prentice-Hall, Inc.

Bertalanffy, L. von: General systems theory: a critical review. In Buckley, W., editor: Modern systems research for the behavioral scientist, Chicago, 1968a, Aldine Publishing Co.

Bertalanffy, L. von: General systems theory: foundation, development, applications, rev. ed., New York, 1968b, George Braziller.

Boulding, K.E.: General systems theory: the skeleton of science. In Buckley, W., editor: Modern systems research for the behavioral scientist, Chicago, 1968, Aldine Publishing Co.

Buckley, W., editor: Modern systems research for the behavioral scientist, Chicago, 1968, Aldine Publishing Co.

Buckley, W.: Sociology and modern systems theory, Englewood Cliffs, N.J., 1978, Prentice-Hall, Inc.

Chin, R.: The utility of models of the environments of systems for practitioners. In Bennis, W.G., et al., editors: The planning of change, ed. 3, New York, 1976a, Holt, Rinehart & Winston.

Chin, R.: The utility of system models and developmental models for practitioners. In Bennis, W.G., et al., editors: The planning of change, ed. 3, New York, 1976b, Holt, Rinehart & Winston.

Duncan, W.J.: Essentials of management, ed. 2, Hinsdale, Ill., 1978, The Dryden Press.

Finch, J.: Systems analysis: a logical approach to professional nursing care, Nurs. Forum **2**(2):176-189, 1969.

Gibson, J.L., Ivancevich, J.M., and Donnelly, J.N.: Organizations: behavior, structure, processes, Dallas, 1976, Business Publications, Inc.

Hall, A.D., and Fagen, R.E.: Definition of system. In Buckley, W., editor: Modern systems research for the behavioral scientist, Chicago, 1968, Aldine Publishing Co.

Hazzard, M.E.: An overview of systems theory, Nurs. Clin. North Am. **6**:385-393, Sept. 1971.

Kast, F.E., and Rosenzweig, J.E.: General systems theory: applications for organization and management, Acad. Management J. **15**(4):447-465, Dec. 1972.

Luciano, P.R.: The systems view of organizations: dynamics of organizational change. In Jones, J.E., and Pfeiffer, J.W., editors: The 1979 annual handbook for group facilitators, LaJolla, Calif., 1979, University Associates, Inc.

Marmor, J.: The relationship between systems theory and community psychiatry, Hosp. Community Psychiatry **26**:807-811, Dec. 1975.

Putt, A.M.: General systems theory applied to nursing, Boston, 1979, Little, Brown & Co.

Stevens, B.J.: Nursing theory: analysis, application and evaluation, Boston, 1979, Little, Brown & Co.

Wiener, N.: Cybernetics in history. In Buckley, W., editor: Modern systems research for the behavioral scientist, Chicago, 1968, Aldine Publishing Co.

This confusion about organization theory is not surprising if we recognize that because large organizations are so complex, researchers usually study only segments and limited aspects of their operations.

Lawrence, P.R., and Lorsch, J.W.: Organization and environment, 1969, Richard D. Irwin, Inc., p. 2.

3

ORGANIZATION THEORY: DESIGN STRATEGIES FOR COPING WITH CHANGE

W. Jack Duncan

The supervisor of Surgery Unit Three in Holy Mother Hospital has just been informed by the hospital administrator that James Britman, a promising young R.N., cannot be granted a leave of absence for advanced graduate work. The reason is simple: the university's quarter begins three weeks before Mr. Britman completes his compulsory one year of service. The rule is that any employee must be in full-time service for one year before a leave of absence can be granted. The options are equally clear. He can wait until the next class is admitted in six months or resign his position. Mr. Britman consequently resigns. The nurse supervisor must now recruit a replacement who will demand as much pay with no experience as Mr. Britman presently makes, and the hospital will lose a valuable and promising employee. "Rules are rules," says the administrator, and if you make one exception the entire system will break down.

What person in a responsible position in any organization has never experienced this type of frustration? "It's the system," some say, and "you might as well adjust to it." Others are not content with the status quo, and they look for new ways of making organizations responsive to changing conditions.

Solutions to this type of problem have as a rule been sought at the interpersonal level, and it has been suggested that improved human-relations skills, altered leadership styles, and sharper negotiating abilities would solve or even prevent such difficulties. The interpersonal level is indeed important. Organization theorists, however, view interpersonal relations as only one part of a larger, more serious question. In fact, the behavior evident at the interpersonal level may be merely a symptom of a more fundamental set of forces resulting from the organization's structure or design philosophy.

Since interpersonal skills are the focus of other parts of this book, the present chapter will approach the management problem from the perspective of organizational design. In doing so, the following objectives will be accomplished:

1. To present the logic of classical organizational design theory
2. To present modern organization theory in a proper perspective by reviewing its historical foundations
3. To highlight real and potential problems of classical theory within the context of modern organizational realities
4. To introduce some contingency arguments that propose to make organization theory more responsive to environmental changes

This is an ambitious undertaking for a single chapter on organization theory. Therefore the overriding concern will be to survey the issues rather than to examine intensively the numerous arguments and controversies that will be uncovered.

HISTORICAL FOUNDATIONS

Organization theory has, as Perrow (1973) puts it, a "short and glorious history." The history is certainly short if we restrict the survey to the existence of "systematic" organization theory or that body of knowledge that has developed from conscious attempts to develop concepts and principles of management. On the other hand, the historical framework would have to extend to early civilizations if we include all attempts to deal with organizational problems. For numerous reasons, not the least of which are time and space constraints, our review will be limited and brief.

Most of the organization theory practiced today can be traced to the early twentieth century. Concern for the theory of organizational design evolved from attempts by the German sociologist Max Weber to describe and improve on the bureaucratic structures he observed in religious, governmental, and military organizations (Henderson and Parsons, 1947). Extension of Weber's work is known generally as the theory of *bureaucracy*. A French industrialist named Henri Fayol contributed to the field through his analysis of administrative aspects of organization. Fayol was particularly interested in understanding and improving the functions managers perform, such as planning, organizing, and controlling (Gulick and Urwick, 1969). In America, an engineer named Frederick Taylor popularized his approach, known as *scientific management,* and emphasized the importance of applying systematic methods to the study of work (Taylor, 1914).

Collectively, these writers formed the basis of the classical theory of organization. That is, these people were important because some aspect of the structural properties of organization was addressed by each. Weber was interested in the structure of organizations, Fayol in the structure of the manager's job, and Taylor in the structure of work. It was not until the mid-1930s, after the famous Hawthorne Studies on the social characteristics of organizations, that a substantial interest in human factors developed among social scientists concerned with management (Roethlisberger and Dickson, 1939). Our initial concern will be restricted to classical theory and practice.

CLASSICAL DESIGN THEORY

It would be a mistake to assume that classical organization theory is a thing of the past. It is very much alive and well. In fact, it is probably the most commonly encountered theory of organizational design in business, education, government, and health care. Therefore we must understand the logic of classical theory if we are to understand the structure and operation of most contemporary organizations.

Logic of classical design theory

We can illustrate much of the logic of classical design theory with reference to Fig. 3-1, which is the organization chart for the Division of Nursing Services at Cooper's Cove School and Hospital (CCSH). CCSH is a state-supported mental retardation facility that has facilities for 600 residents.

Referring to this chart and speculating about some of the things that "go on inside," five basic concepts of classical theory can be illustrated:

1. *Division of work.* Looking across the horizontal dimension of the CCSH organization chart, it is easy to see that most of the nurses in this division are specialized in terms of their job demands. Some nurses are responsible for ward services; others are specifically responsible for coordinating training and development activities, others for emergency services, and so on. The economic specialization principle justifies this type of structure, because efficiency can be increased so long as the degree of specialization is kept within limits (Franklin, 1975).

2. *Hierarchy.* This relates to the vertical dimension of the organization whereby management personnel are stratified by level. The coordinator of emergency nursing stations reports to the head of support services, who reports to the director of nursing services (Kochen and Deutsch, 1974).

3. *Unity of command.* Unity of command means that no employee should have more than one supervisor at any given time. If a nurse in emergency station one is simultaneously accountable to the coordinator of emergency services and the coordinator of unit one, look out! Trouble will follow unless care is taken to specify who has ultimate authority. Fig. 3-1 clearly specifies the appropriate chain of command.

4. *Span of control.* There is a limit to the number of employees any nursing supervisor can effectively manage. The number may vary according to the personalities of the supervisors and nurses and the specific work being done. All things considered, however, a reasonable limit must exist.

5. *Departmentalization.* The way an organization is subdivided is called departmentalization. The approach an organization uses relates to its mission and the other realities it faces. For example, the division of nursing services is broken down functionally into the support and ward operations. Ward nursing, on the other hand, is geographically departmentalized, and psychiatric nursing is divided according to the patients served. Some need counseling while others require more serious treat-

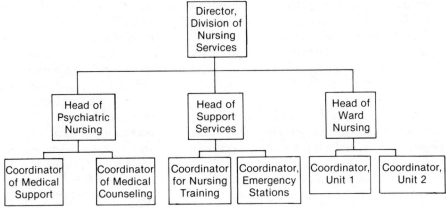

FIG. 3-1
Nursing Services Division: Cooper's Cove School and Hospital.

ment in cooperation with other medical specialists. As can be seen, the exact method used relates to the activities involved.

These five concepts provide the basis for classical approaches to organizational design. Other characteristics are implied but not immediately evident from an organization chart. The CCSH, for example, has a comprehensive system of policies, rules, and procedures to ensure that services are provided in a uniform way, employees are treated fairly, and funds are spent on appropriate items. Most organizations also attempt to develop a procedure for ensuring that promotions are granted to the most qualified contenders. Of course, in reality there are exceptions and deviations from standard practices. However, organizations today have, in general, come a long way from the days when family background, social status, and other such considerations determined promotability.

Results of classical design theory

Surely there must be a reason for placing so much emphasis on design and structure. There certainly is, and this reason can be stated in one word: *efficiency*. The early writers on organization theory were looking for an organizational form that would efficiently accomplish organizational goals.

Imagine the organizational setting created by the principles of classical theory. First, the principles imply that there are absolute guidelines for organization and management. The nurse's job should be specialized and clearly distinct from other health care professionals. Health care facilities should be hierarchially structured with a clear and established chain of command. Spans of control should be kept to manageable sizes and departments should be established on one or more logical foundations, such as functions, geography, or client system.

This absolute orientation appears quite precise. Unfortunately, for this and other reasons several key problems develop with the logic and practice of classical organization theory. These problems are serious but, in all objectivity, are far from sufficient to invalidate its usefulness. To illustrate, let us briefly examine some problems of classical theory.

Theoretical inconsistencies

Anderson and Duncan (1977) itemize several dilemmas or paradoxes of administrative theory. Two are particularly relevant for our purposes.

Dilemmas develop when administrators are forced to choose between actions that appear equally desirable but are mutually exclusive of one another (Aram, 1976). This type of choice is presented to managers in at least two cases when an attempt is made to utilize classical design theory.

First, a manager of a work group dedicated to quality nursing care is told that the span of control should be kept to a minimum so as to facilitate participation and communication; a very common-sense prescription. Of course, the nursing director can better manage six than thirty-six nurses. The same manager is also told to keep the number of levels in the hierarchy at a minimum. Again the purpose is to facilitate communication and participation. However, Simon (1976) notes that the latter principle is in direct conflict with the first.

The dilemma is complex. If the director of nursing has 100 nurses to supervise, the average span of control may be limited to 5. This requires, however, 20 levels in the chain of command. If the average span is extended to 20 the levels can be reduced to 5. The dilemma requires a relatively difficult choice.

A second paradox is perhaps more serious from the standpoint of organizational design. This relates to the conflict between order and the flexibility necessary for change. The efficiency that is the objective of classical design theory is purchased at a price. Highly specialized and structured organizations emphasize the economics of internal operations. The result is often that an organization actually isolates itself from external and environmental forces.

Consider the story of a nurse supervisor who was noted for running the "tightest ship" around. The supervisor's unit was never late with medication schedules, clutter around the work area was never seen, and, as the old saying goes, "there was a place for everything and everything was always in its place." The supervisor, however, was also noted for resisting change. New ideas and concepts just seemed to confuse the work routine. Therefore nurses in the unit were seldom encouraged to participate in the in-service training opportunities because it was necessary to release participants for "more important and pressing duties."

The fact is that the flexibility necessary for

change is often in conflict with the order necessary for efficiency. Thus, as Chamberlain (1968, p. 9) notes, the manager is faced with a paradox because the organization moves toward "a future where the equilibrium it is in the process of achieving will no longer be appropriate. . . . Management is faced with the necessity of tearing apart . . . the very system which it finds equally necessary to bring closer to perfection."

Lack of responsiveness to change

It has been argued that classical design theory works very well in a static environment. In such a setting the future is predictable, innovation is not particularly important, and efficiency is the determinant of organizational success. Unfortunately, few environments today are really static. This is especially true of the dynamic nature of health care delivery.

Think of the introductory example of Holy Mother Hospital. Where procedures and rules become extremely inflexible, the incentives for creativity and innovation are often lost (Duncan, 1981). Rigid structures, firmly established rules, and inflexible chains of command provide the incentive to operate by the book, not to innovate. Since more will be said about change and the importance of the organization structure, no more attention will be given to the subject at this point.

It is important to note, however, that classical theory has been criticized on other grounds that are relevant to our discussion. Moreover, some of these limitations are easily observed by people who have lived and worked in organizational settings.

Everyone who has worked in a large health care organization has probably observed the way in which individuals are sometimes subordinated to the group's welfare. Sometimes this is the result of overspecialization and the routine nature of many jobs. At times, the single individual appears very unimportant and insignificant in the overall scheme of things (Rakich et al., 1977). Moreover, it should be recognized that Weber's ideal bureaucracy was devised as a theoretical model, and often reality deviates significantly. In spite of management's attempts to promote and reward the most talented employees, it sometimes seems as if whom you know is more important than what you know. Nevertheless, attempts to avoid this type of behavior and effectively manage remain an important priority of good administrators (McCool and Brown, 1977).

In any event, the accomplishments of classical design theory are significant. Ford Motor Company, General Motors, and countless other giants of the industrial, educational, governmental, and health care worlds were built on one or more of the principles of classical theory. But the problems constitute limitations. These limitations have been sufficient to provide an incentive for improvement. Many of the potential improvements have been incorporated into what is called contingency or situational design theory.

CONTINGENCY-DESIGN THEORY: ENVIRONMENTAL EMPHASIS

During the late 1920s and 1930s, as noted previously, the famous Hawthorne studies conducted at the Western Electric facilities outside Chicago ushered in what is known as the *human-relations movement* in management. This movement was important and produced significant changes in administrative thought.

Another real change in organizational design theory, however, emerged in the mid-1950s and was initiated by a group of British researchers headed by Joan Woodward. The studies highlighted some problems of classical theory and presented some new solutions.

The types of problems confronted by the Woodward researchers can be illustrated by the experiences of three nurses who share a house but work in different settings. Each of these situations can be briefly compared.

J.M. Courtney, public health nurse practitioner. J.M. Courtney works for the county public health department and runs the neighborhood clinic in Paradise Park. Each head of a neighborhood clinic reports to the director of external services in the health department headquarters. Each nurse practitioner is granted almost total autonomy over the medical decisions in the clinic. Reports are filed weekly on cases reviewed, recommendations, and other activity. Unless specific problems develop, the central headquarters does not become involved in clinic operations.

B.L. Thomas, supervisor of on-site nurse development. B.L. Thomas is employed in a large state vocational rehabilitation center. As supervisor of nurse development, Ms. Thomas is responsible for all on-site educational programs offered to nursing personnel. Because of the requirements of various professional accrediting agencies and state continuing education requirements, specific training activities are required. For this reason, the supervisor of training is given almost no discretion over the conduct and content of the offerings. Primary duties of this position involve scheduling and related logistic details.

H.M. Loring, team coordinator of surgical services. In the large hospital where H.M. Loring is employed, many surgical procedures are performed each day. Most operations are performed by highly specialized teams of physicians, nurses, and support personnel. For this reason, the composition of each surgical team must be carefully planned and monitored. Ms. Loring is responsible for assigning nurses to the various teams through close coordination with the involved physicians. In general, the team coordinator can make assignments, but it is clearly understood that all appointments must be cleared with the surgeon in charge of the team.

The three cases noted above have little in common—little, that is, except one thing: all are extremely successful ways of operating as evidenced by serious evaluation. How can this be? Is it possible that administrative arrangements can be so different yet equally successful? According to contingency theory advocates, it is possible indeed.

Logic of contingency-design theory

Contingency theory "is ultimately directed toward suggesting organizational designs and managerial practices most appropriate for specific situations'' (Kast and Rosenzweig, 1973, p. ix). In other words, the situational differences in the three cases cited could be sufficient to account for the success of the various managerial or organizational philosophies. Therefore, it can be seen that contingency theory is built on the situational foundation and is a highly relativistic view of organization when contrasted to classical thought. There is no talk of optimal spans of control, unity of command, or other such considerations in contingency design theory unless care is taken to specify that comments are directed to a specific case or situation.

Foundations of situational theory

There is a relatively impressive history of contingency theory. The Woodward Studies mentioned above encouraged the development of situational theories by illustrating how management and organizational practices vary when technological differences are important (Woodward, 1970).

The Woodward researchers, for example, selected a sample of firms in an industrial area of England and carefully recorded managerial characteristics such as span of control and levels in the hierarchy. When the sample was divided into three subsamples based on technological differences, some important variations were noted. For example, three primary technologies were evident in the sample. Some of the firms employed unit or small-batch processing and manufactured custom-made items such as individually tailored suits. There were also large-batch or mass-production firms that made internal combustion automobile engines. Finally, there were firms employing continuous processing, as in the petrochemical industry.

"So what?" we might ask! In fact, the results were very significant. A careful review of the data revealed that successful firms in each of these industries appeared quite different organizationally. Spans of control varied, as did average levels in the hierarchy and the ratio of operative to administrative personnel. Interestingly, within the subsamples, successful firms looked similar. In other words, successful unit-production firms were or-

ganized alike, as were successful mass-production and continuous-processing firms. Successful unit-processing firms were not organized like mass-production or continuous-processing enterprises, however. The conclusion: apparently there is no one "best way" to organize as proposed by classical theory. Instead, the situation (in this case technology) was the important contingency that accounted for the difference.

A study by Lawrence and Lorsch (1969) extended the Woodward Studies to include additional aspects of the environment. It is tempting to examine the study in detail. However, in the interest of time and space, we can simply note that the selection of firms in the plastics, standardized-container, and packaged-foods industries to represent varying degrees of environmental dynamism and key management orientations relative to goals, time, interpersonal relations, and formality of structure, resulted in significant findings. Particularly important to note was that the types of organizational structures and managerial practices required for successful coping with the environment varied with the situation faced by the organization. Again the argument emerges suggesting that there is no one best way to organize (Reimann, 1980).

The consistency of the findings on contingency-design theory has suggested that a new importance should be attached to the organizational-environment interface. Although internal efficiency and an adherence to classical principles may lead to economical operations, hospitals, public health agencies, and all other types of organizations must be adaptive as well as efficient if they are to succeed and accomplish their goals. This brings us to the question of how organizations built around contingency concepts might look.

An illustrative design

The recognition of the importance of environmental forces and the necessity for change has resulted in some new and impressive organizational structures. In one sense the structures may be called "deviant" because they violate or at least do not adhere to one or more of the principles of classical design theory. This is not necessarily "bad" in a normative sense, because sometimes the deviation results in outcomes that are valued more than the results achieved by adhering strictly to classical principles.

To illustrate, consider the task-force or project structure frequently found in health care organizations and other sectors confronted with rapid change. This approach was popularized by the National Aeronautics and Space Administration (NASA) as a means of administering America's complex space program but is now freely employed in a number of settings.

The major advantages of the task-force or project structure are its ability to muster relevant talent around a single problem and its temporary nature (Kolodny, 1979). We can illustrate the principle of the project organization by looking at a surgical team as a task force. Let us assume there is a patient, say an infant, with a unique heart problem.

Since the heart problem exists in a child, the surgical team must be carefully formulated. It is decided that for this case, a pediatric anesthesiologist, a surgeon specializing in cardiac surgery, a pediatrician, and two cardiovascular nurses are needed. The task force allows the mustering of unique specialists for a specific problem (case) and can easily be dismantled when the surgery is complete. No single functional department has all the relevant specialists, so the task force (project structure) works well. During the operation the customary hierarchial (vertical) structure is maintained, but the project authority (horizontal) is also operative (Wright, 1979). Because this horizontal and vertical authority exists, project structures are sometimes referred to as matrix organizations to capture the idea of the two-dimensional authority flow. Fig. 3-2 provides an illustration of how one might diagram the project (matrix) set structure.

Fig. 3-2 represents the structure of a state-supported mental retardation facility. The hier-

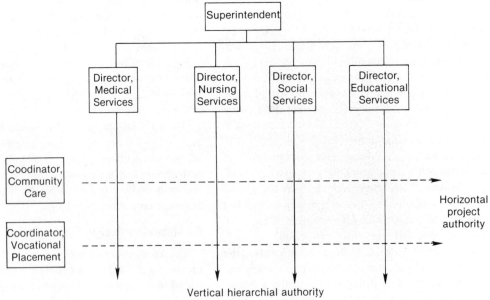

FIG. 3-2
An example of a project structure.

archy is functionally organized into four departments under the superintendent; each department is headed by a director. At the present time there are two experimental projects; the community-care and vocational placement programs. Each project is headed by a coordinator.

The two projects require part of the time of personnel in all four departments. One nurse in nursing services, for example, is assigned half-time to the community care project, and another nurse is assigned one-third time to vocational placement. When the two individuals are doing work related to nursing services, they report to the director of the department involved. When working on the project, each reports to the appropriate project coordinator. Again the task-force idea is useful, because the projects are temporary and should not require a functional department that could not easily be dismantled when complete. Moreover, a range of relevant talents are focused on a single problem.

Of course there are problems with the project structure. The classical principle of unity of command is violated unless care is taken to ensure that the hierarchial boss and project leader do not become simultaneous supervisors and confuse and frustrate a helpless member of the team. Also, employees who get "stuck" on projects for long periods often feel they are out of touch with the line organization and perhaps get passed over for promotions and pay increases.

Finally, project leaders are faced with difficult tasks. They are responsible and accountable for getting specific things done but have little formal authority except for the project itself. In other words, they have no organizational right to demand an employee's time from a line director in charge of nursing, social work, and so on. Consequently, they must become skillful diplomats and learn to lead without any real authority.

We could discuss several other emerging organizational forms that are designed to respond efficiently and effectively to change. A few of the more important would include professional hierarchies, *ad hocracies,* and so on but the point would

remain the same (Mintzberg, 1979). Modern or contingency design theory places relatively more importance on responsiveness to change than classical formulations. However, both must be clearly understood.

SUMMARY

This chapter has reviewed classical design and contingency theory and related each to the overall framework of modern organization theory. It is important to recognize that classical theory was founded on selected aspects of administrative organization (Fayol), bureaucracy (Weber), and scientific management (Taylor).

Classical design theory is based on the absolute assumption that there is one best way to organize. According to this view, work should be specialized, hierarchially stratified, and appropriately departmentalized. The result of this approach is an organizational philosophy based on the principle of efficiency. So important is the efficiency principle that environmental forces are frequently assumed away or acknowledged only as troublesome disruptions to the organizational equilibrium.

In addition to this emphasis on efficiency and resistance to change, classical design theory is characterized by a variety of theoretical paradoxes or logical inconsistencies. These inconsistencies create problems for managers who apply the theory, in that they lead to dilemmas in the guidance system of organizational behavior.

Primarily because of the difficulties experienced by classically designed organizations in responding to change, modern contingency alterations have developed in organization theory. Contingency theory recognizes the importance of operational efficiency but also acknowledges the alterations often required by situational variations confronted by organizations. In other words, it rejects the absolute orientation of classical principles by maintaining there is no one best way to organize.

Contingency theory has encouraged the development of new and innovative organizational forms, one of the most popular being the project structure. Although there are some technical differences, this project design is sometimes referred to as a matrix structure because of its two-dimensional flow of authority.

Organization theory has changed radically throughout the approximately eighty years of its systematic history. Today the importance of efficiency is placed on an equal status with the adaptability to change.

REFERENCES

Anderson, J.P., and Duncan, W.J.: The scientific significance of the paradox in administrative theory, Management Int. Rev. **17:**99-106, 1977.

Aram, J.D.: Dilemmas of administrative behavior, Englewood Cliffs, N.J., 1976, Prentice-Hall, Inc.

Chamberlain, N.W.: Enterprise and environment, New York, 1968, McGraw-Hill Book Co.

Drucker, P.F.: People and performance, New York, 1977, Harper & Row, Publishers.

Duncan, W.J.: Organizational behavior, ed. 2, Boston, 1981, Houghton-Mifflin Co.

Franklin, J.: Down the organization: influence processes across levels of hierarchy, Adm. Science Q. **20:**153-164, 1975.

Gulick, L., and Urwick, L.F., editors: Papers on the science of administration, New York, 1969, A.M. Kelley, Publisher.

Henderson, A.M., and Parsons, T., editors and translators: Max Weber: the theory of social and economic organization, New York, 1947, The Free Press.

Kast, F.E., and Rosenzweig, J.E.: Contingency views of organization and management, Chicago, 1973, Science Research Associates.

Kochen, M., and Deutsch, K.: A note on hierarchy: an aspect of decentralization, Management Sci. **20:**106-114, 1974.

Kolodny, H.F.: Evolution to a matrix organization, Acad. Management Rev. **4:**543-554, 1979.

Lawrence, P.R., and Lorsch, J.W.: Organization and environment, Homewood, Ill., 1969, Richard D. Irwin, Inc.

McCool, B., and Brown, M.: The management response, Philadelphia, 1977, W.B. Saunders Co.

Mintzberg, H.: The structuring of organizations, Englewood Cliffs, N.J., 1979, Prentice-Hall, Inc.

Perrow, C.: The short and glorious history of organization theory, Organizational Dynamics **2:**2-15, 1973.

Rakich, J.S., Longest, B.B., Jr., and O'Donovan, T.R.: Managing health care organizations, Philadelphia, 1977, W.B. Saunders Co.

Reimann, B.C.: Organization structure and technology in manufacturing: system versus work flow level perspectives, Acad. Management J. **23:**61-77, 1980.

Roethlisberger, F.J., and Dickson, W.J.: Management and the worker, Cambridge, Mass., 1939, Harvard University Press.

Simon, H.A.: Administrative behavior, ed. 3, New York, 1976, The Free Press.

Taylor, F.W.: Principles of scientific management, New York, 1914, Harper & Row, Publishers.

Woodward, J.: Automation and technical change. In Dalton, G.W., Lawrence, P.R., and Lorsch, J.W., editors: Organization structure and design, Homewood, Ill., 1970, Richard D. Irwin, Inc.

Wright, N.H., Jr.: Matrix management: a primer for the administrative manager, Management Rev. **68:**58-61, 1979.

> The behavior, attitudes, beliefs, and values of the individual are all firmly grounded in the groups to which he belongs. . . . Whether they will change or resist change will, therefore, be greatly influenced by the nature of these groups. Attempts to change them must be concerned with the dynamics of groups.
>
> Cartwright, B.: Hum. Relations 55(4):387.

4

USING GROUP-PROCESS SKILLS IN CHANGE

Carol Dashiff

All people are social beings primarily concerned with finding their place in the group. Human development is influenced by interaction with many different individuals and groups. Throughout life people modify their behavior as they interact with others.

The purpose of this chapter is to look at the role that groups play in the work setting in making change. To do this, groups are defined, various types are discussed, and the use of groups in an organization is explored. Reasons for group formation are also presented, as well as selected group characteristics and roles people play in groups.

DEFINITION OF GROUPS

Although groups are defined in several ways, common themes emerge. For example, Merrill (1965, p. 43) defines a group as "two or more persons who interact over an appreciable period and share a common purpose." Similarly, Berelson and Steiner (1967, p. 53) describe a small group as a "small number of people who associate together in face-to-face relations over an extended period of time, who recognize something common to their group that differentiates it from others and who have some genuine goals shared by the members." Likewise, Shaw (1971) defines a group as "two or more employees who interact with each other in such a manner that the behavior and/or performance of a member is influenced by the behavior and/or performance of other members."

The common themes in these definitions include social interaction as well as commonly held goals, values, and perceptions. A group cannot be functional unless members have some means of communicating. Without face-to-face contact it is difficult to work toward common goals, which are usually either determined by the members or assigned by other people in the organization. Also, both the group members and those around them must perceive the groups as having a common purpose.

Cartwright and Zander (1968) summarize ten attributes of groups as being situations where members:

1. Participate in frequent interaction
2. Define themselves as members
3. Are defined by others as belonging to the group
4. Share norms regarding matters of common interest
5. Participate in a system of interlocking roles
6. Identify with one another by having set up the same model object or ideals in their superego
7. Find the group to be rewarding
8. Pursue promotively interdependent goals
9. Have a collective perception of their identity
10. Tend to act in a unitary manner toward their environment

DEVELOPMENTAL EXPERIENCES IN GROUPS

In the course of human development individuals proceed through levels of group experience.

Several friends can generally contribute more to the child's socialization than one, because each can contribute something different. One friend may help a child to see why he should act in a sex-appropriate way, another may show him the value of being cooperative instead of aggressive, and still another may help him to develop social insight and learn to be sympathetic.*

A child's membership in groups is a more potent socialization experience than can be achieved with any single friend. Developmental experiences in the group context are illustrated in Table 1.

Another important aspect in assessing human development from a group context is the development of sex antagonism resulting from cultural influences on sex-role development and sex-"appropriate" behavior. Hurlock (1972) summarizes some of the effects of sex antagonism that accompany the increasing cleavage between the sexes when children enter elementary school. Preference for the same sex is accompanied by antagonistic behavior toward the other sex, characterized by bickering,

*From Child development by E.B. Hurlock, pp. 260-261. Copyright © 1972 McGraw-Hill Book Co. Used with the permission of McGraw-Hill Book Co.

TABLE 1
Developmental experience in
the group context

Developmental stage	Experience
Infancy/babyhood	
1-2 years	Family oriented in choice of companion for play (egocentric).
Preschool	
2-4 years	Family siblings, other children from a group with whom child is identified. Companionship with peers. Companions are associates who satisfy needs by being in the observer's play environment. Participates in parallel play (playing independently alongside but not with peers).
4-6 years	More selective in choice of companions. Companions are one or two preferred playmates. Prior to school entry they are likely to be same-sexed children of own racial or religious group. Communication continues to be egocentric, i.e. name calling, boasting, criticizing.
School-age	
Early childhood	Participates in group play with playmates from own neighborhood preferring children of same size, sex, chronological and mental age, social maturity and interests.
Late childhood	Playmates are chosen who can communicate as well as play. Associates with those who are successful and can increase prestige. Girls choose friends who have similar interests and abilities. Boys choose friends who are complementary, i.e. have characteristics they admire but lack.
Puberty	Need for play decreases and need for communication increases due to physical changes and concomitant anxiety. The need for friends peaks and a confidant of the same sex is sought.

Source: Adapted from Hurlock, E.B.: Child development, ed. 5, New York, 1972, McGraw-Hill Book Co. Used with the permission of McGraw-Hill Book Co.

name calling, and quarreling. As a consequence of current cultural pressure, boys are likely to develop unfounded feelings of male superiority and to feel inadequate in social relationships with girls because they are discouraged from learning "sissified" social skills. Girls may develop inferiority or martyr complexes, as well as resentment at being born female. Often boys are ridiculed and called "sissies" for playing with girls; likewise, when girls play with boys they are labeled "tomboys" and may be ostracized by female peers. Because of limited opportunities to develop common interests, difficulties of heterosexual adjustment in adolescence are intensified, and both sexes develop anxieties about their "sex appropriateness." These effects have far-reaching impacts when the dynamics of group functioning are analyzed.

According to McClelland (1975), interpersonal relationships are more important to women than they are to men. Consequently, disapproval in interpersonal relationships may be more anxiety provoking for females. Beland (1980) suggests that within the health profession, women (namely nurses) and physicians (namely men) tend to approach problems from different perspectives. She recommends that, since nursing is a predominantly female profession, the interdependence of its members requires consistent feedback and support to facilitate optimal effectiveness. While some females have been socialized to be more assertive and independent, they too require support because of the reaction they receive in going against the societal norm of female interdependence.

TYPES OF GROUPS

Although there are many different types of groups and various ways of distinguishing them, one classification particularly useful for studying the influence of groups on individual behavior is the primary group as opposed to the secondary group. Primary groups have the most immediate influence on an individual's attitudes, opinions, and behavior. The major distinguishing characteristic of this type of group is the regular, intimate, face-to-face

relationship between members. These primary groups represent all of the small societies with which an individual comes into frequent contact, such as the family, friends, neighbors, and co-workers.

In addition to primary groups, people frequently belong to formal or informal secondary groups. Formal groups are characterized by a specified organizational structure and an explicit outline of functions and duties for each position. Conformity to group expectations is usually enforced by a system of rewards and sanctions. Informal groups are typically less explicit with regard to structure and function, although they are equally real and important.

Formal groups

Formal groups are also called forced-choice or deliberately formed groups. Although all groups have goals, formal groups tend to focus on the attainment of specific objectives.

Members of formal groups do not always seek to work with one another but may be assigned to the group because of the needs of the organization. These formal groups may be of either a command or a task nature. A command group is specified by the organizational chart and comprises subordinates who report to a given supervisor (Gibson et al., 1976). In contrast, a task group comprises people who are assigned to a specific and often time-limited project. An example of a task group would be a committee to plan the social activities surrounding graduation or another significant event.

Informal groups

Informal, spontaneous, or free-forming groups in the work setting are natural groupings of people who tend to get together by choice and for social interactions. These groups are usually not preplanned and the members are neither designated nor assigned; rather, they evolve naturally because the participants like one another and seek out opportunities to spend time together. Examples of this type of group include friendship or interest groups.

Some formal groups form as a result of friendship purposes because members have common characteristics such as age, ethnic background, political or religious beliefs, or similarly perceived attitudes and values, or are participants in an anxiety-arousing situation. The formation of spontaneous groups under conditions of anxiety can be positive when they help participants determine the nature of their emotional upset and provide a mechanism for consciously deciding on appropriate alternatives. Other informal groups form around common interests. When an interest group changes to focus on a common goal, issue, or cause, it has become more formalized and task oriented.

It is important to be aware of the existence of both spontaneously formed groups and deliberately formed groups in professional settings. The sudden proliferation in formation and gathering of spontaneous groups in a work setting may be a cue to rising levels of anxiety associated with lack of support networks and frustration of affiliative needs in the structure and process of the organization. When such conditions persist, the spontaneous subgroups may take over or supersede the functioning of the larger group so as to inhibit or obstruct the task(s) to be performed. This phenomenon is more likely to occur in task groups that persist over time, such as work groups. Intensive care units, where there are high levels of stress, frustrated affiliative needs resulting from the number and complexity of tasks to be performed by an individual staff member for an often verbally uncommunicative individual, and physical proximity of large numbers of staff in a small amount of space constitute settings ripe for formation of spontaneous groups. In the absence of efforts to facilitate mechanisms of support in the system, spontaneous groups (subgroups) will function to meet this need to the obstruction of the unit goals.

Another type of group that influences individuals is the *reference* group. This type of group is often used by the individual as a point of reference in determining judgments, beliefs, values, and behavior. There are several kinds of reference groups:

(1) groups associated with statuses held in the past; (2) groups with which the individual identifies and may aspire to belong in the future; and (3) groups that may provide the individual with a negative reference, thereby providing behavioral modes to be avoided.

MULTIPLE MEMBERSHIP

An important aspect in considering the relationship of the person and the group is multiple membership. The concept of multiple membership is necessary in understanding conflicts that may be generated in an individual's relationship with groups. Membership in two groups that have distinctive yet nonconflicting norms does not usually present a problem. In fact, most individuals, as far as possible, avoid membership in groups with distinct conflicting norms and goals. An individual is not going to be a member of both an Equal Rights Amendment and a Right-to-Life group, or the Ku Klux Klan and the National Association for the Advancement of Colored People. Most people, however, participate to some extent in groups that have contradictory or discrepant norms. When those norms are not central to the functioning of both groups this does not create a problem for the individual.

In many instances contradictions between groups do not create problems. For example, in *overlapping* membership, the same individuals are members of two or more groups (see Fig. 4-1). Overlapping membership can provide an important linkage system, and, depending on the performance of the "linkers," can improve the relation of the groups to one another (Cartwright and Zander, 1968). This is an important principle in community organization, especially in choosing members to serve as advisory boards. When the members of a newly formed group come primarily from *disjoint* groups (see Fig. 4-2)—that is, groups where no singular individual is a member of both groups—the possibilities for conflict, stereotyping, competition and miscommunication are numerous. Such problems are further intensified when the central group norms

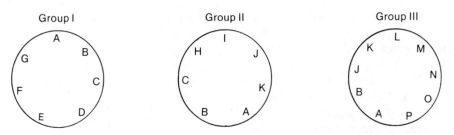

FIG. 4-1
Overlapping membership.

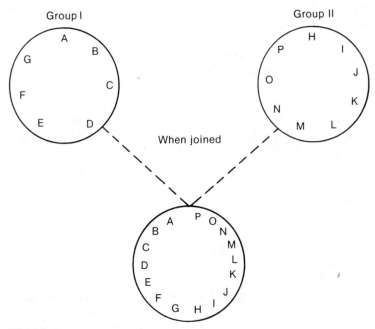

FIG. 4-2
Disjoint groups.

and goals of both groups are conflicting. Under these circumstances, conflict is maintained and facilitated to the point that issues under consideration become polarized without reconciliation. Although polarization of issues is useful to facilitate thinking, as in debates or political campaigns, it is not helpful in situations requiring community action and an agreed-upon solution. In this instance a group comprising individuals with many overlapping memberships in other central community groups will facilitate attempts to reconcile the conflict.

Certain roles have the potential for placing individuals in positions of overlapping membership. Middle-management positions illustrate this. Clinical nurse specialists who occupy line positions as head nurses or supervisors are also in middle-person positions (see Fig. 4-3). Such a nurse often

FIG. 4-3
Overlapping groups with middle person positions.

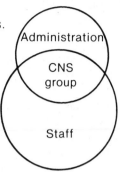

works directly with clients, as do other staff members, but is also responsible for management and administrative functions. When the standards of these groups are in conflict, the clinical specialist will experience role conflict unless this can be resolved by the nurses' adherence to the standards of a third group composed of an association of professional peers. Unfortunately, educational systems that separate clinical nurse specialists from each other in speciality groups do not facilitate the working together of specialists from a variety of clinical areas in agency settings. Cohesion of clinical specialists as a group might facilitate the long-range survival of the clinical nurse specialist role.

An additional application of the concept of overlapping membership is useful in understanding the behavior of "new" employees or group members. It is often said that the addition of a new person to an ongoing group both results in temporary regression of the group to an earlier stage in its development and changes the "group character." When individuals are new to a community or employment situation, conflict is created between their loyalties to their previous groups "back home" and the need to conform to the norms of the current group in order to be accepted (Cartwright and Zander, 1968). Everyone has been in situations where they were treated as "strangers," that is, regarded as members of the "back home" group and labeled as the new employee or community member for

lengthy periods of time. The difficulty of this "in limbo" position is compounded when the standards of the new group contradict or challenge the previously accepted standards of the old. When the difficulty of conforming to current standards is thus magnified, the individual is likely to respond with aggression against the new group, increasing the likelihood of being treated as a stranger, which in turn reinforces the desire to behave in the "back home" manner. A cycle is then created that, if continued over time, will lead either to group expulsion of the stranger or the stranger's terminating the group membership.

Several interventions can be employed to facilitate the new member's integration into an ongoing group. Preorientation interviews allow the identification of grossly discrepant values and beliefs, so that individuals can be counseled regarding the difficulties inherent in moving into a conflictual situation. Orientation phases assist new members by exposing them gradually to the need for adopting the standards of the ongoing group. Further, recognizing the new member's previous experience "back home" for the purpose of tapping a new resource in the group facilitates reciprocal acceptance. Finally, it is important to be aware as a group leader or member that to truly integrate the new member the "group character" will also change, and that this will involve change in the "old" group members as well as in the group as a whole.

REASONS FOR FORMING GROUPS
Satisfaction of needs

As mentioned, everyone needs to feel accepted and respected, and groups provide a mechanism for associating with people who convey these feelings. Seemingly, joining groups is not an innate response of people, but instead is a learned reaction. Children learn early in life that most of their needs are not met in isolation but rather in a group context. The infant is completely dependent on others for food, warmth, and affection, and thus learns quickly that much security can be gained from being with others. This early tendency to form groups is reinforced throughout life as children gain security from family and peer groups. The loneliest child to be found is the class isolate: that one child who because of appearance, intelligence, behavior, or some other factor, just does not fit into any group. In general, voluntary groups are formed to meet the needs of the members and security ranks high on the needs fulfilled by group affiliation.

Location and attraction

When people work in close proximity to one another, there is a tendency for them to interact and come together as an informal group. Physical proximity may be what initially promotes the formation of a group, and attraction and common goals hold the group together. Attraction includes perceptual, attitudinal, performance, or motivational similarities (Gibson et al., 1976). The concept of attraction also implies that a group of which one is not a member can still have a powerful influence on behavior.

Goals and activities

Often people are attracted to a particular group because they like its goals and want to participate in the group's activities. This reason for joining a group is strongly related to social interaction and affiliation needs. For example, several nurses might form a group to engage in activities such as softball or assertiveness training. People gravitate toward these groups based on their personal needs and preferences.

CHARACTERISTICS OF GROUPS

Understanding the role of groups within organizations necessitates discussion of several group characteristics, including structure, communication, norms, cohesiveness, and deviance.

Group structure

Over time, some kind of structure evolves within every group. Group members become differentiated from one another on the basis of competence, knowledge, power, status, and aggressiveness. Each member occupies a unique position in the group and the pattern of relationships among the members comprise the structure. Some members have a certain position in the group based on longevity in the organization. For example, M. Jones may always lead the groups to which she is assigned because she has worked in the institution for fifteen years and seems to know not just the printed rules but also the subtle ones.

Communication

The key factor keeping a group together once it is formed is communication. The efficiency of any group is directly related to the quality and clarity of its communication process. An effective group may generate a great deal of productive discussion; they keep on the subject and allow each person an opportunity to participate. This means not only that members need to speak clearly, but they must also listen to one another. In an effective group, people are not afraid of saying something foolish; they feel assured that they will be accepted no matter what they say.

Productive groups need to be able to say things clearly, listen to hear exactly what others mean, and feel sufficient trust and acceptance to share ideas as well as feelings. This type of group also encourages feedback as to the way others perceive messages. In general, feedback is a way of helping other group members learn how they are viewed. It is a process based on honesty, openness, and kindness. Some general characteristics that describe useful feedback include:

1. It is communication to another person that

expresses your reaction to that person's behavior.
2. It is descriptive, not evaluative. Feedback focuses on your perception of the actions of another and resists making an evaluative judgment.
3. It is specific rather than general, relating to a recent instance that both participants can clearly recollect.
4. It takes into account the needs of both the receiver and giver; the intent is to help the person learn, not to hurt.
5. It is most useful when asked for, not imposed.
6. The timing is appropriate. In general, feedback should be given as soon as possible after the event under discussion but not when the person is overly vulnerable.
7. It is clear. Be sure the recipient of your feedback knows what you meant.

Communication structures in a group refer to the patterns that develop. In centralized communication networks, communication is sifted through one individual. This pattern indicates that one individual receives the majority of communication efforts and, by the same token, initiates the majority of efforts. The centralized individuals are more likely to be satisfied with the group's effectiveness and interaction than are the more peripheral members. Whereas such a structure is beneficial for imparting information and solving relatively simple problems, it is not appropriate when group cohesiveness is needed or problems increase in complexity (Stein, 1975). In terms of overall member morale and satisfaction, less centralized networks are superior. The extremes of *decentralized* and centralized networks are represented respectively by the circle and the wheel. Most groups fall on a continuum between the two (see Figs. 4-3, 4-4, and 4-5).

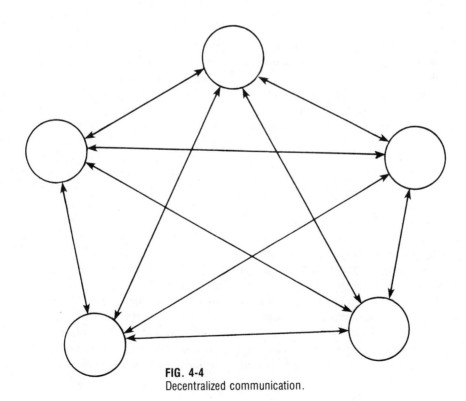

FIG. 4-4
Decentralized communication.

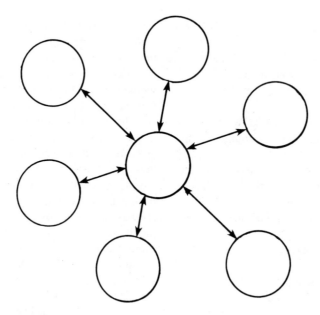

FIG. 4-5
Centralized communication.

It is important in the leader's observance of group behavior to be aware of the patterns of communication. In addition, the leader should assess whether the pattern is appropriate to the task and whether opportunities to foster communication patterns conducive to cohesiveness exist during the group's life.

Norms

Group norms are the standards for behavior that are shared by members of the group. Norms are important in accomplishing goals, maintaining the group, developing reality, and defining the relationship of the group to the environment as well as to the system of which it is a part. The contents of group norms are related to the group goals. A norm is *enabling* if it moves the group and its members toward their objectives and *restrictive* if it obstructs progress toward these objectives.

Norms have certain characteristics that are significant to the members. First, norms are formed only when a matter is of particular importance to the members. For example, if helping other people in order to finish a task on schedule is important, then this will develop as a norm. Second, norms are accepted in varying degrees by group members. Some norms are accepted by all members; other norms generate only partial group acceptance. Third, some norms are applicable to all members but other norms do not universally apply. For example, on a particular hospital unit the norm may be for everyone to be at work by 6:45 AM. The exception may be the nurse who cannot arrive before 7:15 AM because she must wait until a day-care center opens so she can leave her child.

Norms can also be described as explicit or implicit. *Explicit* norms are verbally presented to the members at the outset of group membership, whereas *implicit* norms are grasped through one's experience in a group. Spontaneous groups usually function with norms of an implicit nature, whereas deliberately formed groups function with more explicit norms. Important leadership functions are to assess the need for explicit norms and to evaluate whether explicit or implicit norms in the group are enabling or restrictive. A normative pattern that discourages the open exchange of ideas rather than encouraging openness and conflict will be a restrictive norm, because it prohibits the group from progressing through its developmental stages. For example, meetings that are consumed by announcements often evidence an implicit, restrictive norm. That is, there is an unwritten and unspoken expectation that nothing of significance will ever take place in these meetings.

Cohesion

Group cohesiveness is a concept that refers to the individual members' attractiveness to the group or the degree to which they wish to remain in the group. It is the gel that holds the group together and facilitates movement toward objectives. Cohesiveness has been measured by examining (1) the interpersonal attraction among members, that is, their likingness for one another; (2) an evaluation of the group as a whole by individual members; (3) members' personal involvement or identification with the group; and (4) the members' expressed desire to remain in the group (Cartwright, 1968, pp. 93-94).

An individual's attraction for the group is based on four interacting sets of variables (Cartwright, 1968). With the idea in mind that cohesiveness should be fostered, the group leader can examine these factors and manipulate them in such a way as to foster a cohesive group. These factors are as follows:

1. The individual's motive base for being attracted to the group. What need does the individual hope will be met by the group?
2. The incentive properties of the group, which are significant to the motive base. An individual with a motive base for money is not likely to fit in with a group incentive based on altruism and noncompensatory volunteer efforts.
3. The individual's expectancy that membership

will have beneficial or nonbeneficial consequences. If an individual with a monetary need joins a work unit with the incentive property of high wages, and the individual in question expects that the high wages will be obtained, then 75% of the factors for group attraction exist.
4. The comparison level of the individual, that is, the idea regarding the level of outcome the group will provide based on the person's previous experience. An individual participating in previous groups that had superior outcomes will have a higher comparison level than one who was in a group with a poor outcome.

Cohesiveness is related to the person's motives for joining the group and the extent to which expectations are met in group participation. If people enter groups primarily because of attraction to the group as a social unit, they will generally try to be as friendly and agreeable as possible so as to remain in good favor and be liked by others. Likewise, if people are attracted to a group in order to gain financial incentives, prestige, or other recognition they will work to remain in favor among the members. Similarly, if people are attracted to groups because they value the goals, they will work diligently to meet these goals and to maintain the viability of the group.

Gibson and colleagues (1976, p. 163) postulate that a cohesive group involves people who are attracted to one another, and they summarize five reasons for attraction to a group:

1. The goals of the group and the members are compatible and clearly specified.
2. The group has a charismatic leader.
3. The reputation of the group indicates that the group successfully accomplishes its tasks.
4. The group is small enough to permit members to have their opinions heard and evaluated by others.
5. The members are attractive, in that they support each other and help each other overcome obstacles and barriers to personal growth and development.

As can be seen, each of these factors is related to need satisfaction.

Deviance from the group

Group norms exert a great deal of pressure toward uniformity of behavior and adherence to group goals. Deviance is a departure from something, usually the patterns of rules of the group. Deviance is relative; that is, behavior considered deviant in one group may be perceived as acceptable or even commendable in another group. Each group defines both overtly (openly) and covertly (subtly) its rules, goals, and expectations. In general, the definition of any behavior as being deviant depends on the audience.

In a sense, deviance is the reverse of conformity. In a noncohesive group there is often lack of clarity about roles and expectations. Members have limited investment in whether the behavior of each one follows a designated format, thus deviance is unlikely to be defined. That is, there is a limited commitment to set standards, hence wide variations of behavior are tolerated.

In contrast, in a cohesive group the members identify closely with the group and generally hold firmly to agreed-upon goals and behaviors. Thus members may become anxious when deviance occurs, because this poses a threat to the group's stability.

Individuals who deviate from the group's standards will likely receive many signals that their behavior is unacceptable. Groups, like other living systems, try to maintain balance and a relatively steady state. Members who conform to group goals receive such rewards as acceptance, praise, and promotion. In contrast, those who deviate from the group's expected patterns of behavior are either verbally or nonverbally informed that their nonconformity is unacceptable.

In terms of deviance, groups follow an established pattern whether or not members are aware of it. First, the group defines what behaviors are considered deviant. Second, the group defines those members whose behavior is judged as deviant; and third, the deviant is treated in what is viewed as an appropriate manner such as ostracism or demotion (Merrill, 1965, p. 56). Often an individual is confronted with deviant behavior and given alternatives directed more toward conformity. If the deviant behavior continues after confrontation and/or counseling, the group members will decrease their efforts to change the individual and will isolate or expel the individual from the group.

It should be noted, however, that deviance is not necessarily a negative group characteristic. Deviance involves risk taking which can be an incentive for the process of change. The deviant member becomes a catalyst for fostering the reexamination of group norms. Open communication patterns where dissent is heard minimize the disruptive effects of deviance and maximize the positive.

QUALITIES OF THE EFFECTIVE GROUP

Effective groups often share similar qualities, including an atmosphere conducive to meeting the group's goals, productive interaction patterns, clearly defined goals, effective communication, and a mechanism for decision making. Communication has already been discussed so it is excluded here.

Atmosphere

The atmosphere in an effective group tends to be relaxed and informal, with each member feeling accepted and valued. Members within the group may desire different characteristics in the atmosphere. Some may prefer a friendly, low-key atmosphere; others prefer some lively disagreement. The critical task of both members and leaders is to determine whether all participants seem to be able to function in the group. This does not mean it is necessary to assure that everyone will be happy with the atmosphere, but rather to determine whether the group is functional. In making this determination it is necessary to consider the phase of group development. Conflicts are more likely to become apparent in the early working phase. The process by which conflict is resolved is critical to group process since conflict can destroy group functioning when it is either ignored or exaggerated. Some specific qualities to look for in group atmosphere include:

1. *Formal/informal.* Are people free to say what they please or do they seem wary and constrained?
2. *Antagonistic/friendly.* Are members constantly seeking to take exception with what someone says or is there acceptance and tolerance for differences?
3. *Bored/committed.* Is there little interest in the project or goal or steady progress?

Interaction patterns

It is important to assess a group in terms of the character of its interaction patterns. For example, do a few people do all the talking or is everyone more or less verbally involved in the group? It is also helpful to determine if there are observable subgroups. If a work group splits into two or more subgroups to handle a task more efficiently, the outcome is often positive. In contrast, if the total group splits because of differences or hostilities, their overall effectiveness will generally be diluted.

In looking at interaction patterns, note also any changes in the pattern. Who talks to whom, about what? Is this pattern consistent over time or does it represent a change? Noting who talks to whom may provide information about potential subgroups. It is also useful to note how the quieter members of the group are tolerated. Is silence acceptable, ignored, or viewed as a negative behavior? Group interaction is explored in greater depth in the section on roles people play in groups.

Clearly defined goals and decision-making approaches

Clearly defined goals and a process for making decisions are crucial to effective group functioning. Several questions might be raised here.

Do all members of the group seem to share the same goals? Are the group members' goals consistent with those of the leader or the overall organization? It is generally useful to determine whether the group has a standard written or informally held procedure for making decisions. Many times decisions made in groups meet the needs of rather narrowly defined goals. Such decisions may conflict with overall group or organizational goals. Each group needs someone to clarify the goals and keep the group in touch with what they have agreed to do.

When looking at decision making in a group, assess who makes most decisions. Do all members have an equal opportunity to propose new goals or approaches, or do only selected members assume this responsibility? When the group makes a decision it is important that all members accept the choice in order to facilitate the group's progress. Any criticism of the group's decision should be made openly within the group. What happens in the group when a decision proves to have been a poor choice? Do some members say "I told you . . ."?

ROLES PEOPLE PLAY IN GROUPS

Each person tends to develop a certain way of behaving in a group. The person's behavior may be different in one group than in another, often depending on the level of comfort experienced in the group. For example, some students might be witty people in a group of peers but be virtually silent in a faculty group where they are the only students present. The roles we play tend to move the group forward, block the group's progress, or help to maintain the status quo. In order to help groups function more effectively, it is useful to examine these three types of group roles (Wedgewood, 1967; Larson and Williams, 1978).

Group-blocking roles

Behaviors that block group functioning tend to be directed toward meeting the needs of the individual at the expense of group process.

1. *Aggression*—working for recognition and status by criticizing, blaming others, dis-

agreeing vocally, and generally "bulldozing" the group by hostility and intimidation.

2. *Blocking*—interfering with group progress by stubbornly disagreeing and refusing to listen to the point of view of others; going off on tangents or jumping back to previously discussed topics.

3. *Withdrawing*—usually by silence; acting indifferent or disinterested, doodling on the agenda or writing notes to other group members.

4. *Smoke-screening*—spending time intellectualizing or "talking over the heads" of other members. This is a ploy that makes for the avoidance of real issues by keeping the agenda filled with tangential conversation. Often such behavior is recognition seeking by people who do not know how to do so in more effective ways.

5. *Self-confessing*—use of the group as an arena for airing personal information, opinions, or points of view. This behavior generally reflects anxiety.

6. *Playfulness*—"horsing around" by telling jokes, clowning, or initiating pranks. This disruptive behavior usually reeks of indifference or cynicism.

7. *Sabotaging*—undermining the group's efforts, upsetting others in order to maintain one's own personal comfort. When other persons become upset and lose control, the sabotaging individual is in charge.

Group-building roles

1. *Initiating*—thinking up new ideas and taking the lead with new projects.

2. *Encouraging*—friendly, warm responses to the needs of others; offering praise as well as well-intended critique.

3. *Opinion giving*—stating pertinent beliefs and perceptions about the group's progress.

4. *Clarifying*—seeking to make things as clear as possible; giving relevant examples, listening and detecting lack of clarity in the group.

5. *Listening*—raising questions to test the group's readiness to reach a decision.

6. *Summarizing*—trying to pull the discussion together and review major areas that were covered.

Group-maintenance roles

1. *Tension relieving*—using humor at points of stress; calling for a break when tempers become short.

2. *Compromising*—helping members look at similarities in their points of view; exploring alternate points of view with a willingness to yield for the good of the group.

3. *Gatekeeping*—keeping communication open and moving, and trying to involve all members in the discussion.

4. *Harmonizing*—mediating; resolving differences by helping members recognize and appreciate one another's viewpoints.

In facilitating effective group functioning, it is generally advisable to encourage the group building and maintaining roles, and then to determine what needs are motivating the other members to function in an obstructive manner. Once these needs are determined, the group members and leader can promote an environment for the blockers to try out new, more constructive roles. For example, the silent individual may be angry or apathetic or feel consistently ignored. Note what took place before the person became silent. Was the person cut off in midsentence by a more aggressive member? If so, other group members can do some gatekeeping, calling attention to the occasions when people are interrupted and giving them some assistance in active participation.

Anger is often difficult to deal with in a group because people tend to respond to anger with an angry response that tends to escalate rather than to diminish the hostile feelings. Some useful ways to deal with angry behavior include: (1) recognizing the person's feelings, (2) accepting the angry person's right to these feelings without agreeing or disagreeing with them, and (3) listening carefully to what the person is saying without giving advice or reacting with similar angry expressions (Larson and Williams, 1978).

In responding to people who use smoke-screening or intellectualization in groups, remember they often do so to avoid revealing anything significant about themselves. Smoke-screening also can be used to avoid talking about feelings. Students often use this technique in clinical conferences to avoid talking about their feelings about a particular patient. For example, some psychiatric patients evoke feelings in students that cause pain, as do patients who are terminally ill.

The blocking individual often monopolizes the group by talking incessantly, interrupting when others are talking, or holding steadfast to a minority opinion. Excessive talking often signifies anxiety or insecurity. The individual may not recognize how disconcerting this behavior is to the group's progress. The person may feel left out or inadequate in comparison to other members and may talk to gain attention. The leader might speak to the individual outside the meeting to determine the level of awareness of this behavior. Another approach would be to say to the person who is holding firmly to an opinion, "Joan, you certainly have a point, I wonder what others think about the . . ." In this way, Joan is given recognition, and hopefully the focus is diverted to other members at the same time.

Self-confessing and playfulness can be approached similarly. Basically, individuals need to become more aware of their behavior and provided with some support in trying new ways of relating to the group. They have learned to gain attention via monopolizing, joking, or sharing personal information. Such behavior tends to be perceived negatively; the group becomes angry or irritated and ignores the person who is desperately seeking attention. The key is to give each member acceptance and recognition in a group characterized by warmth and comfort.

Sabotaging is usually more destructive than the other group blocking behaviors. The six blocking roles just discussed are more irritating and distracting than they are deliberately destructive; by contrast, the sabotaging individual often consciously and carefully undermines the group's chances for survival. A common instance is talking about individual group members in their absence and commenting on negative features. Likewise, mumbling to a few members about the "lousy leader" or the "dumb purpose" of the goals tends to thwart progress because people may remain ambivalent about the group. It takes courage and commitment to deal with this behavior, because someone must confront the person and encourage new ways of working together.

HIDDEN AGENDA

Just as it is important to look at roles of group members, so is it useful to look at a process known as "hidden agenda." The main reason for forming a group is to achieve either formally or informally a publicly stated, agreed-upon goal. This is the overt, or public agenda of either a formal or an informal group. On the other hand, there are often "hidden agendas" that operate covertly beneath the surface and are often difficult to recognize. All groups operate at these two agenda levels: the conscious, public, explicit level and the implicit, closed, or hidden level. These levels may also be distinguished as the *content* or task level versus the *process* or emotional level. Addressing only the content or task level of what is happening in a group is likely to lead to a lack of full understanding of the situation. The group can get bogged down through inattention to hidden agendas or process levels.

Each agenda level affects the other. When a group is functioning successfully and making steady progress toward meeting its surface-agenda goals, it is evident that either hidden agendas have been resolved or temporarily "laid to rest." It is important to remember that hidden agendas may not be evident when the group is functioning effectively, but instead will surface when members are under stress. When a group seemingly works hard on the surface agenda yet never seems to get anywhere, it is necessary to examine for potential hidden agendas. This does not mean that hidden agendas are necessarily worse than surface agendas. The problem is that either hidden agendas are not known to all participants, or people know about them but do not subscribe to their intent.

Hidden agendas can be held by any member of the group as well as by the group itself. For example, the leader may hold one goal for the group that conflicts with the priorities of the members. If the leader is able to wait on activating the item, no conflict will arise. In contrast, the leader may subtly mention at frequent meetings the need to attend to the personally held goal. The purpose of repeatedly bringing up the private-agenda item may be to intimidate, to coerce or just to "wear the members down" so they will realter their priorities and comply with the leader's goal.

Likewise, a group may have an assigned task (surface agenda) and a preferred task (hidden agenda). The group may deal with these conflicting agendas by avoiding the surface agenda and secretly working on their own preferred goals. The key to dealing with hidden agendas seems to lie in early detection and clarification. For example, if the leader has one priority and the group has a different one, discussion can often lead to compromise and renegotiation whereby everyone has his or her goals met by a different sequencing or reassignment of responsibilities.

SUMMARY

Groups exist and are instrumental in the change process whether we plan for them or not. From early childhood, people participate in groups, and learn certain roles and behaviors. Primary groups are particularly influential in the development of attitudes, beliefs, and behavior patterns. Each person is born into a primary family group and later becomes associated with friendship and work or school groups. Likewise, most people participate in a variety of formal and informal secondary groups, either by choice or assignment. Each group experience contributes to the development of the participants.

People join groups for many reasons, including attraction and liking for the other members, convenience, or perceived gain from membership. The roles played in each group by the participants contribute to the effectiveness of the group. Some members help the group, whereas others are more of a hindrance. Groups generally exert pressure on members to be positive rather than negative forces, in that each group has a formal or informal structure, norms for behavior, some degree of cohesiveness, and communication. Further, deviance from the group's expectations is usually not tolerated well, and participants are rewarded for helping group process.

REFERENCES

Beland, L.: The burnout syndrome in nurses. In Werner-Beland, A., editor: Grief responses to long-term illness and disability, Reston, Va., 1980, Reston Publishing Co.

Berelson, B., and Steiner, G.A.: Human behavior, shorter ed., New York, 1967, Harcourt, Brace & World, Inc.

Cartwright, B.: Achieving change in people: some applications to group dynamic theory. Hum. Relations **55**(4):387, 1951.

Cartwright, D.: The nature of group cohesiveness. In Cartwright, D., and Zander, A., editors: Group dynamics, New York, 1968, Harper & Row, Publishers.

Cartwright, D., and Zander, A., editors: Group dynamics, New York, 1968, Harper & Row, Publishers.

Gibson, J.L., Ivancevich, J.M., and Donnelly, J.H.: Organizations: behavior, structure, processes, Dallas, 1976, Business Publications, Inc.

Hurlock, E.B.: Child development, ed. 5, New York, 1972, McGraw-Hill Book Co.

Larson, M.L., and Williams, R.A.: How to become a better group leader, Nursing '78 **8**:65-72, Aug. 1978.

McClelland, D.C.: Power: the inner experience, New York, 1975, Irvington Publishers, Inc.

Merrill, F.E.: Society and culture: an introduction to sociology, ed. 3, Englewood Cliffs, N.J., 1965, Prentice-Hall, Inc.

Shaw, M.E.: Group dynamics, New York, 1971, McGraw-Hill Book Co.

Stein, M.: Stimulating creativity, vol. 2, Group procedures, New York, 1975, Academic Press, Inc.

Wedgwood, H.C.: Where committees go wrong, Personnel **44**:62-67, July/Aug. 1967.

Role stress—including role conflict, role ambiguity, role incongruity, and role overload—is probably more prevalent today than ever before. It is reasonable to assume that such prevailing social conditions as inadequate adult socialization, rapid change in social organizations, and accelerated technology contribute to more numerous and extensive role stresses and strains today than in the past.

From Hardy, M.E., and Conway, M.E., editors: Role theory perspectives for health professionals, 1978, Appleton-Century-Crofts, pp. 78-79.

5

ROLE THEORY AND NURSING PRACTICE

Ona Z. Riggin

A discussion of the application of role theory to nursing and to other professionals in the health care delivery system necessitates an understanding of the historical formulation of role definitions, concepts, and constructs, as well as the utilization of these constructs by nurses and other professionals.

In some instances role is viewed from the functional perspective, which encompasses the clinician, teacher, consultant, manager, and research behaviors exemplified by the nurse as an independent practitioner or as a member of the health team. At other times role theory and role constructs are utilized in studying various aspects of the nurse's role and the effect that identified role variables have on the nurse's total function as a person and as a practitioner of nursing.

Behavioral scientists, including sociologists, psychologists, and anthropologists, define role in a manner that is pertinent to problems inherent in their particular disciplines. One of the difficulties that emerges when applying role constructs to nursing results from the multidisciplinary derivation of role theory and its relevance to the diverse functions of nurses. The level of educational preparation of the nurse and the bureaucratic and administrative policies of health care institutions dictate to a great extent the role that the nurse can or must assume in each clinical setting. Two definitions of role are presented to illustrate the diversity that exists.

Biddle and Thomas (1966, p. 29) characterize the striking diversities evidenced in role definitions by noting that role has been used to denote "prescription, description, evaluation and action." In addition, they observe that role refers to "overt and covert processes" and that it may refer to "behavior of self and others or to the behavior an individual initiates versus that which is directed toward him." They define role as "the set of prescriptions defining what the behavior of a position member should be." As will be noted later in this chapter, nurses as individual practitioners and as members of the profession have always functioned under a

set of prescriptions that have delimited their behavior.

Since nurses function almost exclusively in the interpersonal realm, it is worthy to note Scott's definition (1970, p. 58) of role. He defines role as "a set of shared expectations focused upon a particular position; these expectations include beliefs about what goals or values the position incumbent is to pursue and the norms that will govern his behavior."

A major portion of nurses' educational experience focuses on concepts inherent in role socialization. Students learn to identify expectations for various nursing functions and ministrations from a multiplicity of nurses, including faculty, staff nurses, nurse administrators, and advanced nurse practitioners. Additional perceptions of the nurse's role are gleaned from other health professionals and consumers. These shared expectations are internalized by the student nurse and constitute the foundation for a belief system that remains operative throughout the nurse's professional life. Conflict between the student's perception of self as an individual and the internalized values and beliefs that govern the individual nurse's behavior as a professional practitioner creates role conflict, role strain, and role stress. These concepts will be explored later in the chapter.

Additional content will be utilized to depict the historical development of the concept of role and role theory. The relevance of selected role constructs to professional nursing and the socialization process that occurs during the educational process will be discussed. The final portion of the chapter will focus on the effect that the individual's self-view has on the practice of nursing and on the evolution of new roles for nurses.

HISTORICAL DEVELOPMENT OF ROLE

A review of the early scientific writings related to the concept of role reveals that psychologists and social philosophers including Durkheim, Sumner, James, Baldwin, Cooley and Piaget contributed heavily to the perspective of role theory. Although the term role does not occur in their writings, role-related concepts that influence and govern human behavior were studied.*

Three theoreticians who deserve special attention for their work in differentiating various aspects of the concept of role are: (1) Moreno (1945), a psychiatrist who worked with psychodrama and presented the concept of role playing; (2) Mead (1952), a social psychologist who formulated the concept of role taking; and (3) Linton (1936), an anthropologist who struggled with the concept of external constraints and presented his work on role with regard to status (position) and role.

Moreno's concept of role playing

Jacob Moreno began his work in group therapy in Vienna in 1910. In 1930 he came to the United States, where he continued to formulate concepts relevant to psychodramatic and sociometric theories. He augmented modern role-theory literature with his numerous publications from 1930 through 1960. The concepts of "role" and "role playing" were first mentioned in his classic publication, *Who Shall Survive?* (1953); however, subsequent publications provide greater clarity of these concepts.

Moreno identified three categories of roles:

(a) psychosomatic roles, as the sleeper, the eater, the walker; (b) psychodramatic roles as a mother, a teacher, a Negro, a Christian, etc.; and (c) social roles, the mother, the son, the daughter, the teacher, the Negro, the Christian, etc. The genesis of roles goes through two stages, role-perception and role enactment (Moreno, 1960, p. 81).

Moreno's primary interest centered on changing behavior. His contributions to the behavioral sciences and to psychotherapeutic techniques are represented by his utilization of role playing in psychodrama and sociodrama. Moreno defines role playing as "an experimental procedure, a method

*A fuller discussion of the early precursors of role theory is presented in Biddle and Thomas, 1966, Chapter 1.

of learning to perform roles more adequately" (1960, p. 84).

Moreno differentiates between "role playing" or acting out a role in a spontaneous manner and "role taking," which he perceives as "a finished product" or "a role conserve." Moreno states it in this way: "In contrast with role playing, role taking is an attitude already frozen in the behavior of the person" (Moreno, 1960, p. 84).

Psychodrama

The behavioral technology that Moreno formulated and named psychodrama is based on the premise that greater depth of awareness can be obtained through action and dramatic psychotherapy than through verbal measures alone. Although psychotherapeutic concepts such as abreaction, catharsis, and free association are incorporated into the process, interpretation by the therapist is rarely needed. Learning occurs through experiencing and observing interactions with others in a controlled group context (Moreno, 1945).

The process strives to assist the individual in promoting spontaneity and in gaining a fuller perception of verbal and nonverbal responses. A major goal of psychodrama is to assist the individual in achieving self-realization and to gain a realistic perception of the immediate environment (occurrences, interactions, and roles within the controlled group context). Learning responses that occur as a result of greater self-realization are transferred to interactions with others in the world at large (Moreno, 1945).

Role playing in nursing education

Moreno's work in the area of psychodrama and sociodrama is widely used by therapists in the behavioral sciences in an effort to change human behavior. Role playing as a therapeutic modality is employed in a group context as an experimental procedure to assist individuals in establishing role identities and in learning to perform these roles in a more efficacious manner.

Nurses as well as behavioral scientists have benefited from Moreno's formulations concerning role. Although formalized applications of the techniques used in psychodrama and sociodrama are not generally utilized by nurses other than clinical specialists in psychiatric–mental health nursing, the concept of role playing is employed in all phases of nursing education in an effort to assist students and practitioners to learn to perform professional nursing roles more adequately or to learn to comprehend the effect of psychopathological and physiopathological responses in clients. Individual students are assigned hypothetical roles that they act out in a spontaneous manner for their peers; later the performance is critiqued by peers and faculty. The process occurs as a simulated learning experience and utilizes many of the role components that Moreno articulated.

Mead's interaction theory

George Mead's significant work, *Mind, Self and Society,* published posthumously in 1934 by his students at the University of Chicago, contributed primarily to social interaction theory related to self and role. Mead argued that humans are basically social animals. He introduced the concept of "role taking" and differentiated between the "self," the "I," the "me," the generalized "other," and the "audience." Mead defined self as the capacity of mind and organism "to be an object to itself" (1952, p. 136). According to Mead, the self develops through the social process when individuals learn to evaluate themselves as social objects; thus the absence of social interaction precludes the development of self.

Strictly individualistic biological reactions such as elimination, posture, locomotion, and sleep become socialized or conditioned through the actual or perceived responses from others. This process facilitates "role taking" because the individual is able to assume the role of a significant other through an interaction process in which the individual responds to another's gestures in terms of the reaction that individual feels will be elicited in the other (Mead, 1952).

The process is similar to that which is observed in developing children when they learn to react to significant others in a manner that is consistent with the responses that are directed toward them by those individuals. A child learns to call up the significant other's response and in turn assumes or takes on the appropriate role. This phenomenon is readily apparent during children's play when the child acts out the behavior or roles that have elicited favorable responses on previous occasions.

The process of "role taking" is commonly observed in the socialization process of becoming a professional nurse. Students observe the behavior of significant nurse role models; then they emulate those gestures that elicit favorable responses and discard behaviors that provide fewer rewards. Therefore, to a large extent, what nursing students do as developing professionals is conditioned by interactions they have with significant role models in their immediate environment. The reciprocal actions that occur between nursing students and significant role models become organized into role behaviors.

Linton's theory on role status

Ralph Linton (1936), an eminent anthropologist, studied role in relation to culturally and socially determined occurrences. Linton perceived role as an "external constraint" that is socially derived and assigned to an individual. Conceptually, Linton (1936, pp. 113-114) differentiated between role and status (position). "A status, as distinct from the individual who may occupy it, is simply a collection of rights and duties . . . a role represents the dynamic aspects of a status." Therefore, when individuals are assigned to a status (position) that has specific rights and duties, they are performing a role.

Although Linton proposes a distinction between status (position) and role (dynamic aspects), he affirms that in reality, "role and status are quite inseparable, and the distinction between them is of only academic interest. There are no roles without statuses or statuses without roles" (1936, pp. 113-114).

Numerous examples of the application of Linton's conceptualization of role can be evidenced in the development of nursing as a profession and of nursing's status and role among health care professionals. Nurses have historically assumed a subordinate position in the health care delivery system and have functioned in a role auxiliary to physicians and, to a lesser extent, to other health care professionals such as psychologists, social workers, and physical therapists.

The struggle nurses have had in gaining prominence and independence in their profession can be partially explained on the basis of Linton's theory. Nursing is predominantly a woman's profession. In American society women are viewed as being inferior to men; therefore, women become nurses (status) and men become doctors (status). Traditionally, nurses have functioned in a dependent role with relation to doctors because the status (positions) dictates the role (dynamic aspects) of the nurse's function. Societal changes related to the feminist movement and advances in nursing education are partly responsible for changes that have occurred in the traditional roles of nurses and physicians. Nurses with advanced educational preparation, including clinical specialists and nurse practitioners, are delineating new roles for the nurse as an independent practitioner, which necessitates increased status (Simms and Lindberg, 1978; Yeaworth, 1978; Glass and Brand, 1979).

In accordance with Linton's interaction theory, the inherent changes in the nurse's role have occurred partly as a result of culturally and socially determined external constraints (feminist movement, advanced education for nurses, and increased demands on the health care system) that have necessitated changes in the traditional role of the nurse and provided for new positions with increased status. The latter changes, controversial as

they may be, have affected the roles and statuses of not only health care professionals but also consumers of health care.

ROLE CONCEPTS IN NURSING

The concept of role taking as it occurs through the interactional process, as well as its applicability to nursing, have been discussed in conjunction with George Mead's work. Understanding the concepts of role taking as defined by Mead, and role playing as articulated by Moreno, is essential to an appreciation of the process that is involved in role making and role modification.

Role modification

The term role making implies the need for role modification. It appears evident that the need for role modification is more apparent among professionals and patients involved in the health care delivery system than in any other major social system at the present time. The vastness of the system, combined with its increasing complexity and the multitude of reciprocal relationships with other private, social, and governmental agencies, creates problems that lead to role stress, role strain, and role conflict.

The disequilibrium that occurs when previously established roles and relationships are inadequate to meet current health care delivery needs requires evaluation of traditional roles and subsequent role modification. In an attempt to meet the diversified needs within the health care delivery system and to maintain status and positional needs, individuals within the system attempt to carve out new roles. Each new behavior must be tested and validated through a process of role making (Conway, 1978).

Role making

Conway (1978, pp. 24-25) describes five sequential phases involved in role making:
1. "Initiator behavior" involves initiation of a new behavior by a member of the system.
2. "Other-response" occurs when another indi-

vidual responds on the basis of previously established behaviors and expectations; the other individual may or may not be aware of the intent of the initiator's behavior.

3. "Interpretation by action and other" provides an opportunity for each to explore successive symbolic expressions.

4. "Altered-response pattern" helps the initiator and the other individual recognize that the relationship has changed from that which existed initially.

5. "Role validation" confirms the previous steps. The altered relationship is acknowledged by relevant others, and the new behaviors become accepted as acknowledged norms; thus new roles are identified and accepted.

Both role taking and role making occur in the interactional process and involve an attempt on the part of both parties to understand the symbolic gestures of the other. In role taking, as observed earlier, the response patterns occur with a relative degree of consistency, and the interaction of the participants continues with a maximum degree of comfort. In role making the initiated behavior and/or the response pattern are altered or modified. Both the initiator and the participant experience discomfort and attempt to identify new symbolic meanings for their gestures.

Successful completion of the process of role making necessitates passing sequentially through the five phases that Conway has identified. If validation of the altered relationship occurs, a new role is identified and comfort is restored. However, if the process breaks down during any phase, the participants experience tension, and role conflict, role stress, and/or role strain are observed.

Role conflict

Role conflict as defined by Getzels and Guba (1954, p. 164) involves one's being required to "fill simultaneously two or more roles that present inconsistent, contradictory or mutually exclusive ex-

pectations." Role conflict as a conceptual entity has been the subject of several research studies in the social sciences, nursing, and the health care delivery system in general.

Various investigators have hypothesized that the determinants for role conflict encompass a wide array of variables. Most investigators agree that role conflict surfaces more frequently when there is a noted difference between one's educational preparation and the bureaucratic or administrative constraints that militate against utilization of the knowledge, skills, values, and expectations that one holds for oneself as a professional (Corwin and Taves, 1962; Kramer, 1974; Watson, 1977; Chaska, 1978).

Role strain and role stress

Hardy (1978) emphasizes the importance of the social structure in creating role stress and role strain. Role stress is viewed as existing in the environment and is primarily external to the individual; however, it may cause a severe degree of role strain (subjective feelings of discomfort) in others. Hardy notes that in crisis-oriented situations, the effect of role strain may be detrimental to individuals within the system as well as to the organization itself. Workers become drained of energy, and the quality of care as well as commitment to professional values may diminish.

It is not uncommon to witness the presence of role strain during the professional socialization process for health care professionals. The need to accept professional values and beliefs imposed by the educational program conflicts with the individual's existing values and creates role stress and role strain.

Nursing students are especially vulnerable to experiencing role conflict, role strain, and role stress. Chronologically, many of them have not completed the adolescent developmental task of assuming a permanent self-identity or self-image. Therefore they are confronted with the need to adopt nurse-role behaviors that may conflict with their own self-views and value systems before they have had an opportunity to complete their own development.

Lack of role models

The process is further complicated by the fact that consistency in nurse-role models is lacking. Nursing students must reconcile the differences they observe between the faculty's portrayal of the professional nurse as an individual who enjoys independent nursing-role functions and assumes accountability for personal actions on the one hand, and the technical dependent-role functions the staff nurse exhibits in the actual work setting on the other.

Adequate nurse-role models who exemplify the professional nurse role characteristics advocated by the faculty are difficult if not impossible to find in acute care settings, which are crisis oriented. Unfortunately, these clinical settings serve as the primary learning laboratory for nursing students as well as the initial employment centers for new graduates.

Role conflict, role strain, and role stress are inevitable because students and new graduates lack the appropriate cognitions, values, knowledge, and skills to cope with the disparities between the theoretical and real world of nursing. Investigators in the social and behavioral sciences and more recently in nursing have focused attention on professional socialization and professional bureaucratic role conflict in nursing, in an effort to identify ways to minimize conflict and prepare students for moving into the work force (Corwin, 1961a,b; Corwin and Taves, 1962; Kramer and Schmalenberg, 1977).

Role-socialization studies. Mauksch and Corwin completed two of the early studies related to professional bureaucratic role conflict for nursing students and new graduates.

Hans Mauksch (1963) focused on the professional socialization process of student nurses into the nurse role by interviewing and counseling student nurses and staff nurses over a period of ten years. He concluded that socialization of a person into a nurse role requires a "shift of identity from self to role."

Corwin (1961a,b) studied the relationship between nurse-socialization patterns and the magnitude of conflict that occurs by investigating a sample of graduate and student nurses from several hospitals and schools of nursing located in the Midwest. Corwin administered three Likert-type scales designed to assess bureaucratic, professional, and service-role perceptions. His findings revealed that nurse subjects who hold high bureaucratic and high professional orientations experience greater role discrepancies than do those who adhere to other combinations of role organization. In addition, he identified that degree graduates maintain high professional role conceptions more frequently than do diploma nurses; therefore degree nurses experienced a high level of conflict. However, it is interesting to note that the degree nurses in Corwin's study maintained their perception of professional identity after employment, but they also demonstrated loyalty to the bureaucracy.

Reality shock. Nurse researchers Kramer (1974) and Kramer and Schmalenberg (1977) investigated role-socialization problems in nursing. Kramer utilizes the term "reality shock" to explain the conflict experienced by new graduates between school-world values and work-world values in their initial positions as staff nurses. Kramer (1974, p. 4) defines shock, in reality shock, as "the total social, physical and emotional response of a person to the unexpected, unwanted or undesired, and in the most severe degree is intolerable." The research findings revealed that large numbers of new graduates leave their jobs because they are unable to cope with the value disparities, role deprivation, and resultant discord that occur when the neophyte nurse becomes aware that professional nurse-role ideals and values cannot be realized in the work situation.

Kramer's work also focused on identifying a process that would assist students and new graduates in making the transition into the professional work world for the nurse. As a result of her investigations, she developed an "Anticipatory Socialization Program" for new graduates. Follow-up data collected from hospitals who piloted the program revealed positive results for nurses enrolled in the program. Kramer (1977, p. 11) concluded that "more nurses who underwent the program retained their professional beliefs, suffered less reality shock, remained in their jobs longer, were seen as better nurses and initiated more innovations in nursing practice."

Programs to reduce role conflict

More recently the program has been refined and published by Kramer and Schmalenberg under the title, *Path to Biculturalism* (1977). Many hospitals have implemented the bicultural training program for new graduate nurses in its entirety or have utilized selected modules from the publication as a part of their in-service orientation training for new graduates. Likewise, many schools of nursing employ the materials in preparing new graduates for the work situation in an effort to reduce feelings of role deprivation, role conflict, and role stress in the graduates' initial work placements.

Holloran and others (1980) outlined the training program for new graduates that they developed, implemented, and evaluated at the New England Deaconess Hospital. Their findings revealed that the training program was cost effective for the hospital because it resulted in a significant decline in attrition rates for new graduates employed over a period of fifteen months. In addition, increased job satisfaction was experienced by participants in the program.

Other studies have dealt primarily with the conflict that nurses experience between personal needs, desires, values, motivations, and expectations of employers and other health care professionals. Benne and Bennis (1959) identified several "role affectors" with which the nurse must cope in everyday practice. Included in this list are official expectations related to administrative power structures, colleague expectations, external reference groups such as church and fraternal organizations, and political influences.

Watson (1977) noted that the informal power that physicians wield in the institutional care setting is another source of conflict for the nurse. Although staff nurses as employees of the institution are ultimately responsible to the hospital administrator through the director of nurses and supervisory nursing personnel, they must accept orders from physicians who, for the most part, are not responsible for their discipline or promotion. Understandably, a new dilemma arises as the nurse struggles to meet the expectations of the employer, who controls salary and promotion, and at the same time attempts to attain the desired approval from physicians and other colleagues.

RELATIONSHIP OF SELF THEORY AND ROLE

An understanding of the nurse as a biopsychosocial being encompasses two important conceptual role determinants that affect the nurse both as a person and as a member of a profession. The first concept concerns the individual nurse's perception of self as a unique human being; the second relates to cultural values, mores, and norms employed by societal forces in depicting traditional roles for women.

Personality theories related to self

Many personality theories explain the development of self. A common theme in them is the importance of interpersonal forces in influencing and shaping personality. The self-concept, or personal view of oneself, develops as a result of an individual's interactions with significant others. It is formulated either consciously or unconsciously through the perception of one's experiences (achievements, failures, conflicts, embarrassments, and accomplishments) and is constantly reinforced by feedback responses received from significant persons in one's environment.

Sullivan's interpersonal theory

Sullivan's interpersonal theory (1953) has particular applicability to a discussion of role theory and nursing practice. Unlike some of the earlier theorists who emphasized intrapersonal constructs (i.e., ego and superego) in shaping personality, Sullivan ascribed the individual's uniqueness to interpersonal influences. Sullivan identified specific tools and tasks for each developmental period that affect the individual's development of the self-system. According to Sullivan, development of the self-system occurs with the infant's experiences of the "good me," "bad me," and "not me," which set the stage for personality development in subsequent developmental periods.

The individual who is forced to struggle with unconscious conflicts from the past lacks the necessary energy to cope with problems of later developmental periods, and thus is impeded in fulfilling requisite tasks for self-fulfillment. Sullivan (1953) concludes that low self-esteem occurs as a result of certain unfortunate experiences that occur during early developmental periods.

Rogers: the process of becoming

Rogers (1961) believes that the self-actualized person demonstrates an openness to experience in which one attempts to see reality without distorting it. The individual establishes a sense of self-trust and an internal locus of evaluation in which one looks more to self than to others for answers. Perhaps the most important attribute of the self-actualized person according to Rogers is that the individual continues to seek learning experiences in the process of becoming.

Maslow: self-actualization

Maslow (1954) organizes needs into a hierarchy with physiological or survival needs usually taking precedence over higher needs such as love, esteem, and self-actualization. Maslow notes that self-actualized persons are altruistic and self-transcending individuals who hold high regard for others. They recognize and develop their talents, and they continue to learn in an effort to strive for excellence.

As is noted above, most interpersonal theorists emphasize the importance of self-development through the socialization process. Sexual differences as determinants of personality are emphasized to a lesser degree than is evident in some of the earlier developmental theories. However, since nursing is primarily a female occupation, it is important to attend to societal forces that focus on sexual differences during one's developmental years. Society's perception of the role of men and women influences the development of self-concept and affects personal and professional behaviors. The nurse's role as a professional is inseparable from the nurse's role as a woman. Simms and Lindberg (1978, p. 21) state: "The status of nursing reflects the status of females—subordination to males."

Sex-role influences

Several investigators have studied the effect of sex-role stereotyping on the development of an individual's internal valuing mechanisms or self-view. Simms and Lindberg (1978) summarized several studies that identify the effect sex-role stereotyping has on the development of self-concept. Rosenkrantz and colleagues (1968) concluded that sex-role stereotyping influences the perception one has of oneself; however, they noted that it is difficult to identify empirically the specific effect on development of self-concept.

Several investigators have focused on women's use of the educational process to ostensibly enhance self. Horner (1969) concluded that women fear success, and therefore they utilize their intellectual capacity only when they do not need to compete. She notes that women experience psychological barriers that present difficulties in competing with men, despite the fact that many legal and educational barriers have been removed.

Another way of examining self-concept is depicted in McClelland's work (1975), which focuses on power and power motives. McClelland indicates that one of the major difficulties in drawing conclusions from most studies that deal with male-female behaviors is that many investigators have an inclination to view male behavior as the norm and female behavior as a deviation from the norm. He notes that women as a group have a tendency to require more support from others because they have higher interdependent needs; therefore, satisfying interpersonal relationships are more important to them.

Yeaworth (1978, p. 72) observes that men and women achieve power and status in different ways.

Men gain status, power and high salaries by moving up an organization to occupy administrative positions and by being elected to high offices. Women gain status and power by aligning themselves with and pleasing the right man, giving him support and ideas so that he can maintain high position or advance even further.

An understanding of the effect of sex stereotyping on the development of self-concept or self-view is important in role development and negotiation in nursing. Equally important is an appreciation of the means that men and women utilize to achieve power and status. Women who strive for high power and status positions must learn to cope with subtle rejections in interpersonal relationships. Yeaworth (1978, p. 72) states it this way: "Some of the ways this is done include: failing to use titles in introductions (Ms or Mrs. instead of Dr.); referring to the woman as 'our attractive member' or the representative of the 'fairer sex'; or having men greet her with a kiss when she walks into a formal meeting."

Most nurses have been socialized to believe that the white male is superior and that the male ego is fragile and needs protection. They have learned that it is not wise to be too smart, too assertive, or too successful. Bush and Kjervik (1979, p. 48) state: "This is an insult to both men and women because it

negates the personhood, uniqueness, strengths, and self worth of both sexes. But because it is familiar, it is secure." Yeaworth (1978) notes that the professional nurse exemplifies the multifaceted role of the working woman. She assumes the woman's role as homemaker, mother, and wife, and adds to this the responsibilities of job and profession.

Problems related to male-female stereotypes that professional nurses encounter in the institutional setting have been elucidated by Leonard Stein (1967) in his well-known publication, *The Doctor-Nurse Game*. Through various subtleties, Stein depicts nurses as stereotyping themselves as being inferior in an effort to make the doctor feel good. Subtle communication with others supports the stance that nurses assume a secondary role. They are active in providing patient care but passive in claiming just reward for their actions and their knowledge.

Present and future trends

Reflection on the effects of societal dictates for both men and women further emphasizes the complexities that affect role making and role taking by professionals in the health care delivery system. Since nursing is primarily a female profession and medicine is predominantly a male profession, it is apparent that the problems related to role differentiation are approached by each group from their own unique perspective. The diversity of role expectation that exists among nurses who have been socialized in a variety of educational programs adds to the confusion of role negotiation and identification for all concerned.

Newer roles for nurses

Delineating a specific role for the professional nurse is difficult if not impossible. The impact of social change on the health care system has motivated nurses to examine their current status as professionals in an effort to develop innovative roles. As noted earlier, nurse clinical specialists in secondary and tertiary care and clinical specialists in primary care (nurse practitioners) have assumed leadership roles in personifying the nurse as an independent, assertive practitioner who works collaboratively with physicians and other health professionals in providing health care to clients and in attempting to bring about desired changes in the health care delivery system. Acceptance of these new roles has been slow on the part of not only physicians and other health professionals, but also other nurses and consumers who continue to view the nurse in the traditional role as the "Angel of Mercy" or the handmaiden of the physician (Simms and Lindberg, 1978).

The new roles that nurses with advanced degrees are practicing and that nurse educators are advocating lead to role conflict, role stress, and role strain, because nurses as individual practitioners and as a professional group experience difficulty in supporting one another. The reasons for this are intertwined with varying educational patterns and administrative directives discussed earlier in this chapter.

Nurses with strong dependent needs require feedback and support to prevent burnout. Conversely, nurses who are socialized to be independent, assertive practitioners also experience burnout because they refuse to accept the traditional role that society has delineated for them. Simms and Lindberg (1978, p. 9) state: "Laws and other methods have been used to remove some external barriers to independence. Internal barriers concerning attitudes of self and others, are not legislated away."

Cultural influences and societal determinants have made it difficult for women and nurses alike to develop strong positive self-concepts that permit independent and assertive behaviors. The advancement of nursing as a profession is dependent on nurses with advanced degrees and nurses who are being socialized in today's educational programs to accept the responsibility for developing and demonstrating the newer roles for nurses that are operative in select areas at the present time.

APPLICATION OF ROLE THEORY TO THE PROCESS OF CHANGE

As previously mentioned, nurses have functioned largely under a set of prescriptions established by others; changing roles in nursing tend to upset the equilibrium of the system that has been established. As nursing advances as a profession and its practitioners gain knowledge and confidence in their capabilities, repercussions are likely to occur in various areas.

In general, nursing practice is a collaborative set of functions. Only in recent years have nurses ventured into the area of independent practice, and this amid considerable controversy. No doubt the majority of nursing care will continue to be provided within an organizational context that necessitates considerable collaboration and role negotiation. For example, on any unit in an acute care setting, a variety of health care providers interact on a regular basis. Each member of the team has a certain set of functions that both the individual and all other team members recognize. The nurse, not the x-ray technician, gives injections. All participants hold a set of expectations for one another.

The introduction of any change has the potential for disrupting the previously established pattern of role expectations. The specific role expectations attached to an individual are influenced by the nature of the job position, the roles of other members, and sometimes the ability of the person. Hence each participant carves out a specific set of responsibilities, or a niche, that is respected by other group members. When one member of the group changes the prescribed and previously practiced role behaviors, all other members are affected. Other participants may feel threatened by such a change as they see someone else encroaching on their perceived role. For example, if the registered nurses on a particular unit consistently delegate bed baths to the aides, the aides eventually incorporate this task into their perception of their role. Then a new head nurse is hired who believes that baths provide an opportunity for nurses to assess patients carefully for skin condition, mobility, and other important factors. When the head nurse announces that aides will no longer give bed baths, these employees may experience role threat. They may wonder if they will soon become an expendable item on the unit and fear loss of their jobs.

What this means is that any change has potential far-reaching effects on all those involved. Careful planning often decreases the resistance to change, especially when people are given an opportunity to talk about the feared or expected results of the change.

The book *Backstairs at the White House* (Bagni and Dubov, 1979) graphically illustrates the way change is perceived. Historically, the First Lady maintains considerable distance between her life and the everyday details of running the White House. The day-to-day housekeeping responsibilities are delegated to a housekeeper and a sizeable cadre of staff. The staff were in for a major deviation in their role expectations when the Roosevelts occupied the White House. Bagni and Dubov (1979, p. 316) describe the staff reactions when Mrs. Roosevelt suddenly appeared in the kitchen one morning and commented, "Oh my, you are busy here, you can use some help." A speechless group watched the new First Lady pick up a tray and head for the dining room. When urged to forfeit her tray to the butler, Mrs. Roosevelt replies, "I raised a family of five children, I've served a lot of meals." Situations such as the above are often seen in nursing when new nurses do not conform to the expectations and norms of the group. The reactions are positive or negative depending on the perceived value or threat of the new behavior.

SUMMARY

Role theory as a distinct body of knowledge did not gain prominence as a specialty among the behavioral sciences until the 1960s. Behavioral scientists from other specialties, including anthropology, sociology, and psychology, have contributed to role theory since the early 1900s. Precursors of role theory including James, Baldwin, Durkheim, and Sumner date back as far as the late 1800s.

Each specialty defines role to complement the behavioral science it represents. Since nursing employs concepts from all of the behavioral sciences, it is difficult to identify any one role definition that adequately covers all contingencies in nursing. Scott's definition of role was selected for this chapter: "Role is a set of shared expectations focused upon a particular position; these expectations include beliefs about what goals or values the position incumbent is to pursue and the norms that will govern his behavior" (1970, p. 58). This definition of role focuses on interpersonal processes and stresses concepts that are essential components of nursing.

Role concepts articulated by Moreno, Mead, and Linton were presented to acquaint the reader with the formulation of role concepts that are widely utilized by behavioral scientists and nurses at the present time.

The study of role and role concepts in nursing was initiated by social and behavioral scientists in the early 1960s. The uniqueness of nursing as a predominantly female profession provided fertile ground for sociological and role studies concerning role conflict, role socialization, and role strain and stress.

Nurse researchers interested in the findings of the latter studies and troubled by role problems within their own profession were eager to pursue their own research. Simultaneous efforts were made to identify problematic areas in nursing and to find solutions directed toward minimizing role conflict, role stress, and role strain in clinical work situations. Anticipatory guidance programs were initiated to minimize staff turnover and to reduce burnout in new graduates and young staff nurses.

Many problematic areas remain for the profession. Problems associated with role conflict are complex because many of nursing's problems are inextricably intertwined with society's role expectations for men and women. Solutions concerning status, position, and independent functions for nurses necessitate a reeducation and resocialization process not only for nurses, but for all members of the health care delivery system as well as for the consumer.

The work role of the nurse as a professional is further complicated because major differences exist between the theoretical world in which the nurse is educated and socialized into the profession, and the real world in which nursing is practiced.

Society, as well as other health professionals, continue to view the nurse as a nurturing, feminine, self-sacrificing individual who functions in a dependent role to the physician.

Newer roles for nurses (e.g., the clinical specialist in secondary and tertiary care and the clinical specialist in primary care, or nurse practitioner) are not readily accepted by other nurses, health care professionals, or consumers. The newer roles threaten the long-established and accepted roles for nurses as delineated by society and emphasized by the bureaucratic and administrative policies of health care institutions.

The advancement of nursing as a profession is dependent on the willingness of nurses to assume increased responsibility in demonstrating their expertise as professional practitioners of nursing. This will necessitate carving out new roles for nurses and working collaboratively with other health care workers to provide a maximum level of health care for all people. Nurses with advanced degrees and specialty preparation must assume a leadership role in this endeavor.

REFERENCES

Bagni, G., and Dubov, P.: Backstairs at the White House, New York, 1979, Bantam Books.

Benne, K., and Bennis, W.: The role of the professional nurse, Am. J. Nurs. **59:**196-198, 1959.

Biddle, B.J., and Thomas, E.J.: Role theory: concepts and research, New York, 1966, John Wiley & Sons, Inc.

Bush, M.A., and Kjervik, D.K.: The nurse's self image. In Kjervik, D.K., and Martinson, I.M., editors: Women in stress: a nursing perspective, New York, 1979, Appleton-Century-Crofts.

Chaska, N.L.: Status consistency and nurses' perceptions of conflict between nursing education and practice. In Chaska, N.L., editor: The nursing profession, New York, 1978, McGraw-Hill Book Co.

Conway, M.E.: Theoretical approaches to the study of roles. In Hardy, M.E., and Conway, M.E., editors: Role theory perspectives for health professionals, New York, 1978, Appleton-Century-Crofts.

Cooley, C.H.: Human nature and the social order, rev. ed., New York, 1922, Charles Scribner's Sons. (Originally published in 1902.)

Corwin, R.: The professional employee: a study of conflict in nursing roles, Am. J. Sociol. **66:**604-615, 1961a.

Corwin, R.: Role conception and career aspiration: a study of identity in nursing, Sociol. Q. **2**(2):69-86, 1961b.

Corwin, R., and Taves, M.: Some concomitants of bureaucratic and professional conceptions of the nurse role, Nurs. Res. **11:**223-225, 1962.

Erickson, E.: Childhood and society, ed. 2, New York, 1963, W.W. Norton & Co., Inc.

Getzels, J.W., and Guba, E.G.: Role, role conflict and effectiveness: an empirical study, Am. Sociol. Rev. **19:**164, 1954.

Glass, L., and Brand, K.: The progress of women and nursing: parallel or divergent? In Kjervik, D.K., and Martinson, I.M., editors: Women in stress: a nursing perspective, New York, 1979, Appleton-Century-Crofts.

Hardy, M.E.: Role stress and role strain. In Hardy, M.E., and Conway, M.E., editors: Role theory perspectives for health professionals, New York, 1978, Appleton-Century-Crofts.

Holloran, S.D., Mishkin, B.H., and Hanson, B.L.: Bicultural training for new graduates, Nurse Educator **5**(1):8-14, 1980.

Horner, M.S.: Fail:bright women, Psychology Today **3**(6):36, 1969.

James, W.: The principles of psychology, New York, 1890, Henry Holt & Co.

Kramer, M.: Reality shock, St. Louis, 1974, The C.V. Mosby Co.

Kramer, M.: Reality shock can be handled on the job, R.N. **63**(6):11, 1977.

Kramer, M., and Schmalenberg, C.: Path to biculturalism, Wakefield, Mass., 1977, Contemporary Publishing Co., Inc.

Linton, R.: The study of man, New York, 1936, Appleton-Century-Crofts.

Maslow, A.H.: Motivation and personality, New York, 1954, Harper Brothers.

Mauksch, H.: Becoming a nurse: a selective view, Ann. Am. Acad. Pol. & Soc. Sci. **346:**88-98, 1963.

McClelland, D.C.: Power: the inner experience, New York, 1975, Irvington Publishers, Inc.

Mead, G.H.: Mind, self and society, ed. 2, Chicago, 1952, University of Chicago Press. (Originally published in 1934.)

Moreno, J.L.: Psychodrama, New York, 1945, Beacon House.

Moreno, J.L.: Who shall survive?, rev. ed., New York, 1953, Beacon House. (Originally published, Washington, D.C., 1934.)

Moreno, J.L.: Role theory and emergence of the self, Group Psychother. **15**:114-117, 1962.

Moreno, J.L., editor: The sociometry reader, Glencoe, Ill., 1960, The Free Press.

Rogers, C.: On becoming a person, Boston, 1961, Houghton-Mifflin Co.

Rosenkrantz, P.S., et al.: Sex role stereotyping and self concepts in college students, J. Consult. Clin. Psychol. **32**:287, 1968.

Rubins, J.L.: Multiple therapies. In Freedman, A.M., and Kaplan, H.I., editors: Comprehensive textbook of psychotherapy, Baltimore, 1967, Williams & Wilkins Co.

Scott, W.R.: Social processes and social structures: an introduction to sociology, New York, 1970, Holt, Rinehart & Winston.

Simms, L.M., and Lindberg, J.B.: The nurse person, New York, 1978, Harper & Row, Publishers.

Stein, L.: The doctor-nurse game, Arch. Gen. Psychiatry **16**(6):699-703, 1967.

Sullivan, H.S.: The interpersonal theory of psychiatry, New York, 1953, W.W. Norton & Co., Inc.

Watson, J.: Role conflict in nursing, Supervisor Nurse **8**:40-49, July 1977.

Yeaworth, R.C.: Feminism and the nursing profession. In Chaska, N.L., editor: The nursing profession, New York, 1978, McGraw-Hill Book Co.

That leadership is of various kinds, that it works its ways variously under various conditions, that it has its distinctive requirements and its processes, that it has, too, its pathologies—all means that leadership is not simply a mystique. Slowly our understanding of leadership grows and sometime, perhaps, it will emerge from the sociological twilight into the full light of day.

Merton, R.K., Am. J. Nurs. **69**:2618, 1969.

6

CHANGE AGENTS AS LEADERS IN NURSING

Jeanette Lancaster and Carol J. Gray

Leadership is needed in every nursing activity. Traditionally nurses have been educated to give patient care; in recent years increasing attention has been focused on the necessity for including leadership content and practice in curricula. The goal of leadership is to influence people to change, and all areas of nursing practice require some degree of change. If nursing is to continue to develop as a dynamic, effective profession, the quality of its leaders is of the utmost importance.

Because the study of leadership is so critical to nursing, this chapter will discuss leadership by differentiating it from supervision and management as well as by summarizing several key theories of leadership and describing their relative strengths and weaknesses for nursing practice and the change process. The characteristics of successful leaders will also be presented, as will suggestions for new patterns of leadership for changing organizations.

WHAT IS LEADERSHIP?

Stogdill (1974) concluded after four decades of reviewing leadership research that there are nearly as many definitions of the term as there are people who have tried to define it. Additional confusion often arises from the tendency to use leadership and management as synonymous terms. Certainly there are commonalities in the behavior of both leaders and managers, but there are also distinct differences.

What is leadership? Can it be learned or is it an innate characteristic? If it can be learned, how does one go about doing it? These questions are difficult to answer because of the varying definitions of leadership. Some writers claim that leadership is a born trait: you either have it or you do not have it. Others contend that leadership is little more than charm and charisma (Zorn, 1977). More specifically, Yura and others (1976, p. 38) describe leadership as "a concept permeating all organizations and hierarchial arrangements . . . seen in action wherever a person designated the leader is involved with one or more persons who are willing to be influenced in goal setting or goal achievement."

Similarly, Merton (1969) says leadership is a social transaction that involves the attributes of the transactions between the leaders and those who are led. Claus and Bailey (1977, p. 5) define leadership as "a set of actions that influence members of a group to move toward goal setting and goal attainment." Hagen and Wolff (1961, p. 6) describe a leader as "the person who helps the group attain objectives by influencing the members of the group to organize their efforts toward the achievement of their goal or goals." Similarly, Fiedler (1967, p. 11) defines leadership as "an interpersonal relationship in which power and influence are unevenly distributed so that one person is able to direct and control the actions and behavior of others to a greater extent than they direct and control his." In each of these definitions the common thread seems to be that leaders influence people to change, to move toward new goals via a communicative process.

Thus leadership is a process of influencing people to achieve a goal. For the purpose of this chapter the following definition of leadership is offered: Leadership is an interpersonal relationship in which the leader employs styles, approaches, and strategies to influence individuals and groups toward goal setting and goal attainment in a specific situation. The leader is a group member who influences and directs the contributions of other members so that the group goal can be achieved.

As previously mentioned, there is a tendency to use the term leadership as a synonym for management. This practice is confusing because the two terms do not have the same meaning. More specifically, management refers to the coordination and integration of all resources through the processes of planning, organizing, directing, and controlling, in order to accomplish specific goals and objectives. An implicit prerequisite of management is the existence of an organizational setting.

In contrast, the concept of leadership suggests a behavioral process that functions both inside and outside of organizations. Within the organizational context, leadership is primarily concerned with the management function of directing, which has alternatively been called motivating, guiding, stimulating, and actuating. This managerial function is related to the human factors of an organization; it involves an interaction between people, and focuses on the ability of one person to influence the activities of others. Hence, as a major mechanism of the management process, leadership is used to direct the individual efforts of each member of an organization so that objectives may be achieved.

Another term frequently used interchangeably with leadership is supervision. Just as management is not synonymous with leadership, neither is supervision. Instead, leadership is related to supervision in the same way that it is related to management. More specifically, supervisors are first-line managers; they coordinate the work activity of others who are themselves nonmanagers (Donnelly et al., 1975).

Supervisors are in daily contact with their subordinates, coordinating the basic work of the organization in accordance with plans and procedures developed by upper level management. Supervision is a person-oriented activity (Kron, 1976). Consequently, first-line managers are often assigned this task because of their ability to work with people. Thus the effectiveness of supervisors' coordinative efforts will depend as much, if not more, on their leadership skills as on their technical ability.

Therefore it is possible for both supervisors and managers to be leaders depending on the specific qualities of the person filling the managerial role. Likewise, frequently individuals are significant leaders within a group without being acknowledged as such by their title. That is, leaders often exist in informal groups and are recognized by the other members as the person best suited to guide the group. Leadership is described in this chapter as a process involving influence and communication in order to accomplish the designated group goals. Acceptance of the leader's guidance largely rests on either the expectation that a positive outcome will result or the fear that the followers have no other

choice than to accept the leader's directions. In this context, the discussion of power that is set forth in Chapter 7 is applicable. Coercive, reward, and legitimate power are generally included in a person's position in the organizational hierarchy and can be seen in both formal and informal settings. Further, the degree of referent and expert power is based on the individual's abilities and personal characteristics. As will be noted in the following discussion of theories and styles of leadership, power is used in a variety of ways.

The way in which people choose to lead depends to a large extent on the views they hold about others. In general, the assumptions they make about one another have a significant influence on their behavior. For example, if we believe that "everyone outside the family is out to get us," we are not nearly as likely to be open and trusting as are individuals who think that people try to be honest and do their best in life. As a second example, consider your reaction if you were walking down a city street and happened to walk past a middle-aged man who was staggering down the street, grasping at buildings to maintain balance. One reaction might be to think "look at that drunk, what a disgusting sight." In contrast, depending on your perceptions and expectations of others, you might wonder if the man was having a heart attack and gasping for air. Your assumption about the man might influence your actions. You would possibly be more tempted to avoid the person who appeared intoxicated than to deliberately walk past a man who seemed to be having a heart attack.

Douglas McGregor (1960) in his book, *The Human Side of Enterprise,* differentiates between two types of assumptions that managers make about employees. McGregor refers to these assumptions as theory X and theory Y. As will be noted in reading them, they have applicability to nurses in any leadership position where followers are other nurses, students, or patients. Briefly, theory X assumes that:

1. People inherently dislike work and will avoid it whenever possible.

2. People need to be controlled via threats of punishment in order to accomplish the goals of the organization.
3. The average person is not self-directed but desires others to control him or her in order to avoid responsibility.
4. Security and comfort are more desirable than achievement.

In contrast, theory Y espouses an entirely different set of assumptions:

1. People view work as a natural activity.
2. People do not need to be controlled via threats; they have the ability and desire to set goals and exercise self-control in attaining the goals and they will work hard to do their part in meeting the organizational goals.
3. Commitment is associated with rewards for achievement.
4. People wish to and can learn ways to accept responsibility.
5. Many people, not just a selected few, have creative potential.
6. In a number of instances, organizations do not promote the maximal potential of employees.

The mode of leadership that people choose is largely determined by their views of others. For example, the leader who holds a theory X orientation is most likely to adhere to a focus on task accomplishment than to an interpersonal approach for working with people. The reverse would be true of leaders who are more aligned with theory Y views.

OVERVIEW OF LEADERSHIP THEORIES

Harvey (1980) noted that historically some people have found theories to be practical; others have found them impractical; and still other people have not found them at all. This section presents several of the most commonly accepted leadership theories in the anticipation that the reader will be able to make informed choices as to their personal leading behaviors. To date, no one of these theories has gained universal acceptance, but each has certain

valuable components. The following discussion categorizes leadership theories under three broad headings: trait theories, personal-behavioral theories, and situation theories.

Trait theories of leadership

Much of the early work in leadership research was directed toward identifying the characteristics that distinguished leaders from followers. The earliest form of trait theories, referred to as the "great man theory," stated that some people are born with the innate ability to be a leader. This position implies that people are endowed with superior abilities that differentiate them from ordinary people. According to Marriner (1978, p. 13), these leaders are "well rounded and simultaneously display both instrumental and supportive leadership behavior." The instrumental abilities refer to planning, organizing, and managing the work of subordinates in order to meet the goals of the organization efficiently. The supportive behaviors are more socially oriented and include collaboration and participation of others in goal setting. These leaders are purported to be both efficient and nurturant, and they tend to be held in high regard by co-workers. The major drawback to this theory of leadership is its firmly held contention that leadership behaviors cannot be learned but can only be acquired through innate characteristics.

In general, supporters of trait theory attempted to identify those characteristics that seemed to make leaders great. Considerable research was devoted to investigating the intellectual, emotional, physical, and other personal characteristics of leaders. The belief was that if these traits could be identified, then potentially successful leaders could also be identified.

In general, the trait theorists believed that successful leaders should have a striking physical appearance, good speaking ability, insight, and intelligence; further, they should be pleasant, honest, highly energetic, and enthusiastic, with a noticeable sense of purpose. They also stated that leaders should demonstrate integrity, courage, and self-discipline (Bernard, 1926; Tead, 1935). Although trait theory has expanded the knowledge available about the characteristics of successful leaders, it does have its limitations. No one list of traits was universally accepted, and seemingly no attention was directed toward the quality of the followers or the environment. Moreover, trait theory dealt with each variable separately and did not specify relative weightings. That is, was honesty no more important than a striking appearance? Also, the trait approach did not provide for generalizability to other situations, since it was so devoted to leader characteristics that seemed to be person-specific.

Personal-behavioral theory of leadership

Dissatisfaction with the trait approach to leadership led to the investigation of a new way of viewing leadership. The emphasis in the personal-behavioral view of leadership is on the observation of leader performance rather than on categorization of traits. The personal-behavioral theories contend that leaders are best described by their personal qualities in addition to their behavioral patterns. In general, these theories focus on two primary styles of leadership: task orientation and interpersonal orientation.

Three frequently cited leadership theories that have applicability to nursing practice include: the University of Michigan's job-centered and employee-centered view of leader behaviors; the Ohio State University studies, which describe leaders as either initiating structure in the work setting or showing consideration for followers; and the managerial grid, which views the two polar extremes of leader behavior as being a concern for people as opposed to a concern for production. These theories are summarized, and then their applicability, both to nursing practice and the change process, is discussed.

The University of Michigan: Job centered and employee centered

Since the mid-1940s, Likert and his colleagues at the University of Michigan have been studying the behaviors of leaders in order to determine what constitutes effective leadership. Using a questionnaire, they surveyed thousands of employees in a wide range of settings, including workers in chemical and electronic industries as well as employees of hospitals, public utilities, banks, and governmental agencies (Gibson et al., 1976). They identified two general categories of leader behavior: job centered and employee centered. The job-centered leader closely supervises employees and often relies on coercive, reward, and legitimate power to influence performance. In contrast, the employee-centered leader is concerned with people as human beings and seeks to promote job satisfaction and individual achievement.

Evaluation of this leadership view indicates that in the short run, job-centered conditions would yield greater production but would elicit negative attitudes and a feeling of a lack of value to the organization. Likert (1961) concluded that, over time, the employee-centered approach is most effective because workers who feel valued and appreciated sustain a fairly even level of performance.

Ohio State University studies: Initiating structure and consideration

Leadership studies begun in 1945 at Ohio State University's Bureau of Business Research attempted to identify the dimensions of leader behavior. These studies isolated a two-factor theory of leadership that included *initiating structure* and *consideration*. Initiating structure referred to behavior in which the leader organizes and defines the relationships in the group, tending to establish well-defined patterns and channels of communication, as well as ways for getting the job done. In contrast, consideration involves behavior indicating friendship, mutual trust, respect, warmth, and rapport between the leaders and the followers (Gibson et al., 1976, p. 187). That is, the leader assumes responsibility for establishing a supportive environment in which subordinates experience comfort and trust.

These dimensions are measured on two separate

questionnaires. The first, entitled Leadership Opinion Questionnaire, assesses how leaders think they behave in leadership roles; the second, the Leader Behavior Description Questionnaire (LBDQ), assesses the perceptions of others about how leaders carry out their activities.

The initiating structure and consideration scores obtained on the second questionnaire provide a way to measure leadership style. This research indicated that initiating structure and consideration were separate dimensions and a high score on one dimension did not always mean that the same person would have a low score on the other dimension. These studies suggested that leadership style should be plotted on two separate axes rather than on one continuum. Four quadrants, as shown in Fig. 6-1, were developed to show various combinations of the two dimensions. The Ohio State personal-behavioral theory has been criticized for being simplistic, lacking in generalizability, and relying too heavily on questionnaire responses to predict leadership effectiveness. Also, early research indicated that as the leader's consideration level increased, the rate of absenteeism and employee turn-

over decreased. In contrast, initial findings demonstrated that as task orientation increased, employee performance rose. Later research yielded contradictory findings that led to further questioning about the accuracy of this bipolar view of leadership style (Gannon, 1979).

Managerial grid: Concern for people and production

Blake and Mouton (1978) developed the managerial grid concept in the early 1960s. In their scheme, five different leadership types based on concern for production (task) and concern for people (relationships) are presented. Blake and Mouton contend that the assumptions and concerns made about people and production are complementary, not mutually exclusive. They also believe that these two sets of concerns need to be integrated to achieve effective performances. Theoretically, there are eighty-one possible positions on the managerial grid as shown in Fig. 6-2.

The five leadership styles are best described as follows:

1. *Impoverished* (1,1). Minimal effort and con-

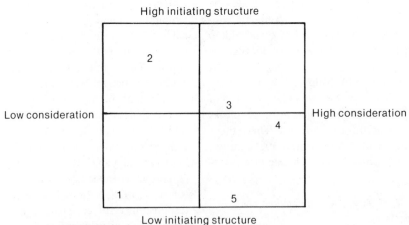

FIG. 6-1
Scores of five different leaders reflecting differences in level of structure and consideration for others.

cern are devoted either to people or to production; the person only does what is required to sustain the viability of the organization.

2. *Country club* (1,9). Minimal attention is given to production and maximal attention to people, as evidenced in thoughtful attention to the needs of others resulting in a comfortable, friendly atmosphere.

3. *Task* (9,1). This style is primarily concerned with production and efficiency and does not let human concern interfere with goal attainment.

4. *Middle of the road* (5,5). Moderate concern for people and production is evident; there is

concern both with getting the job done and with maintaining morale.

5. *Team* (9,9). Viewed as the ideal approach because it integrates maximal concern for people with concern for productivity, this leadership style leads to mutual trust and respect in relationships.

The benefit of the managerial grid is that it allows leaders to identify their own leadership styles and also to examine alternative behavioral styles.

In reviewing the three examples of personal-behavioral theories, several similarities are noted. Each looks at two extremes of leader behavior: a person orientation versus a task orientation. In the

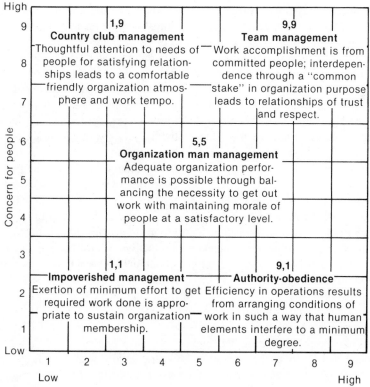

FIG. 6-2
The Managerial Grid.

(From Blake, R.R., and Mouton, J.S.: The new managerial grid, Gulf Publishing Co., 1978, p. 11.)

managerial grid, the continuum from person to task orientation has five dimensions and eighty-one different positions. In general, the similarities among these three theories are greater than the differences. Each offers a way of examining personal leader behaviors; such identification provides information that can enable persons to change their mode of action if their leader behavior is not consistent with their assumptions about people and if they have not had a great deal of success in leading others.

Although people do tend to have a unique style of leadership that they employ in most situations, the strategies of the effective leader generally are modified depending on the demands of the situation. For example, Miss Jones, who is the evening supervisor on the pediatric unit of Happiness Hospital, may be a person-oriented leader who believes that nurses are most effective when they are given considerable autonomy for implementing their roles. She may also think that praise and encouragement are key motivating factors, and her behavior demonstrates this belief in her actions toward all levels of nursing personnel. In general, she is aligned with the University of Michigan's "employee-centered" leader behavior, the Ohio State "initiating structure," and the managerial grid position of about 5,9, which blends country club and team management.

One evening Miss Jones is making her rounds of the patient care units when she walks onto the adolescent unit and finds mass confusion. Two adolescent boys are fighting, all of the ambulatory patients are shouting and urging the fighters on, and the nurse in charge is holding her jaw which was just hit as she tried to step between the boys. The other personnel on the unit are watching helplessly because they are uncertain about how to proceed. Clearly, Miss Jones must implement leader behavior that adds structure and limits to the situation. She must quickly assess the best way to stop the fight, and then clearly and decisively mobilize the staff into action. Although she needs to employ a task-oriented strategy, she will not behave in ways that conflict with her basic approach to leadership. That is, she will demonstrate respect for the capabilities of the staff as she guides their actions.

Situation theory of leadership

Unlike trait theory, which focuses on leader characteristics, and the personal-behavioral approach, which emphasizes a task-orientation versus a human-relations style of leader behavior, the situational view devotes attention to the context or environment in which leadership occurs. From a situational perspective, the successful leader is one who just happened to be at the right place at the right time. Leader effectiveness is considered to be a function of the situation more than of any other single variable. The idea of situational readiness gains support if one considers historical examples in which new ideas were considered heretical at the time they were presented, but a later era considered these same ideas a "stroke of genius." For example, Semmelweiss believed that physicians who were performing dissections should wash their hands before they participated in deliveries in order to reduce the chances of puerperal fever. These ideas were scorned when Semmelweiss stated them, yet now are considered essential aseptic techniques.

In situation theory, leaders are generally more concerned with the needs of the group than with their own needs, in that the best leaders are those who adjust their leadership styles to a particular group at a specific point in time in order to deal with a situation. Hence the primary ingredients of the situational approach to leadership include the leader, the group, and the situation. Symbolically, these ingredients can be expressed as:

$$L = f(LP, GC, \text{ and } S)$$

where leadership (L) is a function (f) of the leader's personality (LP), the group's characteristics (GC), and the situation (S).

Gibson and colleagues (1976) summarize the situational theme by looking at several forces that influence the three aspects of leadership: leader, group, and situation.

1. *Forces on the leader.* The behavior of leaders in any situation is influenced by forces operating within their personalities, including:

    a. *Value system.* Attitudes, beliefs, and behaviors held as important constitute one's value system. For example, in a hospital unit, does the head nurse value participative decision making or prefer to make decisions alone?

    b. *Confidence in subordinates.* How much respect and confidence does the leader have in subordinates? In a public health agency, does the supervisor feel confident that staff nurses are using their time wisely and efficiently to promote patient care? Or does the supervisor maintain constant surveillance on the staff?

    c. *Leadership tendencies.* Can the designated leader supervise the work of others without smothering or ignoring them? Can faculty lead students to try new approaches to patient care by serving as role models?

    d. *Security.* Is the leader secure enough to risk considering the ideas and opinions of others and also to allow others to participate in the decision-making process? Does the supervisor allow staff nurses to try new ideas without constant monitoring of their progress?

2. *Forces in the subordinates.* Each member of a work group is unique and has ideas, goals, drives, and aspirations that the leader needs to consider. Moreover, each member has a set of expectations about how the leader should behave in a given situation. Does the leader attempt to learn about group members' needs, goals, and areas of competency? Can priorities be rearranged if necessary to consider the needs of the group members?

3. *Forces in the situation.* The characteristics of the situation have a definite effect on leadership effectiveness. What resources and constraints are present? What tasks are expected and within what time frame? Specifically, characteristics of the organization, group effectiveness, the task, and the time constraints affect leader effectiveness.

    a. *Organization.* Each organization has goals, values, and expectations that are conveyed in policy statements, organizational charts, job descriptions, and procedure manuals. These factors, in addition to the organization's criteria for evaluating performance, influence leader behavior.

    b. *Group effectiveness.* The degree to which a group accomplishes its goals may influence the way in which the leader interacts with them. For example, a faculty member may need to monitor closely a group of students who frequently argue, disagree, and procrastinate when a group assignment is due. In contrast, a group that runs smoothly and harmoniously and completes the task will need less prodding from the leader.

    c. *Task.* The nature of the task often determines the degree and kind of leadership required. Some tasks are especially difficult, and the members may need technical assistance from the leader. The astute leader seeks to determine the group's ability to accomplish their goals and provides assistance at the first sign of such a need.

    d. *Time.* The urgency of both decisions and tasks influences the kind of leadership required. Participative decision making is usually not appropriate for emergency decisions.

From the situation theory viewpoint, the leader is much like an entertainer who often has to change the act in response to the audience. Some "routines" work with one group and are dismal failures with another. One of the most thorough analyses of situational leadership theory, completed by Fiedler, is the contingency model.

Contingency model of leadership

During the 1960s, Fred Fiedler introduced the contingency model of leadership, which blends concepts similar to those of the personal-behavioral approach with an orientation that emphasizes the situational variables affecting leadership activities. Fiedler (1967) was primarily concerned with how a person becomes an effective leader. The first aspect of Fiedler's contingency model is the differentiation between two leadership styles: the human-relations, or group-oriented, and the task-oriented styles. The task-oriented leader is an authoritarian who is primarily concerned with successful completion of the goal. This person assumes total responsibility for making decisions and directing the activities of the group.

In contrast, the human-relations or group-oriented leader is motivated primarily by a desire for good interpersonal relations with subordinates and uses democratic processes for making group decisions. The foundation for contingency theory comprises three situational components that influence the leader's effectiveness: leader-member relations, task structure, and position power. *Leader-member* relations refers to the amount of confidence members have in their leader as well as their degree of loyalty. *Task structure* describes the degree of routineness involved in the task. Some tasks are well defined and easy to understand; others are ambiguous or lack sufficient structure for participants to understand what is expected. *Position power* consists of the formal authority associated with the leader's position and includes the rewards and punishments associated with the position as well as the support that leaders receive from their supervisors. In general, leadership is easier in situations where considerable position power exists.

Fiedler tested his three-dimensional leadership model in a variety of groups, including military units, basketball teams, and business organizations (Duncan, 1978). He investigated eight possible combinations of these situations to determine whether a task-oriented or a consideration approach was a more effective style of leadership. As noted in Fig. 6-3, task-oriented leadership was successful in five situations, consideration in three.

The key factor in determining which style fits the needs of a situation is the favorability of the situation. Favorability is affected by the quality of (1) leader-member relations in a group, (2) the degree to which a group's task is structured, and (3) the formal power that the leader derives from occupying the position. In general, as leader-member relations improve a situation becomes more favorable, the task becomes more structured, and the leader's position power increases. Fiedler suggests varying leadership styles for situations in which all three dimensions are strong or high (good leader-member relations, structured task, and strong position power), as opposed to situations in which all dimensions are weak or low (poor leader-member relations, unstructured task, and weak position power).

According to contingency theory, task-oriented leaders perform best in extreme situations (either very favorable or very unfavorable). For example, a task-oriented leader would be recommended for handling a disaster such as a fire on a hospital unit. In this example, the leader-member relations are generally poor. The tasks are unstructured even in a hospital with regular fire drills because the same group of staff and patients is rarely present for the practice and the actual situation; often the position power is weak until someone acknowledges a leadership role.

The same leadership style would be reflected in a situation such as the actions of a designated team who consistently respond to cardiac arrests. In this instance the leader-member relations are usually good because each one has a specified agreed-upon role and the tasks are highly structured. Also, there is a designated team leader who holds recognized position power. In both the fire and cardiac arrest, there is little time for consideration because each second is precious.

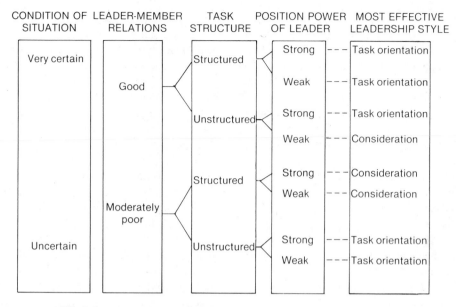

FIG. 6-3

Fiedler's contingency theory of leadership.

(Adapted from Fiedler, F.: A theory of leadership effectiveness, 1967, McGraw Hill Book Co.
Used with the permission.)

The *consideration* style is more effective when the environment or situation is moderately certain. For example, a task force charged with developing personnel policies would generally evidence good leader-member relations, an unstructured task, and weak position power.

Path-goal theory

The path-goal theory of leadership attempts to match the leader's style with certain interpersonal and situational factors. According to this theory developed by House (1971), leaders are effective when they have a positive impact on their followers' motivation, ability to perform, and degree of satisfaction with the job. This theory is designated path-goal because it focuses on how the "leader influences the follower's perception of work goals, self-development goals, and paths to goal attainment" (Gibson et al., 1976, p. 211).

Expectancy theory comprises the foundation of the path-goal view. According to expectancy theory, people are motivated to produce if they believe that their efforts will be successful and will subsequently be rewarded. The concept of *path clarification* is that a key aspect of leader behavior is to clarify the types of activities that are most likely to result in goal attainment. In general, the path-goal approach to leadership has two key propositions (House, 1971):

1. Leader behavior is acceptable and satisfying to the extent that the subordinates perceive such behavior as an immediate source of satisfaction or as instrumental to future satisfaction.

2. Leader behavior will be motivational to the extent that it makes satisfaction of subordinates' needs contingent on effective performance and it complements the environment

of subordinates by providing the guidance, clarity of direction, and rewards necessary for effective performance.

Key concepts in path-goal theory include motivation of subordinates to perform efficiently; the leader's responsibility to clarify activities so that subordinates can be successful; and the value of rewards as a motivating force in performance. Also, it is the leader's responsibility to clarify expectancies and reduce the barriers to goal attainment. Thus a leader can effectively combine task orientation and consideration.

Path-goal theory has considerable potential for nurses. It is basically a human-relations set of activities that recognizes the need to respect others and to provide guidance, encouragement, and clarity of directions. Such behaviors in the long run tend to motivate positive actions from followers. The application of path-goal theory can be seen in the relationship between graduate nurses such as head nurse, to staff nurse, as well as to faculty-student situations.

STYLES OF LEADERSHIP

In addition to looking at the trait, personal-behavioral, and situational views of leadership, it is also useful to examine several leadership styles to determine situations in which the manner of leader behavior has the greatest applicability. Leadership styles can be presented on a continuum ranging from leader domination to the opposite extreme of individual member control of the situation.

Tannenbaum and Schmidt (1973) have developed a leadership continuum that provides a framework for understanding leader behavior especially in regard to decision making. Fig. 6-4 presents the relationship between leader authority and the amount of freedom provided to subordinates in making decisions. The leader behaviors on the left of the figure represent leader-oriented actions that localize control with one person. In contrast, the position on the far right reflects member control in the decision-making process. This continuum can be used to depict the range of the most popularly

discussed leadership styles: autocratic, democratic, and laissez faire. Autocratic leader behavior appears on the left of Fig. 6-4 and is characterized by a leader who makes the ultimate decision and establishes goals for the entire group. In contrast, laissez-faire leader style falls on the far right side of the continuum and is a "hands-off" mode of operation where the leader exerts no direct influence on the followers. The third frequently discussed leadership style, democratic, lies at the midpoint of the continuum and is seen when each group member has freedom to participate in decision making. Each of these styles is described in more detail in the following discussion.

Following the original development of this continuum, Tannenbaum and Schmidt (1973) modified it to take into account the effect that both the social and the organizational environments have on the selection of a leader style. In this context, leadership is seen as an interdependent process between leaders and followers. Interestingly, the term non-manager is substituted for subordinate to reflect the interdependence rather than to emphasize the power difference commonly associated with the terms of manager and subordinate.

Autocratic

The autocratic leader exerts maximal control over followers. In this style the leader makes the ultimate decision and establishes goals for the entire group. This leader actively discourages group participation, especially in decision making, and is task oriented so that goals are accomplished as efficiently as possible. This leader not only decides on which goals will be accomplished, but also how, when, and by whom. The autocratic leader is an order giver; people are told what is expected of them and their opinions are of limited consequence. This type of leader "tends to use non-constructive criticism and praise for personal traits of members rather than for work performed" (Heimann, 1976, p. 19).

These leader behaviors create fear among followers and often lead to hostility, resentment, and

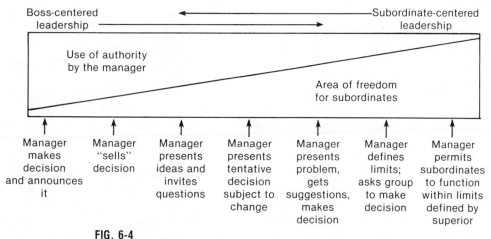

FIG. 6-4

Continuum of leadership behavior.

(From Tannenbaum, R., and Schmidt, W.H.: How to choose a leadership pattern, Harvard Bus. Rev. **51**:164, May/June 1973.)

generally poor morale. The autocratic leader can be ruthless in getting the job done; the feelings and needs of no one are spared. This leadership style is most effective in a crisis or emergency when something must be done quickly.

A variation on the autocratic style is called the *benevolent autocrat*. This type of leader maintains ultimate responsibility but is accesssible to members and listens to their opinions and suggestions. The leader structures the activities of subordinates and makes policies and decisions, yet may encourage participation during the planning phase. The benevolent autocrat maintains power and a position as "chief" while being concerned about the needs of others as well as their attitudes.

Democratic

The democratic leader is "one who makes ultimate decisions about goals and methods of goal accomplishment but allows members to participate in both processes" (Duncan, 1978, p. 208). In this style, group members are treated with respect and valued for their contributions. The democratic leader elicits suggestions and ideas from the group and makes suggestions, but does not usually give orders. The main function of the leader is to stimulate and motivate the group. The members of the group are respected and valued and their opinions and ideas are solicited. When democratic leaders praise members, it is for the work that they performed rather than their personal characteristics. Likewise, criticism of members is matter-of-fact and attempts to help rather than hurt them.

In order to function in a democratic group, members need some understanding of group dynamics so that each participant will recognize the need for shared responsibility. Interactions within the group are predominantly member to member, rather than leader to member as seen in the autocratic group.

Groups that are run in a democratic manner tend to be more cohesive and creative than autocratic ones. The work reflects the ideas of many people rather than just one. The major disadvantage of the democratic style of leadership is that it often takes considerable time to get the tasks accomplished. Members may also struggle to reach agreement or compromise on a goal or plan.

Laissez faire

The laissez-faire leadership style is often referred to as "hands-off" leadership, since the leader exerts no direct influence over the members. The leader simply lets followers pursue their own goals in whatever way they see fit. Laissez-faire style is centered on individuals, whereas autocratic style is centered on the leader and democratic style is centered on the group (Heimann, 1976, p. 20). Basically, the laissez-faire leader is not an actual leader in the true sense of the term, but instead serves as a distributor of information who makes no attempt to evaluate the work of others but merely channels information from one member to another. Frequently this style creates tension and anxiety among subordinates because they perceive that no one is really in charge. In actuality, such a situation is not likely to last long, because the purpose of a leader by definition is to guide and direct. The end result of a true laissez-faire style would most likely be chaos and confusion.

INTEGRATIVE MODEL OF LEADERSHIP

Based on the previous discussion of trait, situation, and personal-behavioral theories of leadership as well as the delineation of four leadership styles, it would appear that no one theory or approach offers a universally accepted explanation of effective leadership. Bennis (1968) contends that new forms of leadership must be developed as rapid social changes alter the organizations in which leadership takes place. He goes on to state (1968, p. 101):

Leadership of modern organizations also depends on new forms of knowledge and skills not necessarily related to the primary task of the organization. In short, the pivotal function in the leader's role has changed from a sole concern with the substantive to an emphasis on the interpersonal.

Bennis further identifies four competencies it is important for leaders to possess:

1. Knowledge of large, complex human systems
2. Practical theories for guiding these systems, including the development and nurturing of participants
3. Interpersonal competence, especially in regard to recognizing the effect one has on others
4. A set of values and competencies that enables one to know the best way to approach others

Similarly, Gibson and others (1976, pp. 213-214) identify variables they consider crucial to an integrative model of leadership as: (1) self-awareness, (2) group characteristics, (3) understanding individual characteristics, and (4) understanding motivation. By self-awareness is meant a recognition of how the leader affects others. Many of us develop inaccurate perceptions of our own personalities and behavior; we think that we are being helpful when actually we are blocking progress. In order to minimize discrepancies, leaders need to diagnose their personal style. It is also helpful to validate your self-awareness with others to see if their perceptions coincide with yours.

The leader also needs to diagnose group characteristics including norms, size, capabilities, communication patterns, maturity, goals, values, expectations, and cohesiveness. If leaders continuously make suggestions that conflict with how the group has worked in the past or with their current goals and plans, resistance is likely to occur.

Just as leaders must recognize and understand the characteristics of the group, so they should work to understand the individual member. Each person in a work group is unique and has a special contribution to make.

Likewise, leaders need to recognize the factors that motivate people. Recognition, praise, and encouragement are usually effective motivators, in that people tend to perform at high levels of productivity when they feel needed and respected.

A workable concept of leadership, then, takes into account the characteristics and abilities of the leader as well as those of the followers; the context or situation in which leadership takes place; and the quality of the interaction among the participants. Merton (1969) refers to the interactions between those who lead and those who follow as transactions. An interactional theory implies that influence between leader and follower flows in two directions: leader behavior affects the responses of followers just as the follower behavior affects the actions of the leader.

When thinking about leadership we tend to emphasize how the leader affects the follower, but we should not discount the follower's effects on the leader. For example, groups can influence leaders by threatening to strike or rebel. Likewise, they can rally around the leader in times of stress or when external pressures build up (Heimann, 1976). Thus the leader is only one component in the complex process of leadership. The process of leadership is complicated when the situation is in a constant state of flux, as often is the case. Goals, priorities, levels of funding, and other variables may be fluctuating, and this requires flexibility on the part of the leaders as well as of the followers. Interaction theory holds that leaders need to consider style, trait, situation, and patterns of interactions.

The following set of characteristics describes the traits needed by leaders who implement an interactional approach:

1. Confidence in one's ability to lead
2. Respect and trust in others
3. The ability to communicate clearly and listen effectively
4. The ability to make decisions
5. Planning and organizing skills, including delegation, providing adequate directions, guiding, and coordinating
6. Lack of overwhelming anxiety; the ability to maintain control in many different situations
7. Good knowledge of the field in which one is a leader
8. Considerable energy and ability to stick to the task at hand
9. Patience and consideration for the needs of others

An integrative model takes components from a variety of leadership theories to build an eclectic approach that emphasizes interaction. Inherent in this leadership theory is a belief in a two-way flow in leader-follower situations, with the leader influencing the followers and vice versa.

SUMMARY

Leadership has been described according to the importance of traits, style, and situations as well as from a personal-behavioral viewpoint. Useful information can be gleaned from each of these ways of viewing leadership. Perhaps the most comprehensive way to describe leadership is through the development of an eclectic model that incorporates aspects of other key leadership theories to build a versatile humanistically oriented strategy. This form of leadership values a mutual working relationship between group members and the leader. It does not discount the contributions of other theories, but borrows from them to develop a flexible, adaptive way to work with others.

REFERENCES

Bennis, W.G.: New patterns of leadership for adaptive organizations. In Bennis, W.G., and Slater, P.E., editors: The temporary society, New York, 1968, Harper & Row, Publishers.

Bernard, L.L.: An introduction to social psychology, New York, 1926, Henry Holt & Co.

Blake, R.R., and Mouton, J.S.: The new managerial grid, Houston, 1978, Gulf Publishing Co.

Claus, K.E., and Bailey, J.T.: Power and influence in health care: a new approach to leadership, St. Louis, 1977, The C.V. Mosby Co.

Donnelly, J.H., Gibson, J.L., and Ivancevich, J.M.: Fundamentals of management: functions, behavior, models, Dallas, 1975, Business Publications, Inc.

Duncan, W.J.: Essentials of management, ed. 2, Hinsdale, Ill., 1978, The Dryden Press.

Fiedler, F.: A theory of leadership effectiveness, New York, 1967, McGraw-Hill Book Co.

Gannon, M.J.: Organizational behavior: a managerial and organizational perspective, Boston, 1979, Little, Brown & Co.

Gardner, J.: No easy victories, New York, 1968, Harper & Row, Publishers.

Gibson, J.L., Ivancevich, J.M., and Donnelly, J.H.: Organizations: behavior, structure and processes. Dallas, 1976, Business Publications, Inc.

Hagen, E., and Wolff, L.: Nursing leadership behavior in general hospitals, New York, 1961, Columbia University Press.

Harvey, J.B.: Innovations in organizations, speech, The University of Texas System Institute of Higher Education Management, Austin, Tex., Jan. 1980.

Heimann, C.G.: Four theories of leadership, J. Nurs. Adm. **6:**18-24, June 1976.

House, R.J.: A path-goal theory of leadership effectiveness, Adm. Sci. Q. **16:**321-329, Sept. 1971.

Kron, R.: How to become a better leader, Nursing '76 **6:**67-72, Oct. 1976.

Likert, R.: New patterns of management, New York, 1961, McGraw-Hill Book Co.

Marriner, A.: Theories of leadership, Nurs. Leadership **1**(3): 13-17, Dec. 1978.

McGregor, D.M.: The human side of enterprise, New York, 1960, McGraw-Hill Book Co.

Merton, R.K.: The social nature of leadership, Am. J. Nurs. **69:**2614-2618, 1969.

Stogdill, R.M.: Handbook of leadership, New York, 1974, The Free Press.

Tannenbaum, R., and Schmidt, W.H.: How to choose a leadership pattern, Harvard Bus. Rev. **51:**162-180, May/June 1973.

Tead, O.: The art of leadership, New York, 1935, McGraw-Hill Book Co.

Yura, H., Ozimek, D., and Walsh, M.B.: Nursing leadership, New York, 1976, Appleton-Century-Crofts.

Zorn, J.M.: Nursing leadership for the '70's and '80's, J. Nurs. Adm. **7:**33-35, Oct. 1977.

So long as we need the services of others, we are never far from the world of power. This is as true in our day-to-day exchanges with loved ones, friends, and employers as it is of more remote exchanges reported in the press between political and industrial leaders. At times we are the targets of power-based influence attempts, and at other times we are the sources—trying to influence others to do something they normally would prefer not to do.

Kipnis, D.: The powerholders, 1976, University of Chicago Press, p. 1.

7

POWER AS A CHANGE STRATEGY

Dalton E. McFarland

Power is an increasingly important form of influence for the nursing profession, for nursing administrators, and for individual nurses who are subject to it or who learn to use it in their work. As an organized profession, nursing exerts power through group processes that link it to society and its health care system. Nursing administrators face power problems in the organizations they serve. Nurses in private practice find power a critical factor in their relationships with patients, physicians, and others in the health care field (McFarland and Shiflett, 1979).

This chapter analyzes the nurse's power within the context of administrative organizations, with special emphasis on the uses of power in bringing about change. Power and change are inevitably present in all organizations, and an understanding of the two concepts is vital to effective nursing performance. The analysis will proceed according to three main aspects of power: (1) the nature and sources of power, (2) the use of power within the health care organization, and (3) the functions of power in the processes of organizational and administrative change.

THE NATURE OF POWER

Power is the ability of a person or a group to require others to act as the power holder desires. Power is the strongest form of influence because the basis for it includes the ability to apply consequences that those subject to it would prefer not to occur. As the strongest form of influence, power is not to be taken lightly. It is generally brought to bear when other forms of influence, such as leadership or delegated authority, are inadequate.

Power is thus a subtle device in an array of strategic methods designed to obtain the desired behavior of others. But power is a two-way street. It cannot function unless those to whom it is directed acknowledge the legitimacy of its use and are willing to act accordingly. The same is true of the use of authority or leadership skill. An important question, therefore, is why do people in an organization acquiesce to the use of power?

The members of an organization accept power when it is the logical expression of the need for order, system, the predictability of behavior, and the achievement of purpose. They expect it to be reasonable and legitimate within the organization's "rules of the game." Latent moral and ethical expectations can also come into play.

Power is so endemic to society that we all learn to respect it, even when resisting it. As we mature from infancy through childhood, youth, and adulthood, we acquire experience by which to judge the legitimacy of power in action. Parents, police officers, teachers, and other authority figures accustom us to the uses of both power and authority. No wonder then that people who work for an organization are not surprised by situations controlled by power.

But acquiescence to power is not automatic or blind. Humans are partly rational and partly emotional; they sometimes react by habit, but often react after carefully considering circumstances. Each situation is unique and each person has a unique personality. Unrestrained, irrational power is therefore unlikely to endure; even legitimate power must be used with discretion and regard for its consequences. In order to understand the nature of power and its use more fully, it is necessary to consider its types and sources.

Types and sources of power

Power derives from multiple sources that may operate simultaneously. Wieland and Ullrich (1976, p. 248) describe five types of power: legitimate, reward, coercive, expert, and referent. *Legitimate* power is the authority vested in a role, position, or office which is accepted and recognized by the members of the organization; it can be called positional authority. *Reward* power is based on the power holder's use of positive sanctions, which may be as simple as a compliment or as complex as monetary benefits. *Coercive* power, the opposite of reward power, involves negative sanctions such as threats of harm, punishment, or withheld rewards; this is the most visible form of power. *Expert* power is founded on the individual's valid knowledge, skills, or information. *Referent* power, the most subtle form, is based on attractive personal characteristics that lead others to emulate or please the attracting person. All of these sources are available to the nurse or nurse administrator. Planned use of these sources of power, called a *power strategy,* requires careful consideration of probable consequences in specific contexts.

Derivative forms of power can also be useful to the nursing administrator. These include *associative* power, which comes from close association with a powerful individual or group. Nurses, for example, acquire power from working with members of the medical staff or with administrators. Another derivative form is the power of lower participants in a hierarchy in relation to higher members. For example, the nursing administrator may have power over the hospital administrator through: (1) control of resources on which the administrator depends; (2) control of others' access to the administrator; (3) control of techniques, procedures, or knowledge that the administrator needs; or (4) personality attributes such as charm, likeableness, or charisma that the administrator considers desirable in a subordinate. Note that this same type of power can be utilized by staff members in relation to the nursing administrator.

We now turn to an analysis of how the types and sources of power apply to nursing administrators and to individual nurses.

Power in the organization

Over ninety percent of today's 1.4 million nurses work for organizations that provide structured job opportunities, resources, planning, goals, and clientele—important elements in the nurse's power base (For new nurse, bigger role, 1980). To increase their power, therefore, nurses need a sophisticated experiential knowledge of organizational processes and the behavior of people within them.

Organizations find professionals notably harder to deal with than other types of workers. They band together through kindred interests, thus gaining the power of alliances and coalitions. Furthermore, they value autonomy, independence, and peer evaluation more than organizational values such as loyalty, conformity, obedience, or subservience. Therefore they cannot be treated like other employees, for their work means more to them than do the tenets of bureaucracy. The struggle between loyalty to the profession and loyalty to the organization presents a dilemma that the nurse can meet by developing a careful sense of priorities.

Although professional and organizational loyalties are both necessary, nurses should recognize that their individual power is enhanced if higher power figures in the institution delegate legitimate authority to them. Thus a route basic to increased individual power consists of advancing through the administrative hierarchy and earning power through effective managerial performance.

It is essential for the administrator to come to grips philosophically and emotionally with the necessity for high-quality nursing administration. Not every nurse desires administrative power, but those who do must accept a new way of life, particularly regarding the eventual decline of clinical skills, but also in the form of new duties that demand new skills. The administrative nurse must come to terms with inner conflicts concerning personality, professional ideals, and the needs of the organization. But for those who are so disposed, the work can be enormously rewarding.

Accepting an administrative role that one dislikes weakens one's power, because the ingredients for leadership are missing. Awareness of the sources, uses, and abuses of power is vital to the nursing administrator, yet some are reluctant to participate in a game played by the rules of power. It is an asset to be able to play the game with skill, although it is helpful to wear the mantle of power lightly, to use it sparingly, and to be cautious about flaunting it. But those who do not have power or are unwilling to use it risk losing the confidence and respect of subordinates. To shun power is to be a weak and ineffective leader.

Legitimate power

The nursing administrator's position and title confer a legitimate power that is generally recognized throughout the organization. There may be disagreement about its precise scope, but it is usually adequate for solving problems within the nursing unit. Beyond the department itself, the nursing administrator's power is less, for a unit is more homogeneous and coherent than the organization as a whole.

Reward and coercive power

Nursing administrators also have substantial reward and coercive power based on their formal rights to hire, evaluate, discipline, promote, or discharge individuals. These activities, of course, are not substitutes for positive leadership and motivation. If the administrator bears in mind that this power is only part of a continuing relationship with those supervised, there is less danger of relying excessively on one power source or of using power for its own sake.

Coercive power contains the seeds of its loss or ineffectiveness, since it generates resentment, anxiety, hostility, and resistance.

Expert power

The nursing administrator gains expert power from two sources: professional knowledge and administrative skill. But this duality poses an inner conflict, for the two types of expertise are not always compatible. The nursing administrator faces the erosion of clinical skills, but at the same time gains in administrative skills. Lambertsen (1972) suggests a compromise: that the nursing administrator need not be an expert clinical nurse but rather should have "an ability to make or to interpret decisions about the nursing needs of individuals, families, or other social groups." However, McFarland (1979) found that nursing administrators have difficulty in resolving the twin pressures of the two roles. They idealize the role for which they have the least time (nursing) and resent the role that makes urgent demands on their time and energy (administration).

One takes up a profession out of fascination for its potentials for fulfillment. The nursing administrator feels, not unrealistically, that administrative burdens interfere with professional interests. Guilt feelings arise over neglect of profession, the erosion of clinical skills, and the loss of close patient contact. For some people, such as a hospital administrator, administration is the profession of first choice; for the nurse it is often the result of circumstances or opportunity. The nursing administrator continues to be filled with nostalgia for the work given up. Unless a compromise that resolves the dilemma can be reached, the confusion will be detected by others, power will be reduced, and leadership will be weakened.

Referent power

Nursing administrators may or may not be attractive persons with enough referent power to induce others to emulate them. If they develop hostile, defensive personality patterns, their referent power is diminished.

Ideally, the nurse with a high power motivation has sufficiently adequate inner resources to feel secure and yet show concern for other individuals. It becomes possible to sublimate personal desires to the good of the institution and to make decisions based on rational evaluation of the total situation. Emotional maturity and self-understanding are thus vital parts of one's power base.

Associative power

The nursing administrator has access to associative power through contacts with general administration and with the medical staff. Physicians are clearly the superordinate power source in the health care field. For effective coordination, it is important that the congruent roles of physicians and nurses be recognized. For this to occur, there must be frequent contact and communication between nursing and medicine at all levels, thus giving the director of nursing an opportunity to utilize associative power.

The nurse administrator also has frequent contact

with higher administration and, in fact, should be a vital part of the top administrative team. Schulz and Johnson (1976, p. 105) suggest:

a participative management scheme, which would also utilize such techniques as management by objectives. Moreover, we suggest that a management team concept would be appropriate for most hospitals. In this arrangement the nurse administrator would essentially function as a partner with the hospital administrator and physician members of the team.

However desirable they may be, coordination, cooperation, and collaboration do not provide lasting solutions in power struggles. As professionals, the hospital administrator, the physician, and the nursing administrator have been trained to preserve their autonomy wherever possible and to give ground grudgingly when that autonomy is under fire. Harmony and conflict can coexist, however; indeed, the hospital may be enriched by power relations that generate innovation, adaptiveness, and change through negotiated conflict.

Lower-participant power

The astute nursing administrator will recognize but not fear the power of subordinates. The power of subordinates is collective, for in a one-to-one relationship the superior wins, though perhaps only in the short run. The nurse administrator must relate effectively to staff members individually and as a group, since the power of a leader, hence the leader's effectiveness, depends on the willingness of subordinates to accord acceptance and support.

Derivative forms of power are less certain to yield results than other forms, and some derivative powers may not be considered legitimate. Wieland and Ullrich (1976, pp. 251-252) state that "lower participants may circumvent or manipulate the organizational hierarchy by using various forms of power that are not legitimate." Also, a derivative power may be legitimate in some circumstances but not in others.

Warren's study (1968) of a public school system provides an excellent view of the interrelationships of the main types and sources of power and derives generalizations about their use. The relationships are depicted in Fig. 7-1, and the generalizations about the types of power and their relative effectiveness in regard to conformity and visibility are as follows:

1. Referent power—especially effective in attaining *attitudinal* conformity (internalization) under conditions of *low* visibility
2. Coercive power—especially effective in attaining *behavioral* conformity under conditions of *high* visibility

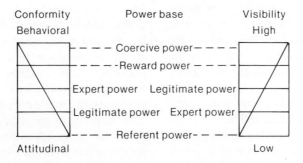

FIG. 7-1
Predicted relationships among social power bases, types of conformity, and extent of visibility.

(From Warren, D.I.: Power, visibility and conformity in formal organizations, Am. Sociol. Rev. **33**:955, 1968.)

3. Reward power—effective in attaining *behavioral* conformity under conditions of *high* visibility
4. Legitimate power—effective in attaining *attitudinal* conformity under conditions of *either high or low* visibility
5. Expert power—effective in attaining *attitudinal* conformity (when used with the expert's knowledge field) under conditions of *both high and low* visibility

Clearly, organizations and change agents should use the types and sources of power in different ways and combinations, depending on specific needs and aims.

Power and the individual nurse

"Nurses are the least political of all the people in health care work." This statement by a nurse reveals the dichotomy between the ideals of service nurtured by professionalism on the one hand and the necessity of coping with bureaucracy on the other. The power game is a game of politics from the point of view of the individual in an organization. Yet few aspects of a nurse's training today teach the strategies for using power. Such training focuses instead on clinical expertise and on competencies for patient care, overshadowing the skills and insights needed for coping with life in an organization. Kramer attributes to "reality shock" the large numbers of nursing graduates who leave the profession. In nursing school they are taught humanism, individual thinking, and treatment of each patient as an individual, but they find that the real world of nursing is much different—even the opposite—from what they were taught. As a result, nurses are shocked at their total lack of control or say in the organization and disturbed by their feelings of powerlessness (Kramer, 1975).

If Kramer is right about these feelings of powerlessness, it may be not just because of a gap in nurses' training, but also because the profession has not brought group power to bear on the use and distribution of individual power, which occurs unevenly in organizations. Those who seek it differ in

their success and in their perceptions as to its sources. Power is also temporary and continually shifting in accordance with pressures and tensions. There are no guarantees of permanent power, though it may last longer if it is earned or sanctioned as legitimate, leading to acquiescence by the less powerful.

Power relationships among individuals are often highly situational; that is, they are contingent on unique factors. For example, a lower participant may have more effective power than someone with greater formal authority and status. In one such case, a nurse felt helpless when an escort employee wheeled a patient to the laboratory and then left the patient there for over an hour. The nurse had no way of seeing that the patient was either treated or returned and expressed intense feelings of helplessness and frustration.

The acquisition of power

Despite the frustrations, the power of individual nurses is increasing, especially that derived from expertise.

In many hospitals nurses have sought and acquired more responsibility and have transferred many routine or clerical duties to others. Moreover, greater autonomy and independence, hallmarks of power, have followed from better education and greater trust by administrators and patients. For example, in many coronary care units, specially trained nurses now have the authority to administer drugs and defibrillation on their own initiative; this has resulted in decreased mortality rates. Patients also accept nurses as the source of primary care in ambulatory clinics, and there are expanded roles for nurses in anesthetic administration and in handling patients with chronic diseases (Rushmer, 1975).

In addition to expanding their expert power, nurses can increase their power in two ways: (1) by accepting it as a normal element of human interaction and (2) by acquiring power from a broader range of sources. Power tactics are important and, whether good or bad, are worth examining. No one can entirely avoid using power tactics; the aim is to use them effectively. This requires practice based on continuing observation and analysis of the interplay of forces in the organization. Martin and Sims (1956) assert that it is neither immoral nor cynical to recognize the actual daily practice of power. They present eight possible tactics: (1) alliances, (2) maneuverability, (3) communication (control of information), (4) compromise, (5) negative timing (withholding action), (6) self-dramatization, (7) confidence (decisiveness), and (8) guarding against friendship or other commitments that limit the acquisition or use of power.

These and other tactical maneuvers should be used with discretion, according to their appropriateness for the individual and for the context. Important as it is, power is a means and not an end in itself. Achieving power for its own sake, without regard for the organization, peers, or patients is a hollow victory. For example, Korda (1975) describes a "jungle" approach to the acquisition and use of power in the manager's self-interest. He sees it as basically a physical matter of domination and territorial control. It helps to be tall, to have some overwhelming physical feature, and to control a strategic space such as a corner office. In meetings, powerful people do not leave early, and they force rivals to sit on their left. A large office is more powerful than a small one, and power figures place furniture between themselves and visitors. Such tactical advice is superficial, and Korda provides few guidelines for answering the ethical questions that are implied. To him the desire for power is what keeps most people working. The power tactics described in Buskirk's manual (1976) are oversimplified.

The matter of ethics is very important in the strategies and tactics used in playing the power game. Nurses must assess the extent to which their actions become undesirably manipulative, calculating, or self-serving, as well as the extent to which they harm others. Power tactics are not inherently or necessarily unethical, but some may be in certain contexts.

The ethical implications of power tactics are difficult to face. The use of any tactic has consequences that affect the game as well as other people and their careers. People in organizations hold strong expectations about the uses of power and will use counterstrategies to limit another's power that exceeds or runs counter to their expectations; power that is primarily directed toward satisfying selfish interests is suspect. Many persons try hard to redistribute the available resources to their own advantage, and the powerful are not always above brutality toward others. Yet power also has its obligations. People expect power holders to help them out and to use power wisely, with judgment and discretion, and in the interests of the organization. A person who flaunts or uses power for its own sake will inevitably run into countervailing forces, including painful stress.

THE USE OF POWER

The holder of power may use it constructively or destructively. Although power pervades the organization and is in fact everywhere in society, it is widely feared and distrusted. Attitudes toward power, hence the propensity to accept or reject its use, vary according to the type and source of power in question.

The determinants of acquiescence or rejection are primarily situational, but they may also include the influence of certain features of the individual's personality and the extent to which an individual's views harmonize with those of other individuals in order that all find support through group processes. Thus a power holder may succeed in using power over an individual, but may experience difficulties in doing so over a group.

Power in action is often not overt, but its very existence rather than its direct use is often sufficient to obtain the desired behavior. It tends to appear in the guise of leadership, authority, or political strategies, luring in the background as a possibility or a threat if other forms of influence do not work. The elusive nature of power follows from the fact that it exists at many levels and in many forms simultaneously, and from the way in which power may be won or lost by individuals according to changing situations. For example, a nursing director in a large urban hospital exercised enormous positional power over 600 nursing staff members, but as these subordinates resisted her authoritarian ways, her power waned and she was ultimately discharged. Thus the way power is used, rather than the amount of power, is significant in maintaining it.

Dependency and the negotiated order

Dependency is a key aspect of power. In this context, nurses and other professionals are relatively dependent on hospitals and other organizations for clients and rewards, as well as for opportunities to develop themselves, continue their careers, and minister to the sick. This is a constraint on the nurse's power. On the other hand, the organization is highly dependent on its nursing staff and the capabilities of individual nurses. Market supply influences the extent to which an organization can regard any individual as dispensable. Nurses derive power from alternative opportunities; they may leave one organization for another, return to nonadministrative duty, avoid organizational life by going into private practice, or even leave the profession.

Administrators often dislike the independence that professionals display, and many of them fear the power that groups can wield in the formal or informal structure. Those who believe in autocratic or even benevolent management styles find it difficult to accept group-participative structures, yet every administrator must work in and through groups as well as with individuals. Therefore nursing administrators' effectiveness depends on their giving special attention to forms of power that derive from group situations. Preferably leaders will use this power responsibly, within appropriate boundaries, and for the good of the organization, rather than for personal prestige and status (Alexander, 1972, p. 205).

Within the organization, power shifts continually among individuals and among groups; it is dis-tributed by negotiation. In addition to a personal role, the individual also has roles in both the group and the organization; intergroup power is a key concept because individual power derives so extensively from membership in a group. For most nurses, the staff of a department or floor unit in a hospital is the primary group, and the hospital as a whole represents a secondary attachment. Both alignments are important and are intertwined to some extent. The route to greater power for the individual nurse, therefore, is to develop strategies for participating in the power negotiations not only within a group but also among different groups.

The three main groups involved in the hospital intergroup power system are the administration, the medical staff, and the nursing staff. An individual, such as a nursing administrator, may belong to more than one group at the same time. The three groups function with each other according to a balance of power that represents a negotiated order. The general character of this order remains generally stable over time, although specific issues or events may cause temporary realignments. Each of the three centers is itself a cluster of power centers that may or may not correspond to departments or other structural units. Here, too, there is a generally stable pattern, but one that reflects realignments of the negotiated order over time.

To participate effectively in this negotiated order, nurses need group leaders who have enough personal and positional power to represent their constituencies. Balance of power among the groups is maintained only by continuous surveillance and by solving the problems of power distribution. If power is not evenly distributed among key groups, it can result in lower morale or the malfunctioning of the groups that are losing ground. The main determinants of intergroup power are: (1) whether a group (such as nursing) can successfully cope with and control uncertainty; (2) whether the group can provide substitutes for the activities and services of another group; and (3) whether the group is important as an integrative mechanism with other groups (Ivancevich et al., 1977, pp. 249-251).

The ability to reduce uncertainty confers power on the group by creating dependencies. If future events are hard to predict, if tasks are relatively unstructured, and if information is uncertain, a group may gain power by developing coping activities that reduce uncertainty for other groups. In nursing, coping activities can be used to achieve an effect on power. Future conditions can be portrayed as uncertain; task performance can be made ambiguous; and normal flows of information can be disrupted or made uncertain. Such coping activities, however, can also provide a positive potential source of power for nursing because of the close working relationship between nursing and other departments of the organization.

There is an inverse relationship between substitutability and power. That is, the more difficult it is to find substitutes for a group's services and resources, the greater that group's power is. In complex systems this power ensues from the effects that occur if services or expertise needed by other units or persons are withdrawn. Withdrawal of services may sometimes be effective as a threat rather than an actuality, but power wanes if the threatened action never occurs. Actual withdrawal is disruptive if there are no satisfactory substitutes for the services denied, causing the target group to try to avoid its occurrence. In nursing there is partial substitutability for the services of RNs to the extent that LPNs, nurses' aides, or candy stripers can fulfill some of their functions during periods of conflict. This substitutability, in addition to questions of professional ethics, makes withdrawal of services a relatively undesirable source of power and therefore one that must be used only as a last resort.

A group's integrative importance depends on the extent to which its resources or activities are connected to the resources or activities of other groups and on the impact on the organization's performance if the group were eliminated or if it performed poorly. From this perspective, nursing has a high degree of integrative impact, which strengthens its power.

The negotiated order resulting from the interaction of groups may be produced through tacit or explicit agreements covering exchanges or interactions expected to take place over time. Another method is structuring a group to include the dissenting or disruptive persons from other groups, thus permitting surveillance of adversaries and providing an opportunity to indoctrinate them or persuade them to go along with the power center. This strategy, called co-optation, risks giving the opposition opportunities for counterefforts that are conducted from the inside. Thus the incorporation of dissenting forces brings with it a price, since those forces must see some advantages in their inclusion.

A third way to negotiate intergroup power relationships is through the political strategy of a coalition; that is, two or more groups join forces to achieve mutually desired goals. An organization almost always requires a dominant coalition to provide direction, control, conflict resolution, and common goals. In a hospital, for example, administrators, medical staff, and nurses may form a coalition to dominate the rest of the organization, or any two groups may attempt to dominate the third. However, coalitions tend to break down as the interests and strategies of the member groups change.

Power within the organization should ultimately be viewed as an influence process that is shaped by the context of the organization, its formal and informal group structure, and the power of individual members. These components are in a state of dynamic equilibrium with interdependent elements; changes in one sector can be expected to produce changes in one or more of the other sectors.

The power of the individual nurse and of the nursing staff is therefore closely related to the nature and goals of the organization. In this connection, King (1976, pp. 51-60) notes that no other group of health professionals provides services in such a wide variety of organizations: schools; industries; official and voluntary agencies; hospitals of various size, purpose, and ownership; nursing homes; extended care facilities; model cities programs; neighborhood health clinics; and crisis, drug, and alcohol abuse centers.

This range of organizational settings poses two problems for nursing in relation to power: (1) for nursing generally, power is highly diffused among subgroups that may disagree with one another over key issues that affect them differently; and (2) individual nurses and nursing administrators must be alert to great differences in the contexts within which power is sought and applied.

The nurse's multiple spheres of influence can provide opportunities for increased power, but they can also lead to diminished power unless the nurse overcomes the problems of communication and physical separation that otherwise may prevail.

Nursing's organizational power base develops from each individual's investment in the goals of the organization; the structure of the organization reflects and facilitates this power base, power taking the form of control over outcomes in which all members of a coalition have an investment. Therefore the decisions of a group or its leader tend to be consistent with its base of power.

As health care organizations lose more and more of their autonomy to external groups such as government agencies, review boards, and planning councils, the sources of internal as well as professional power may be eroded. The organization becomes relatively powerless within its own domain; in attempts to change the domain, the power of nursing in the organization therefore faces the danger of decline. Accordingly, nurses should examine the power relationships that prevail for professionals in society as a whole.

Coalitions provide a balance of power and thus a degree of integration. Balance reflects agreement, if only temporary, about the legitimate distribution of power among constituent groups, and also authenticates the coalition's norms and role prescriptions. An unbalanced relationship is unstable, for it encourages members of an organization to use power in such a way as to reduce the costs of meeting the demands of other power centers. Power networks in a coalition are generally complex;

many variations exist in the interaction patterns, in the relative status and degree of dependency of its members, and in the use of rewards to influence the distribution of power with respect to these elements. Nursing leaders should be aware of the ebb and flow of coalitions and of alignments of the weak and the strong. In coalitions involving physicians or administrators, nursing leadership can be a force for maintaining an effective balance.

POWER, NURSES, AND CHANGE

Changes in society's values and expectations regarding health care services have escalated in the past decade, bringing enormous pressure for change in hospitals, nursing, and other fields of health care. The ability of a profession such as nursing to meet changing needs and expectations depends on learning how to direct and manage change as well as merely to cope with it.

The interaction between nursing and society is mediated through organizational power systems within the profession itself as well as among other health care providers. Efforts to strengthen the power of the profession are useful for shaping and influencing broad changes for nurses in general, but these are focused largely on the external system: the political, legal, and social environment. What counts inside the organization, where goals are to be accomplished in the interests of patient care, is carefully planned change. In order for planned change to be effective, nurses must become involved in the ongoing affairs of the internal power structure. The management of change is one of the supremely important tasks of nursing administration.

Organizational change processes

The basic model for change within an organization is shown in Fig. 7-2. (See Chapter 21 for a more elaborate change model.) This model is an oversimplification of complex procedures, but it usefully depicts the important elements necessary for effective change. The actual processes are not as linear as the model implies. The feedback mecha-

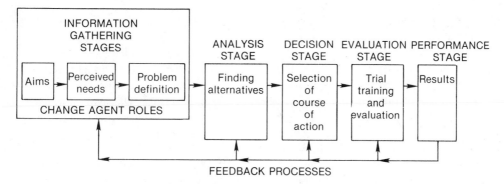

FIG. 7-2
Basic model for intraorganizational change.

nism can result in cutting off the sequence at any stage if observations indicate the need for revision of aims, needs, or problem definitions, or if insurmountable difficulties are encountered at later stages.

The critical elements are at the beginning of the cycle. If aims are misjudged, needs are distorted, or problems are poorly defined, the work at remaining stages will involve considerable difficulties. At every stage, power in its various forms will be evident, along with other forms of influence.

The power to change is often the result of trade-offs as well as of the functioning of an elite. A trade-off occurs when one person gives what another wants only after getting something in return. For example, in one mental hospital a senior nursing staff member accepted a much-hated custodial role ascription in exchange for the power to run the custodial wards with a minimum of interference (Cumming et al., 1973, pp. 344-345).

Control over communications also enhances power. Entrenched informal groups may control information where formal groups abdicate their responsibility. Power comes from withholding information, or from releasing it strategically for purposes of the power holder or the change agent.

The existence of elites, the use of trade-offs, and

the control of information make both power and change a part of the negotiated order.

To explore the role of power in change, let us now consider: (1) change-agent roles, (2) environmental change, (3) innovative change, and (4) resistance to change.

The power of the change-agent role

Any person in an organization may at one time or another be a successful change agent even though it may not necessarily be through the use of formal, positional power. Personal power and influence help the informal change agent achieve results with those who do have the formal power, but for major changes, the change agent must use the whole array of power sources. However, informal change agents find it hard to overcome their lack of practical authority.

In most organizations, formal change-agent roles are built into certain positions either in whole or in part. Staff jobs, such as those in employee training or research work, are examples. While staff persons generally have limitations of authority and hence power, they are expected to initiate plans leading to change. Change agents in the line may enlist the aid of staff units before instituting important changes; staff units in turn need the support of the line, which makes the ultimate decisions.

The limited powers of low-ranking personnel are usually insufficient to produce far-reaching major changes. This kind of change requires considerable formal power. Lower ranking persons have greater influence in thwarting or delaying change. Therefore formal change-agent actions depend on maintaining the goodwill of lower participants. Lower participants find the best source of power in their ability to obtain, maintain, and control access to persons, information, and instrumentalities. Long tenure in a position enables position holders to obtain these controls (Mechanic, 1968, pp. 415-432).

The hierarchy of an organization reflects the intended formal power structure. However, individuals do not necessarily stay within assigned constraints. Many persons like to be independent, creative workers. The opportunity informally or even illegitimately to redesign one's job or role is abundant, especially in nursing and other health care occupations where practice is so complex that supervisors cannot see all that goes on. One form of redesigning a job independently is to expand its power, either legitimately or otherwise. Legitimately, power is expanded by accepting increased responsibility or increasing one's expertise; illegitimately, power is increased by usurping it from others who may be passive, weak, apathetic, or unaware.

In every organization there are power addicts with insatiable greed for power, whose energies constantly focus on acquiring more of it (Gabor, 1972, p. 83). They do so because they enjoy it; they love power for its own sake. In its extreme form this pattern is dangerous for the organization. Ultimately, power addicts too are harmed, as others catch on to their game and introduce counter-strategies of restraint. History is full of the misdeeds of power addicts.

Resistance to change

Change brings fear, anxiety, doubt, and uncertainty. The hold of habit and the "tried and true" is inexorable. There is pain in change whether it is at the level of society, the organization, or the individual. These realities underlie the resulting phenomenon of resistance to change.

The manner in which change occurs influences the kind and degree of resistance. It is tempting for the impatient administrator to use coercive power to bring about change. This use of power may succeed in the short run, but it produces such undesirable consequences in the form of delay, sabotage, and lower morale.

People are more likely to accept change that they perceive as inevitable. Power can be useful in reinforcing this perception. Still, power is probably best regarded as a last-resort method of securing change, used only after other persuading and influencing approaches have failed.

Resistance to change often reflects the power of lower participants. To combat this resistance, the generally accepted techniques are to: (1) pave the way for change as far in advance as possible by carefully communicating problems, issues, and intentions in a timely way; (2) be clear about the need for change and the kinds of change under consideration; (3) involve those affected by potential change in order to inform them and to tap their ideas so as to get more workable changes; and (4) design training opportunities to provide newly needed skills, insights, and attitudes (McFarland, 1979, pp. 192-195).

Environmental change

Changes in the internal and external environments can have a major impact on power, hence on innovative change. Internally, new personnel may come into the organization, altering the power structure and bringing new expectations about what the organization should be doing and how it does it. Technological change such as computerization may affect the way people do their jobs and the rules and procedures involved. Changing lifestyles, values, and expectations may change the preferences of individuals and groups, leading to changes in power relations.

Externally, the important markets for an organization's services may change; legal and political aspects change continuously. There may also be changes in the organization's power position with respect to other organizations in the environment (Zaltman, 1973, pp. 55-58). Any kind of environmental change carries the potential for strengthening or weakening the power positions of many individuals. Power figures in an organization must therefore assess these signs of change and judge their probable impact, deciding whether to ignore, resist, or pursue the changes.

Innovative change

Innovations that are diffused with the cooperation of the target system's power structure generally have a higher adoption rate than innovations that are not (Rothman, 1974, p. 446). Technical knowledge is also an important source of power behind innovative suggestion. Thus technical knowledge is a valuable weapon for an organization attempting to introduce low-threat innovations while maintaining a long-term continuing relationship (Rothman, 1974, p. 479). Technological change can easily be made to appear inevitable on the basis of its inherent merits.

Another factor conducive to innovation is placing a high value on goal attainment rather than on internal distribution of power and status. Organizations focused on internal power relations tend to be conservative and to support the status quo. New ideas are likely to be scrutinized primarily in terms of maintenance issues (Rothman, 1974, pp. 481-482).

Forces for innovative change must be mobilized and given direction, whereas forces resisting change must be overcome, neutralized, or co-opted. Such change is more likely to occur when it is initiated by a respected and trusted source. Such confidence derives from trust in the power as well as the judgment of leaders. Therefore significant change usually requires the support or initiation of highly placed formal leaders. In every organization there is a governing elite that is coterminous with legitimate power centers. A group's elite status, in which its members are viewed with honor, respect, admiration, or esteem, can help to effectuate creative change or to stop or slow unwanted change.

SUMMARY

In a complex organization, power, authority, and control have great impact on nurses' careers and on the performance of nursing functions. Therefore the nurse leader needs to think carefully about such questions as: What is the nature of power in this institution? How is power organized, used, and distributed here? How can I gain sufficient power, control, and authority to do my job? How do I use power and authority? Within a large system, nurse leaders are involved in various kinds of power strategies, so they must be attentive to such organizational phenomena as coalitions, caucuses, power shifts, cliques, and other power ploys. A nurse administrator must seek ways to gain, retain, and even trade off power in order to be an effective member of the organization.

These questions are especially important if the nurse is to be an agent of change for the better. As Alexander (1972, p. 162) has succinctly stated:

The power structure is an important part of our culture that affects significantly the number and range of alternatives that are available to individuals in an organization. There are no easy or even reasonably successful ways to effect a broadening of alternatives available to those in positions of no power. If nurses or other groups have no power within the organizational structure to effect necessary change, they have the alternative of working with external forces to effect these changes. The rational nurse-leaders who are agents of change should recognize its limits and should seek to understand the way those who control the situation organize it to their thinking.

Power, when it takes an exaggerated form, becomes coercive. Psychologically, leaders who receive acknowledgment of power from others often develop a positive self-image that separates them from those others, resulting in feelings of superiority, invulnerability, and a position outside and above commonly held moral standards (Kipnis,

1976, p. 1). The power holder who stays in the game will be one who has recognized these dangers through thorough observation and self-understanding. Power is by no means the sole motivation in the nursing profession, but it is a fact of life that influences the ability of the profession as well as of individual nurses to develop, grow, and achieve the primary mission of patient care.

REFERENCES

Abell, P.: Organizations as bargaining and influence systems: measuring intra-organizational power and influence. In Abell, P., editor: Organizations as bargaining and influence systems, New York, 1975, The Halsted Press.

Alexander, E.L.: Nursing administration in the hospital health care system, St. Louis, 1972, The C.V. Mosby Co.

Blum, H.L.: Planning for health: development and application of social change theory, New York, 1974, Human Sciences Press.

Buskirk, R.A.: Handbook of managerial tactics, Boston, 1976, Cahners Books, Inc.

Cumming, E., Clancey, I.L.W., and Cumming, J.: Improving patient care through organizational changes in the mental hospital. In Bartlett, A.C., and Kayser, T.A., editors: Changing organizational behavior, Englewood Cliffs, N.J., 1973, Prentice-Hall, Inc.

Dalton, G.W.: Influence and organizational change. In Bartlett, A.C., and Kayser, T.A., editors: Changing organizational behavior, Englewood Cliffs, N.J., 1973, Prentice-Hall, Inc.

Emerson, R.M.: Power-dependence relations, Am. Sociol. Rev. **27**:31-41, 1962.

For new nurse, bigger role in health care, U.S. News and World Report, pp. 59-61, Jan. 14, 1980.

Gabor, D.: The mature society, New York, 1972, Praeger Publishers, Inc.

Ginzberg, E.: Health services, power centers, and decision-making mechanisms. In Knowles, J.H., editor: Doing better and feeling worse: health in the United States, New York, 1977, W.W. Norton & Co., Inc.

Gordon, G., and Becker, S.W.: Changes in medical practice bring shifts in the pattern of power, Mod. Hosp. **151**:107-123, Feb. 1964.

Ivancevich, J.M., Szilagyi, A.D., and Wallace, M.J., Jr.: Organizational behavior and performance, Santa Monica, Calif., 1977, Goodyear Publishing Co.

Kemelgor, B.H.: Power and the power process: linkage concepts, Acad. Management Rev. **1**:143-149, Oct. 1976.

King, I.M.: The health care system: nursing intervention subsystem. In Werley, H.H. et al., editors: Health research: the systems approach, New York, 1976, Springer Publishing Co.

Kipnis, D.: The powerholders, Chicago, 1976, University of Chicago Press.

Korda, M.: Power: how to get it, how to use it, New York, 1975, Random House, Inc.

Kotter, J.P.: Power in management, New York, 1979, Amacom.

Kramer, M.: Reality shock: why nurses leave nursing, St. Louis, 1975, The C.V. Mosby Co.

Lambertsen, E.C.: A greater voice for nursing service administrators, Hospitals **46**(7):101-108, July 1972.

Levenstein, I.: Effective change agents, Hospitals **50**:71-74, Jan. 1976.

Martin, N.H., and Sims, J.H.: Thinking ahead: power tactics, Harvard Bus. Rev. **34**:25-29, 1956.

McClelland, D.C.: Power: the inner experience, New York, 1975, Irvington Publishers, Inc.

McFarland, D.E.: Managerial innovation in the metropolitan hospital, New York, 1979, Praeger Publishers, Inc.

McFarland, D., and Shiflett, N.: The role of power in the nursing profession, Nurs. Dimensions **7**:1-13, 1979.

Mechanic, D.: Medical sociology: a selective view, New York, 1968, The Free Press.

Millman, M.: Nursing personnel and the changing health care system, Cambridge, Mass., 1977, Ballinger Publishing Co.

Mulder, M.: The daily power game, Leiden, The Netherlands, 1977, Martinus Nijhoff Co.

Rothman, J.: Planning and organizing for social change: action principles from social science research, part 2, New York, 1974, Columbia University Press.

Rushmer, R.F.: Humanizing health care: alternative futures for medicine, Cambridge, Mass., 1975, M.I.T. Press.

Russell, B.: Power, London, 1938, Unwin Books, Ltd.

Schulz, R., and Johnson, A.C.: Management of hospitals, New York, 1976, McGraw-Hill Book Co.

Siu, R.G.: The craft of power, New York, 1979, John Wiley & Sons, Inc.

Smith, D.B., and Kaluzny, A.: The white labyrinth, Berkeley, Calif., 1975, McCutcheon Publishing Corp.

Swingle, P.G.: The management of power, New York, 1976, The Halsted Press.

Warren, D.I.: Power, visibility and conformity in formal organizations, Am. Sociol. Rev. **33**:951-970, Dec. 1968.

Wieland, G.F., and Ullrich, R.A.: Organizations: behavior, design, and change, Homewood, Ill., 1976, Richard D. Irwin, Inc.

Zaleznik, A., and Kets Devries, M.F.: Power and the corporate mind, Boston, 1975, Houghton-Mifflin Co.

Zaltman, G., Duncan, R., and Holbek, J.: Innovation and organizations, New York, 1973, John Wiley & Sons, Inc.

The meanings of words are not in the words, they are in us.

Hayakawa, S.I.: Language in thought and action, 1949, Harcourt, Brace & Co., p. 292.

8

COMMUNICATION AS A TOOL FOR CHANGE

Jeanette Lancaster

Communication or "the process of passing information and understanding from one person to another" is a prerequisite for the change process (Davis, 1972, p. 344). It is a great deal easier to pass on information than to convey understanding, since this part of communication depends on a complex interaction process involving the message sender, the receiver, the quality of the message, and the context or setting in which the message is transmitted. A change agent must recognize and know how to use both formal and informal communication channels in the organization. The change agent needs also to understand factors that facilitate the communication process, as well as commonly occurring obstacles. Perhaps the most significant factor in communication is being keenly aware of the personal and subjective nature of understanding. People interpret what is said from the perspective of their feelings, needs, hopes, and biases; understanding is only in the receiver's mind. Thus any one who seeks to influence others through communication channels needs a clear perspective on the communication process, including the characteristics of verbal and nonverbal interactions, barriers to effective communication, and ways to improve communication within an organization via collaboration and management of conflict.

The purpose of this chapter is to describe the nature of effective communication as an essential tool for making change. To do this the communication process is described in a simplistic fashion that identifies the role of each participant as well as selected ways to create a climate for communication. Thus trust, respect, and empathy are discussed as qualities that enhance an environment for open, honest communication. Both verbal and nonverbal communication are discussed, as well as barriers to effective communication. Suggestions are provided for dealing with these barriers to minimize their disruptiveness. An additional section specifically addresses communication within the organization in terms of the directional flow of communication, meetings, formal and informal messages, methods for increasing the effectiveness of communication, and patterns of interaction typically seen in organizations. Finally, the three c's of organizational communication are discussed: collaboration, conflict, and confrontation.

PROCESS OF COMMUNICATION

Communication embraces all modes of both conscious and unconscious behavior. It includes both the spoken and the written word, as well as a wide range of body gestures, movements, expressions, and symbols. In many cases an individual's nonverbal communication is more informative than what was actually said.

A wide variety of models can be used to depict the communication process. Commonalities in each model include: a sender, a receiver, a message, an environment, signals, and feedback. From a systems theory perspective the communication process is depicted in Fig. 8-1.

From this perspective, either verbal or nonverbal information enters the system as input that is then processed according to the receiver's perceptual abilities, biases, and cognitive processes, and subsequently expelled back into the environment of the system as output. The output of B is then fed back to A and has an additional effect on the communication. For example, individual A is a nursing supervisor who receives a new policy regarding the institutional procedure for administration of intravenous fluids. The supervisor studies the procedure (*transformation*) and summons six head nurses to explain the new technique (*output*). After carefully going over the procedure with the head nurses, supervisor A asks if there are any questions. No one says anything so the supervisor asks if everyone clearly understands how to implement the procedure on their respective units; all nod in agreement, but the supervisor notices frowns on the faces of three of the nurses (*feedback*). After a few carefully worded questions, the supervisor learns that one part of the explanation was somewhat unclear, yet no one was willing to say this aloud in front of a group of peers. This feedback not only indicated a lack of clarity in the explanation of the

FIG. 8-1
Systems theory view of communication.

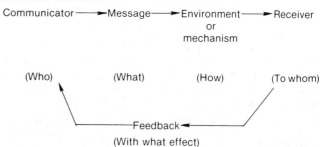

FIG. 8-2
Questioning approach to communication.

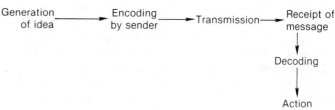

FIG. 8-3
Human relations model of communication.

procedure, but also called attention to group feelings of insecurity and a hesitancy to be open and honest.

A second communication model, depicted in Fig. 8-2, uses the questioning approach of who, what, how, to whom, and with what results to depict the process (Gibson et al., 1976). The questioning approach is essentially a systems model for communication, but the use of simplistic referents aids in the understanding of messages. In Fig. 8-3 the human-relations model of communication is depicted. Although feedback is not shown, it is an integral aspect of all communication. A more comprehensive model of communication is shown in Fig. 8-4. In this composite model, an idea is generated either by an individual or a group and encoded or organized into a series of symbols (verbal-written-pictorial) that are designed to convey meaning clearly to recipients. The sender of the message cannot give meaning to the receiver; instead, the sender conveys a set of symbols to the receiver, who interprets and processes this information in a unique and subjective fashion (*decoding*) and takes action according to how the message

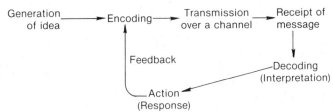

FIG. 8-4
Composite model of communication.

was interpreted. Since nearly every word has more than one meaning, the context in which the communication takes place is a critical factor in interpretation, as are the silent nonverbal expressions that accompany the spoken word.

CREATING A CLIMATE FOR COMMUNICATION

Few people always say the right thing at the right time. In a fast-paced society where change is a continuous process, communication is often rushed and little attention is directed either to what is said or what is heard. Frequently, both time and energy can be saved in the long run if communication is viewed as an integral and critical aspect of any relationship. Such a recognition of the significance of communication begins by establishing a climate that fosters clear straightforward message transmission. This means that the message sender feels sufficiently secure in the relationship with the message receiver to say what he or she truly means. Further, in order to maintain clear communication, those who receive the information (both verbal and nonverbal) must feel free to respond in a similarly straightforward manner as well as to raise questions about the clarity of the message or the consistency between the verbal and nonverbal messages. Creating such a climate requires that concepts such as trust, respect, and empathy be a part of the communication process.

Trust

Trust is an integral part of effective communication; without such feelings, neither the sender nor the receiver will risk the transmission of an honest message. Trust is learned early in life in the mother-child relationship and is reinforced by all future involvements with people. Some people, because of earlier experiences, have reached the conclusion that "you can't trust anyone" or "everyone is out to get me." These individuals have generally experienced relationships in which they felt taken advantage of or discounted as a valuable person. Such individuals are guarded in the information they choose to share, tend to be extremely private about their own lives, and spend considerable energy testing the reliability of others.

In order to gain the trust of those with whom you work, it is important to be extremely careful about what you say, to whom it is said, and where you carry on a conversation. So often we inadvertently pass on information that was given to us in confidence. We may do a great disservice to the person about whom we are talking when we repeat information that was not meant for all to hear. We also invariably reduce the degree of trust others have in us if we carelessly handle messages and information.

Not uncommonly, important and often confidential information is conveyed in a setting that does not provide privacy, for instance in an office with the door ajar or in the hall or restroom.

Another hazard to the building and maintenance of trust is to use real-life examples to illustrate a point without sufficiently protecting the identity of the individual concerned. It is helpful to share examples both with patients and colleagues, but it is thoughtless to be so explicit that the listener can guess about whom you are talking in your illustration. Likewise, information about staff or patients, although it may not necessarily be confidential, should not be discussed in public areas when anyone in the vicinity could hear and possibly repeat the message.

Respect

Each individual is a blend of heredity and experiences, which means that each person is unique. Often we criticize or evaluate others in terms of how much they are like us. If communication is to be effective, each participant must feel accepted and respected as a unique and valuable person. Respect is a nonjudgmental acceptance of other people that implies, "although we are different, we each have good qualities." It is generally easy to respect people who are like us or who have ideas and values consistent with ours. Yet respect means positive regard for people who are different, whose values, beliefs, and opinions are unlike our own. In order to respect people who are different, we each need a clear idea of what we value or hold in high regard. Although it tends to be easier to talk with people who have similar ideas and values, the value of new approaches and different ways of thinking should not be underestimated.

Respect does not mean that you must like or choose to spend time with everyone you meet. It does mean listening to what a person says in order to really hear the good ideas, however. Respecting a person whom you basically dislike requires that you honestly accept your negative reaction to the person. Too often we think we "ought to" like everyone. Then someone comes into our life who is offensive, yet we want to like them. It is not possible for most of us to like everyone, but be honest with yourself about whom you dislike. For example, there might be a supervisor who has many good ideas yet alienates you with her condescending attitude. Rather than avoid her and try to convince yourself that your paths just do not cross often, be honest with yourself. Admit, perhaps, that her at-

titude is offensive and that you would rather not spend much time with her; but also admit that she does have some useful ideas. Listen to her ideas and avoid personalizing her provocative comments.

Respect also includes sharing negative comments with another person in private. If one of your co-workers has made an error, show that person the courtesy of a private audience for this discussion. Reprimands or other negative sanctions can be viewed as a form of two-way communication. People generally do not like to make mistakes, thus the error may reflect good intentions even though poor judgment may have been used. It is useful to help the person who made the error to look at other ways of handling similar situations in the future. Also, a reprimand should take place as soon after the event occurred as possible, while the circumstances are fresh in people's minds. In any discussion of negative content, keep to the topic. This means that you should deal with one issue at a time and avoid bringing up everything the other person did that annoyed you. Remember that the other person also has a perspective on the situation; no one is always accurate. Our information may have been inaccurate or there may have been situations that prompted the person's behavior of which you are unaware.

Empathy

Empathy is the ability to tune accurately into another person's feelings in order to view things from that person's perspective. You try to see the world from the other person's eyes in order to maintain objectivity and increase understanding. Empathy means "feeling with" the other person in contrast to sympathy, which implies feeling (sorry) for the other person. In empathy the other person retains responsibility for personal feelings, whereas in sympathy it is tempting to assume some of the other person's responsibility.

In order to convey empathy you must be attentive to both the verbal and nonverbal messages. Listening is not enough; you need to hear and see the carefully disguised meanings and messages as well as the words. Empathy conveys acceptance of the other person's point of view or feelings, yet it does not mean that you must agree with the other person. The feelings you perceive may be totally different from your own, but you convey that you recognize the other person's perspective and understand the feeling. By sharing with others your recognition of their feelings when those feelings are different from your own, you may open avenues for further discussion that can promote greater understanding of all who are involved.

VERBAL AND NONVERBAL COMMUNICATION

As mentioned, communication takes place on two levels: verbal and nonverbal. Verbal communication includes the spoken word, whereas nonverbal communication includes the signals and cues that are clearly conveyed by a person's actions, expressions, gestures, and tone of voice. It is estimated that, in an average conversation, one third of the information is conveyed by verbal means and two thirds by nonverbal means (Brill, 1973). The meaning of any message is not as much in the words used as in the interpretation the receiver makes. Each person interprets both the verbal and nonverbal aspects of communication based on past learnings, needs, desires, and frame of reference.

Verbal communication

We live in a world of symbols and use words to express our thoughts, needs, desires, attitudes, and feelings to others. Through the use of words or verbal symbols we form mental images of people, places, things, and processes. Communication is a complex process in that words have different meanings for different people depending on their age, level of education, background, experiences, and frame of reference. For example, to a child the phrase, "a lot of money," may be very different from what that phrase means to an adult. Likewise, in nursing we may ask students or staff members to do something "as soon as you can." In truth we may want the item now, but the other person may interpret the words as, "please do this when you

have finished all your other assignments." Communication can be clarified by being as specific as possible in the words we use. That is, if you need something "as soon as possible," tell the listener exactly when you must have the work. It also helps to avoid global pronouns such as they, he, or we unless the listener knows without a doubt who you mean.

Words are used to express as well as to disguise feelings. When people say they are fine, they may mean that they are functioning quite well, or they may be unwilling actually to say how they are. We often use cliches as social amenities; this discourages real communication. Seldom when you ask someone, "How are you?" do you get a response other than "Fine," since the opening phrase is often a substitute for "Hi" or "Hello," rather than a sincere inquiry about the other person's well-being.

Nonverbal communication

Nonverbal communication occurs whenever two people meet; each one sizes the other up and comes to some conclusions about the person. Nonverbal communication takes place continuously, and frequently it is not accompanied by verbal communication. Feelings, attitudes, and thoughts that people are hesitant to share aloud are often conveyed to observers by nonverbal cues. A grimace, twitching mouth, or shaking of the foot frequently indicates that feelings are attached to what is being said to a greater extent than the words indicate.

The adage, "actions speak louder than words," certainly holds true. People can try hard to make a good appearance by dressing appropriately, being punctual, and using the correct words; yet their image can be dramatically affected by their nonverbal reactions. For example, a calm tone of voice and well-planned speech cannot disguise the anxiety evidenced by tapping fingers or a twitching eye.

The eyes are particularly important as a medium for conveying nonverbal messages. It is hard to keep truth and honesty out of your eyes. Many people are described as "smiling from the eyes down."

That is, while they appear friendly and cheerful, if their eyes are not reflecting the same feeling then a different nonverbal message is conveyed. In American culture it is considered polite to look directly at someone when you are speaking to them. This projects honesty and trustworthiness when talking to one another. To avoid eye contact can denote shiftiness, guilt, fear, or lack of self-confidence.

The eyes are also one of the most readily available avenues for quick communication. A glance can alert someone to the approach of another person. A wink can indicate that two people are coconspirators, or it may be a flirtacious gesture. Similarly, a frown can express disagreement with what is being said, or it can mean that the listener did not clearly hear what was said. Closed eyes may mean that the person is bored, sleepy, or has burning eyes, or that he or she is trying to think about something and closes the eyes to decrease distractions. When a person conveys a definite message with the eyes, yet you are uncertain what is really being communicated, clarify the message. For example, if the person is frowning, ask "do you understand (disagree)?" Remember, we frequently say with our eyes what we hesitate to write or speak.

In any person-to-person exchange, it is important to listen carefully to what is being said to determine whether it matches the nonverbal message. Are the words friendly, while the person's eyes or the expression around the mouth are cold or tense? Does the speaker look directly at you or shift eye contact frequently? Whenever the nonverbal and verbal messages are contradictory, further dialogue and exploration are indicated.

The clear receipt of any message depends on the degree of congruence between the message sent and the nonverbal message that was simultaneously conveyed. If a supervisor, Ms. Jones, frowning or in an irritated tone of voice, says to staff nurse Ms. Smith, "You are doing a fine job," Ms. Smith will no doubt receive an incongruent message. These messages establish barriers to effective communi-

cation in that the respondent may not know which level to address. The only way to determine what the speaker actually means is to mention tactfully the incongruence between what was said and the simultaneously conveyed unspoken message. For instance, in the example above the staff nurse could ask her supervisor whether she had any reservations about her effectiveness because the supervisor was frowning while she talked. The supervisor may be quite satisfied with the staff nurse's progress. The frown may have been in response to a fleeting thought about another responsibility.

BARRIERS TO EFFECTIVE COMMUNICATION

The communication process breaks down when the environment is distracting: either the sender's ability to present the information clearly is impaired; the receiver cannot clearly present or hear the information; or the approach used thwarts the conveyance of the message. Such distractions in the environment as noise, other people trying to gain the attention of either the sender or receiver, or visual stimuli can impair the process of message transmission and reception. If something is worth saying, then the environment should be carefully selected. This means that important issues should not be discussed in a hallway encounter, but deserve the privacy of a conference or a telephone call.

Some people have impaired abilities either to speak clearly or to hear all that is said. Impaired speech is generally obvious, but hearing defects may go unnoticed. For this reason, it is helpful for people with hearing impairments to make this known so that the speaker can direct comments to the unimpaired ear or increase the volume of the voice. Also, rapid speech may interfere with a receiver's ability to comprehend accurately the intended message.

An additional communication barrier may arise when participants have differing frames of reference about the topic. Because of past experience, cultural influences, age, or race, two individuals may interpret the same message differently. Communication may also be ineffective when one or more participants only listens partially to what is being said. People have a tendency to "block out" what is being said if they are otherwise pre-occupied, if they are disinterested, or if the new information conflicts with their beliefs.

Source and manner of communication as barriers

Both the source and manner of communication affect its receipt. If the speaker is not deemed trustworthy or competent, or if the message is not clearly conveyed in language appropriate both to the situation and to the receiver's level of under-standing, then the likelihood of an accurate mes-sage being received is decreased. Also, communi-cation can be hampered when the speaker indicates value judgments that may not be held by all par-ticipants, as well as when time pressures limit thor-ough discussion. In addition, when messages are hurriedly sent, someone or some part may be left out, thereby confusing the listener. Biased mes-sages may get in the way of effective communica-tion. All too often people ask for the opinion of another by first inflicting their own opinion. "Questions" such as, "Don't you want to go to lunch now?" or "Don't you think Dr. X is a good surgeon?" often discourage the expression of a different opinion. The speaker's message is clear, and unless the receiver feels comfortable and confident it is easier just to agree than to state a disagreeing opinion. The speaker could gain more information by phrasing the above comments as, "When do you want to go to lunch?" or "What do you think of Dr. X's ability as a surgeon?"

Communication is often affected when one of the participants uses jargon that is unfamiliar to others. Listeners may not wish to appear ignorant or ill-prepared, so they do not ask what the jargon really means, but merely try to nod appropriately and end the conversation.

Also, the frequent giving of advice can block communication by antagonizing the listener. The implication behind unsolicited advice is, "My way is the best way." Thus the words, "If I were you . . ." often serve as communication interrup-ters because the receiver simply smiles and quits listening. Not only does frequent advice giving tend to be offensive, but it also encourages dependency. The receiver may think, "Why bother working out a solution? Joe will tell me what to do."

Defensive communication

Defensive communication can also serve as a barrier to the effective transmission of messages. This form of communication is used as an ego-protective mechanism. It is natural for individuals to protect themselves from either real or perceived threats. The most common reactions to threat are fight or flight. Defensive communication refers to a reaction to perceived psychological threat and can be detected in one or more of three sources: the sender, the receiver, or the actual message (Cross, 1978).

Speaker

Each of us knows at least one other person that we simply do not trust. We may believe from our experience that this person is extremely self-serving and will do almost anything to gain recog-nition. This person is a notorious "brownnoser" who praises superiors frequently and in general spends a great deal of energy trying to look good. Let's call this distrusted colleague Joe. One day Joe comes up and tries to be warm and friendly while discussing a current work project. How do you react? Should you cooperate with him as he is re-questing or should you maintain your usual on-guard position and secretly question, "What's in it for ole Joe?" You have considerable historical in-formation that would interfere with a cooperative venture, but do you give Joe one more chance?

Receiver

Under any circumstance, communication is a give-and-take process between sender and receiver.

Some people have difficulty accepting what is said in a straightforward fashion. They hear every message from a defensive, doubtful perspective and seem suspicious of the sender's motives. These people "take almost any statement, question or remark and turn it into an insult or an attack" (Cross, 1978, p. 442). Such defensive listening interrupts effective communication, in that a clear message is never received. For example, Sue is always responding to statements of praise and encouragement defensively. One day Jane said to Sue, "You look so nice today. That hairdo is very flattering." Sue's defensive comment was, "I guess you mean that I usually don't look good." Such a response by Sue would certainly thwart future attempts by Jane to praise her.

Frequently, no matter what you say, defensive listeners manage to make the speaker leave the interchange feeling guilty. The speaker often wonders, "Why did I say that?" A typical reaction by the speaker is to avoid, whenever possible, any future discussions with the defensive listener. Although a variety of ways are available for dealing with the defensive listener, perhaps the simplest and most effective way is to limit communication to essential job-related topics, thereby minimizing the opportunity for hurt feelings and defensiveness.

Message

According to Cross (1978), defense-arousing messages tend to "maximize the sting effect and minimize concern for others" (p. 442). Defense-arousing messages are sent when the content contains a challenge to the other person's competence; a threat; or a disregard for the listeners' worth, value, or feelings. Several clues can be used to assess whether you are inadvertently sending defense-arousing messages. For example, when listeners ask, "Are you feeling (doing) all right?" "Is this a bad day for you?" or "What's wrong?" you may find that your messages are arousing negative feelings in the other person. On the other hand, the presence of the above questions may not indicate that your message was defense arousing, but may be a clue to how the other person is feeling.

Avoiding defensive communication

Several strategies are available for avoiding defensive communication. The language, tone of voice, and nonverbal messages should be assessed for defensiveness. Some people can speak words that seem like a positive message, but the angry tone of voice or the frown on the speaker's face conveys an entirely different message than the words alone imply. Defensive communication can be avoided by the following methods:

1. *Discuss the problem, not the person*. This means sticking to the issue and avoiding any reference to the other person's ability, appearance, or other personal factors. A problem is rarely solved by casting blame. Instead, time can be more profitably spent in talking about new alternatives to solving the problem.

2. *When something is wrong or a person's behavior seems troublesome, deal with how it affects you*. Avoid talking about the other person's involvement. This can be done by using "I" more often than "you." For example, "I am having trouble understanding the directions for this project," instead of, "You are not making the instructions very clear."

3. *Avoid judgmental statements*. A sure way to activate defensiveness is to offer a judgmental reaction to another person's ability, statements, or projects. From early childhood, each of us has judged other people and things in terms of how we think and act. It is important to remember that there are always many ways to say and do things. That others approach a task differently from us does not indicate that they are wrong. Also, our way may not be the best way for someone else.

4. *Listen*. Defensive communication can be decreased by listening carefully to what the other person is saying. Often we respond to a partially heard

message in such a way as to offend the speaker, who then has to clarify what was really said or has to repeat the message in hopes that we will listen this time.

Responding to defensive communication

If channels of communication are to be kept open and information freely transmitted, then it is necessary to learn how to respond to defensive communication in a way that curtails this form of interaction. It is a fact of life that some people feel defensive much of the time, and all people feel defensive at least part of the time. How, then, can we respond to defensive communication? Several approaches are discussed for handling defensive communication, each of which is based on the assumption that words alone have no meaning. People give meaning to words by the way they speak as well as their expressions and gestures.

1. *Paraphrasing.* This technique is used to repeat to the speaker what *you* heard. In paraphrasing, you restate in your own words the message you received. Such an approach provides immediate feedback to the speaker as to what message was actually heard. For example:

> Head Nurse Agitation: "Where is that IV bottle you were supposed to hang at 1:00 PM? Is it hung yet? Can't you ever get your work done on time?"
> Staff Nurse Calm: "You think I have trouble getting my work done on time?"

Actually the head nurse may think that the staff nurse is quite efficient, but on this particular day nothing is going right on the entire unit. By paraphrasing, the staff nurse can avoid hurt feelings, and this also provides feedback to the head nurse that the message sent is not really what was meant.

2. *Perception checking or validation.* This form of communication is similar to paraphrasing in that it describes what you perceive as the other person's message or psychological state. For example, the head nurse at change of shift says to the oncoming evening charge nurse, "Why are you always five minutes late for report?" Instead of answering defensively, the evening charge nurse could respond with, "Sounds like this has been a rough (long or tiring) day." Such a response avoids getting hooked on the "Why?" and keeps communication open. Perception checking or validation is also useful when the verbal and nonverbal messages are incongruent. Since nonverbal cues are indirect expressions of feelings, it is important that they be put into words and handled.

3. *Voicing the implied.* Like paraphrasing and perception checking, voicing the implied allows the listener an opportunity to call attention verbally to the underlying message. Perhaps a negative evaluation is couched behind a smile and joking comment. It would be helpful to call attention to the negative implication, which may be a major issue that people are reluctant to handle.

4. *Asking for clarification.* Too often we fail to ask for clarification either because we are in a hurry, feel intimidated by the other person, or hesitate to acknowledge that we did not truly understand what was said. Our self-evaluation is sometimes so fragile that the fear of exposing lack of understanding or knowledge deficits is entirely too threatening to risk. In effective communication, clarification is a continuous process.

Defensive communication impairs the productivity of any work group because people respond to one another more often with their feelings rather than with their thoughts. If a problem exists, try to deal with possible feelings of anger or hurt so that you can deal as objectively as possible with the actual or perceived problem. Also, remember that effective communication requires careful planning. Frequent complaints about what another person says are, "It wasn't what he said, but how he said it," or, "I can't stand for people to talk to me in that tone of voice." To a large extent the climate, efficiency, and overall functioning of any organization depends on the quality of the communication (Cross, 1978).

COMMUNICATION WITHIN THE ORGANIZATION
Directions for the flow of communication

Every organization should provide for communication in three directions: upward, downward, and horizontal. Upward communication is essential if those in charge are to make decisions based on valid and accurate information. Also, upward communication gives employees a feeling of belonging and being part of the organization when they know that what they think is important to the effective functioning of the work group as well as of the total organization. Upward communication is of prime benefit to the administrator, who needs extensive and varied sources of information in order to make effective decisions. Communication modes such as group meetings, conferences with individuals or small groups, suggestion boxes, and responses to memoranda tend to encourage upward communication. When employees think that they will receive a fair audience from members of the administration, they are more likely to be open in their messages and avoid "underground" channels such as gossip or anonymous letters.

The most frequent forms of downward communication are instructions, rules, policies, and procedures (Gibson et al., 1976). The effectiveness of downward channels of communication can be determined by how frequently employees complain that they never know what is going on. There are certain behaviors that increase the effectiveness of downward communication. First, the one who has a message to communicate should be well prepared and clearly understand the information to be conveyed. This may mean doing considerable homework before embarking on the communication process. It is also important, once the information is assembled, to plan carefully for the actual communication activity. Some people need to be told about changes that will affect them before massive dissemination of information. The effectiveness of downward communication often depends on the confidence in which the communicator is held.

Mutual respect and trust are integral aspects of effective organizational communication.

Horizontal communication is necessary for the organization and coordination of activities. Time and energy are saved when co-workers readily discuss projects, make plans together, and provide one another with evaluation of ideas or plans. Considerable peer support and a "team spirit" atmosphere can be generated through active, open, and honest horizontal communication. In order for horizontal communication to be effective, participants must trust one another and respect each other's opinions. Also, horizontal communication is enhanced when participants maintain a nondefensive attitude toward suggestions and critiques of their work.

Formal and informal channels of communication

Organizational communication occurs along formal and informal channels, as well as in upward, downward, and horizontal directions. It is usually much easier to monitor formal communication, in that the organizational channels are easily identified. Each organization has procedures for the formal dissemination of information. In some instances, all communication along formal channels is conveyed in a written format, whereas other organizations handle even formal communication in an oral tradition. The important thing to learn is the expected route for formal communication in the organization and how to use it. A great deal of confusion and misunderstanding can be avoided when everyone understands and employs the established formal communication channels.

Although it is generally easier to monitor formal communication channels, the informal medium may have the greatest impact on organizational functioning. Being part of the informal communication network is important for the nurse who wishes to introduce a change. Such inclusion does not generally happen by chance; the nurse must cultivate a role as a participant in the informal communication network by virtue of being trusted, respected, and valued by other group members. Good interpersonal relationships, both within and outside the nursing group, provide an opportunity to become privy to informal channels of communication. Inclusion in this network depends to some extent on the individual being willing to be friendly and responsive, to be respectful of the merits of the "grapevine," and to share information when appropriate. This means that information is always shared both formally and informally with discretion; that is, confidential information is never shared, and that which is passed on is carefully screened in order to avoid bringing harm or embarrassment to individuals, groups, or projects.

The informal communication medium, or grapevine, generally conveys information more rapidly than established channels. According to Keith Davis (1977), the "grapevine moves with impunity across departmental lines and easily bypasses superiors in chains of command. It flows around 'water coolers,' down hallways, through lunchrooms and wherever people get together in groups" (p. 349). If the information carried via the grapevine is reasonably consistent with that which is disseminated across formal channels, then the two modes of communication complement one another.

Occasionally the information carried on the grapevine is a poor representation of reality. When rumors on the grapevine threaten the effectiveness of the organization, action is indicated. It is essential to recognize that rumors are not haphazard occurrences but instead arise from a variety of causes. A major cause of rumors is a feeling that participants lack information. When people do not know exactly what is going on around them, they begin to speculate, and speculation breeds rumors. In addition to lack of information, rumors are caused by insecurity and emotional conflict. Insecure, anxious people are more likely than confident and content persons to perceive situations negatively, and subsequently to talk about fears and worries with others. Likewise, emotional conflict within individuals as well as personality clashes between group members provide fertile ground for the development of rumors. Some people spread rumors to discredit others either because they dislike them, or because the person starting the rumor feels threatened and seeks to "save face" by discrediting others.

Regardless of the reason behind the beginning of a rumor—information gap—emotional conflict and insecurity or dislike among members—each person receives and transmits information in terms of personal biases and vested interests (Davis, 1975). Rumors, like all other forms of oral communication, are subject to filtering. In filtering, the content of the communication is reduced to a few essential details that serve to enhance the effectiveness of the rumor. Rumors are subject not only to being sheared of nonessentials by filtering, but can also be expanded by elaboration. Participants in the rumor will often add new details that may make the situation seem worse in order to reflect their own strongly held feelings and biases (Davis, 1975).

Some rumors are basically harmless and can be allowed to run their course. Others cause untold havoc and confusion in the organization and must be neutralized. In refuting a rumor, never repeat the rumor or refer directly to it, because some people may hear only the rumor and ignore the refutation, thereby reinforcing the negative process. In addition, others may not have heard the content carried in the rumor; repeating it in order to refute it can cause some participants to believe what was being discounted. The first step in interrupting the progress of a rumor is to communicate the truth to all involved as quickly as possible. The truth behind a rumor is more likely to be accepted if the source is considered reliable by the listeners. On occasion representatives from management may be called on to squelch a rumor if they alone are considered credible sources of information.

Although the content of the rumor may be untrue, the feelings behind its generation may convey a great deal about the emotional condition of the organization. Rumors provide valuable information about feelings and existing misperceptions and misunderstandings. Even though the content of the rumor may be untrue, the very fact that it was generated communicates a great deal about underlying worries, fears, jealousies, and motivations.

Organizational meetings as a communication tool

Organizational meetings are typically convened for a variety of reasons: to provide information as well as to allow time for ideas to be generated and decisions to be made. Membership in a powerful committee or task force can provide a rich arena for the transmission of information through both formal and informal channels. The purpose of the meeting may be to convey selected information, yet considerably more messages may be shared through informal channels before, during, or after the meeting.

Critics of the use of meetings as a forum both for communication and decision making contend that meetings are time consuming, expensive, and slow to reap rewards. In addition, organizational meetings may have a leveling effect when group discussion rewards conformity and compromise, and squelches innovation. A further disadvantage of groups as decision-making bodies is that the level of accountability is often diluted. Since no one individual maintains responsibility for group decisions, less critical thought may be given to plans.

In reviewing the organizational meeting as a communication mechanism, several characteristics of productive groups need to be addressed. First, the size of the task group affects its functioning. If there are more than seven people in a group, communication tends to become centralized in that members have limited opportunities to communicate directly with one another (Davis, 1972). Centralized communication in a group gives the leader considerable power that may be disproportionate to the purpose of the group. Any effectively functioning work group needs a leader who can spot trouble areas such as dealing with overparticipators who may dominate decision making by literally "wearing others down" by their excessive communication. Silent group members need also to be drawn into active participation. Silence may reflect apathy and indifference, opinions in opposition to those being expressed, or a behavior pattern of refusal to devote the necessary energy to becoming a participant. The leader needs also to be perceptive in spotting any potential "hidden agendas" among group members. Often factions within a group will have a privately held set of goals that they may subtly attempt to impose on the group. The leader needs to be especially astute at detecting differing viewpoints and encouraging discussion. A great deal can be accomplished by weighing the pros and cons of two opposing positions. It is equally important to remember that the actual leader may not be the person who is designated as chairperson. Leaders within a work group often emerge who serve the useful purpose of monitoring and facilitating group dynamics.

Increasing effective communication

Several factors within the organization, and specifically on the part of the message sender, are useful in increasing the effectiveness of communication. Both what is said and how well participants listen influence communication. The value of actively listening to what is being directly or indirectly said cannot be overestimated in implementing any change process. Good listeners make better decisions than poor listeners because they have far more information on which to base actions. Further, a good listener ultimately saves time because the information gained often saves fruitless attempts. Also good listeners learn how well their messages were received by the quality of the reactions and responses they hear or observe.

Listening is rarely an innate characteristic; rather, it is a skill learned through considerable practice. Listening is more than hearing; it is an active process that demands the person's entire attention and considerable psychological energy. The ability to listen carefully necessitates a commitment to take time to complete the communication without feeling rushed. Listening implies trying to hear what is being said from the other person's frame of reference; this cannot be done if the listener is in a hurry, is disinterested, or is otherwise preoccupied. In order to hear a message from the other person's perspective, a great deal of empathy is necessary. Listening to feelings as well as words means that the covert or subtle as well as the overt or obvious message is addressed. For example, you might ask Ms. Wills, a new nurse on the unit, how her orientation is going. Although she answers "Fine," you notice that her tone of voice is low and that she is avoiding eye contact. The message you "hear" may be that she is basically a shy and hesitant person who is easily embarrassed by direct questions, or that things are really not going particularly well. Ms. Wills may be reluctant to say how things are really going until she finds out whether you want to hear the truth or whether you are just passing the time of day by using, "How are things going?" as a social phrase rather than a sincerely directed question. If you follow up the lack of consistency between the words and the nonverbal message by saying something like, "Are they really doing all right?" you may learn that Ms. Wills is intimidated by the head nurse who speaks loudly and is free with criticism. Listening for feelings means being willing to hear and, perhaps ultimately, to handle the ramifications of an honest message.

Listening also implies being nonjudgmental. Often when we truly listen to messages we "hear" attitudes, feelings, and beliefs that are different from our own strongly held views. Specifically, in the example above you may encourage Ms. Wills to speak with the head nurse and explain how she feels when criticized in front of a group. Ms. Wills may refuse even to consider this alternative saying, "That old witch is just like my mother—you could never talk to her about anything that really mattered." You, on the other hand, may perceive the head nurse to be quite approachable. While it is helpful to point out such a difference of perception, it would not be useful to argue with Ms. Wills about her perception, or to deflate her self-image further by saying, "You are clearly mistaken about Ms. Jones; she is quite easy to talk with." Hence listen-

ing often means hearing more than you would like to know. The Ten Commandments for Effective Listening given on p. 123 may assist you. The effectiveness of communication can be increased if some or all of the following steps are taken (Davis, 1972; Gibson et al., 1976):

1. Use simple words and phrases that are chosen according to the vocabulary and understanding level of the listeners.
2. Convey empathy by being receiver oriented, and consider how the message would be received. When possible use the name of the person to whom you are talking.
3. Use charts, graphs, and illustrations when possible to convey information in the most succinct manner.
4. When writing, use short sentences and paragraphs and active verbs, and avoid excessive adjectives.
5. Utilize feedback; for example, a downward memorandum about a new policy does not always afford much opportunity for back-and-forth communication. In general, face-to-face communication provides greater amounts of feedback than messages sent in written format.
6. Repetition ensures that if one part of the message is not heard, then repeating it is likely to provide the necessary information.
7. Timing is crucial to effective communication. People hear messages accurately only when they are psychologically ready to do so. Hence monitoring the emotional tone of the recipients of information is helpful in order to determine the level of anxiety, comfort, fear, or security.
8. Effective listening has been mentioned as a key factor in communication; this means giving full attention to the person(s) speaking in an environment that is as free as possible from distractions.
9. When possible, use the grapevine. It has already been noted that grapevines are inevitable in an organization, therefore it is im-

TEN COMMANDMENTS FOR GOOD LISTENING*

1. **Stop talking!**
   You cannot listen if you are talking.
   Polonius (Hamlet): "Give every man thine ear, but few thy voice."

2. **Put the talker at ease.**
   Help him feel that he is free to talk.
   This is often called a "permissive environment."

3. **Show him that you want to listen.**
   Look and act interested. Do not read your mail while he talks.
   Listen to understand rather than to reply.

4. **Remove distractions.**
   Don't doodle, tap, or shuffle papers.
   Will it be quieter if you shut the door?

5. **Empathize with him.**
   Try to put yourself in his place so that you can see his point of view.

6. **Be patient.**
   Allow plenty of time. Do not interrupt him.
   Don't start for the door or walk away.

7. **Hold your temper.**
   Any angry man gets the wrong meaning from words.

8. **Go easy on argument and criticism.**
   This puts him on the defensive. He may "clam up" or get angry.
   Do not argue: even if you win, you lose.

9. **Ask questions.**
   This encourages him and shows you are listening.
   It helps to develop points further.

10. **Stop talking!**
    This is first and last, because all other commandments depend on it.
    You just can't do a good listening job while you are talking.

Nature gave man two ears but only one tongue, which is a gentle hint that he should listen more than he talks.

*From Davis, K.: Human relations at work, New York, 1972, copyright by McGraw-Hill Book Co. Used with the permission of McGraw-Hill Book Co.

portant to use them to facilitate change rather than be "used" by the grapevine. Basically the grapevine is a rapid "bypassing" communication mechanism that uses face-to-face contact to circumvent procedures and steps in the organizational communication network.

Patterns of communication

Before designing any strategy for change, it is essential to determine the patterns of communication. As mentioned, according to any organizational scheme, communication flows upward, downward, and horizontally. The organizational chart depicts how communication should flow; the change agent needs to know if the actual pattern of communication differs from or is consistent with that depicted as ideal. Hersey and Blanchard (1977) describe two basic ways in which communication tends to be structured within organizations: the star and the circle.

In these diagrams, shown in Fig. 8-5, the arrows represent two-way communication channels. As can be seen in the star pattern, all communication includes *C,* who is usually a supervisory person. This pattern portrays the amount of control held by one person in the organization. The person holding the *C* position is usually autocratic, and all decisions are made either with *C's* approval or by *C*.

Many organizations function covertly in the form of a star. That is, communication channels are open and free flowing on paper and officially; but the reality is that one person censors or approves all messages, thus vividly controlling organizational behavior.

In contrast, the circle format represents equilateral communication among participants. This communication network tends to be open and democratic in its functioning. Some organizations reflect a combination of star and circle networks, in that typical information related to daily operations is conveyed in circle format, while new decisions and extraordinary communications take place in star form.

It is hard to state which pattern of communication is unquestionably best. There are advantages and disadvantages to both autocratic and democratic channels. For example, communication conveyed according to the star format tends to be faster and more orderly, and there tends to be greater congruence in the messages received by each person. On the other hand, the star mechanism does not tend to enhance group morale and feelings of involvement in the organization. This form may also breed dependence on the person who holds the *C* position.

In contrast, communication according to the circle scheme is slower and potentially less accurate

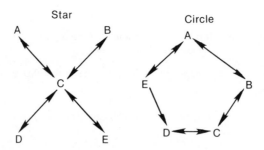

FIG. 8-5
Ways for structuring communication.

(Adapted from Hersey, P., and Blanchard, K.H.: Management of organizational behavior: utilizing human resources, ed. 3, 1977, Prentice-Hall, Inc., p. 285. Reproduced with permission of Center for Leadership Studies.)

because more people have a chance to distort the message as they convey it to others. Circle forms of communication, however, tend to increase morale and independence.

Before implementing a change strategy, it is necessary to recognize the prevalent format for communication. In general, a circle mechanism is used in participative change, while a star format is more consistent with coerced or dictated change strategies. There is no "best" communication strategy for change. The key lies in matching the communication process not only to the organization's pattern and needs, but also to the type of change approach that will best fit the organization.

THREE C's OF ORGANIZATIONAL COMMUNICATION

There are three c's that are often found in organizational communication: collaboration, conflict management, and confrontation. Each communication mode has the capacity to be a positive or negative force in the communication process, depending largely on the participants, the setting, and the way in which the communication is handled. The nurse as a change agent must be a master at handling each of these communication modalities, especially in an era of multiple professional stresses caused by decreasing governmental support of health resources, internal fighting in nursing, and the imminent fear held by other professions that nurses may encroach on their portion of the "health care pie."

Collaboration

Prerequisite to effective collaboration is a basic understanding between individuals or groups as to each other's functions and abilities. Nursing as well as many other health professions is changing rapidly and substantially. Nurses who are graduates from one type of program cannot assume that they know about graduates from other types of nursing programs. Nor can nurses presume to know about the role and competencies of social workers, psychologists, physicians, or health technicians.

There are areas of overlap as well as unique features in the roles of health professionals; thus a first step in collaboration is to learn about the role competencies of other members of the team or work group. Each participant in a collaborative activity has a set of perceptions about the role of the other participants. It is helpful to validate these perceptions with each other to determine what set of tools each person brings to the project or group. Effective collaboration also implies that participants must be skilled communicators who are adept at responding both to verbal and nonverbal cues and who understand and can utilize group-process skills. It is important for participants to recognize hindrances or stumbling blocks to group process and to take responsibility for moving the collaboration forward by clarifying issues or misperceptions, keeping the group on the topic, and respecting one another's opinions and differences. In collaboration it is useful to realize that there is generally more than one way to attain the goals; the way chosen by the participants will not always satisfy everyone.

Collaborative efforts are enhanced if participants feel confident about their skills and contributions, and if they are willing to negotiate, disagree, and compromise when necessary. There may be considerable role overlap, and members may find it helpful if they can comfortably relinquish tasks and perhaps try new approaches. Each member also needs to make a conscious effort to communicate clearly without relying on unfamiliar professional jargon in order to make a point. Effective collaboration requires honest, straightforward dialogue, and often means that participants must take considerable risks in expressing ideas, opinions, and feelings. True collaboration can only occur in an environment characterized by trust and a genuine desire to provide the best possible care.

Organizational conflict

Conflict is an inevitable component of the organizational communication process. Few decisions can be made and implemented without encountering conflicting viewpoints, differing action strategies, and opposing expectations. Since conflict is inevitable in interactions between two or more people, the change agent's goal is to use differing opinions and plans in a constructive way rather than to allow inherent differences to disrupt goal attainment. Too frequently, conflict is viewed as a negative, disruptive force to be avoided at all costs. To gloss over, ignore, or stifle organizational conflict may lead to later problems; open communication is a forerunner to organizational efficiency and change. In order to use conflict as a tool for making or responding to change, several variables need to be considered. First, the nature of conflict must be set forth in order to differentiate positive and negative aspects as well as common sources of conflict. Next, the management of conflict is considered by looking at the reactions of participants and also by describing a variety of strategies for conflict resolution.

Nature of conflict

Although conflict within a group may seem painful and disruptive at the time it erupts, it is important to recognize that conflict is generally useful in that it points out differences that would emerge later in any case, and possibly be even more disruptive. The expression of conflict prevents stagnation and often is a healthy prelude to change. In any successful change activity, it is essential that all participants agree on their goal. Consensus on both a goal and an action plan are basic to the change process. Reaching consensus generally means that a wide range of often different opinions and approaches will be submitted. Consensus is essential when the change will affect each of the participants. Wood (1977, p. 115) maintains that "before a group can achieve consensus, however, the views of different members must be heard, given fair consideration, and critically evaluated."

Conflict can have either constructive or destructive effects on organizational effectiveness. When it is used for personal gain—to achieve vested interests and hidden goals—or when it is expressed to hurt someone or some project, then it is used as a

destructive force. There also does seem to be an optimal level of conflict within an organization; an excessive amount of conflict typically threatens the group and has negative consequences. Too much and too frequent conflict that is poorly managed and never resolved keeps the organization in a turmoil and severely militates against goal attainment and progress. Conflict should be considered a cue that something is amiss, and as such, should generate the need for further dialogue and idea generation (Marriner, 1979). Thurkettle and Jones (1978, p. 39) maintain that "conflict per se has no positive or negative connotations; rather it is the use or misuse of conflict that determines its positive or negative effects." They describe conflict as a dynamic force in any organization that can be considered as the glue holding the group together.

Sources of conflict

Conflict often results from faulty communication, and it is inevitable when participants do not all have the same information. Thus any effective change process requires clear, consistent communication to all participants and influential parties. It is not enough just to discuss the proposed plan with the anticipated participants. Everyone who is likely to be affected, from the administrator to the cleaning personnel, need to be informed in order to decrease conflict, confusion, and angry feelings.

Another source of conflict arises from incompatible goals among participants. People tend to be motivated and to become involved in projects in accordance with their own personal goals and vested interests. The expression of conflict can serve as a useful barometer for measuring clashing goals and personal need-attainment strategies.

A further source of conflict deals with differing opinions about a project or plan. This type of conflict is easier to address than when divergent personal goals and needs constitute the roadblock to the communication process. In hierarchial form, it is easiest to handle conflict that arises from lack of information. Once this gap is noted, an action plan can be formulated to provide effective communication to all persons who are or will be affected by the decision or project.

The next source of conflict in the hierarchy of difficulty in management is that of differing opinions and ideas. When this source of conflict arises, the opportunities for discussion and negotiation are ripe. In actuality, conflict management generally necessitates discussion, compromise, and negotiation. It is often difficult to deal with conflict based on personal interest and one's own needs. Such motives are generally disguised behind one of the other two sources and emerge as "hidden agendas" after several painstaking attempts at resolution have failed.

Reactions to conflict

Nurses are open systems, constantly interacting with the environment. This means that when conflict exists in the external environment, nurses are affected, since the conflict and subsequent tension in the organization serves as input into the nurses' own system. How individuals choose to transform the input (conflict) depends on past experiences, personal coping capacity, and environmental supports or constraints. Each person has a choice between dealing directly with conflict or passively reacting to it, but the choice must be made consciously after considering all possible alternatives and ramifications. Part of the decision about how to handle conflict will necessitate honestly asking the question, "What is the cost to me if I . . . ?" Some situations are extremely resistant to change and cause considerable conflict for participants. When change seems impossible and personal levels of conflict are detrimental, then the only solution may be to leave. The question of utmost importance is, "How much conflict is tolerable for me?"

Positive reasons for conflict

As has repeatedly been pointed out, conflict in and of itself is not a negative force within the change process. It is the motives of the participants that determine the organizational usefulness or destructiveness of conflict. Wood (1977) lists three reasons for encouraging conflict. First of all, conflict calls attention to the need for more communication and dialogue. By discussing divergent and often opposing points of view, all participants have the opportunity to gain a "broadened understanding of the nature of the problem and its implications" (Wood, 1977, p. 116). During this phase of a conflict it may become clear that various people or subgroups hold different notions as to the issue under consideration. Conflict may be automatically decreased once problem consensus is attained.

By encouraging the presentation and discussion of different ideas, a group has far more alternatives from which to choose a problem-resolution strategy. This reason for encouraging the active discussion of conflicting views may ultimately spare the decision-making group (person) the risk of prematurely arriving at a solution without considering all possible options. Choosing from carefully thought out alternatives is the key to successful decision making. Peter Drucker (1973), who has studied organizations extensively, contends that disagreement alone is the precursor to decision making, for without controversy few alternatives are examined.

The final reason that Wood (1977) cites for encouraging the open discussion of conflict is that it serves to stimulate the interest of the participants. "Healthy non-combative disagreement" promotes creativity by providing an arena for idea generation and discussion. In an atmosphere that promotes open conflict, individuals can comfortably offer opinions and ideas without a fear of threat from negative repercussions.

Managing conflict

Whether conflict enhances group action, leads to a stalemate, or causes major hostilities within the group depends on how it is handled. Disruptive or restrictive conflict occurs when those who are involved do not understand the value of conflict and when they either do not know how or choose not to channel differences into constructive channels.

Environments that promote competition at the expense of participants, or that communicate that all conflict must be resolved in a win/lose strategy, do not encourage positive gain from the expression of differences. When a win/lose approach is taken to conflict management, the end result may include personnel resignations, global dissatisfaction, the formation of subgroups or cliques, or a termination to communication. In contrast, constructive conflict resolution develops when participants do not feel threatened by the expression of differing points of view and when there is a commitment to open dialogue in order to reach the desired goals.

Stepsis (1974) notes that conflict-resolution strategies can be categorized into three areas: avoidance, defusing (or cooling down), and confrontation. Each conflict-resolution category has both positive and negative attitudes, and it is important to recognize the advantages and disadvantages to each approach. For the purposes of this discussion, avoidance and defusing are considered as reactions to conflict, while confrontation is seen as a method of conflict resolution. The first two approaches tend to be passive, whereas confrontation requires planning, considerable action, and evaluation. Such an approach to examining conflict management does not imply that an active strategy is always better than a passive one; it does imply that an action-oriented strategy requires more advance preparation because it is a highly sophisticated and sensitive method of communication.

Leininger (1974) discusses nine methods for handling conflict: friendly persuasion; charisma; confrontation; mystical invocation; mutual alliance; mediator arbitration; use of authoritative mandates; revolutions; and feuds or open warfare. While several of these have relevance to nursing practice and there is no question that nurses handle conflict via feuds, mandates, and revolutions, the approach taken in this chapter is that nurses have two principal ways of dealing with conflict: reacting to or resolving the disagreement. Nurses react to conflict when they withdraw or defuse the situation. Withdrawing rarely solves a conflict, but only

postpones the actual impact of the differences. Pent-up feelings remain and often surface in nonconstructive ways; for example, at a later date an angry outburst may be quite out of proportion to the situation, or the nurse may react by somatization.

Defense mechanisms have a beneficial role in handling conflict, although their usefulness is limited. An initial reaction to a conflict situation may be to handle it through a defense mechanism, but successful handling will ultimately necessitate a more direct approach.

Confrontation

Constructive conflict resolution employs a problem-solving communication approach known as confrontation. As noted, many approaches are available for dealing with conflict. This discussion focuses on one approach that is based on the following four prerequisites (Thurkettle and Jones, 1978):

1. Each participant's willingness and ability to identify the issues clearly
2. Open communication, including the ability to listen
3. The maintenance of a focus on the issues, not on the people involved
4. Mutual responsibility for the communication outcome

Smoyak (1974, p. 1632) describes confrontation as a "concept, a process and a technique" that is useful in nursing practice. Confrontation is *not* "telling the other person off" in an angry, hostile outburst of long-held and nourished resentments. It is a problem-solving approach to conflict resolution that relies on preplanning and clarity of all parties as to the intent of the discussion (Tappen, 1978).

Confrontation is essentially a three-stage process: assessment, direct confrontation, and resettlement. The first step in confrontation is to assess the situation. What is the problem? Who seems to be causing the problem? How is it personally affecting you? How does it seem to be affecting others — the total work group? What power structure is involved? What kind of changes can you expect as a result of the confrontation? What might be the cost to you of personally raising the issue? The cost to you of either confronting or ignoring the issue must be weighed. The next series of questions to ask yourself during the assessment stage of confrontation concerns, "Whom do I need to confront?" Is the actual conflict between two people who are members of the same group, or is the total group involved? If the conflict is between you and one other person, then the resolution should take place in private rather than in front of the group. Assessment includes "who" is involved, "where" the discussion should take place, "when" the best time is, and exactly "how" the discussion should be handled.

Confrontation is a direct approach that deals only with the problem. Side issues are not brought in, nor are the participants' personal attributes. Such an approach implies that "you say what you see, hear or experience, directly, forthrightly and clearly" (Smoyak, 1974, p. 1633). No value judgments are included in confrontation; participants must agree to stick with the issues and to present each side of the conflict in a straightforward and rational way.

Finally, during the assessment stage the other participants are apprised of the need for an open exchange about the conflict. A time and place must be decided on, and each participant must know the purpose of the meeting so that preplanning can be done.

The plan is now ready for implementation. In implementing the confrontation, basic skills for good communication prevail. First of all, you stick to the facts, handle only one subject at a time, and avoid interrupting other speakers. No matter how much you want to interrupt to clarify, defend, or refute, it is essential to listen carefully to what the other person is saying. It is a frequent human tendency to "always look good in public." Thus when a colleague is discussing how your actions have affected the group or another person, it is difficult to

"hear" what is said. The tendency may be to begin defending your behavior before you have heard the speaker's complete message.

Once each participant has presented the issues, it is helpful to have each one repeat back what he or she heard the other person say. This form of feedback provides instant clues as to misperceptions or lack of understanding. Perception and accurate hearing may be impaired because of the heightened state of anxiety of the participants. Feedback is essential to clear, straightforward confrontation. During the feedback process, state in your words what you heard the other person say. Simply repeating what they said may not indicate understanding and the ability to find meaning in the other person's message.

The last stage in confrontation, resettlement, includes agreeing that a problem exists and jointly devising a strategy for resolution. Up until this point only one participant may have perceived a problem. The other person(s) may only have agreed to talk about "your" perception of the conflict. Now that both sides have been aired, it is time to agree that a problem exists; what the major aspects of the problem are; and that certain steps need to be taken in order to resolve the conflict. Once these agreements have been reached, participants need to establish goals and priorities for problem resolution, and then outline a procedure to be followed. For example, after a confrontation about inconsistency in evaluation of either students or staff members, two participants may agree that inconsistency does exist, that one participant is not adhering to established evaluative guidelines, and that such behavior is not fair to either the students or the other evaluator. The next step would be to agree on a way to change this behavior and then plan checkpoints. For example, the participants may agree to complete the next set of evaluations individually, then go over them together to assess consistency before informing others of the evaluation. Followup should be built in to monitor continuation of new behaviors as well as to provide ongoing support and encouragement.

SUMMARY

Communication takes place constantly in any organization and serves to both coordinate and control the functioning of the work group (Poole, 1978). The challenge to any organization is to assure that the predominant communication networks will serve to increase the effectiveness of the group, and to avoid communication patterns that undermine, interrupt, or otherwise impede effective functioning. The change agent must be especially astute at assessing the communication mechanism to see who talks with whom and how accurate or destructive the messages are, and then to promote efficient communication or alleviate the causes for disruptive communication.

Communication encompasses far more than what is actually spoken. Inherent in any communication are both verbal and multiple nonverbal messages. Also, each person "hears" a message in terms of personal feelings, needs, wishes, goals, biases, and vested interests. If one participant in a communication dyad feels especially useless, then the words of the speaker will be received within the context of, "I am useless and of no value." For example, suppose speaker A says to B (who feels worthless and useless), "You really did a good job of presenting the goals of your department at the board meeting." Listener B is likely to hear this message as, "You dummy, I could have done a better job of presenting the departmental goals." In addition, B may wonder what A wants, since the compliment is perceived as having a hidden agenda. Thus communication is complex and requires ongoing validation between participants to determine whether the message sent actually reached the listener.

Effective communication is blocked when one or more participants has a hearing or speaking deficit, when speakers have differing frames of reference and do not hear the same message, or when the environment militates against clear message transmission. What participants think of one another also affects the receipt of a message. If one or more parties in the exchange dislikes another one, feels threatened, or is angry, the message is likely to be distorted.

In any organization, people communicate in three directions: horizontal, upward, and downward. In general, people communicate most often with others who are geographically close to them, with those they like best and feel most comfortable with, and with those who can help them achieve their goals. People communicate or fail to do so in order to achieve a goal, to satisfy a personal need, or to improve their situation (Jackson, 1976). Each participant uses the communication process for personal gain and goal attainment. Some are open and honest in their messages, since they view these mechanisms as most consistent with their personal philosophies for relating to other people as well as highly effective for enhancing their position.

In contrast, other people may distort information, leave out parts of the message, or tell only selected group members what should be conveyed to a much larger number of people. It is important to recognize how people communicate in order to detect incomplete and inaccurate information before its transmission causes undue havoc.

Possibly the greatest facilitator of effective communication is listening. Because most people tend to have a great deal on their minds, the ability to actively listen to others often seems a lost art. Frequently, while Sam is talking, Sue is busily thinking about what she will say in rebuttal, her next project, or her dinner plans for that evening. Careful listening usually represents time well spent, as both subtle and obvious cues can be detected.

Within any organization there is a need for collaboration and management of conflict. Effective collaboration requires that participants approach one another with respect for each person's competencies as well as with a sincere desire to maintain open and straightforward communication. Few organizations can maintain communication free from conflict. Whenever two or more people get together, differences in ideas, perceptions, and ways of doing things occur. Confrontation is an open mode of conflict management whereby participants stick to the issues, look at areas of difference, and jointly seek new solutions.

REFERENCES

Brill, N.: Working with people, New York, 1973, J.B. Lippincott Co.

Calhoun, G., and Perrin, M.: Management, motivation and conflict, Top. Clin. Nurs. **1:**71-80, Oct. 1979.

Cross, G.P.: How to overcome defensive communications, Personnel J. **57:**441-443, Aug. 1978.

Davis, K.: Human relations at work, New York, 1972, McGraw-Hill Book Co.

Davis, K.: Cut those rumors down to size, Supervisory Management **20:**2-6, June 1975.

Davis, K.: Organizational behavior: a book of readings, ed. 5, New York, 1977, McGraw-Hill Book Co.

deLodzia, G., and Greenhalgh, L.: Recognizing change and conflict in a nursing environment, Supervisor Nurse **4:**15-25, June 1973.

Drucker, P.F.: Management, tasks, responsibilities, practice, New York, 1973, Harper & Row, Publishers.

Gibson, J.L., Ivancevich, J.M., and Donnelly, J.H.: Organizations: behavior, structure, processes, rev. ed., Dallas, 1976, Business Publications, Inc.

Hayakawa, S.I.: Language in thought and action, New York, 1949, Harcourt, Brace & Co.

Hersey, P., and Blanchard, K.H.: Management of organizational behavior: utilizing human resources, Englewood Cliffs, N.J., 1977, Prentice-Hall, Inc.

Kielinen, C.E.: Conflict resolution, J. Nurs. Ed. **17:**12-15, May 1978.

Jackson, J.: The organization and its communication problems. In Stone, S., Berger, M.S., Elhart, E., Firsich, E.C., and Jordan, S.B., editors: Management for nurses: a multidisciplinary approach, St. Louis, 1976, The C.V. Mosby Co.

Leininger, M.: Conflict and conflict resolutions: theories and processes relevant to health professions, Am. Nurse **6:**16-22, Dec. 1974.

Mariano, C.: The dynamics of conflict, J. Nurs. Ed. **17:**7-11, May 1978.

Marriner, A.: Conflict theory, Supervisor Nurse **10:**12-16, Apr. 1979.

Marriner, A.: Conflict resolution, Supervisor Nurse **10:**46-54, May 1979.

Poole, M.S.: An information-task approach to organizational communication. Acad. Management Rev. **3:**493-504, July 1978.

Smoyak, S.: The confrontation process, Am. J. Nurs. **74:**1632-1635, Sept. 1974.

Stepsis, J.: Conflict resolution strategies. In Jones, J.E., and Pfeiffer, J.W., editors: The 1974 annual handbook for group facilitators, LaJolla, Calif., 1974, University Associates, Inc.

Tappen, R.M.: Strategies for dealing with conflict: using confrontation, J. Nurs. Ed. **17:**47-52, May 1978.

Thurkettle, M.A., and Jones, S.L.: Conflict as a systems process: theory and management, J. Nurs. Adm. **8:**39-43, Jan. 1978.

Wood, J.R.: Constructive conflict in discussion: learning to manage disagreements effectively. In Jones, J.W., and Pfeiffer, J.E., editors: The 1977 annual handbook for group facilitators, LaJolla, Calif., 1977, University Associates, Inc.

Because there has been implanted in us the power to persuade each other and to make clear whatever we desire, not only have we escaped the life of wild beasts, but we have come together and founded cities and made laws and invented arts.

Isocrates, 1966, p. 79.

9

PERSUASION AS A MECHANISM FOR CHANGE

Charlotte Rappsilber

Change and progress have long been a value of the American way of life, and the health care system is no exception. What to change and how to change it have assumed new proportions as the old ways of getting people to do what is wanted are becoming useless in this time of competing persuasions. No longer are the words of leaders listened to as law. Doctors, nurses, parents, priests, politicians, teachers, lawyers, and other leaders have to persuade their listeners in order to influence beliefs and behaviors. Since change in a free society must rely primarily on persuasion, and we could not easily survive if all attempts to influence belief and behavior were suddenly outlawed, it is becoming essential for health professionals to understand this powerful instrument in order to advance the cause of personal, community, and societal health. Persuade or perish is an alarmingly real possibility.

As suggested by the title, this chapter describes how the process of persuasion can be used as a change strategy. It focuses specifically on definitions of persuasion, theories that explain this interactional approach, and techniques of persuasion and application to nursing.

For more than 2000 years, people have been fascinated with the techniques used to influence others. Aristotle was one of the first to study persuasion, and, although his discussion was solely in terms of persuasion in oral communication, it was based on practical theories about human behavior and how to influence human beings' responses to communication. Aristotle defended persuasion to critics as a means of achieving power by asserting that it could be used for either good or bad ends (Larson, 1979). People like Hitler and Machiavelli, in their attempts to deceive others into following ignoble aims, have made persuasion appear to be a tool for the unscrupulous. But for people such as Florence Nightingale, St. Francis of Assisi, Abraham Lincoln, and Albert Schweitzer, persuasion has conveyed noble aims. When the term has negative connotations, it is typically because many of the practitioners of the art have been extraordinarily adept deceivers, flatterers, manipulators, and con

artists, operating under the assumption that people are basically weak, fallible, and gullible. This unflattering view of human nature is typified by Barnum's well-known statement, "There is a sucker born every minute" (Bartlett, 1955, p. 557).

HELPERS AS PERSUADERS

In spite of the often unsavory view that persuasion is a "devil wand" (Simons, 1976), and the reluctance of nurses, educators, scientists, artists, and others to label themselves as persuaders, most helping professions could just as well be called "persuasion professions." Lawyers, physicians, nurses, social workers, educators, and ministers are all involved in tasks of either constructing messages or manufacturing images designed to influence others. Professionals in particular, according to Simons (1976, p. 45), "have an ethical obligation to acknowledge their roles as persuaders." These efforts to influence the beliefs and actions of others often have a moral as well as a pragmatic justification. The individual who, as a result of experience or study, knows what is best for another, has, under normal circumstances, the obligation to keep that person from making a mistake that will jeopardize health or safety. The nurse who understands the dangers inherent in a given diet or a prescribed medicine, but fails to initiate efforts to promote change in a patient's behavior, is clearly delinquent in professional duty. The responses of patients to persuasive health care appeals can exert an immediate, decisive impact on their condition. Of particular interest in this regard is the influence of an initial favorable persuasive communication on a patient's acceptance and utilization of a health facility program. Health professionals' ability to help a patient depends, in part, on the latter's image of the nurse or doctor as the possessor of knowledge with healing powers. However, effectiveness depends not only on training and knowledge but on personal qualities and attitudes, and on persuasive skills.

Just what these personal qualities and attitudes are remains unclear in the literature. What is clear, however, is that "people professionals," whether nurses, teachers, clergymen, or physicians, take pride in thinking that they somehow change the values, attitudes, and behavior of those they serve in some significant way, based on the assumption that such changes are desirable and in their best interests. How they will accomplish these aims is a product of their persuasive powers.

DEFINITIONS OF PERSUASION

The notion of persuasion is difficult to define in a way that includes its characteristics under the many circumstances in which it is used. Simons (1976) constructed a working definition of the term from an examination of the activities of groups most often viewed as persuaders, such as missionaries, lawyers, politicians, casanovas, parents, and helping professionals. One of the common elements observed by Simons was that persuasion involves some kind of human communication, whether written or oral, verbal or nonverbal, explicit or implicit, face-to-face, or through an indirect medium such as the newspaper. Another common element among cases in Simon's study was the attempt to influence others somewhere between the extremes, but excluding physical coercion and reflex response. Even though persuasion is often seen as a manipulative act, it ideally leaves the receiver with some perception of choice. While this is not meant to discount Rokeach's conclusion (1971) that we have the ability to change basic values of others without their awareness, as well as to control the direction of this change by techniques of persuasion, most theorists in the field prefer to believe that freedom of choice is an attribute of persuasion.

In all instances, persuasion seems to be directed at either the modification of attitudes or the alteration of behaviors. Defining persuasion becomes even more difficult when including the notions of range, scope, and flexibility that are so important in the application of persuasion techniques to the variety of situations that a nurse may encounter.

Silvey (1975, p. 13) incorporates these notions into the following comprehensive definition of persuasion:

With a focus on flexibility I would define persuasion to be the single encompassing term in any process of communication which influences thought, beliefs, attitudes, and/or behavior. It is dynamic in nature; a relationship phenomenon; can be either inter-personal or intra-personal; verbal or nonverbal; vocal or nonvocal; intended or unintended; ethical or unethical; conscious or unconscious; have negative or positive results; is context bound; can be transmitted by interaction or transaction; and the recipient can be influenced either knowingly or unknowingly, with the response being either overt or covert.*

This definition of persuasion seems to include most of the ways a person can communicate in any social setting. The many theories about persuasion have emerged as a result of experimental research in a variety of settings and from many perspectives. They are presented in most texts without attention being devoted to any organizing principles of common elements. However, the theories fall into broad categories with common assumptions. This synopsis will introduce six general designs of persuasion theory introduced by Neal (1978), their theoretical bases and major assumptions, and an application to real-life persuasive situations that nurses or other people professionals may encounter.

THEORIES OF PERSUASION

Although persuasion was originally a concept falling within the domain of the humanities, primarily the communication theorists, it has more contemporarily developed as a social science outside the field of speech communication. Persuasion researchers often treat the subject as an independent research topic because it is such a complex and multidisciplinary approach to behavioral change. The concept of persuasion common to all the literature is that it brings about changes in people's attitudes that act as constraints or predispositions to ways of behaving; however, scholars in the various

*From Silvey, L.: Toward a taxonomy for conceptualizing persuasion in the social sciences, Educational Resources Information Center, ED 12S-041, Los Alamos, N.M. 1975.

disciplines operate from a frame of reference common to their discipline. That is, communication scholars view persuasion primarily in terms of rhetorical skills or models that process message development from the source via some channel to the receiver. The complex psychological aspects are not usually emphasized in the communication models. In contrast, psychologists' interests center around motivation, whereas sociologists and anthropologists are most concerned with the social and cultural environment. Those in public relations and politics emphasize theories and means of creating favorable public images in their discussion of persuasion, and marketers aim to apply methods to arouse or trigger buying and consumption behavior. More recently, health professionals have become interested in applying theories and techniques of persuasion to problems of patient education, utilization of health services, and adherence to medical regimens. Such efforts require an eclectic, pluralistic approach drawn from the various social science fields.

Drive-motive design

The needs that are either innate to people or acquired, and the methods in which they are transformed into patterns of behavior, are subject to continued experimentation and debate. The theories represented in this model are probably the oldest in the study of persuasion; and whether drives and motives occur as a result of maturation, learning, socialization, or innateness, the patterns of behavior humans acquire to deal with biologically innate or social psychologically acquired needs are powerful forces that must be considered in understanding the success or failure of persuasion efforts. Two approaches within the drive-motive design are adjustment and growth-motivation theories.

The Freudian concept of motivation contends that all human beings possess libido that can be either directed into sexual activity, or sublimated in some socially approved way, or repressed, thereby resulting in neuroses or some socially undesirable behavior. Through adjustment, human beings'

basic biological needs and primitive instincts are satisfied. The astute persuader would then hope to identify the unmet primitive need and direct a persuasive appeal toward that need.

Maslow views social motivations from a more healthy and humane perspective and also acknowledges that motivation is innate in people at birth. Maslow's hierarchical inventory of needs perceives humans as innately motivated for growth toward self-actualization, and in a search for meaning, as opposed to the Freudian conceptualization of primitive body-based drives (Brembeck and Howell, 1976). The function of persuasion, therefore, operating under these assumptions, is to address human need by demonstrating ways of satisfying it once it is aroused.

Community health workers can easily determine what motivational appeals might be most effective by basing their analyses on Maslow's hierarchy of needs in terms of the client audience they are addressing. For example, the extremely poor are highly unlikely to be influenced by appeals to the needs of self-esteem and self-actualization when food and shelter are their most urgent needs.

Cognitive design

The general theories just discussed have had a significant impact on the development of theories of persuasion, and their effect cannot be discounted. However, the mind as the shaper and holder of experience—in the form of remembered experiences, beliefs, attitudes, values, and habits—is also important in contemporary approaches to persuasion theory and attitude change; and it may be the most popular approach to attitude change. These contemporary theories include balance or consistency theories.

Consistency theories assume that people are capable of processing information in a rational way and have a need for harmony between internal attitudes and beliefs, and all incoming information. If consistency does not occur, the individual experiences tension, which stimulates action. These theories assume that people are rational information seekers who are trying to achieve a psychologically consistent view of the world and stability in their environment.

An example of balance theory applied to a health problem might be a health worker's effort to discourage clients in their smoking habits. The clients, as a result of being exposed to dissonant information, may attempt to reestablish balance by derogating the source of the information, reinterpreting or selectively reevaluating old information, seeking new information to support their position, avoiding the dissonant information, or changing their attitudes or behaviors to achieve consistency with the new information. Recognizing that habitual smokers may sacrifice cognitive consistency and maintain that smoking is not harmful to their personal health, one can persuade smokers that it is quite normal for persons sometimes not to maximize their own interests. Thus they may not need to invent rationalizations or continue to maintain that smoking does not affect their health. Even though some degree of psychological dissonance in the face of smoking would definitely be useful in influencing smokers to stop, if they are too threatened they are unlikely to face the issue realistically. This approach to persuasion is perhaps the most neglected by health care professionals and might be used effectively in many situations involving noncompliant patients and intransigent clients.

Stimulus-response design

Another type of persuasive design includes the stimulus-response theories, which are derived from learning theories applied to the formation and modification of attitudes. Researchers in this area have reported that attitudes can be influenced by classical conditioning as well as by reinforcement and anticipated reinforcement (Neal, 1978). The common elements of these theories are the association of selected stimuli with certain responses. Emphasis on how attitudes are associated with one another can render learning theory a useful tool in explaining and approaching persuasion.

Pavlov's dog, you will remember, was classically conditioned to salivate at the sound of a bell after it was linked to the presence of meat. In the same way, a client might be conditioned to respond to a preventive health measure after it is linked to a prestige source or a physical sign. Examples of this are Betty Ford's effort to encourage women to seek help for drug abuse or to practice regular breast self-examination. The process of prestige suggestion is an example of classical conditioning. Other efforts may be directed toward operant or instrumental conditioning as developed by B.F. Skinner. In this case, a nurse may ask patients how they view a particular health measure. If the response is favorable, the nurse can positively reinforce the behavior by a friendly nod or a "good" response. If the response is unfavorable, the nurse might reinforce successive approximations of the desired response until it is forthcoming. (You reinforce successive approximations of the desired behavior by encouraging the person to continue the effort until the correct response is attained.) This is called "shaping" and it may be more successful than a negative reinforcement to an unfavorable response.

Social-design

The social-design approach to persuasion arises from the assumptions about pressures that impinge on individuals to conform in group situations. Persons experience psychological pressures in group interaction when they care about what others think. Group therapy has been a mainstay of psychological therapy by reducing members' isolation, heightening their hopes, and enhancing their self-esteem. Alcoholics Anonymous has successfully adopted this therapeutic method to the specific problems of alcoholics. More recently, research has demonstrated that peer-group support is more effective in persuading clients to use contraceptives than other appeals, and that hypertensive patients exhibited a higher level of compliance when receiving patient group support than when receiving individual support from nurses (Caplan et al., 1976). This research also identified that what nurses view as support often differs from what patients view as support.

Personality design

Personality-design theories are based on the functional theories about attitudes, which view a person's attitudes as a reflection of total identity. These theories have only recently been introduced into the study of persuasion and are not as widely discussed as the balance or motivational theories. Personality-design theories are oriented to individual differences and personal life-style, and adopt the view that the persuader needs to know the function or role an individual's attitudes serve in that person's realm of experience before developing an appropriate persuasive strategy. Katz is a leading functional theorist who maintains that it is easier to reinforce prejudice than it is to alter it, and that when attitudes serve a social adjustment function they may easily be modified by picturing the advantages of adopting a new position. However, ego-defensive attitudes are often not amenable to change except through psychoanalytical processes (Simons, 1976). The common assumption behind these theories is that knowledge about whether a person's particular attitude serves an ego-defensive, value-expressive knowledge function, or some combination thereof, should suggest the conditions under which change can be expected.

Basing action on this theoretical assumption, nurses would be cautious in the use of strong fear appeals lest they run the risk of waking the ego-defensive function, thus blocking potentially persuasive messages. Intense fear or anxiety tends to cause inattentiveness to communication, aggression toward the communicator, defense-avoidance reactions, and an unwillingness to grapple with the issue. Kirscht (1975) found that public appeals to persuade people to participate in health screening were more useful when the appeals were positive rather than threatening.

Perceptual design

Two varieties of perception theory focus on attribution and self-perception. Attribution theory is concerned with explaining the behavior of others, whereas self-perception theory is concerned with how people explain their behavior. Generally, the theories share the attempt to unite the principles of judgment with the phenomena of attitude change. However, attitude change is first brought about by changing perceptions, not attitudes (Neal, 1978). There seem to be instances in which beliefs, values, and attitudes are inferred from what is said or done.

The changing of attitudes using this assumption is accomplished by inducing a change in perception rather than directly appealing to attitude. Persuasion depends on an innate desire to reorder categories to fit an initial judgment or categorization of behavior.

Neal (1978) cites an example of an application of several designs to the persuasive tactics inherent in the Weight Watchers organization. The motivational design is apparent: the safety, belonging, and self-esteem needs of an individual are compromised, in addition to the physical disequilibrium that is induced when someone is overweight. People join this organization in order to reduce these needs by losing weight. The groups incorporate principles of social reinforcement, group pressure, and conformity to group norms. According to the cognitive theories, persons may hold different cognitive explanations about the relationship between being slim and their own self-image. When the self-image is contrary to ideas about being slim, dissonance may result; thus the person stays with Weight Watchers until the cognitions are congruent. The stimulus-response design is applicable in the techniques of "shaping" used for reinforcement by the group. Approximations of the desired weight loss are always reinforced and negative behavior not reinforced. A variety of harmful health behaviors may be approached using similar applications of persuasion theories, such as an effort to "unsell" and reduce factors associated with heart disease.

Tubesing and others (1977) developed an action-research project focusing on primary care and health education for patients in a group family practice. This project adhered to the whole-person philosophy and used several of the theories just discussed.

TECHNIQUES OF PERSUASION

In this section several techniques of persuasion useful to nurses or other helping professionals are discussed. In addition, two kinds of behavioral influence are distinguished. In one type of influence the objective is to bring about a change in existing attitudes and behaviors; in the other, the objective is to make existing attitudes and behaviors more resistant to change. Since each of these techniques makes several assumptions about behavior, they are essentially eclectic; consequently, one or more designs can be identified as applicable to most persuasive endeavors, each with a different emphasis depending on the source of persuasion.

The persuader as the source

The situation most commonly envisioned when studying techniques of persuasion is the one in which the persuader strives to reverse a behavior of the persuadee, or to change the intensity of the persuadee's attitude. Ideally, the persuader seeks complete conversion; however, success is more likely to be accomplished in terms of the degree of conversion. A major focus for the persuader is study of the ways in which a variety of interacting variables, including the persuader, message, channel, and persuadee, influence persuasive outcomes by facilitating or inhibiting either attitudinal or behavioral change.

Central to this view is the premise that the persuader acts and the persuadee is acted on. The major activity, involvement, and energy emanate from the persuader even though persuadee feedback is solicited and considered important. Helping professionals use this process daily to persuade either a given audience or a single person. Nurses often must persuade clients to undergo painful experiences such as ambulating soon after surgery. Teachers try to persuade students to learn about things that are not seen as directly relevant to their

lives, and ministers attempt to persuade congregations to follow their advice on moral and ethical dilemmas.

A practical strategy traditionally recommended for those interested in persuading others is *coactive* persuasion. Simons (1976) describes this method as a psychological move toward the persuader in order to increase identification and reduce interpersonal distance. The *combative* approach is the analogue to coactive, and although both are manipulative in nature, the combative technique aims to increase the psychological distance by underscoring differences between the participants. In the combative approach the nurse is considered right and the patient wrong; the teacher superior and the student inferior. Threats of punishment and enforced compliance are used as techniques for changing behavior. The combative strategical approach will be described briefly following a more thorough discussion of the coactive position. The assumption here is that, in most circumstances, the coactive approach will most likely bring about the desired outcome in a helping role. Research has tended to support this assumption.

The essential characteristics of the coactive approach are described here in reference to a helper as the persuader.

Identification

The helper emphasizes shared interests and values, as well as demographical similarities. In the case of a hostile client or patient, the helper would move rapidly to topics of agreement. Differences such as expertise, knowledge, special clothing, or trustworthiness are emphasized when they are valued by the clients. However, special clothing such as nurses' uniforms may either serve to increase distances and keep the nurse psychologically removed from patients, or it may actually contribute to patient perceptions of trustworthiness and expertise. Research in this area is contradictory and tends to differ depending on the clinical specialty and geographical area. Clothing is an important aspect of nonverbal behavior that serves a wide variety of communicative functions. People select clothing to help them conform more closely to images of the ideal self. The reasons that nurses do or do not wear uniforms might make for fruitful research findings in that it could be determined whether uniforms are worn to conform to patients' perceived values or to maintain a greater psychological distance from patients.

Avoidance of threats of acts of force

Even though a helper is using the coactive approach, an emotional appeal may be made to the client which may include the use of fear. Threatening or punishing acts, however, are not a part of this strategy. The effective persuasive helper needs to be constantly aware of the possibly unconscious tendency to inflict psychological punishment for noncompliance, such as avoiding and belittling clients. Explaining to a client the consequences of continuing a harmful behavior is an example of this approach; however, care should be taken to ensure truthfulness when implying some future threat.

Seemingly rational persuasion

Even though helping professionals may not always, for reasons of professional expediency, meet the highest standards of candor, they attempt to appeal to the client's need for logical consistency by trying to emphasize rational and reasonable behavior. Operating under this principle, a nurse would gear explanations to patients at the level of their rational understanding and avoid words or behaviors that would upset this balance, if possible.

Attitudes to actions

The persuasive helper's objective is to change a client's attitudes as a precondition for changing behavior. Although this is not always possible, especially in emergency and crisis situations, in most events involving cooperation, patients are brought to the point where their attitudes and beliefs are modified; but it is ultimately their right and decision to modify their behavior. As in the smoking example, many people cannot or do not maximize their own interests.

Equal access

Simons (1976) describes this characteristic of the coactive approach as an effort to ensure that the persuader has no special advantage or access to information. Often this may not be possible in the case of the professional helper, although every effort can be made to ensure that a client is aware of the consequences of different behavioral choices in terms that are understood. A nurse may have access to information or knowledge not available to a patient, but this information can be used selectively and rationally in consideration of the current therapeutic goal.

Persuadee as source

Even though it was suggested earlier that the coactive approach is superior to the combative one, there are two new persuasive techniques that make use of dissonance and perception theories and fall under the general definition of combativeness, because they use some form of forced compliance. However, these strategies appear within the context of the persuadee as the source, and they involve counterattitudinal and role-playing techniques. The important point in these strategies is that compliance to a behavior or point of view can lead to changes in attitude, rather than result from the change. Studies in this area leave little doubt but that there is empirical truth to this notion.

In the role-playing approach, a client may be asked to assume or imagine he has been arrested for drug abuse, contracted lung cancer from smoking, or suffered as a result of whatever behavior the helper aims to alter. This technique can also be used to change attitudes toward the self. The client is forced to take an active stance. In the educational setting, students acquire functionally useful attitudes by simulating interactions in future roles, whether life roles or professional roles. Thus relevance and involvement are instrumental in changing existing attitudes and behavior. Attribution theory is applied in a way that taps an internal self-concept, and it has been repeatedly successful in the research.

Dye (1978) describes an application of this technique with nursing students in regard to attitude change with the elderly. Simulation games, a form of role playing, were developed in which students played the elderly role. Significant changes in attitudes toward the elderly were reported.

The counterattitudinal approach differs in that the persuader is induced to engage in some activity that conflicts with previous attitudes. This, then, triggers a change in attitudes and behaviors, and the persuader becomes more favorably disposed toward the position advocated in the message.

An example of this technique is for a teacher who wishes to induce less favorable attitudes toward pot smoking or alcohol consumption, to have students present antimarijuana or antidrinking messages for some real or imaginary target audience. This has been documented as a powerful persuasive technique; however, there is disagreement among theorists in the interpretation of the phenomena. Festinger accounts for the change in terms of cognitive dissonance; Bem, a perception theorist, interprets the change as a result of people modifying their behavior from external cues when they look at it retrospectively (Simons, 1976).

Inducing resistance to persuasion

The professional helper must devote attention not only to the process of altering existing behaviors and attitudes in clients, but also must teach the client to resist future persuasive attempts that may jeopardize the new-found health behavior or well-being. A review of the persuasion literature yields little on the topic of resistance; however, it can be viewed as an extension of the persuasion process. In simple terms, the persuader receives some kind of message calculated to reduce vulnerability to future persuasive appeals.

Persuasion researcher Hugh Rank (1978) developed a model for training people to be critical receivers of persuasion. Nurses may well use Rank's idea to help clients equip themselves to enhance their critical ability when faced with incoming persuasive appeals from advertising, family, social groups, or well-meaning friends. The basic idea behind Rank's model is that persuaders usually use two major tactics to achieve their goals. They may either intensify and emphasize certain aspects of the appeal, or downplay other points; often they do both. Intensification comprises repetition, association, and composition.

Much of education is based on repetition, and it serves to imprint on the receiver's memory a particular way of responding. Those involved in educating others about health practices often neglect this simple strategy, although advertisers seldom do. Associating or linking an idea with something held in great esteem by the audience is another useful tactic. Overeating and drinking are activities that advertisers consistently link with the good life, family, friends, and other sources of happiness. Composition intensifies messages by contrasting them to a less desirable outcome. For example, the American Medical Association's effort to intensify opposition to national health insurance legislation employs this technique by comparing how comforting it is to have a personal private physician who knows all about you and your family, to the depersonalized physician-patient relationship that would be inevitable with a government-regulated approach. Composition may also intensify messages by introducing logic, statistics, or art in order to highlight certain aspects.

Downplaying is accomplished by the persuader by omission, diversion, and confusion. Key information can be directly withheld or concealed with jargon or euphemism. Diversionary tactics such as humor are also used to drain attention away from the shortcomings of a particular issue. A final tactic in downplaying persuasion is to create confusion. Jargon and technical language often serve to confuse people and overwhelm them in a way that makes them feel stupid and reluctant to ask questions.

Rank (1978) suggests that consumers should

downplay information when persuaders intensify, and intensify when they downplay. Other persuasive resistance techniques involve the use of anchoring and commitment.

Anchoring is a resistance-inducing technique derived from consistency theory. According to Thompson (1975), anchoring involves attaching an attitude or belief to an existing set of values, beliefs, or group norms. A health appeal on television that asks you to see your doctor about your high blood pressure because you love your family is an example of anchoring. The use of support groups for patients is another way this tactic may be directed. For example, Alcoholics Anonymous, Recovery, Inc., and other self-help groups use various aspects of anchoring to help equip group members with tools for resisting persuasive onslaught.

The notion that commitment to a belief increases resistance to future persuasive appeals has been supported by research and reported in the literature. A summary of the prevailing view about this notion is that the level or degree of commitment to an idea is the instrumental force in affecting the tenacity with which attitudes and beliefs are held.

OTHER CHANGES IN NURSING THROUGH PERSUASION

Examples of using persuasive techniques in nursing have generally been oriented toward persuading patients or clients to implement better health practices. Perhaps this is the most cogent application of persuasion theory for nurses and helping professionals in general; however, aspects of professional practice discussed in other sections of this book are concerned with persuasion directly or indirectly.

The nurse in an organization must deal with the role of credibility in maintaining organizational recognition and exerting organizational influence without empirical evidence. The ancients contended that the ethos or image of an individual affected ability to influence or persuade others. Empirical evidence has confirmed the persuasive influence of status or image. It has been shown that if

a person perceives another as more prestigious, there is a greater likelihood that the latter person can influence the former (Brembeck and Howell, 1976).

Although the nursing profession has made considerable progress in the education of its members, their lack of recognition as prestigious health professionals continues to plague nurses within most organizational settings. Nursing has never held the prestige it deserves, primarily because of its predominantly female membership and its dependent relationship to medicine. Although the feminist movement has successfully obtained equal opportunities for women in many other occupations, nursing has not been closely identified with this movement, possibly because of the conservatism of many nurses and the attitudes of many feminists toward nursing.

Therefore one can question whether the persuasive skills of men and women are similar, as well as whether nurses in particular have persuasive abilities similar to women in other professions. There is limited evidence on the comparative credibility of men and women, but the research conducted to date tends to ascribe more prestige, credibility, and expertise to men by both sexes (Brembeck and Howell, 1976). Feminists generally do not view nursing as a prestigious career choice (Kritek and Glass, 1978). This most certainly affects the image of nurses. Female professionals, especially nurses, need to be knowledgeable about principles of persuasion when attempting to exert influence within an organizational setting. They must limit their reliance on prestige or image as the key to persuasiveness and strengthen other techniques of persuasion, such as similarity of attitude between the persuader and persuadee, direct participation by the persuadee, knowledge, and trustworthiness.

The nurse educator has a responsibility not only for teaching students how to be successful health providers, but also influencing or socializing prospective nurses to become committed professionals.

Socialization, as a process, comprises many applications of persuasion. McGuire's inoculation theory plays a major role in both commitment and persuasion (Thompson, 1975). When students undertake a field of study, they commit themselves to the accepted values, beliefs, and reference groups of that occupation. In the case of the nursing student, this means that the profession, as a reference group, becomes an anchor for the individual's opinions and attitudes, depending on the strength of the influence and cohesiveness of the reference group. Cronkhite (1969, p. 150) cites several factors as determinants of the strength of a reference group. Some of the most significant to the nurse educator as a socializer-persuader are the extent that the student:

1. Likes and feels close to the group members
2. Depends on them for social support and respects their opinion
3. Perceives the group as united in opinion and relevant to the reality of nursing
4. Values membership in the group

The nature and quality of faculty interaction with both the student and the larger community directly affect the quality of these determinants and, subsequently, the successful socialization of students as committed professionals.

The political arena is another environment in which nurses and other helping professionals are frequently involved in projecting their influence and persuasive actions. Campaigns for office or for issues and causes are the types of political activity most frequently engaged in by the health professional. Organizing and conducting a political campaign draws on all the principles and practices of persuasion. A number of successful persuasive devices identified by Thompson (1975) are summarized here and applied to issues that may affect the helping professions.

Repetition

Research has indicated that repetition increases comprehension by adding opportunities for shifts in belief. A campaign for passage of a health bill or building a new health facility offers a distinctive opportunity for using repetition. A repeated phrase is often a successful campaign strategy. Other procedures using repetition might include radio or television spots, speeches, or newspaper advertisements.

Prestige and transfer

Through transfer, the political persuader hopes to shift the credibility of a person or an organization toward the political issue. An example described by Thompson (1975) comes from India, where an attempt was made to transfer reverence for a sacred animal to the approval of birth control measures by having an elephant named "Beautiful Flower" distribute family-planning literature and contraceptives.

Glittering generality and name-calling

Common strategies with which the effective campaigner should become familiar are glittering generality and name-calling, although they are ethically dubious.

Name-calling is particularly unjustifiable and serves to short-circuit rational thinking. Campaigns for and against legalized abortion have often resulted in broad evaluations of viewpoints, such as "murderer," without reference to facts, circumstances, or consequences of alternative actions. Generalities likewise tend to obscure rational evaluation on specific issues, such as being for health, for women, for life, or some other general category that leaves more unexplained than explained.

Plain folks and bandwagon

These are two strategies that are designed to obstruct rational analysis; however, the bandwagon approach is used frequently in drives for charitable or health causes, such as muscular dystrophy. The assumption behind this strategy is that success is proof of quality or need, and that certain numbers or names have already joined or donated to the cause. The plain-folks device has been used by successful politicians such as Eisenhower, and might be an effective strategy for a woman in a political campaign to appeal to the female vote.

These are not the only strategies available for the political persuader, but they serve as examples of how all available means of persuasion come together in a political effort.

A PERSUASION CHANGE MODEL FOR NURSES

The model in Fig. 9-1 is based on the persuasion inputs, utilizing the theories and techniques discussed, that nurses can use for planning change interventions, regardless of the purpose or the target population. It is based on an assumption of the multiple causality of a behavior and presents an approach for assessing the determinants of this behavior in the target audience. In this model, adapted from Kar's (1976) diagnosis model, acceptance or rejection of change may be caused by any or all of the target-audience characteristics. The audience determinants may be: (1) political, as in a political campaign or a drive for improved health services in a community; (2) social-structural, as in an effort to create organizational change in a health facility; (3) cultural, psychological, and interpersonal, as in the development of a nurse-patient relationship to

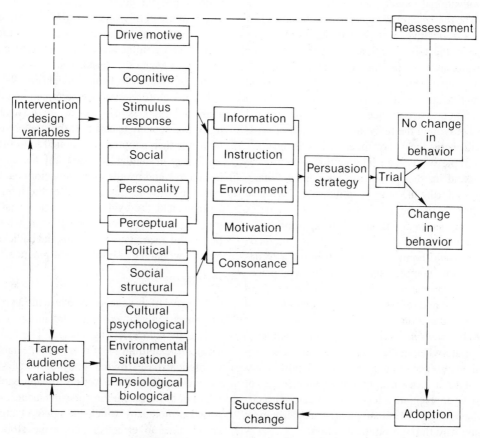

FIG. 9-1
A persuasion-change model for nurses.

encourage acceptance of a medical regimen; (4) environmental and situational, when a particular service is unavailable for a client; (5) physiological and biological, when the change desired is related to a patient's physical disequilibrium; and (6) educational-intellectual, as when a patient-education program is being planned for diabetics. Based on the assessment of audience determinants and an analysis of the intervention variables derived from persuasion theories, an intervention model is selected as appropriate under the circumstances. The five general models for persuasive intervention are the informational model, the instructional model, the consonance model, the situational model, and the motivational model.

1. The *informational model* is appropriate when there is a positive motive and accessibility for change in the target audience, but the person or persons cannot act because of lack of necessary information or skill. An appropriate intervention does not waste effort by trying to create either a motivation or a dissonance, but should be directed toward providing the relevant information or skills that will enable the person to reach the desired goal. An example of such an intervention would be to inform and instruct persons to take precautionary measures during the time of an illness or during an emergency situation.

2. The *instructional model* is appropriate in ways similar to the previous model, but the intervention would be more prolonged in order to develop a more complex set of skills and competencies. An example of such a situation would be a professional and formal program for childbirth and parenting education.

3. The *environmental and situational model* is appropriate when audience nonacceptance is a result of an absence of environmental support or services and not a lack of motivation, knowledge, or skills. An appropriate intervention under such a circumstance would be to manipulate the environment in some way through political action.

4. The *motivational model* is appropriate when the need for change results either from the absence of a positive motive or from the presence of a strong negative motive. An example of this situation is in family planning. Under such circumstances, intervention warrants intensive action to create the desire for a small family and to overcome the negative motives. Social support may be planned as a method of intervention.

5. The *consonance model* is appropriate when the person's reluctance to change a behavior is caused by conflicting motives, values, attitudes, or beliefs. For example, under this circumstance, a woman may be highly motivated to regulate fertility, but also have a high level of anxiety about the ill consequences of various contraceptives. The motivation is present, but it conflicts with other motives. The strategy in this situation would be directed toward reinforcement of the existing motivational system and elimination of the fear and anxieties serving to create the dissonance.

In the persuasion change model (Fig. 9-1), once the approach for action is determined and the persuasion strategies developed, an application is made to a specific instance. If the strategy is effective, it is then adopted and applied to future target audiences in similar situations. If the strategy is ineffective and results in no behavior change, it is returned for a new assessment of the intervention variable and the cycle is completed again. This model aims to present a general approach that can be used in a variety of situations and audiences that nurses encounter in professional practice.

SUMMARY

The goal of this chapter is to provide an overview of persuasion as it exists in contemporary thought and relate it to effecting change. The chapter reviewed the definitions of persuasion, established a theoretical base for the study of persuasion, attempted to describe a variety of approaches and techniques useful for the nurse persuader, and proposed a model by which the nurse change agent could develop effective persuasive strategies in varying situations. Although the surface has only been scratched, variables such as audience attributes, theoretical justification, choice of technique, effort, ethics, and evaluation deserve careful scrutiny by persuasion practitioners. Effective change strategies and practical persuasive success hinge on these and other factors. The quest for developing an understanding about persuasion as a mechanism to facilitate change in nursing has only just begun and can be quite exciting.

REFERENCES

Bartlett, J.: Familiar quotations, Boston, 1955, Little, Brown & Co.

Brembeck, W.L., and Howell, W.S.: Persuasion: a means of social influence, Englewood Cliffs, N.J., 1976, Prentice-Hall, Inc.

Caplan, R.D., Robinson, E.A., French, J.R., Caldwell, J.R., and Shinn, M.: Adhering to medical regimens: pilot experiments in patient education and social support, Ann Arbor, Mich., 1976, Institute for Social Research.

Cronkhite, G.: Persuasion: speech and behavioral change, New York, 1969, The Bobbs-Merrill Co., Inc.

Dye, C.A.: Effects of persuasion and autotelic inquiry methods on attitude change, Percept. Mot. Skills **47**(Part 1):943-949, Dec. 1978.

Isocrates: Nicocles. In Isocrates, vol. 1, Cambridge, Mass., 1966, Harvard University Press. (Translated by G. Norlin.)

Kar, S.B.: A model for communication and intervention: ethical and scientific dimensions, Ethics Sci. Med. **3**:149-164, March 1976.

Kirscht, J.P.: Public response to appeals, Public Health Rep. **90**(6):539-543, June 1975.

Kritek, P., and Glass, L.: Nursing: a feminist perspective, Nurs. Outlook **26**:182-186, March 1978.

Larson, C.U.: Persuasion, reception and responsibility, Belmont, Calif., 1979, Wadsworth Publishing Co., Inc.

Neal, P.W.: A design approach to teaching persuasion: theory and application, paper presented at the 64th annual meeting of the Speech Communication Association, Minneapolis, Minn., Nov. 2-5, 1978.

Rank, H.: Patterns of propaganda and persuasion, paper presented at the 29th annual meeting of the Conference on College Composition and Communication, Denver, Colo., March 30-April 1, 1978.

Rokeach, M.: Persuasion that persists, Psychology Today **5**:68-72, Sept. 1971.

Silvey, L.: Toward a taxonomy for conceptualizing persuasion in the social sciences, Educational Resources Information Center, ED 12S-041, Los Alamos, N.M., 1975.

Simons, H.W.: Persuasion: understanding, practice, and analysis, Menlo Park, Calif., 1976, Addison-Wesley Publishing Co.

Thompson, W.N.: The process of persuasion: principles and readings, New York, 1975, Harper & Row, Publishers.

Tubesing, D.A., Holinger, P.C., Westberg, G.E., and Lichter, E.A.: The wholistic health center project, Med. Care **15**(3):217-227, March 1977.

All of human existence entails a quest for certainty in an increasingly uncertain world.

Anonymous

10

DECISION MAKING IN NURSING PRACTICE

Wade Lancaster and Pat Beare

In the story of *Alice in Wonderland,* Alice was confronted with a problem, so she pleaded with the Cheshire Puss, "Would you tell me, please, which way I ought to walk from here?" "That depends a good deal on where you want to get to," the cat wisely responded (Carroll, 1950, p. 53).

Just like Alice, throughout our lives we are continually confronted with problems. When we awake each morning we face a number of problems, such as what to wear and what to eat. In addition to the many small problems we face throughout our lives, in our chosen professions we are confronted with many larger ones. Many of these problems are long range, others are intermediate in scope, and some are on a day-to-day, or even second-to-second basis.

Decision making and problem solving are integral parts of nursing practice, not only in the normal routine of managing and delivering health care services, but also in the process of planned change. Indeed, the factor that weighs most heavily in the success or failure of nurse change agents is their decision-making ability; the quality of the decisions reached is a yardstick of their effectiveness.

This chapter is about decision making and problem solving. It is the last of those establishing a theoretical framework for understanding advanced nursing practice and the role of a change agent. However, this in no way reflects a lack of importance. If anything, its position at the end of this part points up the importance of problem solving and decision making.

In the preceding chapters, it was suggested that an effective change agent must recognize that people behave not only as individuals, but also as members of groups; and they frequently assume roles within organizations, which act as open systems. It was also established that successful change agents must possess power and exercise leadership skills, as well as be able to communicate and persuade proficiently.

In spite of the multitude of dimensions within our model of change, and the numerous specific skills that the change agent must possess to guarantee

results, effective decision making is the key. Everything else is irrelevant if the change agent fails to take courses of action that ensure success.

These comments may sound like an overstatement of fact so it might be well to dwell on them for a moment. Nursing positions are usually described either from the standpoint of the functions they perform or in terms of their specific duties and responsibilities. Specific knowledge of basic concepts, principles, and procedures is essential, but the knowledge alone is passive; it must be used, applied, and set in motion. It must be made active in terms of applying it to the everyday operation. This requires decision-making skill within the context that it will be developed.

A second reason for stressing the key role of decision-making skill lies in the rapidly changing environment in which today's nurses practice. It calls for today's nurses to put their decision making on a rational basis. No matter what functions they perform or activities in which they engage, the end result—the payoff—is based on the decisions they make. Decisions based solely on intuition and past experience are becoming less effective in dealing with problems, because things are changing at too rapid a pace and because yesterday's experience does not always mirror tomorrow's problems.

For these reasons it becomes necessary to look at decision making as a rational process and to attempt to find an approach that, when applied, can sharpen significantly nurses' ability to make effective decisions.

In this chapter we will examine the various elements of decision making: the problem, the individual or group making the decision, the decision process, the decision itself, and the environment in which the decision is being made. Decision making is one of the principal processes engaged in by individuals, groups, and organizations. While groups of individuals frequently engage in decision making, some individual must select and be responsible for the course of action ultimately chosen. Since the act of choice is frequently accomplished by a single person, the primary focus of the chapter will be on the behavioral dynamics of decision making, rather than the more technical models in the field of decision theory.

ELEMENTS OF DECISION MAKING

Decision making is frequently defined as the selection of one alternative course of action from various alternatives that could be pursued. This definition has the advantage of brevity, it is easy to remember, and it focuses attention on the essential element of decision making—that is, making a choice. This definition, however, is deceptively simple; it is incomplete in that it does not emphasize the making of a decision as only one of several steps that occur in sequence as part of an intellectual process. Nor does it consider the basis for making a decision. The appropriate alternative depends heavily on the setting within which decision making occurs. Moreover, this definition does not indicate that decisions, if they are to be effective, must be executed or translated into a course of action.

Regardless of whether a problem situation is of a crisis or long-run nature and whether it concerns people or things, decision making consists of several elements, including the problem, the decision maker, the decision process, and the decision itself. These elements, as well as the factors that make up the environment for decision making, are depicted in Fig. 10-1. These elements form the basis for discussion in this chapter.

DECISION-MAKING MODELS

Decision theory consists of a group of related concepts and propositions that attempt to either prescribe or describe how individuals as well as groups select a course of action when confronted with a problem. Generally, people who study decision making view it from two distinctive perspectives. The first, the normative or prescriptive viewpoint, focuses on the way people should make decisions. The second, the descriptive or behavioral viewpoint, emphasizes the way people actually solve problems and make decisions (Albert, 1978).

Because of the manner in which general decision theory is discussed, confusion between the normative and descriptive views has often led to misinterpretations of the literature on decision-making processes. One such misinterpretation is the conclusion that these two views compete or conflict with one another. This, however, is not the case (Duncan, 1978). Hence the purpose of this section of the chapter is to examine briefly each of these contemporary views of decision making.

Normative model of decision making

Early approaches to individual decision making focus on a normative model, called economic man, proposed by Adam Smith over 200 years ago (Kotler, 1965). This view of the decision-making process is rooted in classical microeconomic theory and is founded on two fundamental assumptions.

First, all decisions are made with the objective of maximizing some predetermined goal or desired value. Although the original intent of classical microeconomic theory was to prescribe an analytical procedure for achieving optimal profits, a logical extension of this assumption proposed that a major goal of human behavior was to seek pleasure and avoid pain. Hence economic man seeks to maximize pleasure. A prerequisite of the maximization assumption is perfect knowledge. This second assumption endows decision makers with the ability to know every available alternative solution and all of the possible consequences of each (Duncan, 1973; Gibson et al., 1973).

Based on these two assumptions, the normative model of decision making characterizes the decision maker as a completely rational, all-knowing, hedonistic calculator who approaches any given problem in the following manner:

1. The problem is defined and analyzed.
2. All available alternatives are identified.
3. Each alternative is evaluated in terms of its benefits and disadvantages.
4. All alternatives are ranked in the order in which they are likely to meet the desired value or objective.
5. The alternative that maximizes is selected.

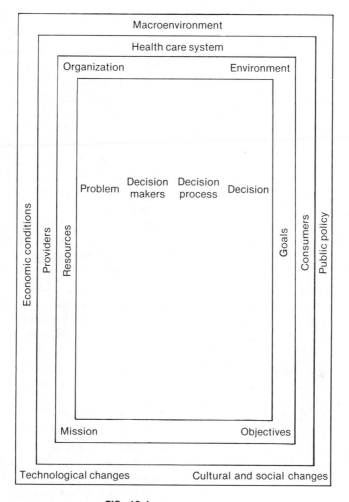

FIG. 10-1
Elements of decision making.

6. The decision is implemented.
7. The decision is followed up.
Fig. 10-2 provides a representation of the normative model.

Although the normative model is analytically precise, the assumptions of maximization and perfect knowledge have been criticized for being unrealistic. Clearly, these are valid criticisms. However, the model should be recognized for what it is, a prescriptive approach to decision making. As such, it prescribes a specified objective and provides guidelines that greatly facilitate the application of analytical techniques in problem solving.

Descriptive model of decision making

As mentioned, the basic assumptions of the normative model have been criticized for being unrealistic. The main quarrel with this model focuses on the notion of perfect knowledge. Critics maintain that people do not really have perfect knowl-

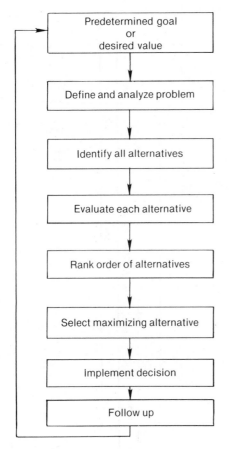

FIG. 10-2
Normative model of decision making.

Simon (1976) developed a descriptive model based on a set of alternative assumptions and called administrative man. According to this model, real-life decision makers cannot possibly be aware of all the alternatives, nor do they always attempt to maximize something as the economic man is presumed to do. Instead, decision makers: (1) are subjectively rational; (2) make decisions on the basis of incomplete information; and (3) are satisficers.

Such a view posits that problems are not always defined correctly, but instead are defined programmatically. It also posits that people do not always solve problems well; instead, they solve them just well enough. Further, the descriptive model recognizes that complete information is not always available, nor is it always sought. It also recognizes the inherent costs involved in the acquisition of information. Consequently, people often consider the cost of obtaining additional information too high with respect to the probable need for the information. Thus decisions are made on the basis of available information. In short, the premises underlying the descriptive model view the decision maker as logically solving problems, arriving at decisions on the basis of known facts about the problem encountered.

The subjective-rationality premise differentiates the descriptive model from the normative model in that people are considered to be rational, whether maximizing or not. Subjective rationality focuses on logical behavior that results from what is believed to be true. Since these beliefs constitute their knowledge of the world, people define problems in terms of subjective perceptions and solve them accordingly. For this reason, decision makers occasionally define problems incorrectly and solve them poorly. They have no real choice; they must either act on their beliefs or not act at all.

The incomplete-information premise, which Simon calls bounded rationality, is based on the assumption that it is seldom possible for decision makers to obtain anything approaching complete information. There are at least three identifiable obstacles to the acquisition of complete informa-

edge. Some critics have argued that if people must possess perfect knowledge in order to make rational choices, then imperfect knowledge must mean imperfect rationality, or even irrationality. Obviously, these views regarding rationality are extreme and are of limited value to understanding decision-making behavior. A more reasonable view accounts for the fact that people do not usually have anything like a complete array of alternatives laid out before them. Such a view is represented by the descriptive model of decision making.

Responding to what he viewed as unrealistic assumptions of the economic man model, Herbert A.

tion. First, people rarely have sufficient time to acquire all available information. Second, the quantity of information available often exceeds the individual's processing capacity. Third, people frequently lack the technical knowledge required to evaluate all of the available information critically.

Faced with these three obstacles, the incomplete-information premise posits that decision makers do not try to obtain complete information. Instead, their attention is directed to gathering information that subjectively appears most relevant to the problem and will provide a satisfactory solution.

The third premise characterizes decision makers as being satisficers rather than optimizers. This notion is based on an observation advanced by Simon, who noted that if people always sought an optimal decision, the number of possible decisions they could make would be reduced to an unacceptable level. Thus instead of seeking optimal solutions, people tend to set some minimum objectives to be accomplished, and they consider as acceptable any alternative that appears capable of satisfying these objectives.

In short, the descriptive model of decision making characterizes people as being subjectively rational: they make decisions on the basis of incomplete information; and they seek satisfactory rather than optimal solutions to their problems.

Fig. 10-3 depicts the descriptive model. An examination of this diagram reveals a number of similarities as well as differences when compared to the normative model. More specifically, the decision maker:

1. Defines the problem in terms of subjective perceptions
2. Identifies acceptable alternatives (the decision maker may either identify several alternatives at this point, before proceeding to the next step, or identify and evaluate alternatives sequentially)
3. Evaluates each alternative in terms of its ability to solve the problem satisfactorily
4. Selects a satisfactory alternative (this may be the first one encountered, or if several have

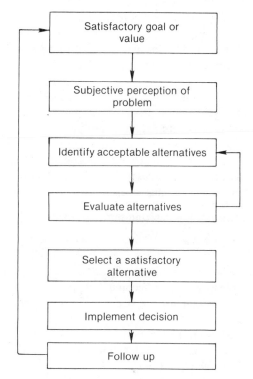

FIG. 10-3
Descriptive model of decision making.

been evaluated, the one that produces the most favorable outcomes)
5. Implements the decision
6. Follows up

In this section of the chapter, two general models of decision making—normative and descriptive—were reviewed. Recall that the normative model specifies the manner in which a person should make decisions; the descriptive model portrays the manner in which a person actually does make decisions. In the next section, the descriptive model will be explored in more detail.

THE DECISION-MAKING PROCESS

When thinking about solving a problem, people often focus attention on finding the right answer. Few situations, however, have only one possible solution. Instead, several feasible alternatives exist for most problems. When multiple solutions are available, the decision maker is confronted with the problem of selecting an alternative.

It should be obvious from the preceding discussion of decision-making models that making a decision, or selecting an alternative, is only one step in a series of acts referred to as problem solving, or decision making as it is called in the management literature. In order to promote better understanding of this process, the steps that precede and follow the act of making an actual decision will be examined.

Overview of the decision-making process

In the years since Dewey (1910) first itemized the steps in problem solving, many conceptualizations of the process have been advanced. These steps, in modified form, have become accepted as the standard paradigm for the decision-making process. They are:
1. Problem recognition
2. Information search and information-processing activity
3. Evaluation of alternatives
4. Decision, selection, or choice
5. Postdecision activities

These steps can be applied to any problem. It is important to understand that a problem exists when there is a goal to be attained and uncertainty regarding the appropriate solution. Further, for a problem to exist there must be more than one alternative solution. These conditions for the existence of a problem are critical because the decision-making process is concerned with designing, evaluating, and choosing from among alternative courses of action. If there is no inherent act of choice there can be no problem solving.

The decision-making process can be characterized as a sequential and reiterative series of psychological and physical activities. Once decision makers recognize a problem, their behavior generally takes the form of collecting and processing information about alternative solutions, evaluating this information, and establishing a preference

order among the various alternatives. The establishment of an initial preference order does not, however, necessarily lead to a decision. Indeed, people often continue to search for additional information and to reevaluate old information until they acquire sufficient confidence that their preference order will not be altered by subsequent information.

It is this reiterative process of seeking and evaluating information in order to achieve the required level of confidence that consumes time and differentiates various types of problem-solving behavior. Obviously, the level of confidence desired before making a decision is affected by numerous factors. When the required level of confidence is reached, the person generally makes a decision.

It has been noted that the stages of the decision-making process are not necessarily unidirectional. In fact, the reiterative nature of the process suggests that a person can move either backward or forward as well as skip stages. For example, search and information-processing activities do not automatically follow problem recognition; nor do these activities lead directly to a decision and postdecision evaluation. In contrast, however, problem recognition will always precede the decision, which is always followed by the postdecision evaluation. In short, the fact that a person is in one stage of the process is neither sufficient nor a necessary condition for progressing to another.

In the sections that follow, each of the stages in the decision-making process is explored in greater detail. For organizational reasons, the stages will be discussed in the order of their normal sequence.

Problem recognition

A necessary prerequisite for decision making is the existence of a problem. Clearly, without a problem there would be little need for a decision. Problem recognition is perhaps the most complex stage of the decision-making process because it is a perceptual phenomenon involving the interaction of social, psychological, and environmental variables. Essentially, the decision-making process begins when an individual believes a problem exists; that is, the difference between what is and what should be is perceived to be significant enough to require that some action be taken.

The ideal state of affairs, or what should be, can be characterized as predetermined goals or desired values. For individual decision makers these values or goals are reflected in their perception of the ideal life, which may include preferred physical, psychological, social, and economic conditions. In organizational settings, the ideal state is represented by established goals and objectives. These may include overall long-run organizational objectives, as well as specific goals for the organization and its various subunits. For example, a private hospital may view its long-run objectives as providing care for the sick and injured, and serving the community through education, research, and public health activities. In order to meet these long-run objectives, several specific operating objectives may be identified. One such objective may focus on maintaining the best possible physical facilities so that optimal inpatient care is possible. This objective provides direction for various subunits within the hospital, such as the housekeeping department, which may have as its ultimate objective maintaining clean and sanitary facilities.

In contrast to the ideal state of affairs, the actual state is characterized as what is actually taking place. For individuals, this represents a perceptual assessment of life as it is currently being lived; it is a performance evaluation of the physical, psychological, social, and economic facets of life. For organizations, the actual state is a manifestation of their activities.

It would seem reasonable to postulate that a perfect situation would exist whenever the ideal and actual states were totally congruent. This condition, however, rarely occurs because both the ideal and the actual states are constantly changing over time. Consequently, both people and organizations are in a continual state of incongruence. In view of this fact, it can also be postulated that the mere existence of incongruence is not sufficient to provoke problem recognition. It would thus seem that incongruence or difference between the ideal and actual states would have to be of considerable magnitude in order to provoke problem recognition.

Having recognized a problem, the decision maker evaluates the situation to determine whether the problem is significant enough to merit solving, and whether there is a feasible or possible solution to the problem (Reitz, 1977). This type of evaluation is important to individual as well as organizational problems.

Since people are confronted with limited resources, such as time and talent, it is often necessary to establish priorities regarding the importance of problems. A problem such as inadequate office space or even the lack of an office may be aggravating to a nurse supervisor, but at the same time this problem may be of minimal importance to the success of the hospital. In this situation, the supervisor may elect just to live with the problem while attempting to solve more important ones.

Not only do decision makers evaluate problems in terms of their relative importance, they also distinguish between those that are solvable and unsolvable. Occasionally problems are encountered that are important but currently not solvable. An example of this situation is a nurse supervisor who is faced with a high turnover of staff nurses. The problem itself stems from the unusual demands of a certain physician who insists on performing surgery at 4 AM in order to accommodate his schedule. Although the administrator sympathizes with the supervisor's problem, he refuses to do anything because the physician is considered to be a valuable asset, providing the hospital with a significant proportion of its patients. In this case, the problem is important to the supervisor, but it is currently unsolvable.

Both of these problem-evaluation decisions are appropriately summed up in a prayer that reads: "O God, give us the serenity to accept what cannot be changed, courage to change what should be changed, and the wisdom to distinguish the one from the other" (Reitz, 1977, p. 188).

In short, one outcome resulting from problem recognition is the postponement of problem-solving behavior because the problem either is not important enough or is currently unsolvable. In contrast, a second type of outcome results when the decision maker believes that the problem can be solved and it is important enough to do so; then problem-solving behavior is activated.

As mentioned, people have limited resources (e.g., time) and cannot solve all problems, nor can they solve all important and solvable problems immediately. Consequently, some priority must be established for dealing with them. In an organizational context, decision makers often prioritize problems in one of the following ways (Reitz, 1977):

1. The first problem encountered is the first problem solved; in other words, problems are dealt with in the order in which they appear.
2. Problems that can be dispensed with immediately are given priority over more time-consuming ones; that is, the easiest problems to solve are given first priority.
3. Crisis or emergency problems are given priority over all others.

Having selected an important, solvable problem, the decision maker is now ready to engage in the next step of the process: searching for and processing information.

Information search and information processing

Seeking and processing information are two separate, yet interrelated activities. Information seeking, which takes place during the second stage of the decision-making process, involves both mental processes and physical activities consciously used to gather information about the problem, possible alternatives, the relative merits of the various alternatives, and the consequences of selecting these alternatives. In contrast, information processing takes place in both the second and third stages of the decision-making process. In the second stage, the function of information-processing activities is to appraise the information being gathered. This appraisal function of information processing assists the individual in determining whether to continue or discontinue information seeking. In the third stage of the process, information processing focuses on discriminating and ranking the various alternative solutions identified. In short, the search process, which takes place in the second stage, serves the function of gathering information about the problem, alternative solutions, and developing criteria for evaluating these alternatives.

No amount of effort in the subsequent steps will resolve the problem unless it is properly defined. Hasty problem analysis often leads to poor decisions when symptoms are confused with the problem itself. For example, if a physician diagnoses chest pain as a duodenal ulcer and the problem is angina pectoris, the treatment will inevitably fail. So it is in organizational settings. If a nurse supervisor fails to identify the real problem correctly and completely, solutions will either fail or temporarily mask the problem.

It is not always easy to differentiate between symptoms and problems, especially those that may be the result of a variety of factors. For example, high nursing staff turnover may be the result of factors such as working conditions, wages, hospital location, or poor in-service training. A good way of getting beyond the symptoms and to the root of the problem itself is first to state specifically what is wrong and what needs improvement. Then the decision maker needs to gather facts, investigate possible causes, and finally identify the real problem. Once this has been accomplished, the decision maker can set forth the requirements of a satisfactory solution and specify any constraints on a solution (Scanlan, 1973).

Having defined the problem, the decision maker is now ready to develop alternative courses of action and assess the potential consequences of each. This is really a search process. At first glance it may seem that search implies the gathering of information not presently available, an assumption that is generally but not always correct. Instead, the extent of search activities will vary depending on the individual as well as the nature of the situation. Consequently, the search process may be instantaneous, or it may involve intensive exploration over a prolonged period of time. Regardless of the extent, the search process normally moves through certain steps.

Internal search

First, the memory will be examined for relevant information. This process of internal search entails recalling stored information, such as the existence of an organizational policy, prior experience and training, and the experiences of others. Organizational policies often provide decision makers with predetermined courses of action for a multitude of problem situations. Similarly, past experience frequently provides the necessary factual information and conceptualizations with which to make a decision. However, there are limits to internally stored information, especially in today's rapidly changing world. Consequently, not uncommonly stored information alone is inadequate and must be combined with additional information gathered from the external environment.

External search

Once the decision to engage in external search is made, the decision maker will begin the process of information acquisition, which involves both physical and mental activity. External search represents a conscious effort to gather new information. Early in the external search process, the individual will perform a preliminary search. The purpose of this activity is to identify alternatives and compare the attributes of these alternatives with a desired set of attributes. This preliminary sampling ordinarily results in a reconciliation of what is desired with what is perceived as being available. When full-scale external search begins, the decision maker makes a concerted effort to match the desired set of attributes with those actually available. To accomplish this goal, information is sought from a variety of

sources. One such source in organizational settings is the data-base information system, which provides management with a timely flow of relevant information. Although these systems provide up-to-date and accurate information, there still remains the need for judgment on the part of the decision maker (Sisk, 1973).

Determinants of search

The extent of search activities depends on the individual problem solver as well as the nature of the problem situation. Numerous factors affect search behavior, and they can be grouped into four categories: the perceived value of search, the perceived cost of search, individual propensities to search, and situational variables.

Whenever people engage in external search activities, they must somehow balance the costs and benefits of search. Essentially, the amount of information sought is a function of comparing the perceived value with the perceived cost of search. Generally, when high value is accompanied by low cost, the individual will engage in extensive information-acquisition behavior. However, when the cost is high and the value of search is low, little search activity will occur.

The perceived value of search is determined by the utility of information, which is influenced by variables such as the amount of information stored in memory, the quality of stored information, ability to recall stored information, and confidence in decision-making ability.

The amount of information stored in memory is a function of knowledge and past experience. The utility of this information is based on the degree to which it is related to a specific problem situation. It would seem that when people encounter familiar problem situations and have clear decision criteria, the perceived value of search is diminished and they would search less. Unfortunately, stored information is not always appropriate for a given problem situation.

The amount of stored information and the resultant perceived value of search are often influenced by the quality of stored information, which in turn is affected by satisfaction with previous experiences as well as the amount of time that has elapsed between situations. When past experience has been less than satisfactory, there tends to be a greater propensity to search for new information when the same or similar problem is encountered. Similarly, the more infrequently a given situation occurs, the greater the probability that a person will search for new information.

Another factor that affects the perceived value of search is a person's ability to recall relevant information. The cognitive process of assimilating new information with old varies among people; some tend to minimize differences in new information in order to assimilate it with stored information, whereas others tend to maximize differences, thereby enabling them to sustain recoverable stored information in an unaltered form over long periods of time. Recall is also affected by the degree to which current problems resemble those that have arisen in the past. Finally, recall ability, like the quality of stored information, is affected by elapsed time. Hence the greater the amount of time between similar problems, the higher the propensity to search for new information.

Not only is the perceived value of search affected by the quantity and quality of stored information as well as by recall ability; it is also affected by the confidence people have in their decision-making ability (Duncan, 1981). As a generalization, search for outside information becomes more important when confidence is low, regardless of the quantity and quality of stored information.

Closely related to confidence is the degree of perceived risk associated with a problem. Perceived risk is individualistic, varying in intensity from one person to another, and also varying over time for a given individual. Though many problem situations activate little or no perceived risk, it is possible for any given problem to contain an element of risk. Perceived risk may be financial, psychological, social, or physical in nature. It may even be a combination of two or more of these forms. While people tend to use a variety of strategies to cope with perceived risk, one of the most important is the acquisition of information. The tendency to acquire information is directly related to the amount of perceived risk. As a generalization, the greater the degree of perceived risk, the greater the propensity to search until enough information has been gathered to reduce the perceived risk to an acceptable level.

As mentioned, whenever people engage in an external search for information, they somehow compare the costs and benefits of search. Just as the perceived value of search is influenced by a number of factors, the same is true with the perceived cost. Included among these are time, effort, and financial expenses, as well as psychological considerations, deprivation of benefits resulting from decision delay, and information overload. In short, all search involves some cost (Stigler, 1961).

Although outlays of time, effort, and the expenditure of money are the more obvious influences on the perceived cost of search, less apparent but of equal or perhaps greater importance are the psychological costs of frustration, tension, and annoyance associated with information acquisition. These psychological costs are often perceived to outweigh the benefits of search.

A similar type of psychological cost is the frustration that results from decision delay. More specifically, the longer a person takes acquiring information, the longer the final decision and the benefits to be derived from the solution are delayed. In view of this perceived cost, people often shorten the search process to minimize delay costs, especially as the alternatives become increasingly clear.

Another type of cost associated with search is information overload. Since there are finite limits on the quantity of information that a person can absorb and utilize, any information gathered that exceeds this limit becomes dysfunctional, causing frustration to mount and deterring decision-making ability.

In addition to the perceived cost and value of

search, the extent of information acquisition is also influenced by an individual's propensity to search, which is a function of several factors. Since the individual as decision maker is discussed later in this chapter, it should be sufficient at this point to note that people differ with regard to their search styles. More specifically, differences exist in the type, intensity, complexity, and duration of search.

Finally, the extent of search is also influenced by a number of situational variables such as the availability of information, the urgency of the problem, and the type of problem itself. More specifically, when information is readily available, as in the case of an information system within an organization, the extent of search is much shorter than in a case where information has to be compiled. Similarly, an urgent situation requiring a quick decision serves to shorten the search process. Last, the type of problem, as will be discussed later in this chapter, often dictates the extent of search. For example, a long-range strategic problem will often require more extensive search than an administrative problem that occurs routinely.

In summary, the search for and processing of information is usually regarded as the central phase of the decision-making process, for it is during this stage that the problem is defined, the need for additional information is determined, and the alternative solutions are developed. Having performed these tasks, the decision maker is now ready to move on to the next step in the decision-making process; that is, the evaluation of alternatives.

Evaluation of alternatives

In every problem situation the objective in making a decision is to select the alternative that provides either an optimal or a satisfactory solution. In order to accomplish this objective, the alternatives that have been developed must be evaluated.

When the objective is to obtain an optimal solution, the decision maker should ideally know all available alternatives, the consequences of each, and their probability of occurrence. In a situation such as this, the decision maker arrays the alternatives, evaluates each in terms of its advantages and disadvantages, and ranks them in the order in which they are likely to meet the objective. Unfortunately, complete knowledge and certainty regarding the consequences and probabilities of outcomes for each alternative are not always possible in optimization problems. Instead, situations often exist where the decision maker is aware of only a limited number of alternatives and has only some probabilistic estimate of the outcomes of these alternatives. In evaluating alternatives under these conditions the decision maker usually relies on the tools of statisticians and operations researchers. These decision aids have made important contributions to decision theory, especially in the analysis and ranking of alternatives (Albert, 1978). Several of these techniques are discussed later in the chapter.

Although they occasionally attempt to obtain optimal solutions to problems, decision makers—operating under the pressures of time, limited resources, and information—more frequently strive for satisfactory solutions. In these situations, rather than conducting an exhaustive search for the optimal solution, the decision maker searches for alternatives that meet a limited set of criteria. Likewise, the search for information about each alternative is also limited. Consequently, alternatives are evaluated on the basis of several crucial criteria, and are either accepted or rejected on this basis (Reitz, 1977).

Even though satisficing appears to be a much simpler approach to problem solving than optimizing, the process of evaluating alternatives should certainly be no less rigorous. Unfortunately, studies have shown that most decision makers do not process information about alternatives very well. Instead, they tend to pay little or no attention to useful and available information.

Obviously, more attention focused on the evaluation of alternatives would yield more effective decision making. Such an approach would involve (Reitz, 1977):

1. Identifying all possible outcomes, both positive and negative, from each alternative
2. Assessing the positive and negative value of each outcome, as well as determining how effectively it will accomplish the objectives or requirements of a satisfactory solution
3. Estimating the likelihood of each outcome for each alternative

Identifying, assessing, and estimating the value and likelihood of each outcome to all alternatives may range from being a relatively simple, straightforward operation to being a complex and detailed procedure. Obviously, the more comprehensive the problem the more difficult the analysis. Fortunately, management scientists and decision theorists have devoted considerable effort to developing various quantitative techniques to assist decision makers in assessing the probabilities of future events, as well as in comparing and evaluating alternatives.

As noted above, every alternative has both advantages and disadvantages, and these must be identified. Identifying disadvantages is probably the most difficult step in the analysis of alternatives because favorable predispositions—either conscious or unconscious—toward an alternative have often been formed. Consideration of disadvantages is, however, extremely important if potential difficulties and shortcomings are to be spotted. The benefit of delineating disadvantages is not that it forces the decision maker to reject the alternative, but rather that it allows for making provisions for these disadvantages in advance of the implementation stage, should the alternative be selected as the appropriate course of action. To the extent that this is done, the decision maker will have a more realistic assessment of the results to be expected (Scanlan, 1973).

Having recognized and defined a problem, and having searched for alternative solutions and evaluated them, what then? At this juncture, the decision maker is now ready to move to the next stage of the decision-making process and make a choice.

Selection of an alternative

The selection of an alternative is an important part of the decision-making process; it involves making a choice between two or more alternatives in order to solve a problem and achieve some predetermined goal. It is important to note that choosing an alternative should not be viewed as an isolated act; instead, it is a means to an end because it rapidly merges into a series of actions designed to implement, control, and evaluate the decision. The critical point is that decision making entails more than selecting an alternative; it is a dynamic process (Gibson et al., 1976).

Rarely are the solutions to problems either black or white, with only one correct decision. Instead, they tend to be various shades of gray. Consequently, selecting an alternative course of action is not always easy. The difficulty encountered in selecting a solution emphasizes the critical importance of the activities that took place during the previous stages of the decision-making process.

Difficulty in making a decision is influenced by such variables as the number and quality of alternatives, the risk, and the interaction effect. Part of the difficulty in selecting an alternative stems from the number and quality of potential solutions available, which is a function of the degree of productiveness and originality employed during the previous stages of the decision-making process (Sisk, 1973). Incomplete and unavailable information often limits the number as well as the quality of alternatives generated. March and Simon (1958) have described the quality of alternatives as being either good, poor, bland, mixed, or uncertain.

Good alternatives have high probabilities of positively valued outcomes and low probabilities of negatively valued outcomes; for poor alternatives the probabilities for positively and negatively valued outcomes are reversed. In contrast, bland alternatives have low probabilities for both positively and negatively valued outcomes, whereas mixed alternatives have high probabilities for both types of outcome. Finally, uncertain alternatives are characterized as those for which the relative probabilities of outcomes cannot be assessed.

Clearly, selecting an alternative from some combinations will be more difficult than others. For example, if one alternative is good and the others are either bland, mixed, poor, or uncertain, then the choice is straightforward. However, if none of the alternatives is good, then the selection becomes more difficult.

Not only is the selection of an alternative affected by the number and quality of potential solutions, but it is also influenced by the element of risk. Part of the difficulty in making a decision stems from the constantly changing environment, which injects uncertainty into the probable success or failure of a projected solution.

Finally, choosing an alternative solution is complicated by the interaction of one activity on another. Rarely does a situation exist in which one activity singularly achieves the desired goal or objective without having some positive or negative influence on some other goal. This is especially true in organizational settings, where a multiplicity of objectives exist. Thus it is not uncommon for short-run objectives to impact on long-run objectives. This is illustrated by the case of the hospital superintendent who attempts to keep a tight rein on maintenance costs at the expense of the hospital's long-run objective of high-quality patient care (Gibson et al., 1976).

Once the decision maker has selected an alternative, it must be converted into action. Obviously, any decision is worthless if it is never implemented. Thus the final phase of the decision-making process, postdecision activities, involves not only implementing the decision, but communicating and evaluating the decision as well.

Postdecision activities

Effective decision making is not limited to skill in selecting good problem solutions; it also includes the knowledge and skill necessary to transform the solution into behavior. This is done by effectively communicating, implementing, and evaluating through individuals and groups. Unfortunately, evidence of postdecision activities indicates that few decision makers are either careful or unbiased in following up their decisions (Reitz, 1977).

In terms of contribution to achieving the objectives for which the choice was made, it must be effectively implemented. In other words, there is no difference between no decision at all and an ineffective decision. Since good decisions may become poor decisions if improperly implemented, the decision maker should follow through and answer the following questions (Scanlan, 1973):

1. What must be done?
2. In what sequence must it be done?
3. Who should do what must be done?
4. How can these activities be most effectively accomplished?

In short, given the importance of implementation, it appears that this activity may be of equal, if not greater value to the achievement of objectives than the actual activity of selecting the solution.

Once a plan of action has been developed, the decision must be communicated to everyone who is involved in implementing it, as well as to those who are directly or indirectly affected by it. A good deal of this section of the book, particularly Chapters 6 through 9, is concerned with concepts and behavior relevant to implementing decisions: leadership, power, communication, and persuasion, for example.

When communicating the decision, every effort should be made to use clear, concise language, pointing out the logic of the decision and stating the reasons for making it. This communication is a measure of the probable success of the decision, since it determines the degree of commitment on the part of those who must participate in the implementation. Clearly, even the most technically sound decision can easily be undermined by those who are dissatisfied and not committed to carrying it out successfully.

Once a decision has been implemented, the decision maker cannot assume that the outcome will meet the original objective. Instead, effective management involves a monitoring system that measures the actual results and compares them with the planned results. If deviations between the actual and planned results exist, then modifications in the solution, its implementation, or the objective are necessary. Obviously, the existence of measurable objectives is an important component of the evaluation and control process, for without them judging performance is difficult. This control and evaluation process is illustrated by the following example.

During the past five years, Woodbrook, a proprietary hospital located in a major metropolitan area, has experienced increasing difficulty in hiring staff nurses. The chief administrator and the director of nursing service have reviewed their current recruiting program, evaluated several new approaches, and decided on hiring professional recruiters to recruit new nursing graduates from NLN-accredited schools across the nation. In order to bring the nursing staff up to an acceptable level, both the administrator and the nursing director agree that a fifteen percent increase per year for the next three years would be desirable. Assume that at the end of the first year employment had increased only five percent; either the original objective was overstated, the use of professional recruiters (the selected alternative) to achieve the objective was not appropriate, or the wrong recruiters were selected (implementation). If the original objective must be revised, then the entire decision-making process will be reactivated.

In this section of the chapter, some of the more significant aspects of the decision-making process were explored. It was established that decision making consists of a series of sequential and reiterative activities that facilitate the decision maker's need to solve problems. Recall that the steps in the process involved:

1. Recognizing a problem, which involves determining whether the problem merits solving and whether there is a feasible solution

2. Searching for and processing information that was obtained so that alternative solutions can be evaluated to develop a plan for problem resolution

3. Evaluating alternatives, focusing on selecting either an optimal or at least a satisfactory solution

There are advantages and disadvantages to choosing either an optimal or a satisficing alternative, which need to be determined and evaluated in order to select the most appropriate alternative under the prevailing conditions. The decision, when made, is converted into an action, which involves the postdecision activities of implementing the decision as well as communicating and evaluating the choice. Now that the decision process has been described, the next step is to discuss the types of problems that typically require decision-making activities and the criteria used to evaluate the decision.

THE PROBLEM

All decisions begin with a problem, which can be either extremely simple or complex, involving many people and variables. A problem can easily be defined as an obstacle to a goal. Such a definition has at least three advantages (Reitz, 1977, pp. 159-160):

1. It helps to distinguish problems from symptoms.

2. It suggests criteria for evaluating the effectiveness of alternative solutions.

3. Defining the problem in terms of the goal may in itself suggest possible alternatives and help avoid restricting the alternatives considered.

The types of problems that decision makers face vary according to the time frame necessary to make and implement them and the degree of structure or routineness that characterizes them, as well as whether they deal with evaluation or allocation and whether they are organizational or individual problems.

One way to categorize decisions is under the subheadings, administrative or strategic. *Administrative* decisions deal with day-to-day activities in the organization and "are concerned with short-range efficiency" (Duncan, 1978, p. 260). The decisions may include who goes to lunch when or who has which holidays off. In contrast, *strategic* decisions refer to long-range problems that affect the organization's survival and that often have some uncontrollable aspects. Examples include economic conditions, supply of nursing work force, and patients needing or desiring services at a specific agency.

Decisions can also be categorized as either *programmed* (structured) or *nonprogrammed* (unstructured). If a situation occurs fairly often, a routine procedure will usually be identified for solving it. "Thus, decisions are programmed to the extent that they are repetitive and routine and a definite procedure has been developed for handling them" (Gibson, 1976, p. 342). Examples of programmed decisions would include a hospital's admitting procedure or a university's standard as to what grade-point average will keep a student in academic good standing.

Other situations arise that are much less structured than the examples cited above, and these necessitate a novel or *nonprogrammed* decision. A nonprogrammed decision requires a creative response to a new problem that has not previously occurred or is of greater complexity than it was previously. Nonprogrammed decisions include the purchase of new equipment or the construction and staffing of new facilities.

Reitz (1977) differentiates decisions as either evaluative or allocative. Basically, all decisions require some degree of *evaluation* in order to sort out and weigh the alternatives. Certain decisions, such as performance appraisal of employees and grading of students as well as program appraisal, are almost entirely evaluative. In both performance and program appraisal either people or activities are measured against a set of objective standards. Just as all decisions have an evaluative component, so also do they generally deal with the *allocation* of resources (time, people, money, physical facilities).

Throughout the health care system, decisions are made at both the organizational and the individual levels. Whereas many of the decisions just mentioned are made at the organizational level, their effectiveness is often dependent on individual decisions regarding participation and production. The most noteworthy organizational goals can become dismal failures if employees fail to implement them. Whether people choose to participate in the implementation of a decision is largely dependent on individual perceptions of the value, risks, and other consequences of their participation. Not only are there several ways of categorizing decisions, but several criteria can be noted that help to classify decisions.

THE DECISION ITSELF

Decisions can be classified according to *efficiency* and *effectiveness* criteria. "Efficiency is a measure of what an organization gets out of a decision relative to what it puts into it" (Reitz, 1977, p. 158). Thus, if hospital A takes three days and four committee meetings of two hours each, and hospital B takes one two-hour meeting to make the same decision, then B has been more efficient. Two major efficiency criteria pertain to cost and time. Cost includes man-hours spent in gathering information, discussing options, and reaching a decision. Other costs include information processing (e.g., secretarial assistance, photocopying, computer time) as well as outside help from consultants. Time is a pertinent factor, since long delays in arriving at decisions may have hidden costs such as patients seeking care elsewhere or staff turnover.

In contrast, "effectiveness in decision making is the extent to which a decision solves a problem" (Reitz, 1977, p. 158). The effectiveness of any decision can usually be measured according to either accuracy or feasibility. *Accuracy* refers to how well the decision correctly evaluates the information, assesses the costs and benefits of alternatives, and determines the best alternative under the prevailing circumstances. Effectiveness can also be measured according to *feasibility* for actually carrying out the plan. The most accurate decision will fall short of its goal if work force or other resources are unavailable for its implementation. Most decisions require support from a wide range of people in order to implement them as planned.

Several conditions affect the implementation of any decision, including degree of certainty, risk, uncertainty, and novelty. Decisions made in an environment where the level of predictability is well known are made under conditions of *certainty;* that is, the probability that a designated outcome will occur is high. This is in contrast to decisions made under *uncertain* conditions, where there is little information or previous experience on which accurate predictions of outcome can be based. "Selection of strategies under uncertainty conditions requires the application of judgment, opinion, belief, subjective estimates of the situation, plus whatever objective data is available" (Scott and Mitchell, 1976, p. 215).

There is some degree of *risk* or chance of failure in all decisions. In a high-risk decision the chances of failure are great, whereas success is far more likely to occur in a low-risk decision. People are generally willing to take more risks in decisions when their outcome is relatively unimportant. Also, people are more likely to take greater risks in certain as opposed to uncertain conditions. Governments, military, sports teams, and some organizations use spies to reduce uncertainty about the activities of their opponents or rivals (Reitz, 1977).

Another important characteristic that affects decision making is *novelty.* Some decisions become routine and the actions attached to them can be almost automatically implemented. For example, students develop a routine response to writing a paper or preparing for an exam. Some students prepare well in advance of the deadline, whereas others are motivated into action only the day before the paper is due or the exam is scheduled. Sometimes a problem or situation may change so dramatically that old established responses are no longer effective and new ones must be developed.

Novel decisions require creativity and innovation and often cause considerable anxiety as old approaches are applied that often fail to provide a solution.

Decision making can be viewed as a type of problem solving that moves through a sequence of steps. The degree to which all steps in the problem-solving approach are employed depends on the amount of predictability associated with the decision. Routine programmed decisions made under conditions of certainty require less focusing on evaluation of alternatives than do novel, nonprogrammed decisions, especially those made under uncertain conditions.

THE INDIVIDUAL AS DECISION MAKER

The outcome of decision-making activities is influenced by the characteristics of the person who is making the decisions. Each individual is subject to a variety of internal and external forces that affect the way in which problem solving is approached. Personal differences are seen in the varying ways in which people perceive problems, the extent of their search for alternative solutions, the quality of the data analyzed to arrive at a decision, and ultimately, the choice that is made. No two people can be expected to view a situation in exactly the same way, since each brings a unique heredity, set of experiences, perceptions, and goals. More specifically, each decision maker is influenced by the following set of factors: perception of the problem; personal value system; ability to process information; various personality factors, including confidence, self-esteem, dogmatism, propensity for taking risks, and the ability to tolerate dissonance; and several personal and physiological factors.

Perception of the problem

Perception is a psychological process that helps people make sense of what they see, hear, feel, taste, or smell. This process blends incoming information with that collected from past experiences to interpret and attach meaning to stimuli. Perception is essentially a selection process by which people choose, organize, and interpret sensory stimulation in a coherent picture. Perception is closely related to observation, which is an active process involving the rating of a fact or event. A person's perception often affects what is observed. Two people rarely witness the same event and perceive its significance in the same way. For example, two women might see a man running down the street carrying a purse. One woman whose home was recently robbed may perceive the man to be a purse snatcher, whereas the other woman may think he is hurriedly taking the purse to someone who inadvertently left it in his office. An individual's perception is usually influenced by:

1. Physiological and psychological status
2. Cultural, social, and philosophical background
3. The accuracy of sense organs
4. Past experiences associated with the present situation
5. Interests, attitudes, and knowledge
6. Environmental conditions/distractions

Thus, perception is crucial at the very beginning of the decision-making process because of the importance of determining what are identified as the problem, alternatives, resources, and constraints.

Personal value system

Values refer to a person's set of beliefs, attitudes, and opinions about the worth or significance of a thought, object, or behavior. The value system develops slowly throughout life and is learned through interactions with others such as family, peers, and teachers. The values an individual holds structure what seems right and wrong, good and bad, pleasant and unpleasant. For example, children raised in families where taking supplies from work is seen as stealing will likely have different values about property than children raised in a family where considerable resources were regularly "brought home."

In the decision-making context, values serve as guidelines that a person uses in making choices.

Values are significant determinants of action at each stage of the decision-making process, since they influence each thought and action. Specifically, values influence (Gibson et al., 1976, p. 349):

1. The statement of the problem
2. The establishment of objectives and priorities for solving the problem
3. The delineation of alternative solutions
4. The prioritizing and selection of an alternative
5. The way in which the alternative chosen is implemented
6. Whether and how evaluation will be conducted

Since values pervade the entire decision-making process, it is important for people to recognize their personal values. Some decision makers value efficiency more than personal satisfaction among employees. It is important to know the most influential values and communicate them clearly to others when necessary.

Ability to process information

In addition to differences in perception and values, decision makers have varying ability and/or willingness to process information. Some decision makers prefer to select choices from a skeleton quantity of information. This type of decision maker may feel confident in the ability to be incisive in determining the "real" problem with minimal peripheral information. This may be a "just give me the facts" decision maker. In contrast, other decision makers desire all possible information before making a choice.

The effect of differences in the ability to process and store information is most evident in the search for and analysis of data and in the development of alternative solutions (Sisk, 1973, p. 246). The breadth of a person's willingness to deal with information is considered to vary from open-mindedness to closed-mindedness. The open-minded decision maker is more flexible and willing to consider more data about the problem as well as a greater number of alternative solutions. In contrast, closed-minded decision makers tend to focus on solutions that support their personal choice.

Not only do decision makers differ in their ability and willingness to entertain information, but wide variations exist in the manner in which they handle information. Some people are outstanding in their ability to collect data, while others excel at the stage of synthesis and interpretation (Sisk, 1973). It is important for people to recognize where their strengths and limitations are, so that deficits can be overcome by such means as collaboration with a colleague who excels in a key area.

Personality factors

A person's personality affects the choices that are made. Three key personality factors include confidence, self-esteem, and dogmatism. In general, self-esteem can be considered the level of regard that people hold for themselves. From this description it can be proposed that self-esteem and confidence are related.

People with high self-esteem tend to weather a failure without an undue lowering of their self-view. They are able to say, "Everyone makes mistakes. My judgment was poor this time, but I can learn from this and make a better decision next time." People with high self-esteem are confident of their overall ability and do not suffer unnecessarily over isolated failures. In contrast, people with low self-esteem are resistant to changing their self-view after successes. They may attribute the positive outcome to chance and be unable to recognize their ability.

People differ in their level of dogmatism, or their tendency to hold firmly to previously conceived beliefs, even in the face of contrary evidence. Highly dogmatic people tend to accept authority more readily than those who are low in dogmatism. People who are highly dogmatic often have difficulty acknowledging that they have made errors and also do not readily accept the suggestions of others. The exception may be seen when suggestions come from acknowledged experts. In contrast, minimally dogmatic people have been found

to discount information from recognized experts (Sisk, 1973). It seems likely that dogmatism plays a role in decision making, but both high and low ends of the continuum demonstrate lack of maximal decision-making effectiveness.

Propensity for risk

People differ dramatically in their willingness to take risks, as seen in the driving patterns of any ten people. Some drivers when trying to move out onto a busy street will attempt to outrun oncoming traffic, whereas others wait until not a single car is approaching before making their carefully gauged entry. Decision makers with considerable ability to tolerate risk will establish different objectives, view alternatives differently, and make a different choice, than will their low-risk counterparts. In fact, some people thrive in high-risk situations where their decisions have a "let's beat the probability of losing" theme. In general, people are more willing to accept risks when they are making group as opposed to individual decisions. The responsibility and accountability is more diluted in a group than in a solo decision. Hence it is often easier to say, "*We* really made a mistake," than "*I* really made a mistake" (Gibson et al., 1976).

Tolerance for dissonance

People differ not only in their predecision behaviors, but also in their postdecision level of comfort. Festinger (1957) labeled the occurrence of postdecision anxiety as "cognitive dissonance," which refers to the lack of harmony among a person's cognitions (e.g., beliefs and attitudes) after a decision is made. This may be seen in a conflict between what the decision maker knows and believes, and what was done. When this conflict exists, the decision maker will have second thoughts about the choice. The level of anxiety is usually greater when (Festinger, 1957):

1. The decision has important financial and/or psychological implications.
2. There are several foregone alternatives.

3. The nonchosen alternatives have a number of positive aspects.

Since each of these conditions is present in a wide range of decisions, postdecision dissonance is common. It can be reduced by acknowledging that a mistake has been made and considering more desirable alternatives for similar future situations. Unfortunately, many people have great difficulty admitting that they made an error. Instead, they try to deal with the dissonance by: (1) seeking additional information that supports their choice; (2) perceiving only selected parts of the available information; or (3) changing their attitude so as to view the alternatives that were initially available in an unsatisfactory fashion or trying to forget and avoid all awareness of the negative aspects by focusing exclusively on the positive elements.

Each of us experiences cognitive dissonance and attempts in our unique way to cope. The potential for dissonance is affected greatly by a person's personality, especially the level of self-confidence and the degree to which one can be persuaded by others. For example, confident people can generally say, "I goofed," and live with the consequences, instead of being consumed with wondering, "If I had only . . ." Further, people who are easily persuaded by others, often from fear of rejection, may suffer dissonance when they realize that the choice made was not what they really wanted to do.

Personal characteristics

Characteristics such as age, sex, and intelligence can have an effect on decision-making ability, although no clear-cut relationship has been found. For example, there are few data to support the notion that people make "better" decisions when they are thirty than when they are fifty. Too many intervening variables must be considered to define a definite relationship between *age* and decision-making ability. The previously discussed variables, including perception, experience, and personality, have a more observable impact on decision making than does age.

Likewise, research does not support the idea that members of one *sex* have a greater innate capacity to make decisions. Although it has been inferred that women, because of their empathy, insight, and compassion, make better decisions, this has not been confirmed with empirical research.

There are few clear-cut data to confirm a positive relationship between *intelligence* and decision-making ability. From past experience, many of us could say that common sense and good judgment, as well as the ability to learn from previous situations, have a greater influence on decision making than does an intelligence quotient (Reitz, 1977).

Physiological factors

Key physiological factors that influence the decision-making process include fatigue, alcohol, and drugs. Everyone has had to make decisions when *fatigued*. After a long day at school or work, especially when everything seemed to go wrong, just deciding what to eat for dinner may seem like a monumental decision. It is not fatigue per se, but the level of fatigue, that is critical to decision making. For example, a moderate amount of exertion, such as in running or swimming, tends to sharpen decision-making capacity, especially when information from short-term memory is required. In contrast, extreme exhaustion impairs the ability to consider the situation carefully because new information is not welcomed at this time.

Both *drugs* and *alcohol* impair cognitive abilities and affect decision-making ability. Alcohol and many drugs are central nervous system depressants and, in moderate amounts, impair perception and mental processing of information. In contrast, drugs such as amphetamines speed up mental processing and often cause the person to ignore key variables.

Thus decision making is influenced by a variety of personal factors. No two people are equally skilled in decision making. Likewise, given the same sets of information, each one of a group of people would arrive at different solutions. The entire group might select the same solution, but there would be unique rationales, procedures, and expectations.

GROUP DECISION MAKING

Although group decision making seems to be increasing, there is debate as to its level of effectiveness. Generally it takes groups longer to make a decision than it would take an individual. On the other hand, because a group can provide greater information, sounder decisions are frequently made by groups than by individuals in that more variables can be considered. All too often, open and honest group discussion is hampered by a feeling of pressure to conform, fear of reprisal, and the influence of a dominant personality or a member who is perceived as having greater status than the other members.

Certain decisions seem to be more amenable to group efforts. In particular, nonprogrammed or novel decisions usually call for pooled talent, whereas routine or more programmed decisions lend themselves to more effective individual decisions. In nonprogrammed decisions, groups are effective in:
1. Establishing objectives since greater knowledge is available
2. Identifying alternatives because a broad range of potential choices can be presented
3. Evaluating alternatives because of the collective information and viewpoints of a group
4. Choosing an alternative; people are more likely to accept a risk when working as a group than when responsibility lies with one person

In contrast, when decisions need to be implemented, whether they are made by individuals or groups, it is the responsibility of individuals actually to carry out the actions. Few organizations function without groups, yet there are both advantages and disadvantages to group participation in decision making.

One of the major advantages of group decision making is that a potentially wider range of knowledge is available in a group than with any single member. Members bring different backgrounds, experiences, and knowledge to the decision process, thus providing an increased number of choices. Also, members are more likely to accept the decision if they have been a participant; further, the chances of having commitment to the enactment of the decision are greater if all members were involved. For example, primary nursing is more likely to be effectively implemented if staff nurses were involved in the decision to try this form of nursing practice, as opposed to being informed by the head nurse that primary nursing will begin Monday.

The disadvantages of group decision making include the amount of time involved and also the potential for some members to pressure others into conforming with the majority view. Additionally, in hospitals as in other organizations, there always exists a superior-subordinate hierarchy. Subordinates may agree to group decisions that conflict with their personal views if they fear the consequences of disagreeing, or if they are seeking to obtain the favor of a superior. The desire for acceptance by other members may also motivate acquiescence. In any group there is the potential for domination by one or two members, which diminishes participation and equality of decisions. Further, some people feel less commitment to a group than to an individual decision.

To date, only one effort has been made systematically to integrate group and individual decision making. Vroom and Yetton's decision theory represents an effort to specify the parameters that influence the decision as to who should be included in the decision process (Scott and Mitchell, 1976). They postulate that managers involved in making decisions have five possible alternatives, ranging from the manager making the decision using available information at the time, to the choice of sharing the problem with subordinates and requesting a group problem-solving effort. They have attempted to identify the properties of the decision that would specify the best approach for effective problem solving. Basically, Vroom and Yetton

(1973) conceptualize the manager's task as determining how the problem is to be solved, rather than as determining the actual solution to the problem. This implies that there is no one best way to handle problems, but the strategy selected should be dependent on the properties of the situation.

THE DECISION-MAKING ENVIRONMENT

Hospitals, like other organizations, are open systems and, as such, are responsive to and affected by a variety of environments. Open systems are affected by their subsystems as well as by interactions with a variety of external environments. The external environment of health care agencies includes the economic, social, and political system. Many of the variables in the external environment cannot be controlled, but they must be understood. Economic conditions affect decision making, as do technological variables. The availability of new machinery and health care aids can make a dramatic difference in the types of services that may be offered.

Political, legal, and regulatory changes also have an impact on the range of decisions that can be made. Many decisions would reflect poor judgment because of the local, state, or federal regulations that affect enactment of certain actions. In many institutions, the guidelines of the Joint Commission on the Accreditation of Hospitals have a tremendous influence on personnel, services, and setting. The decision maker also needs to identify the cultural and social changes that will affect goal attainment (Gibson et al., 1976). For example, consider the impact that the environmentalists have had on many industries, including health care. Similarly, the women's rights movement as well as civil rights activities have greatly influenced the decisions that can be made in terms of personnel.

Within any environment, several *physical* factors affect the decisions made. For example, time pressures as well as physical discomforts and distractions may determine the care and attention that is devoted to decision making. The amount of time available for making the decision often determines how much information can be considered in determining objectives, examining alternatives, and selecting a course of action. Much discussion has involved whether working conditions actually affect decision making. "In general, physical discomforts and distractions can impair decision-making by causing the decision-maker to overlook or ignore relevant information" (Reitz, 1977, p. 181).

DECISION AIDS

Since most decisions involve varying degrees of certainty, a variety of tools or aids have been developed to minimize uncertainty.* Two major developments in the 1960s and 1970s dramatically increased the ability to handle complex problems. First, electronic advancements in data processing expanded decision makers' ability to "record, store, manipulate and call forth vast amounts of information" (Scott and Mitchell, 1976, p. 232). Second, a wide range of decision models aid the handling of information in order to make rational choices. The major categories of aids to be discussed in this chapter include PERT (program evaluation and review technique), CPM (critical path method), and OR (operations research).

The first two techniques were specifically developed for management decision making and they attempt to describe the components of the task, their sequencing, and the expected completion time. An example of these models is seen in Fig. 10-4, where each node at the end of an arrow illustrates the beginning and end of an activity. Each sequential activity is dependent on the successful completion of a prior one. For example, it would not be appropriate to work on activity eight before one and four were mastered.

Specifically, PERT involves identifying key activities, sequencing them in a flow diagram, and assigning the expected duration time for each phase of the project. In regard to the time component, PERT deals with uncertainty in three ways: (1) the

*For a comprehensive discussion of decision aids, see Albert, 1978.

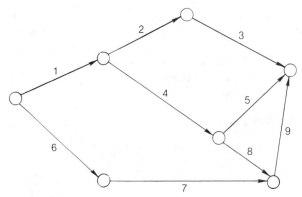

FIG. 10-4
Decision aid model for path analysis (PERT and CPM).

optimistic time (t_o), which refers to anticipated completion time assuming that no complications arise; (2) the most likely time (t_m), which estimates completion time by taking into account the typical range of problems that can be expected; and (3) the pessimistic time (t_p), which estimates completion time with the assumption that the maximal number of problems possible will occur (Marriner, 1980, p. 8). In order to plan in terms of the expected time, the following formula can be employed:

$$t_e = \frac{t_o + 4(t_m) + t_p}{6}$$

If you hope to complete the project in two weeks, the optimistic time is 2. You may know from past experience that delays such as those needed for materials to arrive or subgroups to complete their assignments must be considered, so the most likely time is 6 weeks. Your greatest fear (of encountering major resource or personnel obstacles) could cause the pessimistic time to extend to 12 weeks. Based on these projections, the estimated time is calculated as:

$$t_e = \frac{2 \text{ weeks} + 4(6 \text{ weeks}) + (12 \text{ weeks})}{6}$$

$$= \frac{2 + 24 + 12}{6} = \frac{38}{6} = 6.33 \text{ weeks}$$

Based on this calculation, priorities can be re-evaluated and extra personnel can be employed to move the project forward, or those who will be expecting or waiting for the outcome of the project can be informed of its most likely completion date. Similarly, CPM deals with time calculations, but only handles one estimate rather than the three in PERT. CPM calculates the longest possible time estimate.

In contrast, operations research is defined as: "(1) an application of the scientific method to (2) problems arising in the operations of a system which may be represented by means of a mathematical model and (3) the solving of these problems by resolving the equations representing the system" (Churchman et al., 1957, p. 18). The very term OR, which refers to the analysis of an entire system, calls attention to the greater scope of this tool in comparison with either PERT or CPM. The specific techniques of OR require that mathematical models be used in order to solve the designated problem. Specific OR techniques include linear programming, queuing theory, game theory, and probability theory.

Linear programming is most effective in situations requiring that limited resources be allocated to the best possible advantage. As the name implies, linear programming deals primarily with mathematically determining the linear relationship that exists between parts and the limits that must be calculated. Three conditions must exist before linear programming is needed: (1) either a minimal or a maximal value is desired in order to optimize goal attainment; (2) the variables affecting the goal must have a linear relationship; and (3) some constraints or obstacles can be determined and if no obstacles are present or anticipated, then the process is unnecessary (Marriner, 1980). Linear programming ranges from simple observations to complex computer-handled problems. Examples of nursing activities that may apply linear programming include the determination of a new health clinic within an existing network and the determination of class size based on the number of students who need or desire the course, the number of faculty, and the hours available to teach the course.

Queuing theory, sometimes called "waiting-line theory," is especially useful in determining the correct balance of factors necessary to handle intermittent service. It is particularly useful when the units arriving for service arrive on a random schedule but essentially require the same length of time for service. This can be seen in customers arriving at a restaurant and clients coming to a clinic, such as one devoted to family planning. Queuing techniques could be employed to balance the cost of waiting against the cost of overcoming the need to wait (e.g., employing more personnel).

In many instances, actual observations of the number of units requesting service can be made and a total can be tallied. For example, the number of people seeking services at Planned Parenthood can be recorded and staffing determinations can be made accordingly. In many instances, such observations cannot be carried out for a sufficient length of time to produce a clear picture, therefore the Monte Carlo technique may be applied. This technique is employed to produce a sample of random occurrence of the situation. "Essentially, the Monte Carlo technique provides a large sample of random numbers that may be generated by a computer. From the large Monte Carlo sample, rather precise determinations may be made in regard to the

expected servicing load for each hour of the day" (Sisk, 1973, p. 242).

Game theory is a simulation technique where a model of reality is used to simplify problems by identifying their basic parts and using trial-and-error practices to arrive at a potential solution. A well-known application of game theory is the "war game" approach, which has been widely used in the military. Games allow decision makers to evaluate a variety of alternatives with minimal cost and consequences. Essentially, the game provides a model for simplifying system operations where participants can try to develop strategies that will maximize their gains and minimize the losses or consequences. Management games are more frequently used to train personnel than to solve real problems.

Probability theory is particularly useful for determining the degree of risk involved in each potential solution. The basic assumption underlying probability theory is that factors occur in a predictable pattern. In terms of a coin toss, if a penny were tossed ten times it is probable that heads would occur five times and tails five times.

Limitations of operations research refer to the inability actually to make the final choice. Operations research is valuable because it contributes to the analysis and development of alternatives and potential outcomes. Its effectiveness is limited to the "analyses and comparison of relationships that may be expressed quantitatively and transformed into a mathematical model" (Sisk, 1973, p. 244).

SUMMARY

Decision making is the core of planned change. The capacity of an individual, group, or organization to grow and develop is largely dependent on their ability to use the decision-making process effectively. Effective decision making involves a step-by-step approach in which the nurse: (1) identifies the problem; (2) develops goals, objectives, and outcome criteria; (3) develops, evaluates, and chooses alternatives; (4) implements the decision; and (5) evaluates the outcome of the decision. This chapter explored two general models for making decisions: normative and descriptive. The descriptive model was discussed in depth because it describes how a person actually makes decisions; in order to explore fully the descriptive model, each stage of the decision-making process was discussed so that application could be made to real situations. Several types of problems were mentioned that typically require the application of decision-making skills, and decisions were also classified according to their efficiency and effectiveness.

Since decisions involve people, several behavioral aspects of decision making were considered, including the merits of individuals as opposed to groups as decision-making bodies; human qualities such as perception, values, the ability to process information; and personality factors, including the ability to tolerate risk or dissonance. Further, personal characteristics such as intelligence and selected physiological factors were mentioned, since they play key roles in the effectiveness of the decisions that are made. How people feel and think, as well as their personal needs, goals, and drives affect the choices they make. Most decisions have implications for more than just the one making the choice, hence the importance of a keen appreciation for and understanding of the behavioral aspects of decision making must be emphasized.

The chapter briefly touched on the environment in which decisions are made when it pointed out the need to appreciate the fact that health care organizations are open systems that receive information from multiple sources. Also, the results of decisions have multiple effects in the health care industry. Political, legal, regulatory, and human-relations influences have a tremendous amount of power in determining the decisions that are made.

The last section of the chapter identified several decision aids including PERT, CPM, and OR. Specific types of OR that were mentioned included linear programming, queuing theory, game theory, and probability theory. Each of these aids has useful applicability in a complex decision-making environment such as that in which nurses, especially those acting as change agents, find themselves.

REFERENCES

Albert, D.A.: Decision theory in medicine: a review and critique, Milbank Mem. Fund Q. **56:**363-401, 1978.

Carroll, L. (pseudonym for Dodgson, C.L.): Alice in Wonderland, New York, 1950, Arcadia House.

Churchman, C.A., Ackoff, R.L., and Arnoff, E.L.: Introduction to operations research, New York, 1957, John Wiley & Sons, Inc.

Dewey, J.: How we think, Boston, 1910, D.C. Heath & Co.

Duncan, W.J.: Decision making and social issues, Hinsdale, Ill., 1973, The Dryden Press.

Duncan, W.J.: Essentials of management, ed. 2, Hinsdale, Ill., 1978, The Dryden Press.

Duncan, W.J.: Organizational behavior, ed. 2, Boston, 1981, Houghton-Mifflin Co.

Festinger, L.: A theory of cognitive dissonance, New York, 1957, Harper & Row, Publishers.

Gibson, J.L., Ivancevich, J.M., and Donnelly, J.H.: Organizations: structure, processes, behavior, Dallas, 1973, Business Publications, Inc.

Gibson, J.L., Ivancevich, J.M., and Donnelly, J.H.: Organizations: structure, processes, behavior, rev. ed., Dallas, 1976, Business Publications, Inc.

Kotler, P.: Behavioral models for analyzing buyers, J. Marketing **29:**37-45, Oct. 1965.

March, J.G., and Simon, H.A.: Organizations, New York, 1958, John Wiley & Sons, Inc.

Marriner, A.: Guide to nursing management, St. Louis, 1980, The C.V. Mosby Co.

Reitz, H.J.: Behavior in organizations, Homewood, Ill., 1977, Richard D. Irwin, Inc.

Scanlan, B.K.: Principles of management and organizational behavior, New York, 1973, John Wiley & Sons, Inc.

Scott, W.G., and Mitchell, T.R.: Organization theory: a structural and behavioral analysis, ed. 2, Homewood, Ill., 1976, Richard D. Irwin, Inc.

Simon, H.A.: Administrative behavior, ed. 3, New York, 1976, The Free Press.

Sisk, H.L.: Management and organization, ed. 2, Cincinnati, Ohio, 1973, South-Western Publishing Co.

Stigler, G.J.: The economics of information, J. Political Economy **69:**213-225, June 1961.

Vroom, V.H., and Yetton, P.W.: Leadership and decision making, Pittsburgh, Pa., 1973, University of Pennsylvania Press.

PART TWO

THE ENVIRONMENT IN WHICH CHANGE OCCURS

constraints and facilitating forces

The health care system is often described as either a "nonsystem" or a system in disequilibrium. Critics of the current health care delivery system in the United States contend that the country that has attained the highest level of competence in medical technology and the education of health professionals has fallen far short of meeting consumers' health care needs. Even though the United States has the highest income levels and largest percentage of the gross national product earmarked for health care, as a nation it does not rank in the top ten countries of the world in terms of overall health status of the populace when traditional health indexes are cited.

It is essential that a nurse who seeks to implement a change-agent role be well informed about the status of health care delivery in the United States and also be clearly aware of the constraints as well as facilitating factors for change in the current health care system. The necessity for such documentation will be provided, followed by a brief overview of the content included in Part Two.

SOCIAL AND ENVIRONMENTAL CHANGES

In the United States at the beginning of the twentieth century, the major causes of morbidity and mortality were attributed to infectious diseases. In striking contrast, in recent years chronic diseases, accidents, and the results of human violence have accounted for the major portion of morbidity and mortality instances. In earlier times when infections prevailed, as well as in the current era, health has been derived largely from the complex interaction that occurs between individuals and the multiple environments in which they exist. The environment consists of physical, sociocultural, and psychological components. Because of the confluence of physical, social, cultural, and behavioral factors, all of which play a significant role in the major diseases of today, a multifaceted approach to health care is essential. Moreover, a wide variety of forces in contemporary society influence the national health status.

As Toffler (1979) so aptly points out, "the more change we pump into a system the more strange it becomes to us." He acknowledges that at present Americans are living in a very strange environment that is constantly and rapidly changing. The greater the number of changes, the greater the diversity, which in turn requires increased abilities on the part of participants to keep pace. Because of rapid change and the subsequent introduction of unfamiliar aspects into the environment, individuals are likely to experience greater amounts of stress and therefore find it more and more difficult to make accurate, informed decisions.

The key to keeping abreast of rapid change so as to make the most positive responses possible lies in the clear and careful delineation of goals. Part One dealt with theoretical formulations that provide information useful in the goal-setting process. Part Two goes on to provide information about a variety of social and professional issues that have an effect on the ability to make changes within the health care system. Thus the nursing role is to keep pace with inevitable change and to adapt in a positive manner, as well as to be the producer of additional change that motivates both health consumers and providers toward a positive health orientation.

FAMILY CHANGES

In recent years a variety of changes in both the structure and functioning of the family have had an influence on social, psychological, and physical health. The most visible trend is the increased number of working mothers. Specifically, in recent years a dramatic increase in the work force of women with children under 18 years of age has occurred. More mothers are working now than in previous years, not only because of the high cost of living and the subsequent need for income, but also the escalating numbers of single parents and the awakening of many women to the challenges that can be gained by a career.

Other changes within the family that influence health care include the fact that approximately twenty percent of the population relocate annually. Family mobility means that parents and children alike must establish new support systems, become familiar with entirely new surroundings, and adjust to the loss of friends and established patterns.

Also, as the life span increases more families are called on to make provisions for elderly relatives. In previous generations the home was the traditional site of care for both the elderly and the ill; in recent years more families have turned toward external systems to provide care. Such a trend may ease the day-to-day responsibilities of the family, but it inevitably leads to marked increases in health care costs.

HEALTH CARE COSTS

Since the health care industry is labor intensive, the work force is a valid consideration in any discussion of constraints and facilitators of change. Two major issues in the health care work force deal with the size of the needed pool of providers and how they will be distributed. Over the past three decades the health care industry has expanded exponentially, with vast increases in the work force as well as a constantly increasing proportion of the gross national product devoted to health care. In an era of diminishing resources, the question of who will be reimbursed becomes a key issue. Nursing's challenge is to maintain itself as a viable and essential source for the health work force by astutely responding to the changing times so as to provide effective and efficient care.

To date, hospitals have accounted for the largest portion of the "health care financing pie." The flow of fiscal resources into hospitals is subject to increasing constraints and regulations. Hospitals are being called on by health planning agencies to justify their need for substantial expenditures. As a direct result of the high costs involved in building and supporting hospitals, new modes of care are gaining popularity. A variety of ambulatory services have been developed that may well prove to be highly cost effective. Health maintenance organizations (HMOs), neighborhood health centers, home health care services, and programs for community mental health all promise high-quality care

at lower costs than conventional institutional settings can provide.

GOVERNMENTAL INFLUENCES ON HEALTH

Nurses who are currently involved in the health care system cannot disregard the role the government plays. Although the government neither totally finances nor solely operates the health care industry, its influence is felt in all sectors. Government funds do provide considerable direct as well as indirect health services via local, state, and federally subsidized institutions, including health departments and community mental health centers. Not only does the government provide funds, it also regulates through an array of policies and guidelines. Most governmental funding is provided to local agencies only if they meet certain standards and guidelines.

Hence any attempts to deal with change must consider the impact on nursing that the government exerts. Nurses are becoming more cognizant of their obligation not only to become informed but also to become involved in governmental policy decisions that have phenomenal influence on nursing practice.

PROFESSIONAL AND ETHICAL CHALLENGES

The nursing profession as a collective entity has always been notoriously divided. Such infighting and warring factions can no longer exist if nursing is to assume a vital role in the determination of health priorities. Nurses must work as a unified, informed body through their professional organizations in order to influence health policy. Such a role requires, in addition to professional unity, a well-informed and sophisticated orientation toward the political and legislative process. The time is long since past when nursing as a vital health profession could afford simply to react to change; instead, nursing must initiate change and be well prepared for the expected ramifications.

Nurses must also recognize and become better able to cope with the ethical decisions that will arise as health resources decrease and health care needs increase. The basic concern of the nursing profession is with the whole person. As both an art and science and morally, nursing must be basically concerned with the welfare of clients. Its technological and caring skills are developed to promote and enhance life or provide individuals with the resources to "die with dignity." In order to deal with the rapidly occurring social changes in a fashion that reflects an ethical commitment to oneself, to nursing as a profession, and to the clients who are served as well, each nurse must develop a "personal code which reflects their values and ethics" (Silva, 1974, p. 2007).

REFERENCES

Silva, M.C.: Science, ethics and nursing, Am. J. Nurs. **74:** 2004-2007, Nov. 1974.

Toffler, A.: Focus on the future, Keynote Address, National League for Nursing Convention, Atlanta, Ga., May 1979.

It is a truism that the purpose of health care is to promote health. Yet most observers of the health care system would agree that it deals with disease, not with health.

11

HEALTH AND HEALTH CARE DELIVERY SYSTEMS

Wade Lancaster

Health is a topic of concern—either directly or indirectly, individually or collectively, consciously or unconsciously—to every member of American society. Health, inextricably linked with all aspects of life, is a prerequisite for executing the many diverse chores and obligations that individuals incur throughout life. Conceptually, the term health is related to the notion of well-being; it no longer is an end in itself—if it ever was—but a means for attaining optimal social well-being within the constraints of the physical, social, and biological environment in which people find themselves. Health can no longer be viewed out of context of the social and economic aspects of daily living. Health is not just "feeling good," but a broad concept that embraces the social, mental, and physical aspects of human well-being. It includes the cognitive, affective, and active domains of human behavior as it focuses not only on the individual, but also refers to the functioning abilities of the family, the community, organizations, institutions, societies, and nations. Hence health is important as a concept; it is complex and multidimensional with biological, physical, personal, professional, technical, economic, legal, political, public, social, and cultural components. In other words, health affects and is affected by a multitude of factors, wherever people live.

The purpose of this chapter is to describe the contemporary health care delivery system. In order to do this, an overview of the current health care system is provided, followed by a historical discussion that briefly traces crucial features of health care delivery in order to explain in part the present system. Subsequent to the historical account, selected definitions are presented as preliminary to a discussion of the current health care system and the development of possible models for organization of a delivery system.

OVERVIEW OF THE CURRENT ORGANIZATION OF HEALTH CARE DELIVERY

The vastness and complexity of the contemporary health care delivery system increase the dif-ficulty inherent in its description. At first glance, the health care system appears to be a conglomerate of innumerable public and private providers. In order to discuss the health care system, it is necessary first to consider the debatable topic of whether health is a right or a responsibility. It is then useful to differentiate among three key terms: health, health services, and health care system. Next, a differentiation is made between health care and medical care, as well as among the conceptualizations of health service recipients who are called either patients, clients, consumers, or customers.

Health care as a right or responsibility?

Considerable debate has taken place recently about whether health is a right for all people. Proponents of the "health as a right" position contend that no one should be denied health care; each person is entitled to all of the health care that money can buy. The opposing view holds that health is not a right but rather a responsibility of each individual. As Banta (1977, p. 22) so aptly states, "health is first and foremost the concern of the individual: he can strive for it, but the health care system cannot give it to him."

By virtue of the selection of chapters in this text, including self-care and holistic health, it is no doubt evident that the emphasis is on health as an individual responsibility. It is impossible to "give" health to anyone. Instead, health results from personal choices, actions, beliefs, values, thoughts, and the quality of the environment.

According to the Report of the Surgeon General of the United States, entitled *Healthy People* (1979), the health of Americans is better than ever before in history. There has been a dramatic reduction in infectious and communicable diseases, and a concomitant increase in degenerative diseases such as heart disease, stroke, and cancer. Fig. 11-1 presents the trend in disease patterns from 1900 to 1977. As can be seen, cancer and major cardiovascular diseases have increased markedly.

In December 1977, a task force composed of representatives from all agencies within the Department of Health, Education and Welfare met to

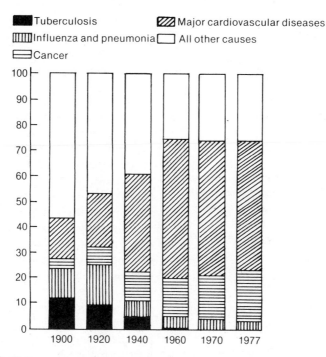

Tuberculosis   Major cardiovascular diseases
Influenza and pneumonia   All other causes
Cancer

FIG. 11-1
Deaths for selected causes as a percentage of all deaths in the
United States, selected years, 1900-1977.

(Source: National Center for Health Statistics, Division of Vital Statistics,
From Healthy people: The Surgeon General's Report on Health Promotion and Disease Prevention,
Washington, D.C., 1979, Department of HEW.)

identify and prioritize problems related to disease prevention and health promotion. This group devised a framework for approaching their task that was targeted in three areas: life-style, environment, and services. The following statements represent three key beliefs inherent in the framework (*Disease Prevention and Health Promotion,* 1978, p. 1):

1. The choices an individual makes about personal *life-style* can increase risk of health problems in a series of behavioral areas.
2. *Environment* represents settings and sources of external hazard that also increase risk of health problems.
3. The third area, *services,* represents the preventive services through which the influence

or course of preventable diseases and conditions can be influenced for any individual.

This task force further identified twelve health status goals and discussed ways to reduce the incidence of disease through increasing the focus on prevention. It seems that these goals (listed below) certainly support the position that health is a matter of personal responsibility.

The term *health* can be viewed from several levels: individual, family, community, organizational, and societal. The World Health Organization defines health as a "state of complete physical, mental and social well-being and not merely the absence of disease or infirmity" (Thomas, 1973, p. H-9). In truth, this statement is more a goal than a definition. Perhaps a more realistic definition of

---

HEALTH STATUS GOALS*

1. Reduced incidence of chronic diseases
   a. Cardiovascular
   b. Cancer
   c. Respiratory
   d. Diabetes mellitus
   e. Arthritis
   f. Neurological
   g. Other
2. Reduced incidence of communicable diseases
3. Reduced incidence of traumatic injuries and deaths (homicide, poisoning, motor vehicle accidents, etc.)
4. Reduced incidence of mental retardation and congenital defects
5. Reduced incidence of morbidity and mortality associated with pregnancy and the neonatal period
6. Reduced incidence of dental disease
7. Reduced incidence of diseases related to vision and hearing
8. Reduced incidence of emotional disorders
9. Reduced incidence of alcohol and drug abuse
10. Enhanced development of children and adolescents
11. Enhanced general physical well-being
12. Enhanced general emotional well-being

*From Disease prevention and health promotion: federal programs and prospects, Report of the Departmental Task Force on Prevention, U.S. Department of HEW, Washington, D.C., Sept. 1978, U.S. Government Printing Office.

---

health would be a state of balance in which the individual is free from disease and is reasonably comfortable in carrying out the activities of daily living. Health has traditionally been viewed as a biological state; although genetic inheritance cannot be discounted, health status results from a variety of interacting factors. It is generally recognized that health is determined by the dynamic patterns of interaction between individuals and the multiple environments in which they live. In this context, environment includes both internal and external components.

One aspect of internal environment that affects health is perception. What may seem like health to one person may be viewed as illness by another. For example, people who have severe orthopedic handicaps may not perceive themselves as being "unhealthy," while those who look at them may not consider them healthy. In many ways health is "in the eye of the beholder," with many people living productive and seemingly normal lives despite severe physical handicaps. Similarly, others view themselves as weak or "sickly" and limit the extent of their activities by assuming a "sick role" that does not clearly correlate with their outwardly obvious health status.

Not only is health affected by genetic endowment and perception; the external environment also plays a key role. The technological accomplishments of the last few decades have extracted a high price. Patterns of disease and adaptive abilities change rapidly in response to environmental conditions. In the past, the microbiological pollution of water was responsible for considerable disease; today air pollution is a far more significant problem. The majority of modern advances have altered health/disease ratios.

To elaborate on Fig. 11-1, it should be noted that in the late nineteenth century, almost half of all hospital admissions resulted from infections, including tuberculosis, malaria, typhoid, dysentery, venereal disease, and puerperal sepsis. All of these except venereal disease are now uncommon or have almost entirely been eradicated, and venereal disease seldom requires hospitalization. Whereas rheumatic fever and rheumatic heart disease have decreased tenfold since 1930, arteriosclerosis and diseases of the heart and blood vessels have tripled. In addition, half of the U.S. hospital beds are used for psychiatric patients and suicide is the tenth most prevalent cause of death. Thus health/disease patterns and ratios seem to be reflective of personal choices regarding life-style as well as genetic endowment and environmental insults such as pollution in the environment and in the foods that are consumed. From this discussion, it can be inferred that health is an individual responsibility. Since financial resources are finite, each person must assume responsibility for maintaining the highest possible level of health so as not to overtax the health care system by expecting always to be "repaired for all that ails mankind." This theme is further elaborated on in Chap. 23, which describes the concept of self-care. Two additional definitions should be set forth before a discussion of the historical and current aspects of the health care system are presented.

Health care system and health care services

The term *health care system* refers to the totality of resources that a population or society distributes in the organization and delivery of health services. The term connotes an organized effort on the part of a variety of health care providers to meet a set of predetermined health goals and objectives. These goals and objectives are attained through the enactment of a varied assortment of health services that include "all personal and public services performed by individuals or institutions for the purpose of maintaining or restoring health" (Levey and Loomba, 1973, p. 4). Health care services can be divided into two general categories: personal and community. Personal health services are directed toward the maintenance of health status of individuals. In contrast, community health services are directed toward groups and tend to reflect a public health orientation of health promotion and maintenance.

Although it is tempting to take such services as solid waste disposal, fluoridation of water, clean air, and food and drug control for granted, the maintenance of these environmental variants plays a key role in health. Thus any discussion of the health care system must acknowledge the social aspects of health, especially in view of the current major causes of morbidity and mortality. Any list that attempted to cite the elements and the commodities, as well as the services, that affect health would be virtually endless. Goods such as food, shelter, recreation, and personal care affect health, as does the general environment including such influences as pollution, crowding, and religion. Although this chapter directs attention to the personal health care component, it in no way denies the significance of community health care and the cumulative effect of the environment on health status.

Health care versus medical care

Health care has often been equated with medical care, yet these terms are not identical and must be distinguished. Health care as the product of health services is delivered through two primary vehicles: personal and public health services. The provision of health care includes the treatment of pathological conditions as well as the promotion and maintenance of health.

In contrast, medical care emphasizes the organization, financing, and delivery of personal health services and includes the services of physicians, dentists, nurses, pharmacists, hospitals, nursing homes, mental health facilities, and other health resources. Thus a major concern of medical care is the diagnosis and treatment of conditions in which health is disrupted.

HISTORICAL REVIEW OF CONTEMPORARY HEALTH CARE SYSTEM

In studying health behavior, anthropologists have found that health needs have varied through time and according to social, economic, cultural, political, and environmental factors. Each culture develops a system of health care that coincides largely with the prevailing conditions in a given country. Similarly, health providers have developed both formal and informal means of carrying out a set of culturally determined practices within a system.

Pre-Christian period

Historical records document that people, even in antiquity, were concerned with birth, illness, and death. With few exceptions, primitive tribes had a certain amount of group and community hygiene sense. In their fight for survival, they gained some knowledge of disease and devised their own measures for coping with it. It should be noted that many health care delivery practices were often based on magic and superstition rather than on health interests. Medicine was practiced in a one-to-one, healer-patient relationship by medicine men, who often were also religious leaders or high priests, held in a revered position in society (Pellegrino, 1963).

Both "the Babylonians and Egyptians" possessed medical skills that are described in their recorded history (Benson and McDevitt, 1980, p. 4). The Egyptians of about 1000 BC were the healthiest of all civilized nations. They also possessed numerous pharmaceutical preparations and constructed some of the earliest public drainage systems. Evidence also indicates that other ancient civilizations, including the Hebrew, Greek, and Roman, were remarkably knowledgeable about personal hygiene, medicine, and community responsibility (Benson and McDevitt, 1980).

The Jews extended Egyptian hygienic thought by stating in Leviticus about 1500 BC what is probably the world's first written hygienic code. Grecian civilization firmly established the delivery of health services as a humanistic responsibility for all people, and the ethics established by the Greeks still guide the medical profession. In addition, the Greeks developed a concern for personal hygiene to a degree that had not previously been approached. They devoted considerable attention to personal cleanliness, exercise, and diet, rather than focusing on environmental sanitation.

The Roman Empire is well known for its administrative and engineering accomplishments. At its zenith, this civilization organized the delivery of health care in much the same fashion as contemporary public health care, including rather sophisticated environmental sanitation measures such as water supply and sewage systems; the Romans also possessed some understanding of sanitation and contagion.

The Middle Ages

With the dawn of the Christian era there developed a reaction to all that was a reminder of the Roman Empire and its attendant paganism. During this period the early Church believed that Roman and Grecian ways of life had focused entirely too much attention on the body with a consequent void in attention to the soul.

During the Middle Ages the Church purported that disease was a result of wrongdoing and as such represented a punishment for wrongdoing. This philosophy of disease as a divine punishment interrupted much of the progressive thinking of earlier ages, which had focused more on a person-environment interaction for maintaining health.

In the Western World, this period was characterized by superstition, mysticism, disintegration of society, the return of political anarchy, and the rigorous persecution of free-thinking persons. Such a milieu clearly curtailed progress in health-related concerns, although this atmosphere did not entirely stifle medical and hygienic developments. This was an era characterized by epidemics, with leprosy and bubonic plague being the most devastating. The busy ports were entry points for many contagious diseases, and the study of infectious diseases became a necessity in order to maintain survival.

The Renaissance

The great pandemics of the Middle Ages caused considerable social and political frustrations, which led to attitudes of fatalism and general disregard for the welfare of individuals. Fortunately, there gradually developed in the minds of a few some doubt as to the teleological origin of disease as a punishment for sin, and the end of the Middle Ages saw a renewed interest in health care (Rosen, 1957).

The people of Europe, coming out of this dreadful depression period of history, slowly and cautiously began to open their eyes and to think as free individuals. During the Renaissance period, which began in Italy in the fourteenth century and lasted about 300 years, medicine began to advance. Characterized by its achievements in scholarship and the arts, and by the rise of commerce and industry, the Renaissance era was also noted for the growing spirit of humanism, and witnessed progress in science and medicine (Benson and McDevitt, 1980, p. 5). Subsequently, the concept of the dignity of humans began to be emphasized more, and the search for scientific truth was at last advocated for its own sake.

The Industrial Revolution

The Renaissance had the effect of influencing political and economic thinking, and paved the way for the development of nationalism, imperialism, and the Industrial Revolution. The false gods of power and profit were placed on higher pedestals than they had ever before occupied, and individual liberties, labors, and lives were sacrificed on a scale probably unprecedented since the building of the pyramids. The onset of the seventeenth century witnessed a reversal of progress in health care delivery. Hepner and Hepner (1973, p. 9) described it as follows:

During the seventeenth century, there was a decline in the quality of hospitals; by the eighteenth century, hospital facilities were abysmal and medical practices deplorable. Infection was widespread throughout the institutions: patients were crowded into large rooms and more than one patient often occupied a single bed. Hospitals were considered pesthouses for the poor and places to die. The wealthy did not use hospitals but were treated in their homes.

The age of modern medicine and health care

It may appear that the conditions and developments discussed thus far have been unduly stressed. However, any discussion of background and development must necessarily emphasize those extraterritorial developments that have exerted the greatest influence on the American health care delivery system. Although many advances had been made elsewhere, the early intimate ties—social, economic, and otherwise—between the North American continent and Great Britain made happenings in the latter of particular significance to the former.

Modern medicine and health care delivery began to emerge during the late nineteenth century. Both can be viewed as integral parts of an overall social reform movement in Victorian England, which was a humanitarian response to the excesses of the Industrial Revolution. At the same time, several major scientific discoveries were made, including anesthesia, the germ theory of disease, and the uses of the x-ray, to name a few (Pellegrino, 1963).

Although formal American medical education began in Philadelphia in 1765 with the establishment, by John Morgan, of the first medical school, it was not until after the Flexner Report was issued in 1910 that medical education's much-needed quality reforms began. During the pre-Flexner period, professional teaching facilities were limited in number and quality. Many physicians were self-designated, self-taught, and itinerant. The prestige of the medical profession was at its lowest ebb, and its ranks were disorganized and split by the development of numerous healing philosophies and cults (Schudson, 1974).

Before the early 1900s, there was not a shadow of a health care system. By and large, physicians were poorly trained in diploma mills or were self-designated and served as apprentices to physicians. Only a small number of American physicians during this era received comprehensive medical education in European schools. Most hospitals were unsanitary places staffed by poorly trained workers; and their chief purpose was to provide a place where people, especially the poor, could come to die. Surgery was conducted under primitive and unsanitary conditions and people often developed infections and died from the treatment that they received in the hospitals.

The gradual change to modern medicine in the United States began in 1893 with the establishment of a medical school at Johns Hopkins University in Baltimore. The growth of medical schools was sporadic between 1893 and 1910, when the famous Flexner study was published. The movement to reform medical education received its greatest impetus with the publication of Abraham Flexner's Carnegie Foundation–sponsored study of medical schools (Schudson, 1974). This report urged that medical schools upgrade the quality of education delivered through more selective admission standards and the closing of schools that were in financial distress. Basically, the Flexner Report heralded the demise of diploma schools and their replacement over the years with approximately 100 medical schools.

The reforms taking place in medical education during the early 1900s had an influence on the development of hospitals, although specialization in medical practice dates from 485-425 BC, when Herodotus reported that "every physician is for one disease and not for several, and the whole country is full of physicians; for there are physicians for the eyes, others of the head, others of the teeth, others of the belly, others of the obscure diseases" (Rees, 1968, p. 182).

By the late 1880s, specialties were well defined at Johns Hopkins and in 1897, Hopkins introduced the French concept of "interne" (which referred to a resident physician in France) to differentiate those serving their first postgraduate year from the senior "residents" who often spent several years in preparation for a specialty. By the 1930s it became customary for almost all medical graduates to serve a year of internship before starting their practice.

As these newly educated physicians moved across the nation, a demand was created for hospitals where such doctors could practice. In 1873, there were only 178 nongovernmental hospitals in the United States, which contrasted with the 4359 hospitals in 1909 (Weinstein, 1968). These early hospitals were seen as havens for the poor and few people of "quality" would enter a hospital unless there was no one else to care for them.

The transition from viewing hospitals as refuges

for the dying poor to that of treatment facilities for people of all social classes was slow to come into being. The Free Hospital for Women, which opened in 1895 in Brookline, Massachusetts, was originally intended as a place only for the poor; yet Edward Everett Hale* proclaimed in his dedication the following statement:

One of the lessons of the Civil War of the utmost importance was that it taught us about hospitals. Some people do not believe it now but they will come to it before the Twentieth Century is over, that it is a great deal better to be sick in hospitals than to be sick in a house only half equipped for the purpose.

Twenty-five years after Hale's address, the Free Hospital for Women fulfilled the dedicatory prophecy. This trend continued with the 1917 construction of the Phillips House at the Massachusetts General Hospital, which was the city's first hospital facility built for the well-to-do (Freymann, 1977). Although hospitals across the United States began to construct special buildings for well-to-do patients, it was not until the 1930s that these patients actually used hospitals for anything but surgery. Thus the transition of hospitals from a treatment facility for the poor to one for all people did not come to pass until the years immediately preceding World War I.

In 1931, forty percent of patient visits by physicians were in the home, whereas in 1966, house calls had declined to approximately two percent of patient visits. By this time, the hospital had come to be a multipurpose facility needing tremendous numbers and types of staff to provide a comprehensive range of services. As specialization has grown, it has become increasingly difficult for people in all geographical regions to secure primary health care services. The nation's health services have not shifted in the direction of the morbidity and mortality indexes. As the major health problems have shifted from acute to chronic diseases the system

*Quoted in First Annual Report of the Boston Hospital for Women, Boston, 1966, p. 10. (Cited in Freymann, 1977, p. 67.)

failed to develop a continuous form of care to re-place that based on episodic treatment. It also failed to shift from the concept of *sick* care to *well* care—from *treatment* to *prevention*.

Health insurance has contributed to greater economic security for consumers of health care, but it has also tended to foster sick care. Frequently, activities considered as preventive, such as screening for cancer, have not been reimbursable by health insurance unless an actual disease can be detected. Also, insurance coverage has reinforced the concept of physician as gatekeeper to the health care system by only reimbursing for services provided by physicians. Nurses, psychologists, and social workers have made considerable advances by qualifying for insurance and Medicare and Medicaid reimbursement, but the process of attaining this acceptance has been slow and tedious.

Now that the general description of the health care system has been briefly traced from its historical origins, several conceptual models of the current system are presented, then selected components of the model are elaborated.

CONCEPTUAL MODELS OF THE CURRENT ORGANIZATION OF HEALTH CARE DELIVERY

The complexity of the contemporary health care system is tremendous. One way to examine such a system is to illustrate its components in a series of models, each of which adds a further layer of complexity. The following section discusses four sequential stages in the illustration of a model of the current health care system. An overall picture of the health care system can be gleaned from an examination of Figs. 11-2, 11-3, 11-4, and 11-5. Each component is introduced and explained in the following narrative. Because of the great variety and complexity of the system, it is not possible to elaborate on each component.

Elementary model

The health care complex is depicted in its most elementary form in Fig. 11-2. The two major components are health care consumers and providers. In

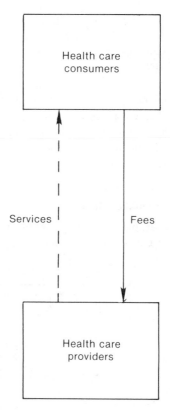

FIG. 11-2
Elementary model of the health care delivery system.

this simplified model, consumers engage in exchange relationships with purveyors.

The system is largely built on a fee or charge-per-service basis. In essence, separate financial transactions take place between consumers and providers following each major event in the health care process. For example, physicians receive fees for each service they render, such as surgical procedures or office visits. The bulk of the physician's charges—determined by physicians themselves on the basis of customary fees—are paid by patients. In contrast, with the exception of certain specialized hospitals, such as those for the treatment of tuberculosis or psychiatric disorders, hospitals typically determine their charges according to full-cost recovery formulas. As will be indicated further on, hospitals levy their charges either on the patient directly or, more commonly, on third parties (Ellwood, 1973).

Hence until a few years ago, the predominant method of financing health care in the United States was personal payment for service—that is, fee (or charge)—by consumers to a physician or hospital. This method still carries most of the cost of ambulatory medical care, dental care, and medications.

Modified elementary model

In Fig. 11-3, one additional component—third-party funding agencies—is added to the elementary model. As previously mentioned, the bulk of health care services produced in this country are paid for by the consumer directly or indirectly. Although there is increasing insurance coverage, it is estimated that about one-third of all health costs come directly out of the individual's pocket.

The national expenditure for health care has increased dramatically in the last few decades. Specifically, from 1960 to 1978 the total spending for health care increased from $27 billion to $192 billion (*Healthy People*, 1979, p. 6). Moreover, in 1960 Americans spent less than 6% of the gross national product (GNP) on health, while in 1979 almost 11% of the GNP was devoted to health care expenses. Between 1960 and 1978 the annual U.S.

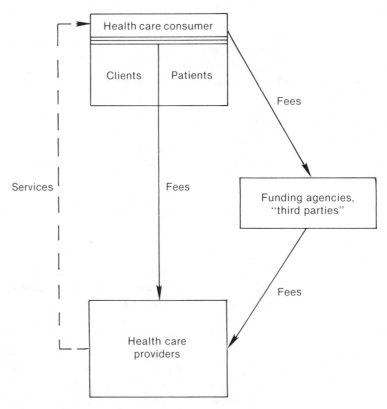

FIG. 11-3
Modified elementary model of health care system.

health expenditures increased over 700%; yet is health care that much better?

According to the Report of the Surgeon General, the majority of health dollars are spent on the treatment of disease and disability, whereas prevention is deemphasized. It may well be time to refocus health expenditures, in that despite phenomenal monetary outlay, the United States continues to lag behind several other industrialized countries in the number of key health indicators, including the following (*Healthy People,* 1979, p. 6):

1. Twelve other countries have a lower death rate from cancer.
2. Twenty-six countries have a lower death rate from circulatory disease.
3. Eleven countries have a lower infant mortality rate.
4. Fourteen countries have a longer life expectancy for men and six others have a higher female life expectancy.

Between 1969 and 1978, personal health care expenditures increased from $57.9 billion to $167.9 billion, which averaged 12.6% gain annually.* It is estimated that 64% of this tremendous growth resulted from inflation in health care costs and about 25% of the increase can be attributed to increased utilization and new or improved health care products. In order to accommodate increasing health bills, consumers are relying heavily on third-party payers to assume a substantial portion of the expense for health care. Although private insurance does defray the cost to the consumer, it also tends to increase utilization. Payments by insurance carriers have increased since 1950 from 9.1% of total health expenditures to 27.0% in 1978.

The methods of payment vary according to different categories of health care spending. This is evident in a comparison of the two major types of personal health expenditures: hospital care and physician care. Hospital costs have traditionally claimed the largest portion of the health care dollar,

*Citations of health care expenditures come from *Health: United States,* 1979, pp. 179-181.

with expenditures increasing from $3.9 billion in 1950 to $39.5 billion in 1978. This represents a percentage increase of total expenditures from 30.4% to 39.5%. Factors that account for this vast increase include inflation, advancements in technology, and increased utilization. Nursing home care has also been increasing its grasp of the health care dollar with expenditures increasing from $187 million in 1950 (1.5% of total health bill) to $15.8 billion in 1978, or 8.2% of the total health expenditures. These increases occurred at an annual average rate of 17.2%.

In contrast, physician care, which constitutes the second largest category of spending, has increased in dollar amounts from $2.7 billion in 1950 to $35.3 billion in 1978, but has actually decreased in the proportion of total health expenditures consumed by this group. That is, in 1950 physician fees represented 21.7% of all health expenditures and only 18.3% in 1978. These figures do understate the impact of physicians on the total health care dollar, since this group controls entry into hospitals and, to a large extent, drug prescription expenditures.

As with physician services, the actual expenditures for dentists have increased substantially (from $1.0 billion in 1950 to $13.3 billion in 1978), while the proportion of total health expenditures going to dentists has decreased from 7.6% in 1950 to 6.9% in 1978.

Other major expenditures and their respective proportion of total health costs are as follows: medication (7.9%); administration of health insurance plans (5.2%); and health-related research and construction (4.9%).

The current literature abounds with descriptions of various methods of health care financing. In reviewing these methods, it is interesting to note that existing financing mechanisms tend to be oriented toward medical care rather than health care. The most notable methods, in addition to direct payments by consumers, include individual prepaid selective insurance schemes, trade union and other large insurance plans, and insurance coverage through government agencies.

Individual prepaid or voluntary health insurance constitutes a major source of personal health care service financing. The American public purchases health insurance from approximately 1800 organizations. Blue Cross and Blue Shield are perhaps most frequently thought of when referring to insurance plans. Together with other insurance plans, Blue Cross and Blue Shield have gained wide acceptance in the last few decades. A variety of health insurance programs are made available to employees and their families through their place of employment. Many organizations finance either the entire program or share the cost with their workers. Trade unions have also been quite active in trying to secure health insurance programs for their members.

Government-sponsored health insurance has now become an accepted part of the health care delivery system. Medicare is a federally sponsored insurance plan, funded by Social Security to provide care to the elderly; Medicaid is financed by federal and state matching funds and provides financial support for medical care to those who are in need.

Since Medicare provides health care to the elderly, this expense has increased as the older U.S. population has increasingly grown. This program went into effect in 1966 as Title XVIII of the Social Security Act. This program has increased almost sixfold in its financial expenditures since 1967. Of the more than $18 billion spent on Medicaid in 1977, 74% went to hospital care, 21.7% to physicians, and 1.9% to nursing homes. Other services, including home health care, constituted 2.3% of Medicaid expenditures in 1977.

Medicaid, or Title XIX of the Social Security Act, went into effect on January 1, 1966. The purpose of this program is to provide medical care to indigent persons. Recipients in cash assistance programs are categorically eligible; this includes Supplemental Security Income (SSI) and Aid to Families of Dependent Children (AFDC). During 1977, 23.9 million people were Medicaid recipients. In terms of eligibility, 15.5% were over 65 years old; 0.4% were blind; 11.9% were disabled; 64.2%

were members of families with dependent children; and 8.0% were other recipients (*Health: United States,* 1979, p. 182). Like Medicare, the total Medicaid program has increased dramatically in the last few years, in that expenditures have increased sevenfold, from $2.3 billion in 1967 to $16.3 billion in 1977.

Thus in the existing health care delivery system, depicted in Fig. 11-3, payments are made directly by the consumer, through some form of private insurance, or through the channels provided by federally and state supported programs. Third-party funding agencies play an increasingly important role in facilitating exchange relationships between health care consumers and health care providers.

Health care delivery model: private sector

As previously noted, the American health care delivery system is very complex. This complexity can be somewhat reduced by first dividing the entire system into two service sectors: private and public. The most important elements of the private sector are shown in Fig. 11-4. Since the public sector has many points of articulation with the private sector, it is shown along with a different conceptual view of the private sector in Fig. 11-5.

The private sector of the health care delivery system, as shown in Fig. 11-4, can initially be broken into three components: personnel, facilities, and suppliers. Taken together, personnel and facilities are the providers of health care in the private sector. Therefore, health care providers include physicians and other health professionals as well as hospitals, clinics, health maintenance organizations (HMOs), nursing homes, medical laboratories, and pharmacies. The final component is made up of companies that supply health products to providers and consumers. Included in this component are distributors of pharmaceutical supplies, medical supply companies, hospital and medical equipment manufacturers, medical furnishing companies, general supplies, and so forth.

The existing health care system, as shown in Fig. 11-4, has been called a "Professional Model" be-

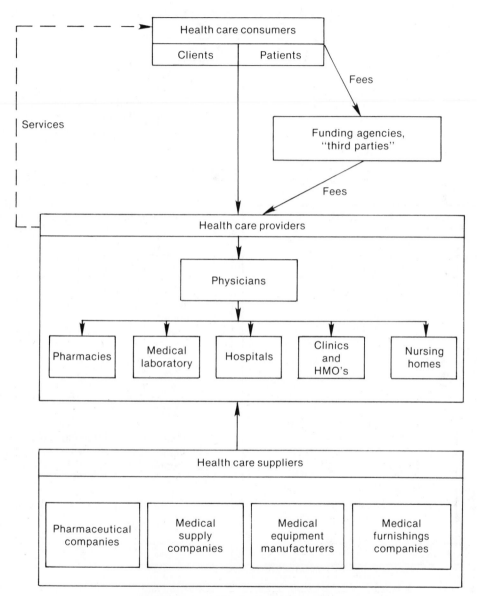

FIG. 11-4
Health care delivery model—private sector.

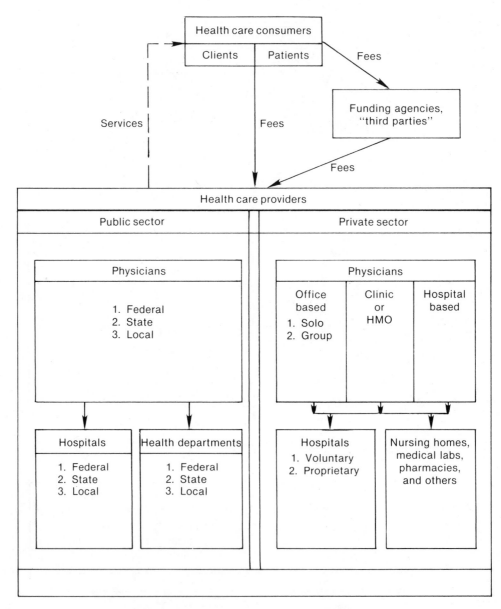

FIG. 11-5
Health care delivery model—public and private sector.

cause its most conspicuous ingredient is the physician. Collectively, physicians and other health professionals influence and dominate this highly elaborate system. This influence and dominance can readily be seen by examining the industry structure. In contrast to many other American industries that have changed structurally, to keep pace with technological and social advances, this nation's health care industry has retained its pre–Industrial Revolution organizational structure. Consequently, it is often referred to as a "cottage industry" because it relies to a large extent on small independent firms (Ellwood, 1973, p. 74).

The central role of physicians is illustrated in Fig. 11-4. Presently, physicians control entry into and the pathway through the health care system. Unless the consumer is providing self-treatment, all health care services are determined by the physician. Drugs, nursing care, x-rays, hospitalization, and specialized medical practice, for example, are selected by the physician. Hence the physician is the point of contact between the consumer and the supply side of health care (Rathmell, 1974).

Health care delivery model: public and private sector

The public sector of the health care delivery system is shown in Fig. 11-5, along with an alternate conceptual view of the private sector. The public health sector consists of various public health agencies, both voluntary and official, which operate at the federal, state, and local levels.

Voluntary agencies are those nonprofit organizations that depend on donations, fees, membership dues, endowments, payments from insurance plans, and contracts. In contrast, official agencies are tax supported. Some voluntary agencies tend to be concerned with the prevention, eradication, or control of certain diseases. Many of these organizations operate on the national, state, and local levels. Such agencies include the National Tuberculosis Association, American Cancer Society, American Diabetes Association, and the American Heart Association.

Other voluntary agencies, such as the Ford, W.K. Kellogg, and Rockefeller Foundations, promote and subsidize rural health programs. In addition, voluntary groups such as the Joint Commission of Accreditation of Hospitals are involved in setting standards, evaluating, and making recommendations concerning care given by hospitals and nursing homes. Finally, professional health and allied health associations are voluntary groups that encourage research, provide for exchange of information among health professionals, and promote high standards of performance.

Among the official public health agencies are the armed forces, Veterans Administration, United States Public Health Service (one of eight agencies within the Department of Health and Human Resources), and certain state and local health departments and health care facilities that provide medical care, preventive services, and environmental control services directly to the public. Collectively, these agencies carry on a variety of tasks. At the federal level, concern is for national and international health and the health of special population groups, such as military personnel and veterans, the aged, the economically deprived, and the physically and mentally handicapped. State agencies tend to be concerned with planning, financing, and assisting local agencies that actually provide direct services to the public.

As previously mentioned, Fig. 11-5 illustrates the structure of both the public and private health care delivery systems. However, compared to Fig. 11-4, the private sector is now viewed differently. According to this alternate view, there are four general types of institutions for the practice of medicine. The first three delivery mechanisms — services that are office, clinic, HMO, or hospital based — reside in the private sector. The fourth includes services provided by health departments, which reside in the public sector.

In terms of health work force, the number of people employed in the health care industry increased 60% from 1970 to 1978, or from 4.2 to 6.7 million. During this period, one out of every seven new jobs created was in the health industry. By far the largest group of health providers are registered nurses, who comprised in 1978 one-half of the total health work force, or a total of 1.1 million nurses.

The number of medical and osteopathic physicians has grown by 51% between 1970 and 1978, to constitute a work force of 424,000. Since the population has been increasing at a slower pace than the number of physicians, the ratio of active physicians to population has increased from 14.2/10,000 in 1950 to 17.9/10,000 in 1977.

From the standpoint of medical treatment, nearly 230,000 physicians in office-based practices function either individually or in groups as private entrepreneurs. For the most part, the nation's 340,000 practicing physicians function independently of one another. Although group practice has been growing, a small proportion of the total supply of active physicians are affiliated with medical groups (*Health: United States,* 1979, p. 158).

In 1975, approximately 24% of active nonfederal physicians were members of group medical practices of three or more physicians, although two-thirds of these groups did not exceed the three- to four-person category. Some medical groups do render their services against an annual prepaid capitation fee; however, less than 20% of all group practices deliver more than one-half of their services on that basis. Thus the fee-for-service solo medical practice or two-person partnerships remain the predominant form of private medical practice in this country (*Health: United States,* 1979, p. 162).

In addition to the office-based physicians, approximately 25% of nonfederal physicians—which includes residents, interns, and full-time medical staff—are based in hospitals. The private-sector portion of the system consists mainly of voluntary nonprofit hospitals, and proprietary profit-making hospitals. From an economic and contractual standpoint, office-based physicians and hospitals function independently, although most physicians, as nonpaying tenants, maintain formal staff affiliations with one or more hospitals.

In summary, the purpose of this section was to present an overview of the vast and complex health care delivery system. It is apparent from the models and narrative that health care delivery currently revolves around the central role of the individual physician and the doctor-consumer relationship. The physician functions as the consumer's point of entry and guide in a complex system of small and often highly specialized provider units that are only loosely related. At the outset, consumers select a physician of their choice, but thereafter most health care choices, including such critical decisions as those involving specialists or consultants, hospital admission, and prescription drugs are made by the physician, not the consumer. Moreover, the commitments physicians and consumers make to one another have no particular time limit and can be quite temporary, even though the relationship ordinarily continues through specific episodes of illness.

In-depth elaboration of these models is limited to three overall categories: mechanisms for delivering health care, which discusses hospitals, public health agencies, and HMOs; work force and prospects; and need for reform in the health care system.

MECHANISMS FOR DELIVERY OF HEALTH CARE

Chapter 19 describes a variety of institutional settings for nursing practice. In order to avoid duplication, this section focuses on three major mechanisms, including hospitals, public health agencies, and HMOs.

Hospitals

Hospitals, as a whole, comprise a large industry, with hospital care accounting for the largest single portion of the health care dollar. There are more than 7200 hospitals in the United States, falling into two general categories of ownership: government and nongovernment. Government hospitals are federally funded (Army, Navy, Air Force, Veterans Administration, and Public Health Service Hospitals), state-level (long-term psychiatric, chronic disease, and state university medical centers), and local hospitals of a county or city type.

Nongovernmental hospitals include two types: voluntary and proprietary. Voluntary hospitals are run on a nonprofit basis and may be church supported or run by a variety of groups such as communities, industry, and Shriners. Proprietary hospitals are run on a profit basis and may be owned by individuals, groups, or organizations such as large corporations. Since proprietary hospitals are designed to make a profit, they must pay taxes from which nonprofit and governmental hospitals are exempt. In general, proprietary hospitals tend to be small, with 70% having less than 100 beds (*Trends,* 1976). They also may provide less outpatient care and community services, although this is changing as more large corporations are becoming involved in the development of major medical centers on a profit-making basis.

A recent innovation in hospitals is the management contract, whereby a corporation may operate several nonprofit and even teaching hospitals. These management contracts aid nonprofit hospitals to improve their efficiency and also increase revenues for the corporation, which may determine that the time is not right for building a new facility because of such variables as high land costs, interest rates, or lack of available personnel.

Historically, hospitals began as institutions to house poor people who were hopelessly ill and had no place to go. Most of the early hospitals were run by religious orders and served an obligation to society (Shindell et al., 1976). Interestingly, the word hospital comes from the word *hospice,* meaning guest room. The oldest hospital in North America is in Mexico City: the Hospital of Jesus of Nazareth, erected in 1524 by Cortez. The oldest U.S. hospital was founded in New Orleans by the Catholic Church and still exists as Charity Hospital (Shindell et al., 1976, p. 301). The oldest voluntary hospital, the Pennsylvania Hospital, was started in 1751 by Benjamin Franklin and a group of interested citizens. This was the first "community hospital" in the United States.

There are two types of specialty hospitals: those that care for a specific type of disease (e.g., psychiatric); and those that provide care for a special category of patients with all diseases (e.g., pediatrics). In general, specialty hospitals are declining in number, whereas general hospitals are increasing. In particular, teaching hospitals are recognized as the core of the U.S. health care system because they provide education, service, and research to a wide variety of people. Several issues facing teaching hospitals include which aspect of their service should receive highest priority and what kind of services they should provide. Because of their highly trained staff, teaching hospitals are best equipped to provide tertiary care for patients with complex health problems. Yet community pressure is also exerted for these institutions to provide both secondary and primary care. "The net result is uneconomic use of the specialized facilities and skills of a teaching hospital and often not entirely satisfactory provision of primary care because the hospital is geared to more specialized care" (*Trends,* 1976, p. 309).

Governance of hospitals

Most voluntary hospitals are run by a board of trustees "who are legally responsible to the community for the operation of the hospital and the maintenance of standards" (Shindell et al., 1976, p. 301). The board hires an administrator to run the hospital. Although businesspeople still comprise a major portion of hospital boards, there are increasing numbers of accountants, engineers, and lawyers on hospital boards. Also, people with political influence are asked to serve on boards to help to influence community spending. Similarly, physicians are often of key significance to boards in dealing with the complex medical judgments that boards are often asked to make. Pressure is being exerted on many boards to include community representation so that public needs will be addressed more fully.

The medical staff is usually composed of community physicians who utilize the hospital's resources. "The principle underlying the voluntary hospital system is self-governance and self-regulation on the part of the medical staff" (Shindell et al., 1976, p. 301). Although hospital boards are legally responsible for governance, they rely heavily on physicians to govern and monitor their professional care. This expectation is often unrealistic, since most physicians utilizing the hospital are in private practice and devote limited attention to participation in hospital activities.

Regulation of hospitals

Although most hospitals function as autonomous self-regulating institutions, they are subject to a variety of rules and regulations from external sources, such as governmental and professional groups, that influence the program of the hospital. Outside regulation comes primarily from the following sources (Shindell et al., 1976, p. 304):
1. City and state health rules
2. The American Medical Association in regard to rules about internships and residency programs
3. Joint Commission on Accreditation of Hospitals (inspection every two years, with emphasis on self-regulation and quality of records)
4. Medicare and Medicaid (governmental review of standards and programs)

Public health agencies

As seen in Fig. 11-5, public health agencies comprise a significant portion of the health care delivery model. The term "public health" is defined in many ways, but in the broadest sense it refers to "those efforts made by communities from the earliest civilizations to the present to cope with health problems that arise as a result of human beings living in groups" (Shindell et al., 1976, p. 304). Public health efforts have been recorded since the days of the Egyptians, with the first clear-cut accounts of acute communicable disease dating from the literature of classical Greece.

In the Western World during the Medieval period, health problems were dealt with by magic and the calling on of supernatural forces. Since disease, sin, and punishment were considered to be related, the Church played an active role in health interests by encouraging prayer, penitence, and good works. In the United States many health problems developed from the poor sanitary conditions caused by overcrowding. Although these early communities lacked an organized system of public health, they frequently had a governing council of influential citizens who were assigned specific responsibilities for health protection. Public health administration was frequently carried out by laypeople, and physicians were employed to treat specific kinds of problems: the poor, prisoners, lepers, and so on.

As cities grew, the need for public health services rapidly outgrew the scope of voluntary, often piecemeal efforts to "cope with the health problems caused by overcrowding, increased mortality and morbidity and inadequate housing and sanitary conditions" (Shindell et al., 1976, p. 306). The 1838 *Report of the Poor Law Commission* revealed in vivid details the desperate health conditions of that era and went on to provide plausible epidemiological explanations that led to a variety of sanitary reforms and public health efforts, both in Great Britain and the United States.

When the AMA was founded in 1847, the National Institute, a distinguished Washington group, urged that a hygiene committee be formed to study the sanitary conditions and to develop a uniform system for collecting health statistics. When this committee was formed in 1848, their surveys revealed the need for an organized public health effort. Throughout the history of public health development in the United States, key concerns have been sanitation, epidemics, communicable diseases, and the health of mothers and children.

Health maintenance organizations

Compared to hospitals and health departments, HMOs are relative newcomers to the health care system, although organizations such as HMOs that offer a broad range of medical services for an annual fee have been in existence since 1929. Until recently, though, few people have known about and had access to such organizations. An HMO is an "organized system of health care that guarantees to provide high-quality physician services, emergency and preventive treatment and hospital services to individuals who have agreed to obtain their medical care from the HMO for an extended period of time" (Ellwood and Herbert, 1973, p. 100). In return for these services, individuals pay a fixed sum of money in advance. In its literal sense the term "HMO" is synonymous with "hospital for the well." As politically defined, the HMO concept has been linked with prepayment.

Although the government has encouraged multiple approaches, HMOs have developed around two organizational patterns (Ellwood and Herbert, 1973, p. 100):

1. A tightly knit organization in which physicians work at single sites as a group and have some sort of working relationship with a hospital. These are usually referred to as "prepaid group practice" and the prototype is the Kaiser Permanente Health Plan.
2. A more loosely knit organization in which physicians continue to work out of their own offices and are paid on a fee-for-service basis. In this arrangement, the entire group of physicians share the risk of patient illness and adjust their fees accordingly. Such HMOs are usually called "foundations for medical care."

HMOs have been developed by consumer corporations, medical society foundations, medical schools, physician group practices, insurance companies, and hospitals. The range of services provided varies, but all HMOs provide, as a minimum, physician services; primary, emergency, and acute care; and care and rehabilitation of chronic disabling conditions for both inpatients and outpatients.

Advantages and disadvantages

The advantages of HMOs relate to their potential ability to address three major problems in the health care system: accessibility of care, fragmentation of services, and the high cost of care. By joining an HMO, subscribers have access to a team of health care providers including physicians, nurses, and a variety of therapists. The HMO guarantees around-the-clock coverage for 365 days a year with a primary care provider who coordinates services. Thus the subscriber has fragmentation reduced by finding all services in one setting. Cost is contained in that subscribers pay a fixed fee for care depending on the range of services offered and the geographical location. Since HMO physicians are on salary, they do not have incentives to run up unnecessary fees for services. The main goal of an HMO is to prevent illness so as to reduce cost to the organization.

An HMO emphasizes preventive care and stresses early detection and treatment to reduce hospital stay. Studies have found that HMO subscribers benefit from these preventive efforts. Two studies completed with the Health Insurance Plan of New York (HIP) examined (1) the health of subscribers in terms of premature birth rates and perinatal mortality; and (2) death rates among elderly subscribers. In the first study, it was found that a prematurity rate of 5.5 per 100 live births existed for white HIP subscribers, versus 6.0 for a matched group of private patients. Further, among nonwhites the spread was even larger, with 8.8 in HIP and 10.8 for private patients. Similarly, the perinatal mortality rate per 1000 births was 22.7 for white HIP patients compared to 27.3 among white private patients, and nonwhites had 33.7 with HIP and 43.8 for private patients.

The second HIP study compared death rates among an elderly population. A group of Old Age Assistance recipients who obtained care from HIP were compared to a similar group that received care in the traditional health system. In the first year, mortality was approximately the same for both groups, whereas during the next 18 months, the annual mortality rate was 7.8 per 100 in the HIP group and 8.8 for the others ("Health Maintenance Organizations," 1975, p. 4).

Hospital and surgery rates are also decreased among HMO subscribers. In one study of 8 million federal employees who could choose between an

HMO and conventional insurance for each 1000 persons covered by insurance, the average hospital days were 924 (Blue Cross–Blue Shield), 987 (other insurance), and 422 (HMO). Also, compared to HMO subscribers, federal participants in the Blue Cross program underwent twice as much surgery as members of the HMO ("Health Maintenance Organizations," 1975).

HMOs, of course, are not the perfect solution to the ills of the health care system. Some major criticisms refer to the possibility that providers may undertreat to save money. Also, in an HMO subscribers may have a limited or no choice of the physician or hospital. Also, some HMOs have limitations on reimbursements for illness or accidents outside the service area. A fourth disadvantage relates to impersonal care and long waits to be seen.

Despite the disadvantages, HMOs do offer a viable means for delivering health care. As with any organization, the quality of care depends on the characteristics of the particular HMO, including the providers who work there.

Work force

The health care industry is labor intensive, and until recent years has enjoyed a long period of expansion and seemingly endless funding from public and private sources. As the U.S. economic situation becomes a more critical factor in determining national priorities, the distribution and utilization of the health work force will receive increasing scrutiny. Since previous sections of this chapter have dealt with issues of the work force such as distribution, this section focuses on selected types of personnel.

In terms of mode of functioning, health care providers can be divided into three major groups: independent practitioners, dependent practitioners, and supporting staff. The independent practitioners include those health care providers who are allowed by law to deliver a designated range of services to anyone who wants them and without supervision or authorization of the practitioner's work by any other party or group (Hanft, 1977). Independent practitioners include physicians (both osteopathic and allopathic), dentists, chiropractors, optometrists, and podiatrists.

To date, the dominant form of medical practice in the United States has been the single physician in solo practice. In recent years, there has been a decline in the percentage of physicians in an office-based practice, especially in a solo practice. This trend has two potential benefits: The utilization of nurse practitioners (NPs) and physician assistants (PAs) is particularly suited to a group-practice setting, thereby increasing the potential efficiency of each member of the health team; and group practice can be more economical in that equipment, personnel, and resources can be shared. Also, groups large enough to hire administrators can free physicians from the many chores inherent in running a private practice. Most group practices are small, ranging from three to six providers, and physicians in groups continue to practice medicine much like those in solo practice. That is, consumers tend to have as little input into the operation of a group practice as they do with a solo practice.

Dependent practitioners, the second category, are "allowed by law to deliver a delimited range of services to persons, under the supervision and/or the authorization of independent practitioners, often of a particular type specified by law" (Hanft, 1977, p. 69). Groups considered to be dependent practitioners include nurses, psychologists, social workers, pharmacists, physician assistants, dental hygienists, and the speech, physical, and recreational therapists. A blurring of roles between dependent and independent practitioners is often seen, since under some circumstances certain members of the designated dependent group can assume independent functions. This is especially true of nurse practitioners and physician assistants, who will be discussed later in the chapter.

The third category, supporting staff, provides a wide range of services to patients and carries out many tasks authorized and supervised by both dependent and independent practitioners. "The work of supporting staff may or may not be regulated by laws directly pertaining to them, but if there are not special laws, they work under the supervision of independent and/or dependent practitioners'' (Hanft, 1977, p. 69). Members of this group include clerical, maintenance, housekeeping, and food-processing workers, as well as researchers, administrators, nurses' aides, dental assistants, and technicians.

Compared to other nations, the United States has an abundant supply of health workers, including one of the highest physician/patient ratios in the world. The total number of physicians in the United States increased 67% between 1950 and 1973, while the population only increased 37%. It is expected that the ratio of physicians to patients will exceed 200 per 100,000 population in 1990, as compared to 141 in 1950 and 171 in 1973. This number is controlled by the 121 medical schools in the United States, including 7 schools of osteopathic medicine. At the present time, medical schools are receiving both state and federal pressures to limit enrollment, so that expensive medical education does not produce an oversupply of highly qualified professionals.

Several factors account for the increased numbers of physicians, including scholarship funds, increased numbers of medical schools, and the favorable immigration procedures for foreign medical graduates (FMGs). The number of FMGs in graduate medical training more than doubled between 1960 and 1973, from 10,000 to 22,000 (Stevens, 1975, p. 11). Likewise, the total number of FMGs in the United States rose from 31,000 in 1963 (one-ninth of all physicians) to 68,000 in 1972 (one-fifth). These figures exclude Canadians, who represent another sizeable portion of physician supply. While FMGs supply a ready source of health care to many underserved areas, they may soon become a problem if the anticipated U.S. work force predictions are accurate.

Another major concern regarding the flood of FMGs is that many may not be fully qualified. Thousands practice medicine without a license and often without supervision (Weiss et al., 1974).

Many FMGs who are currently providing care not only do not have a license, but they may not have even passed the qualifying examination developed by the Educational Council for Foreign Medical Graduates. Passing this exam, which is considered equivalent to the National Boards taken by American students, is supposed to be a prerequisite for admission to an approved internship or residency program. However, the average passage rate for FMGs is only 39%. Since they may repeatedly take this exam, ultimately approximately 67% of all FMGs pass (Weiss et al., 1974).

Despite the escalating rate of production of physicians, certain segments of the population—especially those in rural or urban inner-city areas—still have difficulty obtaining primary care. According to a Health Resources Administration survey, there were over 1000 designated primary care shortage areas in 1978.* Although more physicians are being educated, they are remaining in urban areas. Thus new efforts have been necessary to try to improve access to health care while containing costs. Two new health care providers have emerged that have markedly affected the distribution of health services. The general term "nonphysician health care provider" refers to NPs and PAs who have been trained to perform services that have traditionally been within the purview of the physician. The primary difference between NPs and PAs is that NPs may perform medical functions in addition to their nursing role, whereas PAs are trained solely to assist or substitute for a physician and do not have a unique set of skills. The optimal health care team would not substitute PAs and NPs for physicians, but would use each type of provider in a complementary fashion.

Annual federal expenditures for NP and PA training programs increased from less than $1 million in 1969 to more than $21 million in 1979 (U.S.,

---

*Bureau of Health Manpower, Division of Manpower Analysis, Health Resources Administration: Health manpower shortage areas statistics, unpublished document. (Cited in *Health: United States*, 1979, p. 45.)

Congress, 1979). The first NP program began as a pediatric nurse practitioner program at the University of Colorado in 1965. During the same year, the first PA program began at Duke University. Both of these programs were financed by private funds, and not until 1969 were federal funds used for the education of PAs. At that time the University of Washington began the MEDEX program to "train PAs who would be placed with physicians practicing primary care in underserved rural or urban areas" (*Health: United States,* 1979, p. 46).

In 1971, the use of both NPs and PAs to improve access to and contain health care costs was endorsed in the president's annual message. Subsequently, funding was provided in both 1974 and 1975 by the Nurse Training Act (P.L. 92-63) to train NPs, and the Comprehensive Health Manpower Training Act (P.L. 92-157) provided funds for the training of both NPs and PAs. Further, in 1977, the 1976 Health Professions Educational Assistance Act (P.L. 94-484) was amended by the Health Services Extension Act (P.L. 95-83) to provide traineeships for nurse practitioners who are residents of a health work force shortage area and who agree to practice in such an area on graduation (*Health: United States,* 1979).

Additional support was provided by the Rural Health Clinic Services Act of 1977 (P.L. 95-210), "which provided Medicare and Medicaid coverage for medical services furnished by a qualified NP or PA when such services are rendered in certified clinics located in rural physician-shortage areas" (*Health: United States,* 1979, p. 46).

Approximately 60% of NPs with master's degrees and 90% of those who were educated in a continuing education program were trained in primary care specialties. The majority of PAs and NPs are employed in primary care settings, although more NPs are employed in urban areas than are PAs. Table 2 shows the estimates and projections of nonphysician health providers.

The total range of services offered by NPs and PAs is great, but the scope varies considerably from one setting to another depending on the nature of the practice setting and the type of patients seen. Although they are educated to provide an array of services, constraints on practice exist primarily in the extent to which nonphysician services are reimbursed by third-party payers, as well as by legal restrictions on the scope and independence of practice. In general, NPs and PAs perform medical functions under physician supervision. The identified physician supervisor is then legally responsible; however, states vary considerably in their requirements for physician supervision. In states where requirements are specified, they vary from continuous physician supervision to telephone communication accompanied by written protocols for treatment of specific complaints.*

*For further information about NPs and PAs in regard to reimbursement, quality of care, and acceptance by patients and physicians, see *Health: United States,* 1979, pp. 51-56.

TABLE 2
Estimates and projections of nonphysician health care providers: United States, 1977, 1980, 1990

Year	Total	Type of provider	
		Nurse practitioner	**Physician assistant**
1977	17,280	12,280	5,000
1980	27,720	18,220	9,500
1990	62,520	38,020	24,500

Source: Health: United States, 1979, U.S. Department of HEW Publication no. (PHS) 80-1232, Washington, D.C., 1980, U.S. Government Printing Office.

REFORM OF THE HEALTH CARE DELIVERY SYSTEM

With total expenditures exceeding $100 billion annually, health care delivery has become one of the United States' largest industries. As mentioned, since the early 1960s, the health care system has been criticized for uneven accessibility of resources, high cost of care, and maldistribution of work force. As will be discussed in Chapter 12, health care costs have skyrocketed in the last decade, and no measure to date has been successful in containing costs. Despite vast outlays of money, many people still cannot obtain adequate health care.

In order to remedy the most frequently cited deficits in health care delivery we must consider cost, availability, and accessibility of services. Two chapters in Part Three address these concerns in detail: Chapter 19 describes future practice arenas for the delivery of health care; and Chapter 21 discusses the use of a planning model for the development of a consumer-oriented health care system. What follows is a brief summary of four recommendations that would be included in a reform of the current system. The premise behind these recommendations is that the lack of available primary care providers, uneven distribution of health services, and poor utilization of work force comprise major problems. Although cost is a problem, it is dealt with in Chapter 12. For this discussion, uneven distribution of services is divided into two sections so that surplus resources in some areas can receive some attention.

Recommendation 1: Shortage of primary care

Primary care is defined as "accessible, comprehensive, coordinated, and continual care provided by accountable providers of health services" (National Academy of Sciences, 1978, p. 1). It is generally recognized as the first level of personal health services or the point of entry for the client into the health care system. Frequently, primary care is referred to as care of the whole person rather than care directed toward a specific illness. In the United States, national attention began focusing on primary care in the mid-1960s. At that time, a series of commission reports dealing with comprehensive health care issues began to reflect a conviction that "more socially oriented care, responding to a wide range of patients' problems, was needed to complement the growing medical use of highly specialized services and technological procedures" (National Academy of Sciences, 1978, p. 2). Programs to train physicians for primary care grew, as did the impetus for interdisciplinary teams as well as for other health providers such as NPs and PAs to expand their scope of practice.

Many incentives are built into the present health care system that discourage the practice of primary care. Specialization seems to earn a physician more power, wealth, and prestige than does primary care. Further, those physicians who are considered to be specialists in primary care (pediatricians, obstetricians, gynecologists, family practice physicians) tend to work longer and more irregular hours than other physicians. Efforts are being made both in medicine and nursing to provide incentives for providers to specialize in primary care. The incentives for NPs and PAs have been mentioned. Medical schools are instituting courses in family medicine, and approved family practice residency programs are growing annually. Also, scholarships such as the National Health Service Corps finance the education of providers in exchange for a commitment to work in a medically underserved area for a designated time.

Recommendation 2: Uneven distribution of services

The distribution of health services in various sections of the United States is closely linked to affluence and general appeal to providers. In general, the more affluent states of California, Connecticut, Illinois, New Jersey, New York, and Massachusetts have twice as many physicians as states with low incomes such as Alabama, Arkansas, Louisiana, Mississippi, Tennessee, and South Carolina (*Distribution of Physicians in the United*

States, 1971). It is anticipated that as the provider supply increases in the next decade, it will be necessary for physicians as well as NPs and PAs increasingly to locate in areas distant from major medical centers, which are becoming saturated with providers at the present time. Also, the efforts on behalf of providing primary care to all people should influence the distribution of services.

Recommendation 3: Surplus facilities

In recent years the number of general hospital beds has increased at a greater rate than the population. Many urban areas with large medical centers have considerably more beds than are needed by their population. As mentioned in Chapter 12, certificate-of-need programs are an attempt to halt the development of excessive facilities. What this means is that any institution must document that a need exists before they are approved by their local Health Systems Agency to begin construction or major renovation. (See Chapters 12 and 15 for a further discussion of health system agencies and other forms of regulation.)

Recommendation 4: Poor utilization of work force

The work force in health-related occupations is growing rapidly, yet poor distribution and inadequate utilization, training, and organization have led to shortages in some areas and surpluses in others. Utilization is a particular problem in nursing, where the number of graduates is consistently far greater than the actively employed supply of nurses.

SUMMARY

American medical science has made great advances in curing disease, easing human distress, and prolonging life. Without question, the United States possesses some of the finest hospitals, medical centers, and health providers in the world. Spectacular advances have been made in the last two centuries in sanitation, nutrition, and intervention in disease processes. In recent years there have

been notable decreases in mortality rates and corresponding extensions of life expectancy, even though by these indexes the United States lags behind several other developed countries.

Yet in spite of the strengths mentioned, health levels are no longer rising; in some population groups they may even be deteriorating. The reasons are complex, and at times it appears that the health care system is at a watershed.

The major reason for the lack of effectiveness in the health care system lies in poor coordination. It is contended that the existing provider system, composed as it is of several hundred thousand more or less independent decision makers, is really a "nonsystem" that lacks effective planning and coordination. This lack of coordination has resulted in widespread duplication of costly facilities, equipment, and patient record-keeping systems, as well as a serious maldistribution of resources with a relative abundance of facilities in affluent urban areas and a corresponding lack of facilities in the poorer urban and in the rural areas.

This chapter has discussed the overall composition of the health care system and looked at several key aspects, including facilities, work force, and high-priority problem areas. Each of the remaining chapters in this section will discuss a specific factor that serves either as a facilitator or as a constraint in remedying the ills of the health care system. In many cases, the issues discussed in a chapter will present both positive and negative factors to be considered in looking at the overall system.

REFERENCES

Banta, D.: What is health care? In Jonas, S., editor: Health care delivery in the United States, New York, 1977, Springer Publishing Co.

Benson, E.R., and McDevitt, J.Q.: Community health and nursing practice, ed. 2, Englewood Cliffs, N.J., 1980, Prentice-Hall, Inc.

Distribution of physicians in the United States, Chicago, 1971, American Medical Association.

Disease prevention and health promotion: federal programs and prospects, Report of the Departmental Task Force on Prevention, Publication no. 77-55071B, U.S. Department of HEW, Washington, D.C., Sept. 1978, U.S. Government Printing Office.

Ellwood, P.M.: Models for organizing health services and implications of legislative proposals, Milbank Mem. Fund Q. **51**:76, Spring 1973.

Ellwood, P.M., and Herbert, M.E.: Health care: should industry buy it or sell it? Harvard Bus. Rev. **51**:99-107, July/Aug. 1973.

Freymann, J.G.: The American health care system: its genesis and trajectory, Huntington, N.Y., 1977, Robert E. Krieger Publishing Co.

Hanft, R.S.: Health manpower. In Jonas, S., editor: Health care delivery in the United States, New York, 1977, Springer Publishing Co.

Health maintenance organizations, are HMOs the answer to your medical needs? Am. Lung Assoc. Bull. **61**(2):2-9, 1975.

Health: United States, 1979, U.S. Department of HEW Publication no. (PHS) 80-1232, Washington, D.C., 1980, U.S. Government Printing Office.

Healthy people, the Surgeon General's Report on Health Promotion and Disease Prevention, Washington, D.C., 1979, Publication no. 79-55071, U.S. Department of HEW.

Hepner, J.O., and Hepner, D.M.: The health strategy game: a challenge for reorganization and management, St. Louis, 1973, The C.V. Mosby Co.

Levey, S., and Loomba, N.P.: Health care administration: a managerial perspective, Philadelphia, 1973, J.B. Lippincott Co.

National Academy of Sciences, Institute of Medicine, A manpower policy for primary health care, Washington, D.C., May 1978.

Pellegrino, E.D.: Medicine, history and the idea of man, Ann. Am. Acad. Political Social Sci. **346**:11, March 1963.

Rathmell, J.M.: Marketing in the health sector, Cambridge, Mass., 1974, Winthrop Publishing Co.

Rees, W.D. Personal view: Herodotus. Br. Med. J. **4**:182, Oct. 19, 1968.

Reinhart, U.E.: Proposed changes in the organization of health-care delivery: an overview and critique, Milbank Mem. Fund Q. **51**:171, Spring 1973.

Rosen, G.: A history of public health, New York, 1957, MD Publications.

Schudson, M.: The Flexner Report and the Reed Report on the history of professional education in the United States, Social Sci. Q. **55**:347-361, Sept. 1974.

Shindell, S., Salloway, J.C., and Oberembt, C.M.: A coursebook in health care delivery, New York, 1976, Appleton-Century-Crofts.

Stevens, R.A.: Muddle over medical manpower, Prism **3**:10-63, Feb. 1975.

Thomas, C.L., editor: Taber's Cyclopedic Medical Dictionary, ed. 12, Philadelphia, 1973, F.A. Davis Publishing Co.

Trends affecting the U.S. health care system, Report prepared by Cambridge Research Institutes for the U.S. Department of HEW, Publication no. HRA 76-14503, 1976.

U.S., Congress, Congressional Budget Office, Physician extenders, their current and future role in medical care, Washington, D.C., April 1979, U.S. Government Printing Office.

U.S., Department of Commerce, Bureau of the Census, Abstract of the United States, ed. 96, 1975.

Weinstein, M.R.: The illness process, psychosocial hazards of disability programs, J.A.M.A. **204**:209-213, April 15, 1968.

Weiss, R., Keinman, J., Brandt, U., Feldman, J., and McGuiness, A.: Foreign medical graduates and the medical underground, N. Engl. J. Med. **290**:1408-1413, June 20, 1974.

12

ECONOMIC CONSTRAINTS IN THE HEALTH CARE DELIVERY SYSTEM

Daniel B. Hill

Economics involves the study of how human and material resources are used to meet needs. In the United States, a major economic concern is the rising proportion of the total dollar output of the economy that is produced in the health sector. Table 3 depicts this growth, both in dollars and in terms of health expenditures as a percentage of all goods and services produced; that is, the gross national product (GNP).

Economics cannot provide a definitive standard of how many dollars or what percentage of the GNP should be spent on health care. If the value that the American public places on good health has increased, or if improvements in health care technology have meant that the population's health can be dramatically improved by increasing expenditures for health care services, then it may be appropriate for health care expenditures to grow in relation to expenditures for other goods and services. However, it appears that at least part of the growth in national health expenditures represents inefficiencies in the use of resources, rather than changing value systems or improvements in the efficacy of services.

This chapter will explore reasons for and the consequences of rising health care expenditures. Although rising expenditures are not always synonymous with inefficiency, the emphasis in this chapter will be on health system characteristics that are suggestive of inefficient resource allocation.

BENEFITS AND COSTS

Although economic analysis cannot tell people how much they should spend for health care, it does provide a good general guideline for resource allocation. The benefit (value) derived from using resources for one purpose should equal or exceed the benefit that could have been derived from applying those resources in other uses. The true cost of any use of resources is the benefits foregone from using those resources in other ways. Thus the resource-allocation guideline says that the benefits derived from any use of resources should equal or exceed their cost.

Applied to the health sector, the resource-allocation guideline establishes the following rules for an efficient use of resources.

1. The resources used in the health sector could not provide greater benefits if used in any other sector. For example, a shift in resources from the health sector to the education sector would not increase the total benefits derived by society.
2. Resources are allocated within the health sector in a way that maximizes the total benefits derived from those resources. For example, a shift in resources from acute care services to preventive services would not yield greater benefits.
3. Each health care service is produced using the least costly combination of resources that

TABLE 3
National health expenditures, 1950-1979

Year	Dollars (in billions)	Percentage of GNP
1950	12.7	4.5
1960	26.9	5.3
1970	74.7	7.6
1979	212.2	9.0

Source: Gibson, R.M.: National health expenditures, 1979. Health Care Financing Rev. **2**(1):1-36, Summer 1980.

is technically possible. For example, nurse practitioners, rather than physicians, are used to deliver those services that the nurse practitioner renders in a less costly way than would a physician, assuming the quality of the service that would be rendered by the two health providers is equivalent.

This economic reasoning can be applied to the growing share of the economy's resources that have been devoted to the health sector during recent decades. If this shift in resource utilization has not been accompanied by a commensurate increase in benefits derived from the health sector, then there is cause for concern. Many observers question whether the value derived from health care expenditures have paralleled the growth pattern in these expenditures. This skepticism is reflected in the frequency with which "cost containment" is expressed as a goal within the health sector.

Because much of the emphasis in this chapter will be on health expenditures and costs, it is helpful to consider the appropriateness of applying benefit-versus-cost considerations to health care services. Many health care services are delivered for the purpose of extending life and improving the quality of life. The health professional may oppose cost-containment measures as a threat to the quality of patient care. It might be argued that it is wrong to place a value on human life, yet this ultimately must be done in order to weigh benefits against costs in allocating resources to health services. This contention can be answered by a simple fact: we do place a finite value on human life. A scarcity of resources is an economic fact of life, and every decision reached about resource allocation carries an implicit value judgment about the benefit derived from alternative uses of those resources. When some of the alternative potential uses of resources involve measures that would extend human lives, then the decisions concerning the allocation of resources to those measures place, at least implicitly, values on human lives.

The following example illustrates this concept.

Before the oil embargo of 1974, the highway speed limit in most states was in excess of fifty-five miles per hour. In order to conserve oil, a national speed limit of fifty-five miles per hour was enacted. One of the benefits of this policy was a reduction in deaths resulting from automobile accidents. Because until 1974, the opportunity to save lives was not considered a sufficient justification for lowering speed limits, a finite value had been placed on the lives that could have been saved. The existence of a fifty-five mile-per-hour speed limit, rather than a forty mile-per-hour limit, is further evidence that decision makers do not place an infinite value on human life. Thus a finite value of human life is an economic fact. This is not to say that we all agree on the value that should be placed on saving a life. Even among economists who are skilled in benefit/cost analysis, the value that should be assigned to human life in such analyses is a thorny and unresolved issue.

RISING HEALTH EXPENDITURES: THE COMPONENTS

The health sector contains many components, each of which has its own economic characteristics and expenditure trends. Although it is beyond the scope of this chapter to delve into each component, where possible, those characteristics that are applicable to the health sector in general are described. When specific health sector components are discussed, the hospital industry will receive particular attention. The following statements concerning health sector components clarify the reasons behind this emphasis.

1. Expenditures for hospital services represent the largest component of national health expenditures. This component of health expenditures represents an increasing proportion of total health expenditures in the last several decades, growing from about thirty percent of national health expenditures in 1950 to approximately forty percent in 1980.

2. Expenditures for physicians' services have been a declining portion of national health expen-

ditures since 1950, and currently represent less than one-fifth of total health expenditures.

3. Although only about one dollar is spent for nursing home care for every five dollars spent for hospital care, nursing home expenditures represent the most rapidly rising component of national health expenditures (in percentage terms) since the mid-1960s. This growth has been stimulated by the increased importance of government payments for nursing home care since the enactment of the Medicare and Medicaid programs in 1965.

4. The role of the federal government in health care financing expanded significantly in the mid-1960s, when the Medicare and Medicaid programs were enacted. Government spending currently constitutes over forty percent of national health expenditures. Most government health expenditures are payments for services rendered in the private sector, rather than the direct provision of services in government facilities.

5. *Third-party payers* finance about seventy percent of all personal health expenditures in the United States. The term *third-party* refers to a government program or private health insurance plan that represents a third party in the transaction between a health care provider and a consumer. Thus, on the average, Americans pay for only about thirty percent of their health care expenses directly. Of course, through payments for health insurance premiums, higher prices paid to businesses who pay health insurance premiums for their employees, and taxes that support government programs, consumers pay for those services that are not paid directly, or "out-of-pocket." Hospital services are the most extensively covered under third-party programs, as out-of-pocket (direct) payments by consumers represent less than ten percent of total expenditures for hospital care (Gibson, 1980).

Health care expenditures and cost can also be expressed in terms of the basic relationships shown below:

$$E = (P_1 \times Q_1) + (P_2 \times Q_2) + (P_3 \times Q_3)$$
$$C_1 = c_1 \times Q_1; \quad C_2 = c_2 \times Q_2, \text{ etc.}$$

where E is health expenditures during a year, P_1 is the average price of health service "1," Q_1 is the quantity of health service "1" provided in the year, C_1 is the cost of producing health service "1" in the year, and c_1 is the average cost, per unit, of producing health services "1." Thus the increase in expenditures for physicians' services could be examined in terms of two components: trends in fees charged by physicians; and trends in numbers of surgical procedures, office visits, and so forth. In certain situations, it is more useful to think in terms of the cost equation. For example, the cost of producing inpatient hospital care can be seen as the product of the number of inpatient days times the cost per patient day of producing hospital care. The utilization of inpatient care (e.g., the number of inpatient days) is a concern to people who think that excessive hospital utilization has contributed to the high cost of health care. An issue here is whether costly inpatient care should be utilized when services could be rendered on an outpatient basis or in less costly settings (e.g., nursing homes).

The per-unit cost of a health care service is a function of the quantity of inputs used and the price (for example, wage rate) of those inputs. The quantity of inputs has several dimensions. First, there is the question of production efficiency. Are the services produced using the least costly *mix* of inputs—for example, the right mix of registered nurses, licensed practical nurses, nurse aides, and other types of inputs? Also, is the total quantity of personnel and other resources at an efficient level? The answer to this latter question becomes cloudy when the matter of quality is considered. For example, more intensive use of nurses in providing hospital care might improve the quality of care delivered. On the other hand, the use of more nursing personnel may represent a costly waste of resources. In fact, greater intensity of resource utilization is likely to represent both improvements in quality and some degree of production inefficiency.

We now introduce another factor that complicates our analysis of health care expenditures. Part of the current level of health expenditures includes costs for services that were not rendered ten or twenty years ago. New technology has made possible new diagnostic and treatment methodologies, incorporating new types of equipment, practitioner skills, and so forth.

To simplify our discussion of a complex range of variables, our discussion from this point will focus on three broad dimensions of the cost equation.

1. *Health service production capacity.* Here we consider the implementation of new technology, as well as such capacity measures as the numbers of health care practitioners and the numbers of hospital beds.
2. *Health service utilization.* Here we consider both the level of utilization (e.g., inpatient hospital days) and the relative utilization of various types of health care services.
3. *Per-unit cost of production.* This includes the components of production efficiency and input prices.

In the next section of this chapter, we will examine various factors that help us explain rising national health expenditures.

RISING EXPENDITURES: EXPLANATORY FACTORS

A diverse range of variables have contributed to the rise in national health expenditures in this country. For example, a growing proportion of our population is in the age category of sixty-five years and older. The fact that this segment of our population has health service utilization rates far higher than the rest of the population contributes to the growth in total health expenditures. In this section, we will not dwell on the total range of factors associated with rising health expenditures. Rather, our focus will be on those important variables that are not only associated with rising expenditures, but also raise questions concerning the efficiency with which resources are allocated to and within the health sector. The factors to be considered are listed below.

1. Third-party coverage
2. Third-party reimbursement
3. Input prices
4. Health care technology
5. Nonprofit health care institutions
6. Nature of competition
7. Supply/demand interrelationship

Third-party coverage

A relatively short hospital episode can involve the incurrence of expenses that are in excess of the typical American family's monthly income. The need for hospital care or other expensive health care services is generally not predictable. Thus health care expenses cannot be anticipated in a family's budget in the same way as expenses for housing or food. The purchase of health insurance coverage provides a mechanism for budgeting the unexpected expenses associated with health care needs. For those persons unable to afford private health insurance premiums, government programs such as Medicare and Medicaid provide protection against unexpected health care expenses. Thus public and private third-party payment programs provide protection against the catastrophic financial impact that might otherwise arise as a result of illness and injury.

In addition to the financial protection offered, third-party coverage makes the nature of the health care marketplace different from the markets for food, housing, and other consumer goods and services. In purchasing ground beef, consumers consider their spendable income, the price of ground beef, the price of other foods, and prices of other goods and services that might be consumed with that income. In purchasing health care services, the consumer is also concerned with price, but third-party coverage distorts the *effective price* of health care services. For example, consider a consumer who has a Blue Cross–Blue Shield policy that provides full coverage of all services rendered in a hospital. Under these circumstances, the cost of hospital care will not be a consideration in a decision to enter the hospital or in a decision concerning the date of discharge. If surgery that could be performed on an outpatient basis is involved, the lower cost of outpatient surgery will provide no incentive for the consumer to elect outpatient surgery in preference to inpatient surgery.

Thus third-party coverage can affect both the level of health care utilization and the types of health care services utilized. A further impact on the choice of types of health care services utilized can result from third-party coverage that is limited to certain types of services or that provides more extensive coverage for certain types of services. For example, private health insurance coverage has traditionally provided more extensive coverage of inpatient hospital care than of other types of services. Third-party coverage has also been typically limited to services rendered by, or under the direction of, physicians. Such coverage creates an incentive to utilize expensive services when services rendered in less costly settings (e.g., outpatient clinics) or delivered by other practitioners (e.g., nurse practitioners) might be appropriate.

Third-party reimbursement

As the term implies, third-party reimbursement can affect the behavior of two parties in any health care delivery transaction, the consumer and the provider. Via the consumer, third-party coverage can affect the health care provider's behavior by easing the normal constraints of the marketplace. To the extent that the consumer's behavior is insensitive to prices, controls over provider behavior are weakened. In addition, the terms under which third parties reimburse providers can affect the economic behavior of those providers.

One form of third-party reimbursement that is often criticized is *retrospective cost-based reimbursement*. This procedure is used by Medicare, Medicaid, and many Blue Cross plans in reimbursing hospitals. In its most basic form, retrospective cost-based reimbursement involves paying the hospital for all expenses incurred in caring for patients covered by the third party. In some cases, third parties have employed "cost-plus" reimbursement, where a plus factor, defined as a percentage of cost, is reimbursed to acknowledge that certain costs,

such as bad debts, might not be included in the base figure.

To illustrate the impact of cost reimbursement, consider a business firm that is contemplating hiring three new employees at a total annual cost of $30,000. This decision, in a typical business, would be based on whether the three employees would add sufficient productivity to the business to generate $30,000 in new revenue. Now think of a hospital that is considering hiring three additional nurses at a total annual cost of $30,000. Further, we assume that seventy percent of the hospital's revenues are generated through cost-based reimbursement (a percentage not atypical in many areas). The hospital knows that $21,000 (70% of $30,000) will be added to revenues through cost-based reimbursement, regardless of whether the nurses add to the hospital's productivity.

In this day of "cost containment," it is also appropriate to consider the hospital's financial incentives regarding reductions in expenses. Imagine that a hospital determines that, through improved staffing procedures, it is possible to eliminate three nursing positions. Under the conditions illustrated above, seventy percent of the "savings" that might be generated would be reflected in lower cost-based reimbursement. Thus, in general, retrospective cost-based reimbursement dulls the hospital's incentive to be efficient in the utilization of resources.

The fact that third parties have been slow to move away from retrospective cost-based reimbursement can be better understood by considering an alternative reimbursement formula. The Medicare program and certain private health insurance plans reimburse physicians on a usual, customary, and reasonable (UCR) basis. Under UCR, physicians are reimbursed their established fees, providing the same fees are charged to their other patients and the fees are consistent with prevailing fees in the community. In essence, the third party is paying the "market" price to the physician. However, the problem with UCR is that the reimbursement system itself can exert inflationary pressures on physicians' fees, particularly if UCR reimbursement represents a significant portion of physicians' incomes. At any point in time, the third party's ceiling on fees can become targets for those physicians whose fees are below the prevailing ceilings. The tendency for physicians below the ceiling to raise fees, with no direct impact on their insured patients, will exert constant upward pressure on the ceiling. Assuming that the ceiling is periodically adjusted in response to prevailing fees, an upward spiral in physicians' fees can result. A particular problem can be created when third-party coverage is extended to additional types of practitioners (e.g., nurse practitioners) for which the marketplace has not established guidelines concerning reasonable fees.

Government programs and other third parties have recognized the problems inherent in both cost-based and UCR reimbursement. In many cases, reimbursement systems have been tightened relative to the open-ended systems just described somewhat simplistically. Some of the cost-containment strategies that have been employed by third parties will be discussed later in this chapter.

Input prices

For many years, the provision of health care services in the private sector had a philanthropic tradition, both formal and informal. The informal dimension involved the provision of care to persons unable to pay the full price of that care. Many physicians shared in this philanthropic tradition by using "sliding scales" in determining fees. Under this approach, the fee charged to a patient was dependent on that patient's financial status. The labor force in health care institutions, from unskilled labor to nursing personnel, contributed to this informal philanthropy by working for wages that were below prevailing wages for equivalent skill levels elsewhere in the economy. During the 1960s, as third-party reimbursement grew, wages in health care institutions rose relative to the rest of the economy. In a study of health sector wages, Victor Fuchs (1976) concluded that health sector wages

reached parity with wages in other industries by the end of that decade.

Rising wages have contributed to the growth in the cost of producing health care services. From the broader perspective, however, growing wage rates have not been a particularly important determinant of rising health expenditures. Labor costs have actually been a declining portion of hospital costs in the last decade, and, within the labor cost component, increases in the number of persons employed have had a more significant impact on costs than have rising wage rates. Both increasing employment levels and rising nonlabor costs can be partially explained by the next factor that will be considered, health care technology.

Health care technology

Much of the concern over the rising cost of health care services has been focused on the changing nature of health care services—the rendering of new services and quality-enhancing changes in the way services are produced. In many industries, technological change involves finding ways to produce goods and services at lower cost. This is not typically the case in health care settings, especially in hospitals. Rather, technological change has generally involved new service delivery capabilities associated with equipment, space, and labor requirements.

The dilemma created by the development of new health care technology is illustrated by the controversies surrounding the implementation of computerized axial tomography scanners (CAT scanners). The CAT scanner has created new diagnostic capabilities, but it has also raised questions regarding the adoption of costly technology. Do the new diagnostic capabilities created by the CAT scanner justify its cost? If so, how many CAT scanners represent an efficient use of this technology? In an effective marketplace, this question would be answered by the consumer's willingness to support the employment of new technology. However, third-party reimbursement lessens the incentives for an institution to weigh benefits against cost when employing new technology. Thus benefits, particularly as perceived by the medical staff, become the important determinant.

The number of facilities providing a given service raises concerns about "duplication of facilities." The implications are obvious if there are numerous open-heart surgery units in a community where some of those facilities conduct few open-heart procedures. This condition is undesirable from both a quality-of-care perspective and a cost perspective. However, excess capacity is not the only concern with respect to the diffusion of health care technology. Medical efficacy, cost, and the possibility of excessive utilization relative to the benefits derived are also of concern. A complicating factor is illustrated by the CAT scanner example. Hundreds of CAT scanners had been employed in hospitals when research concerning the medical efficacy of this diagnostic technology was still in its infancy. Although it is not unique to the health sector that millions of dollars can be spent on a new technology of unproved benefits, the economic characteristics of the health sector increase the likelihood of such a situation.

Nonprofit health care institutions

Unlike many other industries in our economy, a significant portion of firms in the health care sector are not organized as for-profit organizations. For example, less than fifteen percent of the nation's acute care hospitals are owned by proprietary (for-profit) firms (AHA, 1979). It is commonly assumed that for-profit firms attempt to produce their product in an efficient manner and produce those products for which market demand is sufficient to assure profitability. The profit test is a mechanism that links the preferences of consumers to the production decisions of business firms. In the absence of a profit motive, a nonprofit hospital has the incentive to utilize least-cost production techniques only as long as demands for resources exceed available resources. Under the influence of third-party reimbursement, it is not clear that hospitals perceive such a constraint on resources. Also, the fine line

between inefficient production and the quality-enhancing aspect of greater levels of resource utilization further confuses the conclusions that we might reach concerning the implications of nonprofit economic behavior. Finally, a nonprofit institution has the latitude to initiate services or programs that are not profitable. Given the fact that social values might not be accurately reflected in the markets that exist for health care services, it cannot be assumed that all unprofitable ventures represent inefficient resource allocation. For example, an emergency room in a remote rural hospital might be an unprofitable venture, yet it may be judged as socially desirable. Likewise, we cannot assume that operating all hospitals on a for-profit basis, given the various characteristics of the market with which we are dealing, would be desirable. However, the prevalence of nonprofit institutions is one more market characteristic that raises uncertainty about the efficiency of health resource allocation.

Nature of competition

The term competition—or, more accurately, price competition—usually refers to a market in which a number of firms produce the same or similar products and vie for the consumer dollar on the basis of the price and quality of their product. Under certain conditions, price competition can be an efficient means of distributing resources. A number of the characteristics of the health care market violate the conditions of efficient competition. One such characteristic is the major role of third parties in paying for health care services. The consumer cannot be expected to be sensitive to the relative prices of alternative health care services if a third party is going to pay the bill. The nonprofit status of many health care providers may also diminish the extent to which these providers establish prices in a manner consistent with price competition.

Two other factors operate to limit consumer choice in the selection of hospital care. First, many towns and smaller cities cannot support more than one hospital of sufficient size to render services in an efficient manner. Second, many physicians either have staff privileges at only one hospital or prefer a certain hospital for admitting patients. Thus once patients have selected a physician, they usually have little, if any, choice concerning the hospital to which they will be admitted, if necessary. To a significant extent, therefore, hospitals compete for physicians, not patients. The economic success of a hospital is a function of the number of physicians on its staff and the propensity of those physicians to hospitalize their patients in that institution. The physicians, in turn, generally prefer to use the hospital that provides the range of services and quality of care that can best meet the needs of their patients. Thus to the extent that competition does exist between hospitals, it is competition to offer the latest technology, the widest range of services, and the highest quality of care possible.

The type of competition illustrated above is often in conflict with the goal of efficient health resource allocation. The economic behavior that may be in the best interests of the individual hospital may result in duplication of facilities and wasted resources from the broader community perspective.

Supply/demand interrelationship

Many observers of the health sector have concluded that a phenomenon exists whereby "supply creates its own demand." This means that the demand for health care services is not independent of the supply of health care resources. The per-capita utilization of hospital beds will be greater in areas with more hospital beds; surgical procedures will be performed more frequently in areas with higher concentrations of surgeons, and so on. Because, in any market, resource supplies tend to gravitate to those areas where demand is the greatest, it is difficult to validate or measure this "demand creation" effect in the health sector. However, the rationale for such an effect can be stated.

The consumer/patient is not usually knowledgeable concerning needs for medical care services, but is highly dependent on professional judgment,

usually that of a physician. Physicians, in reflecting on alternative treatments, consider the availability of resources, including alternative demands on their time. Collectively, then, the decisions of physicians to hospitalize "marginal" patients, or to extend patients' stays in hospitals, can be affected by the availability of hospital beds.

At a minimum, the demand-creation effect can result in higher health care expenditures. An additional concern is the undesirable consequences of providing unnecessary health care services. It has been argued that needless deaths can occur as a result of "unnecessary" surgery. Third-party coverage again surfaces as a culprit here. When providers are paid on a piece-rate basis—that is, on the basis of the volume of services they render—the provision of more services generates more provider income. Thus providers (both physicians and hospitals) have an economic incentive to make use of available capacity.

A number of factors associated with rising health care expenditures in the United States have been discussed. In the next section, several approaches that have been proposed and/or tried in an attempt to control the growth of expenditures are presented.

COST CONTAINMENT

To the extent that health sector resources are allocated inefficiently, people do not get the maximum possible benefits from their health care dollars. Although improved efficiency can be achieved either via measures that enhance the benefits derived from health services or measures that contain the cost of health care services, the major emphasis in today's health sector is on cost containment. With some simplification, cost-containment approaches can be categorized in two ways. First, the *regulatory approach* can be seen as a recognition of inherent weaknesses in the markets for health care services. Second, the *market approach* involves restructuring the marketplace to produce more efficient results. The regulatory approach generally involves an expanded role for government; the market approach can also involve government initiatives aimed at altering behavior in the marketplace.

Regulation

Historically, regulation in the health sector has focused on assuring the quality of health care services. For example, the licensure of both health care facilities and personnel sought to protect the consumer from receiving care from incompetent practitioners and in substandard facilities. Regulatory approaches to controlling health care expenditures are of a more recent origin. Regulatory initiatives can be directed at total health care expenditures, total expenditures for specific types of health care services, or the component parts of expenditures for services: prices charged and/or per-unit cost, the quantity of services rendered, or the availability of health care resources.

Regulation of total expenditures

Regulating total expenditures for any purpose involves some government body determining the amount of money that will be allocated to that purpose. At the national level, such a determination is made with respect to expenditures for national defense. School boards make determinations of public expenditures at the school district level. The closest comparable situations in the health sector are in the areas of expenditures for biomedical research and for certain public health activities.

When decentralized (i.e., marketplace) decision making produces questionable performance in allocating resources, centralized decision making offers an alternative. Some would argue that the escalation in health care expenditures, combined with problems of maldistribution of resources, calls for some form of national system whereby the aggregate level and distribution of health care spending would be under centralized control. While a few of the many national health insurance proposals put forward in recent years have incorporated this approach, it is doubtful that such a comprehensive overhaul of the health care system is forthcoming in the foreseeable future.

Regulation of total expenditures for specific types of health care services is a more realistic possibility. In the late 1970s, President Carter proposed legislation in the ninety-sixth and ninety-seventh sessions of Congress that would have placed ceilings on the rate of increase in expenditures for hospital care. The hospital rate-setting program in Rhode Island has operated within the framework of a statewide "cap" on annual increases in hospital expenditures.

Regulation of prices or per-unit cost

During the 1970s, a number of price controls were attempted in the health sector. The most comprehensive application occurred during the Economic Stabilization Program of 1971-1974, when physician fees and hospital rates were subjected to rate-of-increase ceilings. In a number of states, certain third-party reimbursement rates for hospital services are established through *prospective rate-setting (PRS) programs.* Prospective rate setting involves the establishment, by a rate-setting authority, of reimbursement rates prior to the year during which they will apply. The attractive feature of PRS is the requirement that hospitals justify projected costs before they are incurred, rather than simply being paid what they have spent, as under the more common retrospective plans. Because the implementation of PRS is of fairly recent origin, and the specific features of PRS vary across states, it is hard to generalize on its accomplishments and promise. Additional examples of price regulation include the following:

1. In most states, physician fees and nursing home rates are set at fixed levels or subjected to ceilings under Medicaid.
2. Physician fees paid by the Medicare program are subject to ceilings set at regional levels. It should be noted that when a physician's fee exceeds the Medicare ceiling, the physician has the option of billing the patient for the difference.
3. For the past few years, "routine service costs" payable under the Medicare program

have been subject to ceilings based on comparable groupings of hospitals. Routine service costs include nursing costs and other costs associated with the routine care of patients, excluding ancillary services.

4. Some Blue Cross plans establish cost ceilings for specific categories of hospital cost.

Regulation of quantity of services

Increasingly, third-party payers have attempted to control the cost of health care services by establishing rules about the conditions under which they will pay for care. Private insurers have commonly stipulated that only medically necessary care will be insured. However, it is apparent that medical necessity, as determined by the attending physician, and appropriate care rendered in the most efficient way are not synonymous. Following the enactment of Medicare, hospitals were required to have utilization-review committees composed of members of the hospital's medical staff. These committees reviewed the utilization of services by Medicare patients to assure that appropriate care was being rendered.

The viewpoint that peer review among colleagues on a hospital's medical staff was not a sufficient control over excessive utilization led to new legislation in 1972. This legislation created Professional Standards Review Organizations (PSROs). A PSRO is a regional (statewide or substate) organization composed of a physician review committee that reviews the utilization of institutional services by, at a minimum, Medicare and Medicaid patients. These bodies are charged with the responsibility of establishing standards for appropriate and efficient health care service utilization and for denying payment for care that does not meet these standards. Although PSROs have been established in most areas of the country, their experience in carrying out this challenging mandate is not yet sufficient to draw conclusions regarding their ultimate effectiveness.

Formally, PSROs have usually operated on a retrospective basis, that is, making judgments about hospital episodes after the fact. However, it is intended that the standards established by a PSRO should act as guidelines for physicians as they formulate their treatment plans for patients. In addition, PSROs can establish hospital admission certification programs. For nonemergency admissions, approval for the admission and approved length of stay would be required before admission. For emergency conditions, the certification would be issued shortly after admission. Certification programs have been used for a number of years in some state Medicaid programs.

Regulation of resource availability

One approach to controlling the level and nature of health care utilization is to regulate the number, capacity, and range of services offered by health care institutions. The 1972 Social Security Act amendments established a national *certificate-of-need* (CON) program. In order to receive full reimbursement under federal health financing programs, a health care institution must receive prior approval for major capital expenditures—for example, construction projects and equipment purchases. A number of states have CON programs in operation. Generally, the state programs are stronger than the nationally mandated program because of the more stringent penalties imposed for noncompliance.

Effective regulation of health care resources through certificate of need is dependent on effective resource planning on a regional level. The *health system agency* (HSA) is responsible for planning health resources within its health service area, a region that is usually smaller than a state. Under certificate-of-need programs, HSAs render judgments on capital expenditure proposals. Final approval authority rests with a state agency, often the state health planning and development agency, the state-level counterpart to the HSA.

If a health system agency does effective health planning, renders proposal reviews that are consistent with its plans, and has its judgments upheld by state-level authorities, it may well act as a curb on the creation of duplicative facilities and excessive capacity in the health system. However, the HSA is not an appropriate forum regarding the medical efficacy of newly emerging technology. Concern over the adoption of technology of questionable value may require a separate regulatory mechanism. The Food and Drug Administration provides such a mechanism with respect to pharmaceutical products. In 1978, the National Center for Health Care Technology was created to evaluate new medical procedures and equipment. The center is to issue recommendations that can then provide the basis for determining whether Medicare reimbursement will be allowed for such treatment and equipment.

Issues concerning regulation

Health care regulation essentially represents an acknowledgment of the limitations of the private sector. In a number of sectors in the economy, the performance of regulatory programs has been mixed. One of the most common criticisms of regulation has been the tendency of regulatory authorities ultimately to come under the influence of those with the greatest stake in regulatory decisions—namely, those persons or institutions whose behavior is being regulated. A number of the issues raised by regulation of the health sector are listed and discussed below.

1. *System flexibility.* Regulation requires that standards be established against which the behavior of regulated entities can be judged. PSRO judgments must be based on standards of appropriate care; certificate-of-need judgments must be based on standards of appropriate service availability. Today's standard may or may not be appropriate in tomorrow's health care system. Potentially, standards can act as barriers to the development and implementation of more efficient health care delivery systems. For example, PSRO standards that provide sanctions for inpatient treatment modalities under certain diagnostic circumstances could discourage the development of innovative outpatient treatment methodologies. States establishing defined roles for certain health care practitioners

(e.g., physicians) might stifle the evolution of new roles for alternative practitioners (e.g., nurse practitioners). The key to this issue is the flexibility of the regulatory process, both in reality and as perceived by those persons and institutions who might initiate innovative practices. To the extent that the regulatory authority has had its functions validated through the legal system, it may be reluctant to change standards that have survived legal challenges.

2. *The "spillover" effect.* Some observers have suggested that regulation in the health care system tends to create a spillover effect. For example, control of one element of health care cost may tend to generate greater cost in other elements. This phenomenon was observed in one research study that examined the effect of early certificate-of-need programs. The study concluded that CON programs had been effective in controlling the growth in numbers of hospital beds, yet no impact on the total level of hospital capital investments was observed (Salkever and Bice, 1976). It appeared that the programs, while curtailing one type of capital investment (expansion in bed capacity), resulted in investment funds being channeled into areas that were not subject to certificate-of-need review and/or investments that the review process was less effective in controlling. The spillover effect is also a possible outcome of regulations that apply to only certain types of patients. For example, controls on Medicare reimbursement may, rather than controlling cost, simply transfer the burden of payment to other third parties and self-pay patients.

Under Medicare reimbursement for physician services, reimbursement limits may result in a greater burden on the Medicare beneficiary. If desired, physicians can collect the difference between their fees and the Medicare limit directly from the patient. On the other hand, a physician cannot collect payment from a Medicaid patient above that reimbursed by the Medicaid program. This situation creates another problem, namely, the possibility that fee-level restrictions will limit physician participation in the Medicaid program and, thus, restrict the availability of services to Medicaid beneficiaries.

One response to the spillover effect is to make regulations more comprehensive in scope. Alternatively, the incentives created by regulations can be examined more carefully and dealt with accordingly. For example, if controls on resources and costs associated with inpatient hospital care encourage hospitals to expand outpatient programs, this may be seen as a desirable spillover.

3. *Coordination of regulation.* A single regulatory program cannot be viewed in isolation from other programs. PSROs, HSAs, rate-setting authorities, and other regulatory bodies each make decisions that affect the impact of other regulatory bodies. For example, PSRO judgments concerning appropriate treatment modalities should influence CON decisions concerning resource availability. Rate-review decisions should be made with cognizance of legitimate needs of hospitals to finance approved investments in new services. Under current practices in most states, this coordination must be done by separate, largely autonomous regulatory authorities. This creates the potential for fragmented decision making. The alternative may be to create comprehensive regulatory authorities. This raises concerns as to whether a ''super'' regulatory body would devote sufficient attention to each aspect of its broad range of regulatory activities, whether such an authority could command the necessary diversity of staff expertise, and whether we are willing to rest so broad a mandate in one regulatory body.

4. *Distribution of decision-making authority.* Most management scientists agree that decision-making authority can be too centralized in an organization or system. Those persons responsible for implementing decisions often have the firsthand knowledge of most significance to effective decision making. To the extent that regulation ties the hands of those who administer health care programs and institutions, the potential contribution of those administrators to effective decision making is limited. Centralized decision making tends to create a system that is inflexible and unresponsive to change. On the other hand, regulation can be seen as a way to require accountability on the part of health care providers. A certificate-of-need program, for example, creates an environment in which the medical staff of a hospital must recognize that careful analysis, both financial and medical, must precede decisions about the implementation of new technology. A PRS program, for example, can instill more effective budgetary practices in hospitals.

5. *The state of the art.* The previously mentioned study of certificate-of-need programs raises another issue. The observed emphasis of CON programs on hospital beds might have resulted from a lack of sophistication on the part of regulatory authorities. If thirty percent of the hospital beds in an area are empty on an average day, it may be obvious that approval of additional hospital beds is unwise. On the other hand, setting curbs on the number of CAT scanners to be allowed in the region may be a more difficult matter. The existence of regulations does not assure the existence of the talents and skills necessary for effective regulation. When a regulatory program does not appear to be successful, several responses are possible. First, we can decide that successful implementation of the regulatory mandate was infeasible. Second, we can be patient and hope that the regulators develop the necessary expertise through experience. Third, we can examine the regulatory program to determine whether the resources available to the regulatory body are sufficient to secure the talent and work force necessary for effective regulation.

The market approach

Concerns about the regulatory approach can also be addressed by assessing ways to improve the private marketplace. This basically involves trying to change the incentives that influence the behavior of health care providers and consumers. A number of changes in the way we deliver and finance health care services have been suggested. For example, health education programs have been proposed as a way to improve the health-related behavior of the population (e.g., smoking cessation), giving greater emphasis to preventive health care, and making the consumer a more informed user of health care services. More intensive use of computer technology, expanded roles for nonphysician health care personnel, and development of more ambulatory care centers are seen as desirable ways of improving the efficiency of health care delivery. This section focuses on two basic approaches to altering the way health care services are organized and reimbursed: (1) the restructuring of the health insurance system; and (2) the development of health maintenance organizations.

Restructuring health insurance

As discussed earlier, health insurance, by affecting the relative price of alternative health care services, can create undesirable incentives for consumer and provider behavior. The health insurance system can be altered in two basic ways. First, changes can be made in the nature of health care expenditures that will be paid by the health insurance plan. Second, changes can be made in the balance between the obligations of the insurance plans and the consumer in paying for health care services. In the former case, a number of alternatives are possible. Where health insurance coverage has created biases against cost-efficient care, modifications can eliminate these biases. Outpatient and ambulatory care can be covered on equal terms with inpatient care, and, where appropriate standards can be established, certain services can be covered only when rendered on an ambulatory basis. For example, certain surgical services might be covered only on an outpatient basis, and it may be required that certain types of diagnostic tests be performed only before a patient is admitted to the hospital. Other programs can be established to encourage desired behavior. Some health insurance plans have provided coverage for receiving second opinions when elective surgery has been recommended. Some Blue Cross plans have disallowed payments for routine tests conducted on hospital admission

unless they are justified by the attending physician. In general, the insurance mechanism can be used as a way of reinforcing standards of efficient medical practice as such standards are established.

Another approach to making health insurance a positive force is to make the consumer a more active participant in paying for care. Deductibles (under which the insurance plan is only responsible for expenses above some predetermined amount, e.g., $100) and coinsurance (where the insured individual pays a specified percentage of covered expenses, e.g., 20%) can increase the cost consciousness of the consumer. Another approach is to define the insurance plan's responsibilities in terms of a "fair price" and make insured persons responsible to the extent that they consume more expensive services. A problem with making the consumer a participant in paying for health care services has to do with the consumer's knowledge of prevailing prices and the effective choice available to consumers. For example, the consumer's choice of a physician may be the key factor in the selection of a hospital.

Another deterrent to altering health insurance coverage is securing consumer acceptance of such modifications. One approach to this problem is to change the nature of existing incentives. A major factor here is current federal income tax laws. A significant portion of private health insurance premiums are currently paid by employers, and such payments represent tax-free income to the employee. Changes in income tax legislation could eliminate this incentive to receive income in the form of tax-free insurance premium payments and might result in a reexamination of the value of health insurance coverage versus the true cost of extensive health insurance coverage.

Health maintenance organizations

Persons opposed to further regulation in the health sector often suggest that introducing more competition into the health sector would be a preferred alternative. For over a decade, the federal government has attempted to stimulate market competition by supporting the development of health maintenance organizations (HMOs). An HMO is an organization that provides a comprehensive range of health care services to its members in return for an established monthly enrollment fee.

The oldest HMO-type organization is the prepaid group-practice plan (PGP). The largest of these is Kaiser-Permanente, which has more than 3.7 million members, mostly in plans in the West Coast states. In each Kaiser plan, the physicians are salaried members of the Permanente Medical Group Practice. The Kaiser plan owns and operates its own ambulatory care facilities and hospitals. The need to establish enrollment fees that are competitive with the premiums charged by private health insurance plans creates an incentive to acquire and use resources in an efficient manner. Being paid a salary, rather than fee for service, the physician has no incentive to render unnecessary care. In fact, cost-saving bonuses encourage the physician to provide services in the most cost-effective setting and modality. The most striking impact of PGPs on their members' health care utilization, when compared with experience under traditional health insurance plans, is significantly lower hospital inpatient utilization rates. For the Kaiser plans, this impact is reflected in their planning for hospital facilities, since they have hospital beds to population ratios that are about half that of the national average.

Though the accomplishments of many PGPs have been impressive, the number of people enrolled in these plans has only been significant in a limited number of metropolitan areas. Beginning in the early 1970s, the federal government sought to build on the perceived strengths of the PGP concept. The HMO concept, as it was defined in federal legislation, includes prepaid group-practice plans and an alternative HMO prototype: the individual practice association (IPA). The IPA has certain features in common with the PGP: namely, prepayment income from enrollment fees, comprehensive health care benefits, and physician peer-review mechanisms to assure the appropriate provi-

sion of services. However, in an IPA, participating physicians retain their independent office practices (often solo practices), render services to HMO enrollees as well as other patients, and receive payments from the HMO on a fee-for-service basis (within negotiated constraints on total payments to physicians).

As mentioned earlier, many HMO proponents view this delivery approach as a positive competitive force in the health sector. Competition among HMOs as well as between HMOs and private health insurance carriers is seen as a means of creating more effective cost-containment incentives for these organizations. By including the IPA in the definition of HMOs, it was intended that the HMO concept would be attractive to a broader diversity of health care consumers and providers than those that are attracted to PGP plans.

In the last decade, the development of HMOs has been impressive in both the number of new HMOs and the number of communities in which HMOs have been established. However, HMO enrollment still represents a small fraction of the population. Three major factors will affect the future effectiveness of prepaid health plans as a competitive force in the health system:

1. The financial viability and growth of new and recently established HMOs
2. The ability of the younger HMOs in general, and IPAs in particular, to replicate the performance of the more established prepaid group-practice plans such as Kaiser-Permanente
3. The continued evolution of the prepaid health plan concept into new prototypes that are both cost effective and attractive to health care consumers and providers

SUMMARY

It is an economic fact of life that national resources are insufficient to satisfy all the needs and wants of the population. This fact is realized in different ways. For example, a family is forced to "make do" with their automobile for another year because they cannot afford to purchase a new one. Nurse administrators are not able to convince the hospital's administration that they should be allotted the nursing positions that they believe could provide a higher quality nursing care.

Realizing that resources are scarce, we are able to understand the true costs of using resources in inefficient ways. Devoting resources to uses that are not justified by their productive contribution diverts those resources from potentially more productive uses. The family's inability to purchase a new automobile may reflect poor budgeting of the family's expenditures in the past. Nurse administrators may be forced to live with insufficient staff because the hospital has offered services that unnecessarily duplicate services adequately provided elsewhere in the community.

The growth in national health expenditures during recent decades reflects, in part, inefficiencies in the use of health sector resources. This chapter has discussed many characteristics of the health care system that are conducive to inefficient resource allocation. At the heart of the problem are the incentives created by the ways health care services are financed. The prominent role of third-party payers (government programs and private health insurance companies) creates an environment in which health care providers and consumers do not adequately consider all benefits and costs in making decisions about the utilization of health

care services. Inefficient resource utilization diminishes the availability of resources for more productive applications elsewhere in the health sector and the economy.

Alarm concerning rising health expenditures has led to the development of new regulatory programs. Concerns regarding the impact of regulation have encouraged efforts to improve the effectiveness of private markets. Neither the regulatory approach nor the market-improvement approach has demonstrated considerable success in curtailing health care expenditures to date. Although many dimensions of our future health care system are not clear at this point, continued emphasis on finding ways to control health care expenditures can be anticipated. Increasingly, those who affect the allocation of health sector resources will be held accountable for their decisions.

REFERENCES

American Hospital Association guide to the health care field, Chicago, 1979, AHA.

Fuchs, V.R.: The earnings of allied health personnel—are health workers underpaid? Exploration Econ. Res. **3**(2):408-432, Summer 1976.

Fuchs, V.R.: Who shall live? New York, 1974, Basic Books.

Gibson, R.M.: National health expenditures, 1979, Health Care Financing Rev. **2**(1):1-36, Summer 1980.

Salkever, D., and Bice, R.: The impact of certificate-of-need controls on hospital investment, Milbank Mem. Fund Q. **54**(2):185-214, Spring 1976.

To be sure, if the reader's objective is to find quickly and effortlessly the answers to the problems we have raised, he will be bewildered and disappointed.

From Melden, A.I.: Ethical theories, p. 19. Copyright © 1967 by Prentice-Hall, Inc.

13

ETHICAL ISSUES IN NURSING

Anne J. Davis

The perennial ethical dilemmas confronting nurses have both broad relevance and complex ramifications for all those engaged in the health care industry. The ethical principles involved in the change-agent role cover a wide range of issues and situations; this discussion, however, will be limited to a few selected major ethical principles that are central to that role. The context for the development of these ethical principles has three dimensions: (1) the nurse and the individual patient; (2) the nurse and the system; and (3) the nurse and the nursing profession. Obviously, these categories are not mutually exclusive, but for purposes of discussion they will be dealt with separately.

Although people face many dilemmas, those defined as ethical dilemmas are situations that present conflicting moral claims. For example, there can be a dilemma between an individual's professional role obligation and personal value system. A dilemma can also have approach-avoidance characteristics, where one ethical principle implies an action while a second principle discourages the action.

Every profession has a code of ethics that provides guidance in the practice of that field, and nursing is no exception. The American Nurses' Association (1976) has developed a *Code for Nurses* indicating nursing's acceptance of the responsibility and trust with which it has been vested by society. Once having entered the nursing profession, each person inherits some measure of that responsibility and trust that has accrued to the profession over the years, and the corresponding obligation to adhere to a code of conduct. Although codes of ethics are indispensable for practitioners, they nevertheless have, by their very nature, the limitation of not being able to deal with ethical dilemmas with great specificity. They cannot provide specific actions that should be taken in a complex given situation, but they do provide some general comments on broad issues and suggest general ethical stances.

ETHICAL THEORIES

In order to reason through an ethical dilemma, some understanding of ethical theory is necessary. A thorough discussion of ethical theory remains outside the main focus of this chapter, but numerous sources can be helpful in attempting a more detailed examination (MacIntyre, 1966; Sellars and Hospers, 1970).

By definition, ethics refers to the science or study of moral values, and as such, serves as a code of principles and ideals that guide action. The word "ethics," derived from the Greek term of *ethos*, originally referred to customs, modes of conduct, expected standards, and moral criteria for action (Davis and Aroskar, 1978). In current usage, the term ethics generally refers to character and motives that influence behavior.

Three schools of thought in ethics have been developed: descriptive, metaethics, and normative ethics. Descriptive ethics concerns itself with how people actually behave. A second tradition, metaethics, addresses the semantics of meaning; and the third tradition, normative ethics, raises questions about what is right, what is good, and what is obligatory (Frankena, 1973). Normative ethics is explained by two different theories: (1) deontology or formalism; and (2) teleological ethics or utilitarianism. Approaching an ethical dilemma with deontology focuses mainly on the notion of duty or obligation. In this reasoning, an ethical act is one that is in agreement with an individual's obligation or duty. To know whether an act is wrong or right, it is necessary to determine whether it is in accordance with a valid moral rule. One writer has listed ten valid moral rules: Do not kill, do not cause pain, do not disable, do not deprive of freedom or opportunity, do not deprive of pleasure, do not deceive, keep your promise, do not cheat, obey the law, do your duty (Gert, 1966). These rules form the basis of deontological ethics.

The other normative theory of ethics, utilitarianism, judges an action as morally right or wrong by judging the consequences of the action

(Brody, 1976). The major principle in this theory holds that right action is that which produces the greatest amount of good or pleasure for the greatest number. The act itself is not right or wrong; rather, the consequences are either right or wrong.

A combination of ethical theories often serves to explain, describe, or predict the decisions people make. Realistically, most people are concerned with the means as well as the ends of their actions and thinking. This is called ethical pluralism, and implies that people will gather maximal information in order to examine the complexity of a given situation so as to select the most ethically sound action. Before attempting to change a situation or policy, it is useful to reflect on the ethics of the current situation, as well as to consider the ethics that will be involved as a result of the change itself. In some instances, although the ethics of the situation may not be the best, the change may bring about a less desirable situation.

A change agent ordinarily possesses some degree of power, or domination. The meanings of these words, often used as synonyms, are uncertain, shifting, and overlapping, depending on their context. For the purpose of this discussion, power refers to a generalized potentiality for getting one's own way or for bringing about change in the actions or conditions of others.

THE NURSE AND THE INDIVIDUAL PATIENT

In complex organizations such as hospitals, there is a division of labor in which people enact roles that have different amounts of power built into them. For example, directors of nursing service are usually seen as having more power within their role to change events or people than staff nurses do. However, it is important to realize that, although power is unequally distributed among roles within a system, there are some areas in which the staff nurse may have more power than the nursing service director. For example, staff nurses may have more power in a situation with individual patients, since they have both knowledge about and a relationship with these people. The staff nurse's abil-

ity to influence or have power over the individual patient situation entails some possible ethical dilemmas that require examination. The ethical issues most apparent here are autonomy, paternalism, coercion, and informed consent.

Autonomy

Autonomy, a form of personal liberty, is the ethical principle that values the rights of individuals to determine their own course of action in accordance with some chosen plan. In essence, autonomy is the person's self-reliance, independence, and self-contained ability to decide. Diminished autonomy occurs in situations where individuals become excessively dependent on others and incapable of thinking or acting on their own. In ethics applied to the health care arena, usually referred to as bioethics, certain categories of people have been labeled vulnerable because they are more open to control by others: for example, children, the mentally ill and retarded, the aging and the dying patient. It could be argued that all patients admitted to the hospital have, to some extent, the potential for being vulnerable to control by others and therefore of having their autonomy violated. Basically, the concept of autonomy refers to being one's own person without constraints by another's action or without limitations that result from one's physical capabilities (Beauchamp and Childress, 1979).

Some people believe that autonomy is such a supreme value that it is inconsistent with the authority of the state, social groups, or individuals who enact roles of authority, such as health professionals, who can make decisions over the lives of others. However, generally speaking, this is seen as a radical position because it would imply that, among other things, health care providers could never ethically intervene in the lives of autonomous patients except in those instances where the individual patient has made an autonomous decision. Most people do not agree with this position because it has the potential to unravel the fabric of society, and in some instances, it may indeed cause harm. The task, then, is to find some balance between the rights of the individual and the obligations of the state, or, in bioethics, the obligations of health care professionals.

Although total individual autonomy may not be viewed as an absolute right, autonomy as a general principle is nevertheless regarded as a primary value in this culture. In health care facilities, the patient's autonomy can be easily violated because of the power structure and the roles enacted by those involved, including the change agent. This fact led the American Hospital Association to develop the "Patient's Bill of Rights" (Davis and Aroskar, 1978). This document speaks to the institution's obligation to patients in promoting their rights to certain kinds of care and consideration within an institutional setting. One point in the "Patient's Bill of Rights" is that patients have the right to obtain complete, current information concerning diagnosis, treatment, and prognosis in terms that they can reasonably be expected to understand. This implies that patients have the right to make decisions about their own well-being once they have all the necessary information, and it also implies that health care professionals have the obligation to provide such information and to act in accordance with the ethical principle of veracity or truth telling. The patient's autonomy, in part, is dependent on the health care professional's veracity.

Autonomy and paternalism

One of the ways that patient autonomy can be violated is through paternalistic behavior on the part of physicians and nurses. Paternalism refers to practices that restrict the liberty of individuals, without their consent, where the justification for these actions is either to prevent individuals from harming themselves or to produce some benefit for them that they would not otherwise secure. In the many discussions of this principle, the major ethical issue centers on whether paternalistic justifications are morally acceptable. Those who support paternalism as ethical say it is morally justified only under certain circumstances. They contend that limiting personal liberty is justified if, through their

own actions, people would produce serious harm to themselves or would fail to secure an important benefit. Those who oppose paternalism argue that the principle is not a valid moral principle under any conditions and that it should be used only under extremely restricted circumstances. An example of restricted circumstance can be found in the case of the individual who has a contagious disease and who, if left at liberty, would infect many others—thereby causing harm for many people.

Paternalism, the use of coercion to achieve a good that is not recognized as such by the individual for whom the good is intended, plays an important role in medical and nursing decisions. In the change-agent role, as it is enacted within the context of the nurse-patient relationship, paternalism can serve to limit the liberty and autonomy of the patient. This constitutes an ethical dilemma that should be thought through before any actions are taken. One issue that arises here has to do with the interaction of patient compliance and coercion of that patient by the nurse who is in the role of change agent. In nursing, we speak of patient teaching and the need for patients to comply with the prescribed treatment program. Within our own professional value system we view patient compliance as something that is in their own best interests. But what if that patient refuses to comply or only partially complies? What, if any, ethical obligations does the nurse have in this situation? Is it ever ethically justified to coerce patients even when it is in their own best interests as defined by the nurse?

Autonomy and informed consent

Another major consideration in the ethical principle of autonomy is that of informed consent. The "Patient's Bill of Rights" and the code of ethics for both medicine and nursing either explicitly state or imply that before undertaking therapeutic or research procedures, personnel must obtain informed consent from the patient. Although consent measures have been developed to promote patient autonomy, they serve other functions as well. These additional functions include the protection of patients, the avoidance of fraud and duress, the encouragement of self-scrutiny by health professionals, the promotion of rational decisions, and the promotion of autonomy as a general social value (Capron, 1974). It is usually considered the physician's ethical and legal obligation to obtain informed consent; however, the nurse often becomes involved in this process. For example, nurses may be asked to obtain the signature from patients on the consent form. In undertaking this task, or in just talking with patients about an upcoming medical procedure, the nurse may realize that the patient does not fully understand the implications of the consent. What ethical obligations does the nurse have in this situation? What sort of changes can or should nurses attempt to make if this type of situation continues? What is the ethical response to the situation in which physicians tell nurses that they have been unable to obtain informed consent and ask them to use their relationship with the patient to obtain consent to the medical procedure that is in the best interests of the patient?

In order to answer these questions more fully and to reason through these situations ethically, a clearer understanding of informed consent as a basic principle in bioethics may prove helpful. First, underlying the concept of informed consent lies the moral duty to seek valid consent because the individual is an autonomous person with all the entitlements that status confers (Beauchamp and Childress, 1979). The law has spoken to this moral duty in its statements on behalf of autonomy. Essentially, it says that people who are adults and of sound mind have the right to determine what shall be done with their own bodies because Anglo-American law begins with the premise of individual self-determination. It follows that people are responsible for their own bodies and have the right to prohibit the performance of lifesaving surgery or other medical treatment, except in cases of emergency where the individual is unconscious and where treatment is necessary before consent can be obtained (*Natanson* v. *Kline,* 1960). In these emergency situations, the health professional's ethical

obligation is to obtain informed consent from a family member. If this is not possible, the professional's obligation to uphold the sanctity of life outweighs the patient's right to give informed consent in emergency situations.

Several elements constitute informed consent. The act of consent itself must be voluntary and based on the patient's having received adequate information as to risks, benefits, alternative procedures (including no treatment), and the consequences of all these alternatives to the extent that they are known. Additionally, the individual patient or someone speaking in the patient's best interests, such as a family member, must be competent in order to give consent.

The ethics of the nurse as change agent should be predicated on the ethical principle of autonomy. This may mean that, in some instances, the patient will refuse treatment. According to bioethical literature, refusal in instances that are not life threatening have not created many difficulties. When patients refuse health care in situations that are life threatening, grave difficulties confront the health care providers. These difficulties stem from the nurse's ethical obligation to provide the best care possible and to participate in the saving of patients' lives when medically possible. This raises the issue of sanctity of life versus quality of life. Another, more difficult situation arises when a second party refuses lifesaving procedures for the patient. The issue here is who has the right to make such a decision for the patient?

Autonomy and nursing

Since the principle of autonomy is central to the nurse-patient relationship, nurses need to be aware of this principle as they attempt to enact the change-agent role with patients. The concept of power—defined as the ability to get one's own way or to bring about changes in other people's actions or conditions—which is central to the change-agent role, can be misused in ways that violate ethical principles. Such misuse can flow from a lack of thoughtful consideration for individual patients, who have the right to nursing care that includes respect for their human dignity and their uniqueness, including their decisions (ANA, 1976). Additionally, the violation of the individual patient's autonomy can be an outgrowth of the nurses' belief that their professional, ethical obligation outweighs the right of the patient to autonomous action. In such cases, it is important to think through the situation from an ethical base and to discuss the ethical dilemma with the other involved health professionals.

THE NURSE AND THE SYSTEM

Nurses as change agents are in particularly advantageous positions to stimulate change in the health care facility where they are employed. In undertaking such action, which may have far-reaching consequences, the ethical principle of justice becomes a central concern. Here the actions of the change agent have the potential to change facility policies that not only affect the individual patient but may also affect many, if not all, patients in that facility. Additionally, such a policy change may extend to affect nursing and other staff as well.

Justice

Unjust actions can be thought of as falling into three categories. First, invidious discrimination or arbitrarily unequal treatment in legislating, administering, or enforcing rules, or in the maldistribution of burdens and benefits in a society, constitutes one category of unjust actions. Exploitation or taking advantage of another's trust to gain unfairly at the other's expense, or placing the other at an unfair advantage is the second category of unjust behavior. And finally, unjust behavior arises in those situations where judgmental injustice or the making of false derogatory judgments about the other occurs (Feinberg, 1978).

On the other hand, justice is present when individuals have been given what is their due or owed to them, and therefore have been given what they deserve or can legitimately claim. The more restricted concept, distributive justice, refers to the proper distribution of social benefits and burdens within a society. When we say that people have a right to health care, we need to understand that for every right there is an attending obligation on someone's part. In order to operationalize this right, we need to use the concept of justice so that the benefits can be distributed in a just fashion.

Bases of justice

Most societies have worked out their distribution of benefits by using several principles in their theory of justice. A fairly standard list of the criteria on which decisions are made stipulates the following: (1) to each individual an equal share, (2) to each individual according to needs, (3) to each individual according to merit, (4) to each individual according to societal contribution, and (5) to each individual according to individual effort. The principle of need as a criterion for making just decisions means that distribution is just when it is based on need; but then we must go a step further and determine what we mean by the idea of need. Obviously, such a concept as need is open to several interpretations, therefore the meaning that we use must be made explicit before a change agent can begin to implement any policy concerning the distribution of benefits. Usually when we say that individuals need something, we mean that without that thing they will be at least detrimentally affected, or will be at most harmed. Many of the bioethical issues of justice arise in the discussion of distribution of scarce resources.

Allocation of resources

Problems of justice in the allocation of resources can be divided into two categories: (1) macroallocation and (2) microallocation. Discussing distribution of resources from a macroallocation perspective focuses on issues about how much of society's resources should be exchanged for social goods such as health-related expenditures. Included in this discourse would be a consideration of how priorities are to be established for the distribution of these resources (Beauchamp and Childress,

1979). These sorts of discussions usually occur in large decision-making bodies such as the U.S. Congress, the state legislatures, and similar bodies.

From the microallocation perspective within the health care system, the concern centers on such issues as which person or group of people will receive some scarce preventive or therapeutic procedure or will have extensive nursing services. The intensive care units (ICUs) in major medical centers provide an excellent arena in which to examine the microallocation of resources. Both the machinery and the supply of highly qualified nursing staff in the ICU, CCU, and the intensive newborn nursery are expensive items in the hospital budget. There is always a specific amount of money that, if used for one budget item, is not available for other uses either in that facility or in the health care budget at large. For example, for every dollar spent in exotic curative measures that may or may not cure, less money is available for preventive costs. The three most basic ethical questions that include the concept of justice in these allocations are as follows: (1) Who should receive these services and how does this distribution of resources affect other budget items? (2) Who should receive these resources when not all who need them can receive them? and (3) Is it ever ethical to remove an individual from such resources if such an action will most likely result in the patient's death? Always with such ethical questions regarding microallocation of resources, some larger questions arise as well. These include, but are not limited to: (1) Who will determine the answers to these microallocation questions and on what basis? (2) How will the decision maker(s) deal with the ethical dimensions of such questions? Will the concept of justice be central in the decision? The first set are questions of justice, whereas the second set raise the issue of who will or should dispense this justice.

Sometimes the hospital, or more specifically the critical care unit, has not developed a formal policy for dealing with these issues of microallocation. When this is the case, what often occurs is that the patient with the least probability of survival remains in the critical care unit. Rescher (1969) has designed a selection system for the allocation of exotic medical lifesaving therapy. Some may argue that critical care units are no longer considered exotic or extraordinary; however, this selection system can provide us with some useful ways of viewing the critical care unit situation. Rescher argues that five factors must be taken into account. The first factor is the relative likelihood of success. This raises the question of whether the chance of the treatments' being successful can be rated high, good, or average. Second, assuming the success of the treatment, the question then becomes the life expectancy considering the patient's age and condition. Third, to what extent do the patients have responsibility to others in their immediate family? Fourth, are the patient's past services to society outstanding, substantial, or average? And finally, considering age, training, talents, and past record of performance and assuming adequate recovery, will the patient render future services to society that can be characterized as outstanding, substantial, or average? Obviously, such a list as this one, in and of itself, is insufficient because there is no specific set of procedures for taking all of these factors into account. Importantly, there are no guidelines as to the relevant weight that is to be given to each factor in determining the allocation of scarce resources.

Although the ethical principle of justice is complex and presents many theoretical and practical problems, nurses as change agents must nevertheless give serious consideration to it when they aim to change the system or some part of it. Many decisions that affect the allocation of resources are made by committees. For example, many medical centers have an ethics committee that can deliberate on ethical issues of resource allocation along with ethical issues in specific clinical situations, and can recommend a new policy or a change in policy. Nurses, especially nurses as change agents, need to be members of these committees that have formal input and potential power in changing the system. This means that in some instances the first change that should occur is the reorganization of committees or other recommending or decision-making groups so that numerous departments in the hospital have formal ongoing input into these decisions.

THE NURSE AND THE NURSING PROFESSION

A colleague at the university has a sign on her door that reads: "I want either less corruption or more chance to participate in it." On first blush, that statement is humorous because of the irony involved in its message, but it also says something about our attitude toward power, which we often tend to equate with corruption. Most of us who have been socialized in the middle-class mold in this country, especially if we are professionals and women, have an ambivalent response to the whole notion of power. Power has been, and still is, a word that is tinged with distaste for many who think of themselves as being above such considerations. Perhaps this can be traced to the two basic philosophical stands in this country, democracy and religion, both of which interacted in establishing our social foundations over 200 years ago. It seems that the common perception of power, when reflected in large concerns such as professional issues, contains the idea that power is something not quite democratic and not fitting into the belief that the meek shall inherit the earth. Often we nod knowingly in our discussion of the political process and find ourselves not entirely surprised that power has been abused in high, and not so high, places.

As change agents who hope to alter the larger scene and change the situation for many people, nurses must come to grips with their ambivalence toward power. Personal power can be curtailed by any number of factors, including inability to use the power one has either formally or informally in the larger system. Of course, nurses do need to be politically aware in order to avoid unrealistic expectations of the power structure, which could lead to feelings of defeat when one falls short of the goal.

An individual nurse or a group of nurses representing the profession have the added burden of being, for the most part, women in a women's occupation. The socialization process of women has in the past played into the status quo of the power structure. It may be true that power can corrupt and absolute power corrupts; but we also need to understand that powerlessness corrupts by undermining integrity and inhibiting human growth.

Historically in this country, women have seldom been in power positions at the top of the societal institutions such as the legal, educational, health, religious, and other such institutions. More often, what power women have had could be called informal power. We have at least two sayings that reflect this situation. The hand that rocks the cradle, rules the world. Behind every successful man there is a good woman.

Every profession has an organization that acts both to maintain certain present situations against outside forces and also to change other situations. Both of these activities are done in the name of professional self-interest and the protection of the public. In order to undertake these activities and to have some record of success, the professional organization must exercise power. It does this through various activities, including lobby efforts in Washington, D.C. and collective bargaining at the local level.

Change agent and collective bargaining

Some evidence indicates that where nurses work under contract gained through collective bargaining, their salaries are higher and work conditions are better. However, collective bargaining for nurses is not without some ethical considerations.

Nurses' rights and obligations

Often in the discussion of nursing ethics we focus on the obligations of those in the nursing role. Underlying the concept of change agent is the idea that the nurse has an obligation to correct or make situations better. There seems to be a strain between the notion of nurses' obligations and nurses' rights, and this surfaces in dramatic form in collective bargaining. Indeed, the question of whether nurses have rights at all has been debated (Bandman and Bandman, 1978). One ethical position says that a professional role confers a privilege, not a right, whereas the other ethical position makes the following point. In the best tradition of the nursing profession, the imperative has been to restore or safeguard the rights of individuals by providing the conditions necessary for recovery. This can only be achieved when the nurse, as a professional practitioner, demands conditions necessary to discharge role obligations and responsibilities. The point is further made by raising the question: how can nurses participate in changing social, political, and economic conditions that are major determinants of health care without asserting their professional right and competence to do so? More specifically, this question and related issues lead us to examine the collective bargaining process for professionals and the role of the change agent in this process.

The ethics of collective bargaining

About eighty percent of all working nurses in the United States are employed in hospitals, yet the traditional notion of the professional is one who is not employed in a complex social institution but is either self-employed or works in a small group of colleagues. As this situation changes for numerous professional groups, unionization and collective bargaining will become more of a factor for many of the white-collar worker groups such as lawyers and university professors. The ethical dilemma arises from the inherent strain between the professional's role obligation to the patient or client and the professional's right to certain working conditions. Several questions come into play in any consideration of this strain. How does the professional group balance obligations to patients or clients and their own rights? Is it ever ethically justified to place more weight on the professional's rights than on the patient's rights if and when they conflict? Is it possible that in the name of immediate patients' rights and nurses' obligation, patients may be placed in unsafe positions that can lead to injury? For exam-

ple, when nurses are asked to work two shifts in the name of the patient's right to receive nursing care and the nurses' obligation to put the patient's needs before their own, is this a misplaced, and possibly dangerous, case of calling on ethical principles?

Often the reasons given for nurses entering into collective bargaining is that it will benefit patients. That may or may not be true. One needs to raise the interesting question of what ethical constraints lead us to avoid the notion that nurses who are better paid (which, in this society, means that you are appreciated) and work under better conditions cannot find an ethical base for this situation on its own merit.

The change agent involved in collective bargaining activities needs to think about the complex dimensions of this activity, which has several role strains. Two strains have been identified as professional self-image versus employees' realities of nurses; and the question of nurses' rights versus obligations. Many nurses and other health professionals, including physicians and hospital administrators, will argue against collective bargaining. The change agent, who will be at the forefront of this activity, must be articulate and be able to state clearly the ethics of the bargaining stance that has been taken.

The ethics of the strike

Eventually in some situations the change agent will suggest, encourage, or actually move to declare a strike because the collective bargaining negotiations have broken down. Even if one can ethically justify nurses as employees entering into collective bargaining, the strike presents special ethical dilemmas.

It is clearly impossible to justify a nurses' strike in terms of the traditional ethics of the profession. This ethic holds that nurses' primary duty is to do what will benefit the patient in the immediate care situation. Nurses, as a professional group, have not really fully faced the dilemma of trading off one patient's interests against another's, or of compromising the patient's interests for some other good such as the family, the state, or the countless numbers of people who do not receive adequate health care.

Although organized nursing has a liberal record, as reflected in the stances taken by the ANA House of Delegates over the years, when it comes right down to the possibility of nursing strikes, many nurses view such action as unprofessional and unethical. This, among other things, may reflect this group's lack of awareness of the social dimensions of health care.

The strike forces nurses to come to grips with the traditional patient-benefiting ethics and to take into account in a serious way the long-term social impacts of viewing health care provision entirely in terms of individual interactions. Insisting that nurses should ethically do what will benefit a particular patient or small group of patients who happen to be receiving their services at a particular time, is not only paternalistic and individualistic, it also tends to be an oversimplified reduction of a complex set of social interactions.

SUMMARY

This chapter has examined selected ethical issues in the change-agent role as enacted by nurses in three separate but interrelated contexts. The ethics of change in the situation of the individual nurse caring for an individual patient reviewed the central ethical principle of autonomy, which maintains that every person has the right to make decisions that affect well-being. One major behavior of the health care professional as change agent, referred to as paternalism, shows that the patient's autonomy can easily be violated when the change agent acts to restrict the liberty of choice for another person. Informed consent, as a special instance of autonomy, raised some questions about the ethical dilemma in which the patient's rights conflict with the change agent's role obligation. The elements of informed consent were briefly presented and raised the question of when, if ever, it is ethically justi-

fied for another person to give informed consent for the patient.

The discussion of the nurse and the system, here defined as the health care institution where the nurse is employed, focused on the ethical principle of justice. Definitions of just and unjust acts lead to a question of how the benefits and harms are distributed in just ways in a society. Five different criteria were listed as usual considerations in distributive justice. The problems of justice in the allocation of resources were divided into two categories. Microallocation deals with the allocation of resources in a specific social arena, which, in this case, is the health care system, whereas macroallocation centers on how much of society's resources should be exchanged for social goods.

Finally, the ethical issues surrounding the larger professional organization's mechanisms for change in working conditions for nurses were examined. Specifically, the issue of collective bargaining and the strike were discussed.

The complexities of the change-agent role in all three of these contexts reveal some profound ethical dilemmas and issues. Answers to these problems do not always come easily, but the need to identify the ethical issues and to attempt to think them through ethically remains a central ethical obligation for any change agent.

REFERENCES

American Nurses' Association: Code for nurses with interpretive statement, Kansas City, Mo., 1976, ANA.

Bandman, E., and Bandman, B.: Bioethics and human rights, Boston, 1978, Little, Brown & Co.

Beauchamp, T.L., and Childress, J.E.: Principles of biomedical ethics, New York, 1979, Oxford University Press.

Brody, H.: Ethical decisions in medicine, Boston, 1976, Little, Brown & Co.

Capron, A.: Informed consent in catastrophic disease and treatment, Univ. of Penn. Law Rev. **123**:364-376, 1974.

Davis, A.J., and Aroskar, M.A.: Ethical dilemmas and nursing practice, New York, 1978, Appleton-Century-Crofts.

Feinberg, J.: Justice. In Reich, W., editor: Encyclopedia of bioethics, New York, 1978, The Free Press.

Frankena, W.K.: Ethics, ed. 2, New York, 1973, The Macmillan Co.

Gert, B.: The moral rules, New York, 1966, Harper & Row, Publishers.

MacIntyre, A.: A short history of ethics, New York, 1966, The Macmillan Co.

Melden, A.I.: Ethical theories, Englewood Cliffs, N.J., 1967, Prentice-Hall, Inc.

Natanson v. *Kline,* 186 Kan. 393, 350 P2d 1093 1960.

Rescher, N.: The allocation of exotic medical lifesaving therapy, Ethics **79:**173-186, 1969.

Sellars, W., and Hospers, J.: Readings in ethical theory, Englewood Cliffs, N.J., 1970, Prentice-Hall, Inc.

Woman is an instinctive nurse, taught by
Mother Nature.

Robinson, V.: White caps: the story of nursing,
1946, J.B. Lippincott, p. ix.

14

SOCIAL ISSUES INFLUENCING THE CHANGE PROCESS

Cecilia H. Cantrell and Marion R. Dickens

THE PREDOMINANT SOCIAL ISSUES AFFECTING NURSING

Although there have been many influences on nursing and its development, the predominant influence on all facets of nursing has been that it is a female occupation. Although nursing is as old as humanity, as a profession it is comparatively new, and although male nurses have existed as long as female nurses, the large majority of practitioners have been and continue to be women.

The aim of this chapter is to look at a variety of key social issues that affect the current role of a nurse as a change agent. The scope of this topic is virtually limitless, thus crucial issues are selected for attention. A historical view is provided, since most of nursing's current approaches and problems, and ultimately the outcomes for the profession, have a decided correlation with historical antecedents. This chapter looks at how the profession has changed over time, as well as at the characteristics that have been retained. Issues addressed include nursing as a primarily female occupation, the educational process for nurses, and the work environment. Current issues in nursing are set forth, including economic impact, personnel retention and distribution, power, energy, and time. Finally, recommendations for maintaining the future viability of nursing are presented.

It cannot be denied that nursing suffers from disorganization. The reasons for this state are varied, arise from many sources, and can be attributed to several causes; but fundamentally the problem or issue is that most nurses are women. No other profession so completely embodies the positive and negative attributes of the female sex. Whereas the doctor role connotes the kind, all-knowing, all-wise, loving father-god figure; negative, base, animalistic characteristics are not associated with the role. The nurse-role connotation is the Florence Nightingale/Sairy Gamp images combined, the best and the worst, the "all things to all people." Even the term nursing must be a direct translation of a primitive female function, the suckling of children.

Nursing became an acceptable occupation for women in a society that held as suspect any woman who worked outside the home. Until Florence Nightingale's efforts, it was not considered "proper" for respectable women to have careers, or even to be educated for that matter. Women were mostly dependent on marriage for economic survival, and society depended on women to organize and coordinate the household. Before the "modern" era, nursing functions were performed, but as an occupation nursing was not highly regarded and formal training was nonexistent except for that given within religious orders. The great bulk of nursing care was provided in the home by women of the household. Mothers handed down to daughters special formulas for making salves, lotions, and potions, as well as skills for caring for the sick and injured. Hospitals that existed before the late nineteenth century cared mostly for persons with a dreaded communicable disease, for paupers, or for the insane. Secular nursing in most hospitals was carried on by women who were considered to be from "the lower class" and had to work either because they were unmarried, were widows, or had unemployed husbands. Since workhouses were usually run by the same people who operated the hospitals, the boards tried to save money by using paupers as nurses; the bulk of the women paupers who were forced to give nursing care had neither experience nor the desire to be good nurses. During this era, "respectable" women did not earn their living outside the home.

Nightingale gave impetus to the reform of secular nursing. Her high social position, broad educational background, and vigorous personality enabled her to overcome enormous obstacles, not the least of which was the opposition of her family. The establishment of "Nightingale" schools to train nurses set the stage for the acceptance of "decent" women to work as nurses outside the home. Nursing thus became an acceptable occupation for women because it fit the female role expectations held by society.

In general, the expectations held by society for

the female role have included such attributes as nurturance, home maintenance, compassion, and tenderness. The female sex role also included such attributes as conformity, passivity, selflessness, dependency, fear of success, powerlessness, and a subordinate status; these attributes have handicapped nursing in its development. Because its practitioners have been socialized into the female sex role, which nursing required for its very existence in the society, the nursing profession has been in a dilemma since its inception. On the one hand, nurses have been expected to exercise considerable responsibility for the people in their care, and on the other, they have been denied the autonomy and authority necessary to care for them.

It might be argued that nursing has an advantage over other female occupations (such as teaching), since women have held most of the administrative positions in a nursing hierarchy. Cleland (1971) pointed out, however, that nursing in its isolation from all vestiges of power can be compared to the situation of the blacks in the South. In both groups there could be upward mobility for members to whom other routes were closed, but the top positions were available only with the approval of the power structure, generally white and male. Therefore, even if nurses were motivated to contribute to the advancement of the profession, they have traditionally lacked the power to do so. They have also lacked the attributes of assertiveness and acceptance of responsibility that, although required for advancement, are usually not taught to women. As noted, American women have been socialized into nurturant, passive-dependent roles, and have been taught that they must choose between a job and having a family. Many times such a choice has resulted in the selection of occupations that would provide skills they could use as "homemakers" after marriage. Nursing as a "homemaker preparation" occupation has generally assumed secondary importance to the family.

Other chapters in this book focus on the interdependence of the health care and societal subsystems. This chapter considers the influence of femininity on certain social issues pertinent to nursing and a consideration of their interdependence.

NURSING HAS (AND HAS NOT) CHANGED HISTORICALLY

The conflicts that exist in nursing today have their roots in the society in which nursing has developed. Throughout its history, nursing in America has attempted to evolve from the status of an occupation toward an independent professional status, but progress has been slow. Whereas other occupations have moved fairly quickly toward professional status, nursing has never achieved the autonomy required by most definitions of a profession. Nursing education has played a central role in both the progress and lack of progress toward this goal. Historically, nursing education has been dominated by men, first in hospital schools and then in colleges and universities. In hospitals, schools, and physicians' offices, the men who controlled the budget, set the policies, and managed the institutions were the ones who had the power, and ultimately controlled the system.

It was generally accepted, in colonial America, that women were intellectually inferior to men, and that a woman's preparation for her allotted sphere (the home) was obtained through apprenticeship to her mother. Formal schooling for a girl was considered excessively costly in both time and money. Hence nursing education developed at a time when apprenticeship training was the predominant mode for learning a vocation, when women were agitating for more educational opportunities, and when women were just beginning to be permitted entry to institutions of higher education. After the Civil War, there was a surplus of women in society as well as fewer men to provide for them economically. Thus women needed occupations in order to care for themselves.

The model for nurses' training schools was Florence Nightingale's St. Thomas Hospital in England, but American schools omitted Nightingale's essential ingredients of independence of the school from the hospital and the separation of nursing service from nursing education requirements for students. In American hospital schools, female students were socialized into dependent, conforming, and obedient roles, and were used for service by proliferating hospitals, which opened nursing schools for the purpose of obtaining labor for the hospital wards (Bullough and Bullough, 1969).

Stewart (1943, p. 131) points out that because the early schools were largely philanthropic in purpose, they did not "discriminate clearly" between the aim of supplying a good nursing service for the hospital and that of developing a good education system for students. Initially there was no regulating body to enforce uniform standards for nursing education and so there was a wide divergence in schools and admission requirements for nursing students. As Roberts (1954, p. 61) states, "No other profession has been developed on the assumption that an education can be secured in exchange for service." Nursing students, who may or may not have had high school diplomas, were depended on for all the actual nursing care provided in hospitals and for a considerable amount of other work (such as housekeeping). Many hospitals started schools of nursing primarily for economic reasons and seemingly few had any real interest in the future of the nurses they graduated. Indeed, graduate nurses were employed in hospitals in small numbers as either supervisors or teachers until the depression. Historically, there was no uniformity in length or type of training for students, no set curriculum, and no requirements regarding instructor qualifications; indeed, much of the teaching was done by senior students who also served as head nurses on the wards, and the superintendents of the schools had little power to set standards.

Small wonder, then, that the first national nursing organization was formed in 1894 by superintendents of training schools (the American Society of Superintendents of Training Schools for Nurses of the United States and Canada, renamed The National League for Nursing Education in 1912 and The National League for Nursing in 1952), and

that the primary purposes of the new society were to "advance the best interests of the nursing profession by establishing and maintaining a universal standard of training, and by promoting fellowship among its members of meetings, papers, and discussions on nursing subjects and by interchange of opinions" (Roberts, 1954, p. 25). The new organization promptly appointed a curriculum committee, and a report was published in the proceedings two years later, after the development of a national association of "professional nurses" (the Nurses' Association of Alumnae of the United States and Canada, to become the American Nurses' Association in 1912) to respond to individual practicing nurses' concerns.

Since nursing was not able to set educational standards in hospital-controlled nursing schools, nurses organized and attempted to influence hospital boards regarding nursing education by promoting studies of nursing, promoting legislation for nurse licensure, and eventually introducing nursing education into colleges and universities.

Organized nursing fought "short courses" for partially trained "subnurses," which were proposed as a solution to nursing shortages during wartime. Nursing was forced to accept responsibility for both nursing care and education, and finally brought practical nurses into the nursing organizations when overwhelming numbers of subsidiary nurses forced recognition. In the 1960s, organized nursing encouraged community colleges to open two-year associate degree programs in nursing to produce "bedside nurses" in the mainstream of American education. Getting nursing education out of hospital schools had been recommended by every major study of nursing since its inception (see the Goldmark Report, 1923; the Burgess reports, 1928 and 1934, the Brown Report, 1948; the Lysaught Report, 1970). Attempts to limit hospital control of nursing education produced a multiplicity of educational levels, which has made it difficult for nurses to "climb the ladder" of nursing education in order to advance in the hierarchy.

In addition, nursing curricula have had to be restructured almost continually because of the proliferation of knowledge and the constant evolution of medical and nursing conceptual frameworks. This has added to the fragmentation of educational structures in nursing and the difficulty in articulating the educational levels.

The advent of the nurse practitioner and the push for continuing education have added to the problems that nurse educators needed to solve. The perennial shortage of qualified nursing faculty, especially for university positions, has further complicated the task of providing education for nurses, especially in institutions of higher education, and particularly that which could be identified and accepted as education for a profession. Nurse educators have been running hard to stay in place. Of course, the evolution of nursing practice has paralleled the evolution of nursing education. Nursing practice has a variety of structural features that make it unique. For example, most nurses work in institutions with hierarchial systems of authority, and their functions are not limited to technical nursing skills needed to care for sick people, but include institutional maintenance and managerial functions as well. Women with wide and varied interests have entered nursing, since it grew to be one of the few acceptable occupations for women.

All workers are influenced by elements of their work environment, as well as by social and cultural elements in society. However, it appears that nursing practice has been particularly vulnerable to the influence of external factors. Although nursing was organized early in its history, nursing organizations have been working toward essentially the same goals without having achieved many of them. It appears that nurses and nursing have "borrowed" ideas and goals more often than they have conceived them, and nurses work together in harmony under crisis conditions rather than in planning and furthering goals.

Although the "Society of Superintendents" was the first official organization of nurses, its members almost immediately recognized the need for an organization that would bring all nurses together to focus on their general needs and common welfare, and so the "practice organization" was inaugurated. By having two national organizations instead of one, organized nursing promoted a situation ripe for competition, conflict, and duplication of effort. Many nurses belonged to both organizations, thus expending time and energy that could have been better concentrated on one. Indeed, early nursing leaders worked for both organizations, and felt that their time was well spent because considerable effort was needed to improve both education and practice in nursing.

It was believed by the early nursing leaders that licensure laws were absolutely necessary "to protect the public from the ill trained nurse," and to upgrade and/or standardize the preparation of nurses. In many instances, the battle raged particularly over the issue of membership on the boards of nurse examiners. Nurses believed in and fought for control of nursing by nurses. The stated intent of licensure was to protect the public from dishonest and incompetent practitioners. In effect, however, laws that control who enters the practice have been interpreted as protecting the practitioner more than the public; thus the licensure problem has never been resolved. Medical groups fearing infringement on their territory have mounted efforts to weaken or kill nursing bills designed to expand the scope of practice, unless medical supervision was clearly indicated. However, medical practitioners seemingly have been willing to divest themselves of functions that could be passed on to the nurse without loss of prestige. The functions of the nurse, therefore, have too often expanded as necessity and physicians dictated. In fighting infringement and paternalism from other groups, however, nurses have never seemed to retain any of their hard-won political "know-how" from one crisis to the next, and the lessons have had to be relearned in every crisis situation in nursing's evolution.

Nursing organizations have suffered from a lack of support, a proliferation of nursing specialty organizations, a resulting diffusion of effort and energy, and a lack of power. As a result, efforts to set standards, pass licensure laws, and secure economic welfare for nurses have met with limited success.

The roles and functions of nurses in practice have proliferated to the point of confusion. A wide variety of health care activities are carried out in different settings under different institutional auspices. The majority of nurses have changed from the relatively independent practice of private duty nursing in the community to structured, hierarchical, dependent practice in institutions. Nurses have been urged into supervisory roles in spite of continued protests by individual nurses who wanted to engage in patient care. They have been rewarded, not for providing nursing care, but for directing the care given. Nurses have appeared powerless to direct their practice in institutions, whereas nurses in the community have had more freedom of practice, and nurses dissatisfied with institutional nursing have turned to nursing education, community nursing, or specialty areas. In institutions, hierarchical line authority made it easy for nurses to relinquish responsibility and accountability in practice. Neophyte nurses suffered "reality shock" (Kramer, 1974) on leaving the idealistic educational systems teaching professional nursing skills to work in the bureaucratic system built more for efficiency and technical nursing. Nurses felt they had to do as they were told in their practice setting, or leave, resulting in high rates of job turnover and dropout.

Nursing has been viewed as an occupation by some and as a semiprofession by others. Rarely has nursing been seen as a profession by anyone other than nurses. The image of nurses has wavered, from "loose woman," to "ministering angel," or, sometimes, "trained professional." But most people in the society have seen the nurse as the doctor's handmaiden, functioning as his assistant and carrying out his orders. This has been shown in various studies that have assessed the images of the nurse that have been held by members of society. Most of these studies have shown that society at large just did not see nurses and nursing as nurses saw themselves and their occupation. Even as far back as the mid-1940s, a study completed at the request of the ANA showed a "surprising ignorance" of nurses and nursing functions by various federal, state, and local government officials (Simmons, 1964). Birdwhistle's 1947 study (described by Simmons) was reported in terms of the appraised social class status of the respondents. The upper income bracket viewed the nurse as "a skilled menial, somewhat higher in prestige than a manicurist or hairdresser, but considerably below the social worker." Both male and female members of this group assumed that there would be casual affairs between the nurse and her male patients. The middle income group saw the nurse as a "semi-skilled to skilled individual who was variedly regarded by women as someone who works a while before marriage, who was widowed, divorced, or who was a career woman" (a career woman was someone who couldn't get a husband or who was a neglectful wife). The men of this group saw nurses as "easy marks." The lower income category of respondents saw nursing as one of the noblest of all professions by viewing the nurse as a woman who was in a position that allowed her to make a good marriage and simultaneously give to her husband and children the advantages of her acquired knowledge. However, the men felt that the doctors "probably had a lot of fun with them" (nurses) (Simmons, 1964).

Some women authors have insisted that society has traditionally viewed nurses as the "fallen woman" or as the "ministering angel/mother." The image of the "trained professional" appears to be one that the public was not ready to accept for women, even though that is the way nurses have thought of themselves. Deutscher (cited in Simmons, 1964) showed that there was a consistent trend in the way that nurses were viewed. The lower the respondents were in socioeconomic status, the more favorably they rated nurses; females rated nurses more favorably than did males. The influence of sex and socioeconomic status was not neutralized even for those people who had received nursing care.

In addition, Wolff (1954) surveyed fictional literature to determine nursing's image. She placed the books she reviewed in three categories: the "crusading" literature (or "career books"), "nurse's stories," and "the nurse in general fiction." In the fictional books, the picture of the nurse seemed outdated. Further, the fiction emphasized the hardships, discipline, and duty aspects on the one hand, and on the other the romance—especially with physicians with whom the nurse worked. Twenty years later, Richter and Richter (1974) noted that fiction still was outdated as far as nurses were concerned. Nursing students continued to be portrayed in hospital schools, although colleges and universities were graduating large numbers of nurses. In their review, students and nurses still worked long, hard hours, were often left alone as charge nurses on busy floors at night, lived in dread of cold, harsh supervisors whose edicts they dared not question, worked out psychological approaches to patients' problems by instinct (rather than from educational preparation in sociology and psychology). Further, nurses were viewed as single, living in nurses' homes, and "sighing" over physicians.

Beletz (1974), in surveying hospitalized patients, asked their ideas about nurses and their work role. The composite image that patients held of nurses was that of a "female nurturer, medicator, physician's assistant, maid, and administrator." The medical role model was the one most firmly held by patients, and they knew little about the reality of nursing.

Illustrating the feminine image of the nurse, Babich (1968) suggested that the roles played in the hospital system were similar to, if not the same as, the roles in the primary family system, in which the physician assumed the father role, the nurse assumed the mother role, and the patient became the child. The physician was the most powerful member of the group and the decision maker, whereas the nurse carried out the decisions and was able to exert only minimal authority; and the patient, the child, was the recipient of parental decisions.

PRESENT ISSUES

From the foregoing review of historical issues in nursing, it can be seen that although nursing has changed, the change has often been imposed by others or has resulted from crisis situations. Also, the development of nursing (practice, education, and professional organizations) has related intimately to the social position of women. Recognizing that the past imposes constraints on the present and that it is imperative to learn from the mistakes of the past, current issues in nursing should be considered in light of their interdependence with the "womanness" (or femininity) of nursing.

Since it would be an impossible task to examine all the issues of import in nursing, attention is given to the broad concern of judicious versus capricious professional resource allocation and utilization. Four resources (money or economics, personnel retention and distribution, power, and energy-time) influence and are influenced by the "womanness" (or femininity) of nursing. Resource discussion includes not only the past and present interdependency of nursing femininity with allocation and utilization, but also pertinent recommendations for future achievement of judicious resource accumulation and expenditure.

Economics

At a time when national health expenditures consume over nine percent of the gross national product and health cost outlays represent over twelve percent of the total federal budget, fiscal responsibility is imperative. Successful solicitation of these funds demands not only political savvy, but a demonstration of cost-effective utilization of funds.

In 1976-1977, the 1439 schools of nursing in the United States graduated 77,755 students (NLN, 1979, p. 27). Whereas the annual cost of educating one nursing student ($1500-$2450, depending on the type of program) is well below the annual cost per medical student of $9700, to date almost $2 billion in federal funds (not to mention private funds) have been spent on the education of professional nurses. The staggering attrition rate among the 1,401,633 registered nurses (ANA, 1980) from the nursing labor force both ethically and logically necessitates that future requests for nursing education not only be based on realistic predictions of supply and demand, but on solutions to the problem of retention and reentry of nurses into the profession.

Strategies of retention and reentry must speak not only to the obvious issue of reenticement, but also must weigh the potential costs of reeducation for nurses with outdated skills. Further, the professional implications of encouraging the reentry of large numbers of diploma-prepared nurses without a baccalaureate degree should be evaluated.

Given the ultimate finiteness of economic resources, greater consideration must be given to fund allocation for educating entry-level versus advanced-degree nurses. Attaching credibility to requests for future educational development without reasoned scrutiny of the multifaceted issues of retention and reentry is fiscally irresponsible.

Personnel retention and distribution

Attempts to respond to the issues related to economic and personnel resource distribution require an understanding of not only statistical data regarding the supply and demand for nurses at all levels of need, but also answers to the basic query of why even conservative attrition rates suggest that thirty percent (413,583) of registered nurses are not currently employed (Gortner, 1979; ANA, 1980).

Contrasts in female and male socialization, both culturally and professionally, provide some insight into questions of retention. Culturally, males are socialized to occupy a work role; all other roles are tangential to this self-defining role. Husband, father, community leader are all subsumed under the role of economic provider. Women are socialized primarily to occupy the dual roles of wife and mother, each of which represents a multiplicity of subroles that may or may not be compatible, given the circumstances. For example, the "wife" role connotes an attentive, appealing sexual partner, and

the "mother" role demands may at specific times directly conflict with fulfilling the sexual partner component of wife, as in the case of a sick child and an amorous husband! Divergence of roles and subroles in conjunction with the ambiguity of role expectations places women in a conflict position rarely if ever experienced by males, since culturally their occupational role supersedes all other roles.

As women have entered the job market, they have continued, unlike males, to expect high performance in all designated traditional roles and subroles while accepting the additional occupational role. Society expects and condones male submergence in the educational process in pursuit of his occupational role; women are expected to juggle all their roles simultaneously. There would be fewer male lawyers, physicians, and executives were there fewer wives and mothers to take care of the other necessities of life for them.

Additionally, basic female-male socialization influences the reactions to occupationally related behavior exhibited by females and males. Thus ambitious, competitive, or "tough" behavior in men is considered congruent both with maleness and occupational advancement. Women exhibiting career-advancing behavior are, however, in conflict with acceptable female behavior, so their positive strokes associated with job achievement are counterbalanced with negative reactions related to this conflict (Wahrman and Pugh, 1974).

Lakoff's (1975) explication of a "women's language" further illustrates this insidious separation of males and females. "Women's language" was found to be characterized by precise discriminations (something is chartreuse or lime, rather than green); weak expletives (My goodness!); special adjectives (sweet, charming); tag questions (It's hot, isn't it?); and polite speech in which there is an avoidance of strong expression of feelings and opinions, elaboration of trivial topics, a greater percentage of pronouns, and the use of more fillers, qualifiers, and hesitations (indicating greater expression of uncertainty).

Lynaugh and Bates (1973) documented "The

Two Languages of Nursing and Medicine,'' in which nurses and physicians have developed different words and phrases for the same concepts. The authors pointed out differences in neutral phrases, phrases that indicate different professional orientations, phrases reflecting professional territoriality, and phrases affecting collaboration. For example:

Nurses	Physicians
Gather data	Take a history
Assess	Diagnose
Communicate, suggest	Order
Collaborate	Delegate
Say ''the patient appears to have stopped breathing''	Say ''the patient is dead''

Lakoff (1975) stated that ''women's language'' is a language of powerlessness.

In addition to cultural socialization, occupational socialization differs among male- and female-dominated occupations. Basic to this difference is the diversity of social reasons attributed to work for males and females. Men have been socialized to expect to work throughout their adult life, providing economic support for themselves and approximately 3.3 citizens (a wife and 2.3 children). This expectation mandates organized efforts to control professional economic security. Thus it is not mere coincidence that there are rigorous constraints on supply and demand exercised by the American Medical Association (AMA) or the American Bar Association, nor that students entering those professions receive professional socialization that assures ''party-line'' adherence (Becker, 1961). Inevitable philosophical diversities are set aside by men when economic security is challenged. Conversely, female-dominated occupations, most obviously nursing, do not demonstrate similar devotion to professional socialization with resultant economic security. Again, the explanation is based in the societal value of work for women. Cultural congruence between women and employment outside the home occurs most completely when the job relates to the immediate and direct benefit of the family. The predominant expectation is that working is at best a temporary state from which one will be rescued by ''the Prince.'' Thus even among women who are working, a large percentage—in fact or fiction—do not anticipate lengthy employment. Considering, however, that women now comprise 41.7% of the work force and the Bureau of Labor projections indicate that by 1990, between 53.8 and 60.4% of the women in the United States will work to retirement (Bureau of Labor, 1978), women need seriously to consider their future roles.

The social expectations related to women and work, coupled with a nursing student composite derived from demographic and personal characteristics,* suggests that in contrast to Kramer's supposition (1974) that nursing graduates want to work, but become frustrated when confronted with work conditions and reality, many students only choose to work spasmodically as a supplement to a husband's advancing career. In many cases the nursing student's intent is to obtain an education that provides such advantages as a backup security to their primary expectations: a financially secure marriage, ''an opportunity to meet a doctor,'' and a ''good foundation for the roles of wife and mother.''

Job, not career, orientation exists, such that ultimate decisions to enter and remain in an educational program are often based primarily on self-reported convenience needs such as geographical location and program flexibility allowing family obligations to be met. These same considerations are frequently responsible for decisions of job selection by both staff nurses and nursing faculty. How often it is said: ''I went into teaching so I could have the same time off with my children.'' Students, therefore, entering nursing with job versus career goals and expectations have this attitude

*Adams and Klein, 1970; Nash, 1977; Elliott and Kerns, 1978; NLN, 1978; Gortner, 1979; McQuaid and Kane, 1979; Goldstein, 1980.

reinforced by many of their educational role models.

Certainly, some females enter nursing with every intention of pursuing a career and, encouragingly, this number is increasing (NLN, 1978; Goldstein, 1980). However, because a majority of their nursing colleagues are socially traditional both as women and nurses, and therefore readily accept (1) the existing male dominance, (2) compliance with the general social structure, and (3) the job organizational structure of nursing, career-oriented nurses often experience a "Catch 22" situation.

As previously discussed, because career mobility is fundamentally contrary to the general socialization of women, it is a catalyst for potential stress. Additionally, the different reasons for entering and remaining in nursing generate conflict, confusion, jealousy, and infighting among nurses. Again, in contrast to male-dominated occupations where socialization both minimizes the opportunity for philosophical divergence through methods designed to control quantity and quality (i.e., strict adherence to high-level entry requirements and educational standards), and orchestrates economic security, nursing continues to be its own worst enemy.

Finally, although there is some difficulty in relating as a colleague with other health care professionals because of the divergence between those nurses of traditional female persuasion and those who are career oriented, there is often a lack of support, even hostile rejection, of the career-oriented nurse by nurses with more traditional views.

When nursing is viewed only as a transient state, it seems clear why efforts to unite as a professional group have failed. Expectations and goals of those who visualize nursing from a professional level and those who view it from an individual perspective are at odds. Additionally, for those who see it as a temporary state to be altered by the arrival of "the Prince," time and money are better spent in preparing for his arrival than in promoting career causes. The idea that a nurse is a nurse is a nurse (to paraphrase Gertrude Stein) is nowhere more fallacious than the assumption that nurses all expect or achieve the same things from nursing.

Power

Difficulties in nursing arise from a lack of a coordinated independent professional national vision. Visionary deficiency is consistent with the female position in a male-dominated society. Neither women nor men have questioned the propriety of men in determining either nursing supply and demand requirements, or the methods employed to meet those requirements. Nursing has not been dominated by physicians except to the extent that physicians are predominantly male. Margaret Mead (1949, p. 168) stated:

In every known society, the male's need for achievement can be recognized. Men may cook or weave, or dress dolls and hunt hummingbirds, but if such activities are appropriate occupations of men, then the whole society, men and women alike, votes them as important. When the same occupations are performed by women, they are regarded as less important.

Support for this contention can be found by examining countries in which a significant percentage of physicians are women. In these countries, such as Russia, the medical profession is not afforded the social prestige level or professional independence it enjoys in the United States. Further, women (and thus nurses) in the United States defer to authority figures such as legislators, hospital administrators, and husbands—not just physicians. For example, not only are policemen reported to be treating policewomen as natural subordinates, connoted by teasing banter appropriate to a kid sister relationship rather than collegial one, but policewomen are reported to accept the situation as appropriate. The relative power of medicine and nursing can be compared if one considers the uproar that would have ensued had Congress attempted to rectify deficits in the *physician* supply by establishing a "physician cadet corps" during World War II, as it did with nurses and the Nurse Cadet Corps.

The concerns of male physicians, hospital administrators, and Congress have been to supply *their* needs as well as the immediate needs of the consumer, and since it was not their profession that was involved, but rather a female occupation not considered to be a profession, limited attention was given to coordinating efforts so that the economic security and professional integrity of nurses were not violated. The AMA and the American Bar Association carefully regulated their own professions (especially the number of medical and law schools, the quality and quantity of students accepted and thus produced for the marketplace). The lack of esteem afforded professional nursing, as well as nursing's own failure to manipulate its destiny astutely, are evident.

The times may be changing; unfortunately, they are not changing in nursing. It is not just our failure to provide intraprofessional and intersocietal definitions that would influence supply/demand quotients as well as state and federal funds for education, that allow detrimental federal and state legislation to be enacted against the nursing profession. It is also nursing's continued failure to recognize and reject male dominance from a position of united strength. If the more than one million registered nurses voted as a block, rarely would presidents risk a total veto of nursing support. It is interesting to note that when drastic legislation was proposed by President Carter in 1980, nurses did manage enough unity to prevent a congressional $16 million budget rescission of nurse-training funds; simultaneously, Congress retained the Carter $24 million cut in medical school capitation grants. The victory of nursing places second to the realization that medical schools could experience this $24 million reduction without eliciting the fury of the AMA.

However, the AMA has not, as one might be tempted to assume, lost its clout, especially when one considers that the major health care legislative activity for the 1980 budget was the defeat of Carter's hospital cost-containment proposal (the heart of his antiinflation program). It was defeated by nearly a two-to-one margin in the House of Representatives; the AMA contributed to the campaign funds of 202 of the 234 House members who voted against the Carter proposal (contributions averaging $8157 per member, or a total of $1,647,714). It is obvious, then, that the AMA did not seriously oppose the $24 million capitation cut. Could it be that the reduction in educational programs only heightens the supply/demand security of the physician, whereas the hospital cost-containment strikes at the economic security of practicing physicians?

As women, nurses are a numerical majority, representing a fifty-three percent proportion of the total population, as well as sixty-five percent of the health care provider population. Comparing the 200,020 physicians in the United States to the 1,401,633 nurses, again nurses constitute a numerical majority. Power, however, is not dependent on size alone. Prestige afforded a position endows occupants of the position certain levels of formal and informal authority. Thus, for reasons such as male versus female occupational dominance, differences in educational preparation, professional independence, understanding and utilization of formal and informal power, and unequal income distribution, nurses view themselves—and are viewed by others—as having modest to low power.

If nursing is to correct its past negative commissions and omissions while benefiting from its positive affirmations, professional cohesion, integrity, and planning are required. Nurses must employ the nursing process and develop a care plan for nursing itself if it is to survive as a profession. Germane to this is the realistic assessment of what nurses must do for themselves and consumers, and what they must expect the government, colleagues, and society to do for nurses. Certainly, nursing cannot continue to seek funding to prepare registered nurses without either a clear statement and professional commitment to an entry-level commensurate with a profession, or an accurate supply/demand quotient.

Energy and time

Supply/demand estimates must consider the professional responsibilities related to the distribution of the available nurses in the expanding roles we continue to encourage and develop. If, indeed, a shortage exists and funds for future programs are limited, national decisions must be made concerning the overall value each "position" will contribute to the profession and to national health care. For example, given the 3000 doctorally prepared nurses in the United States, are we wise to continue to proliferate graduate programs that will compete with each other and undergraduate programs for faculty as well as revenue? What alternatives do we have that would assure quality educational preparation for future doctorally prepared nurses while utilizing resources most judiciously? Could universities cooperate to evolve community solution programs that cross political, state, and institutional lines, and share resources rather than compete?

Nursing acceptance in academia is precarious at best. Often large percentages of the nursing faculty fall far below the credentials of faculty in other disciplines. Even as the number of doctorally prepared nursing faculty rises, most are neophytes when compared to their university colleagues; research and theory construction efforts are in their early stages. Yet salaries and rank of nursing faculty sometimes exceed more highly credentialed university faculty.

Academic credibility and recognition are necessary if nursing is to achieve its desired place as a profession in the health care sector. For this to occur, time and space must be available so that faculty can produce scholarly work and interact with the rest of the university on an equal level. As we continue to open new graduate and off-campus programs, we stretch existing faculty to the limit without realistically providing them with the opportunity to mature as university faculty.

Time and energy are vital resources that nurses often ignore in their attempts to expand and respond to the social demands of family and occupational role expectations.

National consolidation and coordination are also imperative for effective responses to other dilemmas of strained time and energy consumption. Unfortunately, just as a diversity of goals and expectations is rampant in the individual and educational sectors of nursing, its national organizations suffer

similar resource-depleting maladies. Extant confusion and jealousy over inter- and intraorganizational territorial issues not only portray nurses as confused and ineffective to society and to each other, but divert attention, energy, and time away from issues of significance. Positive organizational synergy* is imperative if nursing is to attain the professional status it purports to desire.

Currently, nurses are asked to join at least two national organizations (the NLN and the ANA). Participation in these two organizations represents an annual membership cost of approximately $150. Attending local and national organization meetings is often cost prohibitive for individuals and/or their employers. The "spread too thin" syndrome becomes ludicrous in the extreme. Historical understanding of the emergence and divergence of the primary organizations, both from a factual historical perspective and as insight into the female view of power and authority, is essential to future professional development.

Consistent with the failure of nursing leaders to recognize the need for cohesive global problem solving is the lack of forethought related to the interdependence of organizational structuring, the pursuit of national-level professional goals, and organizational productivity evident in the organizational structure of the National League for Nursing.

RECOMMENDATIONS

Innovation is required to contend with the issues facing nursing. No longer can intraprofessional power struggles or peripheral divisive issues be indulged. Rather, nurses must unite on universal concerns; they must become more self-directed and less other-directed, more assertive, and more deliberate in their evolution into viable health care providers and consumer advocates.

Achievement of these major goals hinges not

---

*Synergy is defined as a combination of two or more resources that results in an output different from the sum of the inputs. Thus positive synergy occurs when $2 + 2 = 5$; negative synergy is present when $2 + 2 = 3$.

only on unity, but also on the ability to interpret and apply available scholarly information from all sectors that may assist in solving problems of judicious resource utilization. Phenomenological examination of interdependent relationships is vital.

Future developmental progress must not neglect the examination of the continuing influence of femininity on nursing. Diversity among traditional and nontraditional women will continue to influence social attitudes, laws, and personal self-concepts. Nursing must not only recognize these influences but use them advantageously.

Consciousness raising is imperative for present and future nurses, health care colleagues, and the consumer. Competing for the best potential students for nursing requires a favorable identity, which is dependent on leadership, unity, and utilization of available knowledge from all disciplines.

As theories of change, power, and groups are employed in attempts to impel the profession, recognition that research studies may reflect a male orientation in their findings may be required if these theories are to be effective when used to explain, predict, and control female behavior. Motivations, rewards, goals, and expectations congruent with male-dominated professions may not be effective for females; a paucity of research concerning this possibility exists. Extrapolation, however, from research concerned with cultural socialization and change suggests the potential for this inference (Sears and Barbie, 1978).

Finally, as women, nurses must recognize the socialization tendency to efface themselves while ingratiating themselves to others. Nurses can argue, and often do, the appropriateness of physicians commanding high incomes while agreeing to the low income of nurses. Nurses have held back, allowing others to take first choice on the available resources: a truly female characteristic. What "good" mother ever takes the best piece of chicken or the last piece of anything without guilt? Guilt, of course, depletes the energy needed to solve problems.

SUMMARY

In conclusion, the issue most pertinent to nursing is its predominant femaleness and the obvious subtle influences this femaleness imposes on professional development. Throughout the history of nursing, both health providers and consumers have recognized vast differences between the roles of nurses and physicians. Certainly these differences have been a reflection of the differences in levels of education and the scope of practice; it also seems that the male orientation of the physician role has increased the tendency for this group to have significant control of the health arena. What the future holds for nursing has yet to be determined, but undoubtedly key factors will include economics, education, the effectiveness of practitioners, and public recognition of the value and significance of nurses.

Nurses must gain control of their practice especially by determining its scope, manner of regulation, and levels of education. It is too late to wait for social change that may affect nursing. Instead a significant cadre of nurses must be at the forefront in determining the parameters of change: particularly legislation, economics, the power balance in the health field, and, of great importance, some agreement must be reached within nursing as to level of education for members of the profession. So long as nursing continues as a large, fragmented profession with numerous warring factions, social change will work against any gains that the entire profession can ever hope to make.

REFERENCES

Adams, J., and Klein, L.R.: Students in nursing school: considerations in assessing personality characteristics, Nurs. Res. **19**:363-365, July-Aug. 1970.

American Nursing Association: Fact sheet on registered nurses, Washington, D.C., Feb. 2, 1980, ANA.

Babich, K.S.: The perception of professionalism, Nurs. Forum **7**(1):14-21, 1968.

Becker, H.S., Hughes, E.C., Grier, B., and Strauss, A.: Boys in white, Chicago, 1961, University of Chicago Press.

Beletz, E.E.: Is nursing's public image up to date? Nurs. Outlook **22**:432-435, July 1974.

Blau, P.M.: Exchange and power in social life, New York, 1964, John Wiley & Sons, Inc.

Brown, E.L.: Nursing for the future, New York, 1948, Russell Sage Foundation.

Bullough, V., and Bullough, B.: The emergence of modern nursing, ed. 2, New York, 1969, The Macmillan Co.

Bureau of Labor Statistics: Labor force projections for 1990: three possible funds, Monthly Labor Rev., Dec. 1978.

Cleland, V.: Sex discrimination: nursing's most pervasive problem, Am. J. Nurs. **71:**1542-1547, Aug. 1971.

Elliott, J.E., and Kerns, J.M.: Analysis and planning for improved distribution of nursing personnel and services, HRA 79-16, Western Interstate Commission for Higher Education, National Center for Higher Education Management Systems at WICHE, Dec. 1978.

Future directions of doctoral education for nurses: report of a conference, (NIH) 72-82, Washington, D.C., 1971, U.S. Department of HEW.

Goldmark, J.: Nursing and nursing education in the United States, New York, 1923, Macmillan Co.

Goldstein, J.O.: Comparison of graduating A.D. and baccalaureate nursing students' characteristics, Nurs. Res. **19:** 47-48, Jan.-Feb. 1980.

Gortner, S.R.: Prediction of successful nursing performance Parts III and IV, HRA 79-15, Washington, D.C., 1979, U.S. Department of HEW.

Group, T.M., and Roberts, J.I.: Exorcising the ghost of the crimea, Nurs. Outlook **22:**368-372, June 1974.

Kramer, M.: Reality shock: why nurses leave nursing, St. Louis, 1974, The C.V. Mosby Co.

Lakoff, R.: Language and woman's place, New York, 1975, Harper & Row, Publishers.

Lynaugh, J.E., and Bates, B.: The two languages of nursing and medicine, Am. J. Nurs. **73:**66-69, Jan. 1973.

Lysaught, J.P.: An abstract for action, National Commission for the Study of Nursing and Nursing Education, New York, 1970, McGraw-Hill Book Co.

McQuaid, E.A., and Kane, M.T.: How do graduates of different types of programs perform on state boards? Am. J. Nurs. **79:**305-308, Feb. 1979.

Mead, M.: Male and female, New York, 1949, Dell Publishing Co.

Nash, P.M.: Student selection and retention in nursing schools, HRA 78-5, Washington, D.C., 1977, U.S. Department of HEW, Health Manpower References, December.

National League for Nursing data book: statistical information on nursing education and newly licensed nurses, Publ. No. 19-1751, 1979.

Richter, L., and Richter, E.: Nurses in fiction, Am. J. Nurs. **74:**1280-1321, July 1974.

Robbins, S.P.: The administrative process integrating theory and practice, Englewood Cliffs, N.J., 1976, Prentice-Hall, Inc.

Roberts, M.M.: American nursing: history and interpretation, New York, 1954, The Macmillan Co.

Robinson, V.: White caps: the story of nursing, New York, 1946, J.B. Lippincott Co.

Sears, P.S., and Barbie, A.H.: Career and life satisfaction among Terman's gifted women. The gifted and the creative: fifty-year perspective, Baltimore, 1978, Johns Hopkins University Press.

Simmons, L.: Images of the nurse: theory and studies. Nursing research: a survey and assessment, New York, 1964, Appleton-Century-Crofts.

Stewart, I.W.: The education of nurses, New York, 1943, The Macmillan Co.

Wahrman, R., and Pugh, M.D.: Sex, nonconformity and influence, Sociometry **37:**137-145, Spring 1974.

Wolff, I.S.: As others see us, Nurs. Outlook **2:**408-412, Aug. 1954.

If nurses become serious students of social needs, activists in influencing
policy to meet those needs, generous contributors of time and finances to
nursing and other organizations and to candidates working for universal
good health care, then the future is bright indeed.

Mullane, M.K.: Nursing Outlook **23**:701, November, 1975. Copyright by American
Journal of Nursing Company.

15

POLITICAL
IMPERATIVES FOR
NURSING PRACTICE

Marcia Stanhope and Anne Elizabeth Belcher

Nurses' involvement in politics is receiving greater emphasis in nursing curricula, in professional organizations, and within various health care settings where nursing care is provided. If politics is defined as the art of influencing policy and decision making, then it would seem logical for nurses to be politically active. However, beyond their involvement in decisions directly affecting patient care, nurses as individuals have not consistently participated in local, state, or national policy making. Although their professional organizations have been politically active for many years, their members have often either been unaware of or have chosen not to participate in this function. Why are nurses currently placing an increasing value on their involvement in politics? What is to be gained by the profession's current emphasis on political activity?

The goal of this chapter is to examine the need for political involvement of nurses and to describe ways in which they can become active participants in decision making at the local, state, and national levels. In order to accomplish this, nursing's role in the political system is explored and an overview of governmental structure in relation to health care is given, including governmental impact on health policy, the structure and functions of Congress, the legislative process, and the role of the national government's executive branch in policy making. Finally, intervention strategies for becoming involved in both the regulatory and legislative processes are reviewed, giving specific ways to participate.

Historically, nurses' involvement in politics has been limited. Whereas individual nurses, beginning with Florence Nightingale, have influenced decision making in such areas as sanitation, basic nutrition, birth control, and disaster management, nurses have collectively done less well. However, a national focus on women's rights and the women's liberation movement has resulted in more women, including nurses, addressing health care issues such as child and spouse abuse, care of the handicapped and mentally ill, and abortion. In addition, as more college-educated people enter the profession, they bring to nursing the activism and involvement of the university campus (Deloughery and Gebbie, 1975). Governmental agency and congressional emphasis on such issues as national health insurance and nursing training funds has also stimulated nurses to become more politically active.

The danger of increasing nursing involvement in politics lies in two particular areas. One problem is that nurses who have "suffered in silence" for a long time may be overly forceful, emotional, and/or aggressive when they do become involved, consequently alienating their audience. Another problem is that nurses who are only politically active when their economic welfare is at issue may lose their supporters, who perceive that nurses have a vested interest in their profession and lack concern for the people whom they purport to serve.

NURSING ROLE IN THE POLITICAL SYSTEM

Nurses are still on the outer edge of the health power system. Perhaps this is to some extent a result of the public's assumption that nurses, being predominantly women and traditionally followers, think like and/or agree with physicians, and thus do not need representation on advisory committees and boards. In addition, many nurses seem to be content with "over-the-fence" consultation, offering individual assistance with regard to specific issues but avoiding active political involvement (Deloughery and Gebbie, 1975).

As Ehrenreich (1979) so clearly states, political activism and political commitment must be a part of the professional definition of nursing. Politics must be viewed not as a "dirty" business but as a reality that includes the arts of influence, compromise, and interpersonal relationships. Nurses have played the political game for years in schools of nursing and in health care settings when seeking additional resources, more self-direction, and accountability with authority. It is time to utilize those skills in a "bigger arena" (Burke, 1979, p. 60).

Unfortunately, the present state of affairs is such

that nursing has not yet emerged as a political force. When nurses, either as individuals or within professional organizations, issue position statements, which is an infrequent occurrence, they are often ignored (Ehrenreich, 1979). Perhaps their messages are not delivered forcefully enough or the public and politicians view these nurses as forgetting their place.

So long as nurses avoid involvement in politics, misinformed but skilled outsiders will impose their will on nursing (Kalisch and Kalisch, 1976). Witness numerous attempts by nonnursing groups, often led by other health care providers, to impose institutional licensure, mandatory continuing education, curtailment of advanced nursing practice, and other constraints on a professional group that should have a voice in decisions made in these and numerous other areas. Although nurses have reacted to these situations, often successfully preventing infringement on the profession's self-governance, few efforts have been made to take risks. For example, the reluctance to implement the American Nurses' Association's 1965 position on entry into practice demonstrates the tendency to issue a statement but to avoid implementing any action in its behalf.

Mullane (1975) identifies numerous political arenas for nurses, including the hospital and other agency work settings such as nursing homes, and state and local health departments. In addition, several issues have a potential impact on nursing as a profession, including the equal rights movement, national health insurance, and special programs for the elderly, handicapped, and minority groups. Professional issues that are of increasing political significance include mandatory continuing education, entry into practice, the expanded roles of the nurse, and funding for nurse training.

In order for nurses to effect changes in both professional issues and those affecting consumer health care, they must have a working knowledge of governmental processes.

GOVERNMENT AND HEALTH CARE

A review of the conceptual framework of the legal system shows that there are two categories of law in the United States: federal and state. Each of the two categories has a similar framework of authority for the passage and enactment of laws (Fig. 15-1).

The *Constitution of the United States* provides the legal basis for the passage of all laws through

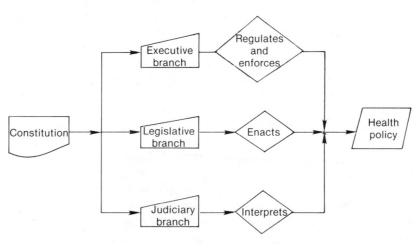

FIG. 15-1
Legal system framework for federal and state government.

the establishment of three branches of government: the executive, the legislative, and the judiciary. The legislative branch has the responsibility for the formal enactment of the law; the executive branch has the responsibility for the enforcement and the regulation of the law. The judicial branch of the government is charged with the responsibility for interpretation of the law's "intent" if the legislative document or the regulations of the law are challenged (*The Constitution*, 1976; "The ABC's," 1977).

A review of the *Constitution of the United States* shows that the states were originally given jurisdiction to enact and enforce laws governing the health of the population (*Health: Special Analysis L,* 1978). However, this power has been returned to the federal government; and it has utilized the power "to regulate interstate and foreign commerce" and "to provide for the general welfare" as a basis for enacting and enforcing health law (Art. I, Sec. 8, *The Constitution,* 1976).

Government impact on health policy

The federal government has become an active partner in health care as established by legislation passed in the last two decades.

With the passage of the Medicare and Medicaid amendments to the Social Security Act in 1965, the federal government established a national and state health insurance program for certain segments of the population. The Medicare program provides for both medical and hospital insurance for a population of 27 million persons over sixty-five years of age and/or persons who are disabled. The Medicaid program provides a joint federal and state health insurance program for a population of 21 million low-income persons who meet specific categorical criteria: families of dependent children, aged, blind, disabled, or medically indigent (*The Social Security Act,* 1976). The federal expenditure for these programs has grown to represent more than sixty percent of the federal health care budget (*Health: Special Analysis L,* 1978).

In 1972, another amendment to the Social Secu-

rity Act became law, one that provides for professional standards review organizations (PSROs) to monitor medical care given to Medicare, Medicaid, and maternal and child health program recipients. The PSRO program was designed to improve quality of care and to provide for appropriate utilization of health care services. Initially, PSRO concentrated on review of inpatient care in the hospital facility.

Once payment mechanisms were established and an evaluation system developed, the government chose its candidate for the system of future health care delivery, the health maintenance organization (HMO). The HMO is defined as an organized program that provides directly, or by contract, comprehensive health services to a defined population on a prepaid capitation basis with the HMO assuming some of the risk of higher costs (Milio, 1975). When the HMO concept was introduced as a mode of health care delivery, a number of advantages were cited: potential for cost containment; introduction of competition into the health care industry; ability to deliver high-quality care by offering comprehensive services—primary, secondary, and tertiary; and a staff of health professionals committed to the HMO. Amendments to the HMO Act of 1973 were passed in 1976 and 1978 to strengthen the HMO concept in the United States. Studies have shown that the cost-saving potential of the HMO is between ten and forty percent of overall health costs reported by other modes of health care delivery. The HMO has shown a reduction in inpatient hospital utilization. The enrollment of some 6 million Americans in HMOs introduces an element of competition into the health care industry (HMO, 1978).

The passage of the National Health Planning and Resources Development Act of 1974 introduced a comprehensive system of health planning (PL93-641). This act brought under one umbrella the previously existing fragmented programs providing for health planning and resource development in the United States: the Hill-Burton program for health facility construction; Regional Medical Programs for categorical health delivery programs; and the Comprehensive Health Planning Act of 1966. This law provided for a network of 205 health services areas (HSAs) throughout the nation. These HSAs are designated by the governors of each state and approved by the secretary of the Department of Health and Human Services (DHHS), according to a geographical distribution of not less than 300,000 persons nor more than 3 million persons. The agencies are composed of a voluntary governing board and a salaried staff of experts, with the board representing a majority of consumers and a minority of health providers (Cavalier, 1976; NLN, 1979a). The act also provides for state health planning and development agencies to be advised on state health planning issues by a statewide health coordinating council. The law also created a national council on health planning and development to make recommendations regarding national health policy to the secretary of DHHS. However, the focal point of planning remained at the HSA level (Judd and McEwan, 1977; NLN, 1979a). HSAs are charged with the improvement of the health of area residents by increasing accessibility, continuity, and quality of services; by restraining cost increases; and by preventing unnecessary duplication of services. To date, reports indicate a savings in health spending and a reduction in service duplication (NLN, 1979a).

Recurrent themes can be identified in the few examples of major health policy legislation discussed here. There is, as a result of national health policy, a greater demand for health services for selected segments of the population. An increase in service demand produces an increase in work force demand. To provide quality health services, there is a need for peer review as well as review of service utilization. Because health care professionals are involved in decision making about both utilization of services and quality of care, they are actively involved in PSROs (U.S., Department of HEW, 1978). To provide for quality and improved service utilization at less cost, planning of innovative modes of health care delivery is required. Not only

are nurses a part of HMO provider teams, but role functions will gradually include increased health planning activities. To date, nurses comprise six percent of the provider members of the HSA boards, whereas representatives of health care institutions comprise thirty-one percent and physicians twenty-two percent (NLN, 1979a). The HSA is a place where nurses can influence health policy if nursing is to influence its own future.

The issues of cost, accessibility, and quality of services have elicited discussion on the national scene about the use of the "new health professional" (NHP)—that is, the nurse practitioner and physician assistant—for health care delivery. NHPs may have an impact on cost, accessibility, and quality because (1) they can be trained in a shorter period of time at reduced costs; (2) they may lower the demand for secondary and tertiary care; and (3) they may increase access to care by providing services now provided by physicians (Fox and Zatkin, 1978).

The Rural Health Clinics Act of 1978 is a piece of health legislation that exemplifies the government's willingness to risk the use of the NHP in primary health care delivery. This act provides for the development of rural health clinics in areas that are medically underserved, the placement of an NHP on the agency staff, and the direct reimbursement of services rendered by an NHP for Medicare and Medicaid recipients. Consequently, nursing is being tapped as a primary source of health care delivery for the future.

In summary, several major laws have been passed in the last twenty years that affect nursing by: (1) increasing demand for nursing services; (2) requiring nursing input into quality assurance and service utilization; (3) providing for positions on health care delivery teams; (4) requiring health planning that affects nursing services; and (5) providing mechanisms for nurses to deliver primary care. Nursing as a profession and nurses as individuals must influence the development of policy issues and legislation that affect the practice of nursing. In order to have an impact on policy issues, nurses must become familiar with the legislative process and the points of intervention in that process.

CONGRESS
Structure and functions

Congress is the legislative branch of government, which has as a major function the enactment of laws. The Congress of the United States is known as the legislative branch of the government and is composed of two chambers: the Senate and the House of Representatives. At present, there are 100 senators, 2 from each state. The term of office for a senator is six years, with one-third of the total membership of the Senate elected every second year.

As of 1977, the House of Representatives was composed of 435 members. Unlike the Senate, members of the House are elected every two years, with the number of representatives from each state determined by the population of the state (Zinn, 1978).

Each Congress is convened for two years beginning in January of the odd year following the biennial election of members. The Congress is divided into two sessions and must assemble at least once annually at noon on January 3 unless changed by law to another day (*The Constitution,* 1976; Zinn, 1978). Both the Senate and the House have equal legislative powers and functions with one exception: the House initiates all bills of revenue (Zinn, 1978).

Committees

The committees, established in the House and Senate since 1789, are known as "the heart" of the legislative process. Because there are 100 senators and 435 representatives, the large number of participants makes it difficult for each member to consider all legislation. Therefore, each congressional chamber has established committees to provide for in-depth consideration of each legislative issue. To allow for further division of the work load, the committees have established subcommittees to consider legislation on specific issues. For example, in the Senate there are three committees, with subcommittees to review all health legislation. Likewise, in the House there are three committees (see Table 4), with subcommittees to review all health legislation (NHC, 1977; Zinn, 1978).

Senate and House committees have related functions and are composed of members representative of the majority and minority parties as determined by a membership ratio established at the beginning of each congressional session. Each subcommittee is responsible to the parent committee, as is each committee responsible to the parent chamber (NHC, 1977).

The Senate Finance Committee and the Subcommittee on Health have responsibility to review

TABLE 4
Congressional committee and subcommittee structure as regards health legislation

Senate	House of Representatives
Finance Committee	Ways and Means Committee
Subcommittee on Health	Subcommittee on Health
Human Resources Committee	Interstate and Foreign Commerce
Subcommittee on Health and	Committee
Scientific Research	Subcommittee on Health and
	Environment
Appropriations Committee	Appropriations Committee
Subcommittee	Subcommittee

all matters pertaining to the Social Security Act. Programs established by amendment to the Social Security Act are maternal and child health, Medicare, Medicaid, PSRO, utilization review, skilled nursing homes, home health care, cost containment, and end-stage renal disease. Similarly, the House Ways and Means Committee and the Subcommittee on Health have responsibility to review all issues related to Medicare, PSRO, end-stage renal disease, black lung, cost containment, and rural health. The House Ways and Means Committee is considered "the most powerful committee in Congress because of the power to tax" (NHC, 1977, p. 26).

The Senate Committee on Human Resources and the Subcommittee on Health and Scientific Research review issues related to the Public Health Service Act; the Food, Drug, and Cosmetics Act; and the Community Mental Health Centers Act. Specifically, the subcommittee considers issues pertaining to health work force (e.g., nurse training), biomedical and ethical research, rural health, HMOs, health planning, mental health and retardation, migrant health, and health research training. Similarly, the House Interstate and Foreign Commerce Committee and the Subcommittee on Health and Environment share responsibility for the Public Health Services Act and the Food, Drug, and Cosmetics Act. The subcommittee reviews health issues pertaining to clean air, environmental protection, HMOs, drug and alcohol abuse, biomedical and ethical research, mental health and retardation, and health planning. This committee also shares responsibility with the Senate Finance Committee for Medicaid and for maternal-child health issues (NHC, 1977).

The four committees just described are responsible for one function of committees: the authorization function. When considering a certain legislative issue, these committees suggest that certain amounts of money are needed to implement a program. This money is said to be "authorized" by the bill if it becomes law (NHC, 1977).

The second function of congressional commit-

tees is that of appropriation. To carry out this function there is one committee in the Senate and one in the House, each of which has a subcommittee. These committees are responsible for the budget of the Department of Health and Human Services (except the Food and Drug Administration and the Indian Health Service), holding the "power of the purse," and are responsible for allocating monies to be spent for programs established by law. The House committee is responsible for initiating all appropriations bills, and allocation cannot exceed but can be less than the amount of money suggested by the authorization committee. In short, these committees, with their appropriations function, can "make or break" a program established by law (NHC, 1977).

At this point, it should be noted that with the exception of national health insurance, each committee has established jurisdiction over certain health programs. All six committees have jurisdiction over national health insurance since the issue involves the use of health work force, the provision of a direct service, and the generation of new revenue.

To review, all health bills go to the House and Senate appropriations committees for allocation of funds. Although the committee structure of the Congress is necessary to its functioning, the national health insurance issue points to the complexity of the use of committees in the legislative process (NHC, 1977).

Committee staff

Again, because of the work load of the Congress and the committees, Congress has employed professional staff to assist committees with their work. The National Health Council (1977, p. 9) reported that in 1969 there were five professional staff members for the six committees on health. By 1977, the number of professional staff members had increased "sixfold." A professional staffperson may be anyone who can contribute to the work of the committees: a physician, a nurse, an allied health professional, or a lawyer, to name a few. The committee staff provides advice and counsel to the senators and representatives of each committee. These persons play an important role in the legislative process by researching health issues pertaining to legislation, holding hearings, and presenting written reports to committee members. The written report on an issue is an invaluable document because the report contains all of the following: a summary of proposed legislation; a history of past legislation; prior program implementation pertaining to the issue; committee views on the legislation; program cost estimates; a definition and analysis of the issue and the legislation; and testimony presented in hearings. When appropriate, the report includes a minority report, or report of dissenting opinions if a group exists within the committee that does not agree with the majority of committee members. When the committee agrees to report the bill to the appropriate chamber, the report further serves to inform all senators and representatives about the issue before a chamber vote takes place ("The ABC's," 1977; NHC, 1977; Zinn, 1978).

A review of the structure of Congress is incomplete if the role of the professional staff of Congress is omitted. The members of Congress employ a number of persons in their offices to assist them in keeping abreast of the issues facing Congress on a daily basis. Just as in nursing, no one person can be a specialist in all clinical areas, no member of Congress can be expected to be a specialist in agriculture, defense, education, health, and economics, at a given point in time. Thus persons who are qualified to become specialists in the above issues are employed to research issues and review legislation in a given specialty area. These staff people work with constituents interested in the specialty issue. For example, a nurse may be employed by a member of Congress to be the staffperson responsible for health legislation; a lawyer may be employed to be responsible for tax issues; a teacher may be employed to be responsible for education issues. Also, staff members may be employed not because of their credentials but because they have the ability to make themselves knowledgeable in a certain issue area (Redman, 1973).

As nursing becomes more involved in the political arena and as nurses begin to pay frequent visits to the congressional offices, they will find that the staffer plays a vital role in the life of the Congress by providing information and advice about legislative issues. To know the staffer is as important as knowing the senators and representatives.

LEGISLATIVE PROCESS

The following discussion focuses on the legislative process, or the mechanism of transforming an issue into a bill.

Issue sources

Ideas for bills of Congress originate from a variety of sources, including those from members of Congress who are fulfilling political promises as well as those from congressional members who have reviewed special programs in their home state or in other countries that show promise for national implementation. Issue ideas may also originate with the congressional staff who, in researching an issue or through constituent contacts, find projects worthy of national attention. The president, in the State of the Union Address, may submit a draft of proposed legislation or promote an issue. Finally, issue ideas may originate with an individual constituent. A prime example of a law that resulted from the suggestion of an individual constituent is the Emergency Health Personnel Act of 1970. This amendment to the Public Health Service Act established the National Health Service Corps. The idea originated with a physician who submitted the idea to a senator. The senator, in turn, supplied a staffer to work with the physician to develop a legislative package (Redman, 1973; Zinn, 1977).

Legislative path

Once an issue idea has been presented, the members of Congress and their staffs elicit the help of the legislative council of the appropriate chamber to write the proposal in legislative language for introduction as a bill. The legislative council drafts the bill in one of four formats: a bill, a simple resolution, a joint resolution, or a concurrent resolution. The bill is the most prevalent format used in both Houses of Congress (AHA, 1978; Zinn, 1978).

Once a bill has been drafted, it is introduced into a House of Congress. Each chamber has an established procedure for "reading" a bill before it is referred to a committee for consideration.

In the House, any member may introduce a bill by placing it in the "hopper" at the clerk's desk in the House chamber. The sponsor of the bill signs it before it is entered into the *House Journal* and printed in the *Congressional Record*. The bill is assigned a number and referred to the appropriate committee by the speaker of the house. The number assigned to the bill indicates the chamber in which it was introduced, and the order in which the bill was introduced into the calendar of the chamber. For example, H.R.1 would be the first bill introduced into a congressional session of the House of Representatives ("The ABC's," 1977; NHC, 1977; Zinn, 1978).

In the Senate, a senator who wishes to propose legislation must be recognized and must state an intent to offer a bill for introduction. If there is no opposition to the introduction, the bill is read by title for the first and second reading. Often, senators obtain consent at that point to have the bill printed in the *Congressional Record*. If there is opposition to the bill by any senator, the introduction of the bill is postponed until the next day. Once introduced, a bill is sent to the appropriate committee for review. It is not uncommon to find the House and the Senate considering similar versions of legislation at the same time. The work begins when the bill reaches committee. The committee assigns the bill to the appropriate subcommittee, where the legislation is reviewed, the issues researched, and hearings held to provide interested groups, the executive branch, and individuals an opportunity to present formally their views on the issue.

On completion of the hearings, the subcommittee or committee will have "mark-up" on a bill, a phrase coined from the committee's review of the bill line by line to change or amend the "intent" of the bill. When the committee has acted on the bill, it

is "reported out" to the chamber floor for debate, amendment, and vote. Once voted on, the bill is sent to the other House for action. Often bills of a similar nature are being simultaneously reviewed by both Houses of Congress. However, when the bills are reported out of the Congress they may have points of dissimilarity. When differences occur, the house originating the bill may request a conference to settle the issue and report out only one version of the bill.

Conferees are appointed by the presiding officer of the Senate and by the speaker of the house. The conferees are usually the ranking members of the committees reporting the bills. During the conference, each House has one vote and must consider only the differences in the two versions of the bill. Once agreement has been reached, the conference report is submitted to both houses for a vote. If either house does not approve the conference report, the bill "dies in conference." If approval is obtained, the bill goes to the White House to be signed into law (see Fig. 15-2).

When the bill is referred to the president for action, the president may take one of several courses of action: (1) Sign the bill; (2) let the bill lie on the desk for ten days while Congress is in session, without objection, whereby the bill automatically becomes a law; (3) let the bill lie on the desk for ten days after congressional adjournment, whereby the bill does not become law (referred to as the "pocket veto"); (4) return the bill to the House of origin with objections (known as a veto). With any of these courses of action, the president is participating in the enactment process by constitutional right. If the president vetoes the bill, it returns to both Houses of Congress, where a two-thirds majority vote of each House is required for the passage of the bill into law. If the two-thirds vote is not obtained, the veto stands. If the bill is passed, it is ready to be published by the U.S. Government Printing Office as a binding statute (AHA, 1978; Zinn, 1978).

Once a bill becomes a law, as in the case of a health law, it must pass once again through the legislative process as a budget request for funds

FIG. 15-2
Legislative path and input for health policy development.

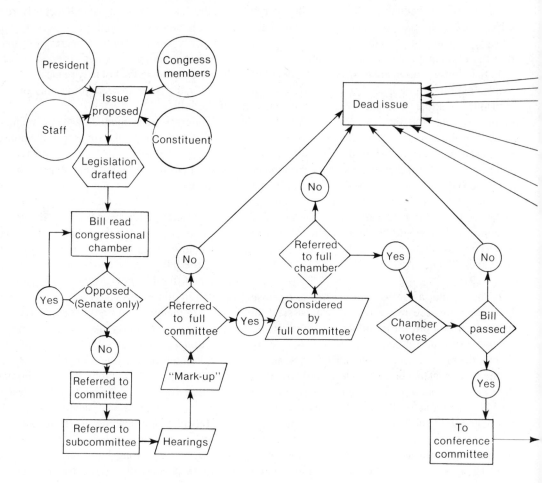

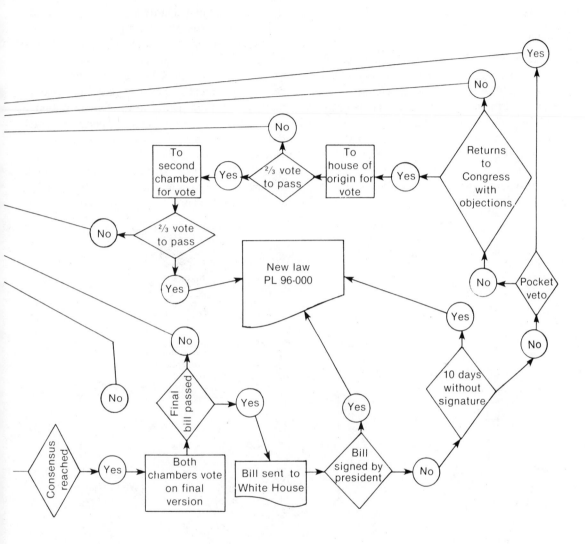

allocation. If funds are not allocated, the program set forth by the law becomes a dead issue.

Budgetary process

The federal budget is a spending and taxing plan for the country for a period of twelve months beginning on October 1 of one year and ending on September 30 of the next year. This is known as the fiscal year. The budget contains the spending and revenue plan for every program of the federal government. It is the budget of the DHHS that reflects monies allocated for the majority of the health-related program activities of the federal government.

A year and a half before the fiscal year, the Office of Management and Budget (OMB) of the administrative branch provides a plan projecting the required funds for all programs of the federal government (see Fig. 15-3). Three months later, the president provides guidelines to the various agencies of government so they may make final funding plans, which they submit to the OMB. Within a two-month period, after submitting budget requests to the OMB, the directors of various agencies meet with the OMB to finalize budget requests. Requests to the OMB are predicated on program evaluation and projected program goals. After the meeting with the OMB and program officials, the OMB pre-

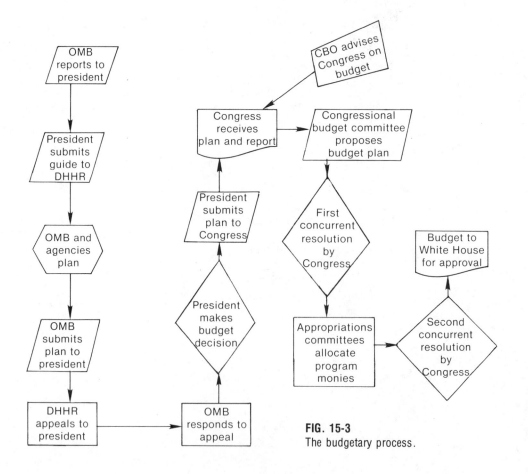

FIG. 15-3
The budgetary process.

sents a budget plan to the president. If an agency is dissatisfied with the plan, it may appeal to the president and the OMB director. The president then makes the final decision about the budget. Within fifteen days after the Congress convenes in January, the president presents his plan to Congress ("The ABC's," 1977; AHA, 1978). While the president is preparing his budget plan, Congress is preparing its own budget proposals.

The Congressional Budget Office, established by law in 1974, assists both Houses of Congress in evaluating costs and economic impact of budget proposals on the taxpayers. Both Houses also have budget committees to set broad spending and tax goals. These committees oversee the process of budget in each chamber. Then there are the appropriations committees, who allocate funding for specific bills within budget limitations.

By April 15 of the year preceding the beginning of the fiscal year, the budget committee proposes a budget plan. By May 15, the two Houses must approve the first concurrent resolution on the budget. The budget plans in the Congress often differ from the proposal of the president. A prime example of the difference in budget plans can be seen in the 1979 Congressional Budget Plan of $270.2 million for nurse training versus the 1979 Presidential Budget Plan of $20.5 million ("The ABC's," 1977; AHA, 1978; NLN, 1979).

From May to September, the appropriations committees review the budget plans set forth in the first congressional resolution and consider bills to raise or lower the taxes in order to allocate monies for new programs as set forth in new laws, and to allocate monies for existing programs for another time period. By September 15, before the beginning of the fiscal year on October 1, Congress must pass a second concurrent resolution to set final limits on spending and revenue.

EXECUTIVE BRANCH

The administrative or executive branch of government comprises the Office of the President, the presidential staff, the cabinet and task forces, as well as the major regulatory agencies of the government. The Departments of State, Defense, Health and Human Services, Education, Treasury, Justice, Labor, Housing and Urban Development, Interior, Agriculture, Commerce, and Transportation are only a few of the fifty-five agencies comprising the "fourth branch" of the government, the regulatory branch. It is with the Department of Health and Human Services (DHHS) that health providers are primarily concerned.

Once a bill has been enacted as law, regulations are written to indicate what can and cannot be done in the day-to-day operations of a program as "intended" by the law. Once a health bill becomes a law, it is assigned to the appropriate office of DHHS. Anyone has a right to petition that office to provide input into the regulations that are written for the new law or to petition for change in an existing regulation for an established law (see Fig. 15-4). Often the office will contact outside sources* to provide input into the writing of regulations for a specific bill. For example, when the Rural Health Clinics Act was passed, the ANA was contacted to provide expertise in writing the regulations for it.

After regulations are written and reviewed within the issuing agency, the proposed regulations are published in the *Federal Register*. After publication, any interested person may submit written comments on the regulations. These comments are then made available for public inspection. An agency may also hold public hearings on proposed regulations, or the hearings may be initiated by a private petitioner. Usually a period of thirty to sixty days is allowed for comment by the public on all proposed regulations. An agency may bypass the publication of proposed regulations, but it must justify the decision when final regulations are published.

After consideration of all comments, the agency publishes final regulations with a statement of their

---

*For example, the American Nurses' Association (ANA); the National League for Nursing (NLN); and the American Public Health Association (APHA).

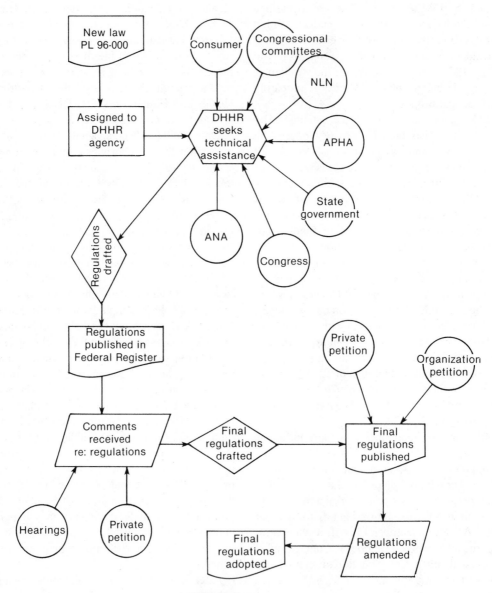

FIG. 15-4
The regulatory process.

basis and purpose. Final regulations appear in the *Federal Register* thirty days before their effective date. This allows another time period for public petition for amendment or change.

Although the role of the judicial branch of the government in health legislation will not be considered here, it is noteworthy to comment that the judicial process allows anyone to challenge the "intent" of the law as set forth by the regulations. The judicial system serves to interpret the intent of the law as enacted and enforced by the Congress and the administration.

INTERVENTION INTO LEGISLATIVE AND REGULATORY PROCESS

As nursing becomes more politically astute and realizes the value of influencing the process of legislation, nurses will also concede the value of intervening at various points in the legislative and regulatory processes. Although an individual constituent may intervene in the process, the value of intervention as an organized body is extremely important for nurses to recognize.

Reviewing the legislative process, it is clear that there are many points of intervention along the path of legislation. As indicated previously, a person or group may initiate an idea for a legislative proposal. Other key points of intervention occur before the time when a bill comes before a committee, as well as before either House considers a bill following committee review.

It is equally important to contact the White House after a presidential speech or press release on a health issue. If the speech or press release relates to existing laws, a communique to DHHS is in order. It may also be worthwhile to contact the White House when a bill has passed both congressional Houses and is on the president's desk to be signed into law.

In the regulatory process, one intervenes directly with the agency assigned to write the regulations for legislation. As previously noted, one can intervene before the writing of regulations, after the draft regulations have been published, or after implementation of the regulations through the judicial process.

Nursing must communicate its views to Congress because others who disagree with nursing's views are constantly communicating with them. One widely practiced method of communicating with Congress is through the organized lobbyists. A lobbyist is "anyone who works to influence decisions by public officials" (Green et al., 1972, p. 30). One who phones a Congress member to influence a policy decision is considered a lobbyist. Many special interest groups, businesses, and consumers have pooled resources to employ a person or persons to serve as lobbyists to influence Congress.

Since lobbying takes a commitment of time, energy, and money, it is practical to have a representative on Capitol Hill who can influence the legislation in process, rather than call up forces after a legislative issue has arisen. As mentioned earlier, the American Nurses' Association, as the professional nursing organization, maintains an office in Washington, D.C., with paid lobbyists and a staff to assist with legislative issues.

Lobbyists serve an important function in Congress. They can assist congressional members to recognize problems with legislation, draft legislation, provide supporting data for an issue, and influence the votes of other congressional members. Lobbyists often intervene with the administration in matters of budget. Organized lobbying is considered to have three major advantages for a person or group: (1) It provides an information network; (2) it provides for an on-the-scene person to influence decisions while committees are meeting; and (3) it provides an effective route for information from the local constituency to the Congress (Green et al., 1972, p. 260).

There are other effective strategies for influencing Congress, which can be initiated by the local constituency. Letter writing is the most common way of communicating with Congress. Telegrams and mailgrams are used to state an opinion on a legislative issue preceding congressional action. Telegrams and mailgrams are also useful to offer "thanks for your support" for work done by a congressional member that benefits a person or organization. Other effective strategies are phone calls and visits to the home office or Washington office of the pertinent member of Congress (Stanhope, 1980).

Before intervening with Congress, it is important to know the issue and to have gathered facts to support an opinion. It is also important to know the records of the officials on health legislation. Regardless of the intervention strategy chosen, be brief, explain the stand in understandable words, be courteous and reasonable, relate the issue to local needs, and contact the Congress members at an appropriate time.

Nurses' involvement in politics

Many health policy decisions are made on the local and state levels; therefore, nurses' involvement in politics is vital to improvement in the health care system.

Humphrey (1979) identified four steps in political activity on the national level, pointing out that the same principles can and should be applied at every level of government. These steps are as follows:

1. Become aware of the importance of nursing communication to current health policy issues.
2. Identify ways in which the individual professional nurse can become more involved personally in the political process.
3. Know the political goals of professional nursing organizations.
4. Understand the governing body's committee system in order to determine how and when information should be channeled to have the maximal effect.

The approximately one million practicing registered nurses in the United States constitute the largest group of health providers in the nation. Their involvement in politics is the most effective means for communicating nursing knowledge and experience to those who legislate policy. This is a new role for nurses, who have "often adopted the public stereotype of a passive rather than action-oriented profession," reacting to policy, being heard and/or seen "only when they want something," being more verbal on issues affecting the profession than those affecting the care that people receive in the health care system (Humphrey, 1979, p. 2).

There are numerous ways in which nurses can become more effectively involved in the political process. One of these is to affiliate oneself with a large organization such as the ANA. The ANA maintains a governmental relations office in the national capitol and is registered as an official lobby. The functions of this office are to evaluate and promote legislation, to advance the goals of the association, to publish a legislative newsletter, to monitor federal and state legislation, and to study trends in government with regard to their implications for nursing practice, service, education, economics, and the goals of the ANA (Billings, 1975). The nurse lobbyist with the ANA is the one who communicates most frequently the professional position of nursing on policy issues. ANA's position statements are based on the decisions of various commissions and divisions of practice, the House of Delegates, and organization officials (Billings, 1975). These statements are then distributed to ANA members, to the press, and to policy makers for their information and consideration. It is the lobbyist who serves as interpreter, clarifier, and supporter of the ANA's positions, effectively bridging the gap between position statement and subsequent policy formulation. Affiliation with such a group enables the individual nurse to become well informed on issues affecting health care. This affiliation increases one's visibility with policy makers, thereby increasing the clout of one's communication.

Nurses Coalition for Action in Politics (N-CAP) and the state political action committees (PACs) constitute the political action arm of the ANA. Established in 1974, N-CAP endorsed and supported political candidates for the first time in 1976. N-

CAP's five main purposes are to: (1) Encourage nurses to take a more active part in governmental affairs; (2) increase nurses' consciousness; (3) assist nurses in organizing themselves for political action; (4) raise funds for these purposes; and (5) make contributions to political candidates whose voting record and statements have demonstrated their interest in the nation's health. State PACs, established by state nurses' associations, encourage political action on the state level, provide political education, and endorse and contribute funds to candidates for state office. To date, there are nurse PACs in thirty-four states (*Facts About N-CAP,* 1979).

Other organizations, such as the NLN and the American Association of Colleges of Nursing (AACN), have staff persons and members who represent the groups' views on both the state and national levels. The NLN has included among its goals for 1979-1981 the promotion of nursing representation on decision-making bodies. Thus the major nursing organizations clearly see political involvement as essential to the future development of the profession. A related way of effecting health policy formulation is to make oneself known as a resource through professional work contacts, hearings, and letters to elected representatives.

Campaigning for and remaining personally acquainted with individual representatives is also important. It is helpful to utilize the representatives' experiences and knowledge in planning or presenting issue-oriented programs to professional colleagues and groups. In turn, one can communicate to the representative the thoughts of colleagues on specific issues. Although the representative may not have a health committee assignment, colleagues' views can be shared by the representatives with colleagues in Congress, and introductions to committee members can be obtained.

In summary, stay abreast of current issues and trends in health care so that communication with policy makers will be relevant and factual. Socialize with legislators, using the informal atmosphere as a means of reaching individuals who may be too busy at work to give the necessary attention to the profession's concerns and ideas. Develop skill in diplomacy and compromise, since these are essential in dealing effectively with those who oppose nursing's point of view or who are as yet uncommitted. Also, learn to address issues in an organized manner, using history, examples, and analogies wherever appropriate.

SUMMARY

In order to be effective change agents, nurses must become increasingly knowledgeable about the political process in the United States. An understanding of both the structure and functioning of governmental processes at the federal and state levels is the first step in developing a continuous involvement with staff and members of Congress. This chapter has emphasized the influence that governmental bodies have on the development and regulation of health policy. Specific examples of major health policies have been cited, especially as they affect nursing. Also, the legislative path has been outlined to provide direction for nurses who seek a more active involvement in health policy decisions.

There are a variety of key points for intervention before the time when a bill comes before a committee, and nurses must provide to congressional staff information about key bills that will affect nursing. This communication, to be most effective, should be regular during both the good times and the hard times. Staff also like to receive unbiased information as well as praise for their efforts, since so often constituents only contact them to plead for an issue in which they have a vested interest.

REFERENCES

The ABC's of how your government works, U.S. News and World Report, 1977.

American Hospital Association: Health specialists' guide to the federal legislative process and to the process of federal program and regulation development, Am. J. Law Med. **3:**2, 1978.

Billings, G.: ANA in the nation's capital, Am. J. Nurs. **75:**1182-1183, July 1975.

Burke, S.: Why nursing has failed. In The emergence of nursing as a political force, New York, 1979, National League for Nursing.

Cavalier, K.S.: Health planning and health resources development, CRS Issue Brief No. IB74081, Washington, D.C., Congressional Research Service, Library of Congress, Oct. 1976.

The Constitution of the United States of America, House of Representatives, No. 94-508, Washington, D.C., 1976, U.S. Government Printing Office.

Deloughery, G.L., and Gebbie, K.M.: Political dynamics: impact on nurses and nursing, St. Louis, 1975, The C.V. Mosby Co.

Ehrenreich, B.: The purview of political action. In The emergence of nursing as a political force, New York, 1979, National League for Nursing.

Facts about N-CAP, Washington, D.C., 1979, Nurses' Coalition for Action in Politics.

Fox, J.G., and Zatkin, S.R.: Third party payment for nonphysician health practitioners: realities and recommendations, Fam. Community Health 1:1, 1978.

Green, M.J., Fallows, J.M., and Zwick, D.R.: Who runs Congress? New York, 1972, Bantam/Grossman Books.

Health Maintenance Organization Act Amendments of 1978, Senate Report No. 95-837, Washington, D.C., 1978, U.S. Government Printing Office.

Health: Special Analysis L, Budget of the United States Government. Washington, D.C., 1978, Office of Management and Budget.

Humphrey, C.: Introduction: mandate for nurses: involvement in health policy. In The emergence of nursing as a political force, New York, 1979, National League for Nursing.

Judd, L.R., and McEwan, R.J.: A handbook for consumer participation in health care planning, Chicago, 1977, Blue Cross Association.

Kalisch, B.J., and Kalisch, P.A.: A discourse on the politics of nursing, J. Nurs. Adm. 6(2):29-33, Mar.-April 1976.

Milio, N.: The care of health in communities: access for outcasts, New York, 1975, The Macmillan Co.

Mullane, M.K.: Nursing care and the political arena, Nurs. Outlook 23:699-701, Nov. 1975.

National Health Council, Inc.: Congress and health, Washington, D.C., 1977.

National League for Nursing: Public Affairs Advisory, New York, 1979a.

National League for Nursing: Public Affairs Report, New York, 1979b.

Redman, E.: The dance of legislation, New York, 1973, Simon & Schuster.

Schneider, A.: Congressional action on health issues: 1978, Clearinghouse Rev. 1979.

Siddall, D.R.: How to prepare a legislative history, CRS 78-48A, Washington, D.C., Congressional Research Service, Library of Congress, May 1978.

The Social Security Act and Related Laws, Committee on Finance, U.S. Senate No. 71-4020, Washington, D.C., 1976, U.S. Government Printing Office.

Stanhope, M.K.: A political initiative, New York, 1980, NLN Publication.

U.S., Department of HEW: PSRO and health care practitioners other than physicians, Washington, D.C., 1978, U.S. Government Printing Office.

Zinn, C.J.: How our laws are made, House of Representatives, No. 95-259, Washington, D.C., 1978, U.S. Government Printing Office.

Nurses need to join together, recognize their legitimate power and influence, and learn how to deal constructively with their roles. . . . Specifically, nurses need personal courage and group solidarity. This does not mean that they should never disagree. There will always be disagreements, but they should be within a unifying framework and set of principles. This framework is especially important when nurses deal with the media, with other professions, and with the organizations within which they work. The main point is that they have to develop positive self-images as individuals and as nursing professionals.

Numerof, R.E.: New roles for medicine and nursing, Health Services Manager, August 1978 (New York: AMACOM, a division of American Management Associations, 1978), p. 9.

16

PROFESSIONAL ISSUES IN NURSING

Cynthia A. Rector

The current decade finds nurses and the nursing profession faced with many problems, including some that are threatening to the survival of the profession as we know it. Yet if one peruses nursing history, this state of affairs is not new. Nurses began to organize to work together near the end of the nineteenth century because they were concerned about the quality of nursing services delivered to the public, the quality of programs for the education of nurses, and the lack of legal status of nurses for practice (Flanagan, 1976). Such organization to work together was essential for nursing to move toward professional status, yet from the beginning problems existed. Nurses were slow to participate in the organizing efforts, and outside people and groups expressed their disapproval and opposition to the early nurses' organizing efforts (Ashley, 1976).

The critical questions of this decade are in many ways similar to the problems identified by nursing leaders in their early organizing efforts. The roles of nurses, their legal status and credentialing, types of educational preparation, relationships with professional colleagues, and the locale and control of nursing practice remain the focus of much attention. Last, but far from least, "The most fundamental problems in nursing are: (1) that it is a woman's occupation; and (2) that the majority of nurses, like the large society, do not perceive this as a problem at all" (Yeaworth, 1978, p. 71). Lavinia L. Dock, an early nursing leader and active feminist, expressed her concern that nurses were not aware of their common identity with other women and did not readily join with the women's suffrage movement (Ashley, 1976). The parallel continues, as nurses are reluctant to support the Equal Rights Amendment. The similarity of these concerns leads to the following questions: Do we know ourselves as individuals and as professionals, and what is our concept of ourselves? Do we have "personal courage" and "group solidarity"? Are our professional disagreements contained within a "unifying framework and set of principles" that enable us to debate the pros and cons of issues, sort out the facts, for-

mulate a plan of action, and move on to achieve our goals? Though we disagree among ourselves, do we speak with a unified voice to others—the public, the media, professional colleagues, and other organized groups?

This chapter will address these questions by assessing the present status of nursing and identifying some of the problems facing the profession. A theoretical framework, Bowen Family Theory, is used to study the problems and suggest possible plans for action. The major issues facing the nursing profession are not new and the profession is not in acute distress; rather, nursing suffers from a chronic condition that requires systematic, long-range efforts to change. No single cause-and-effect diagnosis and treatment will effect a cure. Instead, a systems approach to the problems that suggests multiple courses of action seems indicated to move the nursing profession into a leadership role in health care in the twenty-first century.

A THEORETICAL FRAMEWORK

Bowen Family Theory considers the family as a system and examines individual functioning in the light of family patterns and interactions. Bowen (1978, p. 462) states: "Basic relationship patterns developed for adapting to the parental family in childhood are used in all other relationships throughout life," and he has made an "effort to systematically correlate emotional forces in the family with emotional forces in society" (p. 269). Bowen views people as evolving life forms that are more related to lower forms of life than different from them, and says that people are governed more by instinctual forces than is usually recognized. Bowen (1978, p. 273) believes that systems thinking, which has become prevalent in the physical sciences, also influences people in their relationships with one another and with the society in which they live; but "in an emotional field, even the most disciplined systems thinker reverts to . . . taking action based more on emotional reactiveness than objective thinking."

Bowen (1978, p. 277) speaks of "togetherness-individuality forces'' operating in society, and says that in the absence of anxiety these forces are in balance, with each exerting equal influence on the group. The ''togetherness forces are derived from the universal need for . . . approval, emotional closeness, and agreement,'' whereas the ''individuality force is derived from the drive to be a productive, autonomous individual, as defined by self rather than the dictates of the group.'' However, when anxiety increases there is a move toward togetherness to decrease the anxiety, and a corresponding decrease in individuality. When anxiety is high and conflict is in progress, the togetherness group pleads for more harmony, agreement, and rights, while the individuality group wishes to adhere to principle, self-determination, and staying on course in spite of the increased anxiety. The focus of the togetherness forces on ''rights'' of individuals without consideration of ''responsibility'' leads to a situation where rights of others are violated and ''destroys the goal it is designed to attain'' (Bowen, 1978, p. 279). If the togetherness forces win out, the group reorganizes on a regressed level with less potential for individuality. When anxiety recurs the struggle begins anew, and this cycle continues as an ongoing part of life. If the togetherness forces continue to win out, and there is not a reasonable balance maintained, viable members leave to join other groups. Bowen (1978, p. 279) says that ''a society with higher levels of individuality provides great growth for individuals in the group, it handles anxiety well, decisions are based on principle and are easy, and the group is attractive to new members.'' These emotionally determined togetherness-individuality struggles can be diminished and growth can occur if people learn to use the knowledge and facts available to them to make decisions, rather than regressing to the use of cause-and-effect, emotionally determined decisions in the face of increased anxiety. Emotionally determined decisions usually preserve the status quo and may even intensify the problem. People make far more of their decisions on an emotional basis than most of us care to acknowledge, and the

first step in correcting this problem is to help people develop clearer ideas, opinions, and beliefs about themselves and their values so that they can make decisions based on thinking and use of the intellectual processes rather than feelings. Confusion of thoughts and feelings is prevalent in this society, as the review of any written material will confirm. The word feelings or feel is widely used where the content clearly indicates that the writer means thoughts, ideas, or opinions, and not feelings.

The ''emotional process in society,'' as described by Bowen (1978, p. 426), is an extension of the emotional process as observed in families, and observation indicates how these processes work to impede solving of problems and attainment of goals in professional relationships as well as in other areas of life. The major concepts to be used in this chapter are presented here and briefly defined.

1. *Differentiation of self* is a ''cornerstone'' of the theory and refers to the way an individual handles the intermix between emotional and intellectual functioning (Bowen, 1978, p. 424). Persons who are differentiated are able to live a full emotional life and at the same time make decisions in reality based on their beliefs and knowledge. The less differentiated person confuses emotions and thinking and makes most of life's decisions on a basis of what feels good rather than through consideration of the relevant facts.

2. *Triangles* are the ''smallest stable emotional unit'' (Bowen, 1978, p. 424), and emotional forces in families, groups, and society flow back and forth in predictable ways through the triangles. By identifying the triangles operating in an organization—work, professional, or social—one can make predictions about behavior and can plan strategies with predictable outcomes to deal with problems.

3. The *projection process* occurs in families, where parents project to one or more children problems occurring between the spouses, and the child/children become problematic in some way, such as developing physical symptoms, acting out, or withdrawing. In society, as in the family, pro-

jection is seen when anxiety is present and "two people get together and endeavor to enhance their functioning at the expense of a third" (Bowen, 1978, p. 443). The same principles can occur in groups when two groups get together and project problems onto a third group, often a weak group in the social system, such as minorities and the mentally ill.

4. *Emotional cutoffs* are means used by individuals to deal with increased anxiety and stress in the family system, and these often carry over into work and social situations. There are many variations of emotional cutoffs, ranging from geographical separation to withdrawal into the self even though the individual remains on the scene. Cutoffs are essentially dysfunctional and lead to regression and decreased differentiation in the persons involved (Bowen, 1978).

Based on the principles of Bowen Family Theory, guidelines for changes in families, small groups, and the larger society are offered. It is impossible to change another person or other groups, but the part that self or one's own group plays can be changed, often leading to change in the other. As individuals become more differentiated—or clarify their thinking about themselves as well as their ideas, opinions, and beliefs—and as they calmly and clearly express these beliefs, anxiety in the system increases and efforts are exerted by others to get these individuals to revert to their previous undifferentiated position. When people can maintain their course in spite of the pressures from others, the level of differentiation increases, anxiety decreases, and the others will move to join the differentiated person. Bowen believes that when key people in an emotional system can control their own emotional reactiveness, observe the system, avoid attacking when provoked, avoid withdrawing and becoming silent, and maintain a relationship with other key persons, "the entire system will change in a series of predictable steps" (Bowen, 1978, p. 436). He further notes that "an anxious system is one in which members of the group are isolated from each other, and communication be-

tween group members is in underground gossip" (Bowen, 1978, p. 436). When the leaders of such groups can become more sure of their beliefs and state these clearly, the anxiety in the group will often markedly decrease. Bowen (1978, p. 437) states that "the togetherness opposition to individuation, or differentiation, is so predictable that differentiation does not occur without opposition from the togetherness forces." These theoretical principles and guides for action will be used in examining key questions about nurses and the nursing profession.

WHO ARE NURSES?

Answering the question of who nurses are can immediately result in endless controversy and emotional reactivity within the nursing profession. Are we speaking of registered nurses, licensed practical nurses, or nursing assistants of various types? Who are the professional nurses, nurse practitioners, and nurse specialists? Who defines nursing anyway—the profession itself? The law and courts? The government? It is interesting to note that the American Nurses' Association (ANA) has never officially defined nursing. A draft of such a definition was discussed at the 1980 biennial convention, but not officially sanctioned. Some special areas of nursing (e.g., psychiatric nursing) have been defined by the groups involved, but the absence of a general statement defining nursing provides evidence of the identity problems of the profession. Nurses are different, and it is inaccurate to say that "a nurse is a nurse." Because of the varied educational backgrounds of nurses and the large variety of settings in which nurses practice, their needs and concerns are diverse. The question is: Can we recognize the differences in nurses and respect one another as colleagues?

It is truly a shameful thing that professionally prepared nurses cannot care for and value the lives and experience of nurses' aides, practical nurses, associate degree and diploma graduates. It is shameful that no connection or sense of community exists between these groups of women (Ashley, 1980, pp. 20-21).

Every issue the profession of nursing faces seems to result in deviseveness and nurses fighting with nurses.

Using Bowen Theory to assess nurses, it is noted that nurses seem to get caught in the emotionality of issues and to deal with their frustrations and angry feelings through emotional cutoffs. Many nurses are unable to differentiate feelings from thoughts, which goes along with a poorly differentiated self. Almost any issue elicits strong emotional reactions in groups of nurses, thereby complicating debate and further discussion. Reactions are personalized on the basis of the individuals' feelings, and any attempt at discussion on a rational, factual basis is impossible when nurses get caught up in telling their own particular story or experience from a strictly personal perspective. Broad, sweeping generalizations are often made on the basis of personal experiences, and attempts to look at all sides of the issue, explore the facts, and gather objective data are stymied. Rumors abound and any response to them often flames the emotional fires.

To move to a more differentiated and clearer position as individuals and as a group, nurses must achieve emotional distance from the issues to which they are so reactive. When a professional issue is being discussed and the individual nurse begins to feel "emotional" about the discussion, or notices that the group is becoming reactive, then it is time to consider what evoked the emotional response and try to deal with facts, principles, and knowledge about the issue rather than feelings. As nurses become clearer about their own identity and beliefs—that is, become more differentiated—then they are able to help others move toward similar clarity.

Organized nursing

At this time the "togetherness forces" seem to be operating within organized nursing with a strong focus on "What's in it for me?" with little attention being paid to what the individual nurse's responsibilities are to other nurses and the profession. In talking about the ANA, nurses often indicate that they want and expect the professional organization to take care of them. This theme says a lot about the history of the profession and the fact that most nurses are women. Women in this culture have traditionally been taught that men will take care of them, and nurses are a product of the culture. The history of nursing in this regard is documented by Ashley in *Hospitals, Paternalism, and the Role of the Nurse* (1976). The prevalence of this theme with nurses makes them vulnerable to union organizing efforts. Unions are a male-dominated group, and their literature, designed to attract nurses, gives a strong message of "Come and join us and we will take care of you," which is seductive to nurses. The message given by the ANA, as a professional organization, must be, "Join us in solving your problems." To be considered professional, nurses must join together as individuals and be prepared to take individual responsibility for decision making about the profession and themselves. *Compromise* and *collaboration* are essential ingredients for meeting professional goals. Many nurses who are critics of the ANA remain outside the organization, rather than working from within to change the organization to reflect their beliefs and ideas.

Bowen Theory indicates that leaders in the profession who become more differentiated and who take a clear stance based on their beliefs can expect opposition at first, but if these leaders can maintain a calm, clear course there will be overall benefits and growth for the profession. LaMonica and Siegel (1979) state that ANA leadership is seen by many nurses as representing the interests of nurse educators and managers rather than the majority of nurses, most of whom continue to occupy staff-level positions in hospitals. It has been my observation that the majority of nurses are interested in issues and educational programs that directly pertain to their day-to-day clinical practice. The specialty nursing organizations seem tailor-made to appeal to these interests. The ANA seems remote to many nurses, who do not recognize the effect that governmental health policy decisions and legislative actions have on their practice. Leaders of the profession are charged with bridging this gap and taking into account present needs of potential members and organization goals and programs that must determine the future of the profession. This balance between present and future goals is perhaps reflective of the balance to be achieved between togetherness and individuality forces in the organization.

COURAGE AND SOLIDARITY

When the progress of nursing in its 100 years of growth as a modern profession is considered, there is evidence of considerable courage. The primary goal of nursing has been the care of the sick, and nurses have persevered in this task in the face of tremendous obstacles. It is sometimes difficult to know whether to praise or to blame nurses for the courage they demonstrate in taking on seemingly impossible tasks. Nurses seem to "feel" it is their responsibility to provide care to patients when the level of staffing and other conditions by any objective measures are unsatisfactory. Are they courageous or foolhardy? The courage to work systematically to improve conditions of practice is not easy for nurses to muster, and they often quit and move on to another job when working conditions excessively compromise their standards of practice. Senator Inouye said to nurses at the 1978 ANA convention, "As a politician I find it hard to believe that a huge profession with a positive image sits by quietly and takes all the harrassment that nursing does." He pointed out that nursing is larger than labor unions and has a better image than physicians and lawyers. "Yet for some reason, you decide to remain docile. If you want to take away the phrase 'under physician supervision,' you must flex your muscle" (Educational Services Division, 1978, p. 1).

To flex its muscle the nursing profession must demonstrate group solidarity, and yet the membership of the ANA, after peaking at over 200,000 members in the mid-1970s, is steadily declining with a 1980 membership of approximately 170,000 (*American Nurse,* 1980, p. 1). The number of registered nurses, those eligible for membership, is estimated at over one million, but nurses are not joining the ANA in substantial numbers. Merton (1958, p. 50) defined a professional association as "an organization of practitioners who judge one another as professionally competent and who have banded together to perform social functions which they cannot perform in their separate capacity as individuals." Do nurses generally see one another as professionally competent? It does not seem so when the readiness of nurses to attack one another is observed. Nurses in trouble often do not believe they will receive support from peers, from nursing managers or administrators, or from the professional organization. Nurses often express feelings of powerlessness and helplessness in meeting their own needs, and many indicate that they do not see the ANA as the organization to meet their needs. LaMonica and Siegel (1979, p. 18) have proposed that "to provide services to individual nurses, the ANA could form a consultation consortium of recognized experts in various areas who would offer tangible personal assistance, in the name of the national organization, to any nurse who requests it." Such a proposal seems worthy of consideration because of its potential for increasing nurses' contact with one another and formally acknowledging the different competencies of nurses.

If the ANA is not the professional organization through which nurses will achieve group solidarity, then where is it to occur? The growth in numbers and size of the various specialty organizations for nurses has been astonishing in the past ten to fifteen years (LaMonica and Siegel, 1979), and it deserves careful study. What concerns and issues do appeal to nurses and entice them to join specialty organizations? The degree of participation of individual members in professional organizations varies greatly and is not a problem unique to nursing. Some professional groups have had more success in achieving group solidarity than nursing has, and these groups have exercised more power in society.

ECONOMIC AND GENERAL WELFARE
OF NURSES

In an occupational group as diverse as nursing, disagreements about policies and programs are inevitable and, indeed, are desirable. The manner in which the disagreements are expressed and the methods of resolving the disagreements are crucial to the profession and will determine whether growth or regression occurs.

The Economic and General Welfare Program (EGWP) of the ANA has a long history stemming from its original purpose "to promote the usefulness and honor, the financial and other interests of the nursing profession" (Flanagan, 1976, p. 169). In 1946, *collective bargaining* as a way of meeting the economic needs of nurses was included for the first time in the platform of the ANA, and the ANA through the state nurses' associations continues to be the largest representative of nurses. The employment conditions of nurses have a direct bearing on the quality of patient care delivered. The working conditions, including salary and fringe benefits, affect recruitment of women and men into nursing and influence the decisions of nurses to remain in the profession or to leave for more lucrative employment. Historically, nurses were supposed to be self-sacrificing women who were so concerned with the sick that they put their own needs aside to work long, hard hours for a pittance. This legacy has resulted in much conflict for nurses. Many nurses are more comfortable with the EGWP when the focus is on working conditions that directly affect patient care, rather than on economic issues. For example, the number and qualifications of nursing personnel to be assigned to specialty units, the need for adequate orientation of new nursing staff, and the necessary equipment to give patient care (a group of nurses once had a confrontation with hospital management because there were insufficient sphygmomanometers and wheelchairs on the unit) are items of interest to nurses. These concerns often lead to the most heated exchanges with hospital management because they threaten management's controlling role in the agency and, when

publicized, they threaten the image of "good patient care" that is so important to a health care agency.

Much of the conflict about the EGWP focuses on the use of collective bargaining as a means of meeting the employment goals of nurses. To represent nurses in a formal contract negotiation process, it is necessary for the state nurses' associations to register as labor organizations with the National Labor Relations Board (NLRB); the ANA supports and gives assistance in this activity, but is not itself the labor organization. This activity has resulted in the ANA and state associations being referred to as "unions," which has generated controversy. Chapter 17 details the ANA's involvement in collective bargaining. Using the Bowen Theory framework, I want to consider the effects of this controversy on nursing because of the emotional reactivity generated by this issue.

The mention of the words "collective bargaining" can evoke immediate and strong emotional response in many nurses, such that further discussion of the facts is useless. Because of their socialization into the profession, many nurses think (and feel) that it is inappropriate for them to engage in collective bargaining activities. These same nurses may complain about their working conditions and salaries, yet they do not wish to organize personally to deal with these problems. Their behavior seems to say, "You take care of it," or, "Someone needs to do this for us." The level of differentiation of such nurses is low and they tend to be highly reactive to the responses of others. Their need for approval and acceptance precludes their taking any action that threatens their personal relationships. When the necessity to get involved and take collective action is explained, many nurses back off and decide to tolerate the problems. Then, when they cannot endure any longer, they quit—often with angry feelings that their needs were not recognized—and go find another job. An example is the group of experienced nurses (six to ten years' work experience in the hospital) who complained that new graduates were being recruited to work in their hospital for the same, and in some instances higher, salaries than these nurses were making. When they approached their supervisor about this problem, her reply was, "If you don't like it, you can quit." These women were angry but felt powerless and helpless at this response and were seeking someone to solve the problem for them. They were not anxious to leave their jobs; they liked their work and thought they were good at it. Additionally, this happened at a time and in an area where hospitals were spending thousands of dollars on nurse recruitment! Absolutely incongruous! My response was, "You are right; it's a gross injustice. What are you willing to do about this?" The handicapping feature for them, and they are not unusual, was their fear of standing up for themselves. Any one of them attempting to confront administration alone would likely have been fired, and they knew that. Hence group action of all nurses so affected was needed. Because of their socialization as nurses and women, they found this exceedingly difficult.

As a further example, consider the group of nurses working in a specialized area of practice, who complained of overwork—much overtime, increased patient case loads, decreasing staffing—and then complaints from management about their work performance. They said they were told two years ago that the understaffing and overtime were "temporary" conditions. They stated, "We're tired; how long is temporary?" When they were encouraged to talk with management, they replied that they had tried and an answer was promised but never came. At this point, discussion of the method for effectively registering one's complaints seemed in order, that is, to follow up discussions with memos detailing the understandings reached and to keep copies of all correspondence for future reference. Several of the involved nurses expressed fears about being so direct; they feared being fired or the managers being "unhappy" with them. Yet these nurses said that they were being pushed to their limits, and unless relief appeared, they would quit—not en masse as a protest, but quietly one by one as other jobs were located. Would they better

themselves with new jobs? Probably not appreciably. A careful study of nurse turnover would most likely indicate that many nurses do not geographically relocate or stay unemployed long. Instead, they restlessly seek better working conditions in another setting. Often decision making is based on emotional needs rather than the reality of the situation.

The American Nurses' Association's EGWP and the increasing use of collective bargaining to effect changes in working conditions for nurses have created considerable conflict for nursing administrators. (This term is used to include all supervisors and management-level nursing personnel.) These individuals have often been the leaders in the nursing organization, and by their example have been responsible for the interest and participation of staff-level nursing personnel. The ANA maintains that they can continue the same level of participation, because the EGWP is controlled by the Economic and General Welfare Commission, which is responsible directly to the ANA membership and is not directly controlled by the Board of Directors. However, many hospitals and labor attorneys believe that participation of nursing administrative personnel in a labor organization, which may represent the agency's nursing staff, creates conflict of interest. A number of court cases and hearings before the NLRB have debated this issue. Interestingly enough, it is the hospitals that bring the conflict of interest charges and not the nurses being represented, who would be the logical persons to institute the charges, if they thought that their interests could not properly be represented by the ANA. Truesdale, a member of the NLRB, in a concurring opinion (246 NLRB, No. 25, 1979), stated that he believed the conflict-of-interest charge must come from the nurses being represented and not from the employer of the nurses. He saw the charge by the hospital as a delaying tactic to avoid negotiating with the nurses.

Some hospitals have issued policy statements precluding membership of their nurse administrators in the ANA or state nurses' associations, and many have withdrawn any support of the organizations in terms of time off for meetings, travel expenses for meetings, or allowing meetings on their premises. These actions mean that nurses must recognize who they are and what they think in regard to their own professional activities. The issues are not clear-cut and require much study. The misinformation of many nurses in the area of labor relations is astonishing, and because they are not well informed, these nurses are ready prey for rumors.

There are also nurses who believe the ANA has not devoted sufficient resources or energies to the EGWP. "The percentage of the total ANA budget that has been allocated to the E&GW program has been reduced yearly from 13.5% in 1974 to 5.4% in 1980" (Commission on E&GW, 1980, p. 1). These nurses see collective action, including collective bargaining, as the way nurses exercise their right to professional self-determination. Since the majority of nurses are employees of various health care agencies and are not self-employed, this is the avenue open to them for addressing professional issues in the work situation. Not to be overlooked is the role the ANA has played in other areas to represent nurses and improve their economic status: for example, the suits filed by ANA through the Commission of Economic and General Welfare to protest the sex-based tables in determining insurance benefits used by the Teachers Insurance and Annuity Association (TIAA) and the College Retirement Equities Fund (CREF). After several suits were decided in favor of ANA and the protesting nurse faculty members, the companies changed their policy and these cases are expected to have far-reaching effects in regard to insurance coverage for women, including nurses (McCarty, 1980, p. 1).

Continuation of the EGWP seems essential, and yet the conflict about this ANA service continues. The next few years will be important as nurses decide whether to invest their energies in maintaining a large multifaceted organization to represent the common interests of all registered nurses, or whether a variety of specialized organizations will better serve nursing.

EDUCATIONAL PREPARATION FOR PROFESSIONAL PRACTICE

A major goal of organized nurses has always been "to elevate the standard of nursing education" (Flanagan, 1976, p. 306). Yet the resolution passed at the 1978 ANA convention, which stated "that by 1985 the minimum preparation for entry into professional nursing practice be the baccalaureate in nursing" (Commission on Nursing Education, 1979, p. 5), has been another phase in a continuing controversy. How much education nurses really need and where the educational preparation should be obtained are questions guaranteed to stir deep feelings in nursing groups. This is another issue facing the profession where the emotional reactivity gets in the way of progress and often precludes any lucid discussion of the facts. Given the rapid growth in knowledge and the complexities of the current health care field, anything less than baccalaureate preparation for professional nurses is unsound and puts nurses in a noncompetitive position with other health care providers.

However, the use of "professional" in nursing is so entwined with the legal term "registered nurse" that the "feelings" many nurses have that they are being stripped of their hard-earned status and that their jobs will be threatened makes it difficult to get the facts before nurses and the public. Nurses often have too much emotional involvement in the topic to discuss it rationally. Often impartial groups can review the facts more objectively. For example, a debate entitled "Resolved: The Baccalaureate Degree Shall Be Required for Professional Nursing Practice" was presented by a college debate team, none of whose members were nursing students. Without the emotionality usually seen in discussions by nurses, they clearly presented the facts, and the conclusion was inescapable: baccalaureate preparation is minimal when the responsibilities of a professional nurse are outlined.

As baccalaureate preparation for professional

practice becomes established, the question of "separate licensure for the professional practice of nursing is an issue of major dimension that can no longer be ignored" (Wagoner, 1977, p. 11). A need for some type of credential to distinguish the two categories of nurses has been debated, and the choices seem to be: (1) separate licensure for the technical and professional categories; (2) licensure for minimal technical competence and professional credentialing for professional practice; or (3) a maintenance of the status quo with all the confusion that exists. In many ways, separate licensure seems the more viable of the options, but such a change requires that nurses reach some agreement among themselves and then move to seek public and legislative support for the necessary changes in the law.

The education for the second category of nursing personnel—technical or dependent nursing practice—has been proposed for the community or junior college, and leads to the associate degree in nursing. Such a move would require that existing licensed practical or vocational nursing programs be incorporated within the junior college system and be upgraded to two-year courses of study. A number of junior colleges have already instituted one-year supplemental programs to enable LPNs to move up the educational ladder. As the complexity of health care continues to increase, such a general upgrading of the educational qualifications for nurses seems to fit with social trends. Indeed, nurses are resisting the social trends for more education, especially for professional groups when they fight to maintain the present arrangement for nursing education.

The future of diploma nursing programs, which are still controlled by hospitals, is more difficult to assess. Many of these programs are excellent, but they are outside the mainstream of higher education in the United States. A number of excellent diploma programs have closed as nearby colleges or universities began baccalaureate programs, and the hospitals have made themselves available for clinical practice for the baccalaureate students. Good diploma programs that meet accreditation standards

are expensive to operate, and the question of a service agency (such as a hospital) charging patients to pay for an educational program is open for debate. Some third-party payers have refused reimbursement for that portion of patient care costs attributable to an educational program. Vested-interest groups, both within and outside nursing, are mounting strenuous opposition to the move of professional nursing to upgrade educational preparation for nurses.

The history of nursing education makes the present conflict and dilemma easier to understand. Early schools of nursing were a part of the hospitals with which they were associated, and the director of nursing was often in charge of the school of nursing as well as the hospital's nursing service department. The demands for nursing care of patients were the first priority, and the education of the student nurses was often sacrificed to meet hospital staffing needs. Indeed, hospitals opened schools and recruited students to provide nursing staff and cheap labor. Hospital administrators and physicians often took the stance that nurses did not need much education, and nurses were often the oppressed group in a triangle with these two predominantly male groups (Ashley, 1976). Pleasing these male power figures was important to these women (nurses), and most were reluctant to take a stand on any issue that would result in their disapproval. Unfortunately this state of affairs still exists, and many nurses are still reluctant to examine their own beliefs and principles in order to meet their own needs for fear of reprisal from physicians and hospital administrators. Overcoming this legacy will take time and will require a change in the level of differentiation of nurses. Many nurses want to change "the others" in this situation, but it is unrealistic to expect these groups to institute a change in the status quo that has served them well for a century. As nurses make changes in themselves and their educational system, they can expect strong opposition, but if they can steadfastly maintain the new stance, the outside groups can be expected to change in response.

The ANA Commission on Nursing Education

has clearly stated the historical background and facts that support the change in educational preparation for professional nurses in a booklet entitled, *A Case for Baccalaureate Preparation in Nursing*. Work goes forward through the commission to implement the changes needed to make this goal a reality. If the nursing leaders can maintain a calm, clear course through the storms of protest that are already occurring and that are inevitable if Bowen Theory is accurate, the end result should be an upward move for the profession.

SUMMARY

This chapter has examined from the perspective of Bowen Family Theory why nurses as individuals and as a profession have difficulty in moving ahead to achieve desired goals. Selected issues of the profession have been addressed and various viewpoints explored. There are those who view the challenges and problems facing the nursing profession with a note of alarm about the profession's future. Lysaught (1980, p. 6) has stated that "because the nursing profession is so seriously divided even on the simplest of goals, its ability to survive in its present form by the year 2000 could be seriously imperiled." Others have a more optimistic view. In her keynote address opening the 1980 ANA Biennial Convention, Dumas (Educational Services Division, p. 4) said, "We are about to come together in this profession and we will meet the challenges of the 1980's with renewed commitment to this great profession and with one voice—one audible coherent powerful voice."

REFERENCES

American Nurse: Official Newspaper of the American Nurses' Association. Kansas City: American Nurses' Association, **12**(7):1, July/Aug. 1980.

Ashley, J.A.: Hospitals, paternalism, and the role of the nurse, New York, 1976, Teachers College Press.

Ashley, J.A.: Power in structured misogyny: implications for the politics of care, Adv. Nurs. Science **2**:20-21, 1980.

Bowen, M.: Family therapy in clinical practice, New York, 1978, Jason Aronson, Inc.

Commission on Economic and General Welfare, American Nurses' Association: Resolution rationale: faith and belief in the process of collective bargaining, A statement issued April 17, 1980.

Commission on Nursing Education: A case for baccalaureate preparation in nursing, Kansas City, Mo., 1979, American Nurses' Association.

Educational Services Division: Convention news, Honolulu, Hawaii, American Journal of Nursing Co., June 12, 1978.

Educational Services Division: Convention news, Houston, Tex., American Journal of Nursing Co., June 10, 1980.

Flanagan, L. (compiler): One strong voice: the story of the American Nurses' Association, Kansas City, Mo., 1976, American Nurses' Association.

LaMonica, E.L., and Siegel, F.F.: A professional organization that helps all of us, J. Nurs. Adm. **9**(5):16-18, May 1979.

Lysaught, J.P.: Nursing profession has great potential, Birmingham, Ala., UAB Report, University of Alabama, June 20, 1980.

McCarty, P.: Insurance carriers drop sex-based pension tables, Am. Nurse **12**(2):1, Feb. 1980.

Merton, R.K.: The functions of the professional association, Am. J. Nurs. **58**:50, 1958.

246 NLRB, No. 25. Baptist Hospitals, Inc., Western Baptist Hospital Employer and Kentucky Nurses' Association, Petitioner, Case 9-Re-12492, 1979.

Numerof, R.E.: Management of nursing care: new roles for medicine and nursing, Health Services Manager **11**:8, 1978.

Wagoner, E.F.: The issue of separate licensure enters the nursing arena, J. Nurs. Education **16**:11-13, Jan. 1977.

Yeaworth, R.C.: Feminism and the nursing profession. In Chaska, N.L., editor: The nursing profession: views through the mist, New York, 1978, McGraw-Hill Book Co.

Only by working collectively to define and enforce standards of care will nursing be able to gain the public's recognition of the value of its services and its entitlement to greater personal reward.

Cleland, V.: Am. J. Nursing **75**:289, 1975. Copyright by American Journal of Nursing Company.

17

LABOR RELATIONS AND THE NURSE

Daniel H. Kruger

The mid-1930s saw massive union organization campaigns that management often resisted. Economic conditions spurring union organization activities included high unemployment, low wages, and general deterioration of industrial settings. On the social front, management began to exhibit a change in attitude toward the welfare of employees as a result of the human relations approach to management that was beginning to take hold. Finally, the passage of the National Labor Relations Act (NLRA) of 1935, known as the Wagner Act, and the *Jones and Laughlin* U.S. Supreme Court decision in 1937, which upheld the constitutionality of the Wagner Act and extended the federal government's regulatory powers, lent congressional, legal, and judicial protection to union activity and collective bargaining.

Nurses have used collective actions to improve their wages and working conditions since the mid-1930s. This chapter discusses the effect of *nightingalism,* employeeism, and professional collectivism on collective bargaining, as well as the role of the American Nurses' Association (ANA) in organizing registered nurses. Attention is also given to legislation and selected judicial and administrative rulings of the 1970s that relate to labor relations and collective bargaining by health care employees. The last section of the chapter deals with crucial concerns of today's professional nurses in relation to fulfilling their goals as employees.

COLLECTIVE ACTION AS AN APPROACH FOR IMPROVING WAGES AND ECONOMIC CONDITIONS

The Wagner Act protected employees' rights to organize and to join unions, and specified certain unfair labor practices of employers as unlawful. The focus of this act was on the private sector; it did not extend those same rights to employees of nonprofit and publicly owned hospitals. Although collective bargaining by nurses employed in nonprofit and proprietary hospitals was allowed under the law, legal protections for the exercise of that right were quite limited. Professional nurses were

acutely aware of the inadequacy of their wages, benefits, and conditions of employment. These had deteriorated rapidly during the depression, and failed to improve as the economy began to improve. Thus, in 1936 and 1937, trade unions began organizational campaigns among registered nurses who were covered under the Wagner Act.

Even though the ANA was organized in 1896 to promote the professional interests of its members, this organization had not devoted significant time or resources to furthering the economic interests of nurses (Miller, 1971). Consequently, when the unions began to pursue the economic cause of nurses actively, the ANA saw its organizational purpose as threatened and feared a certain loss of loyalty among its members. The ANA strongly recommended that nurses refrain from joining unions and turn to their state associations to further their economic interests. Specifically, state nursing associations were urged to assume greater responsibility for nurses' employment conditions through educational campaigns to increase the public's knowledge about the services nurses provided and their importance to the economy (Grand, 1973). Public education campaigns were to be carried out at the district level, with special assistance provided by the state and national bodies. Although some state organizations attempted the prescribed activities to improve the nurses' employment standards, they were, for the most part, unsuccessful (Kruger, 1961).

Nursing ideologies as deterrents to collective action

The ANA, adverse to undertaking more forceful action than the educational campaigns, was opposed to union membership for its members because it viewed the strike tactics of unions as incompatible with the service ideal of nursing. In an article in the *American Journal of Nursing* in 1938, the following comment appeared:

No one has yet suggested the organization of mothers' unions, with the standard scale of hours, wages and other safeguards. In a sense, modern nursing is a specialization of certain functions formerly performed by mothers. The nurse serves others. A nurses' union would be almost, if not quite, as absurd as a Mothers' Union (Miller, 1971, p. 135).

Humanitarianism and self-sacrifice have been the most prominent values within the nursing occupation since its inception. The service ideal in nursing is based on a widely held set of beliefs termed *nightingalism* in reference to the values symbolized by Florence Nightingale. According to the ideology of nightingalism, self-sacrifice on the part of nurses has come to mean that "the primary concern of the nurse is the welfare of the patient and excludes a concern on the part of the nurse with her own economic and social welfare (Grand, 1973, p. 30). In her role as the doctor's assistant, the nurse was expected to relinquish home comforts in her service to the patient as well as to accept as a duty the performance of menial or offensive tasks. Insofar as the sick were often poor and could not pay the hospitals for services, nurses were expected to work for minimal wages. Nurses generally viewed unions with their emphasis on "bread-and-butter" issues as incompatible with their belief systems of service and self-sacrifice. Furthermore, the use of the strike as an economic sanction to improve the conditions of work seemed unacceptable, since strikes directed against employers harmed the very patients nurses were dedicated to serving.

Nightingalism was not the only belief system that deterred collective action during the 1930s. *Employeeism*, the belief that "employers of nurses have the best interests of the nurses at heart and will do their best for them," developed during and after the depression (Grand, 1973). Many private-duty nurses were forced to depend on the paternalism of their hospital employers, who offered them a place of employment when the prevailing economic conditions dried up the demand for private-care nurses. Despite the disadvantages of hospital employment and its long hours, low wages, and in-house residency requirements, nurses accepted these adverse conditions along with their ideals of service and self-sacrifice, believing that their employers were concerned about the nurses' welfare, however modest their actions might actually appear. Thus the ideologies of nightingalism and employeeism encouraged and reinforced one another and so acted as major deterrents to the organization of professional nurses into unions interested in the financial betterment of their members.

Nursing's entry into collective action during the 1940s

Improvements in employment conditions were not achieved by the ANA's state organizations' public information campaigns, and the economic position of nurses worsened with the restrictions on wage increases that were enacted in 1942. In 1943, the California State Nurses' Association (CSNA) proposed that a basic (minimum) salary schedule for nurses be adopted by the California State Hospital Association. When the latter organization refused to accept the nurses' demands, they appealed to the National War Labor Board (NWLB) for assistance and were successful in gaining the desired wage improvements. The significance of the NWLB's ruling and the CSNA's success were to demonstrate the usefulness of collective bargaining and to lend support for further group action in nurses' quests for better standards of employment (Kruger, 1961).

The success of the CSNA prompted other state nursing associations (SNAs) to question their roles with respect to spearheading collective action efforts on behalf of their members. With the increased pressure from within its ranks and with the outside forces of trade unions seeking to organize and represent nurses, the ANA resolved actively to assume responsibilities for the collective advancement of nurses' economic interests. At its 1946 convention, the ANA proposed and adopted their economic security program with these express purposes: (1) the protection and improvement of wages, hours, and working conditions of nurses; and (2) the assurance that professional nursing service of high quality and sufficient quantity would always be available to the public. These two objectives were closely related and interdependent, in that the quantity and quality of nursing care were seen as dependent on the wages and working conditions offered nurses. Where poor working conditions existed, the quality of patient care was expected to suffer in that employees would be dissatisfied, and their dissatisfactions would be manifested in their work. Low wages were deleterious to the overall quantity of patient care available in that nurses would neither be easily attracted to nor retained in the profession. The ANA's objective of improved nursing service through improved working conditions was more palatable to nurses, who identified strongly with their profession, than were the economic goals supported and proposed by the trade unions.

The SNAs were chosen to represent the collective economic interests of nurses because they are considered the most knowledgeable about the nursing profession and nurses' abilities, skills, and economic needs (Alexander, 1978). Although SNAs act as exclusive agents for their members, the ANA provides guidance and interpretation regarding the economic security program. The ANA has a policy on membership that permits the nurse to belong to one other organization that has collective bargaining as a primary objective. Although membership in other such organizations was not prohibited by the association, the ANA encouraged its state affiliates to discourage dual memberships on the premise that exclusive jurisdictional rights were just as appropriate for professional associations engaged in collective bargaining as they were for trade unions. The ANA elaborated on the economic security programs in 1950 with its adoption of a "no-strike" policy in accordance with its belief that professional nurses share a responsibility with their employers for providing adequate public health service:

The American Nurses' Association, in conducting its Economic Security Program, (1) reaffirms professional nurses' voluntary relinquishment of the exercise of the right to strike and of the use of any other measures whenever they may be inconsistent with the professional nurses' responsibilities to patients; and (2) reaffirms its conviction that the voluntary relinquishment of measures ordinarily available to employees in their efforts to improve working conditions imposes on employers an increased obligation to recognize and deal justly with nurses through their authorized representatives in all matters affecting their employment conditions.*

The willingness of nurses to abstain from employing the strike as an economic weapon in support of their demands and their reliance on their employers to "deal justly" with them often impeded their collective endeavors to improve their conditions of employment. In 1968, the ANA found it necessary to reassess and rescind its policy prohibiting strike tactics.

ANA structure and membership as deterrents to collectivism

The composition of its membership and the organizational structure of the ANA have hampered the opportunities for nurses to make sizeable gains in their collective dealings with employers. The organizational structure of the ANA below the national level comprises three levels: the local unit, the district level, and the state association. The local unit is composed of the various nurses who work for a common employer; together, local unit members are encouraged to establish standards of employment and develop policies that meet their common and individual employment needs. It is this local group that chooses to be collectively represented by a particular organization, such as the SNA, in their employment relationship with their employer hospital. The ANA looks on the local unit as "a real key to the success of a functioning economic security program" (Boyer et al., 1975, p. 233).

*From Miller, R.L.: Development and structure of collective bargaining among registered nurses—part I, copyright February 1971. Quoted with permission from *Personnel Journal*, Costa Mesa, Calif. All rights reserved.

The district nurses' association comprises various local units within a particular area (i.e., district), and it supports the state association's activities through its informal ties with the local units. Basically, the district association encourages the formation of local units and generally supports their efforts by providing them with information regarding employment conditions within the district and by communicating with the state association on their behalf. Where authorized, the SNA represents the local units' interests to the local employer, be it a hospital, nursing home, or health service agency. The negotiating functions are carried out at the local unit level with assistance from the state association. The SNA represents the grievants in arbitration, collects data for purposes of collective bargaining, organizes new local units, and monitors the collective bargaining activities (Kruger, 1961). The ANA's reasons for vesting the primary responsibility for the organization and implementation of the economic security program with the state association are threefold:

First, the state association's levels of funding and staff size enable it to employ any necessary consultant assistance in the areas of law, labor relations and public relations.

Secondly, the usual location of state associations in state capitals allows them to be aware and knowledgeable about the economic and political forces in various parts of the state which can be expected to influence the successes of the different economic programs.

Finally, the state association will not be subject to local pressures and thereby be enabled to act more objectively during the negotiating process (Boyer et al., 1975, p. 233).

The responsibilities assigned to the organizational levels in conjunction with the composition of their membership (i.e., the kinds of nurses belonging to the local unit, the district association, and the state association) have frequently resulted in economic security programs of a rather weakened nature. Historically, general duty nurses have accounted for about one-third of the membership at all

levels of the ANA's organizational hierarchy, whereas nursing service directors and educators have comprised the majority of members on the state association governing boards (Miller, 1971). As would be expected, the establishment of priorities regarding SNA activities reflects the interests of those in authority. Although the SNA's objectives include the provision of quality nursing care, the promotion of professional self-determination and status, and the advancement of nurses' economic well-being, it places primary emphasis on its various professional programs. In the majority of states, the association's active members—that is, those in authority—are unlikely to support aggressively the economic security programs.

Commitment to multiple goals has impeded many SNAs in taking advantage of their potential strength in collective bargaining functions. Collective bargaining activities are essentially negotiating agreements covering wages, hours, and conditions of employment and their administration; that is, grievance handling, including arbitration. The provision of services by the state association to the local units is often inadequate because of insufficient financial resources and staff.

In July 1976, the registered nurses at Midland Hospital successfully petitioned the National Labor Relations Board (NLRB) to have the Michigan Nurses' Association (MNA) decertified as their collective bargaining agent. The Midland nurses felt that the MNA representative assigned to represent their interests in a dispute with the hospital was "out of touch" with the political and other factors influencing the nurses' relations with their employer hospital; worse yet, he had no labor, medical, or legal experience (Natonski, 1978). Furthermore, the local unit had serious difficulties communicating with their MNA representative as a result of the distance between the state association's office location (in East Lansing) and their hospital, as well as a result of the representative's heavy case load, which kept him on the road and out of direct touch with his clients. The Midland nurses saw the MNA's role as primarily concerned with advancing the professionalism of nursing practice rather than with the furthering of nurses' collective economic interests. Many other professional nurses view their state associations in a similar light.

Positive influence of ANA's new policy of the 1960s

In general, ANA's role in economic security programs until 1968 was limited to making broad policy decisions and providing consultant services. However, at its 1968 convention the ANA initiated a "new approach" by making direct financial and staff support available to local units and state associations as they carried out economic security program activities. The ANA's reasoning for assuming direct involvement in economic security matters was that the association had been only moderately successful in representing nurses at work, which in turn "threatened the future of the profession." The ANA had to take a new approach if the association was to effect positive changes in nurses' economic well-being (ANA, 1968). Although the "new approach" called for the ANA's direct involvement in economic security programs, the SNAs retained both their roles as bargaining representatives and the right to veto any projects in their jurisdictions. Traditionally, SNAs recommended minimum salaries for registered nurses. In 1966, the ANA approved the first nationwide minimum salary on the basis that since hospitals derived their income from a number of sources other than local resources (such as third-party payments), community economic conditions could no longer be advanced as the most important criterion in the determination of wages. Since 1966, the ANA has updated the approved minimum wage levels in response to changing economic and social conditions. The hoped-for result of the ANA's injection of money, staff, and experience into the SNAs' economic security activities was to gain greater confidence in and commitment to collective action by all professional nurses.

In 1968, ANA rescinded its no-strike policy in an effort to strengthen nurses' collective demands.

During the eighteen years when the no-strike policy was in effect, nurses bargained with their employers from a weak position; both public and private employers frequently refused to negotiate issues and instead unilaterally initiated actions. Feeling that their professional dedication was being used to deny them fair and equitable treatment, nurses pressed for the use of coercive tactics against employers instead of relying on public education campaigns and persuasion. Initially nurses supported mass resignation as a more professional tactic than the strike. However, many nurses now recognize the right to strike as a necessary condition for improving their personal well-being and ultimately for improving the quality of patient care. The ANA's revised policy on strikes provides members with the option of invoking coercive sanctions. When strikes are called, nurses generally recognize their responsibility to their patients and permit peers to cross picket lines to provide nursing care to those who are critically ill. Most nurses do not like strikes and instead support fact finding and mediation, as well as voluntary and compulsory arbitration as alternatives. Still, there is definite support, especially among younger nurses, for using strike tactics to obtain economic and other concessions from employers (Donovan, 1978). Moreover, SNAs and local bargaining units are turning to universities for assistance in obtaining needed skills in labor law, contract negotiations, and administration, so that they can be more effective at the bargaining table.

RECENT POSITIVE DEVELOPMENTS SUPPORTIVE OF COLLECTIVE ACTIVITIES

More recently, professional collectivism by nurses has been positively influenced by the growth of unionization among other professionals, the passage of the 1974 amendments to the National Labor Relations Act, and the subsequent successful organization of other hospital employees by national unions. The collective activities of professionals, such as social workers, teachers, and professors has influenced many nurses' attitudes toward the idea of acting in concert to further their professional and economic status. Nurses have witnessed the successes teachers have achieved in negotiating over professional issues and economic matters. Teachers, represented by the National Education Association (NEA) and the American Federation of Teachers (AFT), have bargained over both salary levels and class-size limits because they believe that the "only way (they) can insure that salary improvements they gain are not at the expense of the children's education is to bargain for a package that includes both salary and class size" (ANA, 1969, p. 1894).

The belief that professional initiative and reform may be best served by collective action has made collective bargaining more palatable among nurses today. Professional collectivism is viewed as necessary "not only to redress the balance of power between [professionals] and their employers, but also to give weight to the professional judgment on the standards, performance and quality of the services that they themselves provide, and judgment that frequently conflicts with the bureaucracies that employ them" (Matlack, 1972, p. 41).

The advancement of educational programs for nursing has affected the attitudes of nurses toward collective bargaining. More highly educated nurses are seeking to exercise their professional expertise in order to carve roles for themselves that include greater authority, autonomy, and involvement both in determining their working conditions and in providing patient care. It appears that a growing number of nurses do not consider concerted actions to be "unprofessional." On the contrary, collective bargaining is increasingly viewed as compatible with professionalism.

The increasing complexity of health care institutions also helps to explain the growth of collective bargaining among nurses. Hospitals, the largest employers of nurses, have become bureaucratic and impersonal in their emphasis on efficiency as a way to restrain the exploding costs of health care. Nurses are turning to concerted actions in order to protect their professional interests and identity.

One of the most significant labor relations developments during the 1970s that encouraged collective bargaining among nurses was the enactment of Public Law 93-360, or the 1974 National Labor Relations Act (NLRA) Amendments. On July 26, 1974, this law amended the Taft-Hartley Act of 1947 by extending the rights to organize collectively for matters concerning wages, hours, and working conditions to all employees of nonpublic health care facilities. (Employees of government-owned hospitals and health facilities were still excluded from protection under the NLRA.) By enacting such legislation, Congress sought to ameliorate the low wages and poor working conditions common to the health care industry, which were seen as "retarding the delivery of quality health care" (BNA, 1978, p. E-5). The rights of hospital employees to organize and bargain collectively were seen by Congress as necessary to the achievement of long-term improvements in health care. Hospital employees were brought under the protection of the NLRA, so that strikes and picketing would be eliminated by providing other procedures (elections, petitions) for the resolution of disputes. Although the 1974 amendments include specific strike notice and mediation provisions to forestall the interruption of critical health care services, the right to strike, even where it leads to the disruption of patient care services, was seen as important for the achievement of harmonious employer-employee relations and the long-term betterment of health care services. The Supreme Court upheld the intentions of Congress in its passage of Public Law 93-360 in the case of *Beth Israel Hospital v. NLRB [(SC77-152) (S.C. 1978)]* by affirming the rights of hospital employees to solicit and distribute union organizing literature during nonworking hours in the hospital cafeteria.

While the 1974 NLRA amendments were an important development in the recent growth of collective bargaining among nurses, the original act of 1935 did not specifically exclude charitable, religious, or educational institutions, although it clearly exempted all public employees—federal, state, and local. As will be discussed later, public employees are covered by separate legislation. In 1942, a U.S. district court held (in *Central Dispensary and Emergency Hospitals v. NLRB,* 1942) that the NLRA included nonprofit hospitals. The lower court's decision was affirmed by the U.S. Circuit Court of Appeals on the grounds that the hospital met the interstate commerce interpretation given by the NLRB in terms of sale of medical services and purchase of medical supplies. The U.S. Supreme Court denied review of this decision. However, the 1947 Taft-Hartley Amendments excluded nonprofit hospitals from coverage under the act in Section 2(2) (U.S. Department of Labor, 1979).

Between the 1947 act and the 1974 amendments, certain developments led to congressional reconsideration and repeal of the nonprofit hospital exemption. These included the growth in third-party payment for health care services; the extension of collective bargaining to public employees, which gave rise to a surge in union activity; and the organization of low-wage hospital workers and their ties with the civil rights movement. In addition, the NLRB began to assert jurisdiction in the health field over private profit hospitals, and both private profit and nonprofit nursing homes. The NLRB, however, did not assert its jurisdiction over nonprofit hospitals because they were specifically excluded by Section 2(2) of the Taft-Hartley Act.

Another legislative development in 1966 lent support to a congressional reexamination of extending NLRA to nonprofit hospitals. Congress amended the Fair Labor Standards Act of 1938 to include hospital employees. In addition, in 1950 the Social Security Act was amended to permit voluntary participation by employees of nonprofit and public institutions.

The Taft-Hartley Amendments of 1947 contained an important provision dealing with bargaining units, which are essential in collective bargaining. According to these amendments, the employer negotiates with representatives of the bargaining unit, and responsibility for determining the unit appropriate for collective bargaining rests with the NLRB. The board, in making unit determinations, considers such factors as: the history of bargaining, organization, and representation of employees; interests of employees; desires of employees; and interchangeability of employees. Its decision affects the size and composition of the unit. Thus the bargaining unit determines who will do the bargaining for the employees in that unit, who will represent whom, and the subject matter for collective bargaining.

Under the National Labor Relations Act of 1935, professional employees could be included in bargaining units with nonprofessional workers. In Section 9(b)(1) of the Taft-Hartley Act of 1947, Congress stated that professional employees have the right to vote separately on their desires concerning representation, that is, determination of a bargaining unit. No units of both professional and nonprofessional employees can be established by the NLRB unless a majority of the professional employees vote for inclusion in such unit [1947 Act P.L. 101, 80th Cong., 1st Sess., Sec. 9(b)].

The term "professional employee" is defined in Section 2(12) of the Taft-Hartley Act as follows (NLRA, 1935):

(a) Any employee engaged in work (i) predominantly intellectual and varied in character as opposed to routine mental, manual, mechanical, or physical work; (ii) involving the consistent exercise of discretion and judgment in its performance; (iii) of such a character that the output produced or the result accomplished cannot be standardized in relation to a given period of time; (iv) requiring knowledge of an advanced type in a field of science or learning customarily acquired by a prolonged course of specialized intellectual instruction and study in an institution of higher learning or a hospital, as distinguished from a general academic education or from an apprenticeship or from training in the performance of routine mental, manual, or physical processes; or

(b) any employee, who (i) has completed the courses of specialized intellectual instruction and study described in clause (iv) of paragraph (a), and (ii) is performing related work under the supervision of a professional person to qualify himself or herself to become a professional employee as defined in paragraph (a).

The Senate Labor Committee, in explaining the rationale for Section 9(b)(1) covering the professional employee, stated:

When Congress passed the National Labor Relations Act, it recognized that the community of interests among members of a skilled craft might be quite different from those of unskilled employees in mass-production industry. Although there has been a trend in recent years for manufacturing corporations to employ many professional persons, including architects, engineers, scientists, lawyers, and nurses, no corresponding recognition was given by Congress to their special problems. Nevertheless such employees have a great community of interest in maintaining certain standards. At the hearings, representatives of various professional associations appeared before the committee to protest against the occasional practice of the Board of covering professional personnel into general units of production and maintenance employees or general units of office and clerical employees, despite the fact that their interests in common with such groups was extremely limited. (See testimony of representatives of the American Society of Civil Engineers, American Chemical Association, American Nurses' Association, and the American Institute of Architects, hearings, vol. 3, pp. 1702-1715.) Since their number is always small in comparison with production or clerical employees, collective agreements seldom reflect their desires. Under the committee bill, the Board is required to afford such groups an opportunity to vote in a separate unit to ascertain whether or not they wish to have a bargaining representative of their own. Senate Rep. 105, 80th Cong., p. 11 (*Labor Course,* 1979, pp. 1836-1837).

The NLRB has relied on the community of interest doctrine in its determination of appropriate bargaining units in the health care industry. The NLRB has attempted to establish guidelines that have resulted in the development of six well-recognized bargaining units: registered nurses, physicians, other professionals, technical employees, service and maintenance employees, and office clerical employees (Morales, 1979).

The NLRB has adopted the stance that "registered nurses share interests different from those of most other professional employees in the health

care industry" and has found that RNs should have separate bargaining units because of their particular sorts of responsibilities and "their impressive history of separate representation in collective bargaining." Moreover,

nurse trainees who, although not yet licensed, have either taken or are ready to take the licensing examination have been consistently included in registered nurses' units. However, nurse techs who still lack the training or educational background necessary to perform the functions of the graduate nurses have been included in other types of bargaining units (Morales, 1979, p. 175).

Before the 1974 Taft-Hartley Amendments, twelve states with a high percentage of union membership had enacted legislation covering collective bargaining in health care institutions. This legislation also provided mechanisms for resolving conflict through mediation, fact finding, and arbitration. By 1980, thirty-five states had legislation permitting nurses in public health care institutions and other public employees to engage in collective bargaining. The right to strike by nurses and other public employees under these legislative enactments varies greatly.

Federal employees, including nurses, were first permitted to organize and to bargain collectively in 1962 under Executive Order 10988 signed by President Kennedy. President Nixon amended this executive order by Executive Order 11491 on October 29, 1969, which strengthened and improved collective bargaining in the federal sector. Congress, in 1978, enacted the Civil Service Reform Act of 1978, and Title VII of this Act, the Federal Service Labor Management Statute, became effective on January 11, 1979. This statute replaced Executive Order 11491 as the basic legislation governing labor management relations in the federal government.

The Federal Labor Relations Policy affecting nurses has been shaped by the legislation itself, by court decisions, and by administrative law. Since the NLRB is the administrative agency for implementing federal policy, its decisions are of paramount importance and are subject to judicial review by the federal courts. In 1975 the NLRB ruled that nurses had the right to employ their own professional associations as bargaining representatives and that they need not bargain in combination with other hospital professionals (Mercy Hospitals, 1975). In the same case, the board also defined a nursing supervisor as one who supervises in the interests of providing patient care, as contrasted to supervising in management's interests.

Supervisory status and bargaining

The occupational classification of supervisors deserves additional comment. The 1947 Taft-Hartley Amendments excluded supervisors from the coverage of the act. Section 2(11) of the Taft-Hartley 1947 Amendments defines a supervisor as:

any individual having authority, in the interest of the employer, to hire, transfer, suspend, lay off, recall, promote, discharge, assign, reward, or discipline other employees, or responsibility to direct them, or to adjust their grievances, or effectively to recommend such action if in connection with the foregoing the exercise of such authority is not of a merely routine or clerical nature, but requires the use of independent judgment (NLRA, 1935).

Many state public employment relations acts adopted the language of Section 2(11) of Taft-Hartley in defining a supervisor, but permit supervisors to form separate unions of their own choosing and to bargain collectively with their public employers. The issue of the role of the supervisor as defined in Section 2(11) of the 1947 Taft-Hartley Amendments and applied to nursing was decided by the NLRB in 1975 in *Annapolis Emergency Hospital Association, Inc. d/b/a Anne Arundel General Hospital* (1975). The board recognized that collective bargaining is only one function of a professional nurses' association and that administrators (supervisors, in the language of Taft-Hartley) have the right to belong to the association and to participate in other programs of the association; they, however, are prohibited from taking part in collective bargaining activities. This case was appealed to the U.S. Circuit Court of Appeals.

In August 1977, the U.S. Court of Appeals for the Fourth Circuit refused to uphold the certification of the Maryland Nurses' Association (MNA) as the bargaining representative of the RNs employed at Anne Arundel Hospital in Annapolis (1975). The court came to this decision because nursing supervisors were included on the board of directors of the MNA, who had the authority to make policy, allocate money, and hire staff for economic and general welfare activities. In other words, the MNA was charged with being an inappropriate bargaining unit on account of supervisory domination.

To avoid similar charges of supervisory domination, some SNAs have reorganized their economic and general welfare commissions (which are responsible for collective bargaining) outside of the control of their boards of directors. The Wisconsin Nurses' Association Board of Directors was presented with such a proposal by the nurses it represented, whereby only members eligible to vote for collective bargaining would be able to vote for or serve as members of the economic and general welfare commission, and the commission would have the authority to hire its own staff and set its own budget and policies. The board, however, rejected the proposal, upholding the ANA's "adamant opposition to changes in the SNAs' internal structures" (Beason, 1979). In December 1978, a special convention of the Wisconsin Nurses' Association voted to discontinue collective bargaining activities altogether (with the exception of servicing existing contracts and completing negotiations in process), effective December 31, 1980 (BNA, 1979).

The question of supervisory dominance in SNAs that engage in collective bargaining has been particularly troublesome for the ANA. The NLRB has held that the test for determining whether actions qualify individuals as supervisors hinges on whether they, in addition to directing other employees, also exercise supervisory authority in the interests of their employers (Newton-Wellesley Hospital, 1975).

In November 1978, an NLRB panel overturned a regional director's decision that charge nurses are supervisory employees not entitled to bargaining representation, and ordered an election held among charge nurses at a Colorado nursing home (*Eventide South,* 1978). The panel concluded that "charge nurses perform duties and functions predominantly in the exercise of professional judgment incidental to their treatment of patients" (BNA, 1978a, p. A-3). Furthermore,

their duties and authority are all directed toward quality treatment of patients, and do not constitute supervisory authority in the employer's interest. Further, we find that charge nurses possess neither the authority to hire or discharge, or discipline beyond the state of a minor reprimand, nor the authority to make effective recommendations affecting the employment status of employees. The Board has carefully avoided applying the definition of "supervisor" to a health care professional who gives direction to other employees which is incidental to the professional's treatment of patients.

The panel further cited a previous board decision in *Meharry Medical College,* 219 NLRB 488, 490 (1975):

It appears that charge nurses do not exercise any real supervisory authority on behalf of management over employees. Rather, their duties are for the most part routine, involving the general direction of employees in the performance of their normal patient care duties and, as such, the charge nurses function more in the nature of lead persons. Even assuming the charge nurses may exercise some supervisory authority, the fact they may do so only for a short period of time and on a sporadic basis would not require their exclusion from the unit (BNA, 1978a, p. A-3).

New developments in the determination of bargaining units

When the 1974 amendments were passed, one legislative objective in the determination of bargaining units by the NLRB was to avoid unwarranted fragmentations. Nurses were considered by the NLRB to be an appropriate unit for bargaining for the following reasons: The nurses worked in close and continuous contact with one another; they have similar education, training, and experience; they possess the same license and have highly responsible positions regarding the well-being of patients compared with other professionals who have limited personal contact with the patients; they are administratively separate in a nursing division and are subject to common supervision by head nurses, the assistant director, and director of nursing.

In the *Newton-Wellesley Hospital* case decided in July 1980, the NLRB ruled that bargaining units of registered nurses are not always appropriate. Whether or not nurses are to be a separate bargaining unit depends on the particular circumstances of each situation. The Newton-Wellesley Hospital had sought to have a bargaining unit that included nurses as well as other professional employees, and presented evidence in support of its position. Although the NLRB ruled in this case that registered nurses were an appropriate unit for bargaining, the effect of this case is that the NLRB will not consider automatically a unit of nurses to be appropriate in all situations.

ORGANIZATIONS INVOLVED IN COLLECTIVE BARGAINING FOR NURSES

The legal protection afforded nurses to engage in collective bargaining has stimulated concerted action in various sections of the country. Hospital unionization is primarily centered in three geographical areas: the Northeast, upper Midwest, and the Pacific Coast. At the time of the 1974 Taft-Hartley Amendments, four states (New York, California, Pennsylvania, and Michigan) accounted for approximately two-fifths of all hospitals with labor agreements. After the passage of the 1974 amendments, the same four states accounted for about half of all hospital representation elections for bargaining rights (Miller, 1980).

There are approximately 40 national unions and some 100 employee organizations engaged in collective bargaining activities in the health care industry (U.S. Department of labor, 1979). Of these, the largest are: ANA; Service Employees International Union (SEIU); American Federation of State, County and Municipal Employees (AFSCME); and District 1199 of the National Union of Hospital and Health Care Employees. It has been noted that between August 1974 and December 1977 these four unions accounted for seventy-five percent of all hospital representation elections. The membership of these four unions varies. For example, *AFSCME* is oriented to nonprofessional workers employed in state and local governmental health care institutions. *SEIU* focuses primarily on health care institutions in the private sector and includes, primarily, aides, orderlies, and kitchen and maintenance workers, as well as a significant number of technical and professional workers, including registered nurses.

District 1199 is firmly rooted in New York City, with its major area of bargaining rights in the northeastern states in private-sector institutions. District 1199 has been particularly successful in gaining the right to act as the collective bargaining agent for numerous groups of registered nurses, and about one percent of its membership are RNs (Miller, 1980). For instance, registered nurses at Brookdale Hospital in Brooklyn, New York elected District 1199 over the New York State Nurses' Association (NYSNA) in 1977 as their bargaining agent, in order to gain not only economic and working benefits but also for a governance system similar to that which District 1199 had negotiated for Brookdale's pharmacists, social workers, lab technicians, and housekeeping personnel (Wynne, 1978). The nurses desired more effective representation than they had received from the NYSNA, yet at the same time did not want their interests lost among those of the other hospital personnel represented by 1199. In order to maintain their sense of identity within the union organization, the nurses stipulated that a separate division be established for registered nurses, the League of R.N., which would have its own elections, its own officers, and autonomy. If an 1199 drug division elects to strike, the other 1199 divisions are not contractually obligated to follow.

District 1199 continues to make definite inroads into the organization of professional nurses and other health care and medical professionals throughout the United States. In January 1979, District 1199 organized 1800 health professionals employed by the state of Connecticut. This number is substantial when combined with the 4600 paraprofessional health employees employed at Connecticut public facilities who chose District 1199 as their bargaining agent only three months earlier. Among the types of professionals represented by this union are registered nurses, physicians, psychiatrists, psychologists, dentists, and laboratory employees. The professionals' reasons for electing District 1199 was their belief that the union would address three main areas of concern: broadening the professionals' roles in the care of patients, maintaining the working conditions to which they were accustomed, and obtaining salaries and wage rates comparable to those paid to health professionals in private enterprises (National Union, 1979). Another factor influencing the health professionals to elect District 1199 is the common belief that by joining their fellow employees represented by District 1199 they would have greater bargaining strength when negotiating with their employer than if their interests were represented by an independent union or an employee association.

The *ANA* is the largest organization representing health care professionals. Its membership is approximately 200,000. In April 1978, of this number, an estimated 70,000 professional nurses were covered by collective bargaining agreements administered by state affiliates of ANA (Miller, 1980).

In addition to the "Big Four," there are independent unions of nurses that are not affiliated with any organization. One possible explanation for this development is that some SNAs are reluctant to engage in collective bargaining activities, which has led some nurses to form independent unions. For example, in 1976 in Connecticut, 1500 nurses from ten bargaining units voted to disaffiliate from the CNA and join the new labor organization, the Connecticut Health Care Associates

("Connecticut Nurses," 1976). Also, in Los Angeles, 1500 RNs employed in southern California Kaiser-Permanente medical facilities formed an independent organization called the United Nurses Association ("California Nurses' Contract," 1977).

The *Federation of Nurses and Health Professionals* (FNHP), an affiliate of the American Federation of Teachers (AFT) AFL-CIO, is a newcomer to the groups seeking to organize nurses. In 1977 the AFT amended its constitution to open membership to workers outside the teaching profession. This change seemed to result from actions of nurses, librarians, and others who sought to join an AFL-CIO affiliate (HLRB, 1977). The FNHP, a national union of RNs and other health care employees, views itself as an advocate for health professionals whose primary objective is to promote collective bargaining for members. It also seeks to be a professional organization concerned with continuing education. The FNHP is supportive of its members' right to strike, and the decision to strike in support of its bargaining demands is made by the local unit. The FNHP does not permit supervisors who have the power to hire, fire, or discipline employees to join, because their presence conflicts with the needs and interests of the nurses and other health care employee members.

In July 1979, the FNHP won the right to act as the bargaining agent for nearly 500 nurses at the Lutheran Medical Center in Brooklyn, New York by a 15-1 margin. Since then, the FNHP-AFT has launched successful representation campaigns in Colorado, Massachusetts, Oklahoma, Pennsylvania, Rhode Island, Texas, and Wisconsin. In some cases, the FNHP-AFT has replaced state nurses' associations, whereas in others it has won the right to represent nurses formerly represented by an independent union. Nurses are turning to the FNHP because of its ability to obtain improved salaries, benefits, and working conditions for its members; the union's understanding of and commitment to promoting the professional concerns of nurses; and its commitment to autonomy for the state and local federations.

The AFL-CIO, the national labor federation, has recognized that the number of white-collar and professional workers who have joined unions has increased rapidly and will continue to increase. In 1977 it established a Department for Professional Employees (DPE) composed of twenty national and international affiliates of the AFL-CIO. The DPE was specifically designed to meet the needs and interests of employees in scientific, professional, and cultural fields, and in 1980 represented more than one million workers (FNHP, 1980).

From the foregoing it can be seen that nurses have four courses of action with respect to collective bargaining:

1. They can refrain from concerted activities, and this is a right protected both by the NLRA as amended and by state legislation.
2. They can look to their professional association to represent them.
3. They can join a traditional type of union such as AFSCME, SEIU, and now FNHP-AFT, all of which are affiliated with the AFL-CIO.
4. They can form independent unions as they have done in Connecticut and California.

How many registered nurses are organized for the purposes of collective bargaining? There are no reliable estimates available. In 1972, according to ANA data, there were 1,127,657 registered nurses in the United States, and of this number 795,000 were employed as nurses (ANA, 1977). In 1978 ANA estimated that approximately thirteen percent (141,000) of all registered nurses were organized by all types of organizations (i.e., national and state associations, national unions, and independent unions), as indicated below (Donovan, 1978, p. 64):

Group	Number of members	Percent
State nurses' associations	105,000	74.5
National labor unions	30,000	21.3
Independent unions	6,000	4.2

Thus, as of 1978, the ANA and its state affiliates represented about three-fourths of all nurses covered by labor agreements.

BARGAINING ARRANGEMENTS

The majority of bargaining arrangements involving nurses occurs at the local level, where one unit bargains with one employer. There are, however, multiemployer arrangements where a bargaining unit covering nurses of several employers negotiates with a group of employers who have formed an association for purposes of bargaining. The NLRB will only approve this type of arrangement where both parties voluntarily consent. Either party may terminate this arrangement for any reason so long as negotiations have not commenced for a new agreement.

Multiemployer bargaining for nurses tends to be concentrated in urban areas such as the San Francisco Bay Area, New York City, and Minneapolis–St. Paul. In the Twin Cities, one agreement involves twenty-three hospitals and approximately 5000 nurses. There are both advantages and disadvantages to multiemployer bargaining. The advantages include (1) uniform wages and conditions of employment in all hospitals; (2) elimination of whipsawing—playing one hospital against another; (3) nurses in the employing units can speak in one voice; (4) bargaining power of both the nurses and the hospitals is enhanced; (5) time is saved in that there is one set of negotiations rather than a number of negotiations; and (6) the negotiations provide a forum for the exchange of information on conditions of employment including patient care.

There are also disadvantages: (1) The nurses as well as the employer have to develop a common denominator on their demands and responses, respectively; and (2) a work stoppage can have a devastating effect on the area in that it can lead to a higher turnover among members of the nurses' bargaining team, who cannot negotiate an agreement that satisfies all constituent groups.

Several current forces could lead to a significant increase in multiemployer bargaining. The pressure of rising costs is resulting in shared activities and consolidated functions among the hospitals in a given area (e.g., laundry). The emphasis on health care planning with hospitals specializing in specific areas of patient care could lead to more multi-

employer bargaining. This arrangement could permit temporary assignments of nursing personnel to member hospitals, since wages and conditions of employment are standardized; this, in turn, could result in more effective utilization of nursing resources.

SUBJECT MATTER OF COLLECTIVE BARGAINING

The end objective of bilateral negotiations between employers and employee organizations is to consummate a written agreement covering wages, hours, and conditions of employment for a specified time period. The subject matter of the agreement gives insight into the concerns of the parties, especially the union, since the union is the charging party. As a general rule, the union makes various demands for inclusion into the agreement and the employer responds to these demands. Collective bargaining is a give-and-take process where items may be negotiated, traded, or taken off the table.

To understand the process of bargaining, it is necessary to discuss the types of subject matter of bargaining. Broadly speaking, there are three types of subject matter in collective bargaining. Under the amended NLRA and state laws, the bargaining parties are legally required to bargain over mandatory topics such as wages, hours of employment, and other conditions of employment. Failure by either party to bargain over these mandatory items can result in an unfair labor practice, and the NLRA and state labor relations acts contain a list of unfair labor practices for both employers and unions.

If one of the parties believes that the other party is not bargaining in good faith on a topic that it considers to be a mandatory item, an unfair labor practice can be filed with the appropriate administrative agency—that is, the NLRB or state agency. The agency investigates the charge and then rules on whether it is an unfair labor practice. The parties can, under law, appeal the decision of the administrative agency to an appellate court. If the decision is that no unfair labor practice exists, the parties are not obligated to bargain on the subject. Conversely, if a ruling is made either by the administrative agency or the courts that the actions constitute an unfair labor practice, the parties are obligated to bargain on it; however, it is not mandatory that they reach agreement on the subject in question.

Under the Federal Service Labor Management Relations Statute (Public Law 95-454), the mandatory subject matter for bargaining by federal employees is restricted to conditions of employment [Sec. 7103(a)(12)]. The act defines conditions of employment to "mean personnel policies, practices and matters whether established by rule, regulation or otherwise affecting working conditions" [Sec. 7103(a)14]. Conditions of employment do not include bargaining over job classifications and other matters specifically provided for by federal statute [Sec. 7103(a)14A,B,C]. Over the years, through NLRB and state agencies' rulings and court decisions, the scope of mandatory subject matter for bargaining has expanded significantly.

A second broad area of subject matter of bargaining includes permissive subjects, where the parties may bargain on permissive items if they so choose; they cannot bargain to an impasse on them, however. By contrast, the parties can bargain to an impasse on mandatory topics. The parties cannot insist on the inclusion of permissive items in the collective bargaining agreement, nor can the parties strike or lock out employees in support of these items. It is difficult to cite an example of a permissive topic because topics once considered permissive have become mandatory. Currently, a demand by the union to have a member on the board of directors of the employer would be a permissive subject in bargaining.

A third broad area of subject matter would be illegal topics (i.e., topics forbidden by statute). For example, pay for work not performed or preferential hiring are illegal subjects for bargaining.

In the parlance of actual negotiations, the parties use another classification, namely economics and noneconomic items. The former includes wages, hours, and conditions of employment that have an identifiable cost. The latter includes such items as recognition, duration of agreement, employee organization representatives, and contract administration.

The labor agreement reflects the goals and objectives of the employee organization. One goal of the organization is to survive. The sections of the agreement dealing with recognition and union security (e.g., union shop, agency shop, or maintenance of membership) reflect this concern.

Union security arrangements are extremely important for the employee organization. Under federal and state laws, when the union wins bargaining rights it has the legal duty to represent *all* members of the bargaining unit, those who voted for the union as well as those who voted against the union and those who are included in the bargaining unit but for some reason did not vote. In other words, the union is the exclusive bargaining representative for all employees in the bargaining unit. Accordingly, the employee organization seeks to have all employees of the unit become members of the organization, or, if they do not become members, to pay a service fee to support the organization.

A second objective of the organization is to improve the economic status of the members through seeking better wages, fringe benefits, hours of work, and other conditions of employment. Much of the agreement is directed toward this objective.

A third objective is to develop a system of workplace jurisprudence whereby grievances arising over the interpretation and application of the agreement can be resolved. Another feature of the grievance procedure is to provide a mechanism for protecting the due process of the employees. When an employee is disciplined unjustly by the employer, the employee/union can challenge this managerial action through the grievance procedure. This is an important protection that the employee organization provides to its members. The collective bargaining agreement can be used to protect employee rights in the workplace.

Another objective of the agreement is to achieve power. Nurses are seeking, through collective bargaining, to obtain a meaningful voice in the determination of patient care. Nurses are increasingly recognizing that conditions of employment are inextricably intertwined with standards of patient care. Moreover, collective bargaining gives the bargaining unit the legal right to bargain with the employer, which changes the allocation and distribution of power by making the decision-making process bilateral rather than unilateral. Thus nurses are seeking increased participation in the decision making in three areas: patient care, changes in the health care delivery system, and the actual operation of the health care facility. Nurses are seeking shared governance in the operation of the facility by the professional staff and administration because, in their view, providing quality nursing care is a jointly shared responsibility.

Through collective bargaining, nurses are also seeking individual and collective professional accountability. The state licensing acts spell out the duties and responsibilities of the professional nurse and give nurses the legal right to practice. Nurses, by law, are held accountable for their actions, although they carry out their job duties under supervision of other nurses, including the director of nursing. Because of the individual accountability of the nurse by law, supervision of nurses takes on special significance and must be coordinated with patient care concerns. Accordingly, nurses seek to include in the agreement procedures, criteria, and standards in which staff and administrators share responsibility for legal accountability. They seek to include standards established by accreditation and licensure bodies and to enforce these standards.

The major thrust of collective bargaining activities has been to improve the quality of patient care and to provide nurses with a voice in the provision of health services. Nurses are having some success in bargaining for such subjects. The clauses cited below are illustrative of what nurses have been seeking in their bargaining relationships.*

*Agreement between Michigan Nurses' Association and its affiliate Wayne County Professional Nurses Council Unit 1 and the Board of Commissioners, Wayne County, Mich., term of agreement Nov. 30, 1981, pp. 62-64.

ARTICLE XXI: The role of the registered nurse
Section 1.

Both parties agree that they share responsibility for providing nursing services which are consistent with the needs and goals of the recipient(s) who use the County health care facilities. To this end, both parties further agree to recognize responsibilities of the registered nurse and the Employer within the scope of the *1978 Michigan Public Health Code;* the *Code for Nurses* and the *Standards of Nursing Practice* as adopted by the American Nurses' Association; the *Standards of Nursing Service* as developed by the Joint Commission of Accreditation of Hospitals: *Licensure Guidelines of the Michigan Department of Public Health;* Federal Health Insurance Regulations: *Conditions of Participation,* and other appropriate legal requirements.

Section 2.

Both parties agree that the registered nurse, as provided in the 1978 Michigan Public Health Code, must and shall have authority commensurate with his/her responsibility for directing, teaching and supervising of less skilled personnel in carrying out delegated nursing activities. The registered nurse has the responsibility for assessment, planning, implementing, evaluating nursing care including patient teaching and coordination of services and the primary responsibility of the registered nurse is direct patient care. The Employer continues to recognize its obligation to assist the registered nurse in fulfilling these responsibilities.

Section 3.

Both parties agree that in order to permit the registered nurse to perform the activities associated with his/her responsibility for nursing care, the registered nurse will normally only assume those functions identified as the practice of nursing. The Employer agrees that relief from non-nursing tasks is desirable to further increase the availability of professional nursing care to patients, and will make every effort to implement the transfer of such non-nursing duties to other services or auxiliary personnel.

Section 4.

The parties further agree that it is the Employer's responsibility to make every effort to provide adequate numbers of registered nurses and auxiliary nursing personnel on all shifts as necessary, and to fill vacancies as soon as possible to provide safe and adequate nursing care and to make maximum utilization of the training competencies of all nursing personnel.

Section 5.

It is the responsibility of each registered nurse to maintain and upgrade his/her knowledge and skill affecting the quality of nursing care.

Section 6.

The Employer will continue to accept its responsibility to establish programs and/or provide resources and appropriate opportunities within and outside the County facilities for orientation and staff development; and to support, encourage and equalize opportunity to seek continuing professional development.

Section 7.

The recommendations of registered nurses will be considered in planning decision-making and formulation of policies and procedures that affect the operation of the nursing service, the nursing care of patients, or the patients' environment.

Section 8.

Each Department of Nursing shall continue to assume responsibility for administration and supervision of its nursing personnel covered by this Agreement and shall provide for adequate orientation and in-service education.

Section 9.

Both parties agree that it is the right of the physician to exercise his/her responsibility and authority in the care and treatment of patients; that it is the right of management to exercise its responsibility and authority in directing the affairs of the Health Facility; and that it is the right of Nursing Administration to exercise its responsibility and authority in directing the affairs of the Department of Nursing.

ARTICLE XXIA: The role of the public health nurse

A Public Health Nurse is a registered nurse who is a graduate of a baccalaureate program in nursing, approved for public health nursing and accredited by the National League for Nursing. She has an understanding of the social, medical, and biological factors which influence health and behavior, and which provide her with a basis of preparation for developing the ability to make the independent judgments and decisions demanded by present complex health problems of families.

ARTICLE XXIII: Professional standards
Section 1.

The parties agree that Registered Nurses are governed by a professional code of ethics, and the Employer agrees that it will support the Registered Nurses in compliance with the professional code. In supporting the nurses in compliance with said code, it is expressly understood that the Employer does not relinquish its right to manage the various County Departments, and nothing in this Agreement is intended to replace or abrogate the Employer's right with respect to disciplinary procedures.

Section 2.

The Administration and Nursing Administration in each Health Facility continue to recognize the need for channels through which Registered Nurses will provide information, make recommendations, discuss and be involved in the decision-making process concerning standards of nursing practice as it affects patient care. The Nursing Administration will accept responsibility for seeking methods whereby regular channels of communication will be continued and broadened.

Section 3.

In accordance with Section 2 above, a Professional Standards Committee will be established in the Acute Hospital, composed of three (3) Hospital Management Representatives, one of whom will be the Director of Nurses and three (3) Council Registered Nurse Representatives to be named by the Council, at least one of whom is from Unit II, who are employed in the Acute Hospital.

Section 4.

This Committee shall meet once each month at a mutually agreeable time to consider, study and make written recommendations to Hospital Administration concerning factors affecting Registered Nursing Standards and practice in the Acute Hospital. Meetings of this Committee will not be cancelled except by mutual agreement. Each meeting will have a prepared and prescribed agenda established prior to the meeting. Agenda items may be proposed and placed on the agenda by any member of the Committee in concert with Section 2 above. This Committee shall neither supplant nor abrogate the procedures and policies established for the settlement of disputes in the Agreement between the County of Wayne as the Employer and the Wayne County Professional Nurse Council, Michigan Nurses Association, as the recognized collective bargaining agent for Registered Nurses.

Section 5.

Such recommendations of the Professional Standards Committee shall be considered by Hospital Administration, and a written response will be provided to the Committee within three (3) weeks of receipt of the recommendations.

Section 6.

A committee consisting of association, Nursing Administration, and Civil Service Representatives shall be established to meet, on a regular basis to consider, study, and make recommendations to the County concerning the development of a system for clinical advancement in Nursing Practice.

The Public Health Nurse directs her efforts towards helping individuals and families maintain health and prevent illness as well as obtain treatment and cure. The individual, the family, and the community are separate yet interdependent entities of the Public Health Nurse's concern. Through both preparation and experience she sees her responsibility as family-centered, largely within the scope of the home. By visiting families, she provides health supervision to parents and children, retarded and handicapped individuals, and to persons with communicable and chronic diseases. In her role as teacher and counselor, she assesses needs of the family and its individual members, and helps them to obtain needed services by referral to proper resources. She attempts to help the family recognize its problems and needs and proceed toward acceptable solutions.

The Public Health Nurse is a member of a team working cooperatively with health, social and civic agencies for continuity of services to the family and community. Her services are complementary to medical services and are provided within the framework of the Division of Public Health Nursing. The Division of Public Health Nursing assumes responsibility for the overall adminis-

tration and supervision of all nursing personnel covered by this Agreement and must provide for adequate orientation and in-service education.

In addition, nurses have also been successful in negotiating provisions providing for special conferences to discuss matters of mutual interest, tuition-refund programs for job-related courses at universities and colleges, and expense reimbursement for attending continuing education programs. These types of provisions, which have moved nurses beyond "bread-and-butter" items, reflect the desire to protect and strengthen professional roles and to increase involvement in the operation of the health care facility. Nurses have not consistently made use of these additional provisions once they are in the labor agreement.

In addition to the nurses' failure to use these provisions once they have been negotiated, there is the problem of growing employer resistance to nurses' organizations' proposals at the bargaining table that fall outside the traditional labor contract items (i.e., economic issues). Employers have taken the position that responsibility for quality of patient care is a management right.* Such matters, therefore, in their view, are under management control.

Some employers have accepted the proposals advanced by nurses' organizations on professional concerns and have agreed to include them in the agreement, as in the case of Wayne County, Michigan. Wayne County, the most populous county in Michigan, is a public employer and therefore is covered by the Michigan Employment Relations Act (Act 379, Public Act 1965). The employer decided that these proposals were appropriate subjects for bargaining and therefore negotiated them and agreed to their inclusion in the agreement. The employer did not challenge these proposals before the

---

*In a typical management rights clause in a labor agreement, management retains the right to hire, to assign and to direct its employees, to discipline and discharge for cause, to determine location, and to determine the kinds of services to be provided.

Michigan Employment Relations Commission, the state administrative agency, as being inappropriate subject matter for bargaining.

In another bargaining relationship involving the MNA and a private hospital covered by the Taft-Hartley Amendments, the employer, in 1980, filed an unfair labor practice with the NLRB against the MNA for insisting on the inclusion into the agreement of the ANA *Code of Nurses with Interpretative Statements and the Recommendations of the Joint Commission on Accreditation* (Michigan Hospital Association, 1980). The NLRB determined that these matters were nonmandatory subjects for bargaining and therefore could not be taken to impasse or strike. Accordingly, the association's insistence on their inclusion would constitute a violation of the NLRA as amended; thus MNA, to avoid a finding of refusal to bargain, withdrew these proposals.

The nurses' association had struck this hospital over the issue of patient care, and the hospital filed a subsequent unfair labor practice charge with the NLRB. The NLRB found that the MNA had violated the act and had refused to bargain in good faith when it bargained and struck over the subject of patient care. The NLRB determined that "patient care" matters did not relate to wages, hours, or other conditions of employment and hence were nonmandatory subjects to which the hospital owes no duty to bargain. The MNA settled the matter and posted the required notice that it will not bargain to impasse or strike over the issue of patient care.

The expired agreement between the parties in this example for 1977-1979 continued a provision (Article V) entitled "Role of Registered Professional Nurses," which emphasized the joint responsibility of providing *nursing care* (author's emphasis) that is consistent with patients' needs and that is both adequate and safe.* In view of the NLRB's determination that patient care matters are

*Agreement between Grace Hospital, a division of Harper Grace Hospital, and Michigan Nurses' Association, 1977-1979, p. 4.

nonmandatory subjects for bargaining and the language in the above agreement dealing with nursing service, there is a distinction between patient care and nursing service. Patient care provided by the hospital involves the services of many different employee groups, lab technicians, dieticians, inhalation specialists, physicians, and nurses. The term "patient care" is broad, whereas nursing services refer to only one aspect of patient care.

In a bargaining relationship, such as the example cited, the nurses can negotiate on the role of the nurse and on nursing services, but cannot bargain to an impasse on patient care matters. Hospitals can choose whether to bargain with nurses on patient care matters and to do so without penalty because of the NLRB's decision. It is too early to assess the impact of the NLRB directive on the willingness of hospitals to bargain on patient care matters. This directive is of great importance because it relates to how far nurses' bargaining units can pursue their professional concerns. As a professional association of and for nurses, the state association is rightfully concerned with the professional concerns of nurses relative to the quality of nursing services for patients, which raises another question. If nurses' associations are precluded from insisting on the inclusion of provisions dealing with professional matters and from bargaining to an impasse on patient care matters, then why should nurses' associations be involved in collective bargaining? In other words, if the emphasis in bargaining is to be "bread-and-butter" subjects, then what will be the strategies of the state association in bargaining? It is too early to answer this question, but it strikes at the heart of the professional association's involvement in collective bargaining. It raises questions as to the professional association assuming the functions of a union. On the other hand, the NLRB directive may well result in the nurses' associations developing alternative strategies. It should be noted also that the issue is not finitely resolved by the NLRB directive. This was the directive of a regional office and not the full NLRB. Moreover, the final word will be spoken when the federal courts eventually are called on to rule on this issue. Given the importance of the issue of professional matters to the registered nurse, in all likelihood the issue will be tested in court.

CONFLICT IN COLLECTIVE BARGAINING

Collective bargaining calls attention to conflict between labor and management, since workers in the private sector have the right to strike. The 1974 Taft-Hartley Amendments granted employees in health care institutions covered by the act the right to strike, but mandated that certain procedures be followed before a strike can occur. Section 8(d) requires a party desiring to terminate or modify an agreement to provide written notice at least ninety days before contract expiration. Also, the Federal Mediation and Conciliation Service (FMCS) and state mediation agencies are to be notified sixty days before the expiration date of the agreement. During the sixty-day period, mediation is mandatory; for all other workers in the private sector, mediation efforts are voluntary. Mandatory mediation is unique to health care institutions. In mediation, the mediator attempts to help the parties resolve their differences by making suggestions and keeping open the lines of communication.

Section 8(d)(B) also provides for initial or new contract situations. After being recognized as the bargaining agent, the union, which is negotiating its first contract, is required to give a thirty-day notice to FMCS and to appropriate state agencies. The parties are also required to give a ten-day strike notice before a work stoppage or picketing can take place [Sec. 8(g)].

The amendments also provide for the appointment of a board of inquiry (BOI) by the director of FMCS to conduct fact finding in an effort to help settle disputes before they reach a critical strike state (Sec. 213). The BOI investigates the issues and makes a written report with recommendations for settling the dispute. Within fifteen days of its appointment, the BOI issues its report to the parties and to FMCS, and, for an additional fifteen days, the parties are required to bargain. The BOI's rec-

ommendations are nonbinding and the parties are free to strike providing they have given the proper notification.

Employees in federal health care institutions are covered by the Federal Service Labor Management Relations Statute.* Section 7116 states that a strike is an unfair labor practice and if the labor organization is found to be involved in a strike, work stoppage, or slowdown, the Federal Labor Relations Authority (FLRA) will revoke the exclusive recognition status of the organization and it will not legally represent the employees in the bargaining unit. In other words, the organization will lose its bargaining rights. The FLRA is also authorized to take other appropriate disciplinary actions against strikers, such as discharge [Sec. 7120f(1) and (2)].

Nurses employed in public health care institutions are covered by public employment relations laws if the state has enacted such legislation (U.S. Department of Labor, 1979, pp. 34-47). As a general rule, state statutes declare strikes of public employees to be illegal. These state laws generally provide for mediation and, if mediation is unsuccessful, fact finding to resolve impasses. Under fact finding, the state agency appoints a fact finder to hear the facts in the case on the theory that exposing the facts to the public will facilitate agreement. The fact finder issues a report, usually with recommendations that are not binding on the parties. Minnesota, Washington, New York, and Massachusetts provide for binding arbitration in addition to mediation and fact finding. In binding arbitration, the state administrative agency appoints one or more arbitrators who hear the case and then make an award, either on each issue in impasse or on the entire economic package in impasse. The award of the arbitrator(s) is final and binding on the parties.

Several states permit public employees to strike if certain procedures are followed or certain conditions prevail. Pennsylvania, for example, permits

*See Federal Labor Management Relations Statute, Chap. 71, Title 5, of the U.S. Code.

strikes of public employees if there is no clear and present danger to the health, safety, and welfare of the public. Hawaii permits strikes after certain procedures have been followed, and Montana has enacted a special law covering nurses. Strikes are permitted if there is no hospital strike in effect within a 150-mile radius. In addition, the nurses must give the employer written notice thirty days in advance as to the exact date the strike will begin.

Times are changing and strikes of nurses employed in hospitals are becoming more acceptable to the public. The public has become accustomed to strikes by teachers, police officers, and firefighters; thus strikes by nurses appear to be less objectionable than they previously were.

More importantly, the nurses themselves are changing their attitudes toward the use of the strike weapon. In a survey conducted by the journal *RN* in 1978, fifty-eight percent of the respondents supported the strike as a means to obtain better salaries and working conditions and better nursing services (Donovan, 1978). The editors expressed surprise with the prostrike feelings of the nurses who responded to the survey. The results of the survey also revealed that eighty-two percent of the age group thirty-five to forty-four years suppported the use of the strike, as compared to sixty-eight percent of the nurses under the age of twenty-five. It should be noted, however, that it is one thing to indicate on a survey what an individual will do; it is quite a different situation when an individual is actually confronted with the decision to strike or not to strike. Although this study did indicate wide support by nurses of the strike weapon, it appears that bargaining units of nurses are using the strike cautiously and sparingly. Although there are no readily available data on the number of strikes by nurses,*

*The writer contacted the National Office of the American Nurses' Association in Kansas City, Missouri, in an effort to identify data on the number of strikes each year by nurses. He was told that no such data existed because of the number of different unions representing nurses in collective bargaining. The U.S. Department of Labor, Bureau of Labor Statistics, does publish regularly data on strikes in hospitals, both in the public and private sectors, but these data do not indicate which bargaining units were involved.

there appear to be a limited number of strikes by nurses in any given year.

In considering nurses' participation in strikes, it should be noted that other health care workers are organized for purposes of collective bargaining, and their unions on occasion strike to support their demands. When other health care workers in a hospital strike, the nurses in that hospital appear to have adopted a position of neutrality. Nurses, generally, have declined to honor other unions' picket lines and have reported for work according to their schedules.

THE ROAD AHEAD

There are a number of factors that will influence the future of collective bargaining for nurses. They will be discussed in this final section.

The legal climate

The 1974 Taft-Hartley Amendments cover private hospitals. Many states have enacted legislation providing for public employees to form unions of their own choosing and to bargain collectively with their employers. Many nurses are employed in hospitals and agencies operated by state and local governmental units and thus are covered by these state public employment relations acts. Other states will undoubtedly enact similar legislation. Thus the legal climate permits nurses to form unions or to bargain collectively with employers over wages, hours, and conditions of employment.

The attitude of nurses toward their role and collective bargaining

Even though federal and state statutes have given nurses the legal right to engage in collective bargaining, in the final analysis, nurses will decide the extent to which they will become involved. Attitudes of nurses toward their role in the delivery of health care services are changing. There is a thrust toward more autonomy and "self-determination" by the professional nurse. Increasingly, nurses view collective bargaining as the vehicle or means to achieve a more meaningful role in the delivery of nursing services. The *Harper Grace Hospital* decision by the NLRB underscores the question whether "patient care" is a mandatory subject of bargaining. Given the historical pattern of the interpretations of "other conditions of employment" by the NLRB, state administrative agencies, and federal and state courts, bargaining over nursing service will become a mandatory subject of bargaining. Historically, the scope of bargaining has been broadened to include many items, and this same pattern will develop in collective bargaining for nurses.

Even in the absence of collective bargaining, nurses will be increasingly involved in decisions affecting the delivery of nursing services and patient care. Management literature is replete with references to the positive contributions that workers make when they are given the opportunity to participate in the decision-making process on matters affecting their jobs. Progressive managers of institutions employing nurses may well develop mechanisms for nurse involvement in an effort to minimize unionization.

Who will represent nurses in collective bargaining?

As was noted, there are a number of organizations and unions seeking to represent nurses in collective bargaining ("Unions," 1980). Presently, SNAs have the largest number of nurses covered by collective bargaining agreements. The ANA and state bodies tend to be dominated by administrators and therefore cannot always represent staff nurses effectively (Beason, 1979). Moreover, some nurses believe strongly that their professional association should focus on matters of professional concern (i.e., licensure, nurse practice, and continuing education), rather than on collective bargaining activities (Crooks, 1979). In 1978, the House of Delegates of the Wisconsin Nurses' Association (WNA) voted to decertify WNA as the bargaining agent. Other states like Virginia, Utah, Texas, and Rhode Island have withdrawn from economic and general welfare activities ("Unions," 1980), that is, collective bargaining. The Michigan Nurses' Association, and other state associations, by contrast, have strengthened their collective bargaining activities.

There is much to be said for the professional nurses' association representing nurses in collective bargaining, and thus an argument can be made for SNAs to include collective bargaining activities in their program of activities. As was pointed out, nurses are seeking autonomy in the exercise of their professional job responsibilities. Collective bargaining gives bargaining units the legal right to negotiate with the employer on wages, hours, and conditions of employment. The quality of nursing service is highly intertwined with wages, hours and conditions of employment. Whether SNAs will increasingly represent nurses in collective bargaining will depend on the wishes of the membership and the ability of the associations to meet the needs of the members consistently and over time.

Financial resources will also affect the association's ability to become extensively involved in collective bargaining, in that staff must be employed who are knowledgeable in collective bargaining, and the association must have finances to process grievances through arbitration. Collective bargaining activities require a level of dues higher than if the association focuses only on legislation and continuing education activities. Nurses will decide whether they want to tax themselves to underwrite the costs of collective bargaining activities.

Bargaining units for nurses

The *Newton-Wellesley* decision by the NLRB raises critically important questions about the nature of the bargaining unit. Nurses have been successful in establishing bargaining units composed solely of nurses. In the *Newton-Wellesley* decision, the NLRB appears to be moving away from this historical pattern. The NLRB will not automatically determine bargaining units of nurses, but will examine each case on its merits. It is too early to assess the impact of this decision on bargaining units.

Another series of questions about collective bargaining relates to the bargaining rights of supervisors. Bona fide supervisors are excluded from bargaining units depending on the statute covering them and the interpretation of these statutes by administrative agencies and the courts. The acid test is: what are the specific job duties of the supervisors? Administrative agencies look behind the job titles and carefully examine job duties. There are three approaches to handling supervisors for purposes of collective bargaining: (1) Include supervisors in the bargaining unit; (2) exclude bona fide supervisors from the bargaining unit of general duty nurses; and (3) permit bona fide nursing supervisors to form unions of their own, separate and apart from general duty nurses. Option 3 is more likely under the public employment relations act.

Another problem that may surface and that may affect bargaining unit structure is the increasing specialization in nursing. If a nursing specialty becomes sufficiently unique that it is licensed by the state, there could be a proliferation of nursing bargaining units. Licensure is evidence of a unique community of interest and, therefore, conceivably merits the specialty group becoming a separate bargaining unit.

Growth of third-party payments for health care services and its implications for labor relations

Instead of a simple transaction in which the consumer of a health service pays the provider of the service, payments are most frequently handled by a financial agent or a third party. In fiscal year 1977, 70% of the $163 billion spent for personal health care involved third parties, primarily private health insurers or public agencies acting as insurers, or in some cases, as providers of health service. In fiscal 1977, third-party payments accounted for 94.1% of the personal expenditures for hospital care as follows: public, 55.2%; private health insurance, 36.6%; and philanthropy and industry 2.3% (Gibson and Fisher, 1978).

The growth of third-party payments is already having an impact on the conduct of collective bargaining, especially on the size of the wage increases as they affect hospital costs. Medicare/Medicaid and about half of the states have developed rate-review procedures with respect to hospitals. These procedures, for the most part, call for prospective reimbursement; that is, the rate of reimbursement is established before the costs or charges are incurred. They are designed to provide an incentive to hospitals to control costs, because costs in excess of the established rate of reimbursement will not be covered and therefore must be absorbed by the hospital (Rosmann, 1977). These reimbursement policies, coupled with the possibility of federal legislation on hospital cost containment, will be another factor shaping the collective bargaining relationship in the future.

The changing economic, legal, political, and social environments and labor relations

Labor relations are dynamic in nature. Economic changes such as levels of unemployment, rate of inflation, and the rate of economic growth influence labor relations. The political environment, new legislation, and administrative and court decisions are continuously changing and shaping the legal environment in which labor relations are conducted. The attitudes of taxpayers, as voters, toward supporting social services influence legislators and the budget process, and the budgets of public jurisdictions affect labor relations, both in the public and private sectors. Also, societal changes such as demographic changes, rising educational attainment, and more emphasis on individual involvement and autonomy affect labor relations. Thus labor relations may be viewed as a mirror reflecting economic, legal, political, and societal changes.

SUMMARY

Since change in labor relations is ceaseless, there are no final answers. Problems, once resolved, give rise to new problems evoking new solutions. Labor relations is, therefore, essentially a process of accommodation, whereby employers, employees, and unions—where present—continuously learn to work together if the mission of the employing institution is to be realized effectively and efficiently.

I wish to acknowledge the assistance of Elaine Karle and Jeffrey Lewis, two graduate students in the School of Labor and Industrial Relations, in the preparation of this chapter.

REFERENCES

Alexander, E.L.: Nursing administration in the hospital health care system, St. Louis, 1978, The C.V. Mosby Co.

American Nurses' Association: Collective bargaining: what is negotiable? Am. J. Nurs. **69:**1894, 1969.

American Nurses' Association: Facts about nursing, Kansas City, Mo., 1977, ANA.

American Nurses' Association: The new approach to economic security, New York, 1968, ANA.

Annapolis Emergency Hospital Association, Inc. d/b/a Anne Arundel General Hospital, 217 NLRB 848 (1975).

Beason, C.: Nursing's labor relations crisis, RN **42:**21-33, Feb. 1979.

Boyer, J.M., Westerhaus, C.L., and Coggeshall, J.H.: Employee relations and collective bargaining in health care facilities, St. Louis, 1975, The C.V. Mosby Co.

Bureau of National Affairs (BNA): Decision of Supreme Court in *Beth Israel Hospital v. NLRB* (text), White Collar Rep. No. 121, June 22, 1978.

Bureau of National Affairs (BNA): White Collar Rep. No. 1126, Nov. 24, 1978a, p. A-3.

Bureau of National Affairs: White Collar Rep. No. 1133, Jan. 19, 1979.

California nurses' contract gives 22.8 percent boost, Health Labor Relations Rep. **1:**5, Sept. 19, 1977.

Cleland, V.: The professional model, Am. J. Nurs. **75:**288-292, 1975.

Connecticut nurses reported defecting from association, Health Labor Relations Rep. **1:**4, Nov. 15, 1976.

Crooks, E.: Nurses' associations and collective bargaining: wave of the past? RN **42:**83-88, Apr. 1979.

Donovan, L.: Is nursing ripe for a union explosion? RN **41:**63-65, May 1978.

Eventide South, a division of Geriatrics, Inc. and Professional and Health Care Employees, Retail Clerks International Union, Local 7, 27-R-5700, 239 NLRB No. 34, Nov. 14, 1978.

Federal Labor Management Relations Statute, Ch. 71, Title 5, U.S. Code.

Federation of Nurses and Health Professionals (FNHP/AFL-CIO): Healthwire **2:**1, Mar. 1980.

Gibson, R.M., and Fisher, C.R.: National health expenditures, fiscal year 1977, Soc. Security Bull. **41:**5, July 1978.

Grand, N.K.: Nursing ideologies and collective bargaining, J. Nurs. Adm. **3:**30, Mar.-Apr. 1973.

Health Labor Relations Board (HLRB): Rep. No. 1, Sept. 19, 1977.

Health Labor Relations Report, May 12, 1980. (See also NLRB Region 7 directive relative to Case No. 7-CB-4662, Apr. 15, 1980.)

Kruger, D.: Bargaining and the nursing profession, Monthly Labor Rev. **84:**2-3, July 1961.

Labor law course, ed. 24, Chicago, 1979, Commerce Clearing House.

Matlack, D.R.: Goals and trends in the unionization of health professionals, Hosp. Prog. **53:**41, Feb. 1972.

Mercy Hospitals of Sacramento, 217 NLRB 131 (1975).

Michigan Hospital Association: President's letter, May 15, 1980.

Miller, R.L.: Development and structure of collective bargaining among registered nurses, Part 1 of two parts, Personnel J. **50:**134, Feb. 1971.

Miller, R.U.: Hospitals. In Somers, G.G., editor: Contemporary American experience, Madison, Wisc., 1980, Industrial Relations Research Association.

Morales, G.: Unit appropriateness in health care institutions, Labor Law J. **30:**174, Mar. 1979.

National Labor Relations Act of 1935 as amended (NLRA, 1935): 29 U.S. Code, Ch. 7, Subch. 11, Sec. 151-168.

National Union of Hospital and Health Care Employees, 1199 News **14:**5, Mar. 1979.

Natonski, J.: Why a union contract didn't work at our hospital, RN **41:**69-71, May 1978.

Newton-Wellesley Hospital, 219 NLRB (1975). [See also Trustees of Noble Hospital, 218 NLRB 1441 (1975).]

Newton-Wellesley Hospital and Mass. Nurses' Assn., 250 NLRB #1-RC-166669 (July 3, 1980).

Newton-Wellesley Hospital and Mass. Nurses' Assn., 104 LRRM 1384. (See also Bureau of National Affairs: Collective bargaining negotiation and contracts, July 24, 1980, p. 3).

Rosmann, J.: Hospital revenue controls: their labor relations and labor force utilization implications for the hospital industry, Paper presented at the 30th National Conference on Labor, New York Institute of Labor Relations, May 17, 1977.

Unions intensify organizing efforts among nurses, Am. J. Nurs. **80:**185, 1980.

U.S. Department of Labor, Federal Mediation and Conciliation Service: Impact of the 1974 health care amendments to the NLRA on collective bargaining in the health care industry, Washington, D.C., 1979.

Wynne, D.: A union contract was the only language our hospital would understand, RN **41:**66-68, May 1978.

PART THREE

EFFECTING CHANGE IN THE HEALTH CARE SYSTEM

The position taken in Part One is that nurses are in an ideal position to effect change in the health care delivery system. Not only do nurses represent the largest single group of health providers in the United States, but nursing education specifically addresses a holistic approach to health care. The educational process in nursing focuses on examining the total system in which health care is delivered, so as to provide the most relevant services possible. Thus Part One sought to address theoretical content, which forms the backbone of the change process.

In contrast, Part Two dealt with the varying influential factors in present-day society, specifically within the current health care delivery system, which may either enhance or interfere with the individual nurse's or nursing as a collective's ability to make changes in the provision of health care. In an era of escalating costs, increasing demands for accountability, and accusations of apathy, nursing cannot afford tunnel vision. All nursing care must take into account the social necessity for providing optimal care with both the greatest possible efficiency and at the most reasonable cost.

Thus Part Three takes into account the theoretical foundations essential for implementing the change-agent role, as well as the constraints and motivators for change, in order to explore a variety of innovative and socially timely approaches to the provision of health care. An implicit assumption in the change-agent role is that nursing care cannot be delivered in a vacuum. Nursing is a part of a system composed of an array of other health providers. An isolationist view of nursing practice would hinder the acceptance and subsequent achievement of change in that nursing care is provided in conjunction with many other forms of health care. Hence the future directions for health care described here view nursing as an integral change force working in interdisciplinary relationships to assist consumers in achieving a state of maximal health.

POSITIVE STRATEGY FOR HEALTH

A positive strategy for health is called for (Breslow, 1979), which recognizes that the critical factors negatively affecting health status are as much a result of social and environmental influences as of shortages and inaccessibility of health resources (Ng, and others, 1978). According to Wildavsky (1977), "most of the bad things that happen to people are at present beyond the reach of medicine" (p. 105). Estimates contend that the medical system can make a difference in about ten percent of the usual health indexes, whereas the remaining ninety percent are sensitive to factors beyond the reach of the traditional health care system: social conditions, genetic inheritance, the environment, and—perhaps most important—the American life-style. It is no longer a valid comfort to think that chronic illness results solely from greater longevity. The impact of industrialization and urbanization on the health of the populace cannot be disregarded. It is likely that each advancement and social comfort is bought at the price of its effect on health. Pollution, a sedentary life-style, and the frequent consumption of readily available and often nonnutritious foods all influence health status.

Along with a national trend toward a life-style that militates against health and an environment that often has a negative effect on health comes an urgency for containing health care costs. It is no longer reasonable to expect that the American economy can afford to "fix" everyone who evidences a health disruption. Financial resources are finite, and decisions are increasingly being made as to who should have the benefit of health resources. To date, few incentives have been available to reward individuals who are healthy. The health care system has largely been an "illness care system," whereas the current emphasis focuses on health promotion and disease prevention. Individuals will increasingly receive incentives to stay healthy. A positive health strategy must address ways to prevent disease, maintain health, and extend life through life-style and environmental changes that will promote rather than disrupt health. Individuals will be called on to take steps to maintain their health by changing dysfunctional habits such as substance abuse, lack of exercise, and the consumption of unnecessary, nonnutritious foods.

Nursing can and must take an active role in moving the American public toward a positive health strategy. Health education, self-care teaching, and health maintenance surveillance are only a few ways in which nursing can promote health. Nursing can have an influence on health promotion both by direct service to consumers and through participation in health planning and policy-making decisions. Incentives for the maintenance of health must be introduced into the system, and this will require major planning and subsequent legislative and health policy decisions.

NEW APPROACHES IN NURSING

New models for the delivery of nursing care must be developed in order to assure nursing's continued role in the health care system. Nursing actions directed toward both individuals and aggregates must be based on a careful assessment of the health needs of the client. Programs cannot be developed because providers believe such activities are needed. Instead, critical assessments must be made as to the perceived health needs of a given population. Subsequent program development will depend increasingly on consumer participation, to provide assessment information as well as to make realistic plans for the population being served.

As programs are developed to promote health and encourage consumer participation and responsibility, new methods for evaluating program effectiveness will be essential. In an era of diminishing fiscal resources and increasing consumer health care needs, the benefits of each program must be carefully weighed in order to justify its existence.

A change agent in nursing clearly understands the goals and objectives of each project and works diligently with others who are involved in the change process in a fashion that exemplifies cooperation and interdependence.

REFERENCES

Breslow, L.: A positive strategy for the nation's health, J.A.M.A. **242**(19):2093-2095, Nov. 9, 1979.

Ng, L.K., Davis, D.L., and Manderscheid, R.W.: The health promotion organization: a practical intervention designed to promote healthy living, Public Health Rep. **93**(5):446-454, Oct. 1978.

Wildavsky, A.: Doing better and feeling worse: the political pathology of health policy. In Knowles, J.H., editor: Doing better and feeling worse: health in the United States, New York, 1977, W.W. Norton & Co., Inc.

The construction of a model, as a scientific procedure, is founded on the belief that there can be order and reason in the mind, if not in the real world.

Borko, H.: Automated language processing, 1967, John Wiley & Sons, Inc., p. 39. Reprinted with the permission of Systems Development Corp.

18

MODEL BUILDING AND THE CHANGE PROCESS

Wade Lancaster

Seldom does a day go by when we are not confronted with the inevitability of change. Rapid advances in industrialized nations, world tension, soaring costs of all products and services necessitate actions and reactions directed toward coping with change. Two basic choices of action are available to us: we can plan in advance for the onset of change, or we can wait until change ensues and react to its consequences. Nurses have long been accused of being "reactors to" rather than "initiators of" change.

As noted in the title of this book, an action-oriented approach toward change is purported. The thesis for this text is that nurses must become sophisticated and knowledgeable agents of change in order to maintain a viable role in the health care system. Considerable knowledge of theories supportive to the development of change strategies is essential, as is an understanding of the key factors in the environment that help or hinder change.

This chapter addresses the use of models as a tool for planned change. Few change strategies are simple, clear-cut, and easy to define, thus the use of models allows us to conceptualize situations, problems, and plans by using abstract symbols to depict complex real-world events.

Models are not a recent innovation. The use of models is as old as recorded history and is clearly evidenced in the pictorial language used by early Egyptian and Chinese societies (Lippitt, 1973). Throughout the centuries models have been used in the sciences to aid in the explanation of phenomena in order that scholars can have a greater understanding of their area of study.

Model usage in the twentieth century is an everyday occurrence. Whether we recognize it or not, we are all model builders. In order to deal with the complexity of daily existence people use models as tools in their problem-solving efforts. The systematic inquiry into and analysis of most phenomena is enormously complex; the ability to cope successfully with ever-present change is no exception. In truth, of all the phenomena that could be studied, human behavior is probably the most complex, intangible, and unpredictable. When change occurs, who but humans are generally the initiators, recipients, reactors, or resisters? Hence any examination of the change process is a gargantuan task made even more complex by the myriad of interacting human variables.

The purpose of this chapter is to answer the following questions: What are models? Why are models helpful (essential) to a discussion of the change process in nursing? How are models differentiated from other aspects of theory building such as concepts, conceptual frameworks, and constructs? What factors affect model building? How can models be classified? What are the skills required of the model builder, and what difficulties can ensue from the use of models?

MODELS—WHAT ARE THEY AND WHY HAVE THEM?

In ordinary language, the word *model* means different things to people and has been used in a variety of ways. It can denote a person or thing that represents a pattern of excellence; or a person employed to display items of clothing, or one who poses for various artists such as painters, sculptors, and photographers. The term also refers to a type, design, or style of structure; a pattern of something to be made or tested; a representation of something.

The common usage of the word model is both helpful and injurious to an accurate understanding of the scientific usage of the term. Excluding both the fashion and the artist's model, most people tend to view a model as a structure that replicates, reproduces, or represents something else. Although this notion of a model is consistent with the scientific view, an important distinction between the common view of a model and the scientific view lies in the use to which the model is put.

A model, in the scientific sense, may be used to define or describe something; to assist with the analysis of a system; to specify relationships and processes; or to present a situation in symbolic terms that can be manipulated to derive predictions. There is actually only one common characteristic of the various usages of scientific models, as summarized by Kaplan (1964, p. 263): "We may say that any system A is a model of system B if the study of A is useful for the understanding of B without regard to any direct or indirect causal connection between A and B.''

In engineering, industry, and several of the sciences, models are used to solve both simple and complex problems by focusing on a selected portion or key features rather than on every detail of real life. This approximation or abstraction of reality represents the scientist's idea of a model. As Hazzard (1971) observes, no one segment of the universe is so simple and easy to understand that it can be grasped and controlled without the use of abstraction. Consequently, models do not represent all aspects of reality because of the innumerable and ever-changing characteristics of the real world. Since models employ the process of abstraction, the model builder focuses attention on those details of reality that seem to have the greatest relevance to the inquiry. This feature is consistent with the scientific approach, which includes some aspects of the real system and excludes others.

Stogdill (1970) concisely summarizes models when he states that their purpose is to describe and explain a system of events in the real world. A model, then, is a conceptual representation of reality—not reality itself, but "an abstracted and reconstructed form of reality" (Riehl and Roy, 1980, p. 6). A model does not intend to explain why something does or does not happen, but rather "orders, clarifies, and systematizes selected components of the phenomena it serves to depict" (Bush, 1979, p. 16).

CORRELATION OF MODELS WITH OTHER ASPECTS OF THEORY BUILDING

In an era of increasing complexity and change, nurses must become highly skilled at planning interventions based on sound knowledge and theory. As health professionals, nurses are constantly expected to make sound decisions about health care based on a well-formulated rationale. Too often it is assumed that if an idea is in print or has been stated by a person in authority, then it must be true. Such noncritical acceptance of the ideas, opinions, and procedures of others will no longer be satisfactory in an era where consumers are demanding increasing accountability, and the pressures on professional nursing mount. Nurses must develop a sound basis for practice founded on theoretical formulations rather than intuition or a "we have always done it that way" rationale. It is time for nurses to learn how to evaluate presented knowledge critically so as to make informed judgments. Chinn and Jacobs (1978, p. 1) maintain that "the development of theory is the most crucial task facing nursing today." Indeed if nursing is to gain power and prestige in the health care system, coping with change from a sound theoretical base is imperative.

Relationship between models and theories

In order to describe how models relate to the theory-building process, several key terms must be defined. As mentioned, a model is a "symbolic representation of the various aspects of a complex event or situation and their interrelationships" (Lippitt, 1973, p. 2). The term model is sometimes used as a synonym for theory. Using terms interchangeably, however, leads to their misuse. Certain distinct features differentiate models from theory, and to equate the two without clarification of their differences adds confusion to the precision that nursing is seeking to develop.

Kerlinger (1973) defines theory as "a set of interrelated constructs (concepts), definitions, and propositions that present a systematic view of phenomena by specifying relations among variables, with the purpose of explaining and predicting the phenomena" (p. 9).

Williams (1979) expands on Kerlinger's definition by saying that to qualify as a theory, the phenomena under consideration must be precise and limited, and the concepts must be clearly defined. Chinn and Jacobs (1978) go a step further in defining theory to emphasize the need for prediction and control relative to the relational statements set forth about the phenomena comprising the theory.

Thus whereas a model primarily describes structure, a theory provides substance, not only by stating relationships among the parts, but also through its ability to move beyond description to the advanced level of prediction. In actuality, theories are a subset of models, since all theories can be depicted as models, but the reverse is not true; all models are not theories. Models provide a useful schema for depicting the relationships that exist among the variables of the theory. Moreover, models are assumed to be precursors of theory, and can be used to "display certain structural and functional relationships that are inherent in a specific theory" (Bush, 1979, p. 17).

Models are particularly useful for depicting the relationships that exist among the variables of the theory. The construction of a model allows theorists to illustrate graphically and to explain relationships. In this context, model building is considered an early step in the time-consuming and complex theory-building process.

Although several characteristics differentiate models from theory, they also share certain common qualities. Both vary in their degree of abstractness, and both are isomorphic systems. Isomorphism refers to the similarity between a thing and the model of it (Brodbeck, 1968). A model, in order to be maximally useful, must accurately depict the object that it seeks to represent. In other words, isomorphism requires a one-to-one correspondence between the model or theory and reality. Also, to meet the criteria for isomorphism, certain relations must be preserved in any model of reality. For example, some models do not work on exactly the same principles as the original they seek to replicate. For example, an inert model of a heart is not complete in regard to isomorphism in that a "real" heart continuously serves to pump blood. In contrast, an example of complete isomorphism might be a model of a steam engine that is itself steam propelled (Brodbeck, 1968).

Concepts, propositions, and frameworks

Just as concepts are the building blocks of theory, so are they the basis of models. *Concepts* are words or elements that describe or express an ab-

stract idea. Concepts, like theories and models, vary in their level of abstraction, from highly primitive concepts that cannot be operationalized to concepts that can be clearly operationalized and described. Williams (1979) describes concepts that are not directly observable as constructs, such as ego or intelligence. She points out that whereas the terms concept and construct are often used interchangeably, there are subtle differences. Benne, Chin, and Bennis (1976, p. 135) elaborate on constructs by describing them as "deliberately created ideas or inferences with or without any directly observable reality, but which serve the heuristic function of allowing analysis, and explanation to occur." Both concepts and constructs play significant roles in model building in that models are often highly abstract and not always clearly replicated.

Propositions are statements that specify the relationships between two or more concepts. As such, propositions link concepts and explain the interaction among them. In models of a change process, the propositions often spell out the interaction patterns among the variables.

A *conceptual framework* denotes an entity more abstract than a model, yet less complete than a theory. As such, conceptual frameworks provide broad outlines that support, define, and ultimately relate parts of the whole. Often the terms model and conceptual framework are used interchangeably. This tendency is more true to reality than confusing models with theories, in that the differences between models and frameworks are generally subtle. Like models, whereas a theory can be used as a conceptual framework, the reverse relationship does not hold true. A conceptual framework is generally derived from one or more theories and may ultimately evolve through empirical testing into a theory. Often a conceptual framework is an early stage in model development.

Although models are an important tool for theory construction, not all are designed for that purpose. Classifying models is thus important in order to more fully understand their nature.

CLASSIFICATION OF MODELS

Any model can be classified and described in different ways. The task of categorizing models is complicated, however, by the lack of uniform terminology, since a variety of terms are used to distinguish among the various types of models. Obviously, it is confusing to use a number of terms to describe the same types of models. In the classifications that follow, the basic types of models are identified, and where possible, synonymous terms are noted.

Classification according to level of abstraction

Models are frequently described according to their level of abstraction, which essentially refers to composition or manner of presentation. When models are classified in this way, they can be arranged along a continuum, with mental models at one pole and physical models at the other. In this context, mental models represent the highest degree of abstraction, whereas physical models are specific, concrete replicas of their real-life counterparts. Symbolic models, as shown in Fig. 18-1, are positioned between pure mental and physical models, and they generally employ a set of connected symbols, objects, or concepts to represent a designated problem or project (Hardy, 1974). Thus by starting with mental models and moving toward physical models, all models can be seen to fall on a continuum in which the manner of presentation becomes progressively less abstract.

Mental models, sometimes called images or implicit models, are the pictures of the world we hold in our minds. They consist of thought patterns composed of words and concepts arranged so as to show a meaningful image of reality. These thought patterns can be formulated into language, which ultimately allows us to communicate and describe the abstractions to others. A question arises, however, as to the completeness of any mental image. A mental model is a simplification of the situation it portrays, consisting of a few incomplete and abstract concepts that are considered integral to

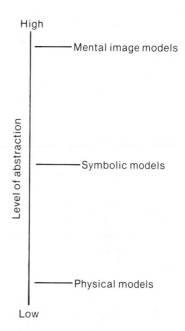

FIG. 18-1
Models classified as to level of abstraction.

forming a meaningful image of reality. Mental models reduce the scope of the situations they portray, enhancing their usefulness by simplifying reality. The real value of mental models comes from their *not* corresponding precisely to the complexity of the phenomena under scrutiny. Instead, the model focuses on the details of reality that have the perceived greatest relevance to the situation.

Not all phenomena can be understood by the use of mental models. Consequently, these highly abstract models may become very explicit in the form of physical models. One type of physical model is the *iconic,* which means that it looks like what it is supposed to represent; it is a physical representation of some real-life object, either in more or less idealized form or on a different scale. Some iconic models are exact replicas of the entities they are designed to represent, whereas others deviate from reality in the number of properties represented. Iconic models are sometimes referred to as *scale* models. Although not all iconic models involve a change in size, many are designed to be either smaller or larger than the entity being depicted.

Iconic models are used widely by engineers and designers. For example, they are used in the design of ocean liners, bridges, water-supply systems, and all sorts of products from automobiles to stage scenery. Aeronautical engineers use miniature models of airplanes to represent full-sized planes in wind tunnel tests. Iconic models are also familiar to nurses in the form of replicas of various body organs such as the heart, kidney, or brain, used for instructional purposes. In each of these examples, the value of an iconic model lies in its ability to duplicate an entity to make it more understandable.

When a model ceases to look like its real-life counterpart, thus becoming more abstract while still retaining physical properties, it is referred to as an *analog* model. In contrast to iconic models, analog models transform properties; that is, one property is used to represent another. In other words, there is a substitution of components or processes to provide a parallel with what is being modeled.

A topographical map in which the property "color" is substituted for "height above sea level" is one common example of an analog model. Another example is a graph, such as an ECG, in which a unit distance along a line is used to represent a unit of time, or speed. The ECG is realistic in behavior (i.e., it reflects what is occurring in the heart), but it certainly does not have characteristic features of any aspect of the processes producing the data displayed.

When a model no longer has a recognizable physical form and takes on a higher level of abstraction, it becomes a *symbolic* model. In this type of model, phenomena are represented figuratively by using a set of connected symbols, objects, or concepts. Symbolic models can be either verbal, schematic, or quantitative.

A *verbal* model is a statement that points out the important aspects of a phenomenon; it is either written or spoken in a standard language, such as English, which is familiar to those who seek to understand the model. A verbal model, such as a poem, can be thought of as a prose description of a mental model. An important virtue of this type of symbolic model is that it is easily constructed and communicated. For example, in medicine, effective verbal models that describe the transmission of disease have been useful in the eradication of many of the epidemic diseases that previously terrorized humanity. Similarly, Harvey's model of the circulatory system, as well as the various models of the reaction of the human body to invading organisms, have influenced the development of the modern treatment of diseases.

Another type of symbolic model is the *schematic* model, which represents a useful next step in the process of symbolizing a verbal model. Many diagrams, graphs, drawings, pictures, and similar schemata are schematic models. This type of model is more abstract than the analog model; it is generally descriptive, but cannot be easily tested for representativeness and may even lack precision. However, schematic models often provide an effective way to communicate with nonexperts and can assemble ideas that will be used in formulating other types of models. One common example of a schematic model is the communications map of an organization, such as a hospital, which shows by the use of arrows how messages and other means of communication are transmitted. The map does not show anyone talking to anyone else, yet one can easily determine from the map who communicates with whom.

A final type of symbolic model is the *quantitative* model, which uses mathematical symbols to represent a phenomenon or certain aspects of a phenomenon. Such a model possesses many useful and desirable characteristics. More specifically, quantitative models are concise and add the potential for certain kinds of precision. Moreover, they are not easily misconstrued; mathematical symbols are easier to see and manipulate than words, in the sense that all of the tools of logic and mathematics

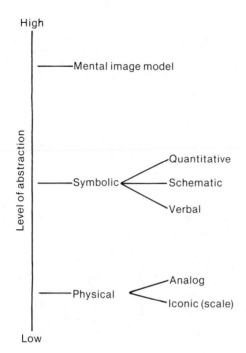

High

Level of abstraction

———Mental image model

Symbolic ———Quantitative
———Schematic
———Verbal

Physical ———Analog
———Iconic (scale)

Low

FIG. 18-2
Classification of models according to levels of
abstraction and including subcategories.

may be brought to bear on the models. Finally,
quantitative models are easier to test and replicate
than other types. There are various types of quantitative models, ranging from the relatively simple
to the extremely complex. One example of a quantitative model is the Health Belief Model, which
has been expressed in the form of several equations
as well as being depicted verbally and schematically. The classifications described in this section
are schematically illustrated in Fig. 18-2.

Classification according to purpose

Not only can models be distinguished from one
another in terms of their level of abstraction, but
one model can be contrasted with another by considering its purpose. The intent of the model brings
into focus a variety of factors that distinguish vari-

ous types of models. A series of bipolar adjectives
are useful for categorizing models according to
purpose. Specifically, models can be classified as
physical or behavioral, static or dynamic, macro or
micro, comprehensive or partial, and descriptive or
decision. Table 5 classifies models according to
purpose. ·

Models are classified as *physical* or *behavioral*,
depending on whether the purpose is to replicate the
structure of a phenomenon or to duplicate its performance. For example, one purpose of using a
model skeleton in an anatomy class is to show the
structural relationship of the various bones in the
skeletal system. In contrast, the purpose of two
people simulating a nurse-patient encounter in the
classroom is to demonstrate a behavioral phenomenon and illustrate a variety of intervention
strategies.

A similar distinction can be made in the differentiation of static and dynamic models. The purpose of a *static* model is to portray a phenomenon
or group of phenomena at a given point in time.
Static models do not readily portray change, although by using several or even a series of static
models, change can be depicted. In contrast, *dynamic* models have time as an independent variable
and emphasize the process by which change occurs.
The life-cycle concept, for example, is a dynamic
model of human growth and development. In contrast, an organizational chart illustrates a static
model, whereas a set of photographs of a child at
different ages represents a series of static models
that could be viewed as a comparative dynamic
model.

Since models can be built at various levels of
detail and complexity, another way to distinguish
among them is based on whether they are macro or
micro. *Macro* models may be more or less aggregated in terms of the variables they contain. The
micro model is the least aggregated in that its purpose is to focus on individual units as well as to
postulate detailed linkages between dependent and
independent variables (Kotler, 1980). By way of
contrast, the variables in macro or aggregated mod-

TABLE 5
Classification of models
according to purpose

Category	Subcategory	Purpose
Physical		Represent structure.
vs.		
Behavioral		Depict performance.
Static		Portray phenomenon at a given point in time.
vs.		
Dynamic		Show time as an independent variable.
Micro		Focus on individual units and detailed linkages between variables.
vs.		
Macro		Use varying levels of aggregation and gross relationships between variables.
Partial		Identify only a few variables, but develop them in detail.
vs.		
Comprehensive		Identify many variables, developed in detail or linked with gross relationships.
Descriptive		Describe things as they are or as they act.
	Communicative	Describe structural arrangement.
	Explanatory	Describe causal relationships.
	Predictive	Forecast future behavior or events.
vs.		
Decision		Find problem solutions.
	Optimization	Find best solution.
	Heuristic	Find a satisfactory solution.

els may be of different kinds. Sometimes macro models use aggregated variables that are measured at the individual level, whereas other macro models use variables that have no counterparts at the individual level. Whereas the micro model focuses on detailed linkages between variables, the purpose of macro models is to postulate two or more variables and link them with a gross set of relationships without explaining the specific mechanisms operating within each variable.

An example of a macro model would be a description of the behavior of various population groups with regard to health care service utilization. In contrast, a micro model would focus on the health care service utilization behavior of an individual rather than an entire group.

Closely associated with macro and micro models are comprehensive and partial models. Though these terms are occasionally used interchangeably, there are substantive differences between them.

Comprehensive models attempt to identify and relate most or all of the variables involved in a phenomenon. These variables are then linked with a gross set of relationships, as is the case with macro models, or the variables are linked with more detailed relationships, as is the case with micro models. Whereas comprehensive models attempt to identify most of the variables, *partial* models are limited to a few variables that are developed in detail. For example, a comprehensive model might examine individual decisions about smoking by considering all possible variables, such as the demographic characteristics of age, race, sex; or sociopsychological variables. In contrast, a partial model would be limited to the examination of selected variables such as attitudes toward smoking. Once again, this examination might take place in either a micro or a macro context.

Another way of classifying models according to their purpose is based on the distinction between descriptive and decision models. This distinction is frequently noted in the literature; however, terms such as positive, systems, behavioral, empirical, and concrete have been used to refer to descriptive models. Similarly, terms such as analytical, normative, goals, optimization, theoretical, and hypothetical are often used to refer to decision models.

The general purpose of *descriptive* models is to describe things either as they are or as they work. Descriptive models can be broken down into three subgroups: communicative, explanatory, and predictive. A *communicative* model seeks to describe the structural arrangement of various elements or components in a system. In contrast, an *explanatory* model is used to describe causal relationships among the elements in a system, and a *predictive* model asserts or describes causal relationships among the elements in a system before the events take place. Therefore, descriptive models serve the purpose of communicating, explaining, or predicting some phenomenon (Kotler, 1980). Freudian psychology and Maslow's hierarchy of human needs are examples of descriptive models be-

cause they discuss human motivation and behavior.

Unlike descriptive models, the purpose of *decision* models is to propose how things should be, and they can be grouped into two categories: optimization and heuristic. Optimization models often use computational routines for finding the best solution to a stated problem, including differential calculus, mathematical programming, statistical decision theory, and game theory. Heuristic models are designed to evaluate alternative outcomes associated with different decisions and to find the best decision when optimization routines are not available or cost effective. Some heuristic models are referred to as rule-of-thumb approaches.

In the preceding classification, models are categorized according to their purpose, in terms of a series of bipolar adjectives. By using one or more sets of bipolar adjectives (see Table 5), any model can be described in terms of its purpose. If both classification schemes (level of abstraction and purpose) are combined, a relatively comprehensive means of classifying models results.

MODEL BUILDING

All of us are model builders as we deal with the thousands of thoughts that pass in and out of our lives daily. Throughout a lifetime we solve perhaps millions of problems that vary from exceedingly simple (such as what to wear) to those that are complex and have far-reaching and occasionally life-or-death consequences. Model building allows for complex, real-world problems to be depicted visually, verbally, or quantitatively in order to assess relations among events, things, or properties. Some of these relational statements made possible by models are of a cause-and-effect nature.

Several factors affect model building, including perception, abstraction, problem-solving ability, an understanding of the model-building process, and the skills of the model builder. Since people are the builders of models, there can be no one best way, best model, or best replica of reality. The quality of any nursing model lies in its ultimate usefulness to nursing practice, which is determined by how well those who seek to implement the model can either devise, modify, or apply it.

Perception

No two people view the same situation in exactly the same way. For example, two nurses could see a patient gasp and then sit down, with his head in his hands. One nurse, because of her experience in a cardiovascular unit, might assume that the patient is experiencing a cardiac dysfunction; the other nurse, who works on the psychiatric unit, might assume that the patient is highly anxious and depressed and is attempting to cope with a high level of stress. Each person views the environment in terms of sensory acuity, past experiences, beliefs, values, and cultural expectations. In this example, both nurses may have 20/20 vision and sharp auditory acuity, yet each viewed the situation from a different experiential basis. Lippitt (1973, p. 5) defines perception as "the process of becoming aware of objects, relationships and qualities outside or inside the individual who is doing the perceiving." Anyone who seeks to use models in planning for change needs to be keenly aware of the multiple factors that influence perception.

Not only does perception vary from one person to another, but the same person may perceive things differently from one day to the next depending on physical and mental health status. For example, consider the usually even-tempered, clear-thinking head nurse who gets up on Monday morning to find one child with an elevated temperature, a husband who is desperately packing to go out of town, and a teenager whose "best jeans" are dirty. After the nurse finds a neighbor to stay with the sick child, she sees her husband and teenager off, and then wearily drives to work to begin a new week on a busy medical unit. No sooner has report ended than she is approached by her supervisor, who says "I have a new project that I would like to implement on your unit; could we talk about it?" Ordinarily the head nurse would welcome a challenge, but on this particular day the supervisor's request is just too much and the head nurse responds, "Why do you

always ask me to be the guinea pig?" The supervisor is stunned because this behavior is highly atypical. Perceptions, then, largely determine how people become involved in change and also the models they develop. Perception is never static but is constantly being altered by internal and external stimuli.

Abstraction

Models are built by abstraction. Since most real-world problems are complex, the most efficient way to begin the problem-solving process is by using abstraction. In order to solve any problem—and much change arises in response to problems—it is necessary to explain, describe, or predict that aspect of reality where the problem exists. Therefore, it is necessary to model the part of reality that is relevant to the problem or change process, and this is done through abstractions.

Thoughts or abstractions about a real situation may seem like three-dimensional moving pictures of one part of the real world. The pictorial abstraction of reality seldom represents the total situation. Just as a photograph cannot capture the total range of hidden thoughts and beliefs, our perceptions of reality are also limited. Often the most significant part of any mental image is that which does not correspond to the actual physical aspects. For example, if we were to look at the picture of a friend we could recall the color of the person's hair, eyes, and general body build as well as his preference for certain styles of clothes. However, many of our memories of the friend, which comprise a private mental image of the person, would consist of a variety of characteristics that could not be captured in a photograph, such as habits, personality, likes, and dislikes. The intangible, nonvisible aspects of people are often the most memorable. Thus the process of abstraction in model building provides a way to represent reality at a given time by depicting complex events so as to delete extraneous factors and only portray essential aspects.

The model builder begins by abstracting several key concepts, which can then be related to a logical

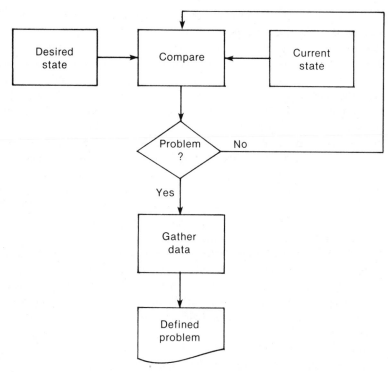

FIG. 18-3
Steps in the problem-solving model: problem definition and data gathering.

whole. The usefulness of abstraction in model building has two key purposes. First, abstraction allows the modeler to select key variables to depict and manipulate while holding other aspects constant. By abstracting out critical parts for review, the complexity is reduced and the model-building process is made more manageable. Second, the use of abstraction ultimately allows greater generalizability when the model is completed.

Problem solving

Modeling helps to expedite problem solving* and change because it forces those involved to conceptualize all the influential factors through visual

*See Chap. 10 for a more detailed discussion of the problem-solving process.

thinking. Although both problem solving and model building employ a set of steps, they are interrelated. Models provide a way to illustrate and depict the steps in problem solving, thereby clarifying and simplifying the process.

Several elements or ingredients must exist before the problem-solving process can begin. Naturally, there must be an identified problem and a person(s) who wishes to act as problem solver. Other essential but less obvious elements include the objectives of the desired state, and information that best describes the current state. Fig. 18-3 illustrates the elements in the problem-solving model.

The objectives describe the desired state and in order to be useful they must be clearly specified. There would be little point in beginning to solve a problem without knowing what the desired outcome is. Most attempts to solve problems involve some type of change; as has been discussed, people tend to resist change, hence it is necessary to plan carefully for change by clearly specifying the expected outcome as well as having considerable information about the current state of the system. If the current state and the desired state are essentially the same, then no problem exists and action is not indicated. By evaluating the differences between the current state and the desired state, you may recognize that more than one problem exists. When this occurs the problems can be prioritized and dealt with one at a time.

The difference between the current state and the desired state represents the solution criteria, or what is necessary to bring about greater congruence between the current and desired states. Implicit in the delineation of a proposed solution to bridging the gap between these two states is the identification of alternate solutions. Several alternate solutions should be identified and evaluated as to their usefulness.

As the alternate solutions are considered, the constraints inherent in each one should be identified. These constraints frequently revolve around finances, work force, and other resources; the majority of constraints result from limited finances. Some alternate solutions can be eliminated because they require resources that are unavailable. Three steps are part of the alternate solution phase: identifying alternatives, evaluating them, and selecting the best solution. A decision must be made regarding each alternative to determine (1) if it is a possible solution to the problem and (2) what constraints exist that would interfere with certain actions. Once the anticipated results of each alternative are established, a decision can be made regarding which one is best under the circumstances.

Not only is the problem-solving process one example of model building, but the value of many models often depends on how accurately the problems they seek to depict are conceptualized. The usefulness of any model depends on the cognitive steps that were taken in its development.

Model-building process

Since model builders are concerned with phenomena that occur in the real world, they must describe the system to be analyzed, and clearly state the implicit assumptions and values in the model and in the society that comprises the model's environment. For example, in a communication model, likely assumptions would include honest, straightforward interaction among participants and the ability to hear as well as to understand the spoken or written word; further, certain mechanisms for interchange would be implicit, including face-to-face contact, telephone, or the written mode of communication.

The model builder needs also to maintain an awareness of the degree of congruence between the model and society at large, or at least that segment of society that is in close influential proximity. For example, a model for open communication among all levels of an agency's hierarchy would be doomed to failure if an overall agency value was, "Never talk to other departments or they will steal your ideas."

Next the model builder should "observe and analyze a system of real events in order to isolate the determining variables that are operating in the system" (Stogdill, 1970, p. 8). To do this, the major components of the model must be clearly defined and must also be identified as separate, observable units that can be related to one another.

In order to discuss the units of any given model clearly and logically, the ultimate goal or outcome of the model must be described. Each variable or subset should be described in clear, easily understood terms that others can recognize and interpret. Next, the actors in the model need to be noted, as well as their expected roles and activities. For example, in a nursing situation the caregiver and recipient comprise the actors in the model; their roles, goals, and expected outcomes must be enumerated.

The next step is for the model builder to describe the goals and actual process of the steps taken or activities selected. The activities should relate to the problem statement, the expected outcome, and

---

STEPS IN DEVELOPING A CHANGE MODEL

1. Describe the proposed system to be analyzed keeping in mind:
   a. The abstract nature of some concepts.
   b. The degree of congruence between the proposed model and reality.
   c. The people who will be involved.
   d. All variables that must be considered.
2. Factor the proposal into simpler subparts where possible to examine and clarify the relationships among the parts.
3. State assumptions and values.
4. Establish a clear set of goals or outcomes:
   a. Determine the symbols to be used.
   b. Seek analogies to clarify understanding.
   c. Write down the obvious.
5. Identify alternatives.
6. Describe the steps to be taken.
7. Establish criteria to evaluate the effectiveness of the change process.

---

to characteristics external to the situation being scrutinized?

3. *Relative importance* — Each variable should be assigned a weight to judge the magnitude of its significance to the total situation.
4. *Outside constraints* — What boundaries exist for the situation? What forces can exert an influence?
5. *Internal constraints* — What limits exist within the situation under consideration?

The steps used in developing a change model are summarized in the box at the left.

SKILLS NEEDED BY MODEL BUILDERS

It is helpful to remember that models do not have to be complex to be useful. The most sophisticated mathematical model is only as useful as the quality of the decisions that determined the variables, significant influencing factors, and constraints. Often it is far more difficult to develop a simple, accurate model than one with numerous interacting variables that may or may not accurately explain reality.

Since those who seek to build models are concerned with accurate description and explanation of a system of events or a process, a certain set of skills are required. First, the model builder must clearly describe the system or process under consideration. Lack of clarity at the onset of model building will snowball into massive confusion. Aspects to be included in describing an action-oriented practice model include defining the actors, the goals, the process, and the expected outcome. No process or event can be pictorially set forth unless the builder knows who is involved, what they hope or expect to attain, how they plan to implement the process, what facilitators and barriers seem likely, and both the intended and potentially unintended consequences (Reilly, 1975).

Though the following list may not be exclusive for all model builders, it does set forth several crucial skills that model builders should have.

1. *Possess a considerable degree of personal security and the ability to make independent deci-*

the characteristics of the actors. The choice of activities includes ongoing awareness both of the model's structure and its functioning, since any alteration in one part of the model is likely to affect all other parts. The last skill for the model builder is that of clearly putting forth a set of defined concepts with statements that describe them, as well as a set of statements that discuss the relationship between the concepts and the constituent parts of the model.

Lippitt (1973, pp. 83-84) elaborates on this last step when he purports that any model builder must describe thoroughly and accurately the situation, problem, or system by identifying the essential variables, components, or subsystems and then asking the following questions about each variable:

1. *Relevance* — Is each variable relevant and necessary for a clear assessment and understanding of the situation?
2. *Relationships* — How are the variables related to one another, to the total situation, and

sions. In order to venture out into the world of model building, an individual must possess a certain degree of confidence in self and willingness to be a risk taker. Setting forth a model opens up numerous opportunities for critique of what a person believes. It is not always easy to work long and hard on a conceptual model to depict the change process on a given hospital unit, only to have the first person who critiques it accurately point out two areas of missing variables. The model builder has to be able to risk saying, "This is how I view the process—what do you think?" It is also necessary to be able truly to *hear* critiques of a model, so as to learn from each experience.

2. *Be able to abstract*. The ability to deal with and understand abstract concepts is a key component in modeling. This means that the model builder must be able to look at a situation and determine the possible variables as well as the likely interactions among them.

3. *Be able to state implicit assumptions and values*. The model builder must be able to state clearly those assumptions and values implicit in the model, as well as those in the part of society that comprises the environment of the model. For example, in a communication model, possible assumptions might include honesty, openness, willingness to change, the ability to accurately hear what is said or to validate any misperceptions.

4. *State the ultimate goal or outcome of the model*. It is useless to begin any change process when the hoped-for goal cannot be clearly stated. Modeling the process clarifies the jump from the start of the process to the outcome. Clearly stating the anticipated outcome helps to determine from the beginning any cognitive loopholes in moving from point A to point G.

5. *Determine the expected variables*. Once the model for analysis is decided on, the model builder must clearly identify the variables. In most instances, the purpose of the model will suggest a provisional set of variables. Once these provisional variables are established, the next step is to examine each one as to its relevance for the model. The

variables must next be defined in terms that are understandable to others. If only the model builder understands what the variables mean, then generalizability will ultimately be severely limited. The variables now should be examined in terms of the relationship between them. How does each variable relate to all others, to the total proposed change, and to the environment? Each variable should also be assessed as to its significance to the total situation. In other words, the variables should be prioritized. Finally, both internal and external constraints must be identified to determine the feasibility of including any given variable.

6. *Describe the actual steps to be taken*. The activities should relate to the problem statement (goal), the expected outcome, the potential intervening variables, and the characteristics of the participants. It is important always to write down the obvious. Leave very little to memory or guesswork because key components can easily be lost. Included in this skill is the ability to write clearly the specific objectives that will generate the list of steps to be taken. In describing the steps it is often helpful to factor the problem or plan into subsets and tackle one subset at a time. This may reduce the tendency to become overwhelmed by the modeling process.

Difficulties in developing change models

Because of the complex nature of change, which invariably involves humans who are at times quite unpredictable, the development of models for this process has inherent difficulties. Lippitt (1973) attributes the majority of difficulties in the change process to three human factors: inadequacy of judgment, lack of skill, and the types of values and beliefs held by the participants. To avoid the potential difficulties the following advice is offered:

1. Lack of clarity in goal development inevitably leads to unexpected and often undesired outcomes.
2. Avoid oversimplifying the change diagnosis or not being thorough in assessing potential obstacles or forces or resistance. As men-

tioned in Chapter 9, resistance to change is inevitable and its occurrence should be built into the change plan.

3. Avoid making the change diagnosis overly complex. Often it is more reasonable to subdivide a complex change process into two or more subplans or stages. Success in achieving the goals of a simplified plan is far more rewarding than failing at an overly complex one.

4. A limited ability to conceptualize is a handicap. It is a well-accepted fact that some people go through life with a more concrete rather than an abstract orientation. The ability to conceptualize requires considerable mental flexibility in order to view a situation from a variety of perspectives.

5. Lack of self-confidence is a handicap. Model builders must feel competent in stating their point of view, accepting criticism, and avoiding feelings of failure and inadequacy when they do not on first try develop a "perfect" model.

6. Resistance to change is the natural human tendency to attempt to perpetuate the status quo. Change is, to many people, frightening and threatening. Fear of the unknown often prevents people from even listening to the ideas presented in a change proposal. The change agent may need to approach the numerous interest groups from a variety of perspectives.

7. The perception of any given situation is dependent on the participants' background, current emotional status, needs, and goals. The adage "he could not see the forest for the trees" frequently holds true when a change is proposed. Some participants invariably have difficulty viewing the situation or plan in its entirety or as the presenter intended.

8. Timing and environmental readiness are important factors. Model building, especially in regard to any plan for change, cannot be forced. The participants must see the need for

the model and the environment must be ready to support its creation. Model building takes time and frequently nurses have difficulty finding uninterrupted opportunities to think carefully through a change model.

ADVANTAGES AND DISADVANTAGES OF MODELS

Both positive and negative results can ensue from utilizing models for a practice-oriented profession such as nursing. At present, a "halo effect" is attached to the topic of models. Models are considered "good," useful, and sophisticated approaches toward looking at nursing practice. Indeed, models have many benefits, but they are no panacea for either nursing or the change process. This means that model building must be approached thoughtfully in order to make certain that the plan and process are compatible.

Lippitt (1973) describes several advantages and disadvantages of change models. The first advantage is that models allow experimentation without risk. It is possible to determine with a model the potential effects of several different patient care approaches without involving a single patient. This approach takes a "what if" orientation. For example, you might be planning to purchase all new furniture for your office. One approach might be to select several items that look good and would really suit your needs—and then to hope they fit your allotted office space. A second approach would be to draw the items of furniture and the room dimensions to scale and actually place the furniture in the scale model or diagram of the room so as to determine the fit accurately. The risk involved in the first approach would include time, energy, and money if the furniture did not fit. Although the entire spectrum of human reactions to any given change cannot be anticipated, many ideas and potential reactions can be gleaned by modeling the proposed change.

A second advantage of using models as an early step in the change process is that they are often good predictors of behavior and performance. In truth, models generally are far more suitable for describing rather than predicting. The reason for this is that change models invariably include people, and human responses are never 100 percent predictable. Certainly models generate ideas about potential responses to a change strategy and allow for the development of new coping approaches.

Third, models promote greater understanding and clarity about the system in which a change is proposed. In order to construct a model that depicts real-world phenomena, careful consideration must be given to selecting the essential elements and disregarding those that may seem tangential to the purpose at hand. In order to delineate the variables to be considered in a change model, a great deal of disciplined attention must be directed toward the system in which a change is proposed. Such a careful assessment of the situation under consideration promotes heightened awareness of the relative significance of each component, which may necessitate that the model builder forfeit old prejudices when they do not hold true under scrutiny.

Model building also helps in deciding exactly what type and amount of data should be collected and analyzed. As people begin to devise pictorial models of change, gaps in information and faulty interactions may become obvious. For example, if a hospital is planning a change in scheduling in the laboratories, and a department that serves as a courier or messenger service is part of the organization, then representatives from this area must be included in any proposed laboratory change. The messengers who deliver the specimen to the laboratory are critical to the change plan.

In considering the disadvantages inherent in model building, Ashby (1970, p. 94) says that "every model of a real system is in one sense second-rate." Ashby's position is that no single model can accurately depict reality and that some aspects are always lost in the development of a model. In addition, the model builder may be tempted for the sake of simplicity and convenience to make the situation fit the model rather than trying to fit the model to the situation. A further criticism of the use of models is that they may induce over-

generalization of the situation. Just as a primary value of models is their tendency to select out key aspects for consideration, this may be a disadvantage in that some important aspects may be lost in the process of abstraction.

SUMMARY

This chapter has described a variety of ways in which models can be useful in nursing practice, education, and research. In order to discuss the usefulness of models, they were differentiated from theory, concepts, propositions, and conceptual frameworks. A system for classifying models was presented to clarify the terminology that is currently used to describe models. The process of model building was also discussed, as were the skills needed by model builders and several advantages and disadvantages of the modeling process.

Currently, nursing models are widely applicable, and the use of analogies, constructs, verbal descriptions of systems, idealizations, and graphic representations is widespread. As nurses become increasingly skillful at developing practice approaches based on sound theoretical information, the usefulness of models will increase. Models by definition allow for complex phenomena to be presented in varying ranges of simplicity. The model builder can conceivably start with a hunch about a designated nursing education or practice problem, and the hunch can then be set forth as a model, which can be applied, revised, and used again.

REFERENCES

Ashby, R.: Analysis of the system to be modeled. In Stogdill, R., editor: The process of model building in the behavioral sciences, Columbus, Ohio, 1970, Ohio State University Press.

Benne, K.D., Chin, R., and Bennis, W.G.: Science and practice. In Bennis, W.G., Benne, K.D., Chin, R., and Corey, K.E., editors: The planning of change, ed. 3, New York, 1976, Holt, Rinehart & Winston.

Borko, H., editor: Automated language processing, New York, 1967, John Wiley & Sons, Inc.

Brodbeck, M.: Models, meaning, and theories. In Brodbeck, M., editor: Readings in the philosophy of the social sciences, New York, 1968, The Macmillan Co.

Bush, H.A.: Models for nursing, Adv. Nurs. Sci. **1**(2):13-21, Jan. 1979.

Chinn, P.L., and Jacobs, M.K.: A model for theory development in nursing, Adv. Nurs. Sci. **1**(1):1-11, Oct. 1978.

Hardy, M.: Theories: components, development, evaluation, Nurs. Res. **23**:100-107, March-April 1974.

Hazzard, M.E.: An overview of systems theory, Nurs. Clin. North Am. **6**:385-393, Sept. 1971.

Kaplan, A.: The conduct of inquiry, Scranton, Pa., 1964, The Chandler Publishing Co.

Kerlinger, F.: Foundations of behavioral research, ed. 2, New York, 1973, Holt, Rinehart & Winston.

Kotler, P.: Marketing management, ed. 4, Englewood Cliffs, N.J., 1980, Prentice-Hall, Inc.

Lippitt, G.L.: Visualizing change: model building and the change process, La Jolla, Calif., 1973, University Associates, Inc.

Reilly, D.E.: Why a conceptual framework? Nurs. Outlook **23**:566-569, Sept. 1975.

Riehl, J.P., and Roy, Sister C.: Theory and models. In Riehl, J.P., and Roy, Sister C., editors: Conceptual models for nursing practice, ed. 2, New York, 1980, Appleton-Century-Crofts.

Stogdill, R.: Introduction: the student and model building. In Stogdill, R., editor: The process of model building in the behavioral sciences, Columbus, Ohio, 1970, Ohio State University Press.

Williams, C.A.: The nature and development of conceptual frameworks. In Downs, F.S., and Fleming, J.W., editors: Issues in nursing research, New York, 1979, Appleton-Century-Crofts.

The inability to speak with precision and certainty about the future . . .
is no excuse for silence.

Toffler, A.: Future shock, 1970, Random House, Inc., p. 5.

19

FUTURE DIRECTIONS: ORGANIZATIONAL SETTINGS FOR PRACTICE

Kathleen G. Andreoli

In the future, nursing practice will be dynamic and responsive to the changing health needs of society. Nurses will continue to assume roles associated with being parent surrogates, technicians, and managers of people and environments (Smoyak, 1975, p. 31). Further, the responsibilities associated with these roles will be modified as technological and scientific discoveries replace or improve on current knowledge. Since the process for delivering health care is based on the same scientific knowledge for all health professions, varying amounts of role overlap will occur. According to Christman (1980), as the growth of mutually shared competencies and tasks takes place, it will be necessary to create organizational models that facilitate the performance of each professional. Thus "shared power models will replace the territorial and monolithic power models" (p. 32) that characterize the current health care system.

Although all health professions make important contributions to health care, the nursing and medical professions dominate the health work force scene. It is especially important, therefore, that these two professions understand and respect one another's expertise. As nursing care does not equal health, neither does medical care. In point of fact, the medical system (physicians, drugs, hospitals) affects about ten percent of the usual indexes for measuring health: whether you live at all (infant mortality), how well you live (days lost due to sickness), and how long you live (adult mortality) (Wildavsky, 1977, p. 105). The remaining ninety percent are determined by individual life-styles, social conditions, and the environment. The nursing system is prepared to assist individuals in attaining health in their own environment.

Christman (1980) forecasts hopeful signs for nursing on the horizon. Good indications are liberalization in many states of nursing practice laws, an improved economic base for nursing, involvement of more nurses in research to provide the profession with a richer scientific base, and more nurses earning graduate degrees. Competent nursing practice will progress with these changes and

will identify and capitalize on opportunities for innovations.

The nature of nursing practice is, and will continue to be, influenced by a variety of factors including census, geographical distribution of the population, age, sex, socioeconomic levels, health indexes, kinds and number of health work force, the national economy, reimbursement structures, licensing laws, government control, and consumer involvement, to mention a few. Discussion of these factors is beyond the scope of this chapter; therefore, the reader is referred to other chapters in this book where these issues have received full attention. The point here is that these data must be considered in defining the great equation of health care. The nature of nursing practice and the settings where it will take place cannot be determined in isolation.

Predicting future settings for nursing practice within the confines of a book chapter will necessitate some generalization and the use of examples for clarification. By no means does this chapter intend to represent an all-inclusive index of possible settings for the next generation of practicing nurses. Accordingly, the material to follow has been divided into two areas. The first approach will be a consideration of the institutional and ambulatory settings that will provide nursing services for sick, high-risk, worried well, and well people. The second section is dedicated to healthy people. The concepts of health promotion and disease prevention will be explored, along with their implications for nursing practice.

INSTITUTIONAL SETTINGS FOR NURSING PRACTICE

Institutionalized health care is a part of the health heritage in the United States. Because of the mystique associated with illness, health institutions have traditionally continued to exist long after the conditions that made them viable and socially useful had vanished (Kalisch, 1978). Such luxury will not be available to future populations. The declining economy, scarcity of resources, and changing patterns of morbidity will force the nation to re-evaluate the existing health care institutions and justify their existence. Although the numbers and locations may be revised, one can safely predict that hospitals and community health institutions will continue to be settings for patient care in the coming century.

Hospitals

It is inevitable that disease and disability will affect individuals at some point in their lifetimes. Contrary to the conviction expressed by Norman Cousins (1976), hospitals will continue to be the most effective place to treat a person who is seriously ill. Emergency care, critical care, specialized diagnostic and therapeutic care, and general and selective rehabilitative care will be offered in community hospitals and highly specialized medical centers, currently known as secondary and tertiary institutions respectively. No matter how splendidly equipped the hospitals, how superb the physicians, and how great the medical research, the welfare of patients will depend on the quality and number of registered nurses working within those institutions. Even now the majority of nurses are employed by hospitals (Aiken, 1979; Moses and Roth, 1979). This is not surprising, considering the trend for shorter hospitalization, which means that the patient population will be more acutely ill. Furthermore, the advancement of biotechnical science continues to expand the content and complexity of nursing responsibilities in intensive care units and other highly specialized services.

Primary nursing as a system of around-the-clock responsibility for care of clients will be maintained and refined. The all–registered nurse team staffing this system, under the leadership of clinical nursing specialists, will devise and test nursing interventions that best serve the individual client, family, and community. With patient classification systems stratifying clients according to categories of nursing needs, planning, accountability, evaluation, and reimbursement will be possible. Nursing's contribution in the hospital setting will be identifiable.

Academic medical centers will offer unique op-portunities for nursing practice development. This is the ideal setting for planning and implementing practice demonstration projects. Such projects are necessary for the purpose of improving the climate for practice, increasing the quality of practice and research in practice, and enhancing collaboration with other health disciplines. Joint faculty practice models between nursing and medical faculties should serve as the foundation for these programs.

Because of the development and implementation of new technology that traditionally occurs in the academic medical centers, this setting will serve to implement and evaluate computer-assisted nursing practice. This technology will provide a mechanism for reducing practice errors of omission and commission, facilitate nursing research, and enhance accountability. Thus hospitals will continue to offer a haven for sick people and provide nursing an opportunity to help people restore their health by capitalizing on the strengths of individuals, families, and community resources.

Depending on the future health needs of the population, specialty hospitals for psychiatric disorders, cancer, other categorical diseases, specialized diagnostic services, and the like will remain as separate entities, be incorporated into existing facilities, or be discontinued. The same fate lies ahead for institutional care outside secondary and tertiary settings. Examples of community health institutions that have future promise are discussed in the following section.

Community health institutions

Future community institutions for short-term and long-term residence with and without linkages with hospitals and home will require nursing services. Such settings include hospices, nursing homes, and childbirth centers.

Hospices

Hospice, a European concept that has become popular recently in the United States, offers a humane alternative in health care delivery for terminally ill patients. Hospice care attempts to make the final period before death as comfortable, dignified, and productive as possible for the patient and family in the familiar surroundings of the home (Amado, et al., 1979). Hospice care is palliative rather than curative and focuses on symptom control, pain management, and psychological support.

There are over 200 developing hospices across the United States (Lack, 1979), and as demonstration projects prove successful, more hospices will flourish. The predicted economic incentive is that a package of reimbursed home health services will reduce the dying patient's utilization of hospital days of care (Amado, et al., 1979). The choice of home versus institutional setting for hospice care will continue to be determined by the psychological and physical readiness of the family and the nature of the terminal disease.

The visiting nurse has been identified as the key health professional in the home hospice setting (Krant, 1978), and this should not change in coming years. Helping the family to assume the responsibilities for giving care through scheduled home visits and providing around-the-clock coverage by way of telephone contact, the nurse, in communication with the physician, organizes a system of caring with a humane concern for the dying and his or her loved ones.

Hospice care cannot always, however, be delivered in the home. Family exhaustion, loss of commitment to responsibilities, and severe complications of the dying person's disease will require hospitalization. As reported by Krant (1978), hospitals can provide selected areas with a homelike environment where patients are encouraged to bring things from home, children are allowed to visit freely, and rooms are set aside for family members to sleep overnight. In this setting the hospital nurse assumes the same responsibilities as the visiting nurse in the collaborative direction of care of the dying person. Providing for a dignified death will never become outdated.

Nursing homes

The aging citizen faces the prospect of a limited life span. Nursing is already involved with this age group, with nursing homes and extended care facil-

ities being the employers of the second largest number of nurses in the country (Moses and Roth, 1979). It is likely that this trend will continue in view of the fact that people aged sixty-five years and older are the fastest growing segment of the U.S. population. This older group, moreover, has a high likelihood of being functionally dependent, physically limited, sick, and socially isolated (Institute of Medicine, 1978a). Functionally dependent elderly are those individuals over sixty-five whose illnesses, impairments, or social problems have resulted in disability, thereby reducing their ability to carry out independently the customary activities of daily living (Institute of Medicine, 1977, p. 1).

Although long-term institutional care for the aged person is expected in some cases, it is important to note that current efforts are being directed toward systems of care that provide for maintenance of maximum possible function and social independence, preserving the dignity of the elderly and providing opportunities for personal choice (Institute of Medicine, 1978a). The nursing implications in these instances will be addressed later in the chapter under ambulatory care.

A new dimension to the institutionalized long-term care of the elderly is assessment of an individual's functional capacity as a part of the overall health status record. This process is currently shared by nurses, physicians, and social workers depending on the financial constraints and work force availability. The most appropriate person for conducting functional assessments is the geriatric nurse practitioner. This professional has the opportunity and responsibility to (1) refine the procedures and instruments for assessing the functional status of elderly persons; (2) identify appropriate levels of care; (3) develop and test standards for the implementation of care; (4) decide on the scope and frequency of assessments; and (5) conduct research on ways to decrease stress and increase quality of life in this group. The outcome of the nursing process is an individualized plan of care that minimizes loss of function while maintaining maximum ability to function with respect for a client's wishes.

Collaboration with physicians in the care of clients in nursing homes is essential because these are high-risk people predisposed to exacerbations of chronic disease, depression, and further deterioration requiring pharmaceutical and other forms of medical interventions. The geriatric nurse practitioner should be the director and coordinator of care in long-term facilities, calling on other health professionals and community resources as indicated. Assuming the federal government provides financial support for long-term care of the functionally dependent elderly, the opportunities for nursing practice and research in nursing homes is boundless. In a society that is characterized as burying its old people alive in nursing homes, nursing can make the future a brighter experience for institutionalized aging senior citizens.

Childbirth centers

Hospital obstetrical units have provided a resolution for the high infant mortality rates associated with unattended home deliveries. Current childbirth plans, however, are evaluating alternatives for hospitalized deliveries that are safe and cost effective. In this regard, the nurse-midwife has expanded her role from that of home delivery to a more formal role in collaboration with other health professionals in settings known as maternity or childbirth centers. Recent research indicates that care can safely be provided to low-risk obstetrical populations in these settings (Faison, et al., 1979).

Although childbearing units are also established sections of many hospitals, it is likely that these will be used for high-risk deliveries, whereas low-risk pregnant women will be referred to maternity centers where care is provided by a team of nurse-midwives, obstetricians, pediatricians, and ancillary health personnel. This health care model responds to the informed consumer and freedom of choice. If freestanding childbirth centers can be demonstrated to be effective and safe, they should be permitted to exist and parents should have the right to whatever data are available to make an intelligent, informed choice about the kind of childbirth experience they wish to have.

Screening patients initially and throughout pregnancy, providing childbirth education to parents, and assisting with the birth process, the nurse-midwife can fill an indispensable place on the childbirth team. As evidenced by the British model, Queenan (1979) noted that in the United States over ninety-nine percent of deliveries are by physicians, and one percent are by nurse-midwives. Alternatively, in England twenty-seven percent of deliveries are by physicians and seventy-three percent are by nurse-midwives, in a system with physician supervision. In the latter setting, the midwife is "inside the system," whereas up until now the midwife in this country has been "outside the system." Although both systems produce good pregnancy outcomes, the U.S. system (traditionally without the midwife) uses more personnel with extensive training and education than does the British system. The incorporation of the nurse-midwife into this system has clear economic and performance implications.

AMBULATORY SETTINGS FOR NURSING PRACTICE

The concept of nurses managing selected ambulatory care systems is not without related precedent. Customarily, when physicians admit acutely ill patients to the hospital, they are not physically present on the unit at all times. This occurs because physicians are assured that their prescribed treatment plan will be carried out, that their patients will be professionally monitored, and that the multiple resources and services required for the management of their patients will be appropriately coordinated and carried out by the nursing staff. Even when the physician is absent from the hospital, the entire process continues. Why this kind of nursing responsibility has not become common to the ambulatory setting as well is a mystery. Although great strides have occurred through the institution of the nurse practitioner, what continues to be uniform to the majority of ambulatory settings is limited autonomy for nursing practice. The variation on this rule is usually predicted by the geographical distance of the ambulatory setting from organized medicine, with the nurse practitioner assuming more responsibilities as the distance from the physician increases.

Ambulatory care of the future will share some of the features of the system as it is known today. As institutional settings provide for cure and restoration of health, ambulatory settings focus on health promotion, disease prevention, and cure of minor illness. The first level of personal health services, called primary care, provides for evaluation, management of symptoms, disease prevention, health promotion, and continuity and coordination of care through appropriate referral. Primary care is holistic in nature and not defined by location of care, providers, or disciplinary training. Services define primary care; therefore, good practitioners can be trained in a variety of disciplines (Institute of Medicine, 1978b). Nurse practitioners have proved their worth as primary care providers. In the present system they are less costly, more accessible, and better prepared in health promotion than the physician. Nurses will be the major general practitioners of the future (Davis, 1979). The concept of health promotion, an important component of primary care, will be addressed later in the chapter. This section, then, will be devoted to future directions in ambulatory care, with emphasis on settings organized around health care providers, the community, and rural and underserved populations.

Care organized around providers

Ambulatory care settings that are primarily located in proximity to health care providers are medical center ambulatory clinics, physicians' offices, and health maintenance organizations.

Medical center ambulatory clinics

Ambulatory clinics in academic medical centers will continue to plan and implement demonstration models of joint practice for physicians and nurses, recognizing each professional's contribution through a service-oriented reimbursement system. These clinics will also remain as a rich environment for nursing research generated through practice. Innovative nursing strategies regarding

health behavior, utilization of health services, compliance to therapeutic regimens, and so on, will be developed and tested. It is interesting to note that Finnerty (1975) reported that the nurses managing his hypertension clinics were better able to motivate patients to remain on medication than the average physician. Since hypertension is a major health problem with a high incidence of patient noncompliance, the implications of nursing success in helping clients comply with therapy include the probability of reducing the incidence of complications of untreated hypertension, decreasing the number of hospital admissions, and lessening the likelihood of premature death. Considering that complications resulting from hypertension cause 150 million disability days and 26 million hospitalization days every year, and cost business and industry 52 million person days of productivity, and account for the largest number of disability claims under Social Security, compliance of hypertensive persons with therapy is a most desirable end (Finnerty, 1978).

All chronic disease clinics with populations of low-risk patients will be managed by nurse practitioners with physician backup. The same system should be implemented for other low-risk patients in need of primary care services, including any age group who feel well, worried, or are experiencing minor illness.

Physicians' offices

Individual physicians' offices will continue to be an important locus of care in a society that prides itself on free enterprise, competition, and independence of the individual (Saward, 1977, p. 202). Depending on the location, population served, and medical specialty, various forms of practice will be available including solo practice, team practice, and corporate or multispecialty practice. The classical fee-for-service payment that has shaped the present form of the medical profession will be available to those who can pay; however, the fees will be directed to the service given, not the provider giving the service. Payments will also come by way of some future form of comprehensive health insurance in an attempt to make health care accessible to all.

The image of the "office nurse" will take on a new meaning. With the tremendous demands anticipated in response to a "paid-for" health service, nurse practitioners are ideal as the first lineup for individuals entering the health care system. These nurses have demonstrated their skill in performing many of the technical procedures in physicians' practices, have managed follow-up for patients with chronic illnesses, and have provided preventive services, health education, and patient counseling. These primary care nursing services have been found to be acceptable to patients and physicians (Institute of Medicine, 1978b). Such a track record supports the rationale for physicians opening their practices to a nurse-partner, thereby satisfying the attributes of comprehensive primary care.

Health maintenance organizations

Another form of ambulatory care established around health care providers that has evolved over the last decade is the health maintenance organization (HMO). As an organized system in a geographical area responsible for the health care of all its members, the HMO provides voluntary, multiple-choice enrollment for its members and is financed by fixed, periodic payments that cover all health care regardless of how often services are used. The HMO provides the services of primary care health professionals, including primary physicians, specialists, nurses, and support services (Saward, 1977, p. 201; Fromer, 1979, p. 32).

The implied promise of health maintenance is that preventive services will result in lower hospital use by subscribers and, therefore, will curb health care expenditures in this country. Unfortunately, this has not been the case to date. Klarman (1977, p. 230) pointed out that the basis for decreased hospitalization of HMO enrollees has not been established. He also noted that HMOs do not provide more preventive services than do other forms of health care delivery.

Another problem with HMOs is that this plan discriminates against the poor, who are either unable to get into the system at standard rates or are forced to accept fewer services than they need. This is incongruous because the needs of the urban poor for health services are significantly greater than those of other urban residents. HMO clients also tend to complain about the difficulty of establishing a personal relationship with a physician who cannot usually be seen quickly when the need arises (Wildavsky, 1977, p. 113). In fact, physicians in HMOs work fewer hours than do physicians in private practice. With a predicted physician oversupply in the future, short workdays may be the pattern of future physician practices.

In spite of the problems, it is too soon to give up on the HMO. As noted by Saward (1977), the HMO is "one of the viable choices for Americans, . . . a constructive alternative to the direct governmental provision of health services" (p. 202). This prepaid system, moreover, provides an accessible environment for the consumer to assume the responsibility for the outcomes of health-related behavior, while making available a wide range of health-illness services suitable for the well, the worried well, the early sick, and the sick (Yahle, 1977, p. 489). The nursing practitioner has a special opportunity in this system by being available when a consumer need arises and by assisting individuals to adopt healthful behavior. The HMO is the only organized health system with the goal of health visible in its name; however, it has not been around long enough to prove its efficacy.

Community ambulatory care

The health care of communities can be envisioned in three ways: aggregate, family, and individual. Examples that encompass these views and dictate nursing practice are public (community) health, mental health, occupational health, student health, and health of the elderly citizen.

Community health

Community (public) health nurses will continue to assess the health and health care needs of populations in collaboration with other disciplines, as well as identify aggregates, groups, families, and individuals at increased risk of illness, disability, or premature death. Responsive plans of action will be consistent with the needs and expectations of the community, the available scientific knowledge and resources, the clients' understanding and participation, and the standards of nursing practice. It is interesting to note that there has been an increase in employment of public-community health nurses in recent years (Moses and Roth, 1979), and this trend will likely continue.

The public health nurse works with community leaders, health-related groups, groups at risk, families, and individuals, and becomes involved in relevant social action to achieve the health goals of the community. Nursing practice in this setting involves community assessment, case finding, and referral to other agencies to ensure comprehensive health and welfare services. In the future, public health nurses will need to become more involved singularly and as a group with government officials at all levels, and also to take responsibility for promoting health of the population by speaking out on such issues as safety and product regulation, firearms regulation, sanitation, and pollution control. Future health care will not depend on individualized health plans, but rather on plans that involve communities, where health changes are seen as vital statistics. In communication with nursing specialists who work with individual/family clients, the public health nurse is the ideal professional to represent the nursing view in policy decisions.

The community health nurse, who practices both in the clinic and in the home, will experience many of the same challenges that face nurses in other clinic settings. One difference is that the clientele of the public health clinic are traditionally of a lower socioeconomic status than populations enrolled in an HMO or private physician's practice. Since clients attend the clinic in geographical proximity to their home, and since the community health nurse is familiar with this environment, individualized and practical health prescriptions can be developed,

evaluated, and revised. The home will likely continue to be the major practice base for the visiting nurse working in collaboration with the community health nurse and other health team members.

Nursing practitioners in community mental health centers have precedence and a promising future. "There is nothing on the horizon to suggest any diminution of life stresses; therefore, psychological and psychiatric disturbances will continue to be a major source of demand for care" (Eisenberg, 1977, p. 241). Over the past twenty years the number of outpatient episodes of care provided for by mental health facilities have increased fivefold, whereas the length of each stay in institutions has been dramatically shortened (Eisenberg, 1977, p. 240).

Reducing the length of stay for patients in mental hospitals does avoid the problem of chronic patienthood, but it also generates the possibility of poor patient adaptation in the community. This problem exists now as reflected in the high readmission rates of former patients to institutions. The challenge, then, is for the institutional psychiatric nurse and the community mental health nurse to work together for the successful orientation of the client to society.

Practitioners in community health centers have a unique opportunity to work with populations at risk, contribute to the resolution of neighborhood crises, and plan for improved mental health for the community (Sherrow, 1977). Nurses will need to increase their sensitivity to the culture, language, values, and traditions of diverse populations and use paraprofessionals who reside in the community to assist them in helping the people accept and use strategies for health. Stress will be a normal part of life in the next century, as it is now, and people will have to continue to learn how to cope.

Occupational health

A safe assumption is that corporations will always be interested in higher employee productivity, increased work attendance, reduction in workers' compensation claims, and improved "health age'' of their workers. Thus the workplace constitutes a site for implementing programs for environmental and physical safety, health screening, disease prevention, on-the-job emergency care, minor illness treatment, and health promotion. Government mandates for occupational safety and growing public awareness of environmental health and human rights support the need for occupational health nursing.

Many of the more than 97 million American workers are exposed to some kind of occupational health hazard such as carcinogenic agents, pulmonary or other physical disease incitants, or job-related pressures including noise, crowding, stress, boredom, and unsafe environments resulting in injuries (*Healthy People,* 1979, p. 107). The impact of the work environment on the health of employees has been known for many decades, and the time has come for increasing efforts to control known hazards, treat those afflicted, and develop techniques to identify and prevent harm from materials and processes not currently recognized as dangerous (*Healthy People,* 1979, p. 110).

Occupational health nursing is not new; it has simply begun to receive more government and public attention. According to a 1977 survey (Moses and Roth, 1979), the number of occupational health nurses has increased by twenty-one percent over a five-year period, suggesting that nursing's role in this setting is expanding. Ideally, the occupational health nurse will assume the major role in planning and evaluating occupational health programs in collaboration with labor and management, the workers, and members of the community health team (Keller, 1979, p. 436). Prevention is the underlying theme. Health hazard appraisals (see pp. 329-330) should be done for every worker at the beginning of employment, with follow-up plans and periodic reassessment. These data plus the information gleaned from the history and physical examination provide the facts for individualized health plans and the baseline against which changes can be measured. As will be discussed later, the worksite lends itself to health promotion–health

education programs including nutrition, weight reduction, exercise, stress management, smoking-cessation programs, and so forth. Nursing's potential impact here is far-reaching.

Student health

A major way to improve the health status of the American people is to begin with the young people. Nursing has already responded to the health needs of this group, as witnessed by the fact that the number of nurses employed in student health services between 1972 and 1977 increased by one third (Moses and Roth, 1979). But numbers do not necessarily represent the scope and depth of practice, and it is toward this end that school nursing must expand.

The current state of student health programs at all levels—elementary, high school, and higher education—leaves much to be desired. Knowles (1977, p. 60) reports:

School health programs are abysmal at best, confining themselves to preemptory sick calls and posters on brushing teeth and eating three meals a day; there are no examinations to determine if anything's been learned. Awareness of danger to body and mind is not acquired until the mid-twenties in our culture . . . children tire of "scrub your teeth," "don't eat that junk," "leave your dingy alone," "go to bed" and "get some exercise." By the time they are sixteen, society says they shall have cars, drink beer, smoke, eat junk at drive-ins, and have a go at fornication.

The health problems of the younger generation are real and, for the most part, preventable. For example, forty-five percent of total childhood mortality is a result of accidents, and common problems in younger people are intellectual, behavioral, and emotional disorders including learning difficulties, behavioral disturbances, and speech and vision problems (*Healthy People,* 1979, p. 33). Common health problems of adolescents and young adults include violent death, injury, alcohol and drug abuse, unwanted pregnancies, and sexually transmissible diseases. Three quarters of all deaths in this age group result from accidents, homicides, and suicides (*Healthy People*, 1979, p. 43).

Public Law 94-142 has guaranteed the availability of free, appropriate public education for all handicapped children and adolescents, thereby putting a severe strain on the existing educational system and its personnel. Under this law, services including counseling, physical recreation, athletics, health services, and recreational activities must be provided to affected eligible students regardless of the handicap (MacDonough, 1979, p. 339). There are important implications for collaborative efforts of the school health nurse with teachers, administrators, families, and community resources.

If resolution of the health problems of school-aged people is to be achieved, schools and communities must take the initiative in establishing a system of primary health care within the school setting, and this must be a national effort if any impact is to be recognized. School nurses educated as nurse practitioners are best qualified for this role. Backed by a supervising physician working in the community, these nurses will be able to manage problems of minor trauma and most episodic acute illnesses. Moreover, nurses can provide physical examinations, screen for health problems, immunize against preventable disease, work with physicians and parents in caring for young people with chronic disease, and offer health education and counseling for students, parents, and teachers.

Students can learn early in life about what health care facilities are available in the community, how to use them, and how to evaluate the services they receive. Moreover, students must learn how to participate in their own health care, how to ask appropriate questions about suggested treatment, and how to make intelligent decisions regarding personal health (MacDonough, 1979, p. 402).

Elderly citizens' health

The geriatric nurse practitioner, described earlier in this chapter, has an important role with ambulatory elderly clients. Fortunately, not all people over

sixty-five years of age in this country are candidates for institutionalization and, therefore, other alternatives for care must be provided. Life expectancy has increased as formerly disabling diseases have been conquered. Accordingly, by the year 2000, the number of persons over sixty-five will have risen by fifty percent (Eisenberg, 1977, p. 241). "Yesterday's victims of tuberculosis are today's geriatric cases. The Paradox of Time is that success lies in the past and (possibly) the future, but never the present" (Wildavsky, 1977, p. 106).

In general, the focus of health care in this country has been to help people add "years to life." Less emphasis, however, has been directed toward the concept of adding "life to years." In short, the older people of our country are a forgotten generation without employment, on limited income and assets, with few personal and social resources, with limited physical abilities, and with a high likelihood of becoming sick. There are valid economic as well as humanitarian reasons for the public to be concerned about these older citizens, and every effort must be put forth to prevent the development of unnecessary dependency (Institute of Medicine, 1977, p. 5).

It must be emphasized that only five percent of the elderly in our country reside in institutions, and those who are recovering from illness will return to the community. The majority of the elderly, moreover, are vigorous and completely independent, whereas approximately forty-five percent have certain activity limitations as a result of physical handicaps caused by heart conditions, arthritis, hearing loss, and visual impairment, and some due to mental disabilities (Institute of Medicine, 1977, p. 74). There is a sizeable population of elderly people who, with professional help, can perform at their highest functional capacity on physical, psychological, and social levels. In this regard a number of laudable health and social efforts have already been initiated on behalf of the elderly, including senior citizens' rehabilitation centers, day hospitals, congregate dining facilities, as well as individual services such as foster care, housekeeping, home health services, and meals-on-wheels (Institute of Medicine, 1978a, p. 17). A relatively new movement for elderly that will receive attention here is the concept of geriatric day care, also called adult day care. The unique feature of this type of center is that it provides for the older citizen as a whole person throughout the day, using a broad range of community services that enable the elderly to remain in their homes for as long as possible, thereby encouraging freedom to exercise individual initiative (Weiler and Rathbone-McCuan, 1978, p. 4).

The staff of the geriatric day-care center may include social workers, adult educators, recreation workers, dieticians, craftspeople, and musicians; however, it is the geriatric nurse practitioner who coordinates the multidisciplinary approach for the long-term needs of each enrollee. Each day is planned for each individual based on functional assessment data, and each service has a therapeutic objective: prevention, maintenance, or rehabilitation. In collaboration with the community health nurse and the physician, the geriatric nurse practitioner can adapt the center to the local health care delivery system and contribute to the quality of life of the geriatric population.

Rural and underserved population health

There are 34 million people in this country who are classified as underserved, half of whom live in urban settings, the remainder in rural areas (Institute of Medicine, 1979). These people fare much worse than the rest of the population, with higher mortality rates, higher incidence of major diseases, and less availability of medical services (Kalisch, 1978). Ways must be developed to help underserved neighborhoods in the inner city to capitalize on their locations and become affiliated with local hospitals that can offer advanced medical and nursing training, provide backup and referral services, and plan projects in collaboration with the community health agency. With local government and hospital support, this is possible. The role of the community nurse planner and practitioner in this setting has already been described.

The rural area presents other problems. For one, physicians are unlikely to locate in these areas, and this trend will continue. One government-sponsored response to this situation is the National Health Service Corps, which through a loan-forgiveness program assigns physicians, nurses, and other health providers to underserved rural areas for a specified limited period of time. Although health personnel change frequently in these clinics, the program does produce a source of health care for the people. This program seems to be progressing well; therefore, there will be no incentive to change it unless a better alternative comes along. Primary care is the focus and the nurse practitioner will continue as the model of practice.

The Rural Health Clinic Services Act of 1977 (PL 95-210) is another recent government response for providing health care to rural people. Instead of reimbursing physicians for health care, this act provides a way for nurse practitioners and physician assistants to serve as the primary health care providers with physician backup, and to be paid for these services through Medicaid and Medicare. In the opinion of an Institute of Medicine Committee on Manpower (1978b), rural populations of 4,000 or less are adequately and economically served by nurse practitioners or physician assistants.

One concern with the rural clinic initiative is that only 353 of the 1,500 clinics in the rural areas of this country are participating, after more than two years of legislative implementation (Lane, 1980). Clearly, more evaluation is needed to assess the type and quality of health services being rendered, reimbursement methods and rates, and clinic availability and accessibility. Rural populations are a high-risk group, with poverty and poor education compounding the problem. Therefore, in addition to bringing health care providers to the people, other innovations must be considered that will bring the people to health care providers. Rotating individuals in a community to come to a teaching hospital to learn about health care, better roads and bus systems, "life" flight helicopters—the exploration of alternatives for rural health care delivery has just begun.

HEALTH PROMOTION

This chapter has thus far focused on the provider-oriented organizational settings for health care delivery, with an emphasis on the scope of nursing practice now and in the future. Nursing's role in disease prevention has been discussed with reference to the concept of health promotion, that is, keeping well people healthy and preventing premature onset of disease. This section is devoted to the concept of healthy people and is divided into three areas. The first section will offer definitions of health; the second will describe the concept of health promotion; and the third will delineate goals and examples of strategies for a nationally organized program for health promotion.

Meaning of health

In the American society, health and illness have become symbols for many positively and negatively valued biological, physical, social, cultural, and metaphysical phenomena (Fox, 1977, p. 14). For example, it is not unusual to hear circumstances described as a "healthy state of affairs," or a "sick system." The concept of health invokes a reality that is regarded as eminently desirable. "When one is in 'good health' it is not even noticed; when one is not, it is desperately desired" (Callahan, 1977, p. 25).

It seems to be taken for granted that everyone knows what health is. Attempts have been made, however, to try and give the term some substance. For example, the World Health Organization defined health as "a state of complete physical, mental, and social well-being and not merely the absence of disease or infirmity." The emphasis on "complete" in this definition puts health care providers and society in the untenable position of being required to attain the unattainable (Callahan, 1977, p. 26). Instead, *health* is an individual phenomenon describing a person's ability to adapt to biological, psychological, and social changes in a manner that allows the individual to function at an optimal level of well-being in his or her environment. Following this thinking, *wellness* is described as a dynamic state in which an individual progresses toward a higher level of functioning, thus maximizing his or her potential in the environment. *Fitness,* then, is simply the attainment of wellness on a continuing basis.

Health promotion concept

If one reviews the health history of the United States, it becomes clear that the major reasons for the improvement in health levels of the people in the eighteenth and nineteenth centuries were improved nutrition and sanitary conditions. In this century immunizations were added to the formula. There is little evidence, however, that shows specific treatment measures as affecting the overall health levels of the population (Jonas, 1979). That is not to say that effective treatments are not necessary. Indeed they are, and they should be made available to those in need. The point here is that modern science has conquered infectious disease through prevention and has been unable to conquer the existence of chronic disease. Thus the people of this country still die of heart disease, cancer, and stroke, as well as catastrophic events.

This does not imply that Americans are a sick lot. Quite the opposite is true. Americans have never been healthier than they are now. For example, this country's infant mortality rate, the mortality rate for children aged one to fourteen years, and deaths from heart disease have been cut dramatically from the rates in former years. Furthermore, the expected life span for Americans has increased in the past decade by 2.7 years (*Healthy People,* 1979, p. 5). Prevention has played a key role in these accomplishments.

Even though this country possesses an advanced technology, substantial financial resources, and a skilled health work force, it still lags behind several other industrial nations in the health status of its citizens (*Healthy People,* 1979, p. 6):

Twelve others do better in preventing death from cancer.

Twenty-six others have a lower death rate from circulatory disease.

Eleven others do a better job of keeping babies alive in the first year of life.

Fourteen others have a higher level of life expectancy for men, and six others have a higher level for women.

There is serious concern over the escalating health care costs in this nation, with a health bill of over $200 billion. Hospitals and medical care account for the major portion of this bill. Alternative models of care within current financial possibilities must be developed, and such models must promote prevention and health and maximize the contributions of nursing care.

More than ninety-nine percent of American people are born healthy and suffer premature death and disability as a result of personal misbehavior and environmental conditions (Knowles, 1977, p. 79). For example, a large percentage of deaths resulting from cardiovascular disease and cancer are premature when they occur in relatively young individuals. Dietary factors, cigarette smoking, potentially treatable but undetected hypertension, and lack of exercise contribute to this premature onset, and these bad habits are preventable. Deaths resulting from homicide, accidents, and suicide are theoretically preventable. This also applies to obesity, alcoholism, improper nutrition, promiscuous sex, and other high-risk states that predispose one to illness.

This means that if health promotion is to occur in the United States, individuals will have to forsake bad habits and adopt a life-style that contributes to health and the enjoyment of living. One study (Belloc and Breslow, 1972; Belloc, 1973) showed that life expectancy and health are significantly related to the following simple habits:

1. Three meals a day at regular times and no snacking
2. Breakfast every day
3. Moderate exercise two or three times a week
4. Adequate sleep (seven to eight hours a night)
5. No smoking
6. Moderate weight
7. No alcohol or only in moderation

This life-style resulted in a difference of eleven years in longevity for men and seven years for women beginning at the age of forty-five (Breslow, 1979). Thus the individual has the power to maintain his or her own health by observing these prudent rules of behavior. The challenge is, and will continue to be, convincing Americans to adopt healthy behavior.

Health promotion goals and strategies

Helping the American people to improve their health is the overall goal of the future. Clearly, such an awesome task will have to be achieved in an incremental and organized fashion through the identification of priority interventions and specification of practical and measurable goals. Such a plan has already been put forth in *Healthy People* (1979). Based on this country's recent mortality trends for each age group, the rates achieved in other countries with resources similar to this country, and the likelihood that a reasonable, affordable effort can make the end points achievable, the following goals were recommended:

1. To continue to improve infant health, and by 1990 to reduce infant mortality by at least thirty-two percent, to fewer than 9 deaths per 1,000 live births (p. 21)
2. To improve child health, foster optimal childhood development, and, by 1990, reduce deaths among children aged one to fourteen years by at least twenty percent, to fewer than 34 per 100,000 (p. 33)
3. To improve the health and health habits of adolescents and young adults, and, by 1990, to reduce deaths among people aged fifteen to twenty-four by at least twenty percent, to fewer than 93 per 100,000 (p. 43)
4. To improve the health of adults, and, by 1990, to reduce deaths among people aged twenty-five to sixty-four by at least twenty-five percent to fewer than 400 per 100,000 (p. 53)
5. To improve the health and quality of life for older adults and, by 1990, to reduce the average annual number of days of restricted activity resulting from acute and chronic condi-

tions by twenty percent, to fewer than thirty days per year for people aged sixty-five years and older (p. 71)

Although the deadline of 1990 may be a little ambitious for the achievement of these goals, the directions are desirable and the end points are necessary. Accomplishing these goals will require thorough diagnosis and planning in order to determine the best strategy for individuals, groups, families, and communities. Moreover, these plans will never be implemented without political, business, and economic support, and positive attitudes about health on the part of consumers. In this regard there are three classifications of strategies that comprise the health promotion effort: (1) preventive health services; (2) environmental protection; and (3) health education. As has been alluded to throughout this chapter, nursing has and will continue to have major responsibilities in these three areas.

Preventive health services

Americans are accustomed to contacting the health care system when they feel sick. Health education programs must be geared to inform the public of the importance of preventive health services, which are designed for different age and risk groups and are continually being modified as new procedures become available and obsolete measures are deleted. In this regard, Breslow and Somers (1977) have recommended a Lifetime Health-Monitoring Program that is age specific, practical, and cost efficient. This program uses clinical and epidemiological criteria to identify health goals and criteria for ten age groups.

Services that promote the health of infants and aim to ensure a good birth weight are primarily directed toward the pregnant mother. In this case, physical, emotional, dental, and social health are assessed, with plans for their restoration or maintenance. Decisions about the necessity for diagnostic procedures such as amniocentesis are made and parents are prepared for the birth event and parenting responsibilities. Examples of postnatal preventive services are instilling silver nitrate in the eyes

of the newborn to prevent eye infection if the mother has active gonorrhea, and administering Rh-immune globin to an Rh-negative mother after the birth of an Rh-positive baby.

Services that are directed toward improving child health include immunization, early dental diagnosis and care, and well-baby care, with emphasis on early diagnosis of developmental disorders related to physical development, learning, vision, hearing, and mental status. Nurses will be especially involved in these services in pediatricians' offices, in clinics, and in schools.

The package of tested preventive health services for the adolescent and young adult is comparatively smaller than that available for the other age groups. As a matter of fact, "adolescents typically see a physician less often than younger children do and much less often than adults do" (Brown, 1979, p. 338). Although the overall mortality in the adolescent age group is comparatively low, health problems occur usually in the forms of unhealthy lifestyles and emotional stress rather than with physical diseases. The school health nurse in high schools and institutions of higher education is in a position to keep in contact with the young people in these settings. The nurse can administer booster immunizations and assess the young person's health risk status.

Appraisal of health risk factors and the counseling of individuals concerning those risks are important components of health care. Although often used as a part of the periodic health examination, *health risk appraisal* has been formalized into a concept based on the fact that a person faces a greater probability than the rest of the population for developing certain health problems because of age, sex, race, heredity, and life-style. When these factors are combined with information from a client's medical history, physical examination, laboratory studies, and x-rays, the health care provider is able to determine the health risk of each patient. When comparing these prognostic characteristics with the experience of other patients, the risk can be quantified and the client may be counseled on how to avoid illness. If the client responds, significant improvement in health (i.e., reduction in health risk factors) can occur. Health risk assessment is important for all age groups. In this regard, health hazard appraisal questionnaires are now available on the open market. It is important to note, however, that further research is necessary on these questionnaires before the instrument can be accepted as a reliable longitudinal measure of risk (Sacks, et al., 1980).

Adults between the ages of twenty-five and sixty-four are considered an at-risk group and health hazard appraisal is an important service. As they grow older these people are affected by heart attacks and strokes; therefore, the primary care nurse must search for contributing risk factors through history and laboratory data. Such factors are smoking, hypertension, elevated cholesterol, diabetes, obesity, physical inactivity, personality patterns, and so forth. Cancer also has a relatively high incidence in this age group. Therefore, risk factors of alcohol ingestion, diet, smoking, radiation, sunlight and occupational exposures, air and water pollution, and heredity are noted. Essential screening services for these people are blood pressure check, breast exam, and Papanicolaou smear. Preventive dental services are particularly important at this time since periodontal disease and tooth loss increase with age. Routine examination and professional removal of tooth plaque by a dentist are necessary services for the maintenance of dental health.

Preventive services for older adults cover immunization for influenza and pneumonia and regular health checkups. Services to maintain independence should be provided. Activities in this regard have been described elsewhere.

Environmental protection

"The American environment today contains health hazards with the potential to kill, injure and disable individuals and substantially affect the health of entire communities" (*Healthy People*, 1979, p. 101). Until political leaders at national, state, and local levels develop and support health and safety standards that protect their citizens, there will be little hope of achieving better health for Americans in spite of outstanding programs of preventive health services and health education.

Environmental measures to provide for healthy infants begin by protecting pregnant mothers from exposure to radiation and chemicals in the workplace, and continue with inspection laws for toys, equipment, and infant clothes. Measures for child health protection provide for fluoridation of the community water supply, as well as safe features for homes, schools, and recreational facilities.

Environmental protection services for adolescents and young adults require improvements in roadway safety, car safety, and firearms control. Athletic equipment with safety features is essential for young as well as older athletes. This action appears especially important in the face of the more than 2 million sports-related injuries a year, with football, baseball, and basketball contributing 400,000 of them (U.S. Consumer Product Safety Commission, 1977).

Worksite safety and health measures are programs designed for the adult population and have been discussed in the section on occupational health. Such measures include control of toxic and infectious agents in the environment and construction of safe places of work that provide sanitary working conditions. Outside of the occupational setting, safe housing, roads, air, food, medicine, water, cars, and equipment at home afford a protective environment for all citizens.

In consideration of older adults, home safety is a prime consideration. Furthermore, as a group that is often victimized by social deviants, these elderly people must be assured of police protection in their neighborhoods and the surrounding area.

Health education

"Health education is any combination of learning experiences designed to facilitate voluntary adaptations of behavior conducive to health" (Green, et al., 1980, p. 7). In other words, consumers are participating under their own direction in determining their health practices. Fromer (1979, p. 23) points out that the uninformed consumer is a threat to the health care system because people who cannot, or will not, accept this responsibility endanger their own health and place a drain on the entire system. "The greatest potential for improving the health of the American people . . . is to be found in what people do and don't do, to and for themselves" (Fuchs, 1968, p. 285).

Although health behavior is considered a voluntary activity, there are circumstances when health behavior should be mandatory, such as providing smoking and nonsmoking sections in public facilities, maintaining a speed limit for cars of fifty-five miles per hour, and requiring immunizations for admission to school. When a behavior has been judged by society as a whole to be hazardous to the common good, curtailment of individual choice is warranted (Green, et al., 1980). Thus the imposition of rigid criteria for appropriate health behavior is justifiable under certain circumstances.

The fundamental objective of health education programs is to intervene in the process of development and change in such a manner as to maintain positive health behavior or to interrupt a behavioral pattern that is linked to increased risks for illness, injury, disability, or death (Green, et al., 1980, p. 10). Such programs, moreover, must take into consideration the beliefs, values, attitudes, socioeconomic resources, educational levels, support systems, and availability of health care resources for the given population. Although many people are aware of the "dos and don'ts" of personal health behavior, their readiness to act on that knowledge can be lacking. Thus motivation is an essential factor in a successful health education effort. Reinforcement of health education must also be incorporated into the program if favorable outcomes are to be achieved (Vickery, 1979, p. 89).

Health professionals have a responsibility to contribute to consumers' education, but so do business and other professional groups (Fromer, 1979, p. 24). Mass media, insurance companies, schools,

industry, and corporations must join together with health professions to ensure desired outcomes of health promotion programs in this country.

All age groups are amenable to health education and a variety of available educational methodologies can be selected and tailored for specific needs. Green and associates (1980, p. 107) provide a list of recommended strategies, including lectures, individual instruction, programmed learning, skill development, inquiry learning, peer-group discussion, modeling, behavior modification, community development, social action, simulations and games, mass media, audiovisual aids, educational television, social planning, and organizational change. These can be used singly or in combination.

In providing for healthy infants, educational programs can be directed toward parents by increasing knowledge about parenthood, genetic counseling, maternal habits, prenatal nutrition, breast-feeding, and pediatric care. Further, safety and accident prevention must be learned and practiced by parents of infants and young children. Informed parents can acquire skills of observation in order to detect early signs of growth and development problems. Follow-up contact with the health care system by concerned parents will give the affected child the benefit of preventive measures or early treatment. Parents and schools also have an opportunity to initiate and reinforce healthy habits in children with special attention to nutrition and exercise.

Adolescents are in desperate need of health education programs that address self-esteem, self-discipline, stress management, and responsibilities for fellow citizens. Other important programs for this age group seek to modify behavior as it relates to smoking, drinking alcohol, eating unbalanced diets, and physical inactivity. With modifications for age appeal, all these health education programs are appropriate for the adult group.

Finally, older citizens can learn ways to remain functionally independent. Exercise and nutrition programs for this group are essential. Recognizing that they are a high-risk group for illness, the elderly should maintain a relationship with the health care system so as to prevent premature onset of disability, or at least facilitate remediation early in the course of the disease.

If the five goals set forth in *Healthy People* (1979) are ever to be achieved in this century and the next, health promotion and disease prevention programs must be initiated, tested, revised, and continued. If the promise of healthy people eventually evolves, new incentives for financing preventive health care will develop, and make this kind of health care available to all. This has particular significance for nursing. The time is coming when health promotion, a traditional activity of nursing, will receive the visibility and recognition it deserves. Financial autonomy is a long-desired goal of nursing, and health promotion is a realistic means to this end.

SUMMARY

This chapter has reviewed broadly organizational settings for nursing practice, with a focus on those that are currently operating or developing and have a high likelihood of continuing in the future. Nursing practice in the settings of hospitals and community health institutions were described. The nursing role in ambulatory settings was presented, including the settings organized around health care providers, the community, rural, and underserved populations. Finally, the concept of health promotion was explored, with a view of its subcomponents of preventive health services, environmental protection, and health education.

Farsighted nurses will recognize the opportunities that lie ahead and will prepare for this time. The future, like the present, will offer nursing challenges, satisfactions, and disappointments. Accepting the former and adapting to the latter will make progress possible. For nursing, progress has been a way of life.

REFERENCES

Aiken, L.H.: Introduction: alternative care models. In Aiken, L.H., and others: Nursing's influence on health policy for the eighties, Kansas City, Mo., 1979, Publication No. G-134 3M, American Academy of Nursing, pp. 13-35.

Amado, A., Cronk, B.A., and Mileo, R.: Cost of terminal care: home hospice vs. hospital, Nurs. Outlook **27:**522-526, Aug. 1979.

Belloc, N.B.: Health practices and mortality, Prev. Med. **2:**67-81, March 1973.

Belloc, N.B., and Breslow, L.: Relationship of physical status and health practices, Prev. Med. **1:**409-421, Aug. 1972.

Breslow, L.: A positive strategy for the nation's health, J.A.M.A. **242:**2093-2095, Nov. 1979.

Breslow, L., and Somers, A.R.: The lifetime health-monitoring program, N. Engl. J. Med. **296:**601-608, March 17, 1977.

Brown, S.S.: The health needs of adolescents. In Healthy people: the Surgeon General's report on health promotion and disease prevention, DHEW Publication No. (PHS) 79-55071A, Washington, D.C., 1979, U.S. Government Printing Office.

Callahan, D.: Health and society: some ethical imperatives. In Knowles, J.H., editor: Doing better and feeling worse: health in the United States, New York, 1977, W.W. Norton & Co., Inc.

Christman, L.: Leadership in practice, Image **12:**31-33, June 1980.

Cousins, N.: Anatomy of an illness (as perceived by the patient), N. Engl. J. Med. **295:**1458-1463, Dec. 1976.

Davis, A.J.: Nursing's influence on health policy for the eighties. In Aiken, L.H., and others: Nursing's influence on health policy for the eighties, Kansas City, Mo., 1979, Publication No. G-134 3M, American Academy of Nursing, pp. 3-17.

Eisenberg, L.: The search for care. In Knowles, J.H., editor: Doing better and feeling worse: health in the United States, New York, 1977, W.W. Norton & Co., Inc.

Faison, J.B., et al.: The childbearing center: an alternative birth setting, Obstet. Gynecol. **54:**527-532, Oct. 1979.

Finnerty, F.A., Jr.: The nurse's role in treating hypertension, N. Engl. J. Med. **293:**93-94, 1975.

Finnerty, F.A., Jr.: Use of paramedical personnel in treating hypertension. In Carlson, R., editor: Future directions in health care: a new public policy, Cambridge, Mass., 1978, Ballinger Publishing Co.

Fox, R.C.: The medicalization and demedicalization of American society. In Knowles, J.H., editor: Doing better and feeling worse: health in the United States, New York, 1977, W.W. Norton & Co., Inc.

Fromer, M.J., editor: Community health care and the nursing process, St. Louis, 1979, The C.V. Mosby Co.

Fuchs, V.R.: An economist prescribes for medicine, Med. Econ. **45:**271-286, Feb. 5, 1968.

Green, L.W., et al.: Health education planning: a diagnostic approach, Palo Alto, Calif., 1980, Mayfield Publishing Co.

Healthy people: the Surgeon General's report on health promotion and disease prevention, DHEW Publication No. (PHS) 79-55071A, Washington, D.C., 1979, U.S. Government Printing Office.

Institute of Medicine: A policy statement: the elderly and functional dependency, Washington, D.C., 1977, National Academy of Sciences.

Institute of Medicine: Aging and medical education, Washington, D.C., 1978a, National Academy of Sciences.

Institute of Medicine: A manpower policy for primary health care, Washington, D.C., 1978b, National Academy of Sciences.

Institute of Medicine: Physicians and new health practitioners: issues for the 1980's, Washington, D.C., 1979, National Academy of Sciences.

Jonas, S.: Hospitals adopt new role, Hospitals **53**:84-86, Oct. 1979.

Kalisch, B.J.: The promise of power, Nurs. Outlook **26**:42-46, Jan. 1978.

Keller, M.J.: Health needs and nursing care of the labor force. In Fromer, M.J., editor: Community health care and the nursing process, St. Louis, 1979, The C.V. Mosby Co.

Klarman, H.E.: The financing of health care. In Knowles, J.H., editor: Doing better and feeling worse: health in the United States, New York, 1977, W.W. Norton & Co., Inc.

Knowles, J.H.: The responsibility of the individual. In Knowles, J.H., editor: Doing better and feeling worse: health in the United States, New York, 1977, W.W. Norton & Co., Inc.

Krant, M.J.: The hospice movement, N. Engl. J. Med. **299**:546-549, Sept. 1978.

Lack, S.A.: Hospice—a concept of care in the final stage of life, Conn. Med. **43**(6):367, 1979.

Lane, N. (President, Small Town Futures, Inc.): Personal communication, May 2, 1980.

MacDonough, G.P.: School nursing. In Fromer, M.J., editor: Community health care and the nursing process, St. Louis, 1979, The C.V. Mosby Co.

Moses, E., and Roth, A.: Nursepower, Am. J. Nurs. **79**:1745-1756, Oct. 1979.

Queenan, J.R.: Two systems appraised, Contemp. OB/GYN **14**:7-8, Nov. 1979.

Sacks, J.J., Krushat, W.M., and Newman, J.: Reliability of the health hazard appraisal, Am. J. Public Health **70**:730-732, July 1980.

Saward, E.W.: Institutional organization, incentives, and change. In Knowles, J.H., editor: Doing better and feeling worse: health in the United States, New York, 1977, W.W. Norton & Co., Inc.

Sherrow, V.: A multifamily approach to neighborhood crisis intervention. In Hall, J.E., and Weaver, B.R., editors: Distributive nursing practice: a system approach to community health, Philadelphia, 1977, J.B. Lippincott Co.

Smoyak, S.A.: Toward a model for future health care systems. In Abdellah, F.G., and others: Models for health care delivery: now and for the future, Kansas City, Mo., 1975, Publication No. 6-119, American Academy of Nursing, pp. 1-43.

Toffler, A.: Future shock, New York, 1970, Random House, Inc.

U.S. Consumer Product Safety Commission, NEISS data highlights, **1**(6):2-3, Washington, D.C., 1977, Consumer Product Safety Commission.

Vickery, D.M.: Is it a change for the better? Hospitals **53**:87, Oct. 1979.

Weiler, P.G., and Rathbone-McCuan, E.: Adult day care, New York, 1978, Springer Publishing Co.

Wildavsky, A.: Doing better and feeling worse: the political pathology of health policy. In Knowles, J.H., editor: Doing better and feeling worse: health in the United States, New York, 1977, W.W. Norton & Co., Inc.

Yahle, M.E.: Distributive nursing practice in a health maintenance organization. In Hall, J.E., and Weaver, B.R., editors: Distributive nursing practice: a system approach to community health, Philadelphia, 1977, J.B. Lippincott Co.

To survive on the earth, human beings require the stable, continuing existence of a suitable environment. Yet the evidence is overwhelming that the way in which we now live on the earth is driving its thin, life-supporting skin and ourselves with it, to destruction. . . . Biologically, human beings participate in the environmental system as subsidiary parts of the whole. Yet, human society is designed to exploit the environment as a whole, to produce wealth. The paradoxical role we play in the natural environment—at once participant and exploiter— distorts our perception of it.

Commoner, Barry: The Closing Circle: Nature, Man and Technology, 1971, p. 11. Copyright Alfred A. Knopf, Inc.

20

TOWARD AN ECOLOGICAL PERSPECTIVE: IMPLICATIONS FOR THE NURSE AS A CHANGE AGENT

Jeanette Lancaster

Few would question that phenomenal technological advancements have been made in the twentieth century. A large number of social and health care advancements have influenced nursing and necessitated rapid changes in the scope as well as in the characteristics of practice arenas. The future of nursing depends largely on how the profession responds to social, environmental, political, and cultural changes. This book focuses on the nurse as an effector of change; simultaneously mechanisms must increasingly be implemented by nurses to deal with changes that they do not initiate. It would be naive to assume that nursing will always be the originator of change, in that the practice of nursing inevitably takes place within an organizational context in interaction with a variety of consumers and providers.

The premise in this chapter is that a new conceptual model can be utilized to allow nursing as a profession to respond to varying pressures and stresses. Nurses must increasingly maximize their coping capacities in order to move forward in the face of rapid societal change. Hence an ecological approach is suggested as one conceptualization of an interactional pattern to promote homeostasis between nursing and society. It is necessary that nursing as a profession continue to progress toward a more refined conceptual orientation. This is not to imply that only one conceptual approach is ultimately the goal of nursing. Rather, an ecological approach is set forth as a viable model for viewing the interaction between nursing and the environment in which practice occurs; such an approach represents progress in understanding the complex arena in which nursing care is provided.

The word progress comes from the Latin verb *progredior,* which means "going forward." Nursing must move forward as a profession in a thoughtful manner while carefully examining the consequences of progress. Frequently actual progress is made after careful assessment and accurate planning, in contrast to vigorous action for action's sake. Kalish (1978, p. 43) maintains that "the critical challenge facing nursing over the next 25 years

will be to acquire a solid resource and power base upon which to move the profession forward." In order to do this, nurses must face the social givens in the next few years: scarcity, frugality, and cost effectiveness will dramatically call attention to the fact that the earth contains finite resources. In an era of economic scarcity the health care industry will experience greater scrutiny from regulatory and fiscal bodies. Such scrutiny will dictate that nursing actions be efficient and cost effective, and that nurses maximize their own resources so as to provide the highest possible care. An ecological model emphasizes the inseparability of internal and external environmental factors in any attempt to maintain equilibrium and simultaneously maximize one's efforts and resources. In an era of rapid social change, new technology, decreasing fiscal resources, and subsequent specialization of health care functions, it is increasingly important to devise models that attempt to explain relationships by depicting the environmental characteristics that simultaneously impinge on every human organism. An ecological model is especially applicable to the analysis of change, as it calls attention to the ways in which people affect and are affected by their environment. Such a model acknowledges the environmental impact by taking into account biological, socioeconomic, political, cultural, and emotional forces, as well as their cumulative and ever-changing impact on the human organism.

An ecological model is not set forth as a panacea for devising nursing theory, in that ecology does not possess its own unique body of knowledge; rather, like nursing, it borrows freely from other social and natural sciences to order its conceptual basis. Ecology's main contribution as a conceptual model that has applicability to nursing practice lies in its emphasis on the human-environmental relationships, paying particular attention to the junctures or interfaces between the living organism and the environment. Interfaces refer to the points at which individuals meet and respond to the environment. Such points of interaction include that which the individual brings to the situation—including values, beliefs, and biases—as well as physical and sociopsychological qualities.

The ecological view holds that people must be considered in their totality, as open systems in dynamic interaction with the environment. An ecological approach recognizes "both the interdependence and uniqueness of people, whatever their level of social organization and the cumulative effects that a single change will have on a family, group, or community" (Bruhn and Cordova, 1980, p. 257). The ecological approach actively seeks to gain as much information as possible about all levels of social organization so that a change at any level can be assessed and its effects accounted for throughout the system.

ECOLOGY'S CONTRIBUTION AS A PERSPECTIVE FOR NURSING PRACTICE

The term ecology was first proposed in 1869 by a German biologist, Ernest Haeckel. The word *ecology* is derived from the Greek root *oikos,* meaning house, and, literally translated, ecology refers to the study of organisms at home. As such, ecology is concerned with both the structure and functioning of organisms. Moreover, ecology includes the surroundings of organisms as well as that which is surrounded with all aspects of the environment, both living and nonliving, being interrelated and interdependent. In human ecology, people are viewed as open systems in continuous interaction with the environment.

Ecology's major contribution as a perspective for describing and analyzing nursing lies in its definition, attitude, and the set of principles that it offers as an explanation of human functioning. By definition, ecology refers to the study of the interrelationships between individuals and their environments as well as among one another. Principles of ecology describe ways in which people live with one another, and are derived from the biological, social, and behavioral sciences. An ecological attitude refers to a respect or appreciation for all parts of the universe in order to recognize the open and interdependent nature of living systems.

Systems concepts

An ecological approach is built with systems theory concepts as its foundation in order to provide "an overall conceptual framework with which otherwise unconnected parts can be integrated" (Roberts, 1976, p. 36). In human ecology each person is viewed as an open system constantly interacting with both internal and external environmental forces in order to maintain stability. The complexity of each person's adaptive capabilities can be appreciated by recognizing that individuals are often bombarded by a variety of simultaneous environmental forces. Noise, conflict, confusion, pain, weather changes, and hunger can all be experienced simultaneously, thereby necessitating sophisticated reactions in order to maintain homeostasis.

Systems differ in terms of their relationship with the environment, in that some are open and in continuous interaction with the environment, whereas others are closed and do not exchange energy or information with the environment. All living systems are open systems, which must maintain continuous interaction with the environment in order to maintain stability. This constant interchange results in ongoing adaptation on the part of the open system as well as by the environment.

The concept of ecosystem is considered by some as the key to an understanding of ecology (Odum, 1971). An *ecosystem* is defined as the sum total of all existing subsystems and includes both the structural and functional components under consideration. That is, ecosystems include both a place and a way of life, and in general the more complex the ecosystem the more stable its functioning. The size and characteristics of ecosystems vary considerably, ranging from a single cell to an entire nation or population group. In human ecosystems the organizational unit for consideration is usually small to intermediate in size and most often refers to families, work groups, or communities. A principle attribute of a human ecological approach is that one can only understand a designated ecosystem by viewing it within the context of the larger com-

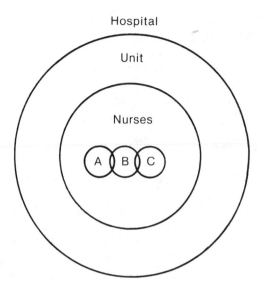

FIG. 20-1
Nurse-hospital interaction.

posite of ecosystems (Bruhn, 1970). For example, any assessment of a stressful situation on a patient care unit must be analyzed in terms of the total hospital ecosystem. Each nurse on the unit represents a single ecosystem within the total unit, which is influenced by the overall hospital system. Fig. 20-1 depicts this example.

If nurses A, B, and C were involved in a disagreement, the impact on both the unit system and the total hospital would need to be considered. For example, the head nurse on this unit might feel threatened by these three nurses, each of whom is especially competent. In order to subtly reduce each of their levels of effectiveness, the head nurse consistently provides different information to each nurse. Thus when the three nurses attempt to coordinate unit planning they immediately get caught up in trying to decide who is "right." From the institutional level, if this conflict and stress continued it would be necessary to assess what maintained or interrupted the behavior. The behavior could be interrupted if an astute supervisor recognized the ever-present level of stress on this unit and made an

effort to locate the causative factor(s). The situation would be maintained if neither of the three nurses was willing or able to step back from the situation, assess the origin, and take actions to ameliorate the cause.

The human ecological approach seeks to look at individual and group behavior in terms of cause-effect relationships that continue through both time and space. "The human ecological approach emphasizes the use of observation in following events and behavior as they develop naturally in an environmental setting" (Bruhn, 1970, p. 39). Although observation lacks the rigor of experimentation, it is a necessary first step in explaining, documenting, and predicting behavior patterns.

Environmental impacts: stressors or adapters

Each individual continuously engages in the process of maintaining equilibrium with the environment. From an ecological perspective, environment includes both the internal environment of the individual and the external physical and social environments. Disequilibrium in either the physical or social component of the external environment can cause changes and alterations in the internal environment. Likewise, internal environmental alterations and imbalances can influence the individual's relationship to the external environment. The degree of success that people attain in establishing a homeostatic balance within and between internal and external environmental influences is evidenced in behavior. The behavior of an individual represents a delicately arrived at balance between environmental stressors and adaptive abilities. Hence the balance attained between adapters and stressors largely determines an individual's position on the wellness-illness continuum. Favorable ecological factors (adapters) push the individual toward health or a state of positive adaptation. In contrast, unfavorable ecological influences (stressors) militate against wellness and press the individual toward illness or maladaptation.

Stressors are internally or externally generated agents that make demands on the individual; they may be perceived as either positive or negative. A variety of events, including the arrival of a baby, the winning of a large prize, or failing an examination, elicit the same type of nonspecific demands from the body for the reestablishment of homeostasis. Unless a balance is reestablished fairly quickly, a state of prolonged stress or frequent, recurring stress attacks cause an observable manifestation. Observable does not mean that all stress effects are visible; rather, the effects measurably change the organism. The body's capacity to adapt is based on finite resources, thus severe stress over a prolonged period may deplete the organism's inherent adaptive capacity.

As mentioned, ecology can be described by its definition, attitude, and set of principles. The foregoing discussion has set forth a definition and ecological attitude. Four primary ecological principles are presented: adaptation, interdependence, succession, and cycling of resources. After briefly describing these principles, we will incorporate them into a discussion of how nurses can maximize their own resources in order to cope more effectively with the environment and ultimately be more effective change agents.

Principles of ecology
Adaptation

The adaptive behaviors of individuals are varied and often complex. People respond to and subsequently attempt to adapt to situations based on their perceptions, attitudes, fears, biases, strengths, and limitations. Moreover, each person has a finite supply and variety of adaptive mechanisms. Although each person continuously attempts to maintain homeostasis through successful adaptation to environmental stressors, the attainment of a steady state does not imply a static, "once attained, always maintained," guaranteed condition, but rather a dynamic, constantly changing state of existence. In order to maintain a state of adaptation, each individual consciously and deliberately influences the environment. Within any human system forces are continuously operational that serve either

to promote or to resist the threat of change. In attempting to maintain homeostasis, forces that seek to resist change can either be beneficial as they maintain stability and the status quo, or these forces can exist as barriers to the potential for positive change. Resistance to change, whether physiological or psychological, is generally undertaken as a protective measure.

Nursing's responsibility in an ecological model is to assist ourselves and others in making creative and adaptive choices for guiding their responses to internal and external stimuli. Both the person and the setting are critical ingredients in an ecological discussion, in that all behavior occurs within an environmental context. Ecology's usefulness lies in its attempt to call attention to the multiple and continuously interacting factors that influence adaptation. As a synthetic approach, ecology maintains that no one stimulant can be isolated as the single causative factor in determining human reactions and adaptations. An ecological model demands that an active effort be made to obtain maximal information about the inputs into a system, their subsequent processing, and the output that is provided back to the total system. It is helpful to note that adaptation is ecosystem specific, in that behavior that is positive and growth producing in one ecosystem may be maladaptive in another. Wilkinson and O'Connor (1977) refer to ecosystem competence as the ability to behave in appropriate ways in a given setting. Whereas shouting at moments of great excitement at a football game is certainly appropriate, such behavior in church might be received in a negative fashion.

Any discussion of adaptation must consider the effect of change on the coping capacity of humans. The rate at which change occurs may threaten a person's psychosocial adaptation. The adage "too much or too little of anything is a bad thing" can be applied to the experience of change. Many people are fairly comfortable with change so long as it occurs at a reasonable rate and does not significantly affect those aspects of life that are most cherished. Whereas too much change, too fast, tends to be disruptive by interfering with the ability to adapt successfully, too little change tends to foster boredom and apathy.

Interdependence

Since all components of an ecosystem are interrelated and interdependent, a change in any one component affects all others. A change in any relationship within an ecosystem affects all other components. In other words, an ecological model calls attention to the fact that we can never just do *one* thing. Since any alteration in one living or nonliving ecosystem component will have far-reaching effects, it is unrealistic to hope that simple solutions can be found for complex problems.

In looking at interdependence within an ecosystem, it is helpful to emphasize the significance of the statement, "everything has its niche." *Niche* refers to both the structural and functional roles that an organism occupies within an ecosystem. In nonhuman ecosystems, niche is limited to a place or structure; in living systems niche includes functional role. A cursory illustration of niche is the introduction of a new pet into a household with one or more pets. It takes little time for each animal to make clear his or her boundaries and roles, especially in regard to territory. Just as is noted with pets, humans stake out their own tenaciously held territory (place, role, status, power) and work diligently to prevent any interlopers from stepping over the invisible boundaries.

Cycling of resources

Within each ecosystem there is a finite supply of resources; that is, tangible physical, or intangible psychosocial supplies. The client-environment relationship should be one that maximizes the efficiency of resources on both sides of the exchange. Historically, people have evidenced limited respect for the notion of cycling of resources by evidencing an attitude of domination over the environment rather than pondering a way to live in greater harmony with the environment.

Succession

An ecosystem is never completely stable or static, but rather is in a constant state of flux in response to changing environmental conditions. An open system continuously reacts to environmental inputs, each one having the potential to alter the previously established state. Succession means that flexibility and openness exist; however, these qualities also render predictability difficult. As each component of a system is altered, demands for responsiveness and subsequent adaptation are placed on each other part.

Utilizing these four ecological principles, a model is presented that describes ways to maximize the relationship between the nurse and the environment. If changes are to be made in the overall health care arena, each professional group must function at optimal efficiency and with a sophisticated understanding of the overall system.

MODEL OF HUMAN ECOLOGICAL INTERACTION: THE NURSE AND THE ENVIRONMENT

An hourglass model is employed to illustrate the interaction between the nurse and the environment. Basic premises for this model include the following:

1. The goal of nurses is to move their profession forward so as to be effective change agents.
2. At present the practice of nursing is taking place within an environment that has a finite supply of resources.
3. Interfaces, or the points at which nurses exchange energy and information with the environment, are critical to the development of a change-agent role.
4. Nurses are open systems in continuous interaction with their own internal environment, an external work environment, and also an external social environment.
5. Resistance to change within an open system can be a protective device.
6. Principles of ecology (adaptation, interdependence, succession, and cycling of re-

sources) explain the relationship between nursing and the environment.

Role of environment

Fig. 20-2 presents a pictorial display of the hourglass model of human ecological interaction. The basic function of an hourglass is the measurement of time; each grain of sand represents one aspect of the nurse-environment ecosystem. The positions of the shifting sands represent the status of the relationship between the nurse and the environment at any given point in time. As can be seen, the environment has physical, biological, socio-cultural, and psychological components. The physical aspects represent the environment's characteristics as a source of shelter and protection, as well as the design, qualities, and limitations of the setting. The biological aspects of the environment include the innate capacities and resources of other living components of the environment. The socio-cultural aspects refer to norms, values, attitudes, and biases that are sanctioned by the environment. Not only are these aspects sanctioned, but they are also supported and conveyed from one group to another as the environment's way of thinking, feeling, and acting. The psychological aspect in-

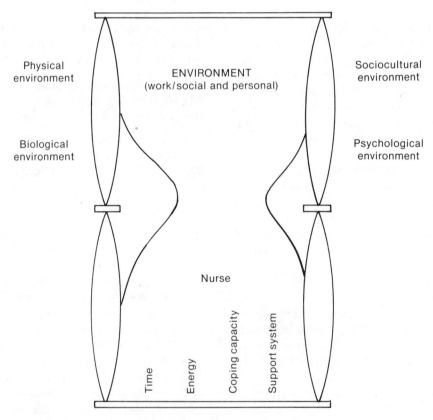

FIG. 20-2
Hour-glass model of human ecological interaction.
(The idea for this model was used with permission of John Bruhn, who is a contributor in this book.)

cludes the personality and interpersonal characteristics of parts of the environment, as well as the overall psychological gestalt. The way in which each of the environmental aspects impinges on nursing depends largely on the capacities of individual nurses to respond to the environment so as to promote professional nursing practice rather than to be limited by the qualities in the environment.

The rationale behind this pictorial model is that nurses have the ability and resources to maintain positive, productive relationships with the environment. In order to maintain homeostasis with an environment that presents numerous and often conflicting demands for time and energy expenditures, the nurse must use time wisely so as to conserve energy and maximize coping capacity. Although many applications could be made to illustrate the relationship of the hourglass schema to nursing, this discussion focuses on the nurse as an open system who uses time, energy, coping ability, and support systems to maintain homeostasis.

Adjustment to any change is a stressful situation. That is, an alteration in the biological, physical, sociocultural, or psychological environment will initially produce a stress reaction. Extensive discussion of the concept of stress and suggestions for management are dealt with in Chapter 22. For the purposes of this chapter, stress is considered a nonspecific physical or psychological reaction to threats to a person's ability to maintain balance. Hence both pleasant and unpleasant occurrences cause stress, which means that the number of possible stressors is unlimited. The key is to learn ways to handle stress in order to function more effectively.

Later chapters in this section provide in-depth treatment of topics such as managing stress, handling time more expediently, becoming more responsible for your own health, using assertiveness as a technique for making change, and initiating and coping with change in new ways as well as in a wide range of settings.

Stressors, either at home or at work, diminish the ability to adapt and deal effectively with responsibilities. Although some stressors are inevitable in daily living, others can be prevented, reduced, or efficiently handled by using principles of time management and delegation of responsibilities. No one person has unlimited capability to do everything for everyone. Responsible and thoughtful decision making allows nurses to apply ecological principles to relationships and responsibilities at work and home.

Role of the nurse in maximizing resources: application to working mothers

Nurses as open, living systems are continuously exchanging information and energy with the environment. As mentioned, the environment offers a wide range of stressors that threaten to disrupt the often precariously held balance. One way to cope with often overwhelming input from the environment is to maximize time usage in order to process the input effectively and to generate output that is appropriate to the situation. This is more thoroughly discussed in Chapter 26. Another way to maximize the positive nature of the nurse-environment relationship is to examine the mechanisms commonly used by individuals in order to handle stress and to describe ways to improve these responses.

Frequently environmental input is stressful because the human system is already overloaded or the input conflicts with other goals or aspirations. For example, Ms. Jones, a nurse with two school-aged children, works the day shift in a large hospital. For the past several weeks the nursing unit has been short on staff and all nurses have been asked to work considerable overtime. About 2:15 PM the head nurse asks Ms. Jones if she can work evenings because the one nurse who was scheduled has called in sick. Ms. Jones explains to the head nurse that she has made plans with her children immediately after work. The head nurse says she understands, but there is no one else who could do as effective a job as Ms. Jones. On hearing this, Ms. Jones sits down and starts to cry. What the head nurse did not know is that Ms. Jones has been experiencing considerable pressure at home already because of the overtime. She has missed several of her son's ball games and also her daughter's ballet recital. This request to work overtime is the "last straw." Ms. Jones feels like everyone is pulling her apart; everyone needs her. At this point, she can respond to the conflict by talking with the head nurse and setting limits on the overtime that can be expected from her, and also negotiating with family or friends to be more supportive. Her other alternatives include quitting her job, transferring the stress into a physical illness, or calling forth a variety of psychological coping mechanisms.

Although all people have the same options available to them as does Ms. Jones, working mothers have considerable role conflict and often utilize selected defense mechanisms to cope with multiple demands. Although the application of ways to maximize one's coping capacities could be applied to many situations, it is applied here to working mothers.

Working mothers all seem to have one thing in common: an abundance of guilt (Lancaster, 1975). This is not to imply that every working mother experiences guilt each day. What it means is that when role expectations collide, the first reaction is guilt. Although the cadre of mothers in the labor force is escalating annually, a cultural norm still seems to prevail that "mothers ought to stay home with their children." Thus when anything goes wrong at home an immediate reaction is, "If I did not work . . ." Just as nurses attempt to help clients adapt to their environment to maintain balance, so should nurses devote time and attention to their own adaptive needs. The way in which women handle guilt resulting from multiple expectations determines their adaptation to the environment.

Several defense mechanisms are commonly used to cope with conflicting role expectations. Although the application given here relates these mechanisms to working mothers, each coping attempt can be seen in varying degrees in most people. Three frequently observed defense mechanisms used by working mothers include rational-

ization, projection, and undoing. Rationalization is used to help people justify their behavior by providing acceptable explanations for what seems like undesirable beliefs or behavior. The working mother may justify a career with such statements as, "If I didn't have a job I would do volunteer work." The use of rationalization here conveys that the speaker has some ambivalent and unresolved feelings about working. Some degree of energy is necessary to maintain ambivalence, so as long as the person feels conflict about working, the supply of available energy is lessened.

The second frequently seen mechanism, projection, occurs when individuals attempt to protect themselves from undesirable feelings by attributing these thoughts or feelings to someone else. The working mother who experiences ambivalence might say, "If only my husband had a better job," or "I have to work to buy the children the kind of clothes they want." A more honest response might be, "I work because I like to" or "I work because I like nice things for myself and my family."

The third mechanism, undoing, is seen when people try to compensate for or negate a disapproved thought or action. Behaviors of working mothers illustrative of undoing include buying numerous "things" for the child to make amends for one's absence, or allowing the child to dictate how time at home will be spent.

Everyone uses defense mechanisms. The three that were discussed as well as others (e.g., identification, sublimation, flight into fantasy, denial, displacement, and regression), are all used unconsciously to protect people from anxiety, lowered self-esteem, insecurity, or guilt. Used in moderation, defense mechanisms serve a useful, protective function; used in excess, they impair effective coping.

What can the working mother do in order to deal with conflicting roles and not overuse psychological coping mechanisms? According to the four ecological principles discussed in this chapter, each person has a finite supply of resources. That is, nurses are not boundless vessels of energy, patience, and tolerance. Since resources are limited, the key to maintaining balance seems to be to increase internal and external support systems. In increasing internal support, the first step is to identify and accept your own feelings about working. If you work because you like to, try to accept this reason as valid. Numerous sources indicate that working as such is not harmful to children. The quality of time spent with children rather than the quantity seems more influential in their positive development (Coopersmith, 1967; Howell, 1973a, b).

The child-care arrangements that a family makes have a great influence on the total level of stress in the family system. Each family must carefully assess what is best for them, bearing in mind expense, convenience, well-being of the child, and congruence between the parental childrearing patterns and those of the caregiver.

Delegation at home is an important way to develop successful coping abilities. It is estimated that if a working woman chooses to do all of the housework, she will work approximately 105 hours weekly (Howell, 1973b). Such an arrangement typically places a heavy burden on one person and provides fertile areas for guilt to develop, when meals are late, the laundry is not done, and the house does not sparkle. Each family can work out alternatives for handling responsibilities. Even small children can participate in homemaking activities, as can husbands and household workers.

SUMMARY

It is important also to remember that no open system remains constant. According to the principle of succession, all living systems are in a continuous state of adaptation and often alteration. This means that each participant in a group (family or work) must maintain an attitude of flexibility and willingness to alter old habits and behavior when necessary. In order to deal with multiple stressors that result from complex problems and multiple responsibilities, effective coping abilities must be either developed, improved, or maintained. Just as nursing as a profession faces constant onslaughts of stress, so do individual nurses. Creative adaptive efforts incorporate the ecological principles of adaptation, interdependence, cycling of resources, and succession. These principles call attention to the "wholeness" of effective coping in that any one change can affect many people.

In this chapter these four principles are illustrated by an application to the multiple roles of the working mother. An hourglass schema serves to describe pictorially the relationship between the nurse and the environment. The position of the sand grains depicts who has control—the nurse or the environment. Creative adaptation implies that nurses will use all potential resources in order to exist and develop in harmony with environmental stressors rather than constantly feeling pressured and constrained by human and nonhuman demands.

REFERENCES

Bruhn, J.: Human ecology in medicine, Environmental Res. **3**:37-53, Jan. 1970.

Bruhn, J., and Cordova, D.: An ecological approach to the practice of community mental health nursing. In Lancaster, J., editor: Community mental health nursing: an ecological perspective, St. Louis, 1980, The C.V. Mosby Co.

Commoner, B.: The closing circle, New York, 1971, Alfred A. Knopf, Inc.

Coppersmith, S.: Antecedents of self-esteem, San Francisco, 1967, W.H. Freeman & Co.

Howell, M.C.: Employed mothers and their families (I), Pediatrics **52**:252-263, Aug. 1973a.

Howell, M.C.: Effects of maternal employment on the child (II), Pediatrics **52**:327-343, Sept. 1973b.

Kalisch, B.J.: The promise of power, Nurs. Outlook **26**:42-46, Jan. 1978.

Lancaster, B.J.: Coping mechanisms for the working mother, Am. J. Nurs. **75**:1322-1323, Aug. 1975.

Odum, E.: Fundamentals of ecology, ed. 3, Philadelphia, 1971, W.B. Saunders Co.

Roberts, S.: Behavioral concepts and the critically ill patient, Englewood Cliffs, N.J., 1976, Prentice-Hall, Inc.

Wilkinson, C.B., and O'Connor, W.: Introduction and overview, Psychiatr. Ann. **7**:10-15, July 1977.

If the field of health care marketing is going to grow and mature, then marketing scholars must accept the responsibility for: educating themselves about the complexities of the health care field; communicating the essence of marketing to health care professionals; and, making meaningful contributions to the health care field.

Cooper, P.D., et al.: J. Health Care Marketing **1**:44, 1981.

21

HEALTH CARE MARKETING: A MODEL FOR PLANNING CHANGE

Wade Lancaster

Over the past decade, health care services have been subjected to considerable criticism and demands for change, especially from the population served. The public insists that health care, especially medical care, is expensive; that its quality is unpredictable; that the availability varies from one geographical location to another and often depends on the ability to pay. Moreover, critics contend that the contemporary health care system has two prevailing orientations. First, the needs of the providers often seem to receive more consideration than those of the health care recipients. Second, the system often seems directed toward sickness, not health, with more incentives being directed toward caring for the sick and fewer incentives for the prevention of illness or at least early diagnosis and prompt treatment.

HEALTH CARE SYSTEM: CRISIS OR NONCRISIS?

The causes of today's health care crisis are varied and the target reasons depend to some extent on who is discussing this issue. Certainly increased birthrates, longer life spans, the introduction of Medicare and Medicaid, and the tremendous growth in biomedical information and technology have made health care services possible for people, whereas the delivery system remains unprepared in its ability to provide increased services.

Perhaps one of the greatest impediments to the delivery of health care services has been the way in which providers have traditionally conceptualized the recipients of their care. The recipients of health care have generally been referred to as *patients,* which connotes a passive, dependent role. The focus of this text is on change, not only in nursing, but also in the entire health care system. Various chapters consider holistic health and self-care, and each one speaks to the need for personal responsibility for health. Also, from an economic standpoint the national economy can no longer support a "fix-it" orientation to health whereby people live as they choose and seek health care to repair ravages to their bodies from poor nutrition and from lack of exercise, disease prevention, or early diagnosis and

treatment. People must increasingly become responsible for health promotion.

Likewise, just as individuals must assume greater self-responsibility, the delivery system must become increasingly accountable for providing services designed to meet the needs of the population served. Historically, health care organizations have decided what services they want to provide, with minimal attention to what the public wants, needs, and is willing to purchase. For too long those who purchased health services have been poorly informed about their needs and have had few choices about where to get care, who will deliver it, and how much it will cost. This trend is changing, and with increased consumer levels of knowledge and self-responsibility must come a receptiveness among health care providers to deliver care that effectively and efficiently meets the needs of the consumer. In order to meet consumer needs, nurses must play a key role in the health care system by consistently implementing the nursing process with *all* client groups. To date the nursing process has been utilized effectively with individuals and families. In recent years this problem-solving approach has been applied to communities. The position taken in this chapter is that the nursing process must be used consistently at all levels of health planning and delivery—for individuals, families, groups, communities, and entire delivery systems.

This means that assessment, planning, implementation, and evaluation comprise a viable way to examine, critique, and, when necessary, modify the health care system in which nursing is provided. Specifically, this chapter deals with the assessment and planning stages of the nursing process or problem-solving approach through the application of a marketing framework. Such a framework, applicable to any organization, provides a way of thinking for nurses as change agents. The following section outlines the marketing framework.

MARKETING PERSPECTIVE IN HEALTH CARE

Marketing is an approach to planning that was developed mostly in business but that is gaining considerable momentum in the health field. Basically, marketing philosophy holds that the organization has an obligation to determine what the public perceives as its needs and to develop plans to meet these needs in a cost-effective way that can be evaluated and modified as needed (Lancaster, 1980). As such, marketing provides a way to examine, predict, plan, implement, and evaluate the exchange process between provider and consumer.

A marketing approach begins with an assessment of consumer needs, desires, and wants. In order to make this assessment, a needs identification must first be completed that is based on various research efforts designed to describe the population for whom services are to be designed. The basic premise of a marketing framework is to design services that are based on consumer needs and desires rather than being solely determined by provider preferences. In general, a marketing approach includes the following steps: problem identification, search for information, development of products or services, implementation of the plan, feedback regarding the plan's effectiveness, and evaluation and control.

The marketing approach employs a consumer orientation to health planning, which focuses on consumer needs, desires, and wants as they relate to what is already available as well as to possible resources. The steps that would be taken in a marketing approach to planning are consistent with the following steps in the decision-making process as outlined in Chapter 10:

1. *Problem recognition.* This entails the process of becoming interested in or concerned about a problem.
2. *Information-search and information-processing activities.* This step includes assembling materials, tools, and/or available knowledge with which to work, and deriving a number of possible solutions to the identified problem.
3. *Evaluating alternative solutions.* It is essential to examine thoroughly potential choices of action before implementation so as to save time, energy, and money.

4. *Decision selection or choice.* This stage narrows the potential choices and makes a decision for action. Chapter 10 describes a variety of decision-making approaches.
5. *Postdecision activities.* During this stage the proposal is objectively tested and revised according to the degree of congruence between the actual outcome and that which was originally expected; essentially this stage is one of evaluation.

OVERVIEW OF MARKETING MODEL FOR HEALTH PLANNING

The model in Fig. 21-1 presents the basic components, variables, and processes essential to the planning of consumer-oriented community health care. Although this model is described in terms of planning for an entire agency (a community mental health center), it can be utilized for both large and small projects. In the illustration, besides increasing the health agency's awareness of actual needs, the model provides for an evaluation of the consequences of the selected strategy. Feedback loops provide the consequences of a strategy over time as well as indicating which factors facilitate and which inhibit success. The steps in the decision-making process are italicized for clarity.

Recognition of need

The starting point in the model, according to the problem-solving process, is the recognition of a need or *problem recognition* for specific services in the community. Several groups can serve as sources from which problem awareness might originate. These groups include the community at large, private health providers, and hospitals, as well as political and power groups within the community; too often, however, only the needs of *each* group that would affect and subsequently be affected by the proposal are considered.

In order to progress from this first step, that of recognition of need, to the stage of information gathering or community analysis, it is helpful to discuss the applicability of a marketing audit, which

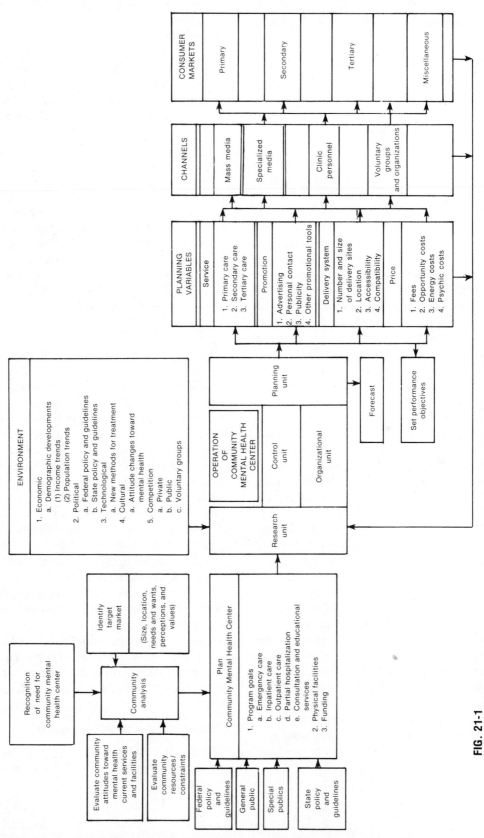

FIG. 21-1
Basic components, variables, and processes essential to planning a consumer-oriented community mental health center.

begins as soon as a need is identified and serves to identify key pieces of information that are essential to the accurate assessment and planning of pertinent services. The *marketing audit* is composed of three overall categories of analysis, each of which has several subcategories for information:

1. *Market analysis*. During market analysis the planning group or organization learns about its present and potential market. During this stage it is important to identify clearly the primary market as well as the segments that comprise the total market. Once the total market and key segments are identified, the next step is to determine the specific needs of each market segment. For example, if the problem relates to planning services for pregnant women, the total market would be all pregnant women in a given area and the market segments might be identified according to the age groups of pregnant women, marital status, race, income, and so forth. The next step in the market analysis would be directed toward learning about the decision-making process of each segment. For example, what factors influence the decisions made by pregnant teenagers in regard to selecting prenatal care? At that point, it would be helpful to learn the current level of satisfaction regarding existing programs. Are teenagers essentially pleased with the prenatal care they receive or do they have ideas for key changes?

2. *Mission analysis*. At this stage the planning group or organization should recall what business they are in, including both who their current consumers are and who they should be. Part of the mission analysis deals with a determination of what needs are currently being satisfied, as well as those that the planning group or consumers wish to be satisfied. Other key information to gain includes what, specifically, each market segment wants to focus on; who major competitors are; and what competitive benefits the planners want to offer to the target market.

3. *Internal resources audit*. During this stage, strengths and weaknesses of staff, existing programs, physical facilities, and resources are identified.

The marketing audit will be elaborated on and applied in the following section, which discusses the gathering of information and information-processing activities by way of a community analysis.

Community analysis

The second and third steps in the problem-solving process require the gathering of information as well as the evaluation of alternatives. Four major inputs comprise the basis for the *information search* or a community analysis. These include assessment of (1) community attitudes toward health care; (2) currently available services, resources, and facilities; (3) contraints; and (4) identification of the target market to be served.

Community attitudes

Specific attitudinal information that is prerequisite to health planning should be gathered from both the professional and lay components of the community. In the professional community, information should be gathered from private practitioners, public and private hospital administrators and staff, social workers, community- and agency-based nurses, and individuals who provide health-related services such as welfare and social agency staff. In addition, attitudinal information should be gathered from special interest groups. For example, if mental health services were being considered it would be essential to determine the attitudes of any organized lay group in the community, such as the mental health association, mothers of mentally retarded children, or selected power groups such as black power groups. Finally, attitudinal information should be gathered from the portion of the community at large that would be affected. A later section will discuss the concept of target market and will amplify the way to determine community attitudes from a designated segment of the total population.

Assessment of community resources

This stage includes an assessment of both available physical resources and work force. This means carefully examining the ratio of agencies to the documented needs of the population. Information gained from local health planning groups such as health systems agencies is valuable at this stage. Such data might include available health work force, hospital beds, nursing home capacity, mental health services, and other social agency resources. In addition, the availability of professionals outside the traditional health disciplines can be surveyed. Included in this group might be counselors; clergy; self-help groups; halfway houses; voluntary community groups such as women's centers; and organizations for special groups such as single parents, chemical abusers, or victims of human abuse. This assessment actually constitutes an audit of existing facilities and services.

Constraints

The audit of existing resources and services generally illuminates deficiencies and constraints on providing relevant comprehensive services. Often major constraints on program planning include lack of funds, limited available work force, inadequate resources, poor coordination of services, and interference from special interest groups. Occasionally a community may actually have adequate services but have a serious lack of coordination, so consumers receive only fragmentary care.

Identification of target market

The purpose behind identifying the target market is making available the needs and desires of the consuming public to be used as guides for planning. A first step in target market identification is to identify a specific geographical area. This limits the market area to a selected group of residents. A census tract may be used, as can other forms of defining geographical boundaries. In some instances the most manageable approach might be to subdivide the heterogeneous target market further into homogeneous subtarget markets.

One way to refine and divide a target market further is through market segmentation. Although there is no one best way to segment a market, three

conditions must be met before beginning the process of segmentation:

1. *Measurability*. Each variable to be studied must be measurable, thus segmentation according to determinants such as values, beliefs, or attitudes is not usually feasible.
2. *Accessibility*. The data about the variables to be studied must be available in a usable form.
3. *Substantiality*. Market segments must be sufficiently large so that they can be measured and, when appropriate, further subdivided.

Markets can be segmented in a variety of ways, depending on the type of program being planned. The resources and information available and the time allotted for data collection must be considered. The following list, though not inclusive, covers a variety of ways to approach market segmentation. Markets can be segmented according to demographic variables, including:

Age	Education
Sex	Occupation
Race	Religion
Income	

Demographic variables alone are not sufficient for a thorough segmentation, but they do provide a starting point or foundation. Segmentation can also be accomplished according to socioeconomic variables, stages in family development, diagnostic categories, and consumer desires for specific services.

Once the target market has been identified, the second stage of the problem-solving process, the gathering of information, nears its completion. The outcome of the second stage is the delineation of a set of possible plans for change or solutions to identified problems. Stage three, evaluating alternative decisions, is synonymous with the planning stage in the nursing process.

PLANNING FOR CHANGE

Once the market has been segmented and a specific group identified or targeted to become involved in a health project, the planning phase begins. The planning phase is a critical step in the problem-solving process and should be approached comprehensively so as to consider all possible alternatives and potential solutions. The planning phase includes the steps in the decision-making process of evaluating alternative solutions and making the decision, selection, or choice. Since all organizations exist for a purpose, the first step in planning is to clarify the purpose. Since the overall purpose of a health program or agency will influence philosophy, goals, objectives, policies, and procedures, this step should be taken seriously (Marriner, 1980).

In general, the planning stage includes activities leading to a definition of goals, as well as a determination of the appropriate means to achieve the goals. Although a variety of theoretical approaches to planning exist, there is a core of planning concepts. Crown (1978) identified three key elements in the planning process: values, goals, and plans.

Values

Values, whether implicit or explicitly stated or written, determine the ends toward which activities are directed as well as influence the actual process of achieving the designated goals. The values of an agency should be reflected in the written statement of philosophy, and these statements should be reviewed periodically so that employees are aware of agency values. The value systems of the members of a work group form a composite set of standards and expectations for evaluating behavior.

Goals

Goals refer to the perceived expectations of ideals, which are established from values. Since goals represent the desired end product or output of an organization's activities, they are influenced by the values of persons who are instrumental in the planning process. The goals can be spelled out more clearly through objectives, which are action statements of the intent of the project or agency. According to Marriner, if the purpose and philosophy "are to be more than good intentions, they must be translated into explicit goals" (1980, p. 17).

Blum (1974) describes goals as "descriptions of aspirations which represent fruition of the ideals established by values" (p. 29). The planner must be cognizant of whose goals are being met, since it is often noted that individual members of a planning group have personal value systems that significantly influence their choice of goals. In any group project, a negotiating process is often essential to arrive at a consensus on goals. Intended outcomes must be mutually agreed on by all participants if the overall organizational goals are to be met. Goals are often defined in terms of time, scope, and degree of specificity. In general, long-range goals extend longer than three years and provide the direction or impetus for organizational activities. These goals typically define the overall master plan of the organization. In contrast, short-term goals tend to be more specific and can be evaluated in accordance to how closely they meet the parameters of the master plan.

The operationalization of overall goals is reflected in the specific action-oriented objectives. Objectives consist of the time, place, quality, and quantity of change that is anticipated and planned (Blum, 1974). In the planning process specific actions are delineated and mechanisms for reaching the end goals are set forth. Implicit in any plan is a determination of the availability of resources such as funds, facilities, and work force.

The development of policies and procedures constitutes that portion of the planning process that serves as a mechanism for accomplishing the defined goals and objectives. "Policies explain how goals will be achieved and serve as guides that define the general course and scope of activities permissible for goal accomplishment" (Marriner, 1980, p. 19). Policies may be implied or explicitly stated. In general, it is easier to orient new employees to written policies. Often the implied policies (e.g., for honesty, fairness, and courtesy) can be observed but are not always spelled out in written communication.

The danger of an organization that functions with a great many implicit, unstated policies is that newcomers have difficulty fitting in simply because they may not understand the rules that seemingly guide the behavior of others. What may happen is that new employees will learn about the unwritten policies after they have been violated. This can become dehumanizing in that new employees may think, "I can't seem to do anything right."

This caution to write policies when possible does not mean to imply that change cannot occur. In fact, policies should change to reflect a reorientation in goals, needs, values, or expectations. Policies not only should be flexible, negotiable, and written whenever appropriate, but they should also reflect consistency within the organization. Also, agency policies should be communicated to all employees. When new policies are developed, information from agency representatives is useful to assure fair decisions that suit the needs of a maximal number of employees.

Procedures are often more specific than policies, and set forth a specific set of guidelines for actions. The establishment of clear, concise, readily available procedure manuals, although initially a time-consuming process, leads ultimately to considerable time saving. For example, a great deal of questions, errors, and misdirected energy can be saved if all ward clerks have a procedure manual that describes how, where, and when they carry out specific duties such as requisitioning supplies or services of other departments. Likewise, such manuals would be equally useful in the academic setting for both faculty and support personnel. Many secretaries can attest to the considerable amount of time they spend asking how to carry out certain tasks that could easily be discussed in a procedures manual.

Plans

Plans reflect the operationalization of organizational goals. These goals thus represent the standards for evaluating the effectiveness of the planning process. As mentioned in the discussion of goals, in the planning process specific actions are delineated and mechanisms for reaching end goals

are developed. Implicit in any plan is a determination of the availability of resources such as funds, facilities, and work force. As will be pointed out later in this chapter, several features in health planning distinguish it sharply from planning in the for-profit sector.

Four external factors are particularly influential in the planning process: the external environment, information, process, and timing. The environment for planning is made up of psychosocial aspects— including the characteristics of the people who are involved—as well as the tangible aspects like materials, equipment, and facilities. In any planning project the attitudes, values, and beliefs of the participants exert a tremendous impact on the ultimate outcome, just as do funds and equipment. Poor morale, lack of motivation, and a desire to disrupt the process are as influential in planning any project as are supplies, space, and equipment.

No planning process can overlook the importance of information in determining goals, communicating them to the involved participants clearly and in a nonthreatening fashion, carefully listening to the ideas and criticisms of others, and then exploring alternatives and ultimately deciding on a course of action (Crown, 1978). Accurate and thorough information is a prerequisite to obtaining an accurate assessment of need or determining participants' real desire to commence and participate in the planning process. Timing is also vital to effective planning. Until participants are ready and able to invest their time and resources in the development and subsequent implementation of a plan, no actions will be effective. Planning should not take place at a time when key participants are feeling overworked, tired, and anxious. If important and unavoidable deadlines are pressing, this is no time for planning except in the case of emergencies, because the persons involved will be distracted in the planning process by the deadlines and pressures of the day.

Moreover, the process of planning must take into account the group interaction that takes place. As mentioned in Chapter 4, group process is an instrumental part of the change process in any setting. Likewise in planning it is helpful to note the group interaction. If certain people do not look at each other or talk with one another, what might be expected regarding their ability to "pull together" in the implementation of a plan? It is always helpful to note in a planning session who looks at whom, how, and when. For example, let us say three colleagues are planning a new approach to patient education in an agency; two are very excited and obviously involved in the planning process, but the third is handling a paper clip and looking at the floor. Significant information can be gleaned from this nonverbal behavior. In no way does it imply what is distracting or disturbing to the third person, but it would seem clear that the individual is not able or does not wish to be involved. The person may be worried about a problem at home, may feel left out of the triad, or may totally disagree with the idea and wish to avoid it at all costs. It would be important to clear the air and find out why the person is choosing not to participate actively in the process. It may be that this particular triad cannot work together; on the other hand, the problem may be stress in the person's personal life and totally unrelated to the plan.

Health planning has many unique features, yet does share a range of commonalities with planning activities in the for-profit sector. For this reason the remainder of this chapter will look at specific planning characteristics in both business organizations and health care. The purpose of this portion of the chapter is to emphasize the point that health care planning has much to learn from past successes in the business sector. The final section considers the planning process in a health systems agency and addresses the question of what similarities are evidenced between planning in a health systems agency and in a business organization.

Planning in for-profit business organizations

Effective corporate planning is not simply a system but rather an administrative process. A critically important task, it involves the management within the corporation under the leadership and direction of the chief executive officer. Planning is an essential business function, of equal importance in the small company as in the large (Gross and Gross, 1967).

Corporations exist for the purpose of achieving certain goals. Through the concerted actions of groups of people, services and goods are provided. Each business is characterized by its unique goal-directed behavior, which is reflected in its influence within society. Customers are created by the business: they are the foundation of the business and maintain its existence. What is bought and valued is not a product but a utility; what is important is the purpose that product or service provides.

Classical economic theory states that the sole mission of a corporation is to maximize profits. This theory has been negated by modern economists, who argue that the specific purpose of a business is instead economic performance. Business management can justify its existence and authority only by the economic results produced. Profits represent a measurement of how well a business is functioning in serving the market and customer (Drucker, 1973).

American managers view the goals of profit, efficiency, and productivity as being of primary importance. These are followed by goals reflecting growth and stability, employee welfare, and social and community interests. Underlying managerial behavior toward organizational goals is the personal value orientation of the manager. In general, today's managers stress pragmatic and practical values. Their values affect not only the perceptions of appropriate goals, but also the appropriate means to attain those ends. Their preference is to achieve desired results through their own efforts, not from the efforts of others (Gibson, et al., 1976).

Managers have a responsibility to obtain a profit for the corporation. Profit is neither a cause nor a goal; rather, it reflects the corporation's performance in marketing, innovation, and productivity. To provide the essential economic functions of the business, profits are necessary. Profitability fails if it does not improve, or at least maintain, the wealth-producing capacity of the economic resources that have been entrusted to the corporation (Drucker, 1973).

Profit planning is based on the interrelated objectives of ensuring access to the capital needed while minimizing the cost of that capital. A business must produce enough profit to enable it to obtain the necessary capital at a minimal cost. The U.S. capital market is structured such that a high "price/earnings ratio" is the key to minimization of capital costs.

Profitability is not only a corporate need but also a limiting factor for business enterprise and activity. When establishing goals and objectives, a business must be cognizant of its expected profitability. Often this requires a balancing of objectives against attainable profitability and against immediate and future demands, as well as against each other—trade-offs being reached between the desired performance in one area with that desired in other areas.

Confusion exists with the mistaken belief that the only motive of an individual or corporation is profit, which explains any behaviors or actions undertaken. As a consequence, a deeply rooted hostility toward profit prevails. Another prevalent belief holds that there is an inherent contradiction between a corporation's being profitable and its ability to make a social contribution. In truth, only if a business is highly profitable is it able to provide a significant social contribution. Profits allow for societal services to be paid for from the surplus of economic production (Drucker, 1973).

In for-profit corporations, marketing is an integral function within the operational plan. According to Kotler and Levy (1969), marketing refers to activities for finding and stimulating consumers for the outputs of the organization. This process involves the four phases of product development, pricing, distribution, and communication. Every business has some type of product, which may be a tangible item, a service, a person, or an idea. Moreover, each organization has consumers.

Planning for nonprofit services—health

Health care planning has certain obstacles and complexities unique to its field. Planning theories must be utilized with a thorough understanding of the organizational and functional characteristics of the health care system. One unique characteristic of significance is that of dealing with social concerns as opposed to profit concerns. Health care planning has been referred to as a social science: planning involves assessing problems, weighing their components and importance, and then evaluating and proposing alternatives that will provide the most desirable solution. The eventual outcomes are heavily influenced by social and political variables, which must be incorporated into the planning process. A "subgovernment" power structure has been identified as a dominant force in the health-industrial complex. Included are members of the American Medical Association and other health professional groups, the American Hospital Association, nursing home groups, pharmaceutical firms, manufacturers of medical care equipment, and insurance carriers. Considerable weight in the future directions of health care delivery is carried in these assorted groups.

McCarthy (1977) identified four steps constituting the planning process in health care: (1) goal formation, (2) program development, (3) implementation, and (4) evaluation. Three assumptions are set forth as guiding beliefs for health planning. First, in health care, resources are scarce; therefore, mechanisms must be developed for optimal utilization of those resources that can be devoted to health care. Second, since health care serves basic needs of humans, it should be valued more than economic or purely social goals. Third, the effectiveness of the health care system correlates directly with its responsiveness to community needs.

Traditionally, health care planning has occurred in both the public and private sectors. However, the majority of the provision and payment systems that were developed to deliver health care have been designed, operated, and defined by institutions within the private sector. As a result, they serve as a valuable resource in providing health care and in exerting pressure for cost containment (Gifford and Anlyan, 1979). Incorporated into health planning is the need to refrain from overutilization of health care services and to reward cost-efficient providers. Through effective planning, resources will be coordinated, costs will be decreased, services will be more effective and efficient, and health care will become more responsive to societal needs.

Kotler and Levy (1969) call attention to the similarity in planning and operationalization between for-profit businesses and organizations whose major purpose is that of service. Classical business planning includes a financial mandate to raise, budget, and expend money efficiently; a production function that seeks to arrange and deal with company inputs so as to maximize outputs; a personnel function that deals with hiring, training, assigning, promoting, and terminating employees; a purchasing function for acquiring resources in the most efficient manner possible; and a marketing function for locating consumers for the organizational outputs. The relevance of these planning functions is clearly evident for increasing the effectiveness of health care delivery.

The current era in health care planning began in 1946 with the passage of the Hill-Burton Act. Officially entitled the Hospital Survey and Construction Act, this was the first U.S. legislation to focus on planning as a major area of concern. The primary purpose of this act was to provide for a more equal distribution of hospital beds, as well as to provide a mechanism for replacing obsolete hospital buildings. Any state that chose to participate was required to submit an annual state plan for hospital facilities, and was also expected to match federal funding of between one third and two thirds of the total cost of each proposed project. The 1954 Amendments to the Hill-Burton Act extended coverage to financing the construction of nonprofit or public nursing homes. In terms of its effects on health planning and health care facilities, many contend that Hill-Burton funds had a deleterious influence on cost containment in health care. Since

monies were made available for inpatient facilities, these types of hospital beds were supported at the expense of ambulatory care facilities.

Following the passage of this act, no further substantial health legislation was enacted for almost twenty years. The Eighty-Ninth Congress enacted twenty-seven major pieces of health legislation; two of these acts had a major influence on health planning. The Health Disease, Cancer, and Stroke Amendments of 1965 (Regional Medical Programs [RMP]) broadened the focus of planners to include "essentially all the medical resources of a region necessary to achieve a particular medical objective" (Crown, 1978, p. 273). Regional Medical Programs were institutionally focused as well as directed toward categorical illnesses with a heavy medical care focus.

In contrast, the Comprehensive Health Planning and Public Health Services Amendments (CHP) of 1966 emphasized regional planning. This act was a landmark piece of legislation, in that it established for the first time each person's "right to health care." The major purpose of this act was to promote comprehensive planning on both state and regional levels and thereby eliminate categorical grants for specific diseases. Section 314 of this act specifies that one state agency be responsible for supervising and administering the planning for health functions in the state. The state-level agencies were designated as 314a.

The National Health Planning and Resources Development Act of 1974 (Public Law 93-641) was set forth as an enactment of the 1966 Amendments. The aim of this law was to coordinate and direct national health policy via state and regional regulatory agencies. The initial development of guidelines that could be utilized to operationalize PL 93-641 has taken at least three years in most regions. To date some regions still have ineffective systems for health planning.

The major purpose of PL 63-641 was for health systems agencies (HSAs) to develop plans (health system plans) that would be responsive to the unique needs of the service area as well as comply with the previously established national health guidelines that address supply, distribution, and organization of both services and resources (Zwick, 1978). The provisions of PL 93-641 were set forth in Titles XV and XVI of the Public Health Service Act. Part A of Title XV was the first federal legislation to require the Secretary of the Department of Health, Education and Welfare to issue national health planning goals based on the health priorities identified in the law. In order to enact this section of the law, a National Council on Health Planning and Development was established. Part B of Title XV created the HSAs. The governor in each state was requested to designate health planning areas within the state that would

1. Reflect consideration of the different health planning and developmental needs of metropolitan areas.
2. Not divide SMSAs and
3. Be coordinated with areas for professional standards review organizations and areas for existing regional and state planning efforts.
4. Contain no fewer than 500,000 and no more than 3 million residents, unless the entire state population was less, or the population of an SMSA more.
5. In each area there must be at least one center capable of providing highly specialized health services.

Under section 1513 of PL 93-641, HSAs were charged with

1. Gathering and analyzing suitable data
2. Establishing health systems plans (long-range) and annual implementation plans (short-range), abbreviated as HSPs and AIPs
3. Providing either technical and/or financial assistance to those seeking to implement provisions of the plans
4. Coordinating activities with PSROs and other appropriate planning and regulating entities
5. Reviewing and approving or disapproving applications for federal funds for health programs within the area
6. Assisting states in the performance of capital expenditure reviews (certificate-of-need)
7. Assisting states in reviewing existing institutional health services with respect to the appropriateness of such services; and annually recommending to states

projects for the modernization, construction, and conversion of medical facilities in the area.*

Marketing concepts

Marketing management concepts provide a thread for linking and comparing the planning functions in for-profit organizations with those applicable to HSAs. Nonbusiness institutions are increasingly utilizing marketing logic in furthering their goals and objectives. Basically, marketing management "examines the wants, attitudes and behavior of potential consumers which could aid in designing a desired product and in merchandising, promoting and distributing it successfully" (Kotler and Zaltman, 1971, p. 4).

The key marketing problems for any business or institution include developing the right product, using the best possible promotion plan, putting the product in the best place for distribution, and setting the right price. This chapter takes the position that HSAs obey many of the rules that have typically been applied to for-profit organizations. Also, the premise is set forth that in order to implement the federally mandated guidelines for HSAs, a sophisticated social marketing function must be an integral part of the agency's structure.

The HSA chosen for study had a reputation as a particularly effective agency staffed by conscientious and informed employees. Three people were interviewed in order to gain understanding of the actual functions of the agency.

Characteristics of the health systems agency

The agency studied was one of the first HSAs in the United States to be conditionally designated in 1976, and at that time was made responsible for a six-county area with a population close to 900,000. The agency is governed by a fifty-five-member governing board that meets quarterly, and a twenty-

*From McCarthy, C.: Planning for health care. In Jonas, S., editor, Health care delivery in the United States, pp. 363-365. Copyright 1977 by Springer Publishing Co., Inc., New York. Used by permission.

five-member executive committee that meets monthly. The members of the executive committee are selected from the board. In order to understand the functioning of the HSA and to assess perceptions of this function, interviews were held with the executive director, a staff member, and a consumer representative on the governing board.

The three interviews provided data that support the contention of the author that the HSA utilizes a variety of marketing approaches in disseminating its product to both consumers and providers in the service area. The four *P*s (promotion, price, place, and product) are used as a framework for discussing the interviews. Moreover, the first descriptive area is that of the environment that sets the stage for the distribution of the agency's product: health planning.

Environment

Six counties comprise the environment in which the HSA studied operates. Possibly few geographical areas could present the diversity typified in this service area. The area varies from rural to the extreme complex urbanization noted in a major health sciences center. In general, the environment of the service area can be described as conservative. The governing body, or board, is selected in such a fashion as to represent the clientele of the community. It is important that the board be representative and also that its decisions be fairly consistent with the overall community sentiment if acceptance of the HSA is to be accomplished. This is not meant to imply that the board avoids efforts directed toward creativity and progress, but they must recognize that their credibility depends on blending progress with a keen sensitivity to how much innovation and change the service area will tolerate.

The environment for the HSA extends beyond the service area to include the state planning agency. At the state level, planning activities are dominated by physicians. If, in the future, the state planning committee includes a more representative mix of providers and consumers, then the environment in which the HSA operates would be different.

The influence on an HSA of a geographically close major university cannot be overlooked. The university has, at times, both positive as well as hindering influences on the functioning of the agency. In a positive vein, the faculty resources provide a tremendous pool of well-informed consultants. In contrast, the university, which serves as a major community power source, may take exception to HSA decisions and provide a negative climate for health planning.

Environment thus includes local and state, as well as national forces. Increasingly, the federal government is pushing for HSAs to control costs within their service areas. The government is asking not just for control of health cost increases, but also that HSAs bring about actual decreases in health spending. In an era of daily rising inflation, such a task seems exceedingly difficult.

Product

The products or goals of HSAs are to carry out the seven designated tasks in order to accomplish the following three overall missions: (1) improving the health of service area residents; (2) increasing accessibility, acceptability, continuity, and quality of health care for residents; and (3) restraining further increases in the cost of health care while avoiding unnecessary duplication of health resources (McCarthy, 1977, p. 365). These three missions are achieved via the development and implementation of a five-year health systems plan for the service area, and by establishing yearly goals in the annual implementation plan. In order to accomplish its overall mission, specific agency goals are set forth in a yearly work program that includes seven performance categories:

1. Agency organization and management
2. Plan development
3. Plan implementation: health systems development
4. Plan implementation: review activities
5. Data management and analysis
6. Coordination
7. Public involvement and education

Health systems agency personnel constitute the change agency designated to implement the work program. Eleven members of the planning staff and six support persons are responsible for discharging the responsibilities of the agency. The planning staff includes an executive director; an associate executive director; directors of research, planning, and project review; four senior planners; and two staff planners.

Product development within an HSA is a long-term project; moreover, the results of the extensive time, energy, and financial expenditures are often difficult to visualize. Product development actually occurs when the community accepts the health systems plan as a guide for planning activities and modifies courses of action in keeping with the tenets set forth in the plan. Change within any community is often a slow and painful process; hence staff in an HSA do not readily see the fruits of their labors. For each of the performance categories of the work program, specific projected achievements are established, as well as specific objectives, time frames, and staff assignments.

Promotion

The advertising and publicity frameworks utilized in an HSA include two major components. First, all promotion begins with soliciting nominations, to the board as well as to the several committees that advise and assist the staff in their endeavors. Both the board and the committees are meant to include consumers as well as providers. The agency publicly solicits nominations for agency service. A five-member nominating committee screens and recommends appointments based on a need to have a board that represents a wide range of groups.

In terms of product promotion of health planning, the HSAs have a monopoly on their market in that they are mandated by law to serve as the official health planning agency for a designated geographical area. The agency promotes its product through widespread community involvement in the development of the plan as well as of the AIP. Each

voluntary participant in the work of the agency potentially can serve as a sales representative.

The HSA markets its product through public advertising in newspapers, as well as through public forums. One staff person is assigned to coordinate public information via radio, newspapers, and distribution of the plan description in publicly accessible locations such as libraries.

Place

The place relative to marketing the product of an HSA is the entire six-county service area. In terms of place, the eleven staff members comprise the principal work group for product development. Since place is more than merely location and physical resources available, attention is devoted to the individuals who participate in the planning process. Kotler and Zaltman (1971) discuss place in terms of channel types, number, size, locations, and compatibility. Each section of the plan is written by a task force who has an interest and some expertise in that component. Each task force is composed of about half providers and half consumers. The participants come to the attention of the HSA in a variety of ways, including volunteering or being recommended. The executive committee of the board votes on the potential participants for each committee. The technical committees of the HSA include health work force, facilities and services, preventive and environment, and plan development.

Price

The price refers to the costs that the buyers must pay in order to obtain the product. As has been mentioned, the primary product of the HSA is the community's acceptance of and adherence to the goals, objectives, and action plans of the health systems plan. Since HSAs are federally funded, the actual buyers are the taxpayers of the service area. The 1979 budget for the HSA here studied is divided according to the seven sections of the work program. Table 6 represents the percentage of the budget for each item, as well as the actual dollar

TABLE 6
Allocation for work plan items

Item	Percentage of budget	Amount (dollars)
Agency management	15.0	45,000
Plan development	23.5	70,000
Plan implementation: resource development	20.4	61,000
Plan implementation: project review	20.0	60,000
Data management and analysis	9.6	29,000
Coordination	5.4	16,000
Public involvement and education	6.1	18,000

allocation rounded off to the nearest thousand.

The process involved in implementing the work program includes delineating a specific product for each item on the budget, with responsibility for completion of each assigned to a staff person.

Consumer participation

The rapid change from a physician-dominated health care model to a system orientation has evolved a whole new language of health care and has served to focus national attention on the considerable need for coordination, planning, accessibility, and the avoidance of duplication. The consumer-participation component of PL 93-641 has significantly influenced the functioning of health planning activities. Until recently, consumers were the forgotten members of the health care delivery system. Now they are sought to identify community needs and interests of their constituencies. Participation in health planning is a visible symbol of having control over factors affecting health and welfare (Hochbaum, 1969).

Although consumers comprise the hub of the health care system, they often are unaware of the importance of their role. Previously they have not been part of the decision-making process as to what health services should be purchased, nor had they an objective basis for judging or comparing quality of services (Rathmell, 1974). Similarly, providers tend to view consumers of health care as passive, uninformed recipients of prediagnosed and deter-mined care. Because they lack education and experience, consumers have been viewed by providers as nonviable components within the health planning arena.

Although a consumer orientation in health care does promise advantages, in that individuals will have the opportunity to become partners in the pursuit of health rather than always being recipients of treatment, such a focus holds numerous risks. It is irrational to think that the majority of consumers of health services are well informed and can make educated choices. A number of crucial questions must be addressed in anticipation of expanded levels of consumer participation. For example, who should be involved in health planning? Should only well-educated consumers be afforded the opportunity to become full-fledged participants in health delivery measures? How should consumers participate? Should they be advisors or part of the actual decision-making process? What are the benefits to be gained by consumer participation? Is this just one more attempt to devise new methods of rhetoric or can consumers actually affect the quality of care being delivered?

In the study HSA there is a strong orientation toward maximal involvement of consumers. Input from community groups is actively solicited, and task forces composed of consumers and providers are frequently utilized to evaluate projects and to help develop new issue positions. Some consumers are found to be easily influenced by providers,

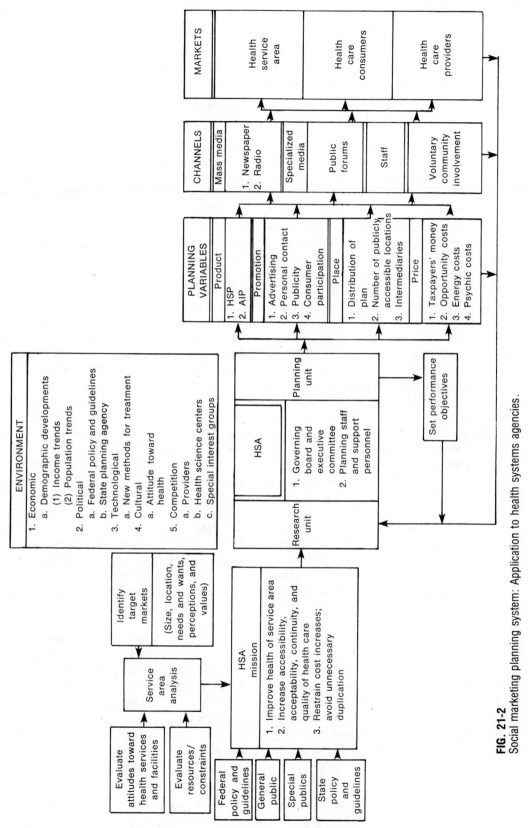

FIG. 21-2
Social marketing planning system: Application to health systems agencies.

whereas others are totally negative and distrustful toward providers. Since consumers serve a term of three years, often they develop confidence in themselves and their ability to think clearly through health issues and play a crucial role in decision making. The majority of consumers are forceful, articulate, and reasonably skeptical. Within the agency the positive environment encourages an open process of discussion, disagreement, and compromise among the consumers and providers.

Consumers view the end products of the HSA as improvement in the capacity and coordination of health services as well as the overall improvement in the health status of the community residents. Because these products are not quantifiable as is a profit, it is somewhat difficult to determine the effectiveness of the agency. Aims may not always coincide with saving money; identifying and fulfilling needs and improving the quality of services may precede cost containment. The lack of definitive cause-and-effect relationships is felt by the consumers, especially when trying to convince others of their planning activities.

Introduction of consumers into the health care planning decision-making process was intended to counterbalance the seemingly irrepressible impulse of providers to expand health facilities. HSAs, because of consumer majorities, could more readily put the lid on expenditures, allocate health resources more rationally throughout the region, promote the interinstitutional sharing of facilities and equipment, and cut health costs. Low approval rates for project requests would be a standard of "success" to federal evaluators. In the past two years, approximately one quarter of the projects submitted for review by the HSA have been disapproved, at an estimated savings of $20 million not added to current health care costs in the service area. The results of consumer involvement and effective, influential input have changed health planning from a rubber-stamping process to an increasingly coordinated, planned process. This does indicate the agency's credibility within the community. Fig. 21-2 illustrates the marketing concept as a planning approach that can be applied to health system agencies.

SUMMARY

The health care system has received much criticism about the quality, cost, and accessibility of its services. Since it is a labor-intensive industry, the nature of the services it delivers are largely dependent on the availability and characteristics of the providers. Traditionally patients as recipients of health care services have played a passive role and assumed that providers would be able to repair their bodies and minds when a need arose. In an era of diminishing resources, such blind faith is no longer adequate.

This chapter addressed the need for a revised view toward health planning based on a marketing orientation, which considers the recipient of care a key member of the health planning and delivery team. The marketing perspective in health care purports that services must be delivered that are based on the identification of consumer needs and wants rather than adhering to the past tendency of deciding on the services to offer based on provider preferences and availability.

Essentially, the marketing orientation utilizes a problem-solving approach to determine the health needs of a group or community based on a marketing audit. The three categories of the marketing audit include market analysis, mission analysis, and internal resources audit. The purpose of the marketing audit is to allow health planners to design services consistent with an accurate determination of consumer needs at any given point in time.

Once a marketing audit has been completed, planning for change can begin. In this chapter, the planning process was outlined, and planning in for-profit organizations was contrasted with planning in the health care arena, which is largely a nonprofit setting. The marketing concepts that seem most critical to health planning were applied to the functioning of a health systems agency, since the operation of an HSA follows many of the principles typically attributed to organizations within the traditional business sector. Certainly the HSP can be viewed as a major and substantial product that ensures the viability of the agency. The primary goal for the agency revolves around the AIP and its subsequent acceptance by significant community decision makers. As has been mentioned, the mission of the HSA is to change community behavior so as to coordinate health planning activities to meet the assessed needs of the service area while maintaining cost containment, avoiding duplication of services, and promoting accessible quality health care.

A wide array of values impinge on the operationalization of the HSP. The myriad of often conflicting values and goals within the HSA studied here is compounded by the diversity of the service area, which ranges from rural to that of a sophisticated and influential health sciences center. Consistently the value systems of providers, consumers, and staff must be discussed, negotiated, and often compromised in order to complete the mission and objectives set forth both by federal mandate and agency delineation.

Decision making within the HSA is often characterized by compromise. Although PL 93-641 was innovative in its dream of ensuring consumer input, perhaps that dream has not been completely realized. Not all consumers, to date, feel comfortable in disputing the recommendations of providers. Hence not all decisions relative to health planning within a service area reflect total freedom of opinion because of hesitancy and possibly fear of exhibiting ignorance or bias.

There has been a lack of investment of resources in the consumer sector, which has produced consumer representatives with incomplete understanding of issues and a knowledge deficit with regard to the legal powers and responsibilities of the boards on which they serve. Consumers tend to be absorbed into the HSA planning process, coalescing into distinct interest groups with definable policies and goals. In conclusion, it seems that the planning process within the HSA has considerable similarity to that which is completed in the for-profit sector. Areas that need continued attention focus on improving the consumer orientation so that participants in the health planning process perceive themselves and are perceived by others as equals in the decision-making process.

REFERENCES

Blum, J.L.: Planning for health, New York, 1974, Human Sciences Press.

Cooper, P.D., Lancaster, W., Mages, P., Robinson, L.M., and Whittington, F.B.: Health care marketing: progress and prospects, J. Health Care Marketing 1(2):42-51, Spring 1981.

Crown, V.: Planning. In Kovner, A.R., and Martin, S.P., editors: Community health and medical care, New York, 1978, Grune & Stratton.

Drucker, P.: Management, New York, 1973, Harper & Row, Publishers.

Gibson, J.L., Ivancevich, J.M., and Donnelly, J.H.: Organizations, Dallas, 1976, Business Publications, Inc.

Gifford, J., and Anlyan, W.: The role of the private sector in an economy of limited health-care resources, N. Engl. J. Med. **300**(14):790-793, 1979.

Gross, A., and Gross, W., editors: Business policy, New York, 1967, The Ronald Press.

Hochbaum, G.: Consumer participation in health planning: toward conceptual clarification, Am. J. Public Health **59**: 1698-1705, 1969.

Kotler, P., and Levy, S.J.: Broadening the concept of marketing, J. Marketing **33**(1):10-15, Jan. 1969.

Kotler, P., and Zaltman, G.: Social marketing: an approach to planned social change, J. Marketing **35**(3):3-12, July 1971.

Lancaster, W.: The application of marketing concepts to community mental health nursing. In Lancaster, J., editor: Community mental health nursing: an ecological perspective, St. Louis, 1980, The C.V. Mosby Co.

Marriner, A.: Guide to nursing management, St. Louis, 1980, The C.V. Mosby Co.

McCarthy, C.: Planning for health care. In Jonas, S., editor: Health care delivery in the United States, New York, 1977, Springer Publishing Co.

Rathmell, J.M.: Marketing in the service sector, Cambridge, Mass., 1974, Winthrop Publishing Co.

Zwick, D.I.: Initial development of national guidelines for health planning, Public Health Rep. **93**:407-420, 1978.

We should at least get on friendly terms with our jobs; ideally, we should try to find "play professions" that are as pleasant, useful, and constructive as possible.

Selye, 1974, p. 137.

22

STAYING WELL WHILE CHANGING: THE ART OF MANAGING STRESS

Lynn W. Brallier

The technology of modern times has allowed us to be aware of distressing situations and events throughout our world and, in a sense, throughout some of our universe. If we focused our attention on such stressors as ecological conditions world-wide, current economic and social conditions in the United States, or our own personal conflicts, we could overload ourselves with distress and not even need a career as a change agent to provide us with adequate reasons to fall gravely ill from attempting to cope with these stressors. Hopefully, however, we can learn to manage work stress well enough so that illness and death are avoided and health and personal growth are enhanced. This chapter will focus on the management of personal stress that is experienced in response to promoting changes in the work setting. The methods outlined are intended to be helpful to the reader in managing distress from other sources as well.

HOLISTIC HEALTH AND STRESS MANAGEMENT

Since the principles of stress management that I use in teaching and in my clinical practice are derived from holistic health philosophy, I will briefly outline that philosophy as background for my later comments on evaluating and managing distress. If readers desire a more comprehensive explanation of holistic health principles, they are referred to the references at the end of this chapter (Travis, 1977; Bloomfield, 1978; Brallier, 1978, 1980).

Holistic health is a model for health care delivery that emphasizes a high level of wellness as a goal for clients and also addresses the wholeness of the individual. The four components of an individual's life that receive attention from a holistic health practitioner are body, mind, spirit, and environment. Whether people seek help because of an illness or accident, or to improve their quality of life, the holistic health practitioner inquires about such diverse areas of living as nutritional status, exercise, interpersonal relationships, and philosophy of life, in addition to gathering the data common to a conventional or medical model approach to health

assessment. Holistic health practitioners emphasize the client's ability to adeptly manage life stressors, including those that originate in the environment, body, mind, or spirit. Stress management for the reader as a change agent is viewed in this chapter from a holistic viewpoint.

IDENTIFYING STRESSORS IN THE WORKPLACE

Professional burnout is a phenomenon that can easily occur in the life of a change agent. A consideration of burnout can begin by looking at the external stressors as well as those that are internal. External stressors include situations that are inherent in professional work, which involve role ambiguity and role conflicts, both qualitative and quantitative work overload, lack of managerial support, estranged relationships with colleagues, and an unclear pathway for career development (Cooper and Marshall, 1978). Since most nurses are women, many of the problems of the woman executive also apply. Dilemmas such as how to schedule time so that work and family both receive the necessary attention they deserve, where to find adequate child care, and how to divide household tasks equitably can easily lead to a woman trying to enact the "superwoman syndrome." This syndrome represents a woman's attempts to carry out her career, family, and other goals perfectly and with little help. This kind of mismanagement of stressors may partially explain why working women are beginning to catch up with men for such health problems as coronaries and alcoholism.

For nurses in positions with sufficient power to create change, these factors and many more specific ones, such as low income for great responsibility, give rise to more than the usual potential for stress-related illnesses. These stressors can be dealt with by such means as time management, renegotiation of one's responsibilities, and assertively confronting interpersonal difficulties. Readings and workshops in various areas of organizational behavior may also be helpful in evaluating and managing stressors from this vantage point. The focus of this chapter, however, is on identifying and effectively managing the internal or more personal aspects of distress. In many ways, caring for oneself by taking responsibility for creation and elimination of personal distress is a more viable way of dealing with stress management than trying to change others or the "system," since change is required of the only person each of us can actually control. Often, managing personal distress reactions in a competent and even graceful way allows other desirable changes to occur in others.

THE STRESS RESPONSE

Before evaluating the types and levels of stress, it is helpful to define stress. Hans Selye, who has done more physiological research into stress reactions than anyone else in history, defines stress as a general nonspecific response by the body to any demand made on it (Selye, 1974). During a stress response, the hypothalamus is stimulated; this, in turn, activates both the anterior pituitary gland and the autonomic nervous system, causing the latter to release epinephrine and norepinephrine. The anterior pituitary gland releases adrenocorticotropic hormone (ACTH), which is a stimulant to the adrenal cortex, to allow release of steroids or antiinflammatory hormones. The other hormone released from the anterior pituitary is somatotropin (STH), which stimulates the adrenal cortex and apparently causes the release of steroids that encourage an inflammatory response. When the sympathetic portion of the autonomic nervous system is activated, our body reflects a "fight-or-flight" mode of operation, which is noticeable to us by an increase in heart rate, an increase in respiratory rate, an increase in blood pressure, and a redistribution of the blood from peripheral areas of the body into the head and trunk of the body. The general adaptation syndrome (GAS), which Selye has identified and researched over the years, is apparently intended to help our bodies adapt to stressors. The real stress involved in the body's reaction to a stressor is the attempt it makes to normalize once it has moved away from a homeostatic condition.

The outline of physiological reactions to stressors represents an awesome coping ability. As with any process so complex, however, parts of it begin to be dysfunctional if overused. Also, Selye (1974) has postulated that each person is born with a particular amount of adaptation energy that allows this process of adapting to stressors to be effective. When this supply of adaptation energy has been exhausted, death ensues. The wisdom, then, of learning to control the effects of the GAS by preventing stress responses and by being able to recover from them quickly should not be discounted.

It is important to clarify here that stress itself is not a negative force. Stress factors include changes, strains, and challenges, which provide much of the richness and depth of human experience. What has to be controlled is the mental and emotional, as well as the physiological response known as distress, or that unpleasant experience in response to a stressor. Technically speaking, then, when people discuss stress and the control of it, they are usually referring to the uncomfortable or even harmful experience of distress. When human bodies are in distress too often or too intensely, the GAS becomes less than optimally effective and a disease process is likely to develop. Over many years, psychophysiological research has shown that in the absence of genetic factors, disease processes such as hypertension, cardiac problems, arthritis, asthma, and various kinds of pain in the musculoskeletal system are common examples of stress illnesses. More attention has been given in recent years to the effects of stressors on the immune system. It is clear that the corticoids released during periods of distress shrink the thymus gland and cause atrophy of lymph nodes, as well as inhibition of inflammatory reactions. If these conditions become too frequent, the immune system becomes dysfunctional to some degree, leaving the person vulnerable to bacterial and viral infections, including some types of viral cancers. In summary, then, it can be seen that although stress is vital, too much distress can cause illness and death. These facts support the notion that those of us who choose to function in high stress roles and are involved in constant changes would be wise to learn how to evaluate our stress levels accurately in order to have maximal control over the stress response of our bodies.

STRESS EVALUATION

There are many methods for evaluating the immediate as well as cumulative effects of stress on the body. One popular way of evaluating past stressors is the Holmes and Rahe Social Readjustment Rating Scale, shown in Fig. 22-1. To utilize this rating scale, read each life event, word, or phrase; if this applies to you within the past year, record the mean value score for that item. When you have finished the checklist, total the mean value scores that apply to you. If your score is above 300, you have approximately a ninety percent chance of becoming seriously ill in the next two years. A score of 150 to 299 indicates approximately a fifty percent chance of a serious illness developing. A score of less than 150 is associated with a thirty percent chance of serious illness.

To evaluate current stressors, consider the concept of energy intake and output. One method of evaluating this parameter is to make two lists. The first list contains ten of the most energy-draining people or activities in your life right now. The second list contains the ten most energizing people or activities in your life. After you have compiled the two lists, rank each person or activity by assigning a number 1 through 5. For instance, if you placed your career on the draining list, assign it a 1 if it is draining only to a minimal extent and a 5 if you are constantly returning home exhausted. A number between 1 and 5 is used to indicate increments from a slight amount of energy to a massive amount of energy. Use the same 1-to-5 ranking scale to evaluate your intake of energy from the people or activities on that list, with 1 being the small amount of energy being taken in and 5 indicating the greatest number of units of energy possible to be taken in. When you have ranked both lists, compare these by totaling the units of energy you take in and the units of energy you put out. If the number of units of

energy discharged in your current life seems significantly greater than the number of units of energy taken in, you are probably subjecting yourself to a potentially damaging amount of stress. In that case, it would be wise to review the two lists while in an open and creative state of mind and see what you can do to bring the energy intake and output into healthier balance.

A third major way of evaluating the effects of stressors in your life is to heighten awareness of your body and its reactions to stressors. One way of doing this is to sit quietly for a few minutes and allow yourself to reexperience a stressful situation fully. As you begin to reexperience the situation, notice carefully how your body departs from its quiet, relaxed state. For instance, many people notice at this time the feeling of "butterflies in the stomach" or an increase in pulse or respiratory rates or a tightening of the neck, upper back, and shoulder muscles. Whatever your particular reactions, try to take note of the subtleties involved so that you can be aware of these areas of your body during your waking hours. When you are aware of one or more of your particular body's reactions to stressors, you can take immediate action to thoroughly relax and minimize or stop the distress reaction. Other typical hallmark signs of stress reactions are perspiring in one or more areas of the body when the physical environment alone is not warm enough to warrant this, and cool or cold hands or feet. As you will recall, during a sympathetic nervous system response, the blood reroutes away from the peripheral areas of the body and the hands and feet may become quite cold. We will discuss the use of hand-warming as a method of combating distress in the next section.

MANAGING STRESS

As stated earlier, stress management is discussed from a holistic health point of view. Managing stress in the environment, stress on the body, stress in the mind, and stress on one's spirit are all considered. Although they are discussed in separate sections, it is important to note that all of these are

Score yourself on the life change test

If any of these events have happened to you in the last 12 months, enter the item value in your score column. The items are listed so that the most stressful situation is at the top and the least is at the bottom.

Item value	Your score	Life event
100	_____	Death of spouse
73	_____	Divorce
65	_____	Marital separation
63	_____	Jail term
63	_____	Death of close family member
53	_____	Personal injury or illness
50	_____	Marriage
47	_____	Fired from job
45	_____	Marital reconciliation
45	_____	Retirement
44	_____	Change in health of family member
40	_____	Pregnancy
39	_____	Sex difficulties
39	_____	Gain new family member
39	_____	Business readjustment
38	_____	Change in financial state
37	_____	Death of close friend
36	_____	Change to different line of work
35	_____	Change in number of arguments with spouse
31	_____	Mortgage over $10,000
30	_____	Foreclosure of mortgage or loan
29	_____	Change in responsibilities at work
29	_____	Son or daughter leaving home
29	_____	Trouble with in-laws
28	_____	Outstanding personal achievement
26	_____	Spouse begins or stops work
26	_____	Begin or end school
24	_____	Revision of personal habits
23	_____	Trouble with boss
20	_____	Change in work hours or conditions
20	_____	Change in residence
20	_____	Change in schools
19	_____	Change in recreation
19	_____	Change in church activities
18	_____	Change in social activities
17	_____	Mortgage or loan less than $10,000
16	_____	Change in sleeping habits
15	_____	Change in number of family get-togethers
15	_____	Change in eating habits
13	_____	Vacation
12	_____	Christmas
11	_____	Minor violations of the law

Total score
for 12 months

Note: The more change you have, the more likely you are to get sick. Of those people with over 300 life change units (your score) for the past year, almost 80% will get sick in the near future; with 150 to 299 life change units, about 50% will get sick in the near future; with less than 150 life change units, only about 30% will get sick in the near future.

FIG. 22-1
The Holmes and Rahe Social Readjustment Rating Scale.

(Reprinted with permission from Psychosom. Res. **11**:213-218, Holmes, T.H., and Rahe, R.H.: The social readjustment scale, © 1967, Pergamon Press, Ltd.)

integrated and intimately related to one another. Luckily, there seem to be as many ways of managing stress as there are stress factors. The methods presented in this chapter are ones that I have found to be highly effective from both my teaching and clinical use of them.

Before turning to a discussion of stress management in detail, let us look at some general issues regarding distress in the workplace. First is the question of what part your career plays in your life. Is it a major source of your personal identity or is it something you squeeze in around other major interests and view mainly as a source of income?

A second, related question is, do you love your work? Let us look for a moment at characteristics of people who do love their work and, in fact, live for their work. These people have been labeled "workaholics" in recent times. In her book about workaholics, Machlowitz (1980) defines a workaholic as one who really desires internally to work hard and to work long hours, rather than wanting to work hard to please someone else or to advance in his or her career. She describes workaholics as intense, energetic, competitive, and driven. These are people who have an overwhelming zest for working and for life in general. Workaholics prefer working to spending time doing nothing, and they can work anywhere, anytime. They also are efficient in the use of their time and tend to blur distinctions between business and pleasure. Workaholics do seem to have strong self-doubts and fears of failure, but they generally are people who, when unencumbered by other demands, do not seem to be terribly distressed but, in fact, seem to be quite happy with life (Machlowitz, 1980). If you fit the definition of a workaholic and there is no conflict in your life about making work your number one priority, you are probably also a successful change agent and may not be in great distress. If you are not a workaholic and, in fact, cannot understand why people would love their work and devote themselves to it, you may be under a significant amount of distress as a change agent, since the demands of the job may exceed the energy you have allocated to carry them out.

Often people will complain about being distressed with their career and say that their distress results from the job description itself. In some instances this may be true and the person is left with a decision about whether or not to continue in that area of work. In many instances, however, the person has not looked at the possibilities creatively enough to allow discovery of new, less stressful ways to accomplish the work goals.

Another frequent complaint of distress at work comes from people who have been in the same position for a long period of time. Distress may then be either a result of boredom or the fact that stressors are ignored or needlessly accepted as part of the job.

Environment

The physical aspects of our environment are often underrated as stressors in our lives. In thinking of both the work and home environment, you may want to ask yourself some questions:

1. Are rooms basically comfortable; that is, can I relax in each room I occupy?
2. Is the furniture comfortable for my height and weight, especially my chair and desk at work and my bed at home?
3. Is there enough space or are too many people trying to occupy this space with me?
4. Can I feel free to come and go easily in my physical environment?
5. Are the colors in the environment stress inducing or stress relieving?
6. Is the temperature supportive to a relaxed state?
7. Is the area quiet enough to allow a low level or absence of distress?
8. Is the environment safe?

Besides the physical space factor in the environment, there are most likely many people in your environment who increase the potential for distress. One way to determine areas of distress in relationships with colleagues at work is to examine the roles people play in their jobs and see if you have received enough support and claimed enough power to carry out your work with ease. Another important interpersonal factor to consider is whether or not there is agreement between you and your colleagues on how much closeness or distance there will be in each relationship. Also, have you helped create a working environment in which people genuinely wish to support each other's ideas and growth, or have you helped create one in which people distress each other by being highly critical or overly competitive? If you notice any patterns of discord with others in the environment, you may want to ask yourself, in essence, what kind of trouble you attract to yourself and if this pattern is a necessary part of attaining your work goals.

Body

As was stated earlier, an excellent way to manage stress is to be acutely aware, at some level during waking hours, of stressful reactions going on in your body. The more aware of the subtleties of body distress you can be, the more you will be able to use the natural biofeedback mechanisms within your body to ease distress. For instance, many people who complain of tightness in the trapezius area of the neck and upper back learn to control that tension by maintaining an awareness of the tightness or strain in that muscle. When they feel that type of tension, they allow their shoulders to drop downward and relax. Practicing this one simple body-relaxation method consistently can reduce a significant amount of the tension that accumulates during the day and causes irritability and exhaustion.

Being aware of the body's energy level is another important stress-management method. Recognizing the times during a day when your body is consistently low in energy and responding by taking even a brief relaxation break will save a greater amount of depletion later. Allowing for a ten-minute period twice a day for deliberate physical relaxation can be of great help in increasing efficiency and lowering distress.

Methods of physical relaxation can be learned in a yoga or meditation course. Other routes to learn-

ing physical relaxation are biofeedback and massage therapy. A good massage therapist not only aids in the actual physical relaxation of various muscle groups, but can educate you as well about physical stress savers such as correct posture and ways of breathing that help relax and thoroughly oxygenate the system so that it can recover from stress more quickly and not be as vulnerable to distress reactions.

In my practice of biofeedback, I find that many people are able to learn relaxation by learning to warm their hands. Hand-warming can be practiced by taking an ordinary thermometer and measuring the palmar skin temperature of the index finger. Skin temperature readings below 85 degrees Fahrenheit may be considered a sign of distress. After recording your skin temperature and while sitting or lying quietly in a relaxed position, simply pay attention to your breathing until you are very relaxed. Then focus on the autogenic training phrase: "My arms and hands are heavy and warm." Your hands will probably begin to warm at this point. You may notice tingling or a sensation of heat in your hands as your skin temperature rises. It is important to relax the shoulders during this hand-warming process. What you will probably discover is that you have become relaxed throughout your body as you focused on and were able to raise the temperature of your hands. Recording your hand temperature before and after a practice session gives encouragement by noting that changes in skin temperature are actually occurring as you intend them to. Once the hand-warming technique has been mastered, you can briefly focus your attention on maintaining warm hands during your waking hours. This will, in most instances, provide an effective way of maintaining a low distress level in the body.

Another important method of managing body stress is to exercise in a regular and disciplined manner. Whether the exercise is in the form of walking, swimming, aerobic dancing, or bicycling, the important point is to reduce stress by maintaining muscle strength and stamina.

Nutrition is certainly another important area of

managing physical stress. So often in the workplace, people attempt to raise their energy levels by consuming caffeine, nicotine, sugar, and/or alcohol. All of these substances can actually cause various kinds of distress in body functioning. Greatly diminishing or stopping the intakes of these substances, and substituting a diet that is high in fresh fruits and vegetables and low in preservatives, gives the body a fair chance of coping with stressors.

Mind

Although environmental and body stressors may elicit the general adaptation syndrome, the major source of distress is the mind. Both mental and emotional processing of data are included in this concept of mind. A whole range of psychological states—including anxiety, depression, chronic frustration, fear, resentment, anger, and worry—can all trigger stress responses, which, in turn, can lead to physical illnesses.

If you find yourself having fairly strong distressing emotional responses to others at work, it is worthwhile to look at your particular patterns of emotional response. Many of our emotional responses are based on old unresolved angers and resentments that become activated in current situations. Since work situations have power structures much like the power structures of family life, unresolved attitudes about authority and affection can be played out in a distressful way. It is important to recognize strong emotional patterns and take responsibility for your reactions, realizing that when the past emotional field becomes clear, you can see people in your present life with a new, uncluttered vision that is not filled with distress. Help in becoming more aware of and letting go of old fears, resentments, and guilts can come from discussions with supervisors and colleagues at work, or with friends, or by getting professional guidance through counseling or psychotherapy.

The basic principle relating to stress management of the emotional nature of ourselves has two components. First, if strong negative emotions are felt, it is wise to express them clearly, quickly, and effectively so that the body can go through the stress response and rebalance as quickly as possible. Second is the importance of increasing one's awareness of the unresolved conflicts that allowed the present strong negative emotions to occur, and working on ridding oneself of these triggers for distress.

Ellis has contended for many years that the most important factor in mental health and low distress emotionally is the ability to think rationally (Ellis and Harper, 1979). Our thoughts do appear to create our feeling states. Some of our thoughts that create distressful states are out of our awareness and are faulty ways of thinking that are habitual and left over from past traumatic situations. We can learn to monitor our thoughts and beliefs in ways that allow us to avoid useless and destructive emotional responses and enhance antistress emotions such as joy and good humor. Besides monitoring your thoughts, consider the idea of retraining your thoughts to permit more positive thinking about yourself and your own ability in the workplace. Retraining yourself to have positive expectations of how projects at work will be carried out is another useful cognitive modification. Keeping your thoughts in a flexible mode is another factor in creating low-distress situations while engendering creativity. Being able to direct your thoughts so that a sense of objectivity is created internally is also important in handling stress. Occasionally asking yourself if this work situation really has any "cosmic" significance may be an important method of creating some detachment and objectivity. Reminding yourself to avoid unproductive criticism of self and others is another key factor in managing thoughts successfully. The more you monitor and retrain your thinking in a constructive, affirming direction, the lower your distress level will be. This leads to greater confidence and assertiveness when presenting ideas, beliefs, and opinions in the workplace. The ability to be assertive with one's thoughts without assaulting others emotionally can certainly be of benefit in lowering distress for everyone involved.

Spirit

The spiritual aspects of stress management are rarely considered in professional literature, yet they are in some respects the most powerful influences on how we manage stressors. By spiritual I am referring to that part of ourselves that is capable of extending past psychological maturity into a state of experiencing a connection with a strongly positive and more powerful force than ourselves. This positive force has been thought of by many names, including God, Nature, and Universal Order, and can be said to connect with the spiritual or "higher self" part of our own nature as human beings. This transcendental experience, or the feeling of connection with a powerful and positive force, gives many people a sense of purpose and a sense of belonging or fitting into an orderly universe. This sense alone provides a strong hedge against experiencing extreme distress.

One's spiritual experience of connectedness to a positive and powerful force leads to the development, even if it is an unconscious process with some, of a series of beliefs or a philosophy about life. Beliefs and attitudes toward oneself and others spring from this philosophy into the realm of everyday life and work situations. If these beliefs and attitudes are firmly positive, it is reasonable to expect that there will be less interpersonal distress in the work situation than if these attitudes are negative. Work standards and personal integrity certainly can be maintained while allowing the positive philosophical stance to prevail. The ability to interact with others in a calm, supportive, and forgiving manner serves to lower the general level of distress at the workplace.

Meditation is a powerful method for handling distress of a mental and emotional nature while supporting the development of joy and lovingness. In the East, meditation has long been a spiritual endeavor, whereas in the West we have associated the practice of meditation more with increases in productivity and decreases in levels of distress. Following are some suggestions for utilizing various forms of meditation to manage distress and to allow for further maturing of your thoughts and spiritual experience.

A meditative state is a state of consciousness in which the mind is focused on one thing at a time. It is usually a condition that is restful for the body. It is a hypometabolic state in which there may be a marked decrease in blood lactate level, which is high in people who are anxious. A meditative state, then, should be of help in fostering a relaxation response that counters the body's distress response. Meditation seems to help calm and integrate the body, mind, and spirit of a person, and this is usually experienced as peace and revitalization. After meditating, people typically report feeling "centered," calm, more loving, and are thus able to demonstrate more productivity and creativity in their work.

In a course I teach on stress management and meditation, I emphasize the necessity of beginning to learn the process of meditating by learning to relax the body thoroughly. I give each person a cassette tape called "Suggestions for General Relaxation" (Brallier, 1978), so that they can assume a passive role while practicing the relaxation of various muscles and internal organs of the body. The tape is designed to help people learn to be profoundly relaxed while staying alert. One may practice thorough body relaxation without the use of a tape for guidance by assuming a relaxed position, either in a comfortable chair or lying down. Focusing first on one's breathing is helpful in beginning body relaxation. Breathing so that the abdomen moves away from the spine during inhalation and toward the spine during exhalation is one way to encourage deep relaxation. You can then mentally review various muscle groups in the body and allow the experience of "letting go" of any tension in these muscles. Next, focus on warming the hands by thinking to yourself the autogenic training phrase: "My arms and hands are heavy and warm." Think this to yourself slowly and repeatedly until you begin to experience some warmth or tingling or some other sensation that indicates you have been successful in allowing the blood to flow into the arms and hands. Your attitude during this relaxation and hand-warming is crucial to success. In biofeedback we speak of passive volition, which means that instead of *trying to make something happen,* one simply lets go and *allows* the hands to warm or the breathing to be full and regular or the heartbeat to be calm and regular.

Imagery is of help in learning to direct the body's reactions in a passive way. For instance, in hand-warming, people might picture in their minds the hands becoming bigger and pink or red in color. They might also visualize the circulatory system and "see" the blood traveling down through the arteries into the capillaries of the fingers and thumbs. "Seeing" this happen rather than trying to force it allows the desired results to occur without achievement anxiety interfering.

Another quieting kind of meditation is carried out by sitting or lying comfortably so that you can breathe easily and deeply, and can count your breaths in a disciplined manner. As you inhale, mentally record the number "one" and as you exhale think to yourself, "and." As you inhale again, think the number "two" and on the exhale "and." This is done with the numbers one through four repeatedly. This meditation is designed to quiet and calm the body and help focus the mind on one thing at a time. Practicing this particular meditation twice a day for ten minutes usually makes a noticeable difference in one's experience of the stress response.

Another meditation that is used for relaxing the body and focusing the mind, but that also supports spiritual growth, is a type of contemplation. After you are seated or lying comfortably and can breathe easily, choose a word that describes a quality that you would like more of in your own character. For instance, you may decide to choose a word such as love, courage, joy, peace, or wisdom. Whatever the word, speak it softly with each exhalation. This process can be carried out for approximately ten minutes, and then another few minutes can be allowed for sitting quietly and thinking about the experiences of the contemplation.

SUMMARY

The suggestions made in this chapter for managing stress in the workplace are but a few of the nearly unlimited possibilities. Making use of methods described here along with others can significantly reduce the experience of distress and the illnesses or even death that can occur when distress levels are too high for too long. Those of us who are creating new roles for ourselves through professional work or who are helping to create change within institutions are a high-risk population for stress illnesses. Learning to control distress, especially through being able at will to initiate a relaxation response, may protect our lives in many ways and enhance the quality of them as well.

REFERENCES

Bloomfield, H.H., and Kory, R.B.: The holistic way to health and happiness, New York, 1978, Simon & Schuster.

Brallier, L.W.: The nurse as holistic health practitioner: expanding the role again, Nurs. Clin. North Am. **13**(4):643-655, Dec. 1978.

Brallier, L.W.: Suggestions for general relaxation, Tape. Stress Management Center of Metropolitan Washington, Washington, D.C., 1978.

Brallier, L.W.: Holistic health practice: expanding the role of the psychiatric-mental health nurse. In Lancaster, J., editor: Community mental health nursing: an ecological perspective, St. Louis, 1980, The C.V. Mosby Co., pp. 219-228.

Cooper, C.L., and Marshall, J.: Understanding managerial stress, Princeton, N.J., 1978, Petrocelli Books.

Ellis, A., and Harper, R.A.: A new guide to rational living, No. Hollywood, 1979, Wilshire Book Co.

Holmes, T.H., and Rahe, R.H.: The social readjustment rating scale, J. Psychosom. Res. **11**:213-218, 1967.

Machlowitz, M.: Workaholics: living with them, working with them, Reading, Mass., 1980, Addison-Wesley Publishing Co.

Selye, H.: Stress without distress, New York, 1974, New American Library.

Travis, J.: Wellness workbook, Mill Valley, Calif., 1977, Wellness Resource Center.

23

CHANGING
HEALTH BEHAVIORS
AND OUTCOMES
THROUGH SELF-CARE

Jean Goeppinger

The lion of Thurber's fable, *The Lion and the Lizard,* lived (and died) within the decaying ruins of a princely castle. He succumbed to the ill effects of sloth, gluttony, and intemperance. So, too, do many Americans! In fact, recent estimates (*Healthy People,* 1979a, p. 9) suggest that perhaps half of the mortality in the United States from the ten leading causes of death is a result of unhealthy life-styles. Individual health practices such as maintenance of a desirable weight, moderate drinking, eating regular meals including breakfast, and engaging in recreational physical activity have been demonstrated to be inversely related to mortality rates (Belloc, 1973; Berkman, 1977). The moral of the fable, "He who dies of a surfeit is as dead as he who starves," is therefore a timely warning to Americans living (and dying) in a society where self-indulgent lifestyles are among the principal known modifiable causes of mortality (Knowles, 1977).

The solutions to life-style – induced health problems involve the exercise of individual and social responsibility—in short, consumer responsibility for self-care at both personal and collective levels. Individuals have to assume responsibility for selecting health-promoting living habits. On the other hand, society has to assume responsibility for facilitating individual members' health-promoting choices. For most people cannot modify their habits alone; they cannot protect their health unassisted. Life-style factors are amenable to change only by individuals who understand the rationale for change and are sustained in their efforts by strong family ties, the assistance of friends, community support systems, and relevant social policy. As Levin (1976a, p. 207)* sees it,

Self-care as a concept, therefore, must be viewed from the levels of both personal health behavior skills and social-political skills. Both levels contribute to individual and family well-being, but the socio-political concept recognizes that the etiology of many health problems is in the community domain and must be solved through social action.

*Cited with permission of the Department of HEW, Public Health Rep. **91**:206-210, May-June 1976, The layperson as the primary health care practitioner.

Yet, self-care is no simple panacea. It presents its own challenges and constraints and may even produce its own iatrogenic effects. Professionals, for instance, have to allow, even foster, patient-provider alliances based more on negotiation than coercion. And since people, despite the best of self-care practices, do become ill, professionals and patients alike must reserve judgment about causation and avoid inflicting "iatrogenic guilt" (Soreff, 1976, p. 1265) and victim blaming (Ryan, 1976, p. xiii).

The chapter begins with a historical overview of self-care, highlighting the reasons for the current renaissance of interest. It continues with a discussion of several frameworks of self-care and the identification of some characteristics common to all frameworks. The public and private dilemmas surrounding self-care are then identified and explored. Finally, the implications of self-care for the health care system and for nursing are examined.

A HISTORICAL PERSPECTIVE ON SELF-CARE

The practice of self-care probably antedates recorded history. Certainly the notion of self-care is not new in the United States. This section includes an overview of the history of self-care, emphasizing the growth of the self-care movement in contemporary American society and the prevailing explanations for the upsurge of interest.

The history of self-care

The concept of people helping themselves in health matters is not novel. Before the advent of specialization, all individuals in primitive societies were responsible for health care: health promotion, disease prevention, and treatment of illness. Rapidly, though, differentiation occurred.

Chinese texts like the *Yellow Emperor's Classic of Internal Medicine* imply that the ancient Chinese had identified individual behaviors essential to health maintenance. The text reveals that the Chinese had also developed an elaborate repertoire of therapeutic skills (cited in Dubos, 1959).

In classical Greece the concurrent proliferation

of disease treatment and health maintenance modalities was equally apparent. The goddess Hygeia symbolized the conviction that men could remain well if they only lived rationally. The god Asclepius typified the more skeptical position that men required assistance to avert disease and recover health (cited in Dubos, 1959). From the fifth century BC, the cult of Hygeia was gradually surpassed by that of Asclepius (Dubos, 1959, p. 114). The trends from lay to professional responsibility and from health protection to disease treatment became pronounced throughout the Western World as better knowledge of the human body and disease mechanisms was acquired.

However, even though societies eventually assigned many health care functions to individuals with specialized training—shamans and witch doctors, priests and physicians—they continued to depend, in varying degrees, on the individual's and family's own health care resources. The nurturance of health and the provision of health care remained, at least in part, individual and family functions (Pratt, 1976).

Such has definitely been the case in the United States. Self-care fits very closely with the traditional American value of self-help. Thomas Jefferson, for instance, was dedicated to laypersons helping themselves. This interest was demonstrated concretely with respect to health when he became provost of the University of Virginia. At that time he instituted a required medical self-help course for entering students (cited in Weiss, 1977).

Frontier American society is as well known as Thomas Jefferson for its commitment to self-reliance. Americans on the frontier not only survived without the benefits of expert advice; they even scorned outside help. In health, as in other areas of life, the frontier custom was that the older, wiser, experienced family members provided counsel and nursed the ill and injured. Of course, they occasionally consulted the medical encyclopedia on the family bookshelf!

The importance of self-reliance, specifically the family nurse's contributions to health maintenance

and disease management, did not begin to diminish until the end of World War II. At that time, the return to a peacetime economy brought higher spendable incomes, all-weather roads, the family car, the proliferation of health insurance schemes, more physicians and paramedical workers, and the modern hospital. Consequently, the dependence on self-health care lessened, and the confidence in professional health care increased. It was assumed that the doctor could and would resolve any and all health problems. The conviction that self-care was useful, important, actually essential, declined. In marked contrast, today there exists a resurging interest in self-care.

The renaissance of interest

The American public has recently developed a lively interest in the topic of self-care. Newspaper articles attesting to the renaissance are published frequently. (See, for example, the articles by Kramer, 1976, and Spiller, 1978.)

Self-care activities, diverse in objectives, methods, and populations reached, have proliferated. For instance, an extensive array of instructional materials designed to enhance laypersons' functioning in health care has been published. It includes health encyclopedias such as *The People's Handbook of Medical Care* (Frank and Frank, 1972), self-treatment manuals (Sehnert and Eisenberg, 1975), and admonitions on *Managing Your Doctor* (Freese, 1975).

The number of organizations with a self-care or mutual aid interest has also grown tremendously, as have their memberships. Several authors (Gartner and Riessman, 1976; Katz and Bender, 1976; Levy, 1976) have developed typologies of self-help groups. Roughly categorized, most of these groups are designed either to modify members' behavior or attitudes, such as Alcoholics Anonymous, Synanon, Recovery, Inc., and Weight Watchers; or to aid members in coping with life crises, such as Parents Without Partners and Mended Hearts. All are examples of voluntary associations of lay individuals experiencing common health problems and seeking peer assistance in problem management (Durman, 1976). They are most frequently viewed as complementary to rather than substitutes for professional care.

Governmental as well as private organizations are becoming involved in self-care. The Bureau of Health Education was established within the Center for Disease Control in 1974. The National Center for Health Education, a parallel but private institution, was also founded in the mid-1970s. Both aim to develop effective strategies and sound programs for health education of the public.

Many individuals display similarly high commitments to self-care. They are exercise enthusiasts, health food gourmets, disciples of stress management, moderate drinkers, and nonsmokers. They jog on city streets, patronize natural food stores, and practice a variety of relaxation techniques in their homes and workplaces.

The reasons for the resurgence of interest in self-health care are multiple. They range from the medical to the social and include the changed nature of contemporary health problems; the inverse relationships between certain risk factors and mortality; the effectiveness of intervention in inducing and sustaining risk-factor modification; the diminishing returns to health from the present system of acute, curative, hospital-based, high-cost medicine; and consumerism, with its associated popular demands for increased self-control in many areas of life.

The first of these, the changed nature of contemporary health problems, has been extensively documented. By the mid-twentieth century the major health problems in the United States were no longer the communicable diseases of childhood but the chronic diseases of middle and later life (Task Force, 1976b, p. 8). Unlike most infectious conditions, heart disease, cancer, and cerebrovascular accidents do not occur as instantaneous events. Each has characteristic precursors that can be monitored and controlled. Heart disease, for example, may take twenty years to result in a fatal myocardial infarct. The infarct requires the additive effect of such risks as cigarette smoking, a sedentary life-style, hypertension, long-term use of birth control pills, and excessive or poorly managed personal stress. Similar natural histories exist for many of the various forms of cancer and for cerebrovascular accidents.

Given the protracted natural histories of major contemporary health problems, cumulative evidence regarding relationships between risk factors and mortality rates is essential. Past assertions that mortality is related to risk have been based largely on correlational data. A dramatic example is the difference in age-adjusted mortality rates between residents of Utah and Nevada. The mortality rate of individuals aged forty to forty-nine in Nevada exceeds that in neighboring Utah by a two-to-one margin (Fuchs, 1974). This occurs despite similarities in climate, per capita income, average levels of educational attainment, extent of urbanization, and numbers of physicians. The hypothesis that the difference is attributable to the Mormon-oriented abstemious life-style of most Utah residents is plausible although not subject to confirmation.

The findings from two ongoing prospective studies lend credence to the argument that risk factors are indeed associated with excess mortality. Belloc (1973) examined the relationship between seven personal health practices and mortality rates among a probability sample of 6,928 Alameda County, California residents. As noted in Chapter 19, five and one-half years after the original health practices survey, mortality rates were determined to be inversely related to the following health habits: eating three meals a day at regular intervals, eating breakfast, sleeping seven to eight hours a night, using alcohol moderately, not smoking, exercising regularly, and maintaining a desirable weight-height ratio. A man of forty-five engaging in six or seven of these habits could expect to live eleven years longer than a man practicing zero to three habits. For women the difference between the life expectancy at age forty-five for those who reported six or seven habits versus fewer than four was seven years (p. 79).

A more recent analysis of factors associated with

respondent mortality nine years after the original survey has both confirmed and extended the earlier findings (Berkman, 1977). The inverse relationship between health practices and mortality evident at five and one-half years was maintained, but mortality was also found to be negatively correlated with the strength of the social networks, that is, marriage, contacts with close friends and relatives, church membership, and ties with informal and formal groups.

The second series of studies that illustrates the effect of different levels of risk exposure on mortality was carried out in Great Britain. British physicians, one of the first groups examined to determine the relationship between cigarette smoking and lung cancer, began to abandon the habit relatively early. A follow-up study showed that the decline in mortality from lung cancer among British physicians paralleled the decrease in cigarette smoking (Doll, 1977).

Though evidence continues to accumulate and confirm relationships between risk factors and mortality rates, some research efforts have been redirected to studies of the effectiveness of alternative techniques for risk-factor control. Examining whether gains in the public's health result from encouraging individuals to modify destructive lifestyles is critical. What, then, is the effectiveness of risk-factor modification techniques? Do any of them result in lessened exposure to known risks? Equally important, do any of them contribute to decreased morbidity and mortality rates?

The findings of three studies suggest that intensive education campaigns can have a positive effect on both the exposure to health risks and the incidence of disease. The biggest "success story" in the United States is the Stanford Heart Disease Prevention Program (Maccoby, et al., 1977). Using two northern California communities as experimental groups and a third as the control, researchers examined the effects of a mass media campaign and a mass media campaign plus intensive face-to-face instruction on three cardiovascular disease risk factors: cigarette smoking, diastolic blood pressure, and serum cholesterol level. After two years, there was a substantial decrease in risk (fifteen to twenty percent) in the experimental communities. Intensive face-to-face counseling was found to be especially effective in inducing, although not sustaining, rapid behavior change. In the control community the total risk of cardiovascular disease increased about seven percent during the same two-year period.

Similar results are emerging from a study in North Karelia, Finland, a largely rural area with an extremely high coronary disease rate (Puska, 1978). In the early 1970s more than half the North Karelian males smoked. They also consumed large amounts of animal fats and dairy products and had grossly elevated serum cholesterol levels. Many suffered from untreated hypertension. Concerned about these risks, North Karelians asked the government for help. A risk-management program was developed to help residents control blood pressure, stop smoking, and decrease cholesterol intake. It included the retraining of professional health personnel, reorganization of public health services, production of low-fat dairy products and sausages by local industries, and patient information services as well as mass public health education. After five years cigarette smoking had declined, more low-fat milk was being consumed, and an increased proportion of hypertension was controlled. The incidence of myocardial infarction had decreased by fourteen percent, while the incidence of stroke among the middle-aged (thirty to sixty-four) dropped by forty percent.

The Multiple Risk Factor Intervention Trial (MRFIT) program is also aimed at lowering risks from smoking, high serum cholesterol, and hypertension. A controlled clinical trial employing counseling as the primary intervention technique is underway in twenty communities (Multiple Risk Factors Intervention Trial Group, 1977). Its aim is to determine whether, for men at high risk, counseling can yield an appreciable decrease in deaths from heart disease. Although the final results will not be available until 1983, preliminary findings suggest that participants in the experimental group have stopped smoking, controlled their high blood pressures, and reduced their cholesterol levels.

Other approaches to the control of disease precursors do exist. One of them, designed for the medical practice, is called health hazard appraisal (Robbins and Egger, 1973). Its aim is to assist physicians in the assessment of total risks to a patient's health based on knowledge of the patient; knowledge of the natural histories of certain diseases; and known causes of mortality for the patient's age, sex, and racial group. With awareness of the risks, it is intended that responsibility for their control can be appropriately apportioned between physician and patient. The patient can reassume personal responsibility for the alteration of everyday personal habits that are health comprising; the patient and the physician can collaborate in the control of certain physiological changes, like cervical dysplasia and hypertension.

All of these examples illustrate that relatively simple, often community-based education programs can contribute to risk-factor reduction and perhaps to decreased premature mortality. They typify the thinking of many self-care advocates today. Equally provocative, however, are the realizations that past medical advances have been minimally related to increased life expectancy, and that current professional health care is limited in both its effectiveness and its appropriateness.

Among others, McKinlay and McKinlay (1977) have participated in the debate over the contributions of medical measures to the twentieth-century decline in mortality. Their secondary analysis of the effect of selected medical measures on the decline in mortality rates from ten major infectious diseases demonstrated that,

In general, medical measures (both chemotherapeutic and prophylactic) appear to have contributed little to the overall decline in mortality in the United States since about 1900—having in many instances been introduced several decades after a marked decline had already set in and having no detectable influence in most instances (1977, p. 425).

If medical measures and services were not primarily responsible for the modern decline in mortality, another explanation is required. The main influences on the decline seem to have been rising standards of living, including a better diet, improvements in sanitation and hygiene, and, consequently, a newly favorable balance in the relationship between human host and infecting agent (McKeown, et al., 1975, p. 391). This conclusion has been related not only to preventable communicable diseases but also to chronic illnesses. Wildavsky (1977, p. 105) writes*:

The best estimates are that the medical system (doctors, drugs, hospitals) affects about 10 percent of the usual indices for measuring health: whether you live at all (infant mortality), how well you live (days lost to sickness), how long you live (adult mortality). The remaining 90 percent are determined by factors over which doctors have little or no control, from individual lifestyle (smoking, exercise, worry), to social conditions (income, eating habits, physiological inheritance), to the physical environment (air and water quality).

Both the comments of McKeown and colleagues and those of Wildavsky substantiate the appropriateness of the public's growing impatience with the emphasis on medical technology and the concomitant neglect of lay responsibility.

The final impetus to the self-care movement to be discussed comes from broad social changes. These changes are exemplified by consumer advocates, civil rights activists, and assertive feminists. They all challenge the authority and correctness of established institutions and articulate public unease about the narrowing scope of lay control.

The health care system, obviously an outstanding example of professional rather than lay control, did not escape the attention of such critics. Illich, for example, confronted the situation directly in the opening sentences of *Medical Nemesis, the Ex-*

*Cited with permission of Daedalus, Journal of the American Academy of Arts and Sciences, Boston, Mass., Winter 1977, Doing better and feeling worse: health in the United States.

propriation of Health: "The medical establishment has become a major threat to health. The disabling impact of professional control over medicine has reached the proportions of an epidemic" (Illich, 1976a, p. 3).

Illich labels the epidemic "iatrogenesis" (p. 3) and discusses clinical, social, and cultural types. Social and cultural iatrogenesis are most relevant to self-care, for social iatrogenesis encourages people "to become consumers of doubtful nostrums rather than changing the morbid social and political conditions that are the major causes of ill-health," (Illich, 1976b, p. 69), whereas cultural iatrogenesis turns "patients into passive consumers, objects to be repaired, voyeurs of their own treatment. . . . It destroys our autonomous ability to cope with our bodies and heal ourselves" (1976b, p. 73).

Illich attacks the medicalization of American society and admonishes individuals to care for themselves. Until less than half a century ago the nation did depend on self-care and emphasized the obligations of the individual toward society. If recently the obligations of society toward the individual and the rights of individuals to the benevolence of the state have been stressed, powerful forces are now agitating for the replacement of the right to health with "the idea of an individual moral obligation to preserve one's own health" (Knowles, 1977, p. 59).

Five reasons for the renewed emphasis on self-care have been examined. In doing so various terms have been employed interchangeably: self-care, self-health care, and self-help. The terms mutual aid and self-reliance have also been used. Since the concept of self-care has not only varied labels but dissimilar referents, the next section presents a lexicon of definitions and an analysis of their meanings.

FRAMEWORKS OF SELF-CARE

A simple, straightforward definition of the concept of self-care is problematic. This is especially true because self-care encompasses activities of daily living usually performed without conscious acknowledgment. To some (Levin, et al., 1976), all lay behaviors—those that merely happen to influence health and those that are intended to do so—can be subsumed under the self-care rubric. Others, particularly professional health care providers, are apt to confine self-care to those discrete or episodic behaviors deliberately selected by the layperson to protect or restore either the individual's or the group's health. This distinction, although perhaps basic to the problem of definition, is certainly no more confusing than several others. Therefore, in the following section the array of terms used to label the concept of self-care is presented. The similarities and differences in definitions are then critically examined. The section closes with a statement of the writer's own definition.

A lexicon of self-care

The concept of self-care may have its antecedents in the term self-help. Self-help, defined by the *Oxford English Dictionary* as "the action or faculty of providing for oneself without the assistance of others" (Murray, 1914, p. 420), originated as a political approach to the solution of social issues arising with the Industrial Revolution (Williamson, 1977, p. 189). It was typified in the United States by the stories of Horatio Alger, who emphasized the importance of working persons, often immigrants, "pulling themselves up by their bootstraps" rather than relying on governmental assistance.

The concept of self-care, arising more recently, shares this conviction and applies it specifically to health. Self-care stresses activity, not passivity, on the part of the "helped" with respect to health matters. The premise that it is reasonable for laypersons to perform unassisted many aspects of health care is common to most definitions of self-care.

Levin, one of the most prolific writers on the subject, proposes the following working definition. Self-care, also termed self-care in health, is "a process whereby a layperson can function effectively on his or her own behalf in health promotion and decision-making, in disease prevention, detection, and treatment at the level of the primary health resource in the health care system'' (1977, p. 115).

Green, also a health educator, defines self-care in a more restricted manner. Self-care is ''the performance by consumers of actions traditionally carried out by health care providers. . . . It does not include basic prevention activities which consumers may and should take which providers have not themselves traditionally provided or controlled'' (1977, pp. 162 and 168).

''Self-care, therefore, is a form of self-control'' (Barofsky, 1978, p. 370). It represents one pole of the continuum from coercion and conformity to negotiation. It indicates that the person is involved in self-health care decisions and actions. Less consensus is apparent with respect to the tasks or functions served by self-care (therapeutic, protective, or diagnostic) and its position vis-à-vis the professional health care system (supplementary, subordinate, or alternative).

Interestingly, nurses have not only emphasized people's natural self-care capacities but even based nursing theory on it. According to one nursing theorist, ''Self-care is the practice of activities that individuals personally initiate and perform on their own behalf in maintaining life, health, and well-being. . . . Self-care is an adult's personal continuous contribution to his own health and well-being'' (Orem, 1971, p. 13). Nursing exists because individuals are not always self-sufficient. When individuals are incapable of self-care, nursing is required. Focusing on nursing people and families rather than simply individuals, Norris writes in a similar vein. ''Self-care is defined as those processes that permit people and families to take initiative, to take responsibility, and to function effectively in developing their own potential for health'' (1979, p. 487).

Other health professionals, particularly those concentrating on primary health care, also espouse self-care. The World Health Organization has defined primary health care as those ''simple and effective measures, in terms of cost, technique, and organization, which are easily accessible to the people requiring relief from pain and suffering and which improve the living conditions of individuals, families, and communities'' (WHO, 1975, pp. 114-115). Certainly these simple, effective, and accessible measures include self-care activities. In fact, Levin and others believe that ''self-care practices are particularly prominent at the level of primary care both in terms of health practices and health judgments'' (1976, p. 14).

However, the definitions of Norris and the World Health Organization emphasize another dimension along which variability exists: the level(s)—societal, community, group, or individual—at which self-care is practiced. The similarities and differences among the definitions on this and other dimensions are elaborated on in the following paragraphs.

An analysis of self-care definitions

Implicit if not explicit in the self-care definitions just presented are several commonalities. The first is that the essence of self-care is increased lay responsibility for health. Laypersons are assumed to be capable of negotiating, perhaps directing, their health care destinies. Another common thread is that self-care is considered to be effective, despite the paucity of evidence. Countering questions as to the reasonableness of this conviction, Levin wrote (1977, p. 116):

There are, however, no firm data to conclude that indigenous health care practices are any less effective than professional care (which is approximately 35% effective), or any less dangerous than professional care (which involves 20% iatrogenic effects and 4 to 11% nosocomial infections).

Third, self-care is thought to be required throughout the life cycle, even if supplemented at critical junctures by mothers, spouses, and nurses. Fourth, self-care is seen as having a grass-roots origin, and remaining, at least to some extent, informal, unsystematized, and thus nonalienating. Finally, self-care is thought to work by the helper-therapy mechanism. That is, the person providing the self-help apparently becomes increasingly committed to the position he or she is advocating. In struggling with self-care needs, the person enters an increasingly deliberate decision-making process that, in turn, decreases dependency and contributes to a feeling of social usefulness (Riessman, 1976).

However, definitions of self-care differ in at least four ways. The extent to which self-care is considered to be purposive is one difference. The level at which self-care is practiced is another. The goal, tasks, or functions of self-care are also viewed differently, as is the relationship between self-care and professional health care.

Children first learn standards for self-care within the family. Hence self-care on a daily basis is established early as an expectation. But it is not a major or even a conscious preoccupation. Only when a unique demand for self-care is experienced does self-care become intentional. Thus a comprehensive definition of self-care must include both continuous and episodic, unintentional and volitional behaviors.

Similarly, a comprehensive definition of self-care must encompass activities related to the individual's own health and to the health of the individual's family and community. It is obvious that self-care cannot be viewed in terms of self-interest alone, since health and health problems are multifactorial in origin. The solutions to contemporary health problems often require concerted action at individual, group, and societal levels. Therefore, consumer responsibility for self-care must be assumed at both personal and collective levels.

For the individual, as for the group, self-care has at least four functions: to maintain health, to prevent disease, to diagnose and treat illness, and to monitor the professional health care system. Self-care need not be restricted to one of these domains; yet at the points of diagnosis, treatment, and monitoring, confrontation with the established system is likely to be provoked.

Lay and professional approaches to health care may most appropriately be viewed as complementary rather than alternative. Certain health care functions are suitable for self-care, like the practice of healthful habits of daily living, management of routine uncomplicated illnesses, and sensible decisions as to when to seek professional advice. Other functions such as the management of chronic illness and decisions regarding health resource allocation are appropriately shared. Still other functions represent professional prerogatives.

A comprehensive definition of self-care, then, must include the elements of continuous and episodic, deliberate and unintentional behaviors; individual, family, community, and societal levels; multiple functions; and complementarity to the professional health care system. Such a definition can now be set forth.

Self-care specified

Self-care encompasses those activities, continuous and episodic, volitional and unintentional, which people can do for themselves, individually or collectively, in a variety of health and illness matters. These activities complement professional health care services.

Even if a single, comprehensive definition of self-care can be derived, other issues remain. They are considered in the following section.

THE ISSUES: A CAUTIONARY NOTE

Several dilemmas surrounding consumer responsibility for self-care do require attention. They may be phrased as questions of ethics, economics, and effectiveness, and posed as public and private concerns. For self-care is not the sole solution to the majority of health care problems; that is, it is not the way to restore the balance between professional and lay control of health care, restrain cost increases, and improve health status.

Ethical questions

The major ethical issues can be reduced to a single basic dilemma. From the far right of the political spectrum, the questions are: Isn't the individual responsible for his own health? Isn't health behavior really voluntary? And, if so, hasn't the individual a "moral obligation" to society to protect his health (Knowles, 1977, p. 59)? On the other hand, at the extreme left, one hears these questions: Isn't individual health determined by social forces largely extraneous to the individual? Aren't the sick merely "society's new scapegoats" (Halberstrom, 1978)? And, if so, isn't responsibility for individual health a "public duty" (Halberstrom, 1978)?

Proponents argue persuasively for each position. The voluntary model that holds individuals personally accountable for their health has a great deal of support. The correlations between life-style choices and health status cited earlier are impressive, if not conclusive. Further, the belief that humans are capable of exercising personal control over their health care destinies has long been appealing. "People have always wanted causes that are simple and easy to comprehend, and about which the individual can do something" (Thomas, 1978, p. 463). This is no less true today than in earlier times. For the tradition of self-help and individual enterprise in the United States, coupled with the more recent loss of personal autonomy attending industrialization and bureaucratization, make the voluntary model especially attractive. Certainly, "No one should rely on some future community action as an excuse for avoiding personal action now for himself or his family" (Higginson, 1976, p. 364).

But what does it mean to hold the individual responsible for smoking, poor eating habits, drinking intemperately, and reckless driving when the government subsidizes tobacco farming, the media inundate the public with advertisements for empty-calorie fast foods, federal farm policy supports record high livestock production, and Detroit continues to manufacture large and uneconomical automobiles? The political difficulties and economic dislocations that would be involved in changing these policies are formidable. It is also uncertain whether, once approved, governmental intervention such as taxing cigarettes and liquor exorbitantly would be effective. Prohibition was not. However, we have even less assurance that

educational campaigns targeted to the individual will be influential without concurrent social change. The recent reduction in automobile fatalities occurred after the speed limit was lowered, not after seat belts were installed!

The well-educated, economically self-sufficient middle class may of course respond to appeals for informed, deliberate choices for health. But blaming the victim, accusing the poor, uneducated central city and isolated rural populations of causing unilaterally their ill health is untenable. Such arguments ignore the structural or social class issues. The poor are not less healthy because they lack motivation, are ignorant, or avoid rational efforts to prevent illness. "The poor are less healthy for the same reason they have less of everything else; they can't afford to buy health" (Ryan, 1976, p. 166). "It is their structural position in society that is truly responsible for their poor health, even if their personal actions may exacerbate the situation" (Kronenfeld, 1979, p. 266).

We may conclude that health is multifactorial in origin, that both the individual and society are responsible. However, although we decide that health risks are, to some extent, voluntarily assumed, the conclusion that the individual is culpable for the ensuing harm, personal or social, is not required (Veatch, 1980, p. 53). The damage done to the health of a police officer or fire fighter, whose work is carried out in the public interest, is probably a nondebatable public burden. Other potentially health-compromising choices are perhaps somewhat less socially ennobling. Traveling fifty miles by car, rock climbing for ninety seconds, canoeing for six minutes, and smoking one and one-half cigarettes all increase an individual's chance of death by one in a million (Pochin, 1974, p. 11). Society may be less willing to bear these costs. Unfortunately, the situations are seldom so clearcut. What about the factory worker whose occupation is less obviously a societal necessity than the police officer's, but which also increases his or her chance of dying by one in a million (Pochin, 1974, p. 11)?

Even if we accept the principle that persons needing health services as a result of truly voluntary, socially irrelevant risks are to be treated differently from those in need of the same services for other reasons, the mechanisms for implementing the principle are complicated. Only certain behaviors can be monitored. Moreover, devices for apportioning the costs may be so crude as to render exact distribution impossible.

Other ethical issues are equally intriguing and irresolvable, if less fundamental. They include questions of risk-producing but cost-saving behavior and the further fragmentation of our communities. To quote Veatch (1980, p. 55), "What ought to be done about a behavior that would risk a person's health, but risk it in such a way that he die rapidly and cheaply at about retirement age?" The demographic and economic effects of disease prevention and consequent delayed mortality may be unmanageable. The projected increase in the retired population will, by the year 2000, necessitate increased taxes for Social Security payments, increased contributions to pension funds, and additional health care costs (Gori and Richter, 1978, p. 1128). The recessive potential is immense. Why, then, not allow cigarette smoking to take its natural toll from lung cancer and cardiovascular disease around the time of retirement?

Another ethical issue concerns the impact of self-care on existing natural groups. Rather than building on existing social networks—families, friendship groups, and neighborhoods—self-care tends to emphasize specific needs, such as widowhood and chronic illness, that cut across natural groupings. This is especially true of self-help groups. Contrary to its historical mission, self-care is now developing new services rather than building on existing strengths. The potentially negative consequences are twofold: the addition of another layer to the established health care bureaucracy and the undermining of the influence of natural support systems. Neither of these consequences was intended. Instead, they are the unintentional effects of a movement aimed at the demedicalization of

society and the restoration of lay control over health and illness.

Economic questions

Still other issues pertain to the economic realm. They relate to the costs of self-care, the aim of self-care (improved health status or increased cost effectiveness of health services), and the distribution of resources—financial, professional—and consequently, power.

The ethical counterparts of questions related to who bears the costs and who reaps the benefits of self-care have already been considered. From a purely economic perspective these questions read: Should additional health insurance fees be paid by those who voluntarily engage in health risk behaviors? Should the benefits of self-care today be experienced as costs by future generations who will be required to support an increasing number of dependents? Who should pay for the health care of those unable, for structural reasons, to engage in protective self-care? Finally, who should bear the costs of the reorientation self-care requires of the professional health care system?

Another economic issue impugns the underlying motives for self-care. Some vow that self-care is just one more in a series of ineffective remedies for spiraling health costs, penalizing most severely those who already are disadvantaged. They see self-care as a second-rate alternative to professional health care, perpetuating the present maldistribution of professional health care resources and denying access to conventional medicine where it is essential. Others, who see self-care as supplementary rather than alternative to the professional health care system, emphasize its potential for improving health status. Both arguments are credible. On the one hand, self-care may contribute to cost containment in the health care industry; on the other hand, it has equal potential for prolonging life. However, it also carries with it the danger that encouraging people to build on their own resources may divert them from seeking and receiving their full measure of the resources of the entire society.

Questions of effectiveness

If self-care is to be widely adopted and used as the basis for social policy, its efficacy has to be demonstrated systematically. Further, questions of its therapeutic value have to be dissociated from ethical and economic issues. The danger here is that self-care can be oversold for ethical and economic reasons so long as rigorous evaluation of its effects is postponed. Only when the results of research have accumulated to the point of confirming which self-care behaviors are effective for which types of persons experiencing which diseases, will the ingredients for comprehensive rational policy formulation exist. At present the data are insufficient to warrant such action.

Yet we cannot simply wait patiently for science to come in with the facts. "The best we can seek is to avoid action based on imprudent interpretation of available data and to promote action against risk factors based upon prudent interpretation of available data, at the same time striving for better and more pertinent evidence" (Breslow, 1978a, p. 456).

All three sets of issues have implications for the health care system in general and for nursing in particular. These implications are discussed next in the final section.

IMPLICATIONS

Self-care, in all of its versions, suggests some sort of connection with the health care system. It focuses, for example, on teaching people how to determine when professional health care is needed and how to work with their health care providers. In other versions self-care is seen as antithetical to the established system. Self-diagnosis and self-treatment, rather than professional diagnosis or collaborative management, are emphasized. In either case, self-care has definite implications for the health care system. If confronted and grappled with, the potential for productive system change is considerable. If avoided, the implications may become limitations. Therefore, some of the consequences of self-care for both the health care system

and professional providers are delineated and explored. Suggestions for constructive resolution are made.

The health care system

The interaction between professional and lay health care systems has at least three readily identifiable implications. One is the dramatic alteration of lay-professional relationships; the second is the possible co-optation of the lay or self-care system by the professional system; and the third is the endangered financial support of the existing health care system. These implications are considered sequentially.

Professional and lay roles in health care are being renegotiated. Professionals are being required to reaffirm their commitment to the caring dimension (Sidel and Sidel, 1976), to experience gratification as teachers as well as therapists (Levin, 1976b), and to work effectively with knowledgeable, confident, empowered patient-clients (Kronenfeld, 1979).

Self-care advocates have viewed professionals as impersonal automatons, but by emphasizing humane care as a particular strength of lay care, they may have inadvertently supported the continued retreat of professionals into technology. Professionals, challenged here directly and indirectly, must not evade their responsibilities for caring. Rather, they must accept new and different modes of caring, those of teacher and consultant. They must become willing to work with the client in the resolution of perceived problems and the realization of goals. The paradox, of course, is whether health professionals, socialized to professional norms, can deliberately restore lay prerogative for self-determination, or whether the public must forcibly reassert its self-care competence.

However, once professional roles are realigned, not an imminent possibility, the danger of professional co-optation of the self-care movement will intensify. Generally (Levin, 1976b; Fonaroff, 1977), it is felt that cooperation will enhance formalization and that with bureaucratization, the antiestablishment tendencies so effective in promoting system change, and probably in improving health status, will be compromised. The lay resource will become a new category of professional.

On the other hand, formalization is necessary for evaluation, and the effectiveness of self-care must be documented if its contributions are to be fully supported. But even establishing the criteria by which effectiveness will be judged can foster co-optation. Professional providers will assess self-care efficacy by the extent to which their services are used appropriately. The most radical self-care advocate will argue for criteria related to decreased usage of the existing system.

This argument leads into the third concern, the issue of economics. Self-care poses a real economic threat to professional health care services on two levels. By challenging the efficacy of the professional health care system and thereby diminishing public support for expansion or improvement of the system, the basic research necessary to support self-care may be compromised. In addition, already inadequate services for poor and rural populations may be more severely restricted.

Secondly, threats are posed to the privileged economic status of health professionals. If effective self-care practices keep people well, the admittedly exaggerated argument goes, what will be left for the health professional, especially the primary care provider, to do—to charge for? And will not the informed consumer decrease provider staffing needs? In fact, are not nurses the most likely provider to be replaced by activated patients? Is not our unique historical mission one of caring and is not our new mission one of providing primary, that is, basic entry-level care? Furthermore, have not nurses always stressed meeting the patients' needs, as the patients perceive them? The apparent vulnerability of nursing to a strong self-care movement is elaborated on in the following paragraphs.

The nursing profession

Although self-care does appear to challenge nursing's goals and priorities, it can be viewed as an opportunity for nurses to reaffirm the basis of their practice and to role model collaborative lay-professional relationships for their fellow health care workers. Nursing practice, at the individual level, involves grasping the patients' definitions of their needs, contracting with them for the achievement of mutually established goals, helping them solve problems more capably, and acting as an advocate when patients' rights seem compromised. At the collective level these same activities translate into nursing practice aimed at defining community health concerns as they are perceived by community members, engaging in community-development efforts to help community members help themselves, and working with or creating the community resources necessary to resolve the identified needs. The correspondence of these activities to those of the self-care movement reveals the potential for alliance.

In reality alliances are already forming. One graduate nursing student, for instance, was able to assist the elderly residents of a low-income high rise in mobilizing to protest the loss of on-site nurse practitioner services. The local government and two health care delivery systems that had withdrawn their support of the nurse's salary were forced to reconsider. Eventually, both salary and services were restored. Another student collaborated with a rural minority to document the need and write a grant for a small health center. Other alliances, less successful in terms of concrete health status or service outcomes, did reinforce the self-care capabilties of lay members. The nurses helped, without co-opting, the people involved to do for themselves. They learned, as professionals must, to play ancillary roles, to wait until their expertise was solicited, and then to have their opinions rejected as often as accepted.

SUMMARY

Having some understanding of the contemporary self-care movement is fundamental to participation in it. Therefore, factors affecting the curvilinear history of self-care were discussed in the first section of the chapter. The various meanings ascribed to self-care were analyzed in the second section. The issues surrounding self-care, despite its current popularity, were then described. Finally, the implications of self-care for the health care system and the nursing profession were explored.

The central theme of the chapter is that although individuals in technologically advanced countries like ours are subject to occasional and minor morbidity, we are basically healthy and can expect to remain so if we do not damage our health by unwise behavior and if our society actively supports individuals' health-promoting choices. Self-care at individual and collective levels, used selectively and with respect for professional health services, will probably result in greater benefits to more people than either lay or professional health care alone. The nursing profession, because of its emphases on client self-determination and basic life-sustaining and -enhancing activities, is in a pivotal position to promote a synthesis of lay and professional health care.

REFERENCES

Barofsky, I.: Compliance, adherence and the therapeutic alliance: steps in the development of self-care, Soc. Sci. Med. **12:**369-376, 1978.

Belloc, N.B.: Relationship of health practices and mortality, Prev. Med. **2:**67-81, 1973.

Berkman, L.F.: Psychosocial resources, health, behavior and mortality: a nine-year follow-up study, paper presented at the annual meeting of the American Public Health Association, Washington, D.C., Oct. 1977.

Breslow, L.: Prospects for improving health through reducing risk factors, Prev. Med. **7:**449-458, 1978a.

Breslow, L.: Risk factor intervention for health maintenance, Science **200:**908-912, July 1978b.

Doll, R.: The prevention of cancer, J. R. Coll. Physicians **II:**125-140, 1977.

Dubos, R.: Mirage of health, New York, 1959, Doubleday & Co., Inc.

Durman, E.C.: The role of self-help groups in service provision, J. Appl. Behav. Sci. **12:**433-443, July-Aug.-Sept. 1976.

Eisenberg, L.: The perils of prevention: a cautionary note, N. Engl. J. Med. **297:**1230-1232, Dec. 1977.

Eisenberg, L., and Parron, D.: Strategies for the prevention of mental disorders. In Healthy people: the Surgeon General's report on health promotion and disease prevention, background papers, Washington, D.C., 1979, U.S. Department of HEW.

Fonaroff, A.: Preface, Issues in self-care, Health Education Monographs **5:**104-114, Summer 1977.

Frank, A., and Frank, S.: The people's handbook of medical care, New York, 1972, Vintage Books.

Freese, A.S.: Managing your doctor, New York, 1975, Stein & Day.

Fuchs, V.: Who shall live? Health economics and social choice, New York, 1974, Basic Books.

Gartner, A., and Riessman, F.: Self-help models and consumer intensive health practice, Am. J. Public Health **66:**783-786, Aug. 1976.

Gori, G.B., and Richter, B.J.: Macroeconomics of disease prevention in the United States, Science **200:**1124-1130, June 1978.

Green, L.W., Werlin, S.H., Schauffler, H.H., and Avery, C.H.: Research and development issues in self-care: measuring the decline of medicocentrism, Health Education Monographs **5:**161-189, Summer 1977.

Haggerty, R.J.: Changing lifestyles to improve health, Prev. Med. **6:**276-289, 1977.

Halberstrom, M.: Society's new scapegoats, The Washington Post, Dec. 17, 1978.

Healthy people: the Surgeon General's report on health promotion and disease prevention, DHEW Publication No. (PHS) 79-55071, Washington, D.C., 1979a, U.S. Government Printing Office.

Healthy people: the Surgeon General's report on health promotion and disease prevention, background papers, DHEW Publication No. (PHS) 79-55071A, Washington, D.C., 1979b, U.S. Government Printing Office.

Higginson, J.: A hazardous society? Individual versus community responsibility in cancer prevention, Am. J. Public Health **66:**359-366, April 1976.

Illich, I.: Medical nemesis, the expropriation of health, New York, 1976a, Random House, Inc.

Illich, I.: Medicine is a major threat to health, Psychology Today **9:**66-77, May 1976b.

Katz, A.H., and Bender, E.I.: Self-help groups in Western society: history and prospects, J. Appl. Behav. Sci. **12:**265-282, July-Aug.-Sept. 1976.

Kinlein, M.L.: Independent nursing practice with clients, Philadelphia, 1977, J.B. Lippincott Co.

Knowles, J.H.: The responsibility of the individual, Daedalus **106:**57-80, Winter 1977.

Kramer, B.: The future revised: wiser living is seen as the key to better health, The Wall Street Journal, March 22, 1976.

Kronenfeld, J.J.: Self care as a panacea for the ills of the health care system: an assessment, Soc. Sci. Med. **13A:**263-267, 1979.

Levin, L.S.: The layperson as the primary health care practitioner, Public Health Rep. **91**:206-210, May-June 1976a.

Levin, L.S.: Self-care: an international perspective, Social Policy **6**:70-75, Sept./Oct. 1976b.

Levin, L.S.: Forces and issues in the revival of interest in self-care: impetus for redirection in health, Health Education Monographs **5**:115-120, Summer 1977.

Levin, L.S.: Patient education and self-care: how do they differ? Nurs. Outlook **26**:170-175, March 1978.

Levin, L.S., Katz, A.H., and Holst, E.: Self-care, lay initiatives in health, New York, 1976, Prodist.

Levy, L.H.: Self-help groups: types and psychological processes, J. Appl. Behav. Sci. **12**:310-322, July-Aug.-Sept. 1976.

Maccoby, N., Farquhar, J.W., Wood, P.W., and Alexander, J.: Reducing the risk of cardiovascular disease, J. Community Health **3**:100-114, April-May-June 1977.

McKeown, T., Record, R.G., and Turner, R.D.: An interpretation of the decline in mortality in England and Wales during the twentieth century, Popul. Studies **29**:391-422, 1975.

McKinlay, J.B., and McKinlay, S.M.: The questionable contribution of medical measures to the decline of mortality in the United States in the twentieth century, Milbank Mem. Fund Q. **55**:405-428, Summer 1977.

Milio, N.: Self-care in urban settings, Health Education Monographs **5**:136-144, Summer 1977.

Multiple Risk Factors Intervention Trial Group: statistical design considerations in the NHLI multiple risk factor intervention trial, J. Chron. Dis. **30**:261-275, 1977.

Murray, J.A.H., editor: A new English dictionary on historical principles, Oxford, 1914, Clarendon Press.

Norris, C.M.: Self-care, Am. J. Nurs. **79**:486-489, March 1979.

Orem, D.: Nursing: concepts of practice, New York, 1971, McGraw-Hill Book Co.

Pochin, E.E.: Occupational and other fatality rates, Community Health **6**:2-13, 1974.

Pratt, L.: Family structure and effective health behavior: the energized family, Boston, 1976, Houghton-Mifflin Co.

Public annual report: multiple risk factor intervention trial, June 30, 1975–July 1, 1976, DHEW Publication No. (NIH) 77-1211, Washington, D.C., 1977, U.S. Government Printing Office.

Puska, P.: North Karelia project: a community programme for the control of cardiovascular diseases, abstract, Conference on Prevention, Institute of Medicine, Washington, D.C., Feb. 1978.

Recommendations for a national strategy for disease prevention, a report to the director, Center for Disease Control, Atlanta, Ga., Center for Disease Control, June 30, 1978.

Riessman, F.: How does self-help work? Social Policy **6**:41-45, Sept./Oct. 1976.

Robbins, L., and Egger, R.L.: Health maintenance. In Conn, H.F., and Rakel, R.E., editors: Family practice, Philadelphia, 1973, W.B. Saunders Co.

Ryan, W.: Blaming the victim, New York, 1976, Random House, Inc.

Sehnert, K.W., and Eisenberg, H.: How to be your own doctor (sometimes), New York, 1975, Grosset & Dunlap.

Sidel, V.W., and Sidel, R.: Beyond coping, Social Policy **6**:67-69, Sept./Oct. 1976.

Soreff, S.: The new medical guilt: who is responsible for being sick? N. Engl. J. Med. **295**:1265, Nov. 1, 1976.

Spiller, N.: His prescription is laugh, laugh, laugh: for Editor Norman Cousins, humor heals all, The Washington Post, May 9, 1978.

Task Force, Preventive Medicine U.S.A.: Health promotion and consumer education, New York, 1976a, Prodist.

Task Force, Preventive Medicine U.S.A.: Theory, practice and application of prevention in personal health services, New York, 1976b, Prodist.

Thomas, L.: Notes of a biology watcher: on magic in medicine, N. Engl. J. Med. **299**:461-463, Aug. 31, 1978.

Thurber, J.: The lion and the lizard, further fables for our time, New York, 1956, Simon & Schuster.

Veatch, R.M.: Voluntary risks to health, the ethical issues, J.A.M.A. **243**:50-55, Jan. 4, 1980.

Weiss, D.: Who has been responsible for our health in the past? paper presented at a workshop of the Kentucky Bureau of Health Services, Lexington, March 22, 1977.

Wildavsky, A.: Doing better and feeling worse: the political pathology of health policy, Daedalus **106**:105-123, Winter 1977.

Williamson, J.D.: Healthward care, Soc. Sci. Med. **11**:187-190, 1977.

World Health Organization (WHO): A report on the promotion of national health services relating to primary health care (Director-General), Geneva, 1975.

Professional consultation is the effective managing of a helping relationship between client and consultant, and as such it is a problem-focused interaction process.

Lippitt and Lippitt, 1977, p. 130.

24

CONSULTATION: A POLITICAL PROCESS AIMED AT CHANGE

Melva Jo Hendrix and Gretchen E. LaGodna

As social systems continue to grow in complexity and potential dysfunction, the health care system is clearly no exception. Nurses have fulfilled a multitude of roles at various levels in the health care system, and perhaps the role least effectively utilized and least well understood is that of consultant. Past literature in the health care field has so perpetuated the stereotype of the consultant as professional male expert and the consultee as quasi-professional help-seeking female, that the terms consultant and nurse evoke almost contradictory images. Therefore, those of us who serve as consultants or teach consultation skills to others are increasingly compelled to reevaluate and redesign the traditional models of consultation. The consultation process is not as all powerful as some of its advocates claim, nor is it an exercise in futility as sometimes suggested by its detractors. It is, however, a process that can result in measurable change when engaged in by those who understand its complexities.

DEFINITION AND CLASSIFICATION

The lack of clarity about consultation is described in a novel way by Lippitt and Lippitt (1977), who say that "consulting, like leadership or love, is a general label for a variety of relationships" (p. 129). All too often, groups or organizations enlist the services of a consultant only to be disappointed and feel cheated at the conclusion of the experience. When this disappointment and inability to work well together occurs, the cause is often traced to a lack of understanding about what a consultant is prepared and willing to do, and what the roles and responsibilities of the consultee are. This chapter seeks to describe principles and concepts about consultation and apply them to an actual situation so that the process, problems, and alternatives can be described.

Although many definitions of consultation exist, most include two common elements: solving a designated problem and helping the consultee(s) improve specific skills or make more effective plans. Caplan (1970, p. 19) describes consultation as a process in which the help of a specialist is sought to identify ways to handle work problems involving either the management of clients or the planning and implementation of programs. In general, consultation is based on a problem-solving approach in which the consultant serves as a catalyst for change. The ultimate goal of consultation is "learning, growth, change" (Lippitt and Lippitt, 1977, p. 130).

Distinguishing consultation from other closely related processes is at times difficult, partially because there are so many different models of consultation and partially because consultation often includes the use of skills and methods basic to other activities as well. Such closely related activities include education, psychotherapy, supervision, and professional collaboration. The distinction between consultation and these activities is determined largely by purpose or goal, as well as by parameters such as setting, role relationships, authority, and responsibility (Haylett and Rapoport, 1969).

Several people have attempted to devise a conceptual classification of the consultation process.* Criteria often used include the nature of the problems presented, the problem area focused on by the consultant, and the method used. Caplan's typology (1970), based on the problem and method approach, consists of four general categories:

1. Client-centered case consultation provides the consultee with expert advice in the handling of a particular client or group of clients.
2. Consultee-centered case consultation focuses on the consultee's work difficulties with clients, which are used as a learning opportunity.
3. Program-centered administrative consultation occurs when an expert provides advice regarding the development of new programs or improvements of existing ones.
4. Consultee-centered administrative consulta-

*Bindman, 1959, 1966; Caplan, 1964, 1970; Haylett and Rapoport, 1969; McClung, et al., 1969.

tion considers the work problems of the consultees in the areas of program development and organization.

For maximal effectiveness, the roles and functions of a consultant in a complex system should be deliberately flexible. Similarly, consultants should be able to move easily between various target levels of the system without disrupting the consultative process. That is, they should have input into and impact on different levels of the system simultaneously. It is increasingly rare to find an example of effective consultation that involves only one consultant and one consultee; it is similarly unusual to identify a problem involving only one level or subsystem of a social system. The consultant must, therefore, work with different individuals or groups of consultees throughout the system. These factors clearly imply that the model needed is one that is process oriented: constantly changing, but with outcomes that can be evaluated.

Signell and Scott (1971) developed an interactional approach to consultation that has considerable promise for utilization in a variety of settings and that best approximates the model used by the authors in the example cited later in the chapter. This model focuses on both the consultant's role and the consultation process. The role is characterized by flexibility in response to ongoing consultee needs and demands, and the major aim of the process is to facilitate constructive change.

ROLES AND FUNCTIONS OF CONSULTANT

A number of variant and flexible subroles are required of consultants, including those of clinician, teacher, group leader, and politician. It is not uncommon for consultants to find greater comfort in certain aspects of their role than in others. Resistance to certain role components may originate internally or may exist in the system itself; resistance is discussed more fully later in the chapter.

Clinician role

In clinical or client-centered consultation, the clinician role is a primary one. Examples abound of consultants from other disciplines who have been "brought in" to solve problems in nursing. Without an understanding of the nursing process or the clinical role of nurses, they more often than not were prone to make inaccurate assessments of the existing problems or to suggest inappropriate solutions.

For the nurse consultant, the clinician role is often the most familiar and comfortable. It is also often the role most essential in establishing initial credibility. Nurse consultants are frequently approached for advice about difficult clinical problems, or they may find their clinical expertise tested in other more subtle ways. Nevertheless, the professional identification that occurs when both consultant and consultee are nurses facilitates trust and confidence on the part of consultees. Consultants who are at ease moving in and out of their clinical role are able to keep in touch with the actual caregiving level of the system and are often able to identify existing problems and alternative solutions in the consultation process.

Teacher role

The nurse consultant may function in the role of teacher. The effective use of teaching-learning principles and strategies enables the consultant to share knowledge and involve consultees in the problem-solving process in such a way that they are better equipped to identify and solve future problems. At times the teaching role of the consultant involves sharing expertise and knowledge or guiding consultees to appropriate resources. Frequently, the teaching role involves helping consultees develop new skills such as problem analysis, determination of power issues, prediction of outcomes, and approaches to influencing policy. One should not underestimate the importance of modeling in the teaching-learning process. As consultants move between the various expected roles, they frequently serve as role models for problem-solving skills and approaches.

The role of consultant as teacher is not an easy one. When the concept of consultation expands from work with an individual consultee to work with individuals or groups of different disciplines and at different levels of the system, learning needs and skill levels may vary widely. The consultant must, therefore, constantly reassess the appropriate teaching approaches required.

Group-leader role

The more frequently expected and readily accepted roles of the nurse consultant are those of clinician and teacher. The roles of group leader and politician are less familiar and often discouraged for female professionals in the male-dominated health care system. In the past, nurses have been well socialized to avoid roles that involve strong leadership or power in interdisciplinary realms.

The nurse consultant may work with a formally identified group of consultees over time or may work with spontaneously created groups as issues arise. More importantly, consultants need to be aware that in the problem-solving phase of the consultation process, they will be looked to for some degree of leadership by a variety of groups within the system. Group membership may be defined by professional identification, department or agency loyalties, status and power, or other commonalities, and individual consultees may be part of more than one identified group.

In any case, the consultant as group leader must be acutely aware of the developing group dynamics and must take advantage of this understanding in promoting the group's growth and productivity. It is imperative to identify the roles individual consultees play in the group, the power and competition issues that exist, and the degree of existing cohesiveness, for only then can the consultant appropriately call on the group strengths in solving the identified problems. Perhaps the greatest error consultants make when in the role of group leader is the inappropriate creation of a "therapeutic" group. As group leader, the consultant is usually dealing with previously existing groups of consultees or specifically designated problem-solving groups, not groups created with the purpose of helping individuals with their special problems. Although some

group techniques may be appropriately utilized in both types of group work, the role of the group leader is clearly different in aim from that of the consultant.

Political role

The conceptualization of consultation as a political process that maximizes the consultant's ability to mediate issues of power, control, authority, and competition, is extremely useful. This approach helps the consultant to anticipate problems that invariably arise, as well as to focus on what is occurring, either overtly or covertly, between actors in a given situation. Clear identification of the political issues assists the consultant in planning appropriate strategies for mediating the problem.

The interaction model proposed by Signell and Scott (1971) places the consultant in a political position within the consultee's system; this political position is influenced by whether the consultant is an insider or outsider. Baizerman and Hall (1977) consider consultation as a political bargaining process and list four social functions fulfilled by the consultant as politician. These functions, all consonant with the interaction model, include the following:

1. *Problem creation.* A situation or combination of facts is defined and legitimized as problematic.
2. *Priority raising.* Attention devoted to a problem may raise the action priority given it.
3. *Legitimation.* Redefinition of problem situations or people allow for resolution or continued bargaining in different decision-making structures.
4. *Interagency linkages.* The consultant acts as a bond or mediator in creating and maintaining linkages of value to both agencies.

Baizerman and Hall (1977, p. 143) describe consultation as a political bargaining process "in which expertise, organizational position, and personal organizational reputation are the currency of the bargaining between consultant and consultee; and in which each actor attempts to maximize his currency at minimum cost." They further suggest that "a change in vocabulary can accompany the change in perspective, and concepts such as 'power,' 'conflict,' 'strategy,' 'tactics,' 'linkage,' 'coalition,' and 'alliance' among others, can be used with advantage in the analysis and discussion of consultation."

Mediation always exists as an integral part of the political bargaining process; thus the role of mediator is an important one for consultants. Mediation by definition means the "intervention between conflicting parties to promote reconciliation, settlement, or compromise" (*Webster's New Collegiate Dictionary,* 1973, p. 714). It is not uncommon for a consultant to be in a position to mediate between various levels of the same system; between agencies that are trying out new models of cooperative planning; between local, state, and federal agencies; or simply between two people who cannot reach agreement about a specific problem.

Professionals have been loath to apply political symbolism and mediation skills to consultation practice. However, the usefulness of such application in analyzing situations and planning effective strategies far outweighs any negative opinion one might hold.

Role stress and strain

Most theorists describe two main orientations to role: a personal dimension that focuses on socialization into life roles and a structural dimension that focuses on given functional positions (Hinshaw, 1978). For the nurse consultant, the occupational and personal roles are most profoundly interrelated and often conflictual. Indeed, as the nurse moves into the relatively unfamiliar role of consultant, and its various subroles, a high level of role stress should be anticipated.

Role conflict—that is, the presence of contradictory and competing role expectations—is a frequent source of role stress. The consultant's expectations of the role may differ sharply from the expectations of the consultees. As the consultant

works with larger systems, this conflict may be sharpened by increased sets of role expectations. For example, expectations among consultees may vary widely depending on their degree of power in the system, their past experience with consultants, their professional discipline, their attitudes toward women, and many other factors. The sheer number of subroles required of the nurse consultant may cause role conflict when the existing subrole expectations are contradictory. Many nurses believe, for example, that the expectations of the clinician role and the political role are mutually exclusive. It is doubtful whether the required behaviors for these two roles are indeed contradictory. However, if consultants believe that roles are in conflict, they will experience role confusion when required to move between them. Likewise, a female consultant may experience role conflict when expectations associated with her role as female are contradictory to those associated with her role as consultant and outside expert.

Another frequent source of role stress for the consultant is role overload. According to Hardy (1978), *role overload* occurs when there is insufficient time in which to carry out all of one's role obligations. Since the consultant role is most often a time-limited one, it is often impossible to fulfill role demands completely. Also, as pointed out by Hardy (1978), this type of role stress may occur more frequently in positions that link one or more systems, which is typical of the nurse consultant.

A number of sources of role stress can be identified. Role conflict and role overload are only two, but were cited because of their particular relevance to the nurse consultant role. Hardy (1978, p. 91) states that role stress, in general, "is more prevalent in some roles and positions than in others. It is likely to be more common in those positions located at the boundary of a system or between systems. It is also likely to be relatively more common in emerging roles and during position shifts."

The individual's subjective response to role stress is often described as *role strain* (Hardy, 1978). Physiological and psychological indicators of stress are quite familiar, and these in turn trigger adaptive responses aimed at reducing role strain. Resolution or reduction of role strain is a complex and situation-specific process. In summary, nurses should anticipate a high degree of role stress as they move into the role of consultant, and should have some available skills with which to combat the resulting role strain.

THE CONSULTATION PROCESS

As mentioned, the consultation process uses a problem-solving approach to assist clients in considering alternatives and, when appropriate, in making changes in their system of operation. One of the first steps in consultation is to determine who the client is. Often the person who contacts the consultant is not the client, but is seeking these services for someone or some group. The identified clients may or may not be aware that consultation is forthcoming; they may not even desire these services.

Once it has been clarified who the consultee is, the next step is to discuss what each participant expects from the consultation experience. Often both consultant and consultee enter the process with different goals and expectations, and each may hold different covert and overt motivations regarding this experience. The perceptions that consultees bring are frequently associated with previous experiences with other consultants; hence it is important to ask a variety of questions in the initial encounter in order to determine past experiences with consultants as well as expectations, hopes, or fears about the process, and also to clarify goals.

The consultation process can be described according to a variety of stages. Torres (1973) and Lippitt and Lippitt (1977) offer models that are similar to the one chosen for this chapter, which includes three phases: (1) entry into the system; (2) problem solving; and (3) exit from the system.

Entry into the system

Before accepting any consultative role, the consultant needs a clear understanding of the system to be entered. This understanding includes not only the structure, organization, and power relationships within the primary agency, but also the primary agency's role, image, and influence in the larger community as well as its relationships with other specific organizations and agencies. Advance preparation for a consultation visit is essential. This includes learning about the city as well as the specific agency if the consultation is scheduled in an area other than the consultant's place of residence.

A crucial task during this first stage in the consultation process is that of establishing the contract. It is essential in establishing the contract to assess the needs of the consultee, the contractor (if different from the consultee), and the consultant. In defining the consultation contract, the consultant must find answers to the following questions:

1. Who is the consultee?
2. What is the purpose (goal) of the consultation?
3. When do the consultees want the consultation to take place, and how long do they expect this relationship to exist?
4. Where is the consultation to take place?
5. How is the consultation to be carried out (group meetings, observation, role modeling, etc.)?
6. Why was consultation sought?

It is not uncommon for a contractor to enlist the services of a consultant to work with a group who may or may not see the need for such assistance. Hence it is important to ask the consultees how they come to the session—that is, by choice or coercion.

During the entry stage, it is important also to orient the consultees to you. They need to know (1) who you are; (2) how you got there—that is, who invited you; (3) why you are there; (4) how you anticipate the meeting will run; and (5) what you expect of them.

When entering a consultation relationship it is important to listen to everyone (Norris, 1977). It will often become evident that each participant has a different perception about the proposed need for consultation. Participants may disagree about whether a problem exists. If there is consensus that a problem exists, members of the consultee group may disagree as to its scope. During this phase, the consultant helps the consultees to explain their personal perception of the problem, the need for change, and the goal of the consultation experience. At this point, the consultant makes an assessment of total readiness for change. When major conflicts surface, the consultant may need to devote considerable attention and energy to helping the consultees reach some agreement on identifying the problem.

Throughout the consultation relationship, the consultant needs to refrain from "taking sides" or seeming to agree with only one segment of the consultee group. It is also important to pay attention to the less verbal members of the group. They may have significant observations and insight into the problem and need for consultation; but because of shyness, lack of motivation, or their perceived position in the group they may hesitate to state their impressions.

The following case illustrates an actual example of entry into the system. The primary agency in this case was the Beckley Appalachian Regional Hospital in West Virginia.* The Appalachian Regional Hospital system comprises ten nonprofit hospitals in three states: Kentucky, Virginia, and West Virginia. These hospitals are located in isolated areas of the Appalachian Mountains, where coal mining is the major industry. Therefore, the hospitals have historically provided service to a clientele composed chiefly of people related directly or indirectly to the coal industry. The fate of the hospitals rises and falls as the economy of the industry rises and falls.

The largest and traditionally most progressive of the ten hospitals is located in Beckley, West Virginia. The hospital is a 220-bed general acute care facility that serves as a major teaching site for the southern part of the state. It has been recognized for

*Example used with permission.

promoting innovative services for a rural mountain population.

The request for consultation emanated from the director of nursing services at the Beckley Appalachian Regional Hospital. As she described what was needed from a consultant, it became clear that in actuality there were multiple problems involved. The first problem was specific: the hospital was under contract with the local community mental health center to develop inpatient psychiatric services. The identification of this problem served to highlight larger and more complex problems. Sources of power and influence were quickly identified within the hospital system and in the larger community.

The procurement of multilevel sanctions is critical to the success of the consultation process. Lack of sanctions at any level may interfere with the consultant's credibility, prevent access to resources, or sabotage implementation of problem solutions.

Sanctions both within the hospital system and outside of the hospital system were necessary in this case. The director of nursing had procured firm sanctions at various levels within the hospital before the arrival of the consultant. She also already had a high level of credibility in her local community and within the state. She identified and arranged meetings with administrative heads of agencies and institutions that would be important with respect to sanctioning a plan, as well as having the potential of needed resources. Together the director of nursing and the consultant met with a wide variety of people within the state to explore ideas, gather information, and gain sanction of planning that might affect and involve their programs. Even at this early stage, the consultant was functioning in her political role by establishing some new and important interagency linkages.

There are two major principles involved in this phase. First, the consultant is an "outsider" brought in as an expert. The consultant must rely on the primary consultee, in this instance the director of nursing, to identify and gain entry to other systems that might be important to the accomplishment of an emerging plan. Second, the consultant must be alert to the existence of territorial boundaries and interagency conflict and competition.

Although the procurement of multilevel sanctions helps to establish the initial acceptance of the consultant, credibility is a status primarily proved and earned by the consultant. In this case, establishing credibility with both nursing staff and members of other disciplines throughout the system was a major task.

The director of nursing explained that the nursing staff were apprehensive about having a nursing consultant with a doctoral degree. It was thus essential that the consultant be viewed as a nonthreatening, nonjudgmental, and at the same time, knowledgeable partner in solving the problems at hand. The other side of the coin was to establish credibility with department heads, the administrator, physicians, and other hospital personnel. These people were not accustomed to having a nursing consultant and were somewhat skeptical of the idea. It was essential that this group view the consultant as knowledgeable, skilled, and equal to the task. In both instances, it was necessary for the consultant to draw on interpersonal and political skills in order to be acceptable to either group. The consultant approached this problem by meeting formally and informally with both groups. The meetings were designed for the purpose of gathering information, assessing attitudes and strengths, and soliciting ideas and suggestions. Equally important was that the consultant be willing to share ideas, impressions, and suggestions. From the beginning, the consultant made it clear that consultees at all levels of the system were to be involved in the initiation and planning of change.

Establishing credibility and acceptance in a new system is a difficult and sometimes time-consuming part of the consultation process. Unless it is successfully accomplished, however, the best of consultation plans may fail. The consultant in this case found that "hanging out" was a critical step in establishing credibility. "Hanging out" describes the interactional process through which the consultant and consultees become familiar with each other.

A frequent response to the anxiety of being in a new role or a new setting is to throw oneself into frantic activity in hopes of being quickly accepted and integrated into the system. Action-oriented behavior may reduce anxiety but does not help in understanding the system.

Moving into an unfamiliar system in order to influence others is a tricky business. Many of us assume that because we have been sanctioned to enter the system as a consultant we can automatically move ahead with our own ideas. This is when the action-oriented person immediately gets into trouble. Permanent enemies can be made by carelessly and thoughtlessly stepping on toes and turf in the process of single-mindedly pursuing one's own ideas and wishes. It is also an indication that there is a lack of sensitivity as well as a sense of what has been done before by individuals within a given organization. This common error, made by many professionals, causes one to pause and wonder what happened when the dust has settled and nothing has changed.

A major missing ingredient for many professionals is the lack of understanding of the concept of "hanging out." Although the slang term "hanging out" has not been a common part of a professional vocabulary, it most accurately expresses what must be done in order to move smoothly into a new system. More importantly, the outcome of using this concept means a better chance for achieving the success that you envision. Many people react to the expression "hanging out" negatively. It is frequently interpreted as doing nothing. However, talking to persons who have developed the ability to "hang out" will reveal that they have a wealth of information about what goes on around them.

Contrary to what one might believe, it takes quite a lot of energy to effectively "hang out." It requires a change in the attitude that "hanging out" is nonproductive and lazy. Furthermore, it means that direct action, or what is usually considered work, is delayed. It takes time and requires that you sit around and talk. More importantly, it requires active listening, since each person holds a unique perspective of the system. An effective "hanger outer" will have a much clearer picture of the strengths and weaknesses of the system by talking with and getting to know a wide variety of people. In other words, "hanging out" provides a road map of the history of the system, the attitudes and values that its workers hold, and the areas where change might occur.

While consultants are gaining information about the system and its workers, they are being evaluated as well. If "hanging out" is approached as a ridiculous task that must be done until one gets on to the "real work," the consultant will not be perceived as a person with a serious intent of learning from others. On the other hand, if "hanging out" is viewed as an essential first step in establishing effectiveness in a system, the consultant will be perceived as a person who can be trusted and valued.

Problem solving

A consultant is usually sought to provide a specific needed service, which is usually to solve a previously identified problem. In analyzing the problem presented, the astute consultant is usually able to identify numerous underlying problems that must also be taken into consideration or addressed directly during the problem-solving phase. These underlying problems are often subtle and frequently interactional in nature. Some examples of underlying problems include unclear goals, ineffective organization, inappropriate programming, power struggles, role conflicts, ineffective leadership, inadequate interagency networks, inappropriate allocation or utilization of resources, lack of knowledge or skills, and conflicts of authority versus autonomy.

When there is ambiguity about the problem or need, the initial step in this stage is to help the consultee to restate or further define or clarify the perceived problem. The identified problem is quite often not the real one. Frequently a superficial problem or issue is serving as a disguise for a more complex or difficult issue. It is the consultant's responsibility to take into account all aspects of the situation and to help the consultee carefully develop the problem or set of problems. If more than one problem is identified, then the consultant serves as a leader in the priority-setting process. Once priorities have been established, the problems or goals should be stated in specific rather than broad terms in order to structure the consultative process more effectively.

A considerable amount of information may have to be gathered in order to understand the problem clearly. Some information can often be sent to the consultant in advance so that valuable time can be saved during the actual on-site visit. Once data have been gathered about the problem and priorities for action established, then the consultant can assist the group to consider alternatives for problem resolution. The preferences of the consultees must be respected regarding alternatives because they will be the ones implementing the plan and living with its consequences.

It is helpful to remember that in the majority of consultation experiences, the problem is people. It may be that leadership is inadequate, or staff are incompetent, unmotivated, or poorly guided. In most instances, consultation is requested long after the problem has become apparent. The consultees may have spent considerable time and energy "fire-fighting" to keep the small crises under control. It is vitally important for the target of the interventions to be included in the planning and implementation of the change process.

As described earlier, the major problem identified in this situation was the need for planning for the care of clients with mental health problems in the general hospital setting. There were indeed many underlying problems. For example, there were no nursing personnel within the hospital who were clinically prepared to develop programs and services for psychiatric patients. In truth, there was a high level of anxiety among all of the hospital staff about the wisdom of having such a service in a general hospital. Various nursing staff had gone to workshops and continuing education programs and came back to report that they still did not feel qualified to tackle such an undertaking. Recruitment efforts outside of the system for qualified personnel had not been successful.

The director of nursing services hypothesized that if nursing staff felt so strongly that they were not qualified to deal with the emotional problems of psychiatric patients, then the emotional needs of the general hospital patient population might be unmet as well. Mental health services had not been well received in this rural community, and a large percentage of staff and patients were more comfortable at that point keeping mental health problems clearly separated from physical health problems.

Also recognized was an initial level of resistance and resentment from other departments within the hospital, who felt it somehow inappropriate that nursing should initiate the planning process in this area. Clearly, these problems were important to recognize and required time, ingenuity, flexibility, and planning to solve.

It is important to note here that as all of this is happening, the consultant is getting ideas, formulating potential plans, and checking them out with consultees at all levels of the system as the consultation process is going on. At this point the plan for change is *emerging,* based on data the consultant is gathering and processing.

In this instance it was obvious that there could be no inpatient psychiatric services without adequately trained people. Further, the traditional method of using workshops and continuing education programs as a means of gaining expertise was not sufficient. Finally, other agencies in the community had expressed similar concerns about meeting the emotional needs of their clients, and a plan was sought that would strengthen these interagency linkages.

After several alternatives were considered and discarded, a solution was developed that was acceptable to the consultant and consultees and realistic to implement in the system. The solution was ambitious and exciting and required long-range planning and commitment at many levels of the system. It was perhaps the ambitious and innovative nature of the plan that facilitated the consultees' commitment to it. The solution was to design and implement a comprehensive training program to teach interpersonal skills to nurses in several agencies in the community. Skills would initially be geared to those necessary to meet the mental health needs of the general hospital patient, and would increase in complexity over time. The program will not be described in detail here, because our purpose is to focus on the consultation process.

Once the solution was arrived at, other problems immediately emerged. For example, the program would have to be designed flexibly enough to be useful to nurses in a variety of settings. It would need to be operative for a long enough period of time to ensure that expertise could be developed within the agencies. In the meantime, it was imperative to recruit a qualified master's-degree prepared psychiatric–mental health nurse to begin the groundwork and coordinate the implementation. Last, and by no means least, funding had to be located to support such a large-scale program.

At this stage the consultant relied heavily on her political bargaining role, negotiating for resources and establishing interagency linkages. She solicited the aid and commitment of an educator with the expertise to take the required ingredients, design an appropriate educational model, and agree to implement it. The consultant also had access to newly graduating students with master's degrees and succeeded in assisting with their recruitment. It was necessary for the consultant to identify appropriate federal agencies with available funds for such a project and to provide technical assistance as well as to participate in the writing of a grant proposal.

The major principle involved in this phase of consultation was that developing a plan was not sufficient for solving the problems presented to the consultant. It was essential that the consultant move beyond the traditional role considered appropriate and become an active partner in carrying out the plan.

In designing and implementing a continuing education model that involved local, state, and federal agencies, as well as an out-of-state university, it was clear from the beginning that issues of power, authority, control, competition, and recognition of differing individual needs would continually influence the process. The consultant must be able to move flexibly among the roles of clinician, teacher, group leader, and politician.

Whether the problem is large or small, as consultants are required to work in social systems that are increasingly complex, the role of mediation can be more clearly defined as an important function. Mediation as a part of the political bargaining process can be brought into sharp focus through a long-term consultation model such as this one. Mutuality of goals is the key to successful mediation. At the base of many conflicts identified in this project lay divergent or shifting goals between individuals or agencies. Signell and Scott (1971) discuss mutuality of goals as a critical aspect of their interaction model of consultation. In this case, it was an essential part of the mediation process for the consultant to help all parties keep sight of the mutual long-term goals of the project. At times, a simple reminder to the project team that whatever was occurring had the potential of undermining the success of the project was enough to pave the way to a resolution. The personal investment in the success of the project was a sustaining force for all participants and allowed maximal opportunity for mediation to be effective.

The importance of the consultant's role as mediator, boundary spanner, group leader, and role model cannot be overemphasized. The following examples demonstrate these roles.

Interagency conflict

Although all of the agencies that agreed in principle to participate in the project had input into the initial continuing education design, the first problem to arise was that some agencies felt that the program as designed did not meet their needs. The consultant was called in to mediate the problem. Because of her previous relationships with the agencies, she had ready access to the systems. After lengthy discussion, the problem identified consisted of the unrealistic expectations that staff would be fully prepared to deal effectively with mental health problems after participating in one workshop. The process was to renegotiate each agency's participation and redefine the specific needs of the various agencies in order for the project to be more responsive. This process of redefining and renegotiating occurred many times over the next six years.

In one instance, it was impossible to renegotiate an agency's participation. A new administrative group had entered the system with a different philosophy. Negotiations broke down permanently when it became clear that the agency wanted control of the federal funding that supported the project. Since that was a nonnegotiable item, the agency discontinued its participation.

Educational needs versus service needs

Although this project was designed as a partnership between education and service in order to meet a specific need, the problems encountered between the two cannot be minimized. In order for agency staff to participate fully in the project, a heavier work-load demand was placed on those staff who were not participating. This was particularly true for staff who were responsible for direct patient care in hospital settings. Furthermore, this problem had a ripple effect throughout the system. Scheduling was problematic for head nurses, and the worry about overall coverage of the hospital increased for supervisors. Ultimately, these problems landed in the lap of the director of nursing.

On the other hand, service demands at times jeopardized the educational design and goals, which created conflict for the people teaching in the project. Pressures to alter the original design of the project triggered off protection-of-turf and vested-interest behaviors of the educators.

The consultant was called in on numerous occasions to mediate these ongoing conflicts. Timetables for the project were altered as it became clear that all outcomes envisioned by the project team could not be realistically accomplished within a specific time period. As problems arose and were resolved, the project became increasingly flexible.

A major stress occurred when two additional universities agreed to participate in the project. New faculty were added to the original project team. Differing educational backgrounds and philosophies had to be integrated into an existing system. The original team, of necessity, had to give up some of the power and control and turn over some of the responsibility for charting new directions to the newer members. These were difficult issues that, on occasion, required direct confrontation between opposing factions. The consultant was called on to facilitate a resolution or compromise.

Interpersonal conflicts between project team members

It should be anticipated that when people work together for a long period of time to accomplish a task, interpersonal conflicts will be a part of the picture. This was true throughout the project period. The needs for power, control, authority, and recognition emerged at various times and among all participants.

The issue of leadership was a constant source of difficulty. Initially the undercurrent existed between fewer people. As the project team increased in size, more people became involved in vying for the leadership position. A later development was the quasi-resolution of competitive issues. That is, different leaders emerged who were most appropriate to handle the specific problem at hand. For example, if the group problem was essentially an administrative one, the administrator, in this case the director of nursing, emerged as the leader. If the problem was an educational one, any one of the educators became the leader.

The consultant again served as a mediator for the team. On occasion a social evening served as a means of regrouping when splintering or conflict had occurred. At other times, encouraging the expression of angry feelings was necessary to clear the air and get back to the task at hand. As the project team developed into a more cohesive and self-confident group, the amount and level of conflict decreased.

Exit from the system

Although consultation has been an accepted process for many years, there have been relatively few systematic attempts to evaluate its effectiveness in bringing about change. Systematic research regarding the process and outcomes of consultation is still in an early stage and is predominantly descriptive in nature. To study the process of consultation is to study the characteristic dimensions of its longitudinal course. Such studies are most frequently based on self-reported opinions and perceptions of consultants and consultees, and on analysis of consultant-consultee interactions. Studies that focus on the outcomes of consultation usually measure changes in the consultees, changes in the client group, or changes in the agency or system, depending on the established goals of the consultation program (LaGodna, 1975).

Ideally, evaluation should be consciously carried out at every step of the consultation process. For those consultants who seek to bring about change in a system, evaluation can be both exhilarating and devastating. Outcomes depend on a number of variables, including the skills of the consultant, the readiness of the consultees for change, the openness of the system to absorb change, and other more subtle factors. Influential in the process of evaluation is the fact that the consultant is one whose role in an organization may be sanctioned, but whose lack of formal authority means that the ideas or advice offered can be either rejected or accepted by the consultees. People who need immediate feedback or clearly identifiable positive outcomes from their work generally cannot tolerate the ambiguity of the consultant role.

Evaluation is critical to the consultation process, however. Outcomes should be measured against mutual goals established early in the problem-solving phase. In the situation described throughout this chapter, expected outcomes had been identified at various intervals along the way and they served as clear evaluative criteria. For example, over the extended consultation period, shifts in roles were important indicators of consultation success. Consultees began to assume the responsibility for political negotiations within and between systems, which had been a major task for the consultant.

Other less obvious cues were important in evaluating the outcomes of consultation. Nurses who at first were suspicious of the consultant and the program were heard explaining and supporting it to others. In the face of a miners' strike that severely affected the hospital, commitment to the program continued. Problems that earlier would have been referred to the consultant were now being handled by consultees and other members of the project team. Some outcomes were in the form of changes clearly growth producing but disruptive to the system. Many nurses were less willing to assume responsibilities abdicated by other professional disciplines and began to seek and demand a more active role in policy decisions affecting working conditions and quality of patient care.

If consultation outcomes are too narrowly defined, one is likely to underestimate the effects. On the other hand, it is usually impossible to trace the specific origin of broad changes that occur in a system.

The ultimate aim of any long-term consultation is planned obsolescence. During the initial phases of the consultation process, it is assumed that the consultant is the expert. It is imperative to begin immediately to establish that the plan initiated by the consultant is based on the information given to her by the various people with whom she has discussed the problem. The consultant is a partner who will assist the consultees in designing a plan that is feasible for them to implement. In other words, the consultant plans how to put herself out of business.

As this project progressed from the initial phase—through developing the educational model, grant writing, site visits, and implementa-tion—people within the agency gradually began to assume more and more responsibility for all phases of the project. The role of the consultant became one of supporting and encouraging greater responsibility, autonomy, and decision making.

As one's consultees question old role expectations or try out new roles, they too are likely to experience role strain. The consultant must help them anticipate and cope with this phenomenon in order to support and maintain the changes that have occurred. Although the consultant does not always receive direct feedback from consultees regarding the consultation process, it is still important for the consultant to provide feedback to consultees regarding their progress, achievements, and contributions to the process of change as part of the termination process. A formal written report is essential for permanently recording goals, progress, and evaluation.

As termination began in this project, visits to the agency were less frequent and consultation was carried on by telephone when consultees needed an outside opinion. Termination occurs over time and seems to happen spontaneously when both the consultant and consultees are able to move beyond their respective roles and simply remain in contact out of mutual interest and commitment to each other and the project they have developed and nurtured as partners. Early clues are fewer telephone calls asking for advice or visits. The nature of the calls change as well. Consultees will more frequently call to tell the consultant about a decision or about a new development. The conversations are clearly between colleagues rather than between an "expert" and a learner. The role of the consultant in this last phase is to accept and encourage independence and to sit back and enjoy what has been accomplished.

RESISTANCE TO CONSULTATION

Even though prospective consultees may desire the services of a consultant and may have been experiencing a great deal of stress and often misery or helplessness, they may nevertheless demonstrate a considerable amount of resistance. Resistance may initially be evidenced in extended tours of facilities, lengthy historical overviews, or social events that exceed the need merely to meet people and establish some degree of warmth and trust toward the consultation. Resistance or disruption of the consultation relationship can occur when the consultant makes any of the following errors:

1. Offers advice or solutions too readily without giving the consultees a chance to use their own problem-solving skills
2. Remains inactive verbally over a series of sessions
3. Comments on too many areas of interaction in a given time, and burdens the consultees with too much information
4. Does not listen for the key problem
5. Becomes distracted with peripheral issues
6. Makes recommendations or gives advice that may conflict with administrative policy of the consultee's organization
7. Assumes the role of supervisor
8. Forces own point of view and biases on consultees
9. Lacks awareness of own limitations, thus promoting the illusion of omnipotence
10. Becomes primarily an educator, trying to tell the consultees what to do
11. Makes a patient of the consultee

SUMMARY

This chapter reviews definitions, classification schemes, and conceptual models of consultation. The interaction model of consultation is described, in which the nurse consultant spans boundaries between levels in a system and between systems in her roles of clinician, teacher, group leader, and politician. Using the example of a long-term consultation agreement, the phases of the consultation process are delineated and described from entry into the system until termination.

REFERENCES

Baizerman, M., and Hall, W.T.: Consultation as a political process, Community Ment. Health J. **13**(2):142-149, Summer 1977.

Bindman, A.J.: Mental health consultation: theory and practice, J. Consult. Psychol. **23**:473-482, Dec. 1959.

Bindman, A.J.: The clinical psychologist as a mental health consultant. In Abt, L.E., and Riess, B.F., editors: Progress in clinical psychology, New York, 1966, Grune & Stratton.

Caplan, G.: Principles of preventive psychiatry, New York, 1964, Basic Books.

Caplan, G.: The theory and practice of mental health consultation, New York, 1970, Basic Books.

Hardy, M.E., and Conway, M.E.: Role theory: perspectives for health professionals, New York, 1978, Appleton-Century-Crofts.

Haylett, C.H., and Rapoport, L.: Mental health consultation. In Bellak, L., editor: Handbook of community mental health practice, San Francisco, 1969, Jossey-Bass Publishing Co.

Hinshaw, A.S.: Role attitudes: a measurement problem. In Hardy, M.E., and Conway, M.E., editors: Role theory: perspectives for health professionals, New York, 1978, Appleton-Century-Crofts.

LaGodna, G.E.: Mental health consultation with community nurses, unpublished doctoral dissertation, University of Kentucky, 1975.

Lippitt, R., and Lippitt, G.L.: Consulting process in action. In Jones, J.E., and Pfeiffer, J.W., editors: The 1977 annual handbook for group facilitators, La Jolla, Calif., 1977, University Associates, Inc.

McClung, F., and Stunden, A.: Mental health consultation to programs for children: a review of data collected from selected U.S. sites, Publication No. (HSM) 72-9088, Washington, D.C., 1972, U.S. Department of HEW, National Institute of Mental Health.

McClung, F., Stunden, A., and Plog, S.: A study of the theory and practice of mental health consultation as provided to child care agencies throughout the United States, 3 vols., Washington, D.C., 1969, Behavioral Science Corporation and Center for Studies of Child and Family Mental Health, National Institute of Mental Health.

Norris, C.M.: A few notes on consultation in nursing, Nurs. Outlook **25**:756-761, Dec. 1977.

Signell, K.A., and Scott, P.A.: Mental health consultation: an interaction model, Community Ment. Health J. **7**(4):288-302, Dec. 1971.

Signell, K.A., and Scott, P.A.: Training in consultation: a crisis of role transition, Community Ment. Health J. **8**(2):149-160, May 1972.

Torres, G.: The consultation process in higher education, Publication No. 15-1508, New York, 1973, National League for Nursing.

Webster's New Collegiate Dictionary, Springfield, Mass., 1973, G. & C. Merriam Co.

History is not made merely through ideas and persons but through their functioning within groups and institutions. These groups and institutions occupy space, and even compete for it in a struggle for power, that is, in a struggle to participate in the shaping of social decisions.

Adams, J.: Union Sem. Q. Rev. **29**(3):246, 1974.

25

MAKING CHANGE THROUGH POWER AND ASSERTIVE ACTIONS

Elizabeth G. Morrison and Paula Purse Pointer

Nursing's efforts to advance itself as a profession have been frustrated by a multitude of internal and external forces. Chapter 14 describes a historical view of the social forces that have affected nursing's development. Specifically, nurses have generally been rewarded and encouraged for demonstrating conformity and a nonthreatening demeanor. Unlike so many other professions—for example, medicine, dentistry, or law—nursing has not established itself as an independent practice. In most other professions, the practitioner works directly with the client. In contrast, most of the practice of nursing takes place within institutions where employers impose a second value system between nurses and patients which complicates nursing practice.

In this context nurses are often considered the "hired help," with physicians and hospital administrators having considerable control over the scope of and environment in which nursing is practiced. Frequently nurses struggle to control their standards of practice and often find themselves torn between the demands of the institution and those of the profession. Nurses often find that their services receive limited recognition by patients who frequently have no basis of comparison for the care they receive. Moreover, nursing care is reflected in hospital charges generally as one component of room and board costs. Such reimbursement mechanisms often discount the worth and value of nursing services.

If nursing is to become increasingly respected and recognized, then the change strategies in this book must be considered as imperatives for action. This chapter considers two somewhat different, yet interwoven ways to negotiate greater recognition for nursing. The acquisition of power and the development of assertive behavior patterns are essential to future change efforts. These concepts are not mutually exclusive; both imply taking responsibility for personal actions. They both necessitate clarity of thinking as well as honest and straightforward communication with others. In essence, assertive actions serve as a useful mechanism for gaining personal, professional, and political power. This chapter looks first at these three types of power and then sets forth assertive strategies for gaining power.

POWER: TYPES, USES, AND IMPLICATIONS FOR NURSES

Few would question that nursing, as a health care profession, faces a decade in which the shaping of social decisions is synonymous with the shaping of the quality of human life. We live in a time when no one issue can be realistically abstracted from the complex web of societal structure and examined in isolation. Nursing, therefore, can no longer continue to focus exclusively on the health and illness care of clients; rather, nurses must participate in and influence the social context in which health and illness care issues are imbedded.

In order to participate in the shaping of social decisions, nurses need both power and space, which are intimately related concepts. Consider, for example, the heads of state who have bodyguards surrounding them and clearing space in their immediate interpersonal environments. Also, consider the power distribution as noted in the size of offices of the heads of companies and department chairpersons in universities. Why would nurses want power and space? Traditionally, as Adams (1974) unwittingly points out, social institutions have been controlled by men. Never in recorded history has there been a time when social institutions have been controlled by women; the farther women get from their particular sphere of influence, the family, the less power and control they are accorded. In fact, it has been said that women are incapable of exercising power and influence because of their passive feminine nature.

Diers (1978) believes that nurses need power in order to take over the health care system. Kalisch (1978) maintains that nurses need power in order to strengthen and develop the profession. The implication seems to be that nurses currently do not have power and should get it, whatever it is. Ashley (1973) states that nurses have had, do have, and will continue to have power; however, they have been misusing, abusing, or failing to use it. If nurses, as the largest group of health care providers in the United States, are concerned about health care for their clients, then it seems ethically consistent with the aims and goals of nursing that nurses should have the power to put their convictions and beliefs about health care into effect.

What is power? According to Jackson and Maughan (1978), power is a value connected to authority and has two important components: legitimacy and coercion. French and Raven (1959) define power in terms of its reciprocity with powerlessness, and list five bases of social power: legitimate, reward, coercive, expert, and referent. To reiterate some of the definitions given in Chapter 7, legitimate power involves situations whereby there is reciprocal agreement between groups or individuals that certain persons have the right to make the rules by which the group will abide. Democratic governments are elected and charged to govern on the basis of legitimacy. Colleges and universities derive power from a combination of legitimacy and expertise. In contrast, the power given physicians is based on expertise, while the foundation of social power is coercion, that is, the means to compel compliance if other aspects of power fail. The salient point is that power ultimately involves coercion, and coercion is the one type of power with which women do not usually have facility. Personal power is the acknowledged ability to control one's own time and space. Women's familiarity with covert, as opposed to overt, expressions of power has led to some deficiencies in the ability to conceptualize, express, and respond to different types of power.

The majority of nurses are, have been, and most likely will continue to be women. If nursing is to increase its sphere of influence and social participation, then nurses must become powerful enough to compete for and hold control of a societal institution, that is, health care. In order to accomplish such a goal, an understanding of and ability to use varying types of power is an absolute necessity.

What is already being done in nursing? What has yet to be accomplished? For purposes of discussion, the remainder of this presentation on power will be divided into three sections: personal power, professional power, and political power. The section on personal power will review some current research on dominance and submission in our culture, and its implications for nursing. The section on professional power will consider the status of accountability and expertise in nursing, and the section on political power will focus on the legislative process and how nursing can use it to advantage. Each section contains suggestions for action to increase nurse power.

PERSONAL POWER

The most effective way to increase the personal power of women is to acknowledge the differences in the ways boys and girls learn to use their bodies. Boys are socialized to use their bodies, not only to defend themselves, but also to exert and assert themselves. In the process, boys also learn to work together physically as a team. They learn both the advantages of individual power and the advantages of group power. Girls have no such sanctioned opportunities to learn what they can do with their physical selves. Certainly, dance is an approved physical activity for girls, but it is concerned with discipline and restraint (gracefulness), rather than aggression and the use of force to accomplish a goal.

What are some of the end results of differences in the ways boys and girls learn to use their bodies? Important differences have to do with the use of personal space. The concept of territoriality is a commonly accepted one. Each person has a certain amount of personal space shared to varying degrees with others. The more power and status an individual has, the more space is likely to be accorded that individual. Also, the more power an individual has, the more likely that individual is to take space and to move into the space of others without seeking permission. Conversely, the less power an individual has, the less space that individual is accorded and the more violable the space by others. Henley (1977) reports that women are acculturated to shrink their personal space (it is more feminine), whereas men are acculturated to expand their personal space (it is more masculine). In addition, Henley (1977) also cites evidence that women's space is more violated than that of men.

What has this got to do with nursing? Certainly we are not going to include courses in physical coercion in nursing curricula in the near future and probably not even in grammar school curriculum. There is promise, however, in the growing number of women taking courses in the martial arts (unfortunately, primarily for self-defense), and in the growing number of girls playing team sports. How can we use this information? The most significant way to use the information that is currently available about personal power and influence is in a consciousness-raising way. Long before Stein (1967) first identified the doctor-nurse game, nurses were able to pinpoint the linguistic basis for dominance and submission, power and obedience in the physician-nurse relationship. Awareness of the use of space can help nurses to get themselves out of powerless positions. How? By not participating in traditionally powerless nonverbal behavior such as shrinking space and allowing violations of personal space, nurses can avoid powerless roles or positions. For example, nurses tend to "give ground" when a physician or other perceived power person appears on the scene. Giving ground can include gathering up belongings to make room for the other, gathering up oneself to provide more room for the other, giving up a chair, or physically retreating to another less desirable space. Nurses permit physicians to touch them with much frequency, and occasionally with more intimacy, than nurses initiate touching behavior.

One obvious way to strengthen a powerless nonverbal position is not to move—that is, do not give up space. Chances are that some consequences will accrue from that behavior and it is important to be prepared to deal with being accused of a variety of things ranging from being inattentive or insensitive to the needs of others to the worst insult of all, being "castrating." However, if nurses decide to hold on to the space they possess and begin to identify certain spaces as belonging to nursing, an interesting phenomenon will occur. Others will believe that, in fact, there is space that belongs to nursing, to which nursing is entitled, and into which others will not move without permission.

A change in the nonverbal behavior of nurses (acculturated to submission and obedience) will not only shock physicians and administrators who have come to expect passive behavior, but also colleagues who also have come to expect the same. If nurses can change their behavior, and maintain that change in the face of pressure to conform to the more expected way of behaving, then gradually the system will begin to change.

The other group of people who need to prepare themselves for a shock are nurse educators. As more and more young women interested in feminism and women's issues enter nursing, they will do much rocking of old boats. Assertive nursing students are neither the norm, nor are they consistently tolerated well in nursing schools where conformity and covert "beating the system" are the keys to educational success.

Randolph and Ross-Valliere (1979) outline a plan for consciousness-raising groups for the specific purpose of dealing with nursing issues. The consciousness-raising process is strongly recommended as a way to identify issues, trace their development, acknowledge the participation of nurses and others in the maintenance and perpetuation of issues, plan alternative behaviors, anticipate consequences, and obtain support and comfort along the way. It is not recommended that change be implemented on a haphazard basis; it should be thought out well in advance.

PROFESSIONAL POWER

Professional power, based on collective personal and expert power, has a variety of dimensions. Those of expertise and accountability will be considered. Jacox (1978) contends that the professional socialization of nurses begins in girlhood and has its roots in stereotypical behaviors such as obedience and servitude. Ashley (1976) describes the nature of the hospital environment, with its assorted personnel, as a hospital family, and equates the roles of nurses in hospital families with the roles of wives and mothers in social families. There is nothing approaching colleagueship in the description. If, in fact, that is so, where is all the literature on competence and accountability coming from? There are possibly two main sources: a concern for the establishment of professional power and women's inhumanity to women. To speak to the latter point first, some women have difficulty allowing other women to achieve because they perceive competition as personal (as they have been taught from childhood) and not as professional (as boys are taught) means to a professional goal. Women tend to see their work as jobs and not as careers until much later in life than men do, if at all (Hennig and Jardim, 1976). This may account, on the one hand, for much of the divisiveness, confusion, and arguing in nursing over issues such as entry into practice, accountability, and responsibility.

On the other hand, professional power is legitimately connected with expertise and accountability. As nurses make an effort to define themselves as a professional discipline, accountable and liable for their practice, they must make an equal effort to take responsibility for their own professional behavior. Accepting the consequences of one's own behavior is a frightening and risky prospect for many women and many nurses who have been protected, comforted, and told not to worry all their lives. An anonymous author ("Facing a Grand Jury," 1976) describes in detail what can and did happen to a nurse who considered herself and was considered by others accountable and responsible for her own behavior and her own nursing decisions. In the instance presented, a group of nurses were investigated by a grand jury on criminal charges related to the performance of abortions in the hospital where the nurses were employed. It is interesting that the author notes that initially no one thought the nurses would be included in the suit because no one thought they would be held accountable for their actions. The legal system thought otherwise and charges were brought. Many of the intricacies and complexities of dealing with the legal system and other systems are well defined. The experience of facing a grand jury was not pleasant, but was useful in that a stand for nursing was taken and a position was won.

McClure (1978) suggests ways to improve or accelerate expertise and accountability. One way is to be more selective about who is admitted to schools of nursing. According to McClure, an egalitarian approach to education limits education to the lowest common denominator. Another suggestion has to do with seizing responsibility before it is either delegated or demanded of nurses, and a third is to establish an effective system of peer review. All three of the proposals are concerned with upgrading nurses as well as serving as a commentary on the development of increased professional power.

Nursing's professional power base lies in its legal definitions as evidenced by the practice acts in each state, in the expertise demonstrated by each individual practitioner, and in the responsibility practitioners take for their actions. Fagin (1975) connects rights and responsibilities and contends that nurses have rights as well as responsibilities and would do well to align themselves with the women's rights movement in its struggle for dignity and equality for all people. There is most assuredly a connection between the image of women and the image of nurses as presented in the public media. The perception of expertise of nurses by the public and by other health professionals is connected to the image of nurses and nursing. The image of nursing should be of concern to every nurse, and a list of specific actions that might be taken is offered by *The American Nurse* ("Nurse Offers Suggestions to Change Media Image," 1980, p. 23):

—Watch the media. If you see or hear a program or advertisement that degrades women or nurses or portrays an untrue image of the profession of nursing,

protest in writing to the network or publication and to the sponsors or advertisers. Offer your services as a consultant to assist them in improving the image they are presenting.
—Boycott products such as T-shirts and bumper stickers that portray a sexy or promiscuous image of nurses and women.
—Watch out for sexual harassment on the job and make written reports to the proper authority documenting incidents.
—Make it known to those who make money from the pornographic display of nurses in sexy and violent films, magazines and porn shops that you oppose them. Send copies of your letters to local legislators and city council members.

Professional power contains two equally important elements: the development of expertise and accountability within the profession and the presentation of the profession to the public and to other health care professions. The fact that most nurses are women cannot be ignored in either category.

POLITICAL POWER

If personal power is achieved via consciousness raising and professional power is achieved through expertise and imagery, political power is achieved through legitimacy. Legitimacy is acknowledged through organizational involvement in the legislative process, which includes getting to know how local, county, state, and national issues affect health care. To be involved, nurses need to make themselves available for lobbying activities, serve on policy-making boards of health care agencies, and familiarize themselves with health care issues at all levels of government. Involvement also means that nurses are running for and being elected to public offices, and that nurses know how power operates at all levels of government.

Nurses are the largest body of health care providers in the country. Do we also realize that that makes us the biggest bloc of health care voters? In conjunction with a growing activist health care consumer movement, nursing could potentially control every health care policy in the nation. It is

frightening to contemplate, not just for nurses, who are unused to the idea of wielding so much power, but also for physicians, who are used to the reality of tremendous power and who are increasingly concerned that nurses might just one day get moving as a group.

Political power involves becoming visible as individuals, as groups, as *nurses,* taking stands on the rights of nurses, the rights of patients, and health issues. The more nurses learn about legislative processes, the less intimidating those processes become. Certainly, not every nurse has the time, the energy, or the inclination to deal with politics. Nurses can, however, support the efforts of others who are invested in the process through such avenues as Nurses' Coalition for Action in Politics (N-CAP) and local committees of their state nurses' associations. Ver Steeg (1979) points out that, for political purposes, size is an important organizational asset. This recognition places a responsibility on each individual nurse to support the professional organization with membership. That is the very least political contribution that can be made to the collective political power of nursing for the future.

One way nurses can gain more personal, professional, and political power is to become skilled in the techniques of assertiveness.

GAINING POWER THROUGH ASSERTIVE BEHAVIOR

Assertive behavior is a well-tested way of gaining power in many diverse situations. People can gain personal power through behavior that enhances self-esteem and projects an image of confidence. The internal and external forces that have frustrated efforts to advance nursing as a profession have been mentioned throughout this text. The purpose of this section is to explore ways in which assertive behavior can contribute to the advancement of personal effectiveness as well as to the advancement of nursing as a profession.

Assertive behavior is defined as "standing up for personal rights and expressing thoughts, feelings and beliefs in direct, honest and appropriate ways which do not violate another person's rights'' (Lange and Jakubowski, 1976, p. 7). Basically, being assertive says to the world: "This is what I think and feel; this is how I perceive and interpret the situation, and I do not need to humiliate or degrade anyone to convey my message."

Behaviors that are nonassertive or aggressive should be contrasted with assertiveness. To be nonassertive is to deny one's own rights by failing to express thoughts, beliefs, and feelings honestly. The nonassertive stance implies, "I am not as important as you are. My thoughts and feelings are not valid. Take advantage of me. My goal is to please others and avoid conflict." In contrast, aggressive behavior involves a pressing of personal rights in ways that infringe on the rights of others. The aggressive stance implies, "What I am thinking and feeling is more important than your thoughts and feelings. You have no right to be different from me. My goal is to dominate and win, no matter what the cost to you."

Basic human rights include being respected as a person of worth; being free to express feelings, thoughts, and reactions; having the right to make choices about the use of resources (time, property, one's own body). Bloom and colleagues (1975) have elaborated on the use of time in professional situations, noting that each person has a right to set priorities and to say no to excessive work demands without feeling guilty. The responsibility to be fair and reasonable accompanies the rights. Professionals have the right to ask for information and help from others and to receive responses. The right to make mistakes, while accepting responsibility for the consequences, is a part of the stance of a professional nurse, as is the obligation to listen to justified criticism. Finally, each has the right to choose when to be assertive and when not to be. Implicit, of course, is the obligation to accept the consequences of these choices and behaviors.

Assertiveness training often focuses on teaching participants what assertive behavior is, and helping them to identify what may be blocking their behaving assertively and to set goals for increasing their own assertive behavior. As in developing any skill, practice is the key to proficiency; thus becoming more assertive demands patience and persistence at practicing specific behaviors.

Nonverbal components of behavior are significant in developing an assertive style. For example, posture plays an important role in how people feel and are seen by others, in that an erect posture with feet firmly on the ground says, "I am a person worth listening to." Eye contact is also essential to assertive communication; dropping the eyes generally accompanies nonassertive behavior. Appropriate voice tone and loudness are aspects of an assertive message and gestures serve to emphasize important points. Assertive body language communicates personal beliefs about occupying space by conveying, "I have a right to be here," thereby inviting others to believe and affirm it!

A primary goal of assertiveness is increasing the range of choices, by increasing the sense of self-control that leads to confidence in dealing with others both personally and professionally. There is certainly no guarantee that the outcomes of assertive behavior will always be what was expected. Indeed, the goal is to enhance self-esteem rather than always to gain a desired end. This is an important factor in a profession whose practice is often defined by others.

DEVELOPING SELF-AWARENESS

The beginning point for growth is knowledge of the present situation. Nurses must become aware of how they see themselves and how they act on that perception. What personal needs, values, and goals attracted them to nursing? What price are they willing to pay to obtain the goals they desire?

Impetus for change toward increased self-confidence can come from within an individual as a result of feelings of vague dissatisfaction, thinking "there is more for me"; or the process of change may begin with feedback from others or from recognition that work performance is not meeting professional standards. Awareness that skill levels fall short of standards is often the first step in a program of growth for adults; adults want to learn skills that enable them to move toward their vision of more effective functioning (Knowles, 1970).

Assertiveness literature is filled with persuasive data about the value of expressing feelings openly, directly, and honestly. Stress, for example, is reduced in the long run by knowing one's feelings and deciding the most effective ways to act on them. Again, decision is the key; people cannot decide how to act on feelings unless the feelings are recognized and validated. Recognition of feelings is not always an easy task in a culture that emphasizes reason and logic. The awareness of an individual's emotions can be heightened by focusing attention on responses to various situations. Seminars, workshops, and books can serve as guides on the journey toward self-awareness.

BLOCKS TO ASSERTIVE BEHAVIOR

It is well documented that Western culture has socialized females into a passive, or nonassertive, role. Mention has been repeatedly made of the consequences that result from the nursing profession's being traditionally female. Female nurses may be blocked individually; and the profession has, in the past, been blocked by the belief system that defines their role as passive and dependent. Though this point has been made repeatedly in this text, it is significant to repeat it in this context. If nurses of either sex believe that they are naturally and properly to play a secondary subservient role (either because of their gender or because of their status in the medical hierarchy), that belief will retard their developing assertive behavior patterns.

The development of an assertive belief system is one element in the process of becoming more assertive. Nurses must believe that "assertion, rather than manipulation, submission, or hostility enriches life and ultimately leads to more satisfying personal relationships with people" (Lange and Jakubowski, 1976, p. 55). Professional relationships as well are enhanced by assertive styles of interaction. Fortunately, individuals can become aware of the thinking patterns that underlie ineffectual behavior and can substitute more productive thought processes through cognitive restructuring.

Ellis (1977) has taken the wisdom of antiquity, "Men's minds are disturbed not by events, but by their interpretation of events," and made a persuasive case that faulty behavior is caused by irrational beliefs. In this context, believing that you are too insignificant to state an opinion or a reaction is a mighty impediment to speaking out. Ellis has demonstrated that irrational beliefs can be challenged and changed to beliefs that support a life-style of more effective functioning.

Another block to assertive behavior is anxiety. Because nurses deal with many high-stress situations, it is important to learn ways to monitor and reduce anxiety—both in immediate situations and in the long run. One useful approach is the deep muscle relaxation methods developed by Jacobson (1938) and Wolpe (1958). These methods utilize the tensing and relaxing of specific muscle groups so that one can develop awareness of early signs of tension and take measures to relax. Some methods (Lazarus, 1971) focus on releasing tensions through deep breathing and imagery, using mental scenes of pleasant places, and visualizing words such as "calm," "relax." On the job a nurse may use modifications of these procedures to prevent anxiety from escalating.

USING CRITICISM FOR PROFESSIONAL DEVELOPMENT

Most people cringe at the thought of criticism, remembering being upbraided as children and recalling their fear of loss of love and acceptance by adults who were their primary "standard setters" and "approval givers." Many carry this anxiety into adulthood and are thus unable to hear and evaluate criticism or to use it for growth and development. Because criticism is frequently a means of manipulation by others, many adults fear it, dread it, and avoid it whenever possible. In general, people respond to criticism either by denying the criticized behavior or by defending themselves—often loudly and aggressively. Such responses usually impede the ability to hear the criticism and may set in motion a cycle of responses that are rarely creative.

When the ego is intact and self-esteem is high, a person is able to hear criticism, evaluate it, use what is helpful, and discard what is not. Most people do not consistently maintain such a high level of self-esteem. It is useful to think of criticism or feedback as a mechanism that keeps behavior in line with intentions, much as a computer gives feedback to a missile to keep it on its course and heading for its target. Without such feedback, nurses at all levels would not know whether or not their performance meets desired standards.

How, then, does one make a friend of criticism? First, by realizing that the critic is operating from a unique, personal frame of reference, and that criticism does not always mean that something is wrong with the person being criticized. This awareness should accompany the important effort to hear accurately what is being said—both the words and the feelings. In a practical, day-to-day sense, this often means checking out what is heard before any response is made. It may mean a deep breath, a pause to gain composure, and a paraphrasing of the criticism to make sure that what is heard is what was intended. An exploration of what was intended may reveal new data about the experience of the critic and how the described behavior fits the operating value system. The criticized person may be assertive by deciding the behavior is appropriate after all.

Assertive nurses who are secure in their competence know both their strengths and their limitations. They can admit their limitations and mistakes and learn from them. This process of admitting mistakes without disparaging oneself as a person is called "negative assertion" by Smith (1975). Such assertion is based on a person's right to be human rather than perfect.

One can prompt further criticism by "negative inquiry" (Smith, 1975) in order to learn more of the expectations, assumptions, and values of the critic. This skill of asking for more information can be useful in enabling people to accept criticism without feeling guilty or unworthy as a person. Through negative inquiry the person who is criticized can learn what the specific behavior in question means to the critic and what is really wanted in the situation.

Effective feedback should describe the specific behavior in question and should be offered with the needs of the receiver in mind. Part of the process of clearly understanding feedback is asking for specifics. When you hear an interpretative statement such as "I wish you would be more cooperative," an appropriate assertive response would be "What have I done that you saw as uncooperative?" or "What could I do to be more cooperative?" Remember, the goal of feedback is to generate an assessment of whether behavior is meeting your intentions. In professional settings feedback can help nurses do their job more effectively, thus enhancing the professional standing of the nurse in question and of the profession in general.

Giving effective feedback is an important part of any supervisory role. Descriptive rather than evaluative terms diminish the need of the criticized person to be defensive. Specific behavior can be mentioned without deprecating the individual involved. Bower and Bower (1976) suggest a method of handling interpersonal conflict that has application to supervisory relationships. DESC scripting (Bower and Bower, 1976) is a way of negotiating for positive changes in a humane, open, and assertive manner. First, you objectively *describe* the unwanted behavior. Next, *express* feelings about the specific behavior. Then *specify* what changes you want in the behavior, including changes you are willing to make; in essence, ask for a contract. Finally, spell out concretely and simply the *consequences* of abiding by the contract. Rewards, rather than penalties, end the script on a positive note and invite cooperation and collaboration.

BUILDING A SUPPORT SYSTEM

Support can be developed within nursing as a profession by assertive expressions of appreciation and personal warmth. Whereas criticism is generally thought of as a negative judgment, the outcome of evaluation of behavior and performance may be positive as well. Indeed, nurses need positive feedback to reinforce and encourage effective behavior with both clients and colleagues. Everyone needs the basic acceptance that is expressed through a smile, a handshake, a pat on the back. Effective supervisors know the value of appreciation expressed with warmth and sincerity in building confidence and self-esteem of employees. Team members know the significance of being recognized as contributing members of the work group.

"The myth of modesty" has conditioned many people to deny their strengths and accomplishments for fear of being seen as conceited. It is now considered a sign of health to recognize and affirm one's talents and skills. The assertive stance includes recognizing and affirming competence and effectiveness, as well as admitting limitations. This attitude has application for the whole profession as well as for each individual nurse.

Giving and receiving compliments is one way people can affirm each other and build an atmosphere of collaboration. Fears of rejection or ridicule may inhibit open expressions of praise, thereby blocking the flow of affirmation. In a high-stress, caring profession, support on the job is one way to minimize burnout. If the work group can build in enough positive reinforcers to buffer the effects of stress, nurses can work more effectively and patients will ultimately receive better care.

THE ART OF NEGOTIATING

Chapter 8 of this text covers confrontation, collaboration, and conflict resolution. It is appropriate here to discuss the role of assertive behavior in the process of resolving conflicts and making decisions through negotiating. Negotiation is defined as bargaining between people to reach an end that is mutually desirable. "Trading off" may be inherent in the process of meeting the goals of all persons involved.

Successful negotiation takes place in an atmosphere of openness and trust. The climate of the workplace may help or hinder the process of "working things out" between professional colleagues. Because each person's perception is unique—based on values, needs, and history—and each has individual goals, conflict is inevitable between professional colleagues. Interprofessional collaboration requires clear goals and skills in negotiation.

A person who feels secure and confident has little need to be rigid in dealing with others. The optimal climate for negotiating includes permission to be tentative while alternatives are being thoroughly explored and each person is being heard. Since the purpose of the negotiating process is to accomplish some task or goal of mutual professional benefit to all, compromise may be necessary and can be done without anyone feeling slighted in the process if the common goal is kept before the group. Also, in dealing with patients in an institutional setting, negotiations about procedures must be based on competence and knowledge.

An assertive stance that places value both on self and others never offers a guarantee that you will get what you want. Indeed, to promote assertive behavior primarily as a means of getting one's own way is to invite manipulation and aggression when what you want conflicts with the goals or values of the others who are involved. Paradoxically, although assertive behavior offers no guarantee, it provides the best chance for a person to build self-esteem, to develop good relationships, and to meet realistic goals.

SUMMARY

Power is an elusive concept, defined differently perhaps by those who have it and those who do not. This chapter has focused on three types of power: personal power in terms of controlling space and developing the ability to coerce directly; professional power in the form of developing acknowledged expert power with its concomitant risks and responsibilities; and political power, which rests on legitimacy in a democratic society. One mechanism for developing each of these three kinds of power is through the employment of assertive behavior.

According to Sovie (1978, p. 373), "Nursing is assuming the responsibility to shape its own future through planned change." Although becoming assertive is not a panacea, individuals may shape their future through planned personal growth. Leininger (1978) says nurses must employ futuristic thinking in order to shape the profession for tomorrow. Included in the definition of futuristic thinking are two attributes of an assertive person. The first is the willingness to take risks, including courage to look beyond security and to try new ways of thinking and acting. This attitude can be characteristic of a person as well as a profession. Second, a futurist "must not be intimidated by popular thinking or by the opinion of the majority" (Leininger, 1978, p. 381). Being assertive is a vital aspect of living in keeping with each one's unique personhood, knowing that one may sometimes stand alone.

If nurses in the future will be the health professionals responsible for primary patient contact, as Schlotfeldt (1978) predicts, it is imperative that they be well skilled in human relations. To be able to listen carefully to patients and to help them articulate concerns when they are sick and worried may be an increasingly vital part of the nursing role. Straight talk about behaviors and their consequences for sickness or health will add power to the nurse's influence. Part of the nurse's role is to help patients recognize and use their own strengths and assets and also understand their limitations. Neither a nonassertive nor an aggressive stance will allow the nurse to be such a facilitator. "In its efforts to shape the future and realize planned change, nursing must remain flexible and prepared to respond to the unexpected" (Sovie, 1978, p. 366). The strength that comes from an assertive stance toward work, others, and self may give nurses the power to create whatever future they can envision.

REFERENCES

Adams, J.: The geography and organization of social responsibility, Union Sem. Q. Rev. **29**(3&4):245-265, Spring and Summer 1974.

Ashley, J.: This I believe about power in nursing, Nurs. Outlook **21**(10):637-641, Oct. 1973.

Ashley, J.: Hospitals, paternalism, and the role of the nurse, New York, 1976, Teachers College Press.

Bloom, L.Z., Coburn, K., and Pearlman, J.: The new assertive woman, New York, 1975, Dell Publishing Co.

Bower, S.A., and Bower, G.H.: Asserting your self: a practical guide for positive change, Reading, Mass., 1976, Addison-Wesley Publishing Co.

Christman, L.: Alternatives in the role expression of nurses that may affect the future of the nursing profession. In Chaska, N.L., editor: The nursing profession: views through the mist, New York, 1978, McGraw-Hill Book Co.

Diers, D.: A different kind of energy: nurse-power, Nurs. Outlook **26**:51-55, Jan. 1978.

Ellis, A.: How to live with and without anger, New York, 1977, Reader's Digest Press.

Facing a grand jury. Am. J. Nurs. **76**:398-400, May 1976.

Fagin, C.: Nurses' rights, Am. J. Nurs. **75**:82-85, Jan. 1975.

French, J., and Raven, B.: The bases of social power. In Cartwright, D., editor: Studies in social power, Ann Arbor, Mich., 1959, Research Center for Group Dynamics, Institute for Social Research.

Henley, N.: Body politics, Englewood Cliffs, N.J., 1977, Prentice-Hall, Inc.

Henning, M., and Jardim, A.: The managerial woman, New York, 1976, Pocket Books.

Jackson, D., and Maughan, R.: An introduction to political analysis: the theory and practice of allocation, Santa Monica, Calif., 1978, Goodyear Publishing Co.

Jacobson, E.: Progressive relaxation, Chicago, 1938, University of Chicago Press.

Jacox, A.: Professional socialization of nurses. In Chaska, N.L., editor: The nursing profession: views through the mist, New York, 1978, McGraw-Hill Book Co.

Kalisch, B.: The promise of power, Nurs. Outlook **26**:42-46, Jan. 1978.

Knowles, M.S.: The modern practice of adult education: andragogy versus pedagogy, New York, 1970, Association Press.

Lange, J., and Jakubowski, P.: Responsible assertive behavior: cognitive/behavioral procedures for trainers, Champaign, Ill., 1976, Research Press.

Lazarus, A.A.: Behavior therapy and beyond, New York, 1971, McGraw-Hill Book Co.

Leininger, M.: Futurology of nursing: goals and challenges for tomorrow. In Chaska, N.L., editor: The nursing profession: views through the mist, New York, 1978, McGraw-Hill Book Co.

McClure, M.: The long road to accountability, Nurs. Outlook **26**:47-50, Jan. 1978.

Nurse offers suggestions to change media image, American Nurse **3**:23, Jan. 1980.

Randolph, B., and Ross-Valliere, C.: Consciousness raising groups, Am. J. Nurs. **79:**922-924, May 1979.

Schlotfeldt, R.M.: The nursing profession: vision of the future. In Chaska, N.L., editor: The nursing profession: views through the mist, New York, 1978, McGraw-Hill Book Co.

Smith, M.J.: When I say no I feel guilty, New York, 1975, Dial Press.

Sovie, M.D.: Nursing: a future to shape. In Chaska, N.L., editor: The nursing profession: views through the mist, New York, 1978, McGraw-Hill Book Co.

Stein, L.: The doctor-nurse game, Arch. Gen. Psychiatry **16:**699-703, 1967.

Ver Steeg, D.: The political process, or, the power and the glory. In McFarland, D., and Shiflett, M., editors: Power in nursing, Wakefield, Mass., 1979, Nursing Resources, Inc.

Wolpe, J.: Psychotherapy by reciprocal inhibition, Stanford, Calif., 1958, Stanford University Press.

Time is a unique resource. It cannot be accumulated like money or stockpiled like raw materials. We are forced to spend it, whether we choose to or not, and at a fixed rate of 60 seconds every minute.

Mackenzie, R. Alec: The time trap: managing your way out, New York: AMACOM, a division of American Management Associations, 1972, p. 2.

26

TIME MANAGEMENT AS A CHANGE STRATEGY

Jeanette Lancaster

Do you have enough time to do what you need or want to do? If your answer is no, then join the ranks of an ever-growing number of nursing students, practitioners, and educators who never seem to have enough time. No matter how hard we wish or hope, there are only twenty-four hours in each day—no more, no less. There is no known way to expand time; each hour consists of sixty minutes, and each minute has only sixty seconds.

Time is perhaps our most valuable resource, and like all other resources it can be managed either effectively or ineffectively. Daily we make decisions, either consciously or unconsciously, about how to allocate our time. We all have the same amount of time, yet some people seem to get so much done whereas others mean to do more but never quite finish their projects.

This chapter presents time management as an essential change strategy for the future. Each of us can and must use our time more effectively because lost time means decreased efficiency and productivity, as well as wasted money or opportunities.

Although there are many ways to structure a discussion of time (self-) management, the nursing process is used as the framework in this chapter. According to this framework, the first step would be to assess what has to be done, including both the resources for and constraints on the task, as well as the best person, place, and approach to use. In the strictest sense of the term, time itself cannot be managed. The clock ticks on at a steady, continuous pace. What this chapter really deals with is managing ourselves. Effective time management is actually effective self-management. In order to consider more effective ways to manage ourselves, it is necessary to spend some time assessing how our own habits, beliefs, priorities, and actions affect the way we use time.

A key part of effective utilization of time lies in planning. Random actions, frequent distractions, poorly made plans, and haphazard follow-up of actions generally consume large amounts of valuable time and yield minimal productivity. Everyone has the same amount of time—168 hours a week—yet

some people use their time to work for them, whereas others seem constantly to lose control of their time. The planning stage includes establishing goals and priorities for attaining them, including delegating responsibilities when possible, and respecting the rights of others to use their time efficiently.

The third stage, implementation, includes an examination of common blocks to managing time well. Careful assessment and planning are worthless if the implementation phase is shortchanged. One block to implementation—meetings—is given particular attention, and suggestions are offered for using meetings more efficiently, if they cannot be avoided. Evaluation is the last stage and includes a review of the outcome of the first three stages and plans for the future.

ASSESSMENT

In order to invest time and energy wisely, you must assess the situations and environment in which you spend time. You need to identify how you use time, what interrupts and distracts you, and what can be done to promote effective time usage. One way to assess how you spend time is to keep a record or time chart for a given period to examine what eats into your time. Questions to be asked when doing a personal time assessment include:

1. How much time was spent on each activity?
2. Was time spent according to preestablished goals and plans or did other factors intervene, such as procrastination or interruptions?
3. Which activities did you like the most; the least?
4. What time of day is your peak period for thinking or working with others?

There does not seem to be a direct correlation between long hours and hard work on the one hand, and productive accomplishment on the other. One of the myths in current society is "the harder you work, the more you will get done." This is not necessarily true; in fact, long hours and carrying home a bulging stack of papers may reflect poor planning rather than great accomplishments.

Everyone has times each day when energy is higher and intellect seems sharper. Some people are "morning achievers" who get up early and work productively until midday, when they begin to lose momentum. This behavior type would use time most effectively by reserving morning hours for activities requiring the greatest amount of attention, for example writing reports or preparing for an important exam or meeting. Afternoon or "slack" times when energy is lower could be used for routine activities or group activities where the stimulation of others might offset the low energy level. These time assignments could be reversed for the person who gets off to a slow start and picks up intellectual momentum as the day progresses.

Need for self-management

Most of us would like to think that we would get a great deal more accomplished each day if other people would not interrupt our plans. When asked to identify our major "time wasters," we invariably list external causes such as the telephone, meetings, interruptions by other people, excessive paperwork, and unclear directions or objectives for a project. After careful analysis of what really gets in the way of our being highly productive, it can often be summarized as *us*. Internal time wasters, such as those listed below, eat away at time and can con-

---

INTERNAL TIME WASTERS

1. Procrastination
2. Socializing
3. "Fire-fighting"
4. Failure to plan
5. Lack of self-discipline
6. Lack of skill
7. Failure to seek clarification
8. An open-door policy
9. Failure to set objectives
10. Lack of prioritizing
11. Inability to say no
12. Acting without thinking

---

sciously be controlled. Although many of these time wasters often originate from external sources, we can control them. Successful time management does not mean working harder — just smarter (Mac-Kenzie, 1972). Although some people seem to have a natural tendency to structure their time effectively, the basic skills can be learned in a step-by-step process. As mentioned, the first step is to assess how you currently use your time. Once you have a thorough list of your activities for a designated portion of time, such as a week, you can categorize the activities according to "essentials" and "wasters." This should reduce the list of activities considerably and make the planning stage more manageable.

Procrastination

As part of your self-examination, determine if procrastination is a major time thief for you. Many people function with the philosophy, "Never do today what you can put off until tomorrow." As can be imagined, successful time usage would reverse this to read: "Never put off until tomorrow, what I can do *now*." Procrastination means putting off until a later date what should receive your attention *now*. Certainly some tasks can realistically be put off and should be in order to adhere to planning priorities; other tasks need to be handled now, and delaying only complicates the situation.

The origins of procrastination can be traced to childhood, when some children form a habit of always waiting until "later" to complete tasks. Parents may nag and complain about the child's procrastination, but if they permit this habit to develop it can become firmly entrenched in the child's later habits as an adult.

Some simple hints on dealing with procrastination can be identified. They are easy to list, yet often difficult to incorporate into daily behavior patterns. It might be helpful first to take the following steps:

1. Identify the tasks you tend to put off. Be specific in making your list so you can see patterns or trends in the kinds of items you avoid.

2. Next, ask yourself, "Why do I avoid this task?" There may be aspects of the avoided task that you could change and thereby make it less repulsive. For example, you may avoid studying for a test until the last possible moment because you dislike spending time alone. A possible solution would be to study with a classmate. Likewise, in the work setting, you might hate serving on committees, yet enjoy writing reports. Again, a possible exchange of tasks with a colleague could be considered.

3. Ask yourself, "What happens to me when I put this task off?" Are you willing to live with the consequences? It is important to consider the worst possible consequence of each of your areas of procrastination. For example, by not studying for a test you could fail. Likewise, lack of fulfilling work responsibilities could lead to (a) no promotion, (b) a demotion, or (c) loss of job.

4. Going hand in hand with question (3) is that of asking yourself, "What benefits do I derive from putting this specific task off?" Some people get psychological gain from seemingly negative situations. For example, Joe, a senior in nursing school, consistently waited until the night before an exam or a paper was due to begin studying or writing. When he scored poorly on the work, he spent a lot of time and got a great deal of attention with comments such as "those dumb teachers, I would have 'aced' that test, but the dummy who wrote the questions never took a course in test construction and wouldn't know a good question from a lousy one."

Now that some key questions have been raised about what you avoid, why, and for what possible reasons, it is time to consider a step-by-step process for interrupting procrastination. A prerequisite is to identify one area where you procrastinate, and work on it now.

1. You might consider *dividing* a large task into two or three subtasks. Often it is motivating to complete a small project, in contrast to working long and hard on a monumental task and seeing few gains and areas of goal attainment.

2. *Set priorities* and focus on one part or problem at a time. This means doing one thing at a time and seeing the task through to completion. The goal is to avoid the loss of time involved in jumping from project to project.

3. *Set deadlines* for yourself and congratulate yourself when you meet them. You may want to ask a classmate or co-worker to check on you, and remember, don't get angry when they say, "How are you doing?"

4. *Do not avoid* the tough projects or plans. Go ahead and tackle them and get them out of the way; then you can do the easy, fun ones!

5. *Do not always expect yourself to be perfect* or all your projects to be the best ones ever, or you will never finish.

The assessment phase of a time-management strategy can be summarized in the following hints for increasing efficiency:

1. Analyze how you spend your time.
2. Identify the essentials for each task, project, assignment, and do them first.
3. Make a daily "I must do" list.
4. Learn to say no gracefully; no one person can be all things to all people.
5. Be aware that it is better to say no at the outset of a project if you are already overcommitted, than to go ahead and do an inferior job.
6. Recognize what your responsibilities are and what someone should or could be asked to do (including family and co-workers).

PLANNING

Before beginning the planning stage of a time-management discussion, be aware that people do not manage time well until they have to do so. That is, unless you feel that time is a precious and rare resource, you are probably not ready to plan time-management activities. The first step in the planning process is to determine the goals for your activities. You need to establish both long-term and short-range goals. Once the goals have been prioritized, you can establish specific action-oriented methods for attaining the goals.

Taking time to plan saves time in the end. "An hour of effective planning can save three to four hours in execution and produce better results" (Schwartz and MacKenzie, 1979, p. 23). Planning principles apply to school, work, and home. According to Schwartz and MacKenzie (1979), most people use about eighty percent of their time performing unimportant tasks and only twenty percent on the most meaningful parts of a task. The most crucial tasks must be identified and listed according to priority. Next, tackle the highest-priority item first. If the highest-priority items are handled first, you can then deal with daily crises without feeling overwhelmed because of your own unmet goals. Planning means getting ready for a task before you start so you can complete each task the first time you work on it, or, stated differently: handle each piece of paper or problem only once. This means that you need all the essential information for completing the task. If you are preparing an in-service education program, know the hoped-for outcome, the characteristics of the participants, time allotment, and setting before you begin developing the program. Then gather all the resources you need for program development, so that when you actually sit down to work on the project you can do so with minimal interruptions.

Setting priorities

When establishing priorities among the list of goals and objectives you have established, identify the items that need to be done now, those that can be handled later, those that are small, and the large, major tasks. Rank your list into categories A, B, C, with "A" items rating top priority for attention. Write everything down when you are devising your priority system; do not trust your memory.

Next you can go over each of your lists (A, B, C) and subdivide these into step-by-step parts. For example, item A might be writing a term paper; if so, A(1) would be selecting the topic—go to library, and so forth. Look back over your list and ask this question: "If nothing else gets done today, what is the one item I have to do?" This should be your

A(1) item, so if a real emergency does arise your daily plan may not be completely destroyed.

Delegating

Planning also includes delegating. "Delegation extends work from what one can do to what one can control" (Schwartz and MacKenzie, 1979, p. 25). A change agent generally needs to devote more time to planning and organizing as well as training and motivating others, than actually to carrying out each and every task. Delegation does not mean "dumping"; rather, it requires follow-through to make sure that the involved persons are clear about the task and have the ability and resources to complete it. It is a good idea to remember that when you delegate the job it will generally not be carried out *exactly* as you would have done it. The key to successful delegation includes matching the person to the project, giving clear instructions, providing support if needed, allowing the other people the freedom to complete the project in their own way, and following through to make sure things were actually handled correctly.

Barriers to effective delegation can arise in the delegator, in the delegatee, or in the situation. For example, some people believe that "the only way to get a job done right is to do it myself." This delegator may feel omnipotent: no one can work as hard, accomplish as much, or be as smart as me. This delegator may instead feel insecure and fear that the only way to be successful is to participate in each and every project. Other delegators are simply inexperienced in the art of delegation. They do not feel comfortable in their ability to give clear directions, so they keep on doing everything themselves.

Delegation can also be impaired when the delegatee is incompetent, inexperienced, or lacks motivation and willingness to learn and try new things. Also, the delegatee may already be overworked and simply cannot take responsibility for anything else.

The situation can impede delegation when there is a history of "one-person shows," in which the one in charge does everything. For example, on program committees for organizations the historical trend may be that the chairperson does all the work, and members are named to the committee only because the bylaws said to do this! Further, some work or academic environments have little tolerance for mistakes, thus people hesitate to delegate. Situations that are continuously characterized by crises allow little opportunity for effective and fair delegation. When everything is always due "yesterday," it is hardly fair to expect others to assume your responsibilities.

In short, delegation requires planning, risk taking, and the willingness to tolerate errors and different approaches to solving problems or carrying out responsibilities.

Consideration of others' needs to manage time

In planning how to maximize your time usage it is important to be considerate of other people's time. This means that when you need information, an answer, or other help, you should call for an appointment explaining what you need so as to allow the other person to be prepared to provide an informed response. When you do need to see or talk with someone, get right to the point, keep on the subject, and leave or terminate the call or appointment as soon as the business has been discussed. We are most likely to be considerate of the time needs of others when we believe that everyone with whom we associate is a busy person with only twenty-four hours in a day.

IMPLEMENTATION

The most critical phase of changing old habits is getting started. It is so tempting and often comforting to respond in old, familiar ways and to put off changing habits. Thus a key step in the implementation phase is gaining control of self. This necessitates a keen awareness of time wasters. As previously noted, internal time wasters seem to be the most difficult to overcome. MacKenzie (1972) suggests two steps in learning new time-usage behaviors. First, *launch* your new practices now. Establish a preplanned routine that contrasts with your

old way of doing things. Second, do not let *exceptions* occur until the new practices are firmly established. Daily at home, work, or school, special situations will arise that tempt you to deviate "just a little" from the new pattern. Someone—a classmate, teacher, co-worker, supervisor, or family member—needs something now. Try to program your responses to the needs of others into your schedule, unless you assess a true emergency or urgency for your assistance that cannot be delayed.

Why do people mismanage time?

According to Davidson (1978), people tend to mismanage time for a variety of reasons, but six general categories of time wasters can be identified. For most people it is not a matter of "Do I waste time?" but rather, "How do I waste time?" In reading these categories, consider which ones characterize you.

1. The *recognition seeker* is the person who constantly seems hurried and stressed. This person dashes around constantly while completing a task, then says, "What a job, I thought I would never finish." These people want others to recognize how hard they work; they need considerable acceptance and acclaim from others. The recognition seeker, in addition to being in frequent motion, may also talk constantly. These are the classmates and co-workers who talk a lot but really have little of importance to say.

2. *Complainers* not only waste their time, but that of the people they capture to hear their complaints. These people frequently blame their faults and shortcomings on others or on the organization. Their typical response to queries about their progress is, "I would have finished that if. . . ." The complainer generally has a negative effect on any group by constantly arousing uneasy feelings and dissatisfaction among the group.

3. The *I will show you* person is often motivated by hostility and resentment and deliberately interferes with group work. For example, Joan and Sue had both been hired on a surgical unit two years ago

after graduation from school. The head nurse resigned, and the supervisor indicated that either Joan or Sue would be offered this position. After careful deliberation, Sue was offered the position. Subsequently, Joan made numerous efforts to block Sue's effectiveness, constantly undermining her by providing key information late so that Sue looked uninformed. Rather than dealing directly with her anger, Joan channeled the anger into an "I will make Sue look inept" attitude. Such passive handling of feelings seldom is effective because everyone suffers. Joan carries around a bundle of unused anger; Sue's effectiveness is undermined, and the entire unit usually feels the tension created by an "I will show you" attitude.

4. The *spontaneity-loving* worker also wastes a great deal of time with an attitude of "let's not plan too much, lest we miss a great opportunity by being committed to a schedule." In truth, this person is seldom committed to any one task long enough to complete it. The spontaneity-loving student or nurse often misses deadlines, frequently asks for exceptions to be made, and generally seems confused about goals and actions.

5. The *fearful* nurse or student wastes time by the inability to make decisions. These people often lack self-confidence and fear rejection because of what they do. Their behavior is characterized by ambivalence: "Should I do this or that?" They may frequently ask for clarification of instructions, and often go from teacher to teacher or from one supervisor to another trying to determine if they really understand what is expected of them.

6. The *"I don't care"* personality type is often bored with school or work and finds few challenges or excitements. This person does the minimum; as a student, the "I don't care" person writes a marginal paper or barely passes exams. In employees this attitude is noted as, "I only do what I have to do."

As Davidson (1978) points out, each of the above six personality styles feels like a loser. Most people are not winners all the time, but do want to enjoy some winning experiences. It may be helpful to ask

yourself, "What made me feel like a winner last week at school (work or home)?" Then ask, "What made me feel like a loser?" If the loser category equals or outweighs being a winner, then try to re-create mentally what those "loser" situations were like.

Meetings as time wasters

Meetings can constitute major time wasters if they are not handled efficiently. Meetings should only be called when they are more efficient than using the telephone or a written communication. Often meeting time is used for announcements that could easily be written and circulated to all concerned parties. MacKenzie (1972, p. 98) states that meetings are most frequently convened to coordinate activities, exchange information, build morale, and solve problems.

If a meeting is inevitable, there are two essential ingredients: an agenda and a time limit (Davidson, 1978). The agenda, a typed list of items for discussion, is distributed before the meeting. The reasons for advance distribution of agendas include:

1. Members know what materials to read in advance as well as what they should bring with them.
2. Members can think about the items for discussion in advance and formulate their opinions and suggestions.
3. Priorities can be assigned more easily when dealing with written as opposed to oral information.

It is important to establish a time limit so that members can structure their day, learn to clarify thinking, speak with thoughtfulness, and stick to the subject. Since people become restless and tend to ramble when engaged in long meetings, the time should usually be limited to one or two hours. Just as meetings should end on time, so should they begin at the designated time. It is unfair to penalize the members who were prompt by asking them to sit and wait on laggards.

Recorders should make note of the decisions reached at meetings, as well as assignment of

---

SAVING TIME AND MAXIMIZING YOUR OWN RESOURCES: TIPS FOR SURVIVAL

1. **Eliminate time wasters from your daily schedule.**

2. **Set goals and list priorities.**
   a. Set life goals and work goals.
   b. Use an A, B, C priority system.
   c. Start with As, not Cs.
   d. Avoid procrastination; do it now.
   e. Write down the important things to do; do not trust your memory.
   f. Keep one organized list, not a handful of scraps of paper.
   g. Set deadlines for yourself and others; adhere to them.

3. **Plan every day by using a "to do" list.**
   a. Give your total attention to the one task you are working on.
   b. Complete each task the first time you deal with it; stick with it until the finish.
   c. Remember that planning saves time in the long run.
   d. Learn to say no graciously.
   e. Remember the worst disappointment to others is to say yes and do an inferior job.

4. **Schedule your day.**
   a. Use your peak energy times for the most intense and detailed activities.
   b. Block out periods of time that will be free from interruptions for completing priority tasks.
   c. Leave some free or "slop" time in your daily schedule for handling the unexpected.

5. **Delegate whenever possible.**
   a. Avoid tendencies to "do it myself."
   b. Never put off until tomorrow what you can ask someone else to do today.

6. **Be considerate of others' time.**

7. **Minimize meetings.**
   a. Ask yourself, "Is this meeting necessary?"
   b. For all necessary meetings, prepare and distribute a written agenda in advance.
   c. Expect something positive to result from each meeting.
   d. Limit attendance at meetings to smallest number possible to get the job done.
   e. Set a time limit and stick to it.
   f. Record the actions and decisions of the meeting and circulate minutes.
   g. Keep meetings brief.

---

follow-up responsibilities. Often it is helpful for all members of the group to have copies of the minutes or decision summaries.

The person who convened the meeting should be responsible for summarizing. A summary focuses attention on the critical elements, the decisions that were made, what goals were either established or accomplished, and who agreed to carry out post-meeting activities. In order for a meeting to be maximally effective, it should end with a brief oral summary followed promptly by a concise set of written minutes. The value of accurate minutes should not be underestimated, since poor minutes are often useless and consume a great deal of time of anyone trying to understand what actually took place.

The scheduling of meetings is important and often affects their usefulness. Those scheduled at high-stress times may accomplish little, since participants may be preoccupied with deadlines, conflicts, or personal needs or goals. Also, afternoons tend to be better times for meetings than do mornings. For many people, mornings are times of peak individual productivity and should be reserved for tasks requiring concentration and attention to details. In contrast, many people suffer a psychological lag in the afternoon, and meetings scheduled during this time can stimulate participants. Further, if some participants have difficulty ending the meeting on time, it is helpful to schedule meetings just before a key event such as lunch or the end of the day.

Each person plays a unique role in meetings; some people encourage goal attainment, whereas others serve as a hindrance. It is important for participants to recognize how they behave in groups. Behavior that is aggressive, rambling, or joking when humor is not warranted can hamper the progress of the meeting. The usual outcome of a meeting is to plan or carry out an activity; when problems arise in attaining the designated goal, it is important to ask if there are inherent factors in the organizational structure that impeded progress. Such impediments may be people, location, policies and procedures, or resources.

It is also necessary to look at the process in an activity. Who helped and who hindered goal attainment? What alternatives exist for future improvements in the process? Often subtle, covert behaviors, discussions, and feelings influence the process of goal attainment more than outwardly observed activities.

The total outcome of an activity needs attention to determine whether it actually met the predetermined goals. Was the outcome what you wanted or expected? If not, what would you do differently next time?

SUMMARY

This chapter has looked at time management as a way to relate more effectively. Few people make the most of the time available to them and each of us has habits that interfere with the effective use of our time. The nursing process has been used as the framework for discussing time management. That is, assessment, planning, implementation, and evaluation are viewed as key steps in the development of a time-management strategy. The essence of the chapter can be summarized in the accompanying list of time-saving tips.

REFERENCES

Davidson, J.: Effective time management, New York, 1978, Human Sciences Press.

MacKenzie, R.A.: The time trap, New York, 1972, American Management Association.

Schwartz, E.B., and MacKenzie, R.A.: Time-management strategy for women, J. Nurs. Adm. **9**:22-26, March 1979.

It is often observed that the reason little is known from the evaluations of many health care programs is that the right questions are frequently not asked in the first place.

Shortell, S.M., and Richardson, W.C.: Health program evaluation, 1978, The C.V. Mosby Co., p. 16.

27

EVALUATION STRATEGIES FOR NURSING PRACTICE IN A CHANGING HEALTH CARE SYSTEM

Anne Elizabeth Belcher

Do organizations or professions such as nursing evaluate their own activities in the manner described in the introductory quotation? What are the external pressures and internal constraints affecting the role of evaluation in nursing practice? What principles and techniques of evaluation have applicability to nursing? What role do objectives play in the evaluative process?

The purpose of this chapter is to answer these and other questions about evaluation strategies for nursing practice by describing the external and internal factors influencing the evaluative process, defining the components of the process, and providing an overview of evaluation techniques.

Health service administrators, program planners, and health care providers "must be more directly concerned with the consequences of their actions as they seek to change health care organizations and to improve health care practices" (Shortell and Richardson, 1978, viii). Evaluation provides the factual basis for making decisions about such issues as priorities in health care and allocation of limited resources. Evaluation can provide an objective examination of the problems and issues involved, the strengths and weaknesses of programs, and the unmet needs in all areas of health care, including nursing practice.

Schulberg and Baker (1979) postulate that evaluation of health services is and will be increasingly influenced by the following groups, "all of whom use differing philosophies, value structures, and judgmental criteria" (p. 5):

1. *The public,* who are demanding health care professionals' accountability for services rendered
2. *Governmental agencies and bodies,* which are increasing the use of fiscal criteria in decision making
3. *State and federal courts,* which are setting standards of quality care more in line with those of plaintiffs than providers
4. *Health care providers,* who are more critical of colleagues' actions and of traditional clinical practices than ever before

Certainly in nursing there is increasing evidence of leaders' concern with the pressures being applied from without and from within for accountability, quality assurance, and maintenance of standards of care. No longer will professional groups enjoy unquestioning public trust and professional autonomy in the provision of health care services. With a tightening economy and greater demands for health care, nursing, like other health care professions, will do well to place greater emphasis on the quality of practice provided to its consumers.

EVALUATION PRINCIPLES

Evaluation is both a judgment of the impact of a program, procedure, or individual, and the process whereby that judgment is made. To evaluate means to place a value on or to derive the worth of an action, decision, or experience. An essential component of evaluation is the identification and examination of values so as to approach decision making rationally.

When evaluation is done with or for those involved, it is more acceptable than when done to them. Evaluation is also more readily accepted when it has favorable prospects such as improved position in the professional hierarchy, increased resources, or goal attainment. Thus people are more likely to view evaluation as a valuable procedure if they are included in the process and if they anticipate some beneficial rewards as a result of their participation.

Evaluation as a process is the collection and interpretation, through a systematic and formal means, of relevant information that serves as the basis for reasoned decision making.

Evaluation consists of some or all of the following components (Dressel, 1976):

1. Identification and examination of the values inherent in a program, policy, or procedure
2. Formulation or clarification of program objectives, goals, purposes
3. Determination of criteria for measuring success

4. Definition, gathering, analysis, and interpretation of data
5. Determination and explanation of the extent of success and failure
6. Indication of relationships between experiences during the program and outcomes of the program
7. Identification of unplanned and undesirable (side) effects
8. Determination of the impact of program and of external uncontrolled variables
9. Recommendation of alteration, replacement, or discontinuance of a program or of individual features
10. Development of continuing review of program results
11. Assessment of the value, benefits, and/or social utility of programs, objectives, and processes, as well as of the evaluation itself

Evaluation may, in summary, be defined as "a decision-making process that leads to suggestions for action to improve participant effectiveness and program efficiency" (Staropoli and Waltz, 1978, p. 83). It should lead not only to the discovery of better ways of accomplishing existing objectives, but also to alteration of the objectives themselves (Wildarisky, 1979).

OVERVIEW OF TECHNIQUES: CONCEPTS AND PROCESS

Staropoli and Waltz (1978) describe the principles governing evaluation in nursing as being the same as those applied to any programmatic endeavor:

1. Determine who is to be involved and assure that data will be collected from everyone affected by the resultant decision making.
2. Clearly delineate the purposes of the evaluation.
3. Prepare a description of the program to be evaluated.
4. Select the evaluation methodology.
5. Make a decision as to when evaluation will occur.

The following processes should be included in any nursing evaluation program (Schweer and Gebbie, 1976):

1. Statement of objectives
2. Statement of specific changes to be expected as outcomes of reaching each objective
3. Provision of adequate sampling of experiences representative of desired behaviors
4. Selection of evaluation methods appropriate to the desired behaviors
5. Selection of evaluation criteria in accordance with established criteria
6. Assignment of criteria for measurement
7. Appraisal of data
8. Interpretation of data

In general, evaluation includes two basic phases that help one to plan and conduct effective evaluation: formative and summative.

Formative evaluation involves looking for potential problems, identifying areas for program improvement, describing and monitoring program activities, and periodically testing for progress toward change. The emphasis is on assessing the worth of a program still capable of being modified. It is the process of gathering information about and judging the merits of the various aspects of a program sequence in order to make it better. The assessment of an early version of a set of patient education materials to determine their readability before having them printed would be an example of formative evaluation. Use of a proposed audit procedure on a sample of patient records and analysis of the data obtained before widespread adaptation of the procedure would also exemplify formative evaluation.

Summative evaluation calls for the production of a summary statement about program effectiveness. It should describe the program, state the degree to which the program has achieved predetermined goals, note any unanticipated outcomes, and perhaps make comparisons with other programs. According to Fitz-Gibbon and Morris (1978, p. 13), the "best summative evaluation has all the characteristics of the best research study." The critical characteristic is that it "provide the best possible information that could have been collected under the circumstances.'' The primary purpose of summative evaluation is to determine effectiveness of a program after it has been completed. The use of the accreditation process by the National League for Nursing is an example of summative evaluation in that its chief goal is to assure the quality of both the educational process and the graduates of the program. Determination of patients' satisfaction with nursing care in a particular health care setting would also exemplify summative evaluation.

Effective use of formative evaluation aids in the decision making that occurs during the planning and development phases of a program, whereas summative evaluation occurs at the end of the program and may influence decisions about future activities. Both are useful concepts in the evaluation of nursing services.

What happens to the results of evaluation activities is of critical importance in that misuse of such information can have far-reaching and often destructive consequences. Three ways in which evaluative information can be misused are unintentional misutilization, intentional abuse, and premature use of information (Rich, 1979).

1. *Unintentional misutilization* is widespread because it typically occurs when information is not clearly understood before being shared with others. Policy makers may draw unwarranted conclusions on the basis of data presented or on the data's levels of statistical significance. For example, the controversial nursing shortage in the United States has been interpreted as an indication for new program development, whereas such factors as maldistribution, working conditions, and lack of incentive must also be considered.

2. *Intentional abuse* has most often occurred when the organizational incentive system encourages such behavior. Statistics are used for agency or other interests, for example, falsifying results to show things as being better than they actually are, not collecting or acknowledging information that could prove harmful, and storing information in an unretrievable form. Although evidence of such

abuse has been infrequently documented as having occurred in nursing, one can see the temptation to use statistics to support one's position on a controversial issue such as patient/nurse ratio for safe care; or to hide potentially damaging data, for example, students' evaluation of faculty and courses from accrediting bodies.

3. *Premature use of information* refers to presentation of evaluation results in a preliminary or incomplete form, often as a political strategy, by persons or agencies seeking publicity, support, or advantage over other persons, groups, or agencies. In order to gain attention at a certain time, inconclusive information based on incomplete or preliminary results of evaluative activities is "leaked" to the press or to persons in authority. For example, preliminary findings of patient neglect in a long-term care facility might be used as evidence of the need for additional financial support, whereas further evaluation reveals the need for better-prepared providers.

EVALUATION BASED ON OBJECTIVES

The field of evaluation was the "birthplace" of the behavioral objective, which was originally intended as a guide for accumulating evidence to document that goals had been attained. A behavioral objective is "a statement of certain behaviors that, if exhibited . . . , indicate that the students (nurses, clients, etc.) have some skill, attitude, or knowledge" (Morris and Fitz-Gibbon, 1978). Objectives are descriptive of the cognitive, psychomotor, and affective behaviors that the evaluator will accept as evidence of change having occurred.

The decision to use precisely stated behavioral objectives rather than generally stated goals is based on the purposes and methods of evaluation in a particular setting. Behavioral objectives are essential when a test or attitude instrument will be used to measure program outcomes. Goals usually are general statements that give direction to an activity or program. Both goals and objectives should meet the following criteria:

1. Their meaning should be clear to participants,

evaluators, and consumers of the evaluation.
2. They should be agreed on by the program planners and implementers.
3. They should be clearly defined as dealing with either ends (outcomes) or means (i.e., materials, activities).
4. They should be realistic in terms of time and money available for attainment.

Sources from which to derive objectives for use in evaluating nursing practice include (a) standards of practice developed by the American Nurses' Association and other nursing specialty organizations; (b) National League for Nursing program accreditation criteria; (c) state or federal mandates and legislation; (d) local, state, and national concerns expressed by nurses, other health care providers, and consumers through a variety of communication channels; (e) records and reports; (f) employer requirements; and (g) needs assessment of learners.

Correctly written behavioral objectives should be measurable; that is, the action identified must be observable either directly or indirectly. Its purpose is to specify what the individual or program must do or perform; for example, demonstrate, articulate, formulate, assist, utilize, apply. In nursing education programs, behavioral objectives refer to student characteristics necessary to meet the community's needs for nursing service. Likewise, this definition could be used in a variety of nursing practice settings to delineate the criteria for evaluation.

Once objectives have been identified, a decision must be made as to which ones will serve as the focus for evaluation. Morris and Fitz-Gibbon (1978) describe a variety of techniques that may be utilized:
1. *Random sampling* is the quickest, simplest method; all objectives are treated as equally important and selection of those to be used for evaluation is based on assigning sequential numbers to all objectives, then using a table of random numbers to select the desired proportion.
2. *Sampling the important objectives* requires

that two or three raters select objectives they think are most important; objectives may then be randomly selected from this pool.
3. *Matrix sampling* involves random assignment of students to take parts of a single large test; for example, you might write a test item for each of many objectives on cards, then have individual students draw one or more cards and answer the item(s) selected; the students' scores could be used as an indication of group performance on the entire test.
4. *Assigning priorities through ratings* (retrospective needs assessment) involves having a group of raters rank all objectives on a scale, with mean ratings being used to determine priorities.
5. *Assigning priorities through objectives hierarchies* makes it possible for the more complex or "terminal" ones to receive priority.

Objectives guide the evaluator in determining the who, what, where, when, and how of gathering the data that are needed to make judgments about the worth of a program.

FOCUS ON QUALITY ASSURANCE

As has been mentioned in a previous section of this book, the public is demanding health care professionals' accountability with documented evidence that the health care to which they are entitled is available, accessible, and cost effective, and that it produces the desired outcomes. Quality assurance, which refers to commitment to excellence in care, like many other "new" ideas, has actually been sought for many years. In the 1800s Florence Nightingale proposed a registry of all surgical operations that was to include the patient's age, sex, and occupation, the disease or reason for the surgery, recovery date, and explanation of any postoperative complication. Thus more than a century ago the basic criterion of quality evaluation was recognized: "the need to know what was done for a patient, as well as by implication the importance of outcome as a [criterion] for what should have been done" (Baker and McPhee, 1978, p. 187). However, as described by Donabedian (1968), outcome is not the only approach to evaluation of quality care. Other approaches include evaluating the process of care and assessment of structure.

In the particular context of evaluating the performance of practitioners in caring for individual patients, Donabedian focused on the process of care, considering structural attributes and outcomes as indirect evidence of quality.

The accreditation process has been the primary determinant of the quality of health care, with the focus on structure evaluation. Although the standards employed are generally developed by consensus of experts, they often lack objective, quantifiable criteria. In addition, competing professional values and opinions are a chronic barrier to the determination and application of standards of care, for example, the role of the nurse in nutrition as opposed to that of the dietician.

Another aspect of quality assurance is the use of peer review, in which professionals are evaluated by other members of the same profession. The concept of peer review has become more complicated in recent years because state and federal governments, health insurance carriers, and consumers are increasingly concerned about the cost and quality of care. Symbolic of these concerns is the professional standards review organization (PSRO), a provision of Public Law 92-603, the Social Security Amendments of 1972. The PSROs are in actuality concerned with elective hospital admissions, lengths of stay, and the upgrading of inadequate care. The retrospective audit has frequently been used as the method by which to measure this aspect of quality care.

Weed (1969) developed the problem-oriented medical record with the goal of ensuring quality of care. This system includes the components of (1) a data base, (2) a problem list, (3) a treatment plan, and (4) follow-up. It is a problem-oriented system that can provide an efficient and effective way of evaluating the health care provider's performance but is not *the* answer to assuring quality care.

Another indicator of health care quality is the patient and family's opinion about the services received. Not only is the consumer's perspective helpful to professional groups in evaluating quality of care, but patient satisfaction or lack of it affects such variables as compliance with the health care provider's orders. As Baker and McPhee (1978) point out, not only patients' satisfaction with outcome of service must be addressed, but also such factors as satisfaction with cost, accessibility, professional skillfulness, staff-patient interaction, and physical surroundings.

Professional health care providers are still the major source of data for quality assurance. With the pressure on providers to comply with increasingly complicated demands for information should come rewards for compliance with record keeping and cooperation with professional review.

SUMMARY

The last stage in any approach to change as a problem-solving process is evaluation. Yet, for a variety of reasons, this crucial step is often forgotten, ignored, or treated far too briefly to be consistent with its significance. This evaluative phase in any change cycle provides immediate information about the reception to the change and how well it was adopted, as well as providing clues as to future revisions, since change is an ongoing process in most organizations.

The demands for thorough evaluation are being increasingly heard as the general public, governmental, and other regulatory bodies, as well as health care providers, utilize evaluative information to make decisions about future health care needs, priorities, and plans. This chapter has identified key evaluative principles that need to be incorporated in the early planning stages for any project or plan. Evaluation begins at the outset of a change strategy; it is not added or devised when the project is finished. The goals and objectives of the change plan serve as a blueprint for developing the evaluation scheme. Further, frequent misuses of evaluative information were cited to warn the potential change agent against falling into one of these traps. Evaluation must be taken seriously and plans must be developed that will provide valuable and key information about the success or failure of a change process.

REFERENCES

Baker, F., and McPhee, C.B.: Approaches to evaluating quality of health care. In Schulberg, H.C., and Baker, F., editors: Health program evaluation, St. Louis, 1978, The C.V. Mosby Co.

Donabedian, A.: Promoting quality through evaluating the process of patient care, Med. Care **6**:191-202, 1968.

Dressel, P.L.: Handbook of academic evaluation, San Francisco, 1976, Jossey-Bass Publishing Co.

Fitz-Gibbon, C.T., and Morris, L.L.: How to design a program evaluation, Beverly Hills, Calif., 1978, Sage Publications.

Morris, L.L., and Fitz-Gibbon, C.T.: How to deal with goals and objectives, Beverly Hills, Calif., 1978, Sage Publications.

Rich, R.F.: Emerging issues for evaluators and evaluation users. In Datta, L-E., and Perloff, R., editors: Improving evaluations, Beverly Hills, Calif., 1979, Sage Publications.

Schulberg, H.C., and Baker, F.: Evaluating health programs: art and/or science? In Schulberg, H.C., and Baker, F., editors: Program evaluation in the health fields, vol. 2, New York, 1979, Human Sciences Press.

Schweer, J.E., and Gebbie, K.M.: Creative teaching in clinical nursing, ed. 3, St. Louis, 1976, The C.V. Mosby Co.

Shortell, S.M., and Richardson, W.C.: Health program evaluation, St. Louis, 1978, The C.V. Mosby Co.

Staropoli, C.J., and Waltz, C.F.: Developing and evaluating educational programs for health care providers, Philadelphia, 1978, F.A. Davis Publishing Co.

Weed, L.: Medical records, medical education, and patient care, Cleveland, Ohio, 1969, Case Western Reserve University Press.

Wildarisky, A.: The self-evaluating organization. In Schulberg, H.C., and Baker, F., editors: Program evaluation in the health fields, vol. 2, New York, 1979, Human Sciences Press.

We make our times; such as we are, such are the times.

St. Augustine

28

COPING WITH CHANGE: PROFESSIONALLY AND PERSONALLY

John G. Bruhn and F. David Cordova

CHANGE: WHAT IS IT?

For better or worse, change is usually painful. It alters our way of doing and thinking about things. It often forces us to make choices, to reexamine goals and priorities, and to relinquish the familiar and comfortable.

In our society, we value progress highly and we believe that to get ahead frequent movement is necessary. Although the direction of any change is a matter of judgment, forward change is generally valued and backward change is discredited. Thus people who make lateral occupational moves or accept jobs at lesser salaries than they are currently earning are often regarded with pity or scorn.

To seek to better oneself is, in general, highly valued. As a consequence, our society fosters the development of persons who can be characterized as seekers of change. Seekers of change believe that being satisfied with how things are at any time is to be satisfied with mediocrity. The opposing view, held by individuals we might characterize as resisters of change, is that change of any type or magnitude is destructive and perpetuates a cycle of change. They argue further that once begun, change is hard to stop, and since its consequences cannot often be predicted accurately, the chance of change is too risky.

Each of us has sought or resisted change at different times in our personal lives, depending on our assessment of the costs or benefits to us. What is important to remember is that change occurs whether we want it to or not, whether we plan for it or not, and whether we can predict its consequences or not. No matter what we do to hide the effects of aging, we all continue to age. Whether we view growing old in a negative light and resist it by enormous efforts to look and act young, or whether we let aging happen and grow old gracefully, change inexorably brings us all to a common outcome.

The thesis of this chapter is that change is inevitable. Few things among living systems remain constant, so adaptation within the health care system requires continuous monitoring in order to plan timely and effective strategies for coping with change. This chapter sets forth several key issues that affect personal and professional coping capacity, including the ability to identify the overall changes within the health care system, recognition of the implications of change on nursing, and examination of factors in the development of nursing as a profession that parallel milestones in human development. Coping with change is a major personal and professional responsibility for nurses, since inability to cope inevitably reduces progress and effective functioning.

TO COPE IS TO CHANGE

All individuals and groups of individuals cope with or adapt to change in some way, and whether the coping is effective is a matter of judgment. Health professionals often judge behavior as healthy or unhealthy by how a person has coped, or is coping, with change. Our criterion for this judgment often is how we would cope with that same change in our lives, and the coping behavior that most closely approximates what we would do in a similar situation, we label as healthy.

Change, and the meaning of change, is intricately bound up with the culture and value systems of groups and societies. In some cultures, to advocate the status quo would elicit the same accolades that we give to progress and getting ahead in the United States.

To cope is necessary for human survival, which involves maintaining identity, self-esteem, or integrity when they are threatened. Coping does not mean that a situation has been mastered or conquered, nor is it limited to one way or one set of ways of coping. Rather, coping is the ability to reduce a threat or to solve a problem, as well as to create opportunities that allow an individual, group, or society to function at its maximal potential.

To some, effective coping implies working toward an acceptable compromise ("Competent Coping," 1973). Yet, since compromise implies a fairly even trade-off between costs and benefits, it is not enough if the goal is to improve or enhance self-esteem or integrity. In coping that is directed at improvement, one would hope to gain more than one would have to give up in the long run.

What constitutes competent coping, therefore, is dependent on the *goals* of the individual, group, or society, as well as the *outcome* of the effort to cope at any one time. Viewed in this light, the ways that we have of coping are also subject to change. We develop new and different ways of coping over time, and with experience, we perceive people and situations differently and take new risks that yield both new problems and new opportunities.

Change, coping, and human growth and development are, therefore, intricately related to each other. Whether we change, cope, and age are not decisions we make, but how we do it and whether we are pleased with who we are and where we are going are matters of choice. Too often, we view ourselves as victims of change, uncertain about how to cope, and we justify our views and actions by our chronological age. It is the authors' view that health professionals and the health care system are currently drifting in a "sea of change."

In the last decade, the lay public has created new demands on health professionals and, in some instances, has become an active adversary. Bombarded by these demands and confrontations (which appear to be increasing in number and frequency), health professionals have become skeptical, resentful, and even pessimistic. Indeed, the coping behavior of health professionals as a group has become almost totally defensive.

The growth and development of our health care system has not kept pace with change, especially with the increasing efforts of individuals to enhance their life-style and health in line with the promises held out by new technologies to treat disease. As a result, the health professions are the recipients of new forces of change for which old coping patterns appear to be ineffective. The effects of the external forces of change are being experienced in different ways within each health profession, and each is confronted by new needs and demands and beset by

new problems. These forces of change appear to be having more negative than positive effects on the individual lives of health professionals as the topics of turnover, dropout, and burnout become more common.

The purposes of the present chapter are to discuss the types of changes occurring in the health care system in the United States and the effects of these changes on nursing, to discuss change as it relates to professional growth and development, and to outline methods for coping with change as an individual and as a member of the nursing profession.

FORCES OF CHANGE ON THE HEALTH CARE SYSTEM IN THE UNITED STATES

The various forces pressing the health care system to change are shown in Fig. 28-1. Most of the forces for change are external to the system, although individuals and groups within the health care system also contribute to the call for change. Certainly health professionals must temper their advocacy to some extent lest they be labeled as disloyal and, perhaps, separated from the mainstream of decision making in their profession or place of employment.

The forces for change may vary in type and number from time to time, depending on what the health care system does or does not do. For example, a hospital's refusal to provide care to a pregnant woman near delivery because she cannot guarantee a source of payment may rally together individuals and groups who are advocates of the right to health care for everyone. On a national scale, the rising cost of health services may consolidate individuals and groups who advocate limits on physicians' incomes. Issues overlap, as do the memberships of groups advocating change in the health care system. What is important to emphasize is that these forces have become large in number and more persistent in their appeal for change, so that the issues can no longer be ignored nor the appeals dampened by lobbying efforts.

Since problems in the health care delivery system have not reached a crisis stage, reforms in this sys-

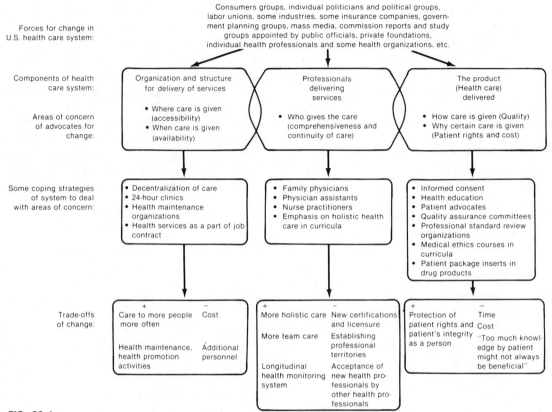

FIG. 28-1
Flow chart of effects of change on U.S. health care system, coping strategies, and trade-offs.

tem are given a low priority at the national level. Although health care costs continue to rise, care is primarily curative rather than preventive, and care is not accessible or available to all segments of our population, these issues have not been seen by a large enough number of people (or perhaps have not affected the right people) to elicit the crisis atmosphere that would spur federal action. Furthermore, health care has become a political football. Unfortunately, health is highly valued in the United States only after it is lost.

The areas of concern regarding the health care delivery system involve its three esssential components: organization and structure, personnel, and the product delivered (Fig. 28-1). Concern about the accessibility and availability of health care relates to where and when health care is administered. In general, it is available in hospitals, through private practicing physicians, and in government-supported institutions and clinics, and it is accessible to those who have transportation to the site of care during weekdays and day hours. The emergency room has become an alternative source of routine care for those persons who cannot get to the health care source during the day, have no usual physician, or do not know where else to go for health care.

Concern about who delivers health care services

is centered around the issues of comprehensiveness and continuity of care. Health professionals are generally experts in delivering care for illness and are not always educated to foster health maintenance because they see most clients when they are sick. Indeed, many health professionals are not interested in health education because health is not as professionally interesting as illness, nor are they prepared with the full armamentarium of skills to teach health as they are with those to treat illness. Thus the U.S. care health system does not offer comprehensive health care, but rather offers comprehensive illness care. Furthermore, for those who do not have a private physician, the chances are great that they will not see the same physician often, and even greater that an illness will not be followed carefully over time, because in public sources of care, turnover of health care personnel is great.

Concern about the kind of care delivered is growing. The often-heard statement, ''We have the best health care system in the world,'' implies that expertise, technology, and so on are such that the *product* delivered is the best. The kind of care delivered, however (i.e., quality of care), goes beyond the provider's knowledge and skills. The set of skills for relating to sick or well persons is the same set of skills that is used in relating to people in general. Certainly sick people have some new needs by virtue of being unable to function as usual, but personal integrity remains intact. It is this respect for integrity during the process of providing technical assistance that is a source of concern by many advocates for change, who feel we have let our technology overshadow our humanity.

To whom are these concerns directed? The health care system? Collectively as health professionals, we are the system. We are the organization and structure for providing health services and we deliver the product. What has been our response to the calls for reformation? We have made numerous changes to correct problems in where, when, who, how, and why health care is delivered (see Fig. 28-1). These changes have all involved positive and negative trade-offs. For example, in order to make health care more available and accessible, neighborhood clinics and round-the-clock clinics have been established in some areas, but this has often required additional staffing, space, and equipment. Also, new types of health professionals have been trained to educate and counsel persons in wellness activities, but this has required new certifications and licensure, as well as the establishment of new working relationships within the health care team. To change the system for delivery of health care means that we must change the way we do things and think about things now. Although we have indeed been making adaptations to change until now, we still were so comfortable with the way we were delivering health care that the small changes we made in the way we did things were outpaced by the rapidly changing needs and demands of our clients. What we can offer our clients lags behind what they expect and feel they need. Therefore, to bridge the gap between the health care system and the public, greater change will be required on our part. This congruence can never be complete, as our needs and expectations are in constant flux. For a health care system that has enjoyed high status, prestige, affluence, and relative stability to take such giant steps is indeed threatening and painful.

IMPLICATIONS OF CHANGE FOR NURSING

In considering the forces of change that act on the health care system, one might mistakenly deduce that the forces of change and the areas of their concern are perceived and evaluated in a similar way by all of the health professionals who make up the health care system. Rather than expressing a coordinated approach to coping with external forces of change, however, health professionals have tended to react to specific criticisms, proposed regulations, and new laws as separate vested-interest groups. This has caused health professional groups to work sometimes at cross-purposes, and at other times to propose separate but similar solutions to problems.

The degree to which health professionals do not work together collectively, and are protective of their territories, statuses, and power, is often fuel for the fire of advocates for change who are not health professionals.

In addition to the forces of change external to the health care system, forces of change are also at work within professional groups and within the health care system as a whole. Therefore, the pressures for change, or the responses to them, do not occur in concert among the members of a group or among the groups that make up the system. This is especially true if there is no overall planning for change in the system. Although the implications of change on any one professional group at any one time are speculative, our purpose is to explore the effects of change on nursing as a professional group.

It is the authors' view that change has had two major effects on nursing that have resulted in part from initiatives for change within nursing itself. One effect is a greater attempt by nursing to become independent and autonomous, especially from medicine and from physicians' leadership; the other is a greater attempt by nurses to enhance their degree of professionalization and specialized skills (as evidenced by the large number of nurses who are acquiring doctoral degrees or certification as nurse practitioners). Change has created new opportunities as well as new ambiguities for nursing.

The nurse has been a key member of the traditional health care team, especially in hospital settings. As many nurses have assumed administrative roles or acquired specialized nursing skills, however, the nurse is no longer seen by other health professionals as an essential member of the health care team. Indeed, in some settings, physician assistants have assumed health maintenance and counseling duties often reserved for nurses. Also, vocational nurses and nurse's aides in hospitals now carry out routine nursing care previously reserved for registered nurses. Therefore, although nursing has broadened its opportunities for professional growth and greater independence and autonomy

from the physician-nurse dyad, other health professionals see the nurse moving away from direct patient care and the hospital setting. This is in part a consequence of the perception by other health professionals of one role for the nurse, namely that of delivering inpatient care, rather than several roles. In turn, health professionals with whom the nurse has not usually worked in the past, ponder how the introduction of the nurse or nurse practitioner will affect the status, authority, and responsibility lines in their traditional teams. In some instances, furthermore, where nurse practitioners and physician assistants might be working in the same health care setting, debates about who is in charge and who is responsible to whom, as well as some overlap in skills, can be disruptive to the provision of patient care.

Ambiguity is a by-product of change until role realignments and reassessments can be made to establish a new *modus operandi*. When we introduce change, our expectations are that the effects or consequences will be positive. What might appear to be benefits at one time, however, might become liabilities. All change brings a price. We often must give up the familiar and comfortable to satisfy new needs. Nursing, as well as all health professions, is currently experiencing uncertainty and ambiguity about professional status and power position vis-à-vis the other health professions. We often see one professional group initiating change in an attempt to gain status and power over others.

If we are to have an effective health care system, we need to plan and organize that system around the needs of those it is designed to serve. Needs change, and so the system should be responsive to these changes. The needs of health professionals should not determine patient needs. In periods of uncertainty and rapid change, it is not unusual for individuals and groups to work to ensure the security of their own positions and protect their own interests. It seems that health professionals have devoted more time and energy to such efforts than to learning how to work together for the benefit of the patient.

CHANGE AND PROFESSIONAL DEVELOPMENT

We have discussed changes occurring in the health care system and in nursing and how changes in each interrelate and create new types of change. While change is going on in the larger society and in professional groups, we are also changing as individuals. How we are changing affects how we perceive and evaluate the changes occurring in society, in the health care system, and in our professional groups—which, in turn, influences our responses to change. Viewed in this perspective, change can create opportunities for us. It is true that change is often created by crises, so we tend to think of our reactions to change as defensive or protective, rather than as opportunities to make choices and change directions. Some change occurs normally or routinely without crises, and is often the result of positive initiatives by individuals or groups. Just as people often change as they move through youth and adulthood, a parallel can be seen in the professional growth and development of the health professional. It is our purpose to examine the key choice points for change in the growth and development of the nurse.

Becker has pointed out that perceptions of the effects of change are unique to the eye of the beholder. He stated that when a change occurs, an outside observer sees it as quite different in kind and degree and magnitude from what it really is. Health professionals, for example, have a perspective quite different from the patients with whom they relate. He stressed that as changes take place in people, the outsider interprets the change from a different perspective. Just as nurses acquire new perspectives and ideas as a result of nursing school, we all acquire new perspectives and ideas at times in our lives (Becker, 1964).

Becker (1964) listed two mechanisms in the development or change of the growth and development of a person: situational adjustment and commitment. With respect to *situational adjustment,* we learn adult roles (or new roles) by moving in and out of social situations and becoming sensitive to the kind of person each situation demands. As experience in social situations broadens, we analyze sequences of smaller and more numerous situations. Thus we must look to the character of the social situation for the explanation of why people change as they do. What is there in the situation that requires the person to act in a certain way or to hold certain beliefs?

Commitment is a second major mechanism in personal change. We say that a person is committed when we observe him pursuing a consistent line of activity in a sequence of various situations. Consistent activity persists over time. If, for example, a person refuses to change jobs, even though the new job would offer a higher salary and better working conditions, we would suspect that his decision is the result of commitment, although there may be trade-offs to the higher salary and better working conditions such as a pension plan he has invested in, the cost of moving and establishing new friends, and the current status of his children in school. It is important, therefore, to consider the "side-bets" we all make in order to fully understand why people do or do not change.

Situational adjustment and commitment are closely related, but not identical processes. Situational adjustment produces change: the person shifts his or her behavior with each social situation. Commitment produces stability: the person subordinates situational interests to goals that lie beyond the situation (Becker, 1964).

Applying Becker's concepts (1964) of situational adjustment and commitment, let us examine the options for change in the professional development of the nurse. Just as there are key developmental stages or phases in our psychosocial growth as persons (infancy, childhood, adolescence, young adulthood, and so on), there are phases in our development as professionals. Obviously, personal and professional development are not independent of one another, but emphasis is given to professional development in this section, and to the times in professional development when we make conscious choices regarding the type and direction our professional development will take.

The factors affecting change and stability at various stages in the professional development of the nurse are illustrated in Fig. 28-2. For purposes of discussion, the stages of career development can be categorized broadly as early, middle, and late. Certain factors are unique to each stage of professional development, so that each stage builds upon the previous stages. The predominant theme of early career development is to form an identity as a professional nurse, a necessary step before moving on to midcareer development where contributions can then be made to nursing. Finally, in the late stage of career development, the nurse has reached maturity and fulfillment, so as to create new opportunities for growth and development.

Numerous positive and negative factors affect change and stability at each of the three broad stages of development. Indeed, these factors are complexly interrelated and sometimes in constant flux. Nonetheless, the degree of balance or imbalance between the factors pressing for change and those pressing for stability elicit a certain type of professional outcome. If the factors of change and stability are positive and equivalent, professional satisfaction is a likely outcome, although others are possible (Fig. 28-2).

Herzberg (1966), in a classic study of attitudes toward work and job satisfaction in a Pittsburg industry, pointed out that five factors stood as strong determinants of job satisfaction—achievement, recognition, the work itself, responsibility, and advancement—the last three being of greater importance for lasting change in attitude. These five factors (called *motivators*) were seldom mentioned when employees complained of job dissatisfaction. It would seem that these five factors would also be

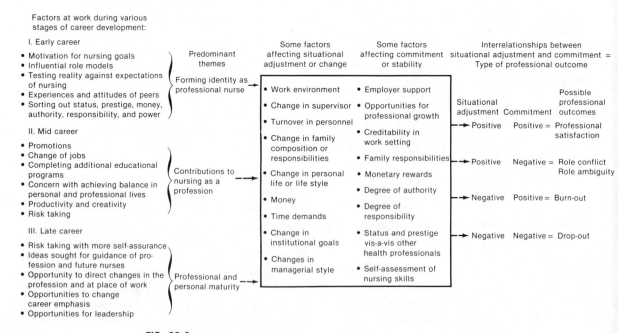

FIG. 28-2
Factors affecting change and stability at various stages in the professional development of the nurse.

important influences in determining professional satisfaction. Certainly no profession or job can provide all five motivators at any one time, but workers (professionals) and management (educators of future professionals as well as employers of health professionals) need to be aware of these five factors that promote personal and professional growth.

Cartwright (1979) has reviewed the sources and effects of stress in health careers. She noted that considerably more attention has been paid to the early stages of career development than to the later stages involving establishment, maintenance, and retirement. A more holistic approach to work, acknowledging the relationship between personal, family, and community life and professional development, offers promise for a better understanding of how to develop health professionals who are able to cope with change and its effects (Wolf, et al., 1978; Bruhn, 1979).

COPING AND PROFESSIONAL DEVELOPMENT

As health professionals, we understand coping as a professional tool. We assess how well our patients are able to cope with their illness (in our judgment), and this influences how much and how we give them information about their illness. We assist patients and their families to cope with the aftereffects of illnesses by providing counseling and support services. Although we learn coping techniques as part of our professional training, many of the techniques we apply to assist patients are those we have found to work for ourselves. As we grow and develop as professionals, and as our experience broadens, our repertoire of coping strategies also widens. Thus how well we cope with change as individuals and as professional helpers will depend on the stage of growth we have reached at any given point in time.

This fact of growth is important to consider in evaluating the degree of appropriateness or workability of another's way of coping with a situation; awkwardness in coping may reflect lack of experience or it may mean that the person is trying out a new coping technique, which does not necessarily signify difficulty in coping or indicate that the strategy will be ineffective. Coping is what works best for each of us. What is important is whether we are receptive to learning new coping techniques or modifying old ones. Change usually forces us to look at how we cope. Our receptiveness to changing our ways of coping will be reflected in the degree to which we welcome or resist change.

Antonovsky (1979) points out four major variables that enter into every coping strategy: rationality, flexibility, farsightedness, and emotional affect. *Rationality* is the accurate, objective assessment of the extent to which the change is a threat. *Flexibility* refers to the availability of options and a willingness to consider them. *Farsightedness* is related to rationality and flexibility, but goes beyond them in that it seeks to anticipate the response of the total environment to the coping strategy. The way in which a person goes about coping (i.e., the type of *emotional expression* or lack of it) also conveys information about the intensity of the situation and the person's degree of investment in it.

Coping involves both ego and functional components. Morowitz (1977) stated, in his book on ego niches in organizations, that each of us plays a dual role: a functional role determined by our job description in the overall activity of the organization we work for, and an ego role determined by our own demanding psychological needs. The ego role leads us to make an ego niche for ourselves in the structure of the organization that might be independent from the normal activities of the organization and often may conflict with them. Egos are unstable entities. They continually feel threatened by change and they need constant support and reassurance. In an organization of egos, each person's ego is regarded by him to be significant, irrespective of others' assessments. Ego security is linked with job security. In addition, each individual brings all of the ego problems into the organization that he or she has spent many years acquiring. Thus how a person has coped outside the organization, in the

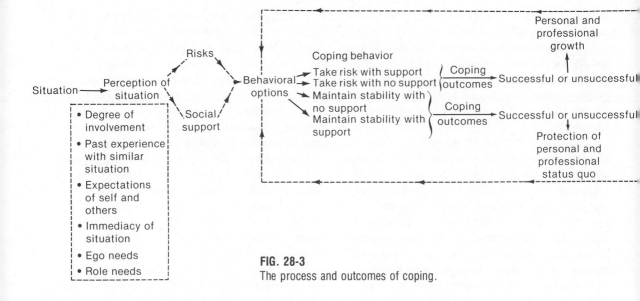

FIG. 28-3
The process and outcomes of coping.

past, continually influences how that person is currently coping inside the organization.

The steps or phases in the process of coping are shown in Fig. 28-3. How we perceive a situation will be a blend of many factors, including ego and role needs and the degree of perceived risk and support for possible options we might take in the situation. On the basis of this perceptual assessment, we decide to change (take risks) or to defend the status quo. Taking risks that result in a successful outcome is more likely to lead to personal and professional growth and the willingness to take risks in the future (Viscott, 1977).

COPING AS A NURSE: PROFESSIONALLY AND PERSONALLY

We tend to think of coping as the action or behavior of an individual. Coping behavior is also evident in large groups of individuals, however, such as professional groups and organizations, and we can even observe coping by societies, especially during crisis periods, war, recession, inflation, coups, and elections. How people cope is in part

influenced by what options are acceptable in the society in which they live, the social and professional groups of which they are members, the community in which they live, and the pressures to conform as exerted by family and peers. Thus it is appropriate to examine the coping process from a systems perspective.

A systems view of coping acknowledges that there are progressively wider circles of forces, pressures, and influences acting on each individual. Factors at all levels — the society, the community, and the family — affect the ways in which each of us copes. Similarly, one's professional identification and associations as a nurse, for example, will have a bearing on how a person copes in the role of a nurse.

Perhaps the best way to illustrate the interaction between professional and personal coping is to consider an example of an innovation in health staffing that arose outside of nursing, but that has enormous implications for the nursing profession as well as individual nurses. The physician assistant is a new health practitioner created in the 1960s, in large part to free physicians' time from tasks that could be carried out by competent assistants, such as taking medical histories and conducting physical examinations. The impetus for the development of such a practitioner was, in part, from the public. Complaints that it was difficult to get to see a physician, that they did not spend enough time with their patients, and that they were not geographically located in places easily accessible to the sick, helped to stir concern about our society's health work force pool. Public pressures, particularly as reflected in increased political activity, led to pressures on health professionals to find solutions to the inadequate number and distribution of various kinds of health professionals. It was in this context that medical corpsmen became a valuable pool of assistants to help relieve public pressures.

The role definition, authority, and responsibility of this new health professional, however, had direct effects on the profession of nursing. Debates within nursing about levels of education (ADN, BSN, and MSN), as well as long-term concerns within nursing about long hours, low pay and status, and the desire to become more independent from physicians, were already going on during the time the physician assistant (PA) was introduced as a new practitioner who would work closely with and under the direction of physicians. The PA was a new member of the health care team. Licensure of these professionals gave them credibility to the medical profession, and acceptance of them by the lay public was positive.

The amount of authority and responsibility the PA can legally be given varies from state to state and from physician to physician. Although mobility as a PA within medicine is extremely limited, they enjoy higher salaries than most nurses and relatively high status in the eyes of patients. These factors have created strain and tension between nurses and PAs. The nursing profession has a practitioner comparable to the PA, namely the nurse practitioner (NP). Although the NP's emphasis is more on health maintenance, wellness care, and patient

counseling than that of the PA, overlap exists in their skills and activities. Role confusion and ambiguity have created new concerns on the part of nurses about what role they are expected to play in patient care, how the role of the nurse interfaces with the roles of other health professionals in the new and enlarged health care team, and the future role of the nurse in the health care system. These concerns have caused some nurses to become dissatisfied and to leave nursing, others to leave patient care for administration or to become full-time educators, and others to cope by narrowly defining their role and carefully selecting jobs where role conflict with others is minimized. Several authors have described techniques to cope with job change and job stress (Kanner, et al., 1978; Shubin, 1978).

PERSONAL GROWTH AND PROFESSIONAL GROWTH

As noted earlier, how we cope or function in nonwork roles cannot be separated from how people cope and function in the work role. If we are unhappy in our personal lives, it affects our work, and vice versa. If we are to continue to grow and develop professionally and personally, we must periodically stop to assess both where we are and where we are going. Are the goals we set for ourselves a few years ago still realistic? Growth can only occur if we want it to occur and if we give ourselves chances to learn. Carl Rogers (1961) has observed that as individuals strive to discover and become themselves, they seem to be more content to be a *process* rather than a *product*. Coping and growing, therefore, are interrelated processes. Change can become a positive aspect of our professional and personal lives if we direct and guide it.

SUMMARY

We all cope with or adapt to change in some fashion. Coping does not mean that a situation has been mastered or conquered, nor does it mean that one is limited to one way or one set of ways of coping. Coping is the ability to reduce a threat or to solve a problem, as well as to create opportunities to grow as a person. Change, coping, and human growth are thus related to one another. How we change and cope are matters of choice. Too often, we see ourselves as victims of change and we resist it, usually because change requires learning new ways of thinking about and doing things.

The health care system in the United States is undergoing change, in part because of pressures outside the system, and in part because of changes within the various health professions that make up the system. Some of these changes have created struggles to preserve professional territories, power, and status. Indeed, these inter- and intra-professional struggles have at times overshadowed concerns about who the health care system should serve: professional or client. When referring to changes in the health care delivery system, we often refer to "the system" as if we as professionals were not a part of the system. We are the system, and the type and direction of change it takes in the future will depend on whether we assist in guiding which way the system should evolve or whether we let change take its course.

The forces of change acting on the health care system have many implications for nursing and for nurses. Nursing is in the process of assessing the future role of the nurse, especially in light of efforts of nurses to become more independent, autonomous, and professionalized. These changes will alter how clients and other health professionals see the nurse and what they expect of nurses. The needs of clients have changed and so have the professional needs of nurses. The challenge before us is to assemble a way to serve clients such that it is personally and professionally satisfying to the nurse.

Change and coping constitute a process that parallels professional development. We learn to cope in a variety of social situations, and when coping becomes patterned and predictable in certain situations, we say the person is committed. Numerous factors affect change and stability at various stages in the professional development of the nurse. There are also options for coping that exist at these devel-

opmental stages. The options chosen can lead to professional and personal maturity as a nurse, or to burnout or dropout from the profession.

Coping is a professional tool of nursing. We are experts in assessing how well our patients cope with illness. How we cope with change in our personal lives will affect how we see our patients cope. Thus we must guard against making value judgments about the effectiveness of another person's methods of coping until we know the patient as a person. Coping involves both ego and role components. Egos and work roles become easily tangled. How we choose to cope on the job may be more a function of ego needs than professional needs. This is an important fact in understanding how and why a colleague adapts in a unique way.

If professional and personal growth are high priorities, we must take periodic inventories of where we are and where we are going. We must be willing to take risks to grow. Growth is a process. Change can be a positive factor in our professional and personal lives if we accept change and focus the direction of change. Viewed in this way, change need not be feared, even change over which one has no control, if one is willing to extract what is potentially good from it and to consider its negative effects as a part of the trade-off for taking forward steps.

REFERENCES

Antonovsky, A.: Health, stress and coping, San Francisco, 1979, Jossey-Bass Publishers, Inc.

Becker, H.S.: Personal change in adult life, Sociometry **27:** 40-53, 1964.

Bruhn, J.G.: Square pegs and round holes: job satisfaction and the health of workers, Health Values **3:**310-315, Nov./Dec. 1979.

Cartwright, L.K.: Sources and effects of stress in health careers. In Stone, G.C., Cohen, F., and Adler, N.E., editors: Health psychology: a handbook; theories, applications, and challenges of a psychological approach to the health care system, San Francisco, 1979, Jossey-Bass Publishers, Inc.

Competent coping, No. 2 in series, The question of coping, Nutley, N.J., 1973, Hoffman-LaRoche, Inc.

Herzberg, F.: Work and the nature of man, Cleveland, Ohio, 1966, World Publishing Co.

Kanner, A.D., Kafry, D., and Pines, A.: Conspicuous in its

absence: the lack of positive conditions as a source of stress, J. Hum. Stress **4:**33-39, Dec. 1978.

Morowitz, H.J.: Ego niches: an ecological view of organizational behavior, Woodbridge, Conn., 1977, Ox Bow Press.

Rogers, C.R.: On becoming a person: a therapist's view of psychotherapy, Boston, Mass., 1961, Houghton-Mifflin Co.

Shubin, S.: Burnout: the professional hazard you face in nursing, Nursing **8:**22-27, July 1978.

Viscott, D.: Risking, New York, 1977, Pocket Books.

Wolf, S., Bruhn, J.G., and Goodell, H.: Occupational health as human ecology, Springfield, Ill., 1978, Charles C Thomas.

GLOSSARY

accreditation a process for evaluation of educational programs that attempts to promote and ensure quality in education.

administrative decisions deal with day-to-day activities in the organization that are concerned with short-range goals.

administrative organization the element of organization theory developed by Henry Fayol with content built around the functions managers perform.

aggressive behavior pressing of one's own behavior in such a way as to infringe on the rights of others.

American Federation of State, County, and Municipal Employees (AFSCME) union oriented to nonprofessional workers employed in state and local governmental health care institutions.

American Nurses' Association (ANA) the national professional organization of registered nurses in the United States and its territories.

analog model uses one property to represent another; does not look like its real-life counterpart.

anchoring attachment of an attitude or belief to existing networks or beliefs. This increases resistance to persuasion.

anxiety a usually unpleasant feeling varying in degree from mild to panic, which is experienced by everyone when the self is threatened.

appropriations the actual amount of monies approved for a program authorized by law.

assertiveness standing up for one's personal rights, thoughts, and feelings in a direct and honest manner that does not violate the rights of others.

assertiveness training teaching people how to express themselves honestly and directly by identifying what is blocking such behavior and by setting goals for increasing personal assertive behavior.

associative power power that has its source in one's close association with a powerful person or group.

authority a form of power attached to an organizational position and made legitimate by delegation with respect to tasks, duties, and sphere of influence.

authorization the process of placing a ceiling on monies to be requested for a program.

autocratic leader one who is task oriented and expects obedience from members of the group so that goals can be accomplished.

autonomy personal liberty to determine one's own course of action.

bargaining unit a group with whom an employer negotiates in the process of bargaining. The NLRB determines the unit appropriate for bargaining; the unit, itself, determines who will do the bargaining for the employees, who will represent whom, and the subject matter for collective bargaining.

barriers obstacles to movement or progress.

benevolent autocrat a type of leader who maintains ultimate responsibility yet is accessible to members and listens to their opinions and suggestions.

bill the most common format used to introduce legislation; all contain an enacting clause prescribed by law in 1871.

bioethics ethics applied to the health care field.

biofeedback a process in which delicate physiological

442

monitoring instruments serve as teaching tools by helping people become aware of and learn to consciously control many physiological variables previously thought to be automatic.

boundary a real or imagined line that separates any given system from the environment that surrounds it.

Bowen Family Theory an approach to human behavior developed by Dr. Murray Bowen, which views the family as a system and examines individual functioning in the light of family patterns and interactions.

bureaucracy a theory of organization that was systematized by German sociologist Max Weber; emphasis is on the structure of organizations.

capitation payment of tax of a fixed amount per person.

certainty a situation in which the level of predictability about the outcome is high.

certificate of need determination in a given community of the need for new health care facilities based on the currently available resources and the anticipated demands for utilization.

chamber the legislative division commonly known as the House and Senate, or both.

change agent a person filling an organizational role that has the purpose of initiating or effectuating change.

childbirth center a health facility where prenatal care and delivery services are provided to low-risk pregnant women by a team of nurse midwives, obstetricians, pediatricians, and ancillary health personnel.

classical design theory collection of administrative organization, bureaucracy, and scientific management that proposed an absolute, principles-based philosophy of organization.

client-centered case consultation attempts to provide the consultee with expert advice or alternatives to be considered in the delivery of care to a client or group of clients.

closed system one that neither admits any matter or energy from the environment, nor expels matter or energy into the environment.

coactive persuasion a method that employs movement by the persuader closer psychologically to the persuadee.

coalition alliance or union of people usually for the purpose of achieving a goal.

coercive power use of negative sanctions such as threats of harm, forms of punishment, or withheld rewards.

cognitive dissonance mental state in which there is a lack of consistency among a person's various cognitions once a decision has been made.

cognitive redefinition looking at a problem from a different perspective.

collaboration mutual sharing and working together to achieve a common goal in such a way that all are recognized and growth is encouraged.

collective bargaining negotiating activities that generally cover agreements regarding wages, hours, and conditions of employment.

combative persuasion persuasive method employing techniques of increasing the psychological distance between the persuader and persuadee.

communication process by which messages are transmitted from source to receiver.

communication model a type of descriptive model that seeks to describe the structural arrangement of the various elements or components in a given system.

community analysis gathering of information and evaluation of alternatives for action based on identified aspects of the community under study.

community health services directed to meet the needs of groups; tend to reflect a public health orientation of health promotion and maintenance.

compatibility degree of congruence between the innovation and existing values, beliefs, habits, past experiences, and needs of participants.

complexity in the change process, describes the amount of difficulty that participants have in understanding and subsequently using an innovation.

Comprehensive Health Planning and Public Health Services Amendments of 1966 (CHP) emphasized regional planning and was a landmark piece of legislation in that it acknowledged for the first time each person's "right" to health care.

comprehensive model identifies and relates most or all of the variables involved, which are then linked with a set of macro or gross relationships.

compromise two or more persons or groups have a goal(s) that cannot be met without modification of the positions of each person or group; implies a "give and take" in the negotiating process.

concepts words or elements that describe or express an abstract idea.

conceptual framework a group of concepts plus a set of propositions that spell out the relationships between them.

concurrent resolution document expressing principles, opinions, and purposes of the Congress on matters affecting the operation of both houses. They originate separately in either chamber, and are not usually legislative.

confrontation problem-solving approach to conflict resolution that includes assessment, direct response to a difference, and resettlement or a state of agreement on problem resolution.

Congress composed of the Senate and the House of Representatives.

Congressional Budget Office advises Congress and assists in evaluating costs and economic impact of budget proposals on the taxpayers.

Congressional Record document published daily by the Superintendent of Documents reporting on public proceedings whenever at least one house of Congress is in session.

congruence amount of agreement between a verbal and nonverbal message.

consciousness raising increasing a person's or group's awareness or interest in a specific topic or issue.

consensual validation verbally "checking out" your impressions with someone else to determine if your perceptions are accurate.

consideration as a concept in the Ohio State University leadership studies, refers to leader behavior involving friendship, mutual trust, respect, warmth, and rapport between the leader and followers.

constraints limitations on achieving the desired objectives; often involves finances.

constructs conceptual components that are not directly observable; deliberately created ideas or references that are not actually seen but that allow for explanation and analysis.

consultation interactional or communication process between two or more persons; one of these is a consultant and the other(s) are considered consultees, and the consultant seeks to help the consultee solve a problem or improve skills.

consultee person seeking the help of an outside, usually impartial person in problem resolution.

consultee-centered administrative consultation focuses on a specific work problem that consultees are having in the general areas of program development and organization.

consultee-centered case consultation focuses on the current difficulties that a provider is having in the delivery of care or services.

contingency design theory a relativistic or situational view of organization emphasizing adaptation to environmental forces.

contingency model of leadership includes three basic components—leader-member relations, task structure, and position power—all of which determine the effectiveness of the leader.

contingency theory a leadership theory holding that the effectiveness of a given leadership pattern is dependent on the demands imposed by the situation.

continuous reinforcement acknowledging or rewarding behavior each time it occurs.

coping the ability to reduce a threat or to solve a problem, as well as to create an opportunity that allows individuals, groups, or societies to function at their maximum.

counterattitudinal advocacy a persuasive method in which the persuadee role plays an attitude counter to the one actually held by the persuadee.

critical path method a decision aid similar to PERT that only considers one time, which is the longest possible time interval.

cybernetics science of communication and control.

decision making a multistep process that has the primary goal of selecting one best course of action from a variety of alternatives.

decision models seek to propose how things ought to be rather than describing how they actually are.

decision theory consists of a group of related concepts and propositions that attempt either to prescribe or to describe how individuals as well as groups select a course of action when confronted with a problem.

decoding a mental process that the receiver of a message goes through to decipher what is meant by the message.

defense-arousing message the message content contains a challenge to the other person's competence, a threat, or a disregard for the listener's worth, values, or feelings.

delegation enlisting others to perform a work task; this includes giving clear, complete instructions as well as following up to make sure that the task was completed effectively.

democratic a type of leader who makes the ultimate decision but encourages considerable group member participation in the establishment of goals and the selection of methods for goal accomplishment.

deontology ethical theory based on rules of conduct.

departmentalization principles involved in logically dividing the organization into operational units.

descriptive ethics deals with how people actually behave.

descriptive model of decision making believes that decision makers do not always know all the facts in advance but solve their problems as best they can under the prevailing circumstances.

descriptive models explain how things are, how they function or work. Includes three categories: communication, explanatory, and predictive models.

DESC scripting a way of negotiating for positive changes in a humane, open, and assertive manner by *describing* the unwanted behavior, *expressing* feelings about it, and *specifying* what changes you are willing to make, as well as spelling out the *consequences* of abiding by the contract.

developmental change that which occurs as an individual, group, or organization progresses from infancy toward maturity.

differentiation of self a term used by Bowen to refer to the way an individual handles the intermix between emotional and intellectual functioning.

dilemma a situation that requires choosing between two equally unsatisfactory alternatives.

disjoint groups where no singular individual is a member of both groups.

distress avoided emotional and physiological response to a stressor; usually harmful and unpleasant stress.

District 1199 a labor union involved in health care, based in New York City and including about one percent RNs in its membership.

division of work economic principle of specialization that was the foundation for classical theory.

dogmatism tendency to hold firmly to previously conceived beliefs even in the face of contrary evidence.

driving forces those that move participants in the change process in the direction desired by the change agent.

dyad two people or objects.

dynamic model can be used to depict change because it includes time as an independent variable and can show movement.

ecology study of the continuous complex interplay that occurs between living organisms and their environment.

economics study of how human and material resources are used to meet human needs.

ecosystem sum total of all existing subsystems including both the structural and functional components.

ecosystem competence the ability to behave in appropriate ways in a given setting.

effectiveness extent to which a decision solves a problem.

efficiency a measure of the difference between what an organization gets out of a decision relative to what it puts into solving it.

emotional cutoffs terms used by Bowen to explain behavior when a person or group ceases to interact with another person or group as a means of avoiding the anxiety evoked when interaction occurs.

employeeism belief that employers have the best interests of their employees at heart and will do their best for them.

encoding converting of an idea into an understandable message.

energy ability to do work; as such, can neither be created nor destroyed but can be changed from one form to another; can change its form or be transduced.

entropy measure of disorder in an open system.

equilibrium sense of balance toward which all living systems strive; the attempt to resist system instability.

ethical dilemma situation of conflicting moral claims.

ethics science or study of moral values; a code of principles and ideals that guide action.

evaluation placing a value on or deriving the worth of an action, decision, or experience.

excess mortality premature death; that is, death occurring before the average life expectancy for persons of the same sex.

expert power that which accrues from the possession of expertise, information, or professional skills.

explanatory model a type of descriptive model that seeks to discuss the relationships among the parts of a given system.

farsightedness in the change process, includes the anticipation of the response of the total environment to the coping strategy necessary to deal with an innovation.

Federal Register a document published each official federal working day to inform the public of executive regulations, presidential orders, organizational changes, hearings, meeting schedules, and other administrative matters.

Federation of Nurses and Health Professionals (FNHP) an affiliate of the American Federation of Teachers whose primary objective is to promote collective bargaining for RNs and other health employees.

feedback energy output of an open system that serves to promote stablity; may be either positive or negative.

filtering reducing the content of communication to a few essential details.

fiscal year annual operating year of the government, October 1 to September 30 of the following year.

fitness attainment of wellness on a continuing basis.

flexibility availability of options and a willingness to consider them.

forces pressures toward movement.

formative evaluation takes place throughout the process of program evaluation and looks for potential problems that can be remedied without waiting until program completion.

function in systems theory, refers to the dynamic interaction among parts of the whole.

functional dependency state of health characterized by a reduction in ability of a person to carry out independently the customary activities of daily living.

game theory a form of operations research that is a simulation technique where a model is used to simplify problems by identifying their basic parts and using trial-and-error practices to arrive at a potential solution.

general adaptation syndrome (GAS) manifestations of stress in the whole body, as they develop in time. Happens in three stages: alarm, resistance, and exhaustion.

geriatric day care an ambulatory health care facility for elderly people that uses a broad range of professional and community services in order to maximize functional independence for this age group in the home and community.

goals perceived expectations or ideals that are established from the set of values held by individuals, groups, or organizations.

grapevine informal communication channel that often exists in organizations for the purpose of short-circuiting the formal structure for message transmission.

Great Man Theory leadership view holding that certain people are born with the innate ability to be leaders.

gross national product (GNP) equals the total value of all final goods and services produced in the economy in one year.

group three or more individuals functioning interdependently to meet a common goal.

haphazard change generally random with no effort made by the participants to prepare for the onset of the change cycle.

health a person's ability to adapt to biological, psychological, and social changes in a manner that allows the individual to function at an optimal level of well-being in his or her environment.

health care system the totality of resources that a population distributes in the organization and delivery of health services.

health education any combination of learning experiences designed to facilitate adaptations of behavior conducive to health.

health hazard appraisal a quantitative technique for risk-factor appraisal and, perhaps, modification, based on an assessment of an individual's health hazards and the initiation of life-style modification and medical therapy to control or decrease the hazards.

health maintenance organization (HMO) an organized system of health care in a geographical area providing voluntary, multiple-choice enrollment for its members and financed by a fixed periodic payment that covers all health care regardless of how often services are used.

health promotion advancement of activities, such as disease-prevention services, environmental protection, and health education, which are devoted to the attainment of optimal physical, social, and emotional well-being for individuals, families, communities, and society at large.

health-risk appraisal a process that allows for data gathering, analysis, and comparison of an individual's prognostic characteristics of health with a standard age group, thereby providing a prediction of a person's likelihood of developing prematurely the health problems that cause high morbidity and mortality rates in this country.

health services the totality of personal and provider services performed by individuals, groups, or organizations for the purpose of maintaining the highest possible level of health.

health systems agency (HSA) a federally funded agency that plans and approves the development of health care facilities in a community.

heuristic model a type of decision model that attempts to evaluate alternative outcomes that seem to be associated with distinct decisions in order to find the best decision, when optimization models are either not available or too costly.

hidden agenda a covert level of interaction or purpose of group members.

hierarchy vertical stratification of organizations according to authority levels.

Hill-Burton Act first U.S. legislation to focus on planning as a major area of concern. Its primary purpose was to provide for a more equal distribution of hospitals across the nation by providing federal matching funds for between one and two thirds of the total cost of a facility.

HMO Act legislation enacted in 1973 to provide a demonstration program for the development of health maintenance organizations.

holistic health an integrated state of wellness, which includes the mind, body, spirit, and environment.

hospice a palliative system of health care for terminally ill persons that takes place in the home with family involvement under the direction and supervision of health professionals, especially the visiting nurse. Hospice care takes place in the hospital when severe complications of the terminal illness occur, or when there is family exhaustion or loss of commitment.

human ecology study of the interrelationships between individuals and their environment, as well as among the individuals in the environment.

human relations movement social science view of organizations popularized by the Hawthorne studies.

iatrogenesis illness induced by the health care provider or institution. Clinical iatrogenesis, the most familiar, includes illnesses created as by-products of medical intervention (e.g., infections caused by antibiotics that alter the body's normal bacterial flora).

iatrogenic guilt guilt engendered at a time of illness as a result of assignment of blame for the illness by the care provider to the patient.

iconic model a direct representation of the subject, event, or process that it seeks to depict; looks like what it is designed to represent.

imagery creation of pictures through the use of mental processes; can be spontaneously or deliberately created and used for many purposes.

impersonal forces come from the environment rather than from people.

incongruence lack of agreement between a verbal and nonverbal message.

individuality forces forces that come from within the person to become a productive, autonomous individual.

induced forces forces that come from another person and impose pressure toward a particular behavior.

influence the act of producing an effect without obvious force or direct authority.

information seeking assembling materials, tools, and available knowledge with which to work toward problem solution.

initiating structure those leadership behaviors in which the leader organizes and defines the relationships in the group; tends to establish well-defined patterns and channels of communication, as well as ways to get the job done.

input information or energy or matter that is taken into a living system.

intent of law legislative language of a law that provides general guidelines for the writing of specific regulations.

interagency linkages in consultation, these refer to situations where the consultant acts as a bond or mediator in creating or maintaining linkages of value to two or more agencies.

interface juncture at which individuals meet and interact with the environment.

intermittent reinforcement noncontinuous or periodic acknowledgment or reward for behavior.

internal resources audit during this stage of the marketing audit, the strengths and weaknesses of resources and existing programs are identified.

isomorphism degree of similarity between a replica of reality and the reality it seeks to portray.

joint resolution a form of legislation similar to a bill. All joint resolutions contain a resolving clause as prescribed by law in 1871. The term joint does not signify simultaneous introduction by both houses; such resolutions become law like a bill does.

justice giving a person what is due or owed.

laissez-faire a type of leadership in which the leader exerts no direct influence over the members; they are simply allowed to pursue their own goals as they see fit.

Lawrence and Lorsch studies led to a formalization of the modern contingency theory by illustrating the importance of adapting to change.

leader-member relations in contingency theory, refers to the amount of confidence that members have in their leader, as well as their degree of loyalty.

leadership an interpersonal relationship in which the leader employs style, approaches, and strategies to influence people to attain mutually established goals.

leadership continuum presents the range of leader behaviors from one extreme where control is localized with the leader, to the other where members control the decision-making process.

legislative counsel consultants in the House and Senate available to assist in the framing of ideas in suitable legislative language and form for introduction.

legitimate power power made legitimate through delegation of authority or the acceptance of it by those over whom it is exercised.

legitimization sanctioning by the people in control of new projects or proposals.

life space psychological environment of a person.

life-style – induced health problems diseases whose natural history includes conscious exposure to certain health-compromising or risk factors.

linear programming a form of operations research that is most effective in situations requiring that limited resources be allocated to the best possible advantage; mathematically determines the linear relationship that exists between parts and the limits that must be calculated.

link in systems theory, refers to the person(s) responsible for making connections between two or more systems.

living systems always open and involved in exchange of matter and energy with the environment.

lower-participant power power that subordinates may have over those higher in a hierarchy, by reason of their knowledge, personality, or other factors.

macro models link the concepts or constructs in gross rather than finely defined explanation.

majority party political party holding the most seats in the House and Senate.

management planning, organizing, staffing, directing, and controlling of time, money, material, and human resources.

managerial grid a way of looking at leadership that identifies five different leadership types based on concern for production (task) and concern for people (relationships).

mandatory bargaining topics areas that parties are legally required to bargain over according to the NLRA amendments; includes wages, rates of pay, hours, and other conditions of employment.

market analysis the first step in the marketing audit, which identifies the primary market as well as the segments that comprise the total market.

marketing a set of human activities directed at satisfying needs and wants through the exchange process.

marketing audit evaluation of an agency's activities; begins as soon as a need is identified and serves to specify key pieces of information that are essential to accurate assessment and planning of services.

mark-up a line-by-line review of a bill by a committee for the purpose of changing the wording or amending the "intent" of the bill.

matrix organization a structure based on a two-dimensional flow of authority. Known for its ability to muster relevant talent around a single problem and its temporary nature. Also known as a project structure.

mediation in collective bargaining, refers to efforts of the mediator to help the parties resolve their differences by making suggestions and keeping open the lines of communication.

Medicaid federally and state-funded insurance plan that provides financial assistance for health care for people who are handicapped or can otherwise demonstrate a need for financial assistance.

Medicare federally funded insurance plan whereby Social Security funds are used to provide health care services to people over sixty-five years of age.

meditation a state of consciousness in which stimuli are eliminated from awareness so that the mind can focus on only one thing, thus providing for rest and relief from stress.

mental models pictures that people hold in their minds; a simplification of the situation that is being portrayed.

metaethics addresses the semantics of meaning.

micro models models that include considerable detail and finely delineated aspects of the content or model to be presented.

minority party political party holding the least number of seats in the Congress.

mission analysis reminds the planning group of their basic purpose by determining what needs are currently being satisfied as well as those that the planners or consumers wish to be satisfied.

models analogies that help to depict complex situations in a relatively simple fashion.

motivation intrinsic and extrinsic factors that are the determinants of choice, persistence, and vigor of goal-directed behavior.

National Health Planning and Resources Development Act of 1974 (Public Law 93-641) set forth to coordinate and direct national health policy via state and regional regulatory agencies; its major goal was to establish a nationwide network of health systems agencies.

National Labor Relations Act (NLRA) passed in 1935 and known as the Wagner Act, protected employees' rights to organize and to join unions, and also provided for what constituted unfair labor practices of employers.

negative feedback the process by which an open system continuously adjusts to the difference between ideal and actual functioning; the tendency toward stability.

negentropy energy in an open system that can be utilized by the system; it represents order in the system and is available for carrying out the work of the system.

negotiated order relative degrees of stability and conflict in organizational relationships that result from bargaining strategies in power settings.

negotiation bargaining between people to reach a mutually desirable goal; takes place in an atmosphere of openness and trust.

new health professional (NHP) nurse practitioners and physician assistants.

niche both the structural and functional roles that individuals occupy within their environment.

nightingalism an ideology that emphasizes self-sacrifice on the part of the nurse when the primary concern is for the welfare of patients with minimal attention to personal economic and general welfare.

NLRA Amendments of 1974 (Public Law 93-360) amended the Taft-Hartley Act of 1947 by extending the rights to organize collectively for matters concerning wages, hours, and working conditions to all employees of nonpublic health care facilities.

NLR Board administrative agency for implementing federal policy affecting labor relations.

nonassertive behavior denial of one's own rights by failing to express thoughts, beliefs, and feelings honestly.

nonprogrammed decisions decisions that deal with novel or infrequent situations and require a creative response.

nonverbal communication that part of a message which includes signals and cues conveyed by a person's gestures, actions, facial expression, and tone of voice.

normative ethics deals with questions of what is right, what is good, or what is obligatory.

normative model seeks to depict the ideal version of an entity; that which is most desired, such as a "model child."

normative model of decision making characterizes the decision maker as a person who is rational with perfect knowledge of all variables that could affect the decision.

norms prevailing or generally accepted standards of behavior in any group.

nurse practitioner (NP) a new nursing role that includes a primary care component focusing on health maintenance, disease prevention, and patient counseling.

Nurses' Coalition for Action in Politics (N-CAP) political action arm of the ANA.

objectives statements of the goal or purpose that is being pursued.

observability in the change process, refers to the viability that a project or innovation has for the onlookers.

occupational health workers' ability to function at an optimal level of well-being at the worksite; reflected by higher employee productivity, increased work attendance, reduction in workers' compensation claims, and increased longevity in employment status.

occupational socialization orientation into a given job-related set of behaviors, that is, the set of expected behaviors that accompany a specific job.

Office of Management and Budget (OMB) White House office that advises the president on the budget and financial affairs of the nation.

open system one that is in continuous interaction and interchange of energy and information with the environment.

operations research (OR) uses a mathematical model to solve decisions or designated problems.

optimization model a type of decision model that is generally mathematical in scope and seeks to use computations to determine the best possible solution to an existing problem or change proposal.

optimizers attempt to make perfect decisions based on optimal amount of information.

optimizing alternatives those that have as their end goals the best possible or maximally effective course of action.

osteopath(y) a doctor trained in one of the two schools of medical practice in the United States. A complete physician, who receives a doctor of osteopathy degree (D.O.). The osteopath receives training in the manipulative healing art originated by A.T. Still. This school of medicine is based on the theory that the normal body is a vital mechanical organism whose structural and functional states are of equal importance, and that the body is able to rectify itself against toxic conditions when it has favorable environmental circumstances and satisfactory nourishment. Therefore, it is the osteopathic physician's responsibility to establish and remove any internal or external peculiarities to the system. Although using manipulation for the most part to restore structural and functional balance, he also relies on physical, medicinal, and surgical methods.

outcome changes in patient health status that can be attributed to their care.

output information, matter, or energy that is expelled from a living system as a result of its functioning.

overlapping membership in groups, this means that the same person is a member of two or more groups.

paradox of administration logical inconsistencies in administrative theory resulting in a dilemma for managers.

paraphrasing restating in your own words the message you received.

partial models limited to a few variables that are fully developed.

passive volition a state of being in which the body is relaxed and the mind holds an idea that is an intention or willing toward a particular outcome such as warm hands.

paternalism practices that restrict the liberty of individuals.

path connection between two or more regions that makes it possible to move from one to another.

path-goal theory based on expectancy theory; contends that leaders are effective when they motivate followers, coordinate their work so that they may achieve the designated goal, and experience job satisfaction from this success.

peer review process in which professionals are evaluated by other members of the same profession.

perception an individual's personally held views of the environment; what is seen, heard, felt.

permissive bargaining topics parties can bargain on these topics but cannot come to an impasse on them; they change often as more areas become included in mandatory bargaining.

personal behavioral leadership theory believes that leaders are best described by their personal qualities; often referred to as style theory.

personal health services those directed toward maintenance of individual health.

personal power ability to control oneself.

persuasion human communication designed to influence others by modifying their beliefs, values, and attitudes.

PERT see program evaluation and review technique.

PERT chart a schematic representation of activities, which identifies key activities, sequences them in a flow diagram, and assigns the expected duration time for each phase of the project; calculates three possible time intervals: optimistic, most likely, and pessimistic.

physician assistant (PA) new health practitioner created in the 1960s to free physicians' time by completing tasks such as history taking and conducting physical examinations.

plan the operationalization of goals; action-oriented approach to solving identified problem or obtaining designated goal.

planned change action designed to intervene in the ongoing state in order to produce a new state or situation.

pocket veto president allows a bill to lie on his desk for ten days after Congress adjourns without his signature; bill dies.

policy principles that govern action toward given ends.

politics art of influencing policy and decision making.

position power formal authority associated with a person's position in an organization.

power ability of people to require others to act as the power holder desires.

power strategy planned use of the various forms of power available to an individual or group.

power tactics forms of behavior useful for acquiring power or for using it effectively in the pursuit of a strategy.

predictive model a type of descriptive model that seeks to describe the causal relationships among the parts of the events actually taking place.

price costs that buyers must pay in order to obtain the product.

primary care first level of personal health services, which provides for evaluation, management of symptoms, disease prevention, health promotion, and continuing and coordinated care through appropriate referrals.

probability theory a form of operations research that assumes factors occur in a predictable pattern; used to determine the degree of risk involved in each potential solution.

problem-oriented medical record (POMR) a system for recording patient information, which includes a data base, problem list, treatment plan, and follow-up.

problem recognition the point at which a person becomes interested in or concerned about the problem.

procedures a specific set of guidelines or steps to be used for accomplishing a designated action.

procrastination putting off to a later date those things that need your attention now.

product the item or service that an individual or organization is attempting to market.

professional collectivism collective bargaining activities taken on by professional groups.

professional power based on collective personal and expert power; refers to the cumulative amount of influence that a professional group holds.

professional socialization process by which a person acquires the knowledge, skills, and sense of occupational identity characteristic of members of a given profession.

professional standards review organization (PSRO) reviews the utilization of institutional services by physicians to determine if health care meets predetermined standards.

program-centered administrative consultation occasions when the consultant provides expert advice or sets forth (elicits) alternatives regarding the development of new programs or improvements in existing ones.

program evaluation and review technique (PERT) management technique that uses a network or series of related events and activities to design a flow chart of events complete with an estimation of the duration of each phase of the work.

programmed decisions deal with situations that occur often and for which a routine for resolution has been established.

projection ego-defense mechanism whereby people attribute their thoughts, impulses, or actions to someone else.

promotion utilizes all the tools in the marketing mix whose major role is persuasive communication.

propositions statements that specify and describe the relationships between two or more concepts; they serve to link concepts and demonstrate the relationships between them.

prospective rate setting involves the establishment of reimbursement rates before the year during which such rates will be in effect.

public health those efforts made by communities to cope with health problems that arise as a result of human beings living in groups.

quality assurance a commitment to excellence in care; procedures to evaluate in a systematic way the characteristics of the care that is being provided.

quantitative models generally more precise than verbal models and often written in mathematical format.

queuing theory also called "waiting line theory"; used in determining the correct balance of factors necessary to handle intermittent service.

rationality in the change process, refers to the accurate, objective assessment of the extent to which any change is a threat.

rationalization ego-defense mechanism whereby the person justifies behavior with a socially acceptable reason for the action.

referent power based on aspects of the power holder's personality that induce others to accept it.

refreezing according to Lewin, this is the third stage in the change process and occurs when the newly acquired behavior is integrated into the participant's personality.

region in field theory, refers to the life space of the group and includes both an area and activities that take place in the area.

Regional Medical Programs (RMP) called the Health, Disease, Cancer, and Stroke Amendments of 1965; broadened the focus of planning to include all medical resources available in a region considered essential to meet specific medical objectives.

relative advantage degree to which a new idea is considered superior to an old one.

replica model one that re-creates as exact a version of reality as possible.

resistance an inevitable reaction to change that seems to stem from fear.

restraining forces those that impede the change process as designed by the change agent.

retrospective cost-based reimbursement involves paying the hospital for all expenses incurred in caring for patients covered by the third party.

reward power derives from the power holder's control of positive rewards such as money or job perquisites.

risk factor a disease precursor whose presence is associated with higher than average mortality (e.g., demographic variables, certain health practices, family history, and some physiological changes).

risk management intervention designed to induce or sustain changes in health-compromising behaviors, such as counseling, mass media campaigns, or increased production of low-fat dairy goods.

role conflict presence of contradictory and often competing role expectations.

role overload occurs when there is insufficient time in which to carry out all of the expected role functions.

Rural Health Clinics Act legislation enacted in 1978 to provide for the development of rural health clinics, staffed by NHPs in existing medically underserved areas.

satisficers choices that are made because a decision maker has limited knowledge or inability to establish criteria that will most effectively provide choices to meet the needs of the situation.

satisficing alternatives the selection of alternatives that are adequate or "just good enough," but do not reflect the maximal effective decision.

scanning seeking information about potential options from a variety of sources.

scapegoating occurs when a group singles out one person as the object of conflict; this person is not the one toward whom the feelings are actually held.

schematic model type of symbolic model that may be a diagram, graph, drawing, picture; is abstract and generally descriptive.

scientific management an approach to administration founded by Frederick Taylor that concentrated on the microstructure of work.

Second Law of Thermodynamics a measure of the disorder of a closed system; will always increase toward a maximum, attained in equilibrium.

self-care those activities, continuous or episodic, volitional or unintentional, that people can do for themselves, individually or collectively, in a variety of health and illness matters.

self-diagnosis lay assessment of individual health/illness status.

self-esteem level of regard that people hold for themselves.

Service Employees International Union (SEIU) a labor union that focuses primarily on health care institutions in the private sector; includes primarily aides, orderlies, and kitchen and maintenance workers.

simple resolution a document used by only one chamber of Congress to deal with issues affecting the operation of the house in which they are introduced.

situational adjustment adaptation on the part of a person to behave in ways that are consistent with the expectations of a given setting.

situational theory of leadership states that effectiveness of any leader is a function of the situation or context in which leadership takes place.

socialization the interaction process whereby a person's beliefs and behaviors are formed or altered by virtue of experiences with others and their expectations.

solution criteria those steps necessary to bring about less difference between the desired and actual states.

span of control the number of employees that a manager can effectively supervise.

spontaneous change occurs as a response to natural, uncontrollable events outside the system being considered.

static model portrays phenomena at a given point in time; is stationary and does not readily portray change.

strategic decisions deal with long-range problems that affect the organization's survival and that often have some uncontrollable aspects.

stress a general nonspecific response by the body to demands made on it.

stressors internally or externally generated agents that make demands on people.

structure in systems theory, refers to the arrangement and characteristics of the parts.

summative evaluation calls for the production of a summary statement about program effectiveness.

superwoman syndrome attempts by women to carry out a multitude of roles with little help and with the expectation that they can excel at everything.

symbolic model does not have a recognizable physical form and represents figuratively by using symbols, objects, or concepts.

synergy a combination of two or more resources that results in an output different from the sum of the inputs.

system assemblage of objects, parts, or pieces that are organized or united in some way to form a whole.

systems theory the organization of knowledge about the world or specific phenomena that focuses on the interaction among the various parts of the system.

Taft-Hartley Act passed in 1947; was a revision of the Wagner Act of 1935; included a provision that professional employees should not be organized in the same bargaining unit with nonprofessionals unless a majority of the professionals voted for such an inclusion.

target market the particular group of consumers toward whom attention is focused.

task structure in contingency theory, refers to the degree of routineness in a task.

territoriality the amount of space afforded to or needed by an individual.

theory a set of interrelated concepts, definitions, and propositions that represent a systematic view of phenomena by specifying relations among variables in order to explain as well as predict occurrences.

Theory X a view of human behavior developed by McGregor that perceives people as inherently unable to be "self-starters," but rather that they need continuous monitoring to get their work finished.

Theory Y a view of human nature presented by McGregor that essentially considers people as committed and able to complete work for which they are responsible.

third-party payer a government program or private health insurance plan that represents a third party in the transaction between a health care provider and a consumer.

time management using time in the most efficient way possible to gain maximal results from the time and energy expended.

togetherness forces a term used by Bowen to explain behavior based on the universal need for approval, emotional closeness, and agreement.

training phrase a series of words that, when repeated aloud or mentally, can elicit a desired body response.

trait theory of leadership states that there are certain recognizable characteristics that all good leaders possess.

transference attitudes toward a group leader that are based on earlier attitudes toward previously important people; not necessarily based on the reality of the current situation.

transformation the process by which living systems handle information, energy, and matter that is taken in from the environment and subsequently expelled back into the environment as output.

triad three people or objects.

trialability the degree to which a new idea can be pretested or tried in advance.

triangles a term used by Bowen to define the smallest stable emotional unit; the "building blocks" of emotional relationships in families and society.

UCR reimbursement payment to physicians of medical fees providing the same fees are charged for all patients regardless of mode of payment.

uncertainty a situation with a high level of unknowns regarding the outcome.

undoing ego-defense mechanism whereby the individual performs actions to atone for previous deeds or behaviors.

unfreezing according to Lewin, the first step in the change process; includes motivating participants in the direction of the change objective.

unity of command a classical principle stating that no employee should be simultaneously accountable to more than one boss.

utilitarianism ethical theory based on rightness or wrongness of consequences.

validation describing what is perceived as the other person's message or psychological state.

values beliefs or standards that serve as guidelines when selecting choices in any decision-making situation.

verbal communication the spoken part of a message.

verbal model the written or spoken version of a mental model.

veto when the president returns a bill to the chamber of origin without a signature; accompanied by written objections.

victim blaming the ideology that attributes an individual's defects or inadequacies to the surrounding social conditions, such as poverty or injustice.

voluntary agencies those nonprofit organizations that depend on donations, membership dues, endowments, payments from insurance plans, and contracts for their support.

wellness a dynamic state of health in which an individual progresses toward a higher state of functioning, thus maximizing potential in the environment.

whipsawing playing one employer off against another in multiemployer bargaining arrangements.

Woodward studies early contingency theory studies conducted in England and based on the analysis of technological impact on organizational structure.

workaholic a person who desires and derives great satisfaction from hard work, with long hours spent on work-related activities.

INDEX